3

"The world is a street."

Cahiers du cinéma

4

5

PILLARS OF THE ROMAN EMPIRE

THE SILENCE OF THE LAMBS

1991 - USA - 118 MIN. - THRILLER

DIRECTOR JONATHAN DEMME (*1944)
SCREENPLAY TED TALLY, based on the novel of the same name by THOMAS HARRIS **DIRECTOR OF PHOTOGRAPHY** TAK FUJIMOTO
MUSIC HOWARD SHORE **PRODUCTION** GARY GOETZMAN, EDWARD SAXON, KENNETH UTT, RON BOZMAN for STRONG HEART PRODUCTIONS (for ORION).

STARRING JODIE FOSTER (Clarice Starling), ANTHONY HOPKINS (Dr Hannibal Lecter), SCOTT GLENN (Jack Crawford), TED LEVINE (Jame Gumb), ANTHONY HEALD (Dr Frederick Chilton), BROOKE SMITH (Catherine Martin), DIANE BAKER (Senator Ruth Martin), KASI LEMMONS (Ardelia Mapp), ROGER CORMAN (FBI Director Hayden Burke), GEORGE A. ROMERO (FBI Agent in Memphis).

ACADEMY AWARDS 1992 OSCARS for BEST PICTURE, BEST SCREENPLAY based on material previously produced or published (Ted Tally), BEST DIRECTOR (Jonathan Demme), BEST ACTOR (Anthony Hopkins) and BEST ACTRESS (Jodie Foster).

"I'm having a friend for dinner."

Clarice Starling (Jodie Foster), daughter of a policeman shot in the line of duty, wants to join the FBI. At the FBI Academy in Woods, Virginia, she races over training courses, pushing herself to the limit. Wooden signs bear the legend "HURT-AGONY-PAIN: LOVE IT" – they're not just there to exhort the rookies to excel, they also reveal the masochism involved. The movie goes through the whole range of this theme, from heroic selflessness to destructive self-hate. Jack Crawford (Scott Glenn), who is Starling's boss and the head of the FBI's psychiatric department, sends her to Baltimore to carry out a routine interview with an imprisoned murderer who is resisting questioning. As well as being a psychiatrist, the prisoner is also an extreme pathological case who attacked people and ate their organs. For eight years

Dr Hannibal "The Cannibal" Lecter (Anthony Hopkins) has lived in the window-less cellar of a high security mental hospital. Crawford hopes the interview will provide clues to the behaviour of a second monster, a killer known as "Buffalo Bill" who skins his female victims and has so far skilfully evaded the FBI. Crawford's plan works, and the professorial cannibal agrees to discuss the pathology of mass murderers with his visitor Clarice – on one condition. Lecter will give her expert advice on Buffalo Bill in exchange for the tale of her childhood trauma. "Quid pro quo" – she lays bare her psyche, he gives her a psychological profile of her suspect. The gripping dialogue that develops between the ill-matched couple can be understood on many levels. On one hand, we see a psychoanalyst talking to his patient, on the

> ## "It has been a good long while since I have felt the presence of Evil so manifestly demonstrated..."
> *Chicago Sun-Times*

1   The naked man and the dead: "Buffalo Bill" (Ted Levine) uses a sewing machine to make himself a new identity from the skin of his victims; above him are butterflies, a symbol of that metamorphosis.

2   The staring matches between Starling (Jodie Foster) and Lecter (Anthony Hopkins) are a battle for knowledge: Lecter is to help the FBI build a profile of the killer; Starling is to surrender the secret of her childhood.

3   The pair meet in the lowest part of the prison system, a basement dungeon from the underworld.

4   The eyes have it: in the serial killer genre, eyes become a tool for appropriation, destruction and penetration.

other, a young detective interrogating an unpredictable serial killer, and that ambiguity is the determining quality in Lecter and Starling's relationship. Both follow their own aims unerringly, refusing to give way, and the struggle that results is one of the most brilliant and sophisticated duels in cinema history. The daughter of a US senator falls into the hands of Buffalo Bill, and suddenly the FBI is under increasing pressure to find the murderer. Lecter's chance has come. In return for his help in capturing Jame Gumb alias Buffalo Bill (Ted Levine), he asks for better conditions and is transferred to a temporary prison in Memphis. He kills the warders and escapes in the uniform of a policeman, whose face he has also removed and placed over his own. His last exchange with Starling takes place over the telephone, when he rings from a Caribbean island to congratulate her on her promotion to FBI agent and bids her farewell with the words: "I'm having a friend for dinner". After hanging up, Lecter follows a group of tourists in which the audience recognise the hated Dr Chilton (Anthony Heald), director of the secure mental hospital in Baltimore, who clearly will be Lecter's unsuspecting dinner "guest".

The Silence of the Lambs marked a cinematic high point at the beginning of the 90s. It is impossible to categorise in any one genre as it combines

several. There are elements from police movies (where crime does not pay), but it's also a thriller that borrows much from real historical figures: the model for both Gumb and Lecter is Edward Gein (1906–1984), who was wearing braces made from his victims' skin when arrested in 1957.

But *The Silence of the Lambs* is also a movie about psychiatry. Both murderers are presented as psychopaths whose "relation" to one another forms the basis for criminological research, even though their cases are not strictly comparable. The movie was so successful that it became one of the most influential models for the decade that followed, enriching cinema history to the point of plot plagiarism and quotation.

Suspense and Deception

Hannibal Lecter had already appeared on the silver screen before *The Silence of the Lambs*. In 1986, Michael Mann filmed Thomas Harris' 1981 novel *Red Dragon* under the title *Manhunter*. Five years later, Jonathan Demme refined the material, and the changing perspectives of his camera work give what is fundamentally a cinematic re-telling of *Beauty and the*

"*The Silence of the Lambs* is just plain scary – from its doomed and woozy camera angles to its creepy Freudian context." *The Wahington Post*

Beast a new twist. Demme films his characters from both within and without.

The director plays with the fluid border between external and internal reality, between memory and the present, as when we see Clarice's childhood in two flashbacks for which we are completely unprepared. Jodie Foster's eyes remain fixed on the here and now while the camera zooms beyond her into the past, probing her psychological wounds. During the final confrontation between Clarice and Jame Gumb, the perspective changes repeatedly. We see the murderer through Clarice's eyes but we also see the young FBI agent through the eyes of Jame, who seeks out his victims in the dark using infrared glasses.

This changing perspective in the movie's final scenes emphasises the extreme danger that Clarice is in. Other sequences are straightforward trickery, like the changing perspectives in the sequence which builds up to the finale. A police contingent has surrounded the house where they expect to find Jame Gumb, and black police officer disguised as a deliveryman rings the bell. On the other side of the door, we hear the bell ring. Jame dresses and answers the door. The police break into the house, whilst we see the murderer open the door to find Clarice standing before him – alone. In the next take, the police storm an empty house. This parallel montage combines two places that are far apart, two actions with the same aim, two houses, of which one is only seen from outside, the other from inside. We are made to

5 | 6

5 The cannibal clasps his hands. Cage and pose are reminiscent of Francis Bacon's portraits of the pope.

6 Lecter overpowers the guards with their own weapons: one policeman is given a taste of his own pepper spray.

7 The monster is restrained with straitjacket and muzzle; the powers of the state have the monopoly on violence for the time being.

8 A policeman is disembowelled and crucified on the cage. With his outstretched arms, he looks like a butterfly.

7

think that both actions are happening in the same place. The parallel montage is revealed as a trick and increases the tension: we suddenly realise that Clarice must face the murderer alone.

More than one film critic assumed that this ploy meant that even Hollywood films had moved into an era of self-reflexivity. Instead of consciously revealing a cinematic device, however, the parallel montage serves primarily to heighten the movie's atmosphere of danger and uncertainty. Nevertheless, *The Silence of the Lambs* works on both levels, both as exciting entertainment and as a virtuoso game with key cultural figures and situations. Some critics went so far as to interpret the perverted killer Buffalo Bill as Hades, god of the underworld, and although analyses like that may be interesting, they are not essential to an understanding of the film or its success.

At the 1992 Oscar awards, *The Silence of the Lambs* carried off the so-called Big Five in the five main categories, something which only two films (*It Happened One Night* (1934) and *One Flew Over the Cuckoo's Nest* (1975) had managed previously. Ten years after his escape, Hannibal Lecter appeared again on the silver screen (*Hannibal*, 2001). Jodie Foster refused to play the role of Clarice for a second time and was replaced by Julianne Moore (*Magnolia*) and Ridley Scott took over from Jonathan Demme as director. RV

8

"I go to the cinema because I feel like being shocked." *Jonathan Demme*

10

9 In "Buffalo Bill's" basement lair, Starling is just about to be plunged into total darkness …

10 … where she has to feel her way blindly, straining to hear, while "Buffalo Bill" watches her through infra-red goggles.

PARALLEL MONTAGE	A process developed early in the history of cinema. Editing enables two or more events happening in different places to be told and experienced at the same time. The best-known kind of parallel montage in movies is the "last-minute rescue", where images of an endangered or besieged character are juxtaposed in rapid succession with those of the rescuers who are on their way. Action movies use such sequences over and over as a means of increasing the tension, and the device has remained basically the same from David Griffith's 1916 film *Intolerance* to today's thrillers. Parallel montage allows us to be a step ahead of the figures in a film. We are allowed to know things that the characters do not themselves realise, and we are also in several places at the same time, an experience which is only possible in fiction.

BOYZ N THE HOOD

1991 - USA - 112 MIN. - DRAMA

DIRECTOR JOHN SINGLETON (*1967)
SCREENPLAY JOHN SINGLETON DIRECTOR OF PHOTOGRAPHY CHARLES MILLS MUSIC STANLEY CLARKE PRODUCTION STEVE NICOLAIDES
for NEW DEAL (for COLUMBIA).

STARRING CUBA GOODING JR. (Tre Styles), ICE CUBE (Dough Boy Baker), NIA LONG (Brandi), MORRIS CHESTNUT (Ricky Baker), LAURENCE FISHBURNE (Furious Styles, Tre's father), TYRA FERRELL (Mrs Baker), ANGELA BASSETT (Reva Styles), META KING (Brandi's mother), WHITMAN MAYO (Old Man), DESI ARNEZ HINES (Tre as a 10-year-old).

"Increase the peace."

One in every 21 black Americans is murdered — almost always by another black American. Tre Styles (Cuba Gooding jr.) is a black American, but he is lucky. Growing up in a ghetto in south Los Angeles, he becomes acquainted with the daily violence of the lower-class Afro-American neighbourhoods at an early age. However, in contrast to his friends, most of whom are brought up by drug-addict or alcoholic single mothers, Tre's father prepares him for life in a hostile and violent society. After one of many fights at school, Tre's mother admits she no longer knows what to do with him and hands over his up-bringing to Father Furious (Laurence Fishburne) who drums three basic values into the boy: "Always look people in the eye, then they'll respect you more. Never be frightened to ask for something then you'll never have to steal. Never respect anyone who doesn't respect you." He

teaches the boy to take responsibility: whilst the father makes sure that the bills are paid and that there is something to eat on the table, the son takes care of the housework. The difference between Tre and his peers is the self-esteem that this responsibility gives him.

Furious, who according to Tre's friend Dough Boy (Ice Cube) is "some kind of fucking Malcolm-X-King", has his own explanation for why most murdered Afro-Americans are killed by their own people: nowhere in the world are there more drugs, more whisky bars and weapon stores than in the black neighbourhoods — according to Furious' theory, this is part of the whites' strategy to force down the prices of real estate in the ghettos so they can sell it again for a profit. For this reason, the blacks' property has to be defended.

2

NEW BLACK CINEMA   In 1991, 19 films by black directors were released, marking the break-through of "New Black Cinema". Afro-American reality as portrayed in the fresh film idiom of young directors such as John Singleton, Bill Duke (*Rage in Harlem*, 1991) and Mario van Peebles (*New Jack City*, 1991) does- n't just hit a nerve with black audiences. The world is full of troubled areas where it is necessary to take a stand against racism, which is one rea- son for the international success of black film-makers. One of the greatest pioneers of New Black Cinema was Spike Lee. Movies like *Do the Right Thing* (1989), *Mo' Better Blues* (1990) or *Jungle Fever* (1991) portray a section of American society which the film industry has largely ignored except in crime movies and the Blaxploitation movies of the 1970s.

Tre's aims are of a more private nature: he mostly thinks about the girl-friend he longs for and his college entrance exam. But one night, while a constant stream of police helicopters thunder over the neighbourhood and searchlights flash down into the streets, violence breaks directly into his life: Ricky (Morris Chestnut), Dough Boy's brother, is murdered by members of a street gang over a trifle. A talented footballer, Ricky was one of the few who would have had a chance of getting out of the ghetto, and he had taken the college entrance exam along with Tre. In a poignant moment, his mother dis-covers after his death that he would have just scraped into college. Tre is faced with a terrible dilemma: should he avenge his friend and perpetuate the spiral of violence, or should he find a way to break out of the deadly cycle?

Singleton's drama about violence, responsibility and life in the ghetto is a political lesson about America at the end of the twentieth century. The tran-quil, almost lethargic rhythm of the tale reflects the agony of a world where unemployed black youths drink beer on the veranda all day or sit around on the plastic covers of sitting-room couches and have nothing but cynical comments to make about life. With its clear dialogues and realistic observa-tions, the movie is addressed above all to the people it portrays. When the movie opened in Los Angeles, it sparked off riots amongst black youths that left two dead and thirty-five wounded, but the movie can hardly be blamed for that. Its appeal for peace, brotherhood and responsibility is absolutely unmistakable. Some critics considered its "intellectual simplicity" a weak-ness, but that simplicity is more like the film's main strength.   SH

4

"Singleton dispenses with explanations. He shows people as they are, bluntly and brutally; he shows what they have become, but not what made them that way." *epd Film*

1 Survival of the fittest is all that counts, even for a simple meeting on Saturday night.

2 Blacks shooting blacks. A human life isn't worth much in Afro-American ghettos.

3 Local lads. Dough Boy (Ice Cube, right) and his mates cannot escape the spiral of violence.

4 Furious Styles (Laurence Fishburne) reaches for his weapon only in extreme emergencies. He faces the daily misery of the ghetto with a radical social philosophy and iron principles.

POINT BREAK

1991 - USA - 122 MIN. - ACTION FILM, DRAMA

DIRECTOR KATHRYN BIGELOW (*1953)
SCREENPLAY W. PETER ILIFF, based on a story by RICK KING, W. PETER ILIFF DIRECTOR OF PHOTOGRAPHY DONALD PETERMAN
MUSIC SHARON BOYLE, MARK ISHAM PRODUCTION PETER ABRAMS, ROBERT L. LEVY for 20TH CENTURY FOX.

STARRING PATRICK SWAYZE (Bodhi), KEANU REEVES (Johnny Utah), GARY BUSEY (Angelo Pappas), LORI PETTY (Tyler Ann Endicott), JOHN C. MCGINLEY (Ben Harp), JAMES LEGROS (Roach), JOHN PHILBIN (Nathanial), BOJESSE CHRISTOPHER (Grommet), JULIAN REYES (Alvarez), DANIEL BEER (Babbit).

"Fear causes hesitation, and hesitation will cause your worst fears to come true."

It's clear from the outset that *Point Break* is about a collision between two different ways of life; as the opening credits roll, the names of the movie's two stars are intermingled. Special Agent Johnny Utah (Keanu Reeves) comes to L.A. fresh from the Academy to help out in the investigation of a series of bank robberies. The members of the gang in question disguise themselves with masks of US Presidents, and Johnny's new partner Angelo Pappas (Gary Busey) suspects that they come from the surfing scene. Johnny is sent to work there undercover. Tyler (Lori Petty) teaches him to surf and introduces him to Bodhi (Patrick Swayze), for whom surfing is a way of life.

Bodhi fascinates Johnny and draws him into the surfing scene, but the investigation is beginning to get out of control. Johnny and his partner make a rushed attempt to bust a suspicious group of surfers and ruin months of work by their colleagues in the Drugs Department. In a moment of high spirits during their next surfing trip together, Bodhi thrusts his naked behind at his fellow surfers. This defiant gesture is exactly what the masked presidents do for the police security cameras at the end of their raids, and Johnny realises that his surfing friends are the gang he has been looking for all along. He and his partner decide to confront them during their next robbery, but the plan goes wrong. His cover is blown, and the next day the surfers stand at his door and challenge him. First they take him parachuting then they force him to take part in the next bank raid. They take Tyler, now Johnny's girlfriend, as hostage.

During the getaway from the bank, Johnny's partner and one of the surfers are shot dead. Johnny himself is forced to get into the plane. The surfers jump out over the Mexican desert and leave him. In despairing rage, he jumps out after them without a parachute and catches up with Bodhi in free fall. Once again they test each other's daring – neither of them wants to pull the ripcord – but Johnny loses once again. He lands in the desert and Tyler runs into his arms.

He has one last chance: the storm of the century has broken out in Australia and all the surfers flee the beaches except Bodhi, who stands waiting to take up Johnny's challenge. They fight, and this time Johnny manages to defeat Bodhi and handcuffs him, but he can't resist when Bodhi asks to be allowed to ride one last gigantic wave before Johnny's FBI colleagues arrive to take him away. The foam closes over the surfer, Johnny leaves the beach and throws his agent's badge over the cliff.

"*Point Break* makes those of us who don't spend our lives searching for the ultimate physical rush feel like second-class citizens. The film turns reckless athletic valor into a new form of aristocracy." *Entertainment Weekly*

Kathryn Bigelow's *Point Break* is a celebration of speed and movement. During the opening sequences when Johnny goes to his new office for the first time, he is filmed in a long steadycam take which follows him down the hall and is directed – as is Johnny – by the pointing fingers of the other employees. In the surf scenes, the camera glides through the crests of the waves parallel to the boards in images that capture the absolute freedom of movement on water. The film's real climax is a chase scene through gardens, sitting rooms and children's paddling pools, where Johnny pursues Bodhi in his Ronald Reagan mask. Johnny sprains his ankle, and his only hope is to shoot Bodhi down, but he can't bring himself to do it. The fascination and intoxication of speed brings the power of the state to its knees.

Bigelow's *Point Break* is one of the best action movies of the 90s. Its excitement doesn't just come from its fantastic camera work and visuals, but also from the acting achievement of its two stars and their electrifying duel.

M

1   Bodhi (Patrick Swayze) dreams of a single overwhelming wave that will sweep him away far beyond the reach of the justice of this world.

2   By disguising themselves as Ex-Presidents, the surfers express their contempt for a meaningless establishment.

3   Macho initiation rites: who'll be the last to pull the ripcord of his parachute?

4   The different careers of Keanu Reeves and Patrick Swayze make them an ideal choice to portray a tense and exciting friendship between two men.

5   The contrast between land and sea in this film represents the contrast between law and crime, and discipline and excess.

6   Like many other film gangsters, the Ex-Presidents are ultimately defeated by their increasing arrogance and self-styled image.

7   Hyper-motivated FBI agent Johnny (Keanu Reeves) lurches from one disaster to another.

STEADYCAM

In the early 70s, cameraman Garrett Brown developed a portable tripod and vest which attaches a camera to the cameraman's body in such a way that all his movements are countered by a system of suspended rotating balancing weights. This made it possible for the first time for movies to be full of movement without the characteristic jiggling of the hand-held camera. The steadycam can also produce running pictures in restricted spaces (for example, stairwells) without additional aids such as runners or cranes. One result of such filming – used for the first time in 1976 in *Rocky* and later in Kubrick's *The Shining* – is the pictures' independent dynamic. The camera seems freed from its limitations and is able to circle the action from all angles in one take so that place and time can be experienced in unbroken continuity.

THE BEAUTIFUL TROUBLEMAKER
La Belle Noiseuse

1991 - FRANCE - 240 MIN. (abridged version *DIVERTIMENTO*: 126 MIN.) - DRAMA, LITERATURE ADAPTATION

DIRECTOR JACQUES RIVETTE (*1928)
SCREENPLAY PASCAL BONITZER, CHRISTINE LAURENT, JACQUES RIVETTE, based on the short story *LE CHEF-D'ŒUVRE INCONNU* by HONORÉ DE BALZAC DIRECTOR OF PHOTOGRAPHY WILLIAM LUBTCHANSKY MUSIC IGOR STRAVINSKY PRODUCTION PIERRE GRISE, MARTINE MARIGNAC for FR3 FILMS, PIERRE GRISE PRODUCTIONS, GEORGE REINHART PRODUCTIONS.

STARRING MICHEL PICCOLI (Edouard Frenhofer), JANE BIRKIN (Liz), EMMANUELLE BÉART (Marianne), MARIANNE DENICOURT (Julienne), DAVID BURSZTEIN (Nicolas), GILLES ARBONA (Porbus), BERNARD DUFOUR (hand of the painter), MARIE-CLAUDE ROGER (Françoise), MARIE BELLUC (Magali), LEILA REMILI (maidservant).

IFF CANNES 1991 JURY PRIZE (Jacques Rivette).

"A cruel game."

"When I take art to its limits, there's blood on the canvas."

Art has always been about pushing back boundaries. It certainly is for artist Edouard Frenhofer (Michel Piccoli), once a famous painter, but now almost forgotten. Although he excels at the technical aspects of his art, he knows he has never succeeded in creating a masterpiece. When the film opens, we see that he has withdrawn to a solitary country house in Burgundy together with his partner Liz (Jane Birkin), and has more or less stopped painting altogether. Liz is no longer his muse: now she merely looks after him. She modelled for Frenhofer's last picture "The Beautiful Troublemaker", which lies unfinished and hidden in his studio, and as a result she embodies his failure as much as the work itself. Both now live a life without art, locked into human and artistic stagnation.

The situation changes when their friend the art dealer Porbus (Gilles Arbona) comes to visit accompanied by the young painter Nicolas (David Bursztein) and his girlfriend Marianne (Emmanuelle Béart). Nicolas and Porbus insist on seeing the "Beautiful Troublemaker". Frenhofer refuses, but eventually they reach a compromise: Frenhofer will continue the work with Marianne as model and Porbus will buy the finished picture.

Outrage is followed by hestitation, until finally Marianne agrees to the deal which soon becomes a gruelling test of endurance for both parties. Painter and model struggle with art and with themselves until they teeter on the verge of self-destruction.

For three of the total of four hours, director Jacques Rivette represents the finishing of the "Beautiful Troublemaker" as an existential challenge for

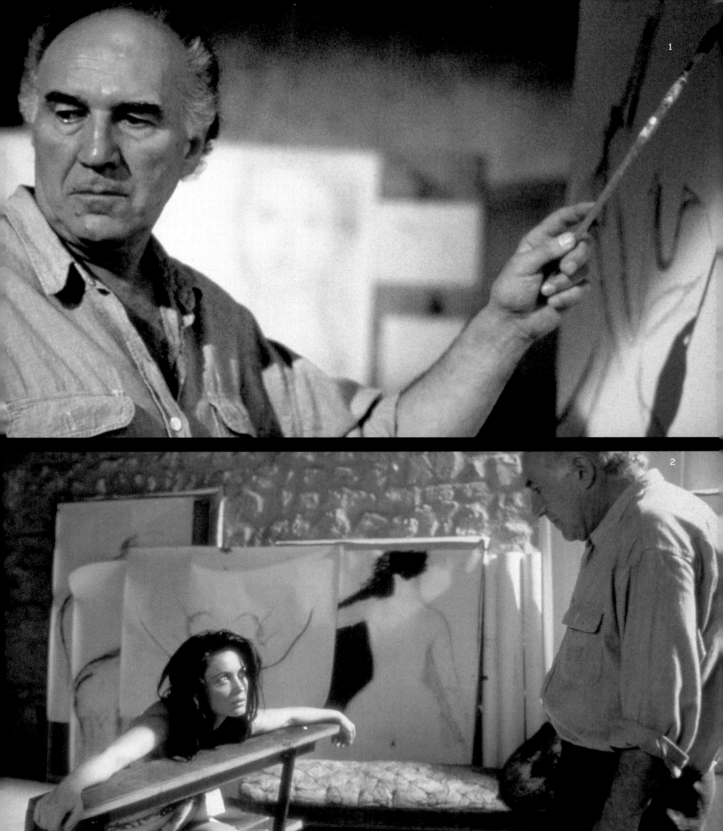

1 Edouard Frenhofer (Michel Piccoli) is in search of the ultimate masterpiece. After a lengthy period of artist's block, he accepts the challenge one last time.

2 Painter and model. Marianne (Emmanuelle Béart) has to suffer numerous humiliations at the hands of the eccentric artist. But she ends up the stronger.

3 The creative process begins by overcoming a fear of the empty canvas.

4 The beautiful muse. Marianne reluctantly agrees to the experiment.

"Whereas in his films about theatre Rivette looked for the truth in the set, the acting and the costumes, in *La Belle Noiseuse* he directs his search towards nakedness, gestures, line, as well as material and flesh." *du*

"We made every effort to produce a film that comes close to painting, rather than talking about it."

Jacques Rivette in: Der Spiegel

painter and model. Frenhofer wrestles to assert himself as an artist, and his naked model is forced into painful poses by the sulky and despotic painter as she fights to defend her personality and her self-esteem.

"Let me be how I am" Marianne demands. In the end, she has to encourage the despondent painter to continue. But, by the time the painting is finished, Marianne has become the "Beautiful Troublemaker" herself, and can no longer bear the sight of the picture and the truth it reveals.

Liz's face on the canvas is replaced by the younger woman's naked buttocks; the creative process is, she concludes "a cruel game". For her, the real obscenity is the question of whether a whole life can be fixed in a couple of brushstrokes. She has sacrificed her life for Frenhofer's art and now she knows the price of such presumption.

Rivette's film is based on Honoré de Balzac's tale *The Unknown Masterpiece*, but whereas for Balzac, blood on the canvas was a reference to the idea that under the painted skin, the observer should be able to imagine blood flowing, coming from Frenhofer it sounds like a threat of mental or physical violence. Balzac's Frenhofer, who is a kind of Pygmalion, comes to believe that the picture he is working on is a real woman. Everything else is a confusion of lines and colours under which the "unknown masterpiece" is hidden; only a perfectly painted foot can be seen in the corner of the canvas.

In the movie, the finished painting is walled up in Frenhofer's studio and no one ever sees it apart from those immediately concerned, and the public are fobbed off with a hastily produced replacement. Rivette's movie can also be taken as an eloquent commentary on literary models: if there is such a thing as creative truth beyond self-centred arrogance and artistic hubris, then it is only accessible to those who appreciate how painful the link between reality and the artistic imagination can be.

SH

FILM ADAPTATIONS OF LITERATURE

Some of the best films of the 90s were adapted from literary models, like *The Silence of the Lambs* (Jonathan Demme, 1990) taken from the novel by Thomas Harris or *L.A. Confidential* (Curtis Hanson, 1997) based on the book by James Ellroy.

Many movies from the 90s also show that filming best-sellers is a lucrative business, as the film versions of John Grisham's books (including *The Firm* by Sydney Pollack, 1993 and *The Jury* by Joel Schumacher, 1996) undoubtedly demonstrate.

When directors choose an older literary model, they must first decide whether to make a historical movie or a modernization. Whereas films such as *Hamlet* (Kenneth Branagh, 1996) concentrate entirely on historical authenticity, modernizations such as Al Pacino's *Looking for Richard* (1996) explore the contemporary aspects of historical material.

THELMA & LOUISE

1991 - USA - 129 MIN. - ROAD MOVIE, DRAMA

DIRECTOR RIDLEY SCOTT (*1937)
SCREENPLAY CALLIE KHOURI DIRECTOR OF PHOTOGRAPHY ADRIAN BIDDLE MUSIC HANS ZIMMER PRODUCTION PERCY MAIN, MIMI POLK, RIDLEY SCOTT for PERCY MAIN PRODUCTIONS.

STARRING SUSAN SARANDON (Louise Sawyer), GEENA DAVIS (Thelma Dickinson), HARVEY KEITEL (Hal Slocumb), MICHAEL MADSEN (Jimmy), CHRISTOPHER MCDONALD (Darryl), BRAD PITT (J. D.), STEPHEN TOBOLOWSKY (Max), TIMOTHY CARHART (Harlan), LUCINDA JENNY (Lena the waitress), MARCO ST. JOHN (truck driver).

ACADEMY AWARDS 1992 OSCAR for BEST ORIGINAL SCREENPLAY (Callie Khouri).

"You've always been crazy, this is just the first chance you've had to express yourself."

The movie's first image is of a broad landscape that slowly brightens and then immediately sinks back into darkness. Two friends, Thelma (Geena Davis) and Louise (Susan Sarandon) are treating themselves to a weekend away. Thelma has to get ready in secret, as her helpless husband would never let her out of the house if he knew, as he needs her to make his coffee and fasten his gold bracelet every morning. The unfamiliar freedom is a revelation to her, and at the first stop she orders a drink and takes up a cowboy's invitation to dance. Things turn nasty and he tries to rape her, only giving up when Louise holds a pistol to his head. The crisis seems to have passed when the cowboy starts shouting unbearable obscenities after the two women. Louise turns round and shoots him dead with the words "You watch your mouth, buddy". Horrified at their own actions, the friends flee,

convinced that no one would believe their version of events. Thelma's self-confidence has been sapped by long years of marriage and she reacts at first with childish despair, whereas Louise coolly organises their escape to Mexico.

The film then develops a double perspective. The first follows the two women, who become more daring, more independent and less tolerant with every obstacle that crosses their path. Thelma begins to get the hang of being free and getting her own way. She locks a policeman into his own trunk at gunpoint when he tries to arrest them, and then blows up a petrol tanker when the driver directs a stream of sexist comments at them as he drives by. The second perspective shows us the police investigations. Detective Hal Slocumb (Harvey Keitel) is a sensitive cop who suspects the

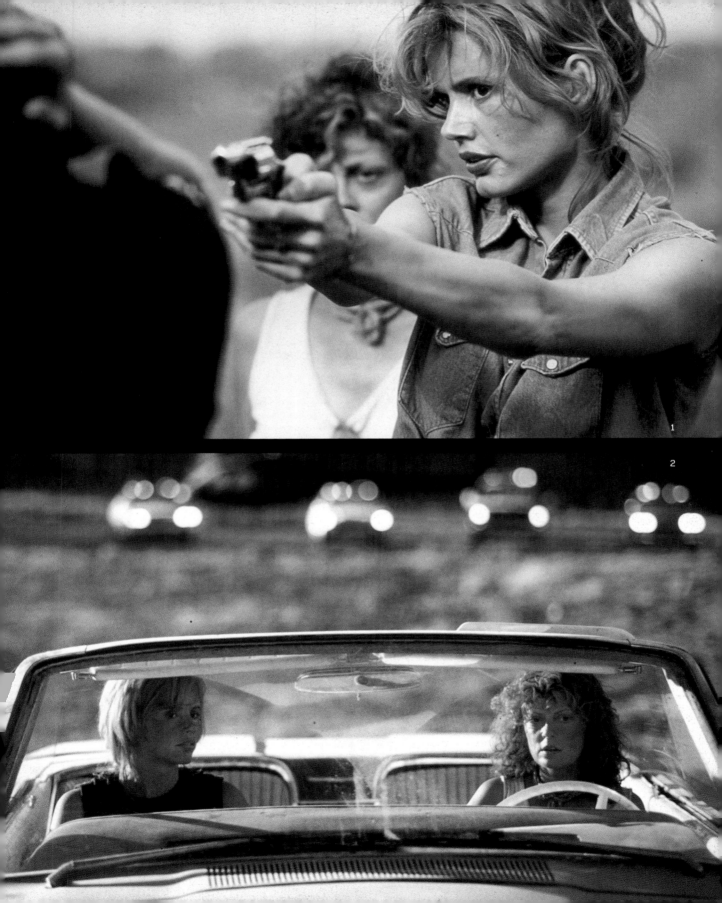

ROAD MOVIE   From the earliest days of the movies, train travel was a popular motif, due to cinema's fascination with movement. When cars and motorbikes became more widespread, movement could be intimately connected with a character's individual development, and from the 40s onwards, outsiders and dropouts were continually portrayed as motorised nomads. The enormous success of Dennis Hopper's *Easy Rider* (1969) helped turn the Road Movie into a recognisable genre.
Similar to the Western, the Road Movie genre generally concentrates on solitary men who only feel free if they are in constant and restless movement. Alongside *Thelma & Louise*, other 90s movies which depict social conflict in the form of epic journeys through the country include David Lynch's *Wild at Heart* (1990) and Oliver Stone's *Natural Born Killers* (1994).

truth about the murder and tries to mediate, but he is powerless to stop the machinery of the FBI once it begins to roll. Thelma spends a night with con man and playboy J. D. (Brad Pitt), who puts the detectives on the trail of the two women. Eventually, an entire flotilla of screeching police cars catches up with Thelma and Louise at the brink of a canyon. A standoff develops and the policemen cock their guns. In a moment of high emotion, Thelma urges Louise to drive on. Louise puts the car in gear and floors the pedal, and they roar off over the edge of the abyss to certain death. The picture freezes as the car hovers high over the canyon and gets brighter and brighter until all we see is pure white light.

Thelma & Louise is the story of a liberation. As the journey progresses, the frightened and helpless Thelma develops into a smart, strong woman. The more critical the friends' situation gets, the more assertive she

becomes. Looking back on her married life, she realises how her husband tyrannised her, and the tragedy of her seemingly normal life becomes clear.

Thelma & Louise is also a story about a journey into the light. In the course of the movie, the exterior scenes get brighter and brighter until they are almost over-exposed. In jarring contrast, the interiors where the police carry out their interrogations are filmed in cold blue and green. Scott's movie doesn't map out an exclusively female pattern of behaviour for the two friends, but rather lets them take on roles that are usually reserved for men. Reviewers in the US criticised the movie for its man-hating attitudes and glorification of violence, but in fact Thelma & Louise makes no generalisations about the sexes. It is one of the few movies where lines and actions were applauded or booed aloud during cinema screenings. Seldom does cinema tread so provocatively on society's fault-lines.   MS

"These great 'heroines' bring Callie Khouri's furious screenplay to life with totally infectious energy."

Cinema

6

5

7

1 Farewell domesticity: Thelma (Geena Davis) forces a policeman into the boot of his car.

2 Pursued by hundreds of policemen, Thelma and Louise (Susan Sarandon) stare resolutely towards the future.

3 Portraying these two radically different women had a formative influence on the careers of Susan Sarandon and Geena Davis.

4 A sensational moment from the film: a tanker, the symbol of masculine power, is blown sky-high.

5 Brad Pitt came fresh from the world of advertising to star as a sex symbol in this film.

6 Composed and resolute, Louise reaches for her gun, having no other option.

7 The film repeatedly offers the two women a fleeting respite in the still of the night.

DELICATESSEN
Delicatessen

1991 - FRANCE - 99 MIN. - BLACK COMEDY

DIRECTORS JEAN-PIERRE JEUNET (*1955), MARC CARO (*1956)
SCREENPLAY JEAN-PIERRE JEUNET, MARC CARO, GILLES ADRIEN **DIRECTOR OF PHOTOGRAPHY** DARIUS KHONDJI **MUSIC** CARLOS D'ALESSIO
PRODUCTION CLAUDIE OSSARD for CONSTELLATION, UGC, HACHETTE PREMIÈRE.

STARRING DOMINIQUE PINON (Louison), MARIE-LAURE DOUGNAC (Julie Clapet), JEAN-CLAUDE DREYFUS (The Butcher), KARIN VIARD (Miss Plusse), TICKY HOLGADO (Mr Tapioca), ANNE-MARIE PISANI (Mrs Tapioca), EDITH KER (Grandmother Tapioca), MICKAEL TODDE, BOBAN JANEVSKI (young rascals), JACQUES MATHOU (Roger).

"How much do you weigh?"

Something terrible has happened to the world. Everything is in ruins and permanent darkness reigns. Somewhere, a solitary apartment block remains standing. It must have been quite a distinguished residence at some point in the past. Now, the people here are better off than elsewhere – the downstairs of the house is butcher's shop, run by an ingenious master butcher (Jean-Claude Dreyfus) who keeps the occupants supplied with fresh meat. The wares on offer at his 'Delicatessen' are the former neighbours, but this no longer seems to bother his customers: in times like these they can't afford to be choosy. When provisions run short at her funeral, Grandmother herself provides the refreshments – giving a whole new meaning to the expression "funeral bake-meats".

Louison (Dominique Pinon), an unemployed clown, strays into this apocalyptic horror-idyll. The butcher, sharpening his knives, takes him on as a caretaker, and the rest of the gruesome crew look forward to a glut of fresh meat.

Despite the difficult times, Louison has retained his sunny character and he entertains the occupants of the house with his tricks – but that isn't enough to get him taken off the menu. Luckily for him the butcher's daughter Julie (Marie-Laure Dougnac) falls in love with him, and she does her utmost to save him from her father's meat grinder. In her hour of need she turns to the archenemies of the house's bizarre inhabitants: the vegetarians, who indulge their repulsive preference for corn and wheat in the Paris sewers …

Delicatessen was the first full-length movie by Jean-Pierre Jeunet and Marc Caro, French directors who had made their names with distinctive shorts. The film is a showcase for comic figures like Mrs Interligator (Silvia Laguna), who constantly hears voices encouraging her to attempt suicide with a series of daredevil contraptions that are as inventive as they are unsuccessful. Then there's the elderly gentleman (Howard Vernon) who has turned his apartment into a pond to keep himself in frogs and snails: the plot is really just an excuse for the succession of peculiarities and monstrosities that Jeunet and Caro parade before our eyes.

The film's impact also depends on the details of its fairy-tale comic scenery, which is loving created. We learn to expect the unexpected from the walls, pipes and shafts of the house, which, rather than providing shelter for

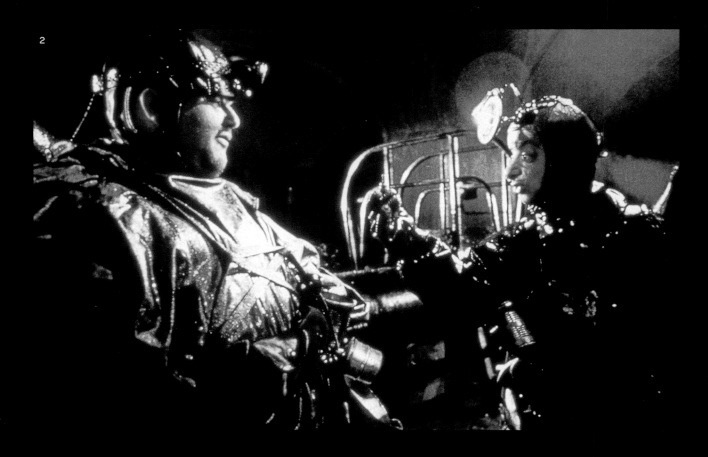

its inhabitants, shifts and stirs like a prehistoric creature and seems to have swallowed them whole. Its crooked staircases and hallways mark it as a surreal motif with many forerunners in the history of the cinema, like the Bates Motel in Hitchcock's *Psycho* (1960) or the Overlook Hotel in Stanley Kubrick's The *Shining* (1980). But more than anything *Delicatessen* is a slapstick version of Roman Polanski's apartment house horror film *Le Locataire* (*The Tenant*, 1976) based on the novel by French writer Roland Topor.

Both the 'living' house and the hero of the film call to mind Terry Gilliam's alarming apocalyptic vision *Brazil*. Like the wilful civil servant Sam Lowry, Louison is a naïve revolutionary who has remained human in an inhuman world and is therefore bound to antagonise the people who surround him. Louison forgives his tormentors by constantly reminding himself that it is the circumstances which have turned them to the bad. He respects his fellow men despite their cannibalism, and the fact that they kill his pet ape, who winds up in their stew-pot.

Delicatessen does far more than push back the boundaries of bad taste. It's also an eloquent plea for humanity, solidarity and – vegetarianism.

SH

SURREALISM – CINEMA AS DREAM The poet Guillaume Apollinaire used the term "surréel" for the first time in 1917. Following the ideas of Sigmund Freud, Surrealism tries to make man's internal reality visible. Motifs from dream experiences and intoxicated states distort the surrealists' view of the world and transform objective reality into a reflection of the soul. As surrealism coincided with the early days of film, it is not surprising that its images and ideas have influenced cinema history since its very beginnings. An early example is *Der müde Tod* (*Destiny*, 1921) by Fritz Lang. Surrealist set pieces can be found in all movie genres, although not always as explicitly as in Alfred Hitchcock's *Spellbound* (1945), whose dream sequences were designed by Salvador Dalí. Variations on surrealist themes and motifs have found their way into in a range of different genres, from horror to science fiction.

---

1   Will that be all, sir? Butcher Clapet (Jean-Claude Dreyfus) always seems to have the welfare of his fellow inhabitants at heart.

2   Living on rabbit food: militant vegetarians barricade themselves in the basement to fight for a meat-free diet.

3   Nobody is safe from the butcher's razor-sharp knife.

4   A Little Night Music … Louison (Dominique Pinon) and Julie (Marie-Laure Dougnac) meet and fall in love.

5   Circus artist Louison tries to survive in an inhuman milieu by using imagination and humanity.

"There's nothing remotely like the world of *Delicatessen*. It's a fragment of childhood miraculously intact. A mirage. A scrap of eternity. It's heart-breakingly lovely." *Le nouvel observateur*

TERMINATOR 2: JUDGMENT DAY

1991 - USA - 137 MIN. - ACTION FILM

DIRECTOR JAMES CAMERON (*1954)
SCREENPLAY JAMES CAMERON, WILLIAM WISHER DIRECTOR OF PHOTOGRAPHY ADAM GREENBERG MUSIC BRAD FIEDEL
PRODUCTION JAMES CAMERON, GALE ANNE HURD for CAROLCO PICTURES, LIGHTSTORM ENTERTAINMENTS, PACIFIC WESTERN.

STARRING ARNOLD SCHWARZENEGGER (Terminator T-800), LINDA HAMILTON (Sarah Connor), EDWARD FURLONG (John Connor), ROBERT PATRICK (T-1 000), EARL BOEN (Dr Peter Silberman), JOE MORTON (Miles Bennett Dyson), S. EPATHA MERKERSON (Tarissa Dyson), CASTULO GUERRA (Enrique Salceda), DANNY COOKSEY (Tim), JENETTE GOLDSTEIN (Janelle Voight).

ACADEMY AWARDS 1992 OSCARS for BEST VISUAL EFFECTS (Dennis Muren, Stan Winston, Gene Warren Jr., Robert Skotak), BEST SOUND EFFECTS EDITING (Gary Rydstrom, Gloria S. Borders), BEST MAKE-UP (Stan Winston, Jeff Dawn) and BEST SOUND (Tom Johnson, Gary Rydstrom, Gary Summers, Lee Orloff).

"You gotta listen to the way people talk. You don't say 'affirmative' or some shit like that. You say 'no problemo'."

In the year 2029, war rages between intelligent machines and the last human survivors of an atomic attack launched against mankind by the computer network Skynet in 1997. But strangely, the outcome of that war is to be decided in our day, as both sides have sent a Terminator back in time to manipulate the course of history. The scene is the city by night, where two naked bodies materialise in quick succession. Unimpressed by attempts to stop him, the hefty T-800 (Arnold Schwarzenegger) robs a Hell's Angel of his leathers, motor bike and shades. T-1 000 (Robert Patrick) appears less muscle-bound, and he takes a policeman's car and uniform. Both set off in search of the ten-year-old John Connor (Edward Furlong), who will lead the human resistance forces in the year 2029, but is at present still living with his long-suffering foster parents. His mother Sarah (Linda Hamilton) has been institutionalised in a mental hospital. Her fearful tales of brutal fighting robots in human form – who the movie's audience recognise from the first Terminator film – are considered the ravings of a madwoman.

The two Terminators find John Connor practically at the same time in the dark corridors of an amusement arcade. T-800 rips out a pump-action shot gun from the gift-wrapped box under his arm, grabs John, deflects T-

"Visceral to the point of overkill (and beyond), a berserk blizzard of kinetic images, it doesn't even give you time to be scared." *The Washington Post*

MORPHING   Of all the special effects used in *Terminator 2*, computer-generated morphing is both the simplest and the most original. Transformations from one form into another (the Greek word *morphe* means form) are shown as a seamless process. Two different images – for example, a man and an animal – are computer-manipulated to produce further images, enabling a seamless transition from one figure to the other. Previously, directors had to rely on the audience's imagination; the original figure was shown, then the successive shape, and the transformation took place in the audience's head. Since *Terminator 2*, the process can be shown in its entirety. Morphing has a surprisingly uncanny effect on screen. It interferes with our preconceptions of material stability and suggests that everybody and everything is interchangeable.

1   Clad head to toe in leather and armed to the teeth, the Terminator (Arnold Schwarzenegger) is the epitome of the action hero.

2   In contrast to the angular figure of Schwarzenegger, Robert Patrick embodies a slippery, cynical liquid metal terminator.

3   The film's explosive chase scenes are also always conflicts between different modes of transport …

4   … the T-800's stolen motorbike enhances Schwarzenegger's "image".

1 000's shots with his bare torso and fires back. T-1 000 is thrown back by the force of the gunfire, but instead of gunshot wounds, his upper body shows nothing but scratches which glimmer metallically and close over instantly.

T-800 escapes with John on his motorbike, but he only explains what is happening after they have blown up the tanker-truck which the T-1 000 is using to follow them. He explains to John that he is an old-fashioned robot (a mechanical skeleton covered with organic tissue) re-programmed by the people of the future, but that the machines of the future have sent a more highly developed cyborg made of fluid metal who can fit itself to any shapes it touches. The glimmering metal figure of T-1 000 emerges from the flames of the burning truck unharmed, and takes on the shape of a cop before our very eyes.

Once John has discovered that T-800 is programmed to obey his every instruction, his first act is to forbid him from killing people, and then orders him to free his mother Sarah from the mental hospital. The robot and Sarah have their hands full saving John from the attacks of T-1 000, but Sarah goes one step further: she wants to stop the coming atomic war single-handed, and goes to find Dyson, the scientist who is developing the technology which will make the machines' domination possible. John and T-800 only just make it in time to stop her killing Dyson, but by cutting open the flesh of his arm to show the mechanics underneath, T-800 manages to convince the sci-entist of the dangers to come. He lets them into the compound of the Cyberdine Corporation, where they steal the remains of the Terminators from

the first movie, without which the deadly future developments will not be possible.

T-1 000 remains hot on their heels, effortlessly gliding through iron bars and transforming his arm into steel spikes in a fraction of a second. They finally destroy him in a steel works, in a fight to the death the likes of which have seldom been seen on the screen. They blow up another tanker truck, but this time it is full of fluid gas, which freezes the amorphous Terminator. A shot from T-800 shatters the metal into millions of splinters. But as they begin to warm up, the drops of metal flow together to re-form the familiar figure of T-1 000. In the fight that follows on the stairways and metal grids of the steel works, he is almost split in two and then grows back together, he takes on the shape of Sarah Connor and tries to deceive John, and the real Sarah fires at him until her bullets run out. At the last moment T-800 appears on a conveyor belt and hurls the badly damaged metal hulk into a furnace full of glowing steel, where T-1 000 runs through all its possible transformations with ear-splitting cries and screeches until it is mixed with the liquid metal forever.

One last test awaits Sarah and John. The chip in T-800's head could also be used for military research and as a departure point for future wars – it too must be destroyed. As the Terminator is incapable of self-destruc-tion, Sarah has to push the button that sends him into the steel bath which swallowed up his enemy. Shortly before he disappears completely, he gives the thumbs-up sign, a "cool" greeting that John taught him during their escape.

A record budget

Terminator 2 is a movie that set standards for years to come. Although it was the most expensive movie of all time when it was made in 1991, it still made an enormous profit. Its effect relies on a continual assault on the senses. The opening credits are underscored by the pulsating music that structures the whole film. The action spectacle contains very few quiet moments, but even in the scenes reserved for developing the comic-sentimental relationship between John and T-800, the mood is dark and overshadowed by the final battle to come. The audience is spared none of the details of Sarah's vision of atomic fall-out with a fireball, burning bodies and disintegrating skeletons. But the apocalyptic mood comes above all from the special effects. The computer technology used was brand new in 1991, and rumour has it that the production crew were still not sure that some of the movie's scenes were actually possible when the filming started. But, despite their spectacular nature, the effects are so well integrated in the movie's plot that they never become a mere end in themselves. *Terminator 2* not only sketches a vision of the future, its special effects themselves are part of this future. The struggle between T-800 and T-1000 is the conflict between two different stages of technological development. While the mechanical skeleton and computing chip of T-800 are still materially fallible, T-1000 represents post-material technology thanks to the use of unprecedented special effects: its mimetic polyalloy allows it to "morph" between metallic machine and human form giving it an unnatural shapelessness. The two Terminators mirror the ambivalent relationship between the human beings and the technology they have created. On the one hand, we fear that research that has run out of control and that technology is becoming self-sufficient – the computerised defence network Skynet in *Terminator 2* is a reference to the SDI project. On the other hand, T-800 represents the fantasy of technology that compensates for the deficits in human society. As Sarah Connor says: "Of all the would-be fathers who came and went over the years, this thing, this machine, was the only one who measured up. In an insane world, it was the sanest choice."

MS

5   Being on the run with John Connor (Edward Furlong) teaches the Terminator how humans behave. On the orders of his protégé, fatalities become a thing of the past.

6   Linda Hamilton was one of the first female actors allowed to bare visibly trained muscles in a Hollywood movie.

7   No other film has ever shown off Arnold Schwarzenegger's face and body to such impressive effect.

5

6

8 As is often the case in Hollywood films, the strong woman is never far from hysteria.

"After *Terminator 2,* Hollywood will have to think twice about making still another car chase movie." New York Magazine

THE LOVERS ON THE BRIDGE
Les Amants du Pont-Neuf

1991 - FRANCE - 126 MIN. - DRAMA

DIRECTOR LÉOS CARAX (*1960)
SCREENPLAY LÉOS CARAX DIRECTOR OF PHOTOGRAPHY JEAN-YVES ESCOFFIER MUSIC VARIOUS, including LES RITA MITSOUKO, DAVID BOWIE, IGGY POP, ARVO PÄRT, GILLES TINAYRE PRODUCTION CHRISTIAN FECHNER, ALBERT PRÉVOST, HERVÉ TRUFFAUT, ALAIN DAHAN for FILMS CHRISTIAN FECHNER, FILM A2.

STARRING JULIETTE BINOCHE (Michèle), DENIS LAVANT (Alex), KLAUS-MICHAEL GRÜBER (Hans), DANIEL BUAIN (Alex's Freund), MARION STALENS (Marion). CHRICHAN LARSSON (Julien).

"I want to be drunk with you, so I can see you laugh."

The first scenes of Léos Carax's movie *The Lovers on the Bridge* are like a documentary shot in cinéma vérité style: a young man staggers along on the central reservation of a road, oblivious to the cars which roar past him. One of the cars knocks him over. A young woman, with a lost air, observes how he is finally picked up by a bus that takes homeless people to a night shelter. Later that night the two meet again on the Pont-Neuf, the oldest bridge in Paris, which is closed for renovation. And there begins Carax's love story, a tale of two outsiders whom life has not treated well.

The young woman is called Michèle (Juliette Binoche) and is a painter who is almost blind in one eye. She is haunted by her bourgeois origins and by an unhappy relationship that forces her to keep a pistol in her paint box. Alex, the young man (Denis Lavant), is hyperactive, antisocial and permanently under the influence of drugs. He occasionally works as a fire-eater. One other memorable character is the old vagabond Hans (Klaus-Michael Grüber), the man who has lived on the bridge for longest. Alex falls in love with Michèle but has no words to express his love. In order to discover something about the woman he loves, he breaks into her apartment and reads her letters.

Léos Carax went to great lengths for the production of his movie and the recreation of the homeless milieu in which it is set. He had the bridge copied and built almost in an almost life-size replica near Montpellier, complete with sham house fronts on the banks of an artificial Seine. The filming of the movie was dogged by misfortune. First the producer died and then the relationship between Léos Carax and his long-time partner and leading actress Juliette Binoche broke down. The movie took three years to finish and by the time it reached the movie theatres it was three times over budget. Its 160 million francs production costs made it the most expensive French movie ever made up. Although strictly speaking it was not a box office success, the critics loved it, perhaps because its strengths lie in its opulent images rather than in its sparing dialogues. Visually, the movie is

1 Painter Michèle (Juliette Binoche) looks more intently at the world inside than she does at the real world.

2 Home as crossover and in-between world: the famous Pont-Neuf bridge in Paris.

3 Michèle asleep.

immensely stylised, but at the same time it also gives a strong impression of realism, so that the audience is never sure whether what it is watching is the product of a fertile imagination or simply an intelligent and realistic film. There are two murders in the movie, which may be real or may just have taken place in Michèle's mind. The empty eye socket, which Alex sees when he lifts Michèle's eyelid, is probably only a figment of his imagination. *The Lovers on the Bridge* is an uncomfortable movie, compellingly filmed and open to many different interpretations.

Léos Carax has never been one for conventional cinematic idioms. The movie is a kind of cinematic litmus test which shows a great number of dif- ferent visual layers and shades of emotion and mood. Some of its more exciting scenes have an almost hypnotic quality, as when Michèle and Alex dance wildly during the firework display commemorating the 200th anniversary of the French Revolution or when Michèle waterskis behind a stolen police boat.

The source of Carax's inspiration becomes clear in one of the last shots in the movie. The two lovers are shown in a pose which reminds us of the figurehead of a ship, a homage to Jean Vigo's film *L'Atalante* (1934), a masterpiece which combines a dream-like atmosphere with the realities of Parisian life. APO

4   The people who live on the bridge have the
    fireworks celebrating the bicentenary of the
    French Revolution in their front room.

5   A love without words: Alex (Denis Levant)
    and Michèle on their bridge.

"This wounded tarantella of a film is unique. The emotion wells from its form not its core, and is as pure and direct as the great never-to-be-forgotten pre-war melodramas. Few words, music of every denomination, and so many breathtaking images that one drowns in them." *Le Monde*

JULIETTE BINOCHE   Juliette Binoche won her first Academy Award in 1997 for her supporting role as the nurse in *The English Patient*. The daughter of an actress and a sculptor, her career as an actress began in the mid-80s in her native land with movies such as Jean-Luc Godard's *Hail Mary* (*Je vous salue, Marie*, 1983) and Léos Carax's *Bad Blood* (*Mauvais Sang*, 1986). She and Carax were partners for many years until their relationship broke up during the filming of *The Lovers on the Bridge*. Her roles in Philip Kaufman's film of Kundera's novel *The Unbearable Lightness of Being* (1987), Louis Malle's *Damage* (1992) and Krysztof Kieslowski's *Three Colours: Blue* (*Trois Couleurs: Bleu*, 1993) won her an international reputation as the archetypal French actress. She has recently consolidated her position at the forefront of European cinema with roles in Michael Haneke's cool, distanced *Code Unknown* (*Code: Inconnu*, 1999) and in Lasse Hallström's sugary romance about confectionery, *Chocolat* (2000).

THE COMMITMENTS

1991 - IRELAND / GREAT BRITAIN - 117 MIN. - MUSIC FILM, COMEDY

DIRECTOR ALAN PARKER (*1944)
SCREENPLAY DICK CLEMENT, IAN LA FRENAIS, RODDY DOYLE, based on the novel *DUBLIN BEAT* by RODDY DOYLE
DIRECTOR OF PHOTOGRAPHY GALE TATTERSALL **MUSIC** PAUL BUSHNELL, VARIOUS SOUL SONGS **PRODUCTION** ROGER RANDALL-CUTLER,
LYNDA MYLES for BEACON COMMUNICATIONS.

STARRING ROBERT ARKINS (Jimmy Rabbitte), ANDREW STRONG (Deco), MICHAEL AHERNE (Steve Clifford), ANGELINE BALL
(Imelda Quirke), MARIA DOYLE (Natalie Murphy), DAVE FINNEGAN (Mickah Wallace), BRONAGH GALLAGHER (Bernie
McGloughlin), FÉLIM GORMLEY (Dean Fay), GLEN HANSARD (Outspan Foster), DICK MASSEY (Billy Mooney), JOHNNY
MURPHY (Joey "The Lips" Fagan).

"The Irish are the Blacks of Europe"

Anyone who grows up in the Catholic north of Dublin has three possible ways of escaping the rubble-strewn wastelands and washing lines. He can be a good boxer, a good footballer or, best of all, play music like U2. This is what Derek and Ray hope to do, although they start out by giving their best renditions of popular favourites at family get-togethers. They are still calling themselves "And, And, And" when Jimmy Rabbitte (Robert Arkins) offers to be their manager. Jimmy has narrow sideburns and knows all about music. He always has the latest records, but most of all, he is a man on a mission: to found the best Soul band that Ireland has ever seen. Musicians are recruited through a small ad which reads "Have you got soul? If so, the hardest grafting band in the world is waiting for you!"

The next day, half of Dublin is lined up outside Jimmy's parents' kitchen and an endless parade of hopefuls show off their talents with the bagpipes, tin whistle and banjo. The Commitments start to take shape, from the 16-year-old bus conductor Deco (Andrew Strong) with his Joe Cocker voice to Joey "The Lips" (Johnny Murphy), the trumpeter, who assures then that God has sent him to come to their aid. When that doesn't work he swears that he once played with Wilson Pickett. After a few weeks of rehearsals, The Commitments bring miserable community halls to their feet and the commercial breakthrough is not long in coming, and Jimmy founds his own record agency.

Alan Parker's *The Commitments* continues the rags-to-riches theme of his earlier movie *Fame* (1979). Both films are based on the "a star is born" ideology. Despite their slum backgrounds, his characters show remarkable wit and intelligence, and considering that they are a group of amateurs at the beginning of the movie, they develop a professional sound with admirable speed. Their musical success is guaranteed by cover versions of Soul classics like "When a Man Loves a Woman" and "Respect". Two years later Parker's fellow countryman Stephen Frears produced another Irish version of the same recipe for success. His portrayal of Dublin's working classes in *The Snapper* was also based on another novel by Irish writer Roddy Doyle, whose book *Dublin Beat* was the model for *The Commitments*.

Parker doesn't stint on sit-com elements and entertaining details. Jimmy, the manager's father, has a picture of the Pope hanging in his kitchen to show his loyalty to the Catholic Church, but as he is also an Elvis fan, there has to be a picture of Elvis as well. And as Elvis is God, not just his representative, Elvis hangs over the Pope. In one key scene in the film, The Commitments wait for Wilson Pickett who has promised to come to one of their concerts. Jimmy has spread the word and so the local press are out in full force. They wait in vain and Jimmy is accused of being a con man. After the premiere of *The Commitments* in Los Angeles, Wilson Pickett himself really did appear on stage. Cinema lives from such stories.   RV

1   A white Prince of Soul surrounded by swinging
    sides of pork – an Irish dream of freedom through
    music.

2   The Commitments' backing singers at their
    first gig in a Roman Catholic community centre:
    "Heroin(e) kills" can just be read in the back-
    groundprint.

3   The sax and trumpet are called Gina (Lollobrigida)
    and Kim (Basinger); when they are played, the
    result is the coolest working rhythm in the world.

4   Deco (Andrew Strong), the heavyweight lead
    singer, hogs the limelight, but when he's pounding
    out Wilson Pickett's "Mustang Sally", Soul reaches
    the Irish working class.

"Alan Parker's *The Commitments* is a loud, rollicking, comic extravaganza." *Chicago Sun-Times*

MUSIC MOVIES	Two new genres telling tales of life in the big city were established with the arrival of the talkies: The gangster film (*Little Caesar*, 1931) and the musical. There is a key difference between film music that accompanies the plot of a movie and a musical per se: film music is a second kind of cinematic language whose score programmatically follows the action of the movie, whereas musicals create their own reality, interweaving dreams and reality and setting aside the conventions and rules of everyday life.
	In the 1980s musicals returned to the beginnings of the genre. Alan Parker's *Fame* (1979) and Richard Attenborough's *A Chorus Line* (1985) renewed the classic backstage music film in modern settings. Unusual, daring and risky combinations of music, dialogue and plot characterised the 90s, like Alain Resnais' *On connaît la chanson* (*The Same Old Song*, 1997) and Lars von Trier's *Dancer in the Dark* (2000).

BASIC INSTINCT

1992 - USA - 127 MIN. - EROTIC THRILLER

DIRECTOR PAUL VERHOEVEN (*1938)
SCREENPLAY JOE ESZTERHAS DIRECTOR OF PHOTOGRAPHY JAN DE BONT MUSIC JERRY GOLDSMITH PRODUCTION MARIO KASSAR
for CAROLCO, LE STUDIO CANAL+.

STARRING MICHAEL DOUGLAS (Detective Nick Curran), SHARON STONE (Catherine Tramell), JEANNE TRIPPLEHORN
(Dr Beth Gardner), GEORGE DZUNDZA (Gus), DENIS ARNDT (Lt. Walker), LEILANI SARELLE (Roxy), BRUCE A. YOUNG
(Andrews), CHELCIE ROSS (Captain Talcott), DOROTHY MALONE (Hazel Dobkins), WAYNE KNIGHT (John Correli).

"She's the fuck of the century."

Sweaty bodies, rough sex, an ice-axe and lots of blood – from the opening shot of the movie, Paul Verhoeven makes it clear what the audience should expect for the next two hours. The director's third film appeals to our animal nature, although it's unclear whether the 'basic instinct' of the title is a reference to hunting or the reproductive instinct. The story unfolds in a totally macho world where there is no place for weakness. Unfortunately, the hero, disillusioned cop Nick Curran (Michael Douglas), is powerless to resist temptation of any kind. Hot-tempered and partial to provocative women, he's also burdened with a past he would rather forget: ever since killing two innocent bystanders as part of a raid, he has struggled with an alcohol problem and had to endure the jibes of his colleagues. Douglas plays the role with his jaw clenched, but behind the foul temper and tough exterior lies a deeply insecure

character whose private and professional life are constantly on the verge of breakdown, He comes across as thoroughly unlikeable, but Curran's weaknesses make him into a character with whom the audience can sympathise.

Despite his personal problems, he's given the job of investigating the murder shown so memorably at the beginning of the movie. The trail of clues leads him to Catherine Tramell (Sharon Stone), a crime writer who is as sexy as she is mysterious, who seems to have already anticipated the brutal act in one of her books. Could she have turned her evil imagination into reality? That solution is a little too obvious even for the police department. No one could be so stupid as to advertise a murder they were planning in a book in advance. Unless of course that is exactly what the murderer wanted the detectives to think.

1 Is she or isn't she? The public were more interested in whether or not Sharon Stone was wearing panties in this scene than they were in working out the whodunnit.

2 Detective Nick Curran (Michael Douglas) does battle with alcohol, nicotine and sharp-tongued women writers.

3 Why would a woman who has everything commit such a senseless murder?

4 Intelligent, beautiful and – lethal? Catherine Tramell (Sharon Stone) is always a few steps ahead of the investigators.

2

3

"The film is like a crossword puzzle. It keeps your interest until you solve it. Then it's just a worthless scrap with the spaces filled in." *Chicago Sun-Times*

Catherine Tramell certainly seems to be capable of such a calculating trick. Breathtakingly seductive, uncompromising in her search for sexual satisfaction and rolling in money, she is a monstrous combination of male wish-fulfilment and castration anxiety: a sex-hungry feminist and man-murdering vamp, intellectually far superior to the men who surround her.

The fearless detectives are helpless in the face of their provocative prime suspect. When they take her in for questioning at the police station, in what is undoubtedly the film's most famous moment and one of the main reasons for its success, she totally confuses them by crossing her legs and letting her skirt ride right up. The pressing question as to whether Catherine murdered her partner during sex is effectively overshadowed by the even more pressing one as to whether Stone was wearing panties during this

scene. Debate raged in the press, and there were even claims that during the love scenes, viewers were witnessing unsimulated sex. Such bizarre slippage of the boundaries between cinema and reality, between actual events and their interpretations is typical of Verhoeven's movies and ultimately part of their attraction.

Appropriately, given this double game with reality, there is also a female psychologist in *Basic Instinct*, in what seems to be the last straw for the beleaguered male characters. Dr Beth Gardner (Jeanne Tripplehorn) plays a large part in the undoing of Curran. Her job is to test his psychological fitness for active police service, but he becomes hopelessly entwined in a labyrinth of sex, lies and psycho trickery when he tries to use sexual humiliation to get his own back for this professional degradation. Eventually the

inevitable happens and Curran succumbs to the charms of the prime sus- pect. Needless to say this does him no good whatsoever either as far as his resolve to give up smoking and drinking is concerned, or in his professional judgement. It is also highly dangerous, and to the very end the audience is kept guessing which trap the hero will finally fall into.

Sharon Stone's striking presence as woman and as actress makes Joe Eszterhas' plot seem more complex to the viewer than it actually is. Verhoeven's strength – as his first two Hollywood films *Robocop* (1987) and *Total Recall* (1990) show – lies in the calculated exaggeration of stereotypes – men crash through his films as city cops steaming with an excess of testosterone. They swill whisky, slap each other on the back and always have a pithy remark on their lips. His women are the complete opposite: unfathomable, and, when there is no 'real' man to be had, lesbians. They

invariably spell disaster for the men. Verhoeven's characters are artificial fig- ures that fall apart when confronted with the complexity of reality, precisely because they are nothing but clichés. They are either figures to identify with, helpless prey of their own appetites like Curran, or they are victims like Curran's dumb colleague Gus (George Dzundza). Gus spends the whole film shooting his mouth off before he is forced to a direct, physical realisation that reality is much more complicated than he imagined. Verhoeven plays the double game even further, and behind the cool superficiality of his cinemat- ic world there are always threatening depths. In a world of sex and violence, voyeurism becomes the most genuine form of perception, but at the same time – as in the scene at the police headquarters – the pleasure of seeing is revealed to be a complex trap. Verhoeven's movies are reflections on film- making. They do not just portray pleasurable illusions, but are themselves

"In Hollywood it's all down to nerve, not originality." *epd Film*

5 Nick Curran has more than the current case on his mind – he's a man preoccupied by his past.

6 Weak in the face of temptation of any kind. Catherine Tramell turns Detective Curran's head.

7 An ice pick is a useful implement if you like drink- ing cocktails. But it has other uses too.

8 After his fall from grace, Curran is hard-pushed to keep a cool head.

lusion as films. Verhoeven ensures that this self-reflexive level doesn't get lost in all the sex and violence by peppering his movies with allusions and quotations from the entire history of cinema. In *Basic Instinct*, for instance, Michael Douglas' role can be taken as an ironic commentary on the prototype of the good cop he played in younger years in *The Streets of San Francisco*.

Above all, Verhoeven quotes from Alfred Hitchcock's movies, so much so that *Basic Instinct* is almost a homage to the great director, with long drives along coastal roads, dialogues inside cars interspersed with meaningful glances in the rear-view mirror – these all nice touches taken from the master. Hitch is also present in the Freudian motives and explanations that give the film an unexpected comic aspect – above all in the home-baked, slap-dash psychology of Dr Beth Gardener, a cardboard cut-out psychologist

if ever there was one. Verhoeven is not however the kind of director to create such an effect unintentionally.

Besides all that, he shows his mastery of the art of suspense. The audience may feel that they are a couple of steps ahead of the hero all the time, but the real danger is always unpredictable.

Some critics saw *Basic Instinct* as a mere glorification of sex and violence, but that fails to do it justice. Verhoeven and Eszterhas clearly intended to do much more than that: Catherine Tramell is presented as a highly intelligent woman who would be unlikely to describe in her books crimes she intended to commit. If the makers of *Basic Instinct* had really only been interested in serving their animal natures, they would have used their craftsmanship and knowledge of film history to conceal it far more skilfully. Unless of course, that was what they wanted film critics to think … Sh

PAUL VERHOEVEN Born in Amsterdam in 1938, Verhoeven first indulged his liking for explicit scenes of sex and violence in Dutch movies like *Keetje Tippel* (1974/75) and *De vierde man* (1983). His first international production, *Flesh and Blood* (1985), which was set in the Middle Ages, continued the trend. Verhoeven then made his name in Hollywood with the Science Fiction spectaculars *Robocop* (1987) and *Total Recall* (1990). In both movies, he uses action cinema stereotypes to reflect on the voyeurism of the film industry and its inherent imbalance of illusion and reality. Reactions to his erotic thrillers *Basic Instinct* (1992) and *Show Girls* (1995) were typical: the first was a great box-office success, but unleashed a wave of enraged protest from the homosexual community, while the second was a flop derided by the critics which went on to become a cult film for the gay scene. The futuristic *Starship Troopers* (1996), based on a Robert Heinlein novel, was a grim parody of totalitarianism.

UNFORGIVEN

1992 - USA - 130 MIN. - WESTERN

DIRECTOR CLINT EASTWOOD (*1930)
SCREENPLAY DAVID WEBB PEOPLES DIRECTOR OF PHOTOGRAPHY JACK N. GREEN MUSIC LENNIE NIEHAUS PRODUCTION CLINT EASTWOOD for MALPASO.

STARRING CLINT EASTWOOD (Bill Munny), GENE HACKMAN (Little Bill Daggett), MORGAN FREEMAN (Ned Logan), RICHARD HARRIS (English Bob), JAIMZ WOOLVETT (Schofield Kid), SAUL RUBINEK (W. W. Beauchamp), FRANCES FISHER (Strawberry Alice), ANNA THOMPSON (Delilah Fitzgerald), DAVID MUCCI (Quick Mike), ROB CAMPBELL (Davey Bunting).

ACADEMY AWARDS 1993 OSCARS for BEST PICTURE, BEST DIRECTOR (Clint Eastwood), BEST FILM EDITING (Joel Cox) and BEST SUPPORTING ACTOR (Gene Hackman).

"Is it true, Pa used to shoot people?"

The story begins with the ultimate affront in a male-dominated society: a young horse-trader goes to town with a friend looking for a good time, but when he drops his trousers in front of prostitute Strawberry Alice (Frances Fisher) she bursts out laughing. tragic consequences follow. The humiliated man slashes Strawberry Alice's face with a knife, robbing her of her good looks, which are all she has. As far as Little Bill Daggett (Gene Hackman), the tyrannical sheriff of Big Whiskey is concerned, the only injured party is the owner of the brothel. The cowboys have to pay him horses in compensation and the disfigured whore comes away empty-handed. But the girls she works with are not prepared to leave it at that, and they scrape together their savings to put a prize on the head of the cowboys.

News of the whores' plot reaches former gunslinger-turned-farmer Bill Munny (Clint Eastwood) at exactly the right, or rather, exactly the wrong moment. His pigs are dying in scores from an epidemic, and the widowed father of two children, now a convert to pacifism and godliness, can see no way out other than taking up the immoral offer.

Despite the fact that he can no longer hold his hand nor his horse steady, he sets off to Big Whiskey together with his old friends Ned Logan (Morgan Freeman) and the almost blind would-be gunman Schofield Kid (Jaimz Woolvett). Little Bill is waiting for them, determined to make an example of every bounty hunter who turns up.

The first man to suffer is English Bob (Richard Harris), who is also attracted by the money offered by the whores. Little Bill crushes him physically, before humiliating him and exposing him as a fraud.

Meanwhile, Munny and his accomplices begin their sorry work. Munny has never shot anyone sober but he soon realises that death is a wretched business that has nothing to do with heroism. Schofield Kid is forced to the same conclusion after shooting his unarmed victim on the lavatory. Horrified

"A moral film which comes over as an allegory of the increasingly violent world in today's large American cities."

film-dienst

by his own deed, he drowns himself and we begin to realise why Munny had to drown his past in alcohol.

In *Unforgiven*, the time of the great Western heroes is long gone. The sagas of fearless settlers and liberty-loving outlaws glorifying American history appear instead as a collective illusion, covering up a seemingly endless spiral of murder and slaughter. There is no forgiveness in this world: when the two cowboys offer Strawberry Alice a pony as compensation out of court, they are pelted with horse dung by the outraged whores.

If institutionalised violence in the shape of the sheriff is a mere tool in the machinations of the powerful, killing in the name of justice is also nothing but a farce. Munny and his friends magnify Strawberry Alice's mutilation in their imagination until they have convinced themselves that her injuries are appalling enough to justify their return to their ways of old.

"Is it true, Pa used to shoot people?", asks Munny's youngest daughter. The truth is he can hardly remember himself. All he knows of his past

identity comes from the tales that others tell, and so he has become a legend even to himself. His return to action – and this is the movie's real adventure – is a journey into his own past.

A freak show of lost souls

Eastwood bought the screenplay for *Unforgiven* in the early 1980s but let it lie so he could "grow into the role". The movie was originally to have been directed by Francis Ford Coppola. It is the quintessence of Eastwood's previous Westerns and at the same time a swan song for the part of the solitary avenger he played so often; he dedicated the movie to the directors who 'spotted' him, Sergio Leone and Don Siegel. Although he has been accused – by critics like Pauline Kael for example – of reactionary views and of excusing rough justice, in *Unforgiven* he tells a sad tale of the senselessness

4

1 A man at the end of the road: Bill Munny (Clint Eastwood) sets off on a journey into his past and has to drown the memories of his own misdeeds in booze.

2 A powerful misanthrope: Sheriff Little Bill Daggett (Gene Hackman) has built himself his own little realm of terror.

3 The Big Whiskey whores are up in arms, demanding vengeance for the mutilation of one of the girls.

4 Old partners. Bill Munny and Ned Logan (Morgan Freeman) on their way to Big Whiskey. Once they sowed fear and terror in their path, now they are shadows of their former selves.

5 His wife reformed Bill Munny's ways. But after her death, illness, poverty and an immoral proposition force the gunslinger-turned-pig-farmer to reach for his gun once again.

of violence and of the existential and moral desperation of individuals. The casts of what Georg Seesslen termed 'phantom westerns' like *High Plains Drifter* (1972) or *Pale Rider* (1985) – the solitary avenger, the cowardly small town citizens, the corrupt town mayor – all come together here in a freak show of lost souls whose last resort for survival is cynicism. At times like these there is nothing left worth fighting for. All the protagonists seem to have reached their final destination and even the whores' revenge will not change their fate. Men like Little Bill are incapable of laying the solid foundations necessary for a home, and not meant for a settled existence. The movie's tragic irony is that the characters who have found their place in life set off once again to repeat the mistakes of their past. They got away with their lives the first time round, but the relapse is unforgivable, and this unholy crusade ends fatally for Munny's accomplices.

The boundless desolation of the movie is reflected in its scenery. The endless expanse of the American West is no longer a grandiose setting for

adventure, but is transformed instead into a barren wasteland, a never-ending desert of stones and dust whose limitlessness implies the pain of homelessness and desertion rather than a sense of freedom. Even the prairie has become a melancholy reminder of a time that maybe never even existed. Those who embroider their own legend, like English Bob, end up even more ridiculous than the rest.

The famous feats of the 'Duke of Death' are shown to be the embarrassing appearances of a ham actor. English Bob is shadowed by a writer called Beauchamp (Saul Rubinek), whose aim is to conserve the memory of a supposedly heroic epoch, but his efforts are as hopeless as the sheriff's attempts to patch his leaky roof. "Maybe you should hang the carpenter", a hapless visitor suggests as the master of the house tries in vain to catch the drips in pails and bowls. A remark like that might have cost him his life in the 'good old days', as a grim look from Little Bill tells us: now it almost passes unnoticed.

"I thought it was about time there was a film showing that violence not only causes pain, but is also not without consequences for the perpetrators as well as the victims."

Clint Eastwood in: film-dienst

THE ANTI-HERO   Whenever and wherever the hero suffers an identity crisis, the hour of the anti-hero has struck. This was how spaghetti Westerns reacted to the Wild West clichés propagated by Hollywood in the 70s, for example, when the anti-hero appeared on the scene as an assault on stagnant genre conventions. As anti-heroes don't need moral justification, they can help break up stereotyped story-telling mechanisms, as in Quentin Tarantino's *Pulp Fiction* (1994). This also explains why anti-hero figures are often used when formal innovation is a director's first priority, as in Oliver Stone's *Natural Born Killers* (1994).

---

6   Unforgiven: Ned Logan has walked into the brutal sheriff's trap.

7   An ill-matched trio: the almost blind Schofield Kid (Jaimz Woolvett) joins forces with his heroes and has to learn the meaning of killing someone.

8   Bill Munny says goodbye to his children.

9   A startling finale: contrary to the conventions of the genre, the showdown is no storm that clears the air, and the hero is denied salvation.

The dime novel writer Beauchamp is Eastwood's merciless portrait of everyone who propagates the myth of the Wild West. Beauchamp panders to criminals' vanity by shrouding their deeds in mystery and praise, but literally wets himself at the first sign of real violence. In settling the score with the myth itself, *Unforgiven* also settles with all those who helped to create it. This extends of course to naturally the actor/director Eastwood himself, who has the self-same legends and clichés to thank for his fame and has often embodied and glorified them on the silver screen. Eastwood does not allow himself a nostalgic look back, however, and his most famous role of solitary avenger has lost all its moral justification in *Unforgiven*.

In the end, the movie's deconstruction of old-style heroes amounts to a thorough de-glorification of violence and its perpetrators. In classic Westerns the final show-down is like a storm which clears the air and allows justice to emerge triumphant. The finale of *Unforgiven*, by contrast, brings no salvation, and Munny is forced to realise that his past has caught up with him. He returns home victorious and yet defeated: a hero who has lost his mask, and one who is even denied a hero's death at the end.

SH

TWIN PEAKS: FIRE WALK WITH ME

1992 - USA - 134 MIN. - MYSTERY DRAMA

DIRECTOR DAVID LYNCH (*1946)
SCREENPLAY DAVID LYNCH, ROBERT ENGELS DIRECTOR OF PHOTOGRAPHY RON GARCIA MUSIC ANGELO BADALAMENTI
PRODUCTION GREGG FIENBERG for LYNCH-FROST PRODUCTIONS, CIBY PICTURES.

STARRING SHERYL LEE (Laura Palmer), RAY WISE (Leland Palmer), KYLE MACLACHLAN (Dale Cooper),
MOIRA KELLY (Donna Hayward), CHRIS ISAAK (Chester Desmond), DANA ASHBROOK (Bobby Briggs),
KIEFER SUTHERLAND (Sam Stanley), DAVID BOWIE (Phillip Jeffries), HARRY DEAN STANTON (Carl Rodd),
PEGGY LIPTON (Norma Jennings).

"A freaky accident."

When Laura Palmer is murdered in Portland, Oregon, FBI Agent Chester Desmond (Chris Isaak) and his young colleague Sam Stanley (Kiefer Sutherland) are not sent to investigate. But the case (a young girl wrapped in a plastic tarpaulin found murdered on a riverbank) bears a clear resemblance to the murder which happens months later in the small town of Twin Peaks. In the course of the investigation Agent Desmond disappears without trace and Agent Dale Cooper (Kyle MacLachlan) is sent to replace him. Several inauspicious signs, including a letter of the alphabet found under a fingernail of the victim, convince Dale Cooper that the murderer will strike again. But who knows where and when …

The film of the television series begins appropriately with an imploding television set, followed by the famous place name sign from the series' opening credits and Angelo Badalamenti's atmospheric film music – we're back in Twin Peaks alright. Laura Palmer is still alive, and what we see are her last days, in the hope of finding out what the series left unclear.

Lynch claimed that his main reason for developing the TV series *Twin Peaks* (1990–1991) into a lengthy feature film was the feeling that he had

not yet finished with the material. The series' creators, David Lynch and Mark Frost, had originally hoped that the crime story of *Twin Peaks* would gradually fade into the background and eventually become completely unimportant. The unexpected success of the series meant that they were eventually forced to present their audiences and producers with a murderer. As Lynch had warned, viewer numbers then fell and he ended up suffering for a mistake that was not his own.

However the bizarre, imaginary world of Twin Peaks and the inconsistencies of its main characters continued to haunt Lynch, and before long he began work on the movie *Twin Peaks: Fire Walk With Me*. Accusations that he was trying to cash in on the success of the TV series are unfair. The movie brings together some of the plot strands which had been lost in the increasingly complex weave of the story. The incest theme, which only emerged slowly in the series, is one of the main elements in this process, and Lynch was also able to give more space to the sexual aspects of the story in general, as he no longer had to worry about TV regulations in the many countries where *Twin Peaks* was broadcast. Numerous hints and questions left

open in the series are explained, and in the movie Lynch does his characters more justice by working on their psychic conflicts and making them more convincing. As obscure hints and contradictions were the lifeblood of the series, clarifying matters in the movie was a risk. In the final edit, a number of scenes were omitted, some off-beat marginal figures were cut to fit the material to film length and a more clearly defined plot framework was provided. Many ironic allusions fell by the wayside, and so for instance regular viewers of the TV series were disappointed to see that the frequent references to doughnuts and cherry pie had disappeared. Much of what was cut

were the elements that served to lighten the mood of the series, and so the movie turned out much darker than its TV model. The bizarre atmosphere of Twin Peaks and the threatening presence of the forest condense into a claustrophobic nightmare. Audiences unfamiliar with Lynch's earlier work are unsure how to react, but, the movie remains a monument to Lynch's single-mindedness and versatility. He did more than continue the series: he fitted his material to the demands of a different medium. The message makes uncomfortable viewing, but his treatment of it is clear.

SH

FILM AND TV   The wide distribution of video and DVD players means that movies are no longer viewed solely on the wide screen, but often at home on a television screen. The two different media and picture formats are therefore easily compared and discussed. Television's means of expression often influence movie making, as is the case for the aesthetic of the video clip and the quick editing techniques used by directors such as Oliver Stone (*Natural Born Killers*, 1994). Other directors like Britain's Peter Greenaway have experimented with new technical possibilities such as high definition TV (*Prospero's Books*, 1991). A further example is David Lynch's *Twin Peaks* (1990–91), a TV series which also complies to the more sophisticated requirements of cinematic art. Despite subsequent efforts to reconcile TV and cinema – for example Oliver Stone's three-part TV series *Wild Palms* (1993) – such ambitious projects remain the exception rather than the rule.

---

1   During his investigation, Agent Dale Cooper (Kyle MacLachlan) visits a bizarre dream world, where he is given puzzling tip-offs by a dwarf.

2   Beautiful but flawed: before her murder Laura Palmer (Sheryl Lee) did not lead the completely blameless life she would have had people believe.

3   *Twin Peaks: Fire Walk With Me* is a prequel to the TV series. The viewer is given insights into Laura Palmer's double life and in the end finds out who the real killer was.

4   There can't always be cherry cake: many ironic allusions fell victim to editorial cuts, including Dale Cooper's fondness for local specialities.

5   The cryptic dream symbolism has a clearer role to play in the much darker film version.

"People want to forget the world around them, but at the same time they're scared of it. Watching a film at home is much safer. There are worlds I'd rather not experience — but if I go to the cinema, I want to be right in the middle of the action." *David Lynch*

4

5

THE LAWNMOWER MAN

1992 - USA - 108 MIN. - SCIENCE FICTION, THRILLER

DIRECTOR BRETT LEONARD
SCREENPLAY GIMEL EVERETT, BRETT LEONARD, based on the story of the same name by STEPHEN KING
DIRECTOR OF PHOTOGRAPHY RUSSELL CARPENTER **MUSIC** DAN WYMAN **PRODUCTION** GIMEL EVERETT for ALLIED VISION, LANG PRINGLE.

STARRING PIERCE BROSNAN (Dr Lawrence Angelo), JEFF FAHEY (Jobe Smith), JENNY WRIGHT (Marnie Burke), JEREMY SLATE (Pater McKeen), AUSTIN O'BRIEN (Peter Parkette), MARK BRINGELSON (Sebastian Timms), ROSALEE MAYEUX (Carla Parkette), GEOFFREY LEWIS (Terry McKeen), JOHN LAUGHLIN (Jake Simpson), COLLEEN COFFEY (Caroline Angelo).

"I am a God here!"

From loser to ruler of the world: mentally retarded assistant gardener Jobe Smith (Jeff Fahey) discovers the blessings of modern technology – until his flight into virtual reality becomes a trip to hell.

Based on a short story by Steven King, *The Lawnmower Man* is a re-telling of the old tale of the sorcerer's apprentice who calls up spirits he cannot control. "Virtual Reality Specialist" Dr Lawrence Angelo (Pierce Brosnan) is conducting research into ways of increasing the intelligence of apes with the help of computer simulations until the government blunders in on his work. They aren't interested in intelligent primates, but they do want expendable fighting machines, so they start to manipulate his experiments until one day Angelo's ape runs amok and has to be killed. The research project seems doomed to failure.

By chance the scientist then happens upon Jobe, who leads a miserable existence exploited and abused by his foster father and the local min-

ister, and is a butt for the jokes and spite of his fellow men. Jobe is known as the Lawnmower Man not because he mows the doctor's lawns, but because he also has a talent for repairing machines of all kinds. He knows that a broken lawnmower doesn't just need mending, but that it also needs a few words of encouragement now and again. This innocent, naive relationship to machines foreshadows of Jobe's fate as a man-machine. Professor Angelo sees in Jobe a chance of saving his work. Attracted by colourful cyber trips and the professor's promise to make him more intelligent, Jobe becomes his apprentice.

In this movie computer games increase the intellect, and Jobe's trips into the world of bits and bytes turn him to an intelligent beast in a literal sense: but unbeknownst to the professor, the military still have an evil hand in the game. Jobe soon overtakes his master and throws to the wind his warnings that the human spirit should not be over-taxed – a

3

"A modern version of *Frankenstein*, which attempts to put across new visual experiences using computer graphics." *film-dienst*

principle which in the eyes of some critics the movie itself also failed to heed.

In no time at all, like everybody too clever for their own good, Jobe wants to rule the world. Disappointed with cyber sex and the limitations of the human race from which he has become completely alienated, he wants to be exalted as the immortal god of cyber space in the form of a world-wide network: the internet as global techno-divinity.

The makers of this movie were not primarily interested in either realism or a critique of technological progress. Their main concern was spec-

tacular video animation, so for example there is no explanation of how all the multicoloured 3D effects make Jobe into a super-brain. Critics loathed *The Lawnmower Man,* and had a field day tearing it to pieces. But at a time when only a small minority used the internet, words like cyber space and cyber sex had a far more mysterious ring to them than they do today, and the idea of being able to have sex without touching someone was particularly attractive in the face of AIDS. As an early example of the fascination with new digital production possibilities, *The Lawnmower Man* is thoroughly worth the journey to the land of computer dreams. SH

1   A brave new multi-coloured cyber-world? In the early 1990s *The Lawnmower Man* made a strong impression with vivid computer animation, warning of the dangerous temptations presented by technology.

2   The computer as weapon. Those who stood in the way of the Lawnmower Man were shot off into the void of cyber-space without further ado.

3   What began as a seemingly harmless computer game soon became deadly serious.

4   Between worlds. Soon nobody can tell what is real and what is simulated.

5   From gardener to superhero: as ruler of cyber-space, the Lawnmower Man Jobe Smith (Jeff Fahey) then turns his attentions to domination of the real world.

CYBER THRILLER   In the 1990s, computers were no longer simply tools used in the process of making movies, but featured more and more often as their subject matter too. The idea of fusing man and machine emerges as particularly fascinating, as in movies such as *The Lawnmower Man* (1992), *Johnny Mnemonic* (1995) or *Strange Days* (1996). Portrayals of how computers or the internet actually change particular aspects of everyday life don't come until later and remain exceptions (for example, *The Net*, 1995). *The Matrix* (1999) can be seen as a provisional climax of the computer theme: the decade ends with the idea that the whole world surrounding modern man is nothing but a vast computer animation.

THE PLAYER

1992 - USA - 117 MIN. - SATIRE, THRILLER, LITERATURE ADAPTATION

DIRECTOR ROBERT ALTMAN (*1925)
SCREENPLAY MICHAEL TOLKIN, based on his novel of the same name DIRECTOR OF PHOTOGRAPHY JEAN LEPINE MUSIC THOMAS NEWMAN
PRODUCTION DAVID BROWN, MICHAEL TOLKIN, NICK WECHSLER for AVENUE PICTURES, SPELLING ENTERTAINMENT, DAVID BROWN-ADDIS WECHSLER PRODUCTIONS.

STARRING TIM ROBBINS (Griffin Mill), GRETA SCACCHI (June Gudmundsdottir), FRED WARD (Walter Stuckel), WHOOPI GOLDBERG (Detective Susan Avery), DEAN STOCKWELL (Andy Civella), PETER GALLAGHER (Larry Levy), VINCENT D'ONOFRIO (David Kahane), DINA MERRILL (Celia Beck), SYDNEY POLLACK (Dick Mellen), RICHARD E. GRANT (Tom Oakley).

IFF CANNES 1992 BEST DIRECTOR (Robert Altman), BEST ACTOR (Tim Robbins).

"No stars!"

"I hate your guts, asshole!" Griffin Mill (Tim Robbins), executive at a big Hollywood studio, is not exactly popular. He's known this for a long time, and he doesn't need the anonymous death threat he gets at the end of the eight-minute opening sequence of *The Player* to spell it out for him. In a single take, a reference to Orson Welles' *Touch of Evil*, director Robert Altman introduces twenty characters and outlines what his movie is all about: the every-day madness of Hollywood studio life. In the faceless machinery of Hollywood, there is no place for personal preferences or artistic ambition – although that thesis is flatly contradicted by Altman's extraordinarily mannerist opening.

However, as long as people like Griffin Mill have a say in whether an idea becomes a movie or not, the only things that matters are internal power games and perhaps, at a pinch, box-office success. Mill is an obstacle which screenplay writers have to surmount on their way to fame. It's his job to get rid of the authors of "witty yet touching political thriller romances" or "High-School Graduation, Part 2", and no-one does it as cold-bloodedly as, smooth career-man Mill. His own life is like a farcical movie: "I guess they must breed guys like him some place", says Burt Reynolds (in the role of Burt Reynolds) at one point in the second half of the film. People like Mill have no friends. They only have contacts and victims.

The anonymous letter seems to point – unsurprisingly – to a disgruntled writer who hates Mill. Mill goes to find him to offer him a "deal", but this time it is the offended and somewhat drunken writer who gives the studio parasite the brush-off ("What would you do if you were out of a job? I can write at least, but what can you do?") In the heat of the moment, Mill kills him, only to discover the next day that he has murdered the wrong man. "Surprise" says the fax. Mill then realises that there were witnesses to his crime.

Although not unduly troubled by the fact that he has killed a man, the murder is the beginning of a downward turn in Mill's life, and things get worse by the minute. Intrigues brew behind his back and suddenly even his own plotting and planning threatens to blow up in his face. The slide continues until finally his whole career is at stake, by which point it is clear to the movie's audience that the end of his career would be the end of him. To make matters worse, cynical police inspector Susan Avery (Whoopi Goldberg) is on his case.

The Player does more than question the divide between screenplay and reality where its main character is concerned. Altman plays a sophisticated game; he does not even present himself from the outside as an uninvolved bystander, but as a worker in the dream-factory from which there is no ultimate escape.

"This film uses Hollywood as a metaphor for our society. It shows greed and corruption, and these are not exclusive to the film industry."

Robert Altman in: Der Spiegel

5

"No stars!" is the demand of a young screenplay writer naive enough to want to make a realistic film. But when Bruce Willis rescues Julia Roberts from the electric chair at the end, he's the one who applauds the loudest.

Increasingly, Griffin Mill's life seems to follow the sort of trajectory to be found in one of the screenplays he rejects in their dozens every day. In the bizarre parallel universe of Hollywood, no one cares whether life imitates art or art life. Seeing movie stars on the street is an everyday occurrence. Around fifty well-known Hollywood greats, including actors, many directors,

writers and studio people appear in *The Player* in small cameo roles, but in a setting like that, the only people who stand out are the ones who aren't famous.

It's only logical that the studio bosses in *The Player* eventually have the bright idea of saving money by getting rid of screenwriters altogether. After all, movies only quote from each other, and real life provides the best stories, as the wonderfully ironic, double bind at the happy end of *The Player* shows.

SH

1   The usual suspects? Producer Griffin Mill (Tim Robbins, no. 5) gets into trouble not only with crazy screenplay writers and the authors of anonymous threatening letters, but also ultimately with the police.

2   Inside Hollywood's High Society, Griffin Mill has forgotten that there's another world out there.

3   "No stars!" Rarely has there been such an array of famous names in a movie. Even Bruce Willis and Julia Roberts got a chance to mimic themselves in *The Player*.

4   A relationship seems to be in the offing between the murdered writer's partner, mysterious Icelander June Gudmundsdottir (Greta Scacchi), and Griffin Mill.

5   Walter Stuckel (Fred Ward) philosophises at great length about classic and contemporary cinema.

A FEW GOOD MEN

1992 - USA - 138 MIN. - THRILLER, COURTROOM DRAMA

DIRECTOR ROB REINER (*1945)
SCREENPLAY AARON SORKIN, based on his play of the same name **DIRECTOR OF PHOTOGRAPHY** ROBERT RICHARDSON
MUSIC MARC SHAIMAN **PRODUCTION** DAVID BROWN, ROB REINER, ANDREW SCHEINMAN for COLUMBIA PICTURES,
CASTLE ROCK ENTERTAINMENT.

STARRING TOM CRUISE (Lt. J. G. Daniel Kaffee), JACK NICHOLSON (Col. Nathan R. Jessup), DEMI MOORE
(Lt. Comm. JoAnne Galloway), KEVIN BACON (Capt. Jack Ross), KIEFER SUTHERLAND (Lt. Jonathan Kendrick),
KEVIN POLLAK (Lt. Sam Weinberg), JAMES MARSHALL (Priv. Louden Downey), J. T. WALSH (Lt. Col. Matthew Andrew
Markinson), CHRISTOPHER GUEST (Comm. Doctor Stone), J. A. PRESTON (Judge Col. Julius Alexander Randolph).

"We're supposed to fight for people who couldn't."

Lieutenant J. G. Daniel Kaffee (Tom Cruise) is a defence attorney with the American army. His speciality is settling cases with the public prosecutor out of court to avoid them ever having to come to trial. For him, law is not a matter of justice, but of pragmatism; he only has a cynical smile to spare for moral issues. This is also all Lieutenant Comm. Galloway (Demi Moore) gets from him when she is assigned to work on a case with Kaffee: at Guantanamo Bay, an American base in Cuba, two members of an elite troop of marines have bound, gagged and beaten a comrade. He dies as a result of the attack and those responsible stand accused of murder. It soon becomes clear that the victim suffered from poor health and had asked for transfer to another base. Galloway suspects that a Code Red was behind the attack, a disciplinary measure carried out by the marines themselves. At first, the accused stand together against Kaffee's efforts as defense attorney. He wants to get them the mildest possible sentence on the condition that they admit their guilt. The two marines admit to the deed, but claim that they acted on orders. Although they risk the heaviest penalty, it is a matter of honour for them to bring the truth to light. Initially, smart Kaffee cannot understand this attitude at all, but the two marines are supported by their other attorney Galloway, who also begins to influence her partner Kaffee.

Rob Reiner's movie addresses the fundamental dilemma of the justice system within the military: does an order free a soldier from personal responsibility? In the course of the investigations, the young attorney is gradually forced to ask himself such questions. The son of a famous lawyer, he has always stood in his father's shadow, and now he has to reconsider his strategy of trying to keep cases out of court: in court it is at least possible to lose. When he finally takes on the challenge of a trial, it is partly because he wants finally to be worthy of his dead father.

His opponent is Colonel Jessup, the commander of the marine base, played by Jack Nicholson with the arrogance of someone who believes himself to be morally irreproachable. Kaffee is only able to live his carefree yuppie existence because he, Jessup, looks after things down in Cuba with his boys. He feels quite safe from this inexperienced upstart, who in his eyes has no right to be in the army anyway. When all's said and done, his orders and his daily struggle with the enemy uphold national security – who cares if they are legal are not. Kaffee discovers Jessup's weak point – his self-satisfaction.

The investigations are difficult and full of unexpected turns, they prepare the young lawyer for the final test, the trial. The two accused marines come to understand that even within the chain of military command, moral

"A dramatically and technically gripping courtroom thriller, which passes harsh judgement on the army and rigorously resists action for its own sake."

film.de

1 Col. Nathan R. Jessup (Jack Nicholson), arrogant, powerful and narrow-minded.

2 Lt. J. G. Daniel Kaffee (Tom Cruise): a photo fit for a job application.

3 Jessup is the victim of his own arrogance. Titles and military decorations count for nothing in the courtroom, where reason free of prejudice triumphs.

4 Lt. Commander Galloway (Demi Moore) finds it hard to persuade the jury. Rob Reiner gives us a series of penetrating portrait shots.

responsibility still has to lie with he who acts. Only the seemingly all-powerful Colonel Jessup remains unaltered and eventually gets his just deserts. At their best, courtroom movies are show cases for the leading actors. Both Tom Cruise and Jack Nicholson throw themselves into the verbal battle with all guns blazing and the result is real movie-star cinema. The film as a whole

also gains by resisting the temptation to involve Tom Cruise and Demi Moore in a love story following their initial disagreements about legal theories and defence strategies. Even if the moralistic undertone is unmistakable at the end of the film, *A Few Good Men* remains a straightforward and exciting courtroom thriller.

"Reiner falls back on a tried and tested formula and creates first rate cinema." *epd Film*

| 5 | Nice people must play baseball, at least they have to if they are American. | 6 | The army is a man's world. JoAnne Galloway's outfit during a conversation after work is evidence of this. | 7 | She's in uniform and is carrying out her duty; he's wearing casual clothes and has given up the case up for lost. Hardly a basis for good communication. |

TOM CRUISE Born in 1962 in Syracuse (New York), Thomas Cruise Mapother IV has always been considered a successful actor. However, it was only after the respect he won with his work on Stanley Kubrick's marital drama *Eyes Wide Shut* (1999) that his earlier roles were reappraised. In *Rain Man* (1988) he took on the thankless task of playing an objectionable yuppie alongside Dustin Hoffman's Oscar-winning performance of the autistic brother – a role not calculated to endear him to the public, but Cruise took it anyway. Previously often seen purely as action star or sex object – for example in *Top Gun* (1986) or *Mission: Impossible* (1996) – his courage in accepting unpopular roles is only just beginning to be appreciated (*The Color of Money*, 1986; *Jerry Maguire*, 1996; *Magnolia*, 1999). Playing smarmy, career-obsessed characters seldom makes an actor popular in the press, but sooner or later the critics realise what great acting talent lies behind the macho roles.

ARIZONA DREAM

1992/1993 - FRANCE - 142 MIN. - COMEDY, TRAGICOMEDY

DIRECTOR EMIR KUSTURICA (*1955)

SCREENPLAY EMIR KUSTURICA, DAVID ATKINS **DIRECTOR OF PHOTOGRAPHY** VILKO FILAC **MUSIC** GORAN BREGOVIC **PRODUCTION** CLAUDIE OSSARD for CONSTELLATION, UGC, HACHETTE PREMIÈRE, CANAL+.

STARRING JOHNNY DEPP (Axel Blackmar), JERRY LEWIS (Leo Sweetie), FAYE DUNAWAY (Elaine Stalker), LILI TAYLOR (Grace Stalker) VINCENT GALLO (Paul Leger), PAULINA PORIZKOVA (Millie), CANDYCE MASON (Blanche), ALEXIA RANE (Angie), POLLY NOONAN (Betty), ANN SCHULMAN (Carla).

IFF BERLIN 1993 SILVER BEAR (SPECIAL JURY PRIZE).

"Wake up Columbus!"

Strange people have strange habits. Some take doors for a walk in the desert; others put dozens of wrecked cars on stilts and sweep sand under them. We are in the land of liberty and adventure, Arizona, USA. Axel (Johnny Depp), a 20-year-old Parsifal, runs away from this place of solitary obsessions to New York, where he counts fish for an obscure research project. His cousin Paul (Vincent Gallo) gets him drunk and takes him back home.

Axel is an orphan and was brought up by his Uncle Leo (Jerry Lewis), who is about to marry for the umpteenth time and would like Axel as his best man. The bride, who is as young as Axel, bursts into tears when she claps eyes on her future husband's nephew. Leo tries to get Axel to stay. He has made a fortune as a car salesman and wants Axel to work for him although his nephew is violently opposed to the idea.

Solitary obsessions again: Leo's father, who started up the car sales business, dreams of a ladder to heaven completely made up of cars. Leo dreams of big business and young women. Paul dreams of being a famous actor as he sits in the movie theatre and repeats all the lines of the films by heart while dogs pee on the screen.

One day, the stylish widow Elaine (Faye Dunaway) appears on the scene with her stepdaughter Grace (Lili Taylor). Axel instantly falls in love with Elaine. They have dinner, and he discovers Elaine's great passion: fly-ing. The couple are constantly disturbed by the moody daughter, who is lost in her own obsessions – accordion music, her love of tortoises and her hatred of her stepmother. Nevertheless, Axel decides to stay and allows himself to be carried away by a passionate affair and numerous breakneck attempts at flying. He has strange visions, but he is the only one who has no dreams and his naivety and innocent curiosity make him irresistible to the others. But day to day life with an egocentric woman gradually takes its toll, and Axel loses his naturalness and eventually falls in love with the neurotic daughter.

At a talent-spotting evening they go to together, Paul makes a fool of himself. To prove his acting talent, he chooses the scene from Alfred Hitchcock's *North by Northwest* (1959) where Cary Grant is strafed by a crop sprayer. As he doesn't have a plane at his disposal, he tries to reproduce the scene alone amidst the mocking laughter of the audience. Leo also breaks down: he takes an overdose of sleeping pills shortly before his wedding and Axel promises him in the ambulance that he will go back to New York.

They all celebrate Elaine's birthday together, giving her a flying machine that really works. In the meantime, the stepdaughter Grace has let her tortoises go and bent a lampshade into an antenna to kill herself with a lightning bolt during a violent storm: in Arizona, even death is a strangely

"The true greatness of American cinema is revealed in the panoramic shot, says Kusturica." *Der Spiegel*

comic affair. Axel often quotes his mother who used to wake him up every morning with the words: "Wake up, Columbus!" He thinks she meant to tell him that America has already been discovered.

All European directors who work in America seem to feel the need to dissect America's most sacred values and lay them bare to the bone. The Bosnian Emir Kusturica takes as his theme the promise anchored in the Declaration of Independence that all Americans are free to seek their happiness in the way they see fit. Visually, *Arizona Dream* is one of the most powerful movies of recent years. But portrays a grotesque world filled with unhappy people and we are not sure whether we should laugh or cry about the abyss that separates American reality and the American dream.

SL

4

JOHNNY DEPP

Born in 1963, Johnny Depp actually wanted to become a rock star, and managed to get as far as Iggy Pop's support band before landing an acting part in the TV series *21 Jump Street*. In 1990 he played the title role in Tim Burton's movie *Edward Scissorhands* and one of the most beautiful couples of the 90s was born: he and Wynona Rider appeared as vulnerable, droll and misunderstood. Johnny Depp had found his place outside mainstream cinema and he went on to play roles such as the Buster Keaton imitator in *Benny & Joon* (1992), *Don Juan de Marco* (1994), and drug-obsessed weapon fanatic Hunter C. Thompson in *Fear and Loathing in Las Vegas* (1998). Johnny Depp embodies like no one else the sensitive, bewildered loser who finds himself in the wrong place at the wrong time.

1 A strange flying machine: dreams come true if you stretch out your arms.

2 Even if you pose as a pro (Faye Dunaway, Johnny Depp), you're still a complete amateur.

3 People's spiritual wounds can be seen when they look you in the eye.

4 Even threats only arouse pity in those involved.

5 Breaking every rule of cinema, all the actors (Lili Taylor) look directly at the camera. They seem as confused as the viewers.

6 Rather than stunning landscapes, the panorama with cars on stilts features weird and impossible things.

6

BAD LIEUTENANT

1992 - USA - 96 MIN. - DRAMA, CRIME FILM

DIRECTOR ABEL FERRARA (*1952)
SCREENPLAY ABEL FERRARA, ZOË LUND **DIRECTOR OF PHOTOGRAPHY** KEN KELSCH **MUSIC** JOE DELIA **PRODUCTION** EDWARD R. PRESSMAN for BAD LT. PRODUCTIONS.

STARRING HARVEY KEITEL (The Lieutenant), VICTOR ARGO (Bet Cop), ZOË LUND (Junkie), PAUL CALDERON (Cop One), LEONARD L. THOMAS (Cop Two), ROBIN BURROWS (Ariane), FRANKIE THORN (Nun), PEGGY GORMLEY (Wife), ANTHONY RUGGIERO (Lite), VICTORIA BASTEL (Bowtay), PAUL HIPP (Jesus).

"Forgive me, please! Forgive me, Father!"

The Lieutenant in question (Harvey Keitel) lives with his wife and children in a suburb of New York. He's a man who can't find peace – and has long been part of the urban hell of violence, drug dealing and prostitution in which he works every day. As a corrupt, competitive junkie cop, he thinks nothing of abusing his power. He's a cheat and a bully, and has given up fighting against temptation of any kind. He is inextricably enmeshed in a life of gambling, drug taking and sexual excess. When a nun (Frankie Thorn) is raped and the Catholic Church offers a high reward to anyone who tracks down the perpetrators, the Lieutenant sees a final chance to pay off his debts to the mafia. Although the nun remains silent, she knows who did it. She has forgiven her rapists – an act of mercy which the cynical cop cannot even begin to understand.

Bad Lieutenant is a journey into the darkness of existential despair. Like Martin Scorsese's *Taxi Driver* (1975), Abel Ferrara's movie presents New York as an inferno where ideas like justice or the difference between right and wrong have no place. A world abandoned by God, where the anonymous protagonist – a "fuckin' Catholic" as he describes himself – has lost all faith and where there is no hope of redemption. The lieutenant suffers terribly. He is a driven man who tries to deaden his despair through sex, drugs and gambling. The lower he sinks, the more he seems to disappear into the gloomy chaos of the city, in the hysterical tumult of a techno disco, or in dark back rooms and stairwells. Increasingly he feels like an alien in the comfortable bourgeois world of his family, and he staggers through the clean sterility of his home in a daze. The coldness of his family life makes it clear that they can never help him, and that they are in fact one of the reasons for his fall. The few moments of real warmth and intimacy he experiences are elsewhere, with prostitutes and a junkie friend (Zoë Lund). Ferrara directs the story in uncompromising, almost documentary-style pictures which he only interrupts when the nun appears or when the cop experiences religious visions under the influence of drugs and his moral crisis. The rape of the nun uses the artificiality of a video clip as though it were just one more of the cop's nightmare hallucinations. The appearance of Jesus shortly before the end of the movie is made in the same way. Here, the religious dimension hinted at various points of *Bad Lieutenant* is made visible: the nun heralds the divine principle against which the Lieutenant has sinned and without which he has no hope of forgiveness. Only when he realises this can he find redemption.

The movie's provocative intensity comes above all from Harvey Keitel's outstanding acting, without which the powerful directness of Ferrara's production would not be possible. Keitel's grotesque howl when faced with his own guilt is so overwhelmingly heart-felt that it seems laden with all the tragedy of our human existence.

JH

1

1 Confession of a sinner: face to face with the capacity to forgive, the lieutenant acknowledges his guilt (Frankie Thorn and Harvey Keitel).

2 The film has a clearly religious dimension: a Christ figure (Paul Hipp) appears to the shattered cop.

3 Acting that reaches the limits of self-revelation: Harvey Keitel's performance makes the lieutenant's existential despair almost physically tangible.

4 A nightmare-like sequence: director Abel Ferrara stages the rape of the nun in video-clip style.

5 A showpiece role for Harvey Keitel: the corrupt cop as a mirror image of a violent society.

HARVEY KEITEL After training at the famous 'Actors Studio' in New York and appearing in various theatre productions Off-Broadway, Harvey Keitel, who was born in New York in 1939, made his film debut in Martin Scorsese's *Who's That Knocking At My Door* (1968). He made four further films with Scorsese, including *Taxi Driver* (1975). Keitel was long considered an excellent character actor thanks to numerous appearances in American and European films, but the 90s heralded the beginning of a new era in his career, and roles in a series of spectacular artistic and commercial successes turned him into a star. The movies of this period include Ridley Scott's *Thelma & Louise* (1991), Quentin Tarantino's *Reservoir Dogs* (1991), Jane Campion's *The Piano* (1993), Abel Ferrara's *Bad Lieutenant* (1992) and finally Quentin Tarantino's *Pulp Fiction* (1994).

"Make no mistake, Ferrara and his *Bad Lieutenant* are on a trip that's nothing to do with transport; out of phase, rude but by no means routine, their philosophy of cinema is one of borderline aesthetic and human experience. They're playing with fire, by turns unsettling and inspiring, and it's a pleasure to see." *Cahiers du cinéma*

BATMAN RETURNS

1992 - USA - 126 MIN. - COMIC, SCIENCE FICTION

DIRECTOR TIM BURTON (*1958)
SCREENPLAY DANIEL WATERS, based on a story by DANIEL WATERS, SAM HAMM and characters by BOB KANE
DIRECTOR OF PHOTOGRAPHY STEFAN CZAPSKY MUSIC DANNY ELFMAN PRODUCTION DENISE DINOVI, TIM BURTON for WARNER BROS.

STARRING MICHAEL KEATON (Batman/Bruce Wayne), DANNY DEVITO (The Penguin), MICHELLE PFEIFFER (Catwoman/Selina), CHRISTOPHER WALKEN (Max Shreck), MICHAEL GOUGH (Alfred Pennyworth), MICHAEL MURPHY (Mayor), CHRISTI CONAWAY (Ice Princess), ANDREW BRYNIARSKI (Chip), PAT HINGLE (Commissioner Gordon), VINCENT SCHIAVELLI (The Organ Grinder).

"I guess I'm tired of wearing masks."

There are some dreadful parents around. A wealthy aristocratic couple in Gotham City, seeing that their babe is born with flippers instead of hands and is generally far removed from human ideals of beauty, summarily dump the deformed offspring along with its black perambulator in a nearby riverbed. The baby disappears down the sewers and nothing more is heard of it. Years later, tycoon Max Shreck (Christopher Walken) is about to turn on the lights on the biggest Christmas tree that Gotham City has ever seen when an enormous Christmas present to the City turns out to be a horrific joke, concealing skeletons armed with machine guns who jump out and gun down bystanders and municipal dignitaries. Naturally, there's only one man to call:

Batman (Michael Keaton), who confronts not just that abandoned mutant son who has become The Penguin (Danny DeVito), but also the seductive yet easily ruffled Catwoman (Michelle Pfeiffer). As inscrutable as her animal model, Catwoman first makes the hero's life difficult and then completely turns his head. Tycoon Shreck quickly turns out to be the baddy and soon nobody seems to know whose side they're really on.

Tim Burton's second *Batman* film is a desolate comic opera that owes more to Sigmund Freud than it does to the characters invented by Bob Kane. Flashy effects and scenic spectacle aside, it is the psychology of the main figures that most interests Burton. As in *Batman* (1989), the city-scape of

1

2

4

5

"*Batman* isn't a film, but an American state of trance. A monologue of the collective subconscious."

Der Spiegel

1   Batman (Michael Keaton) and the Penguin (Danny DeVito): a meeting between creatures of the night. The dividing line between good and evil is not at all clearly defined in *Batman Returns*.

2   Something is brewing in the nether regions of Gotham. The city itself takes one of the lead parts in the second Batman movie.

6

Gotham City is one of the real stars of the movie. The production designer Bo Welch creates a comic nightmare version of Manhattan where cinematic predecessors such as Fritz Lang's *Metropolis* merge with expressionism and borrowings from fascist architecture to form a threatening artificial world. Gotham City was completely remade for *Batman Returns*, and the scenery left over from the first *Batman* movie remained untouched, a clear sign that Burton wanted to use the sequel to correct what he saw as the mistakes of his first *Batman* film – mistakes caused above all by too many concessions to the production company.

Batman Returns is something like an artistic liberation: Burton is not interested in constructing a consistently logical plot and the actual story is

3 Super-villain with a giant rubber duck: Burton skilfully mixes fantastic childhood images and imaginary terrors to form a comic nightmare.

4 The Penguin, a son disowned by his aristocratic family, subjects Gotham to a reign of terror, when all he really wants is to be loved.

5 From goody-goody secretary to horror vamp with bloody claws: Michelle Pfeiffer makes a fascinating, erotically feline Catwoman.

6 Stop that: Batman goes into action.

7 The queen of the cats with her subjects. Whose side is the enigmatic Catwoman on?

8 Sometimes the real villains are hard to be found: Christopher Walken as tycoon Max Shreck, who has everything except the welfare of his employees in mind.

COMICS AND MOVIES The links between comics and movies are often underestimated. Both are dynamic media that depend on a series of exciting pictures where the right attitudes or perspectives are just as important as dramatic events. From their earliest days, comics have always taken up cinematic motifs and themes, and they have also always served as inspiration for new movies. The same is true of their characters. Cinema is particularly interested in the world of the super hero: Superman, Spiderman, and above all Batman have fired the imaginations of film-makers for generations now.

marginal to the movie. The real plot is the story that lies behind the bizarre main characters. Catwoman and the Penguin are lost souls who have been turned into horrific figures by unkind fate and the actions of their fellow men. The Penguin is really only looking for his parents and some recognition, Catwoman is actually a frightened secretary who has seen too much of her boss's affairs. It is hardly surprising that these fantastic figures are what interest Burton most in the Batman story; his favourite cast members have always been the misunderstood, like the subversive freak Pee-Wee Herman in *Pee-Wee's Big Adventure* (1985), or outsiders like the 'recently departed' Adam and Barbara in *Beetlejuice* (1988) and the deformed, benevolent monster who is *Edward Scissorhands* (1988).

The Penguin and Catwoman are the result of their own internal contradictions: the salvation they long for would ultimately rob them of their identity. That is also true of the figure of Batman himself. Ironically, given the title of the movie, Batman himself retreats into the background and his adversaries take centre stage. Michael Keaton plays his sparing appearances with an air that varies from laconic to melancholic, giving the impression of a superhero tired of his job who would like nothing better than the chance to hang up his mask forever. Batman witnessed the murder of his parents as a young boy, and in this film he's left behind the idea of hero as amazing role-model: like Catwoman and the Penguin, he's just another restless phantom searching for the identity he has lost forever.   SH

HUSBANDS AND WIVES

1992 - USA - 108 MIN. - DRAMA, COMEDY

DIRECTOR WOODY ALLEN (*1935)

SCREENPLAY WOODY ALLEN DIRECTOR OF PHOTOGRAPHY CARLO DI PALMA MUSIC GUSTAV MAHLER ("9TH SYMPHONY"), various jazz numbers PRODUCTION ROBERT GREENHUT, JACK ROLLINS, CHARLES H. JOFFE for TRISTAR.

STARRING WOODY ALLEN (Gabe Roth), MIA FARROW (Judy Roth), JUDY DAVIS (Sally), SYDNEY POLLACK (Jack), JULIETTE LEWIS (Rain), LIAM NEESON (Michael), LYSETTE ANTHONY (Sam), BENNO SCHMIDT (Judy's ex-husband), BLYTHE DANNER (Rain's mother).

"Do you ever hide things from me?"

Judy and Gabe (Mia Farrow and Woody Allen) are absolutely convinced that Sally and Jack (Judy Davis and Sydney Pollack) are a happily married couple. They are completely taken aback when their two friends take the opportunity of a dinner party to announce their planned separation. They do not seem to have argued and are calm, almost cheerful about it. They explain to their friends how they have grown apart over the years. Separation seems the best solution, as their children are now almost grown up. Judy and Gabe needn't worry, as it's nowhere near as bad as it sounds. Needless to say, once they taste freedom again the harmonious atmosphere between Sally and Jack doesn't last long, and when Sally discovers that Jack is living with a young aerobics instructor (Lysette Anthony) she is completely distraught. This confirms Judy and Gabe's negative view of the whole affair, but gradually it becomes apparent that their friends' separation has also shaken up their own marriage. Judy tries to match Sally with her attractive colleague Michael (Liam Neeson) but eventually has to admit that she is the one who is really in love with him. Gabe, a literature teacher, may have been outraged by Jack's new relationship, but the friendship which he develops with a talented student called Rain (Juliette Lewis) is neither platonic nor mere professional interest.

The cinema release of *Husbands and Wives* was overshadowed by the scandalous circumstances of Woody Allen's separation from his long-term partner Mia Farrow. The media saw the film as a depiction of the director's failed relationship, and the desires and problems of the couples in the movie were equated with those of the real-life couple. This interpretation is undoubtedly justified to some extent as Allen's figures are always closely related to his own personality and he is regarded as synonymous with the New York neurotics who populate his films. Meditations on the relationship between fact and fiction are a constant feature of his movies, as in the fictional film biographies *Zelig* (1983) and in *Sweet and Lowdown* (1999). In *Husbands and Wives* he treats this aspect in playful documentary fashion: the protagonists and those who have accompanied them in important phases of their life as a couple are interviewed by a television team, as if they were being psychoanalysed. The television team never appears on camera, but this interview triggers a series of flashbacks in which hectic handcamera work captures the action in a seemingly lifelike way. We get the impression that the main figures are being shown to us directly from various perspectives, as if the film really could give us an objective view of events. This is an ironic construction, as the movie's plot reveals subjective truth as essential to interpersonal relationships. Each individual has a completely different view of what is happening, and fact and fiction are inextricably combined in that view. Personal bitterness on Allen's part aside, *Husbands and Wives* is much more than a complex, sensitive and amusing look at the relationship between the sexes. It is also an illuminating commentary on the media's fatal tendency to drag private matters into the public sphere, forcing them into wholly unsuitable categories of guilt and innocence.

JH

3

"The best scenes in *Husbands and Wives* are between the characters played by Allen and Farrow. If we can judge by the subsequent events in their lives, some of this dialogue must have cut very close to the bone." *Chicago Sun-Times*

WOODY ALLEN The director, actor, author and musician Woody Allen was born in 1935 in Brooklyn (New York) as Allen Stewart Konigsberg. He began his career in the 50s as a joke writer for the New York press and – a little later – for television, before he appeared in person as a stand-up comedian. His first film role was in Clive Donner's *What's Up, Pussycat?* in 1965. He made his debut as a director in 1969 with *Take the Money and Run.* Since then, with impressive regularity, he has directed a movie virtually every year, most of which are comedies. The main theme of his films is the eternal struggle between the sexes, which he presents from many different perspectives. His works are almost exclusively set in New York. Allen acts in most of his own movies – most often as the vulnerable urban neurotic with which his personality is also identified in real life. His most famous films include *Annie Hall* (1977), *Manhattan* (1978), *Stardust Memories* (1980), *Hannah and Her Sisters* (1986), *Husbands and Wives* (1992) and *Mighty Aphrodite* (1995).

1 A typical city-dwelling neurotic: writing is a poor
   form of therapy for Gabe (Woody Allen).

2 A relationship that is over: as so often in Allen's
   films, the woman is the first to realise that her
   partner is drifting away from her (Mia Farrow).

3 A richly cast film with outstanding actors: Judy
   Davis (left) received an Oscar nomination for
   her portrayal of the highly-strung Sally.

4 Two master directors in dialogue: the conversation between Jack and Gabe (Sydney Pollack)
   is typical of the film's pseudo-documentary style.

5 In comparison to earlier Allen films, Mia Farrow
   as Judy comes across as much more egotistical
   and ambitious (Mia Farrow and Liam Neeson).

6 Juliette Lewis was still at the debut of her career
   in Allen's film. Shortly beforehand, she had had
   a breakthrough in Martin Scorsese's *Cape Fear*.

JURASSIC PARK

♟♟♟

1993 - USA - 126 MIN. - ACTION FILM

DIRECTOR STEVEN SPIELBERG (*1947)
SCREENPLAY MICHAEL CRICHTON, DAVID KOEPP, based on the novel *DINOPARK* by MICHAEL CRICHTON
DIRECTOR OF PHOTOGRAPHY DEAN CUNDEY **MUSIC** JOHN WILLIAMS **PRODUCTION** KATHLEEN KENNEDY, GERALD R. MOLEN
for AMBLIN ENTERTAINMENT.

STARRING SAM NEILL (Dr Alan Grant), LAURA DERN (Ellie Sattler), JEFF GOLDBLUM (Dr Ian Malcolm),
RICHARD ATTENBOROUGH (John Hammond), SAMUEL L. JACKSON (Arnold), BOB PECK (Robert Muldoon),
MARTIN FERRERO (Donald Gennaro), B. D. WONG (Dr Wu), JOSEPH MAZZELLO (Tim), ARIANA RICHARDS (Lex).

ACADEMY AWARDS 1994 OSCARS for BEST VISUAL EFFECTS (Dennis Muren, Stan Winston, Phil Tippett, Michael Lantieri),
BEST SOUND (Ronald Judkins, Shawn Murphy, Gary Rydstrom, Gary Summers), BEST SOUND EFFECTS EDITING
(Richard Hymns, Gary Rydstrom).

"You should have more respect."

John Hammond (Richard Attenborough) has a vision: he wants to build the biggest and most unusual theme park in the world. As is so often the case in mainstream cinema, his vision compensates for a personal shortcoming – he has a pronounced limp. On a secluded island off the coast of Costa Rica, his idea is to present the public with the most extraordinary thing imaginable: living dinosaurs. Thanks to advances in genetics, such a thing is now possible, and by reactivating the DNA of dinosaur blood from mosquitos trapped in fossilised tree resin, Jurassic Park's scientists clone dinosaurs back into existence after millions of years of extinction.

Unfortunately, the plan begins to go wrong when a park employee is fatally injured by particularly dangerous species of dinosaur as it is being unloaded. His family claims for compensation and the park's insurers and investors commission a safety report. To carry out the investigation, Hammond invites a group of experts to the park including palaeontologist Alan Grant (Sam Neill), his girlfriend Ellie Sattler (Laura Dern) a biologist who specialises in extinct plants of the dinosaur age, an insurance expert, and chaos theoretician Ian Malcolm (Jeff Goldblum). Hammond hopes that the giant lizards will impress the scientists so much that they will abandon their critical attitudes and leave filled with enthusiasm for his project. When the helicopter with the scientists approaches the island and the movie's memorable theme tune is heard for the first time, the audience is also convinced that they are about to see something really amazing. Grant and Sattler are only used to dealing with

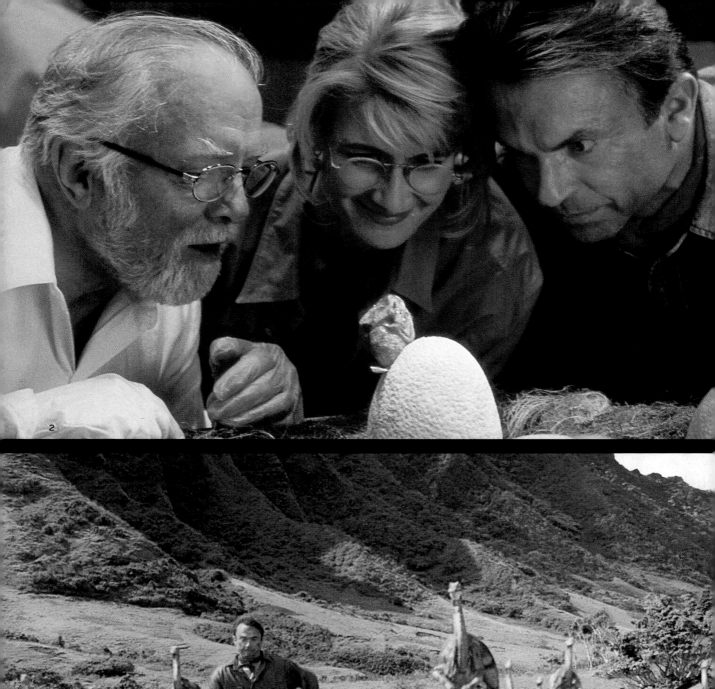

"Spielberg plays like a virtuoso on the keys of the visual arts industry. He takes our longing for the miraculous, and then makes the miraculous accessible to people like you and me." *epd Film*

the dinosaurs' excavated skeletons and they fall in love with the prehistoric creatures at first sight. The insurance expert is positively bursting with enthusiasm and greed. Only Ian Malcolm takes a pessimistic view of the park and predicts that messing around with nature can only bring catastrophe.

It's hard not to be impressed with the computer animated dinosaurs of *Jurassic Park*, which stride majestically across the screen. Spielberg knows how to make the most of them and builds an exciting plot around them.

Before *Jurassic Park*, dinosaurs had only ever been seen on the screen when scientists took a trip back in time or discovered lost continents in the earth's interior where primitive nature survived. But when Steven Spielberg came to make his movie, advances in genetics had added a new motif to the dinosaur story. If it's possible to decipher the human DNA code, why not the genes of an animal which lived on the earth many millions of years ago? The explosive potential of such experiments when combined with human greed soon become all too clear to the protagonists of the movie.

Disaster strikes on the island when Robert Muldoon (Bob Peck, a greedy Park employee), decides to sell embryos to the competition and deactivates the security system for a few minutes to carry out the theft.

Muldoon chooses a weekend when the security staff are on the mainland. As in a traditional horror film, all the prerequisites are prepared, and preparation for a night of spectacular terror, the weather forecast predicts violent storms. The nightmare begins: fences are ripped up, high-voltage cables tear and flail, bridges are flooded, mudslides sweep away the sides of the mountains, there's thunder and lightning, the heavens send forth fire and brimstone and there's also a tyrannosaurus rex, one or two velociraptors, a poisonous dilophosaurus and a herd of brachiosauri. The electricity fails and the visitors' computerised jeeps come to a standstill. Alan Grant, Ian Malcolm, Hammond's two grandchildren and the insurance expert are in extreme danger. The latter falls victim to a tyrannosaurus attack. The chaos theoretician survives, but is wounded and has to be left behind. Grant escapes with the two children.

One of the movie's most memorable scenes is the second attack by the tyrannosaurus. We see vibrations in a puddle of water which become stronger and stronger until it is filled with small waves and the earth trembles under the creature's claws. The hunted visitors try to escape in the jeep, but it can't get up enough speed on the swampy ground.

1   "What used to fascinate me even as a child was King Kong." *Steven Spielberg*

2   Man playing God. Their eyes (Richard Attenborough, Laura Dern, Sam Neill) may be shining, but they are blinded by their enthusiasm.

3   Nature unleashed. Rarely a recipe for success.

4   What looks like a hermetically sealed world turns out to have a few loopholes.

Most impressive of all is the precarious balance that Spielberg maintains on the knife-edge between horror film and family entertainment. He carefully avoids showing the dinosaur's brutal and horrific behaviour in any great detail, while still managing to keep up the tension to please the horror and animation fans. *Jurassic Park* once again proves the cinematic truism that it is more effective to show the consequences of horrific happenings than to show the events themselves. Rather than seeing the blood spurt when a cow is devoured by a velociraptor, we see the waving grass and then hear ear-piercing bellows of fear followed by slurping noises and the sound of bones.

In the morning after the night of terror it seems as if nothing has happened: Alan Grant has found a safe haven in the tree tops with the children. A brachiosaur peacefully grazes under their feet and even allows itself to be stroked. It shows its appreciation by grunting like a walrus and the children feel they could befriend this extinct giant.

But the peace does not last. A small group fights its way into the command bunker of the park. In the meantime the others have managed to re-boot the park's computer and have telephoned for a helicopter to come and take them off the island. They await their rescue in the Jurassic Park museum, where fossilized dinosaurs are exhibited to whet the visitors' appetite for the real thing. Finally, past and present clash for one last time. Two murderous velociraptors attack the group, but a tyrannosaur appears which fights back and saves the survivors. The dream ends, and once again humans and dinosaurs are separated by a distance of millions of years.

SL

SOUND DESIGN   The simulated dinosaurs seem so overwhelmingly convincing because they are the result of a combination of many different hi-tech techniques. The model animators worked closely with computer animators, blue screen experts and animal trainers. Spielberg often uses sound to reinforce the impression of terror and danger, so boffins and sound engineers were kept particularly busy on this movie, where they found themselves on completely new acoustic territory. The dinosaurs had to sound life-like, but no one could say what an enraged dinosaur attacking two children in a kitchen might have sounded like: the solution they finally arrived at was to mix dolphin noises with walrus grunts until the whole thing sounded sufficiently aggressive. Another challenge was to produce an acoustic effect to mirror the optical effect of dinosaur's footsteps making rings in a water glass. Sound engineers solved that problem by placing the glass on a guitar and plucking the strings. Effects like that provided plenty of acoustic thrills for the new sound systems of the multiplex cinemas.

---

5   Sceptics (Jeff Goldblum) may not be heroes, but in the end they are usually right.

6   The hunt for the kill in a shiny chrome kitchen. The boy (Joseph Mazzello), rigid with fear, is trying to hide from the dinosaurs.

7   An American nightmare: the monster doesn't even respect the cars.

FOUR WEDDINGS AND A FUNERAL

1993/1994 - GREAT BRITAIN - 117 MIN. - COMEDY

DIRECTOR MIKE NEWELL (*1942)
SCREENPLAY RICHARD CURTIS DIRECTOR OF PHOTOGRAPHY PHILIP SINDALL MUSIC RICHARD RODNEY BENNETT
PRODUCTION DUNCAN KENWORTHY for WORKING TITLE (for POLYGRAM, CHANNEL FOUR).

STARRING HUGH GRANT (Charles), ANDIE MACDOWELL (Carrie), KRISTIN SCOTT THOMAS (Fiona), SIMON CALLOW (Gareth), JAMES FLEET (Tom), ANNA CHANCELLOR (Henrietta), CHARLOTTE COLEMAN (Scarlett), CHARLES BOWER (David), SARA CROWE (Laura), TIMOTHY WALKER (Angus).

"Marriage is just a way of getting out of an embarrassing pause in conversation."

It's just another normal Saturday morning. At a shrill ring from the alarm clock, Charles (Hugh Grant) falls out of bed, staggers into his tailcoat and rushes off to church. Hardly a weekend goes by when he and his friends are not invited to some wedding or other. Charles is always late. He may be invited to lots of weddings, but he has no intention of marrying himself. As his friends get hitched one by one, the shy and chaotic bachelor remains a "serial monogamist" as he says himself, apparently unable to sustain any serious relationship. But at this particular wedding reception he meets Carrie (Andie MacDowell) – the woman of his dreams, and it's a classic case of love at first sight. Carrie seduces him and they spend the night together. The next morning, Charles hesitates a moment too long and suddenly the American beauty has disappeared from his life – if not from his thoughts.

Of course they meet again – at the next wedding. Before Charles can pluck up the courage to speak, Carrie introduces him to her future husband, who she marries at the movie's third wedding. The fourth, which is only stopped at the last minute by the courageous intervention of Charles' deaf brother, is Charles' own – but the bride's name isn't Carrie.

The succession of wedding celebrations is interrupted by a burial: one of Charles' friends, the bon-vivant and cynic Gareth (Simon Callow), dies of a heart attack at Carrie's wedding. When his friend Matthew holds the funeral speech, Charles suddenly realises that despite the absence of a wedding certificate and the accompanying celebrations, Matthew and Gareth had also made a real commitment for life.

These four weddings and one funeral are the main events of Mike Newell's light-hearted satire on the fossilized code of conduct and behaviour of the British upper classes. The only couples held together by true love are those who will never marry. If Gareth is to be believed, marriage is simply a way of dealing with the embarrassing pauses in conversation which become more frequent as a relationship progresses. Charles' other friend Tom (James Fleet) is equally pragmatic: he hopes to find a nice girl who won't feel nauseous when she looks at him and with whom he can simply be happy.

The script of *Four Weddings and a Funeral* was written by Richard Curtis, one of Britain's most productive film writers and the creator of many successful television series and feature films. He wrote the series

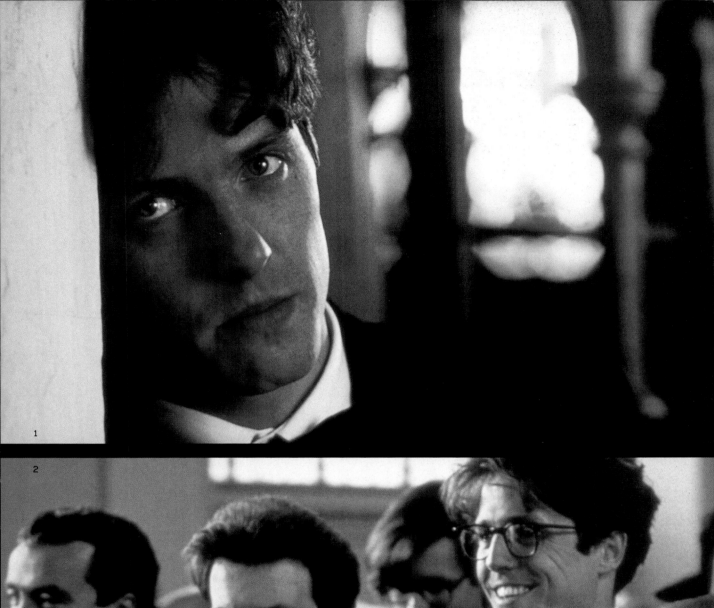

"Mike Newell's film finds its premise in one of modern life's minor truths: if you are a sociable specimen of the yuppie breed, you spend much of your spare income suiting yourself up for friends' weddings." *Time Magazine*

3

4

5

6

Blackadder and *Mr. Bean* together with Rowan Atkinson, who plays a small but hilarious role in this movie as a stuttering priest. *Four Weddings and a Funeral* was a small budget production, but it became Britain's s most successful movie to date and was only knocked off the number one spot when Roger Michell's romantic comedy *Notting Hill* came along in 1999, also starring Hugh Grant and written by Richard Curtis. Mike Newell's movie shows as little of the everyday life of its characters as it shows of the real social conditions in Britain. His protagonists all come from "good" families and we only see them in their Sunday best, either at weddings or on their way there. The audience's gaze sweeps through the party like that of a curious guest. Interesting people catch the eye, and the witty dialogue catches the ear. From the very first ring of the alarm clock to the last kiss, the timing of this brilliant farce is perfect, and it combines all the best elements of comedy and melodrama. APO

BAFTA AWARD The British Academy of Film was founded in 1947 by a committee of 14 people under the director David Lean. Its aim was to promote excellence in the British movie industry. In 1958 it fused with the professional body of television producers and directors and in 1978 it was renamed the British Academy of Film and Television Arts (BAFTA). The BAFTA award is the most important film and television prize in Britain and is awarded yearly in various categories. The golden mask that commemorates each award was designed by the artist Mitzi Cunliffe.

---

1 The role of the shy young bachelor who attends wedding after wedding turned British actor Hugh Grant into a super-star.

2 David (Charles Bower, centre), the speech- and hearing-impaired brother of Charles, saves him at the last minute from making the biggest mistake of his life.

3 Hats off: the role of the independent and self-assured American lady Carrie could have been tailor-made for Andie MacDowell.

4 Suffering in silence: Fiona (Kristin Scott Thomas), who's been in love with Charles for years, is just a "good friend" as far as he's concerned.

5 Last minute rush: Charles and his flat-mate Scarlett (Charlotte Coleman) dash from one wedding to the next.

6 An arch commentator: the long drawn out parties wouldn't be half so much fun without Gareth's (Simon Callow, left) witty observations.

RAINING STONES

1993 - GREAT BRITAIN - 91 MIN. - DRAMA

DIRECTOR KEN LOACH (*1936)
SCREENPLAY JIM ALLEN **DIRECTOR OF PHOTOGRAPHY** BARRY ACKROYD **MUSIC** STEWART COPELAND **PRODUCTION** SALLY HIBBIN
for PARALLAX, FILM FOUR.

STARRING BRUCE JONES (Bob Williams), JULIE BROWN (Anne Williams), GEMMA PHOENIX (Coleen Williams),
RICKY TOMLINSON (Tommy), TOM HICKEY (Father Barry), JONATHAN JAMES (Tansey), MIKE FALLON (Jimmy),
RONNIE RAVEY (Butcher), LEE BRENNAN (Irishman).

IFF CANNES 1993 JURY PRIZE (Ken Loach).

"When you're down it's raining stones seven days a week."

Bad things don't just come in threes. Bob (Bruce Jones) has seen enough of life to know the truth of these sayings: he's forty, unemployed, supports his family with state allowances and occasional labour and lives in a comfortless council flat somewhere in the north of England. You could live and die here, and no one would notice, as his wife Anne (Julie Brown) says.

Despite these miserable living conditions, Bob always bounces back. His family is sacred to him and his Catholic faith a rock in stormy seas. They give him the strength to keep his humour and his self-respect despite the continual bad luck. When he and his best mate Tommy (Ricky Tomlinson) steal a sheep, things go badly awry – they can neither slaughter it themselves nor sell it to a butcher. Bob's old delivery van is stolen from the yard whilst they are trying to get rid of the sheep in the pub, and finally, having tried in vain to get paid work cleaning drains with borrowed tools, he finds himself up to his neck in filth at the church – and that for free!

Bob's daughter Coleen (Gemma Phoenix) is about to celebrate her First Communion, and he wants to buy her a new dress, even though the full outfit with the shoes, stockings and veil costs over 100 pounds. The priest (Tom Hickey) tries and fails to talk Bob into buying a second-hand dress – after all, it's a very important family occasion.

Bob borrows the money from a loan shark, who sells the IOU on to Tansey (Jonathan James), a professional debt collector. When Bob can't pay the money back and Anne and Coleen are threatened at home by Tansey's brutal hitmen, Bob can't take it any more. During the resulting showdown between Bob and Tansey in an underground garage, Tansey is killed. Although Bob is not directly responsible, he feels guilty and wants to turn himself in to the police. He can find no peace until the parish priest, an exceptional man, grants him absolution, saying "You only want justice." He realises that Bob won't find it in secular society and offers him the forgiveness of the church instead.

Despite its grimness, *Raining Stones* has many comic moments. When Bob, Tommy, and a couple of mates see a perfect lawn outside a Conservative Club one day, they neatly take it up and sell it as turf. But most of the humour is extremely black. The daily humiliations these men have to face often make it difficult for the audience to laugh. When someone is as

desperate as Tommy, we don't laugh when his daughter gives him pocket money, as that would be too much like a kicking a man when he's down.

Raining Stones is the opposite of a Hollywood movie. Ken Loach filmed it in a 16mm format and worked with a hand camera and original sounds instead of expensive technology and synchronisation, and like most of his movies, *Raining Stones* is cast with amateur actors drawing on their own experiences. What counts for Loach in front of the camera and the microphone is not appearance, but the reality behind it.

For that reason, he's often been labelled "the social conscience of Great Britain". The name suits him: all of his movies criticise the political system, even if they don't all have the effectiveness of the BBC television film *Cathy Come Home* (1966), which had a part to play in influencing changes made to British vagrancy laws ten years later. He has often had problems with censorship. In the 80s, almost all of his works were banned on the order of the IBA (Britain's Independent Broadcasting Authority) and even as late as 1997, Channel 4 refused to broadcast his film *Ladybird, Ladybird* (1994).   APO

"The credit sharks' heavy boys lurk in front of the social security office, to collect overdue debts. Social imagination seems to be infinitely inventive only when it is a case of exploiting those in serious difficulties even more cruelly." *epd Film*

CO-PRODUCTION	Co-production refers to joint projects carried out by producers and production companies. This form of co-operation arose due to financial and material difficulties in Europe in the years following the Second World War. Production companies and producers in other countries joined together to finance expensive European films and to gain access to newer, larger markets. Co-production is still general practice today for the same reasons.

1   Her big day: Bob's innocent young daughter Coleen (Gemma Phoenix) has no idea that her First Communion dress costs someone their life.

2   Guilt and expiation: Father Barry is a human being first and the Church's representative second. He acquits Bob (Bruce Jones) of the death of the debt collector.

2

3 Dogged by bad luck: while Tommy (Ricky Tomlinson, right) is trying to off-load the worthless mutton on the man in the pub, his car gets stolen.

4 Sympathetic: the pulpit is the only place where Father Barry (Tom Hickey) speaks to his people with raised forefinger.

5 Up hill and down dale: survival artists Bob and Tommy struggling to bring someone else's flock into the dry.

PHILADELPHIA

1993 - USA - 125 MIN. - DRAMA, COURTROOM DRAMA

DIRECTOR JONATHAN DEMME (*1944)

SCREENPLAY RON NYSWANER **DIRECTOR OF PHOTOGRAPHY** TAK FUJIMOTO **MUSIC** HOWARD SHORE **PRODUCTION** EDWARD SAXON, JONATHAN DEMME for COLUMBIA TRISTAR, CLINICA ESTETICO.

STARRING TOM HANKS (Andrew Becket), DENZEL WASHINGTON (Joe Miller), JASON ROBARDS (Charles Wheeler), MARY STEENBURGEN (Belinda Conine), JOANNE WOODWARD (Sarah Becket), ANTONIO BANDERAS (Miguel Alvarez), RON VAWTER (Bob Seidman), JEFFREY WILLIAMSON (Tyrone), CHARLES NAPIER (Richter Garnett), LISA SUMMEROUR (Lisa Miller).

ACADEMY AWARDS 1994 OSCARS for BEST ACTOR (Tom Hanks) and BEST SONG (Bruce Springsteen, "The Streets of Philadelphia").

IFF BERLIN 1994 SILVER BEAR for BEST ACTOR (Tom Hanks).

"Forget everything you've seen on television and in the movies."

Andrew Becket (Tom Hanks) and Joe Miller (Denzel Washington) are two ambitious young lawyers. They have just presented opposing sides of a civil law case; afterwards in the elevator they simultaneously tear their dicta-phones out of their pockets to record the case results; somewhere a cell phone rings and without interrupting their dictation, both search for their phones. Youth, ambition and lots of energy – that's what they have in com-mon, but nothing more: Joe Miller is black, a legal eagle who advertises his work in local TV commercials; Andrew Becket is a WASP, graduate of an elite university and employed by one of Philadelphia's most prestigious law firms. He is also gay. A few days later things start to happen: Becket is made a se-nior partner of the firm by his mentor Charles Wheeler (Jason Robards) and is entrusted with a very important case. A blood test shows that he has AIDS. No one in the firm is supposed to know about his illness. But when a vital document disappears under mysterious circumstances and he is fired for

incompetence, he suspects his disease is the real reason for the dismissal and decides to sue his former employers for discrimination. Unfortunately, there is not a single lawyer in the city who is prepared to take on his case – apart from Joe Miller, who as a black man knows what it's like to be dis-criminated against. After a long period of hesitation he decides to help Becket, above all because the case will bring both money and publicity.

1993/94 seemed to herald a new trend in Hollywood. Two films were released which confronted audiences with historical and social reality. Hard on the heels of Steven Spielberg's Holocaust movie *Schindler's List* came Jonathan Demme's *Philadelphia*, and more than ten years after "gay cancer" first became public knowledge, the first big budget movie about AIDS had appeared.

The interesting thing about *Philadelphia* is that it is not what it claims to be. It is a complete failure as a film about gays and AIDS. It succeeds how-

2

3

"It is, at the very least, a giant step forward for Hollywood, which tends to portray homosexuals as either psychopathic cross-dressers or the giddy fruitcakes who live next door." *The Washington Post*

4

5

6

ever as a tension-filled and exciting courtroom drama about deep-seated social prejudices against those who think, look and love differently. In this respect it resembles Stanley Kramer's movie *Guess Who's Coming to Dinner?* (1967) where parents Spencer Tracy and Katharine Hepburn have to get used to the idea of a black son-in-law. Becket's lawyer Joe Miller, convincingly portrayed by Denzel Washington, is the prototypical normal person. His hatred of gays is deep-rooted and his ignorance of the disease astonishing. When Becket goes to visit him for the first time in his office, they shake hands. A few moments later, Miller discovers that Becket has AIDS. The camera reveals his fear, it follows his eyes to the objects Andrew has touched like the cigars Miller keeps for his clients and a photo of his new-

born daughter. When Andrew has left, he immediately makes a doctor's appointment. But the irony is that Becket could not wish for a better lawyer: Miller forces the jury to examine its own prejudices, just as the cinema audience is forced to do.

Philadelphia was classified as suitable for children. No bodily fluids are exchanged between gay men, and there is nothing more explicit than a peck on the cheek. The same fears demonstrated by Joe Miller's dealings with gays are mirrored in the movie's treatment of what is supposed to be its main theme. Despite, or perhaps because of this, Demme's attempt to make contact was rewarded with a clutch of international film prizes, including two Oscars. APO

HOMOSEXUALITY IN THE MOVIES	Homosexuality hardly appeared at all in the movies from the very beginning of cinema to recent years. Social acceptance was extremely limited and pressure from the industry was too great. One of the very first movies ever made is called *The Gay Brothers* (William Dickson, 1895) and shows two men dancing a waltz. From the mid1930s onwards, the portrayal of homosexuality in film became virtually impossible in the USA thanks to the industry's self-imposed production code. If homosexuals appeared at all, they were presented as ridiculous camp characters. Homosexuality in movies has only ceased to be an issue since the 1980s.

1 The courage to play an outsider: the role of the attorney (Andrew Becket) suffering from AIDS presented a real challenge for Hollywood star Tom Hanks.

2 Worried he might catch something: homophobic attorney Joe Miller (Denzel Washington) knows all about discrimination.

3 Faithful unto death: Andrew's partner Miguel Alvarez (Antonio Banderas) knows he caught the disease by playing around.

4 A plausible façade: as long as Andrew can keep up appearances, the partners in his chambers still think he's the best.

5 Overstepping the mark: Denzel Washington is outraged when someone in a supermarket thinks he's gay.

6 Andrew's mentor Charles Wheeler (Jason Robards, left) holds the ambitious young attorney in high esteem – perhaps because he recognizes in him something of himself. He is inconsolable when he learns the truth about his protégé.

GROUNDHOG DAY

1993 - USA - 101 MIN. - COMEDY

DIRECTOR HAROLD RAMIS (*1944)
SCREENPLAY DANNY RUBIN, HAROLD RAMIS DIRECTOR OF PHOTOGRAPHY JOHN BAILEY MUSIC GEORGE FENTON PRODUCTION TREVOR ALBERT, HAROLD RAMIS for COLUMBIA PICTURES.

STARRING BILL MURRAY (Phil Connors), ANDIE MACDOWELL (Rita Hanson), CHRIS ELLIOTT (Larry), STEPHEN TOBOLOWSKY (Ned Ryerson), BRIAN DOYLE-MURRAY (Buster), MARITA GERAGHTY (Nancy), ANGELA PATON (Mrs Lancaster), RICK DUCOMMUN (Gus), RICK OVERTON (Ralph), ROBIN DUKE (Doris the waitress).

"I Got You Babe ..."

"I Got You Babe" thunders from Phil Connors' (Bill Murray) radio alarm at six in the morning. Connors, the embodiment of the cynical, streetwise modern city dweller, is a TV presenter who has been sent to cover an annual event in weather prediction. In Punxsutawney, deep in provincial America, a groundhog is taken out of its cage at the end of every winter and asked what the weather will be like in the following weeks. This curious ritual is broadcast across the land. Regardless of the predictions of the groundhog, everyone has a good time and enjoys the celebrations. Connors on the other hand considers the whole thing to be the annually recurring height of stupidity. He reports the event without any vestige of enthusiasm and even cuts the last few sequences so he can go home early. However a blizzard stops the television team from leaving and they have to spend another night in Punxsutawney. Phil is awakened the next morning by the sound of his radio playing "I Got You Babe". The other guests and the landlady greet him with the same friendly, conventional phrases as the day before and everyone is

looking forward to the groundhog. Connors realises that he is stuck in a time loop with no way of escape: stuck in everyday life in the provinces.

While everyone around him experiences the day for the first time, from now on everything is repetition for Connors – every morning, the same presenters' voices boom out from the radio to begin the day with "I Got You Babe".

The movie develops the funniest situations out of this idea of endless repetition. One day Phil does his work professionally, the next he refuses completely. He meets his old school friend Ned (Stephen Tobolowsky) again and again and reacts to his offensive cheerfulness differently every time, he shouts at him, strikes up a friendly conversation, or takes the stupid jokes right out of his mouth. Every time, though, the scene ends the same way: Phil runs away from Ned and without thinking steps into an ankle-deep puddle of ice-cold water, so that Ned has the opportunity to call one last joke after him. The running gag is an important element in comedy and a movie whose

"Director Harold Ramis stage-manages these days with a wealth of ideas and precision timing, and after his initial shock the hero enjoys his lack of responsibility." *epd Film*

structural principle is repetition can been seen as a virtuoso play on the running gag. Even when Phil commits suicide, it has no effect on the next morning: "I Got You Babe". Again and again he meets the same people, but he always treats them differently: at first he is curious, then bored, until finally he becomes, compassionate. For Connors it may be sheer repetition, but the audience witness a rebirth, as his hatred for the provinces disappears as he grows to appreciate the people of Punxsutawney. Slowly his cynicism begins to dissolve and eventually the self-satisfied egocentric has to admit that he is in love with his producer Rita (Andie MacDowell). Every day he tries repeatedly to conquer her affections and for each new attempt he is better prepared. Naturally it is this love which saves him in the end.

The movie promotes virtues like genuine sentiment and rural simplicity so blatantly that it could be disregarded as kitsch. However, it's also possible to enjoy the gradual conversion of the arrogant, smug Connors, who at first believes he has everything under control. His sarcasm is shown as a mask that he can only lay aside if he is prepared to break out of the vicious circle of self-importance and throw himself into life with no regard for the consequences. *Groundhog Day* is one of the most intelligent comedies of the 90s. It is one of the few romantic comedies to give us a love story and leave something over for the viewers who will find this too sugary: some will find Phil Connors most entertaining when he is obnoxious and shrugs off every human feeling with a mocking grin.   SL

BILL MURRAY Born in 1950 in Wilmette (Illinois), Murray was popular as a radio and TV comic long before his movie career began. He made his movie debut in 1979 in Ivan Reitman's *Meatballs*. In the years that followed, Murray became a popular star of the so-called "animal comedies", movies characterised by anarchic humour. He landed his first big hit with Reitman's *Ghostbusters* (1984) and proved his talent in a more serious role in John Byrum's *The Razor's Edge* in the same year. *Quick Change* (1990) was his first and only attempt at directing to date. Murray continued his 80s successes with the romantic comedy *Groundhog Day* in 1992. In Wes Anderson's *Rushmore* he played a depressed millionaire and showed once again that he knows better than most US comics how to give depth to his roles. Other well-known movies featuring Bill Murray include Sydney Pollack's *Tootsie* (1982), *Little Shop of Horrors* (1986) by Frank Oz, John McNaughton's *Mad Dog and Glory* (1993) and finally *Ed Wood* (1994) by Tim Burton.

1   The sceptical face of presenter Phil Connors (Bill Murray), before the miracle starts to happen.

2   In films, shower scenes are always moments on the brink of madness.

3   American holidays have strange heroes: groundhogs, turkeys and pumpkin heads.

4   Dancing never fails to bring people (Andie McDowell) closer together.

5   Happiness is only possible if you lay yourself completely open.

IN THE LINE OF FIRE

1993 - USA - 128 MIN. - POLITICAL THRILLER

DIRECTOR WOLFGANG PETERSEN (*1941)
SCREENPLAY JEFF MAGUIRE DIRECTOR OF PHOTOGRAPHY JOHN BAILEY MUSIC ENNIO MORRICONE PRODUCTION JEFF APPLE for CASTLE ROCK ENTERTAINMENT, COLUMBIA PICTURES.

STARRING CLINT EASTWOOD (Frank Horrigan), JOHN MALKOVICH (Mitch Leary/John Booth/James Carney), RENE RUSSO (Lilly Raines), DYLAN MCDERMOTT (Al D'Andrea), GARY COLE (Bill Watts), FRED DALTON THOMPSON (Harry Sargent), JOHN MAHONEY (Sam Campagna), GREG ALAN-WILLIAMS (Matt Wilder), JIM CURLEY (President), SALLY HUGHES (First Lady).

"Why not call me Booth?"

America is traumatized by its dead Presidents, from Abraham Lincoln, murdered by J.W. Booth in 1865 while watching a play from a box at the theatre, right up to JFK, whose death became one of the most disturbing and macabre events in the history of television. The amateur film of Kennedy's murder in 1963 is probably the most minutely analysed pieces of celluloid of all time, and the pictures were broadcast repeatedly in a constant re-examination of the murder, an early example of reality TV.

In the Line of Fire uses that idea as a plot mechanism, but Petersen's movie is really about the ancient duel between good and evil. At first glance the divide seems simple enough: undercover cop Frank Horrigan (Clint Eastwood) is tough and hands-on, his evil opponent Mitch Leary (John Malkovich) thoughtful and intellectual. They are both cynics. But at a second glance another perspective begins to appear. We see Frank play beautiful ballads on the piano and tenderly court his colleague Lilly (Rene Russo), whereas Leary murders two women in their apartment and kills two hunters in cold blood while practising his aim.

Clint Eastwood plays ageing bodyguard Frank Horrigan, a man who feels he failed President Kennedy. The role goes against his image as an unscrupulous supporter of lynch justice, which he owes above all to the "Dirty Harry" movies. The impatient individualist of In the Line of Fire also hates bureaucrats but he has a kindly side too. Eastwood's Frank Horrigan doesn't hide the signs of age or the unhealed wounds on his soul. Leary, his diabolic opponent, also suffers; the system that taught him the art of perfect killing suddenly no longer wants him. Once part of a special unit that planned and carried out assassinations on the government's orders, he has now been discharged. Malkovich's Leary is an intellectual killer who carries out his plan to revenge his dismissal by assassinating the President of the USA with super-cool precision. His sudden outbreak of rage when Frank manages to talk with him on the telephone only makes him seem even more dangerous and unpredictable. Eastwood's stony face contrasts with Malkovich's changing disguises, from eccentric hippy to smart software manager.

Combined with Petersen's fine sense for the right dose of suspense, this constellation carries the movie throughout its length despite occasional narrative shallows. Leary sometimes calls himself Booth after Lincoln's murderer, and plays a gripping cat and mouse game with Frank who sees the case as a chance to make good his previous failure. Booth's real concern is

2

1 Frank Horrigan (Clint Eastwood): patriotism is
a question of honour.

2 The horrors of the past keep catching up with
Officer Horrigan, who is as uncompromising as he
is fearless.

3 Loss of honour to be avenged: John Malkovich
as the demonic adversary Mitch Leary.

4 If Frank Horrigan ever smiles …

5 … it's only because of his good-looking
colleague Lilly (Rene Russo).

not the President's personal safety. The movie distances itself from politics and reveals a clear satirical undertone when it presents an election campaign as a carnivalesque parade, and when the President is removed from the line of fire of a presumed assassin during a public appearance there are strong overtones of slapstick.

The movie concentrates instead on the duel between Leary and Horrigan and plays with the closeness between criminal and victim. Whenever Frank and his colleagues try to locate him, Leary is constantly one step ahead. Leary is a brilliant strategist, and can even manipulate the telephone wires to cover his tracks.

Thanks to the extreme economy of John Bailey's camera work (*Silverado*, 1985) and Anne Coates' (*Lawrence of Arabia*, 1962) masterful editing, Petersen manages to balance and combine the two diverging halves of the movie, its hectic action scenes and the romance between Frank and Lilly. He constantly inserts ironic breaks, as when the CIA and the FBI attack each other in Leary's empty apartment as they have no idea that the other would be there. In the end, however, after a last minute showdown where Frank throws himself in front of the President and saves his life, there can only be one winner.

BR

WOLFGANG PETERSEN   *Das Boot* (*The Boat*) is Petersen's best-known project, made in 1979–1981 as a television series and as a feature film which was eventually nominated for an Oscar. He began his career in 1960 as a director's assistant at the Ernst-Deutsch Theater in Hamburg. After his studies at the Berlin Film and Television Academy, he made a name for himself with television productions, particularly with *Reifezeugnis* ("High School Graduation", 1977), a feature-length episode of a crime series. In his first English-language movie *The NeverEnding Story* (1984) Petersen made a surprising departure from his usual direct style. Since *Enemy Mine* (1985) Petersen has worked in Hollywood, where *In the Line of Fire* was an important breakthrough for him. His latest work is the largely computer animated shipwreck spectacle *The Perfect Storm* (2000), starring George Clooney in the leading role.

3

5

"Thrillers are as good as their villains, and *In the Line of Fire* has a great one — a clever, slimy creep who insidiously burrows his way into the psyche of the hero." *Chicago Sun-Times*

4

THREE COLOURS: BLUE
Trois Couleurs: Bleu

1993 - FRANCE - 97 MIN. - MELODRAMA

DIRECTOR KRZYSZTOF KIESLOWSKI (*1941; 1996)
SCREENPLAY KRZYSZTOF KIESLOWSKI, KRZYSZTOF PIESIEWICZ **DIRECTOR OF PHOTOGRAPHY** SLAWOMIR IDZIAK **MUSIC** ZBIGNIEW PREISNER
PRODUCTION MARIN KARMITZ for MK2 PRODUCTIONS, CED PRODUCTIONS, CAB PRODUCTIONS, TOR STUDIO.

STARRING JULIETTE BINOCHE (Julie), BENOÎT RÉGENT (Olivier), FLORENCE PERNEL (Sandrine), CHARLOTTE VÉRY (Lucille), HÉLÈNE VINCENT (Journalist), PHILIPPE VOLTER (Broker), CLAUDE DUNETON (Doctor), HUGUES QUESTER (Patrice), YANN TRÉGOUËT (Antoine), EMMANUELLE RIVA (Mother).

IFF VENICE 1993 GOLDEN LION for BEST FILM, SILVER LION for BEST ACTRESS (Juliette Binoche).

"If I have all knowledge..."

Like so many artists, Krzysztof Kieslowski likes to use motifs that allow him to work inside a wider framework. His earlier work for instance includes a series of films about each of the Ten Commandments. His movie trilogy on the French Revolution is also based on underlying motifs. Liberty, equality, and fraternity are the driving forces behind each film. Kieslowski uses the tricolour as his guide and defines blue as the colour of liberty. His main concern is with how those revolutionary principles affect our private lives. How can we free ourselves from tragic, shocking, terrifying experiences? How can we become free to live again?

Julie (Juliette Binoche) is the only survivor of a car crash in which her husband Patrice (Hugues Quester) and daughter die. In the hospital she half-heartedly attempts suicide. When she is discharged she gives her house to

a broker (Philippe Volter) to sell and tries to rid herself of all her memories. Patrice was a famous composer and had been working on a symphony for the unification of Europe. Julie was his co-worker rather than his muse, and she destroys all the drafts of it. When Patrice's assistant, Olivier (Benoît Régent) visits her, she sleeps with him to prove to herself how unmoved she is by the tragedy. Nothing matters anymore.

But her protective shield is scratched again and again. A flautist on the street plays a melody from the Europe Symphony which he can't even know. An old woman strains to throw a glass bottle into the recycling bin. A mouse moves into the larder of Julie's new apartment and gives birth. Julie borrows the neighbour's cat to eat up the naked mice which symbolise life and reproduction. Afterwards however she can't bring herself to return to the apart-

ment, and her only friend, a prostitute, offers to go in and clean up. In contrast to Julie, she suffers from too great a hunger for life, too much sex and too many contacts. When she sees her father in the first row at the live sex show where she works, she can't go on and asks Julie for help. The two women sit opposite each other, neither knowing which way to turn. A documentary about Patrice and his work on television shows her dead husband embracing a young woman tenderly, and when Julie makes contact with this secret mistress, she sees that she is pregnant and begins to understand. However much she tries to shut out the past and stop her loss from tearing her soul in two, she will never be able to wipe it out: Patrice's music and his child will live on. She decides to give the house to the child and together with Olivier, whom she loves, she finishes the symphony for the unification of Europe. The final chorus of the work is also the final scene of the film, the words of the apostle Paul to the Corinthians: "If I have all knowledge and if I can move mountains but am without love, I am nothing." Julie sleeps with Olivier again. She can cry for the first time. By making peace with the wounds inflicted by fate, she finds the strength to live on.

SL

KRYSZTOF KIESLOWSKI Kieslowski, born in Warsaw in 1941, described himself as an "optimistic fatalist", perhaps as the result of many successful documentary films he made about Eastern Europe. It was only when he met the defense lawyer Krzysztof Piesiewicz (who much preferred to write screenplays) that he turned his attention to feature films. Together they made ten films about the Ten Commandments for Polish television, including *A Short Film about Love* (*Krotki film o milosci*, 1988) and *A Short Film about Killing* (*Krotki film o zabijaniu*, 1988), which were also cinema successes in the West. In 1990 he went to France, and it was there that he made his later films. He dreamed of showing 17 different montage versions of the movie *The Double Life of Veronique* (*La double vie de Véronique*, 1991) simultaneously in 17 Paris cinemas. The themes of his next trilogy were to have been heaven, hell and purgatory, but Kieslowski died during heart surgery in 1996.

1 Turning your back on everything always makes you more vulnerable.

2 An almost dream-like image.

3 When those who have stumbled talk to those who have fallen, there's no place for glamour.

4 The camera has to love a person's face in order for people to understand the person: Juliette Binoche as Julie.

3

"It's the tenderness in the eyes of someone who is beginning to be sure of themselves and their freedom." *epd Film*

SCHINDLER'S LIST

1993 - USA - 195 MIN. - HISTORICAL FILM, DRAMA

DIRECTOR STEVEN SPIELBERG (*1947)
SCREENPLAY STEVEN ZAILLIAN, based on the novel of the same name by THOMAS KENEALLY DIRECTOR OF PHOTOGRAPHY JANUSZ KAMINSKI MUSIC JOHN WILLIAMS PRODUCTION STEVEN SPIELBERG, GERALD R. MOLEN, BRANKO LUSTIG for AMBLIN ENTERTAINMENT, UNIVERSAL PICTURES.

STARRING LIAM NEESON (Oskar Schindler), BEN KINGSLEY (Itzhak Stern), RALPH FIENNES (Amon Goeth), CAROLINE GOODALL (Emilie Schindler), JONATHAN SAGALL (Poldek Pfefferberg), EMBETH DAVIDTZ (Helen Hirsch), MALGOSCHA GEBEL (Victoria Klonowska), SHMULIK LEVY (Wilek Chilowicz), MARK IVANIR (Marcel Goldberg), BÉATRICE MACOLA (Ingrid).

ACADEMY AWARDS 1994 OSCARS for BEST PICTURE, BEST DIRECTOR (Steven Spielberg), BEST ADAPTED SCREENPLAY (Steven Zaillian), BEST CINEMATOGRAPHY (Janusz Kaminski), BEST FILM EDITING (Michael Kahn), BEST ART DIRECTION – SET DECORATION (Allan Starsky, Ewa Braun) and BEST MUSIC (John Williams).

"It is said that he's a good man."

Can the horrors of the Holocaust be filmed without trivialising them? Can life under fascism be filmed without showing images which everybody has seen before? Steven Spielberg came up with one solution in his film about the German industrialist Oskar Schindler. The story he tells is unique, eccentric even, but the message is crystal clear: responsibility cannot be passed on to someone else, but is always a matter for the individual.

When the film starts, the German army has occupied Poland. The occupiers make a ghetto for the Jews in Krakow, and force them to register. We see their faces, one by one, individual people in great distress, many of whom are later tortured and murdered. This is no anonymous mass.

When we see Oskar Schindler (Liam Neeson) for the first time our eyes are drawn irresistibly to his Nazi party badge. He is an opportunist woman-iser, and is building an enamel factory in Poland for the German army. Jewish workers are cheaper than Polish ones, so he takes Jews. His accountant Itzhak Stern (Ben Kingsley) turns out to be an organisational genius and becomes the real director of the factory. Schindler's job is to bribe the Nazi officials. He is more hard-bitten businessman than hero, and at first his humanity is a more a question economics than it is of morals: happy work-ers, he reasons, produce more than discontented ones.

In 1942, the ghetto is destroyed and all the Jews are deported to a work camp in Plaszow. Schindler observes the harrowing events. A little girl wan-ders silently through the chaos, seemingly oblivious to events around her. Her red coat is the only spot of colour in this film, which is shot almost exclu-sively in documentary black and white. We later see her corpse in Auschwitz.

Through a bizarre friendship with sadistic Lager commandant Amon Goeth (Ralph Fiennes), Schindler manages to keep his workers although they are forced to live in the detention centre. This protects them from being tortured by the guards and means that they can trade on the black market, without which it is impossible to survive. Eventually Plaszow is dissolved and all its inmates are transported to Auschwitz, so Schindler has to make a decision. He uses his entire capital to bribe the Nazis and buy the lives of his workers. He saves over 1100 people, who he transports with two trains, one for men, one for women, to his hometown of Brünnlitz to open a munitions factory. Since the factory produces goods for the war effort, his workers are considered indispensable and their lives are saved. Even when the women's train arrives in Auschwitz by mistake, through fearlessness and bribery

Schindler manages to get the women out again. His strengths are his stubbornness and deviousness. He pretends to be a money-grabbing business man long after his motivation has changed and he has a real desire to help as many Jews as possible to survive. His weaknesses for drink, women, pleasure and luxury lead the Nazis to think of him as one of their own, but his factory in Brünnlitz produces munitions of such poor quality that the army has no use for them. With the rest of his money, he bankrupts himself making sure that all of "his" Jews survive until the end of the war. As he is listed as a collaborator and Nazi Party member, he is forced to flee to Argentina before the Allies arrive. Today, the descendants of his Jewish workers outnumber the total population of Jews living in Poland.

SI

1 An inscrutable face (Liam Neeson as Oskar Schindler) – is this scepticism or self-assurance?

2 Camp commander Amon Goeth's (Ralph Fiennes) uniform matches his facial expression. His lips are pinched and his gaze is haughty.

3 Horrific pictures, like snapshots in some satanic photo album.

4 Hands cannot type as fast as they would like to in the attempt to prevent disaster.

"I just want to tell an interesting and true story." *Steven Spielberg*

STEVEN SPIELBERG   When Spielberg announced that he wanted to make a movie about the Holocaust, everyone was appalled. The Jewish World Congress forbade him to film on the Auschwitz site. Spielberg's image as a maker of successful entertainment movies was too strong (*Jaws*, 1975, *Raiders of the Lost Ark*, 1981, *E.T. – The Extra-Terrestrial*, 1982 and *Jurassic Park*, 1992), and he was considered too lightweight. Today his Holocaust Foundation is the biggest archive of materials on Holocaust survivors in the world. And his second 'serious' film *Saving Private Ryan* (1998) is considered a prime example of how to make a moving and yet commercially successful movie about war. Not only has he managed to bridge the gap between entertainment and intellectually demanding cinema with extraordinary success, but he is now also considered to be the most successful director of all time, as he has managed to get serious without losing his audience.

4

The film deals with survival, where it ought to be talking about death,' is an objection raised by Claude Lanzmann against Spielberg. 'But the Jewish people and Jewish culture survived Hitler,' is Spielberg's response." *epd Film*

5   The broken and traumatized prisoners are momentarily disorientated after their liberation.

6   Itzhak Stern (Ben Kingsley) is an organisational genius. Many Jews owe him and Schindler their lives.

A PERFECT WORLD

1993 - USA - 138 MIN. - DRAMA, CRIME FILM

DIRECTOR CLINT EASTWOOD (*1930)
SCREENPLAY JOHN LEE HANCOCK DIRECTOR OF PHOTOGRAPHY JACK GREEN MUSIC LENNIE NIEHAUS PRODUCTION MARK JOHNSON, DAVID VALDES for MALPASO (for WARNER BROS.).

STARRING KEVIN COSTNER (Butch Haynes), CLINT EASTWOOD (Red Garnett), LAURA DERN (Sally Gerber), T. J. LOWTHER (Philip Perry), KEITH SZARABAJKA (Terry Pugh), LEO BURMESTER (Tom Adler), BRADLEY WHITEFORD (Bobby Lee), JENNIFER GRIFFIN (Gladys Perry), RAY MCKINNON (Bradley), LESLIE FLOWERS (Naomi Perry).

"I don't know nothing."

We are in Eastwood land. The themes of the movie are masculinity and the question of how to live a responsible life in a world that is far from perfect. Butch Haynes (Kevin Costner) breaks out of jail with the help of a cellmate he despises. Looking for a getaway car, the cellmate climbs into the kitchen of a single mother who is busy making breakfast for her family. He tries to rape her, but Haynes intervenes and knocks him down. A neighbour with a gun tries to overpower the convicts, but they take eight-year-old Philip as a hostage and flee.

Philip is an unwilling outsider. His mother, a Jehovah's witness, and his two sisters do everything they can to stop him having fun. Haynes himself feels that he too has been cheated of a large portion of his life and he starts to feel increasingly responsible for the small boy with the big brown eyes. When his cellmate begins to harass Philip, Haynes kills him.

The other focus of the story is Sheriff Red Garnett (Clint Eastwood). He is under pressure: the governor is in the middle of an election campaign, and has assigned a young criminologist (Laura Dern) to track down Haynes together with some agents from the FBI. Years ago, it was Sheriff Garnett who ensured that Haynes was given several years' youth custody for a petty crime. His idea was to save him from his violent father, but now he's not sure if he didn't lay the foundations for his criminal career instead. Garnett has no faith in carefully planned police actions, and knows all too well that even the best-planned chase can end in bloody failure. "In the end, all it's about

is who has the stomach ulcer and the regrets", he snaps at his young colleague.

In the course of their flight, Haynes and Philip become friends. The man encourages the boy's growing self-confidence, and the boy dares to do more and more things which his mother would never allow. He also helps Haynes get out of tricky situations, and Kidnapper and victim slowly become father and son on their journey through rural America. They meet a black farming family who take them in for the night. But when Haynes forces the loveless and brutal grandfather to apologise to his grandchild next morning, the situation escalates. Philip thinks he has been deceived in Haynes, and shoots at him and flees.

The two meet again in the middle of an open field. They are now surrounded by a ring of police who are closing in, and Haynes is gradually bleeding to death. Sheriff Garnett, unarmed, tries to calm the situation, and Haynes gives himself up. But an FBI agent misunderstands his gestures and shoots him dead. At the end of the movie, the only real victim is the criminal himself. There are no winners in Eastwood land.

This was the first film in Clint Eastwood's career where he gave up the main role to another star, and like *Unforgiven* (1992), his previous film, it was another melancholy swan song on the end of innocence. Kevin Costner took the opportunity to give a little more depth to the persona of the bad-tempered boy with a heart of gold that we first saw in *Bodyguard* (1992).   SL

"This film by the mature Clint Eastwood, like numerous other road movies, is also about the father who was lost and then found." *Der Spiegel*

1 Despite appearances, this couple are sadly not father and son (Kevin Costner and T. J. Lowther).

2 The viewer feels liking shouting, "What are you all staring at? Do something!"

3 Waiting for a better world. Butch Haynes and Philip Perry are standing at the side of a road to nowhere.

5

CHILD STARS No serious research has been done on the subject, but some form of inverse relation seems to govern the fate of child stars. Children who reach megastardom in childhood almost invariably disappear, whereas child stars who have average careers while under age often go on to exceptional success in later life. Examples for the second alternative are Elijah Wood, Christina Ricci, Natalie Portman, Edward Furlong and Anna Paquin; tragic examples of a single, roaring success are David Bennent (*The Tin Drum/Die Blechtrommel*, 1979), Adam Hann-Byrd (*Little Man Tate*, 1991) and Macaulay Culkin (Kevin, *Home Alone*). Drew Barrymore, child star in *E. T.* (1982), said of herself that she must have been Hollywood's youngest heroin addict. It took many years and countless therapies before she could continue her career as a mature actress.

"This isn't the first time that Eastwood has turned the tables on our expectations, but he's never been this bold in the past, or this sure of himself." *The Washington Post*

4 The wide-open eyes of children seem to look into our souls.

5 There's real affection here, despite the chain-smoking, the guns and the many misdemeanours.

Sydney Pollack's *The Firm* is as elegant as it is exciting. The movie has John Grisham's brilliant novel to thank for most of its excitement, while the elegance comes from the combination of Dave Grusin's music and the masterful editing, so much so that one of the key features of the film is the way in which the music determines the rhythm of the images. With breathtaking speed we are introduced to the life of Mitch McDeere (Tom Cruise), a Harvard student who is about to take his final law exams. Many law firms have contacted him and made enticing offers.

We see Mitch at job interviews, playing basketball with his lecturers and working as a waiter. His father is dead, he has no contact to his mother and his brother Ray (David Strathairn) is in jail. Unsurprisingly, the job that he accepts is with the company that offers the most money. Bendini, Lambert & Locke in Memphis, known as 'the Firm' for short, don't just offer 20% more pay than the competition but also favourable loans for buying a house and leasing a Mercedes-Benz. Mitch and his young wife are amazed by so much wealth. After years of living in a modest student apartment and suddenly they have a spacious house, a big car, membership of the Country Club and everything that makes for a comfortable, bourgeois existence. The Firm helps Mitch prepare for his exam but also expect him to begin work right away. He is assigned a mentor, Avery Tolar (Gene Hackman), who is as friendly as he is experienced – a replacement father for the fatherless lawyer.

Whilst Abby (Jeanne Tripplehorn) finds some of the customs and principles of the Firm strange, particularly the exaggerated, studied friendliness of its employees, Mitch only wants to see the best in everything, the big career and the rosy future. In this way trust and mistrust are held in balance. It soon becomes clear, however, that the new job has its price. Their life together has a mere veneer of normality – in fact they are completely under the control of the Firm. The house is bugged, Mitch is being watched, and colleagues die in mysterious circumstances. What seemed like a serious law firm turns out to be a Mafia organization. Finally, Mitch is blackmailed by the FBI to appear as chief witness against his firm.

Director Pollack manages to tell two stories at once. On the one hand we see a young lawyer struggling to manoeuvre between professional idealism and corrupt practice, and on the other we see how these difficulties increasingly threaten his previously happy relationship with his partner Abby. Mitch is pressured into a one-night stand on a business trip and then blackmailed. The plot constantly twists and turns to maintain the tension until the very end. As the threats get bigger and his enemies start to mount up, Mitch becomes ever more inventive. He fakes a deal to get his brother out of prison and defends himself against the killers that the Firm sends out to get him. But Mitch's real struggle is with himself, until he understands the greatest danger is the temptation to betray his profession and join the side of the lawless. SL

1 Trust is the name of the game, and knowing what to do when all is not what it seems – even in a marriage (Jeanne Tripplehorn and Tom Cruise).

2 The betrayers betrayed: a frantic search (Ed Harris, left) for Mitch McDeere's brother, who is on the run from the FBI.

3 Appearances can be deceptive: Tammy Hamphill (Holly Hunter) is anything but a naive secretary.

4 Even successful men (Gene Hackman as Avery Tolar) lose their way: he doesn't know friend from foe anymore.

5 Faking it: sophisticated furniture and elegant clothing notwithstanding, this is the Mafia's advocate (Hal Holbrook as Oliver Lambert).

JOHN GRISHAM Born in 1955, the American novelist John Grisham studied law and worked primarily as a criminal lawyer from 1981–1991. For a while, the commercial potential of his novels remained undiscovered, but now all of them have been filmed: *The Chamber, The Client, The Firm, The Pelican Brief, The Rainmaker* and *A Time to Kill*. Grisham's main preoccupation is the relationship between justice and the authorities. His novels always revolve around the same questions, but look at them from different perspectives, wondering about integrity in the workplace, the boundaries of corruption, and constantly asking whether the law still has anything to do with our moral conception of justice.

"The good thing about the film is that Mitch doesn't have to be an idealist in order to carry out his plan."

epd Film

4

5

FAREWELL MY CONCUBINE
Bawang Bie Ji

1993 - HONG KONG / CHINA - 169 MIN. - COSTUME FILM, DRAMA

DIRECTOR CHEN KAIGE (*1952)

SCREENPLAY LILIAN LEE, WEI LU, based on the novel by LILIAN LEE DIRECTOR OF PHOTOGRAPHY GU CHANGWAI MUSIC ZHAO JIPING
PRODUCTION HSU FENG for TOMSON FILMS, CHINA FILM, BEIJING FILM STUDIOS.

STARRING LESLIE CHEUNG (Cheng Dieyi), ZHANG FENGYI (Duan Xiaolou), GONG LI (Juxian), LU QI (Guan Jifa), YING DA (Na Kun), GE YOU (Master Yuan), LI CHUN (young Xiao Si), LEI HAN (old Xiao Si), TONG DI (the eunuch Zhang), LI DAN (Laizi).

IFF CANNES 1993 GOLDEN PALM.

"How will we survive the days of real life with real people?"

A woman hurries through the streets of a Chinese town, dragging her small son behind her. In a square, pupils of the Peking opera school demonstrate their virtuoso talents. The mother is a prostitute whose son can no longer live with her in the brothel. She tries to get the director of the school to take the boy and when he refuses, displeased by a vulgar finger gesture the child makes, the furious mother is beside herself with despair and chops her son's little finger off. This is the first of many injuries that Cheng Dieyi (Leslie Cheung) has to suffer before he becomes a star of the Peking opera playing female roles.

The movie gets its title from the opera of the same name, a story of faithfulness and unconditional love: when Xiang Yu, the great king of Chu, finds himself surrounded on all sides by his enemies in battle, his concubine Yu dances the sword dance for him one last time before slitting her own throat with his sword.

In this world, anyone who wants to become an outstanding artist must suffer. The pupils at the opera school are abused and tortured, both physically and mentally. Most of them are orphans or foundlings, and they have no prospects other than the dream of an opera career. When Dieyi can bear it no longer and runs away with a friend, the two go to see a real performance of a Peking opera and are so moved that they return to the school. His friend hangs himself to escape future punishment, but for Dieyi, the self-punishment of the daily routine soon becomes normal. He makes a new friend in Duan Xiaolou (Zhang Fengyi), who also becomes his partner in the theatre, playing king Yu to his concubine. When an opera house owner visits the school and his eye falls on Dieyi, an uproar ensues. As a performer of female roles, he makes the mistake of talking of himself as a man, and therefore immediately loses the visitor's favour. Duan, normally straightforward and relaxed, is overcome with rage and thrusts his king's sceptre into

2

GONG LI   Chinese actress Gong Li was born in 1965 and is one of the few Asiatic actresses to build a successful career without playing in martial arts films. Her longstanding partner, director Zhang Yimou, made her a star with his film *Red Sorghum* (*Hong Gao Liang*, 1987), and her subsequent films include *Judou* (1990), *Raise the Red Lantern* (1991), *The Story of Qiu Ju* (1992) and *To Live* (*Huozhe*, 1994). Gong Li mostly plays serious, self-confident women, who are never victims and are in charge of their own lives. She combines a strong will with intelligence and sex appeal. After her separation from Yimou she has also worked on American films. In 1998 she was jury president at the Cannes Film Festival. She is that rare thing in the West – a genuine Chinese star.

1   Things aren't what they seem, especially in Chinese opera.

2   Audiences see a man playing a woman in love with a man. In reality, it's a man playing a woman so that nobody finds out he's in love with a man.

3   Even on stage and behind a mask, reality catches up with you.

4   Everyone knows they are being watched. The question is, by whom?

Dieyi's mouth until he performs the concubine's part enchantingly and flawlessly.

Eventually they both become stars of the Peking opera, although their friendship fails due to their differences and the situation in 20th century China. Dieyi lives only for the opera. He turns to opium in moments of crisis, and the life of his best friend, his king on stage, puzzles and repulses him. Duan meets a high-class prostitute called Juxian (Gong Li) in a brothel and marries her. To Dieyi's horror the couple try to build a bourgeois life together, but the political situation in China will not allow this. The new revolutionary government disapproves of all artists who previously performed under other rulers. But the Japanese occupying forces, Chinese liberators and Communist masses all agree about the quality of the opera and are keen to let it continue. The private and political story of obsession and treachery escalates in the Cultural Revolution. No one is safe; Dieyi denounces his friend (the lover he aspires to), Duan his wife and his wife Dieyi. A decade later, years after they have both left the stage, they perform the final scene from 'Farewell My Concubine' one last time. Dieyi takes the king's sword at the end of his aria and beheads himself. This is his answer to the recurring question: "How will we survive the days of real life with real people?" The road to becoming an artist was tortuous and inhuman, and the final answer for Dieyi can be "Not at all". Few viewers will be familiar with the music and stylised masks used in this movie, but it is impossible not be moved by the despairing pessimism of human being whose only real home is the stage.

SL

"Chen Kaige's take on cinema makes no claim to solve the problems of humanity. Instead, it helps to make them bearable, not by dreamy escapism, but by bringing to the everyday a component of dreams, ideals and grace." *Cahiers du cinéma*

4

THE PIANO

1993 - AUSTRALIA / FRANCE / NEW ZEALAND - 120 MIN. - DRAMA, HISTORICAL FILM

DIRECTOR JANE CAMPION (*1954)
SCREENPLAY JANE CAMPION DIRECTOR OF PHOTOGRAPHY STUART DRYBURGH MUSIC MICHAEL NYMAN PRODUCTION JAN CHAPMAN for MIRAMAX, CIBY 2000.

STARRING HOLLY HUNTER (Ada McGrath), HARVEY KEITEL (George Baines), SAM NEILL (Stewart), ANNA PAQUIN (Flora McGrath), KERRY WALKER (Aunt Morag), GENEVIÈVE LEMON (Nessie), TUNGIA BAKER (Hira), IAN MUNE (Reverend), PETER DENNETT (sailor), PETE SMITH (Hone).

ACADEMY AWARDS 1994 OSCARS for BEST ACTRESS (Holly Hunter), BEST SUPPORTING ACTRESS (Anna Paquin), BEST ORIGINAL SCREENPLAY (Jane Campion).

IFF CANNES 1993 GOLDEN PALM, SILVER PALM for BEST ACTRESS (Holly Hunter).

"The voice you hear is not my speaking voice but my mind's voice"

A woman's fate around 1850, at the other end of the world and on the edge of civilization. In the days when fathers were still able to decide what was to become of their daughters, Ada McGrath (Holly Hunter) is married off in New Zealand. There is a chronic lack of womenfolk on the island, and her husband, settler Stewart (Sam Neill), has never clapped eyes on her before the wedding. But doesn't seem to mind her nine-year-old daughter, and nor does he care about the fact that Ada has not spoken at all for six years. The good Lord loves mute creatures as well as those who speak, as he writes to her father in Scotland. But he is more puzzled by the piano that she brings with her, and it remains on the beach where she lands as he doesn't have enough men to carry all her luggage. The instrument is Ada's real voice, and Stewart fails to understand how much it means to her. Her playing has an intensity which expresses the whole force of her personality. Stewart is not a cruel man, but for him Ada represents a level of civilization which is a different

realm to the wild nature he hopes to tame and cultivate, worlds apart from the forest fires and land clearing which are the settlers' main concerns. Mother and daughter, clad entirely in black with bonnets and crinolines, appear to have arrived from another planet as they wade through the mud of the impenetrable New Zealand bush.

In her despair at the loss of her piano, Ada turns to George Baines (Harvey Keitel) who lives a little way outside the settlement in a forest hut. We discover nothing about the illiterate Baines other than the fact that he has abandoned his British roots and gone native. He is covered with tattoos and speaks the Maori's language, and is therefore useful to the settlers as a negotiator and translator. Baines is what Fenimore Cooper would have called a frontiersman. He bridges the gap between two cultures; and despite his familiarity with the wilderness he also transmits his native culture. Ada comes to trust Baines because like her he is an outsider. Unlike Stewart, he

stantly realises what the piano means to her. Stewart accepts immediately when Baines offers him a stretch of forest in exchange for the instrument. He doesn't ask Ada.

Outraged, she rushes to Baines, who has had the piano carried to his house. "The piano belongs to me!" she scrawls in desperation on a page of the notebook which hangs around her neck. Holly Hunter won an Oscar for her portrayal of the role of Ada, and it is extraordinary how much aggression she manages to inject into the diminutive person of the unbending, contrary, small-lipped mute.

Ada demands that Baines return the instrument, but he suggests a deal: she can earn it back key by key with piano lessons. Ada beats him down to just the black keys, but George doesn't want to learn to play; he wants to listen to Ada, watch her and "do certain things" to her as she plays.

They agree on a rate of exchange. The closer he gets to her, the more keys he has to let her have. Finally she agrees to lie naked next to him for the last ten keys, and the piano is hers once more. But she still returns to Baines.

Ada is strengthened by her feelings for Baines and excited by the sensuality of their erotic meetings, which gradually free her from the fear of her own body that her Victorian upbringing has given her. She attempts to win her husband's affection and one night even tries to seduce him. Up until then, she had always remained distant when Stewart tried to claim his marital rights, but now it is he who pushes her away. Ada belongs to him, but now she wants him as a sexual object.

Stewart is annoyed. The movie's audience was also unsettled, accustomed above all to the primacy of male desire in American cinema and the male gaze on the female body. Jane Campion sees her story with the dis

"*The Piano* is a miracle of violence and repose, refinement and cruelty, passion and restraint." *Positif*

1 A surreal moment: washed up on a deserted beach in the wilderness with only music as a comfort.

2 People take familiar cultural objects with them to foreign lands – but why? (Holly Hunter and Anna Paquin).

3 For contact between different cultures to be successful, it must be gentle (Harvey Keitel as George Baines).

2

3

tance of 20th century eyes. Her literary inspirations, like the love triangle in Emily Brontë's *Wuthering Heights*, are not just set in an atmosphere of Victorian narrow-mindedness, they are also products of it. A story like *The Piano* in which the reality of society's sexual drives is revealed would have been absolutely unthinkable at the time in which it is set.

When Ada's daughter Flora (Anna Paquin) tells her step-father about her mother's secret meetings with Baines, Stewart is beside himself with jealousy and rage. He follows his wife to Baines' house and tries to rape her. Stewart cannot help himself, he is a man of his times whose mental limitations "border on the tragic" as critics were keen to point out. He hacks off one of her fingers, so that she can no longer play the piano. He has finally understood her, or at least has realised how he can hurt her most. He sends Baines the finger – and gives up.

Ada leaves the island together with George on the boat in which she arrived. The piano is now nothing but ballast to her, and she wants it thrown overboard. As the rope holding it unwinds, she puts her foot in one of the loops and is nearly dragged down into the depths: She manages to break free, and at the end is shown sitting at the piano again with a metal finger which Baines has forged for her. The clacking of the artificial finger on the keys lends an ironic distance to the emotions of the music. And she begins to learn to speak again.

SL

4

"These characters don't have our 20th century sensitivity as far as sexuality is concerned. They aren't prepared for its intensity and power."

Neue Zürcher Zeitung

HOLLY HUNTER

Holly Hunter's collaboration with Ethan and Joel Coen began unusually for an actress. In their debut movie *Blood Simple* (1984) she doesn't appear at all – we only hear her voice on an answering machine. Her break-through as a film actress came in one of the Coen brothers' wild, anarchic comedies. Alongside Nicolas Cage, she played the charming police woman who yearns for a child in *Raising Arizona* (1987). A year later she appeared as a bubbly journalist in *Broadcast News* and was nominated for an Oscar for the first time. At only 1.57 meters with thin lips and a some-times pinched facial expression, Holly Hunter doesn't fulfil Hollywood's conventional expectations where female beauty is concerned. She was so keen to have the role of Ada in Jane Campion's movie *The Piano* (1993) that she applied for it unbidden with a stream of faxes.

Holly Hunter was born in Georgia in 1958 and grew up on a farm, the youngest of seven children. Her career began on Broadway in 1980, and today she still alternates theatre and film roles. In the comedy *O Brother, Where Art Thou?* (2000) she plays the faithless Penelope who has long stopped waiting for her husband George Clooney to return from his crazy odyssey.

4   Love finds its voice first and foremost in music.

5   A picture beautiful enough to be a painting by an Old Master.

THE FUGITIVE

1993 - USA - 127 MIN. - THRILLER, POLICE FILM

DIRECTOR ANDREW DAVIS (*1946)
SCREENPLAY JEB STUART, DAVID N. TWOHY, based on characters by ROY HUGGINS **DIRECTOR OF PHOTOGRAPHY** MICHAEL CHAPMAN
MUSIC JAMES NEWTON HOWARD **PRODUCTION** ARNOLD KOPELSON for WARNER BROS.

STARRING HARRISON FORD (Dr Richard Kimble), TOMMY LEE JONES (Samuel Gerard), SELA WARD (Helen Kimble), JULIANNE MOORE (Dr Anne Eastman), JOE PANTOLIANO (Cosmo Renfro), JEROEN KRABBÉ (Dr Charles Nichols), ANDREAS KATSULAS (Sykes), DANIEL ROEBUCK (Biggs), L. SCOTT CALDWELL (Poole), TOM WOOD (Newman).

ACADEMY AWARDS 1994 OSCAR for BEST SUPPORTING ACTOR (Tommy Lee Jones).

"This could be his lucky day."

Dr Richard Kimble (Harrison Ford) is a successful and well-loved children's surgeon, married to a beautiful, wealthy woman and popular among his influential colleagues. He is warm-hearted and interested in the well being of his patients; all in all, he's a good person and a happy man. One day, when he is on his way home from a charity function, he is called to the hospital to perform an emergency operation, and when he finally gets home that night, he finds his wife murdered. Although he pleads his innocence and claims to have struggled with the murderer, a man with an artificial arm, all the evidence seems to be against him. The court's decision is that Dr Richard Kimble be sentenced to death by lethal injection.

This plot was the starting point of one of the most successful TV series of the 60s, and it's also the 15-minute opening of one of the cleverest action movies of the decade. The TV series *The Fugitive* was an updated version of Victor Hugo's novel *Les Misérables*. In every episode Kimble tried once more to settle down, taking on a new job or starting a relationship with a new woman. According to the rules of the series, after 45 minutes his attempts invariably failed. It was hugely popular, and the last episode, in 1967, had a record audience of 72%.

The movie concentrates on two central questions – how Dr Kimble always manages to evade his pursuers, and whether he will ever find the actual murderers. A balance is created between his escape and his search for the real culprits. The fugitive doctor is locked in a gripping ongoing struggle with investigating police marshal Samuel Gerard (Tommy Lee Jones). Driven by his will to succeed, the obsessive marshal will brook no criticism of his strategies in chasing the doctor. Gerard may work in a team, but this only gives him more scope to live out his unrelenting ambition. When the two meet for the first time, Kimble shouts: "I didn't kill my wife!' Gerard roars back "I don't care". Kimble, at least, then knows what he's up against. He always has to be a step ahead, always a shade cleverer than his pursuer. In the end, the marshal is eventually forced to admit that his usual methods are not enough. Whether he likes it or not, he has to feel his way into the case, constantly trying to predict Kimble's next move. Eventually he has no choice but to join forces with Kimble in the search for the real murderers.

The audience's attention gradually shifts away from Kimble's escape as his intelligence and creativity increasingly impress the police and awaken the marshal's sense of justice, until eventually their joint efforts to find the real criminals become the central focus of the movie. Everything leads back to Kimble's original workplace at the hospital and to his influential friends. The movie ends with the discovery of a network of intrigue so exciting it can do without the scenes of violence featured in most action films. SL

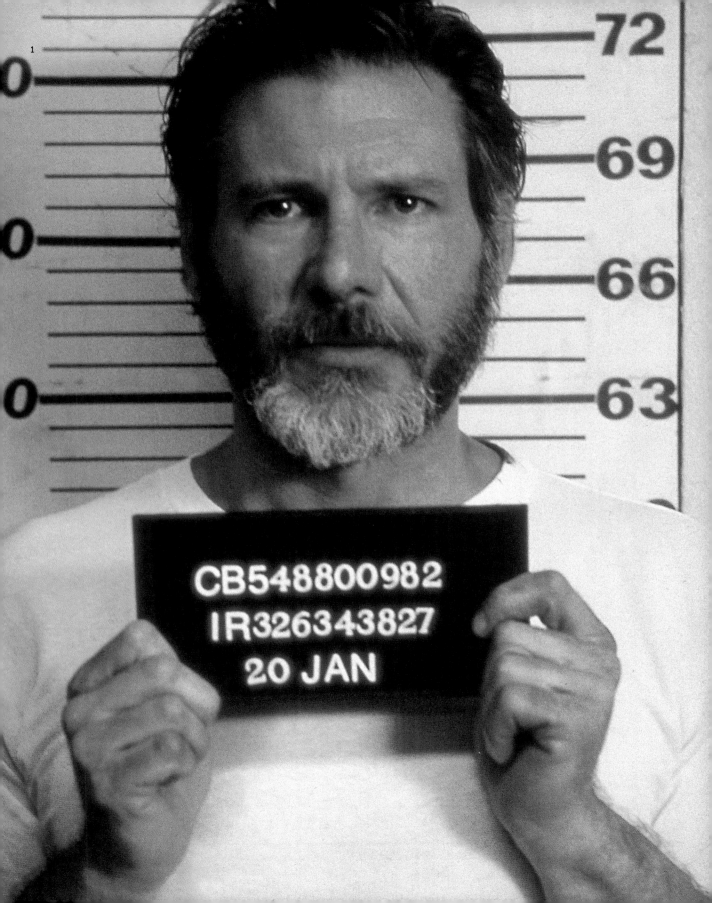

"The way in which Tommy Lee Jones extracts a proper person from a stereotype role, overbearing, lightning quick, cunning and cold (...) is a minor work of art." *Der Spiegel*

HARRISON FORD Harrison Ford trained as a carpenter, and had some film producers got their way, he would still be hammering and sawing. Born in Chicago in 1942, he is not spectacularly good looking; he was never an angry young man or an intellectual. But he doesn't shy away from controversial films like *Mosquito Coast* (1986), and he doesn't try to hide his age. His second marriage to scriptwriter Melissa Mathison (*E. T.*) doesn't seem to be enough for the gossip magazines. They are more interested in seeing him as the actor whose movies have earned the most money: the *Star Wars* trilogy (1977, 1980, 1983), the *Indiana Jones* trilogy (1981, 1984, 1989) and the Tom Clancy films *Patriot Games* (1992) and *Clear and Present Danger* (1994). Harrison Ford represents the triumph of unspectacular solidity over glamour and superficiality.

1 Strange things are afoot: Harrison Ford as Dr Richard Kimble with a criminal record.

2 An unusual hero who knows how to defend himself.

3 A final attempt to kill: Dr Charles Nichols (Jeroen Krabbé) tries to escape arrest.

4 On the run: Dr Kimble manages to escape the police time and again.

5 A false ID card: Samuel Gerard (Tommy Lee Jones) tracking down clues. Dr Kimble has managed to gain access to the hospital archives.

SHORT CUTS

1993 - USA - 188 MIN. - DRAMA, EPISODIC FILM

DIRECTOR ROBERT ALTMANN (*1925)
SCREENPLAY ROBERT ALTMAN, FRANK BARHYDT, based on short stories by RAYMOND CARVER DIRECTOR OF PHOTOGRAPHY WALT LLOYD
MUSIC MARK ISHAM PRODUCTION CARY BROKAW for AVENUE ENTERTAINMENT, FINE LINE FEATURES, SPELLING FILMS.

STARRING ANDIE MACDOWELL (Ann Finnigan), BRUCE DAVISON (Howard Finnigan), JACK LEMMON (Paul Finnigan), MATTHEW MODINE (Dr Ralph Wyman), JULIANNE MOORE (Marian Wyman), ANNE ARCHER (Claire Kane), FRED WARD (Stuart Kane), JENNIFER JASON LEIGH (Lois Kaiser), CHRIS PENN (Jerry Kaiser), ROBERT DOWNEY JR. (Bill Bush), MADELEINE STOWE (Sheri Shepard), TIM ROBBINS (Gene Shepard), LILY TOMLIN (Doreen Piggott), TOM WAITS (Earl Piggott), LILI TAYLOR (Honey Bush), FRANCES MCDORMAND (Betty Weathers), PETER GALLAGHER (Stormy Weathers), LORI SINGER (Zoe Trainer), LYLE LOVETT (Andy Bitkower), HUEY LEWIS (Vern Miller).

"Is this a war which can be won?"

A movie usually tells the story of one person, or maybe several. This is what we're used to. We get to know them, we understand them, we suffer and rejoice with them, and at the end we join them in overcoming some kind of final challenge. Robert Altman's *Short Cuts* is different. The plot seems to lose itself in an endless chain of different stories and characters, there is no time to get to know the protagonists, and we are immediately confronted with closed scenarios. The brevity of the episodes stops us from identifying with the characters, and we can do nothing other than sit back and watch as they lead their unhappy, depraved and solitary lives.

Their fates are shown in such fragmentary fashion that it seems impossible to discover the real motivations for their actions, But the abiding impression is still one of precise observation, coupled with a laconic attitude which Altman has preserved from Raymond Carver's brilliant short stories.

From the very beginning we find ourselves in the midst of the action. The Shephards are having another in a series of family arguments. Gene (Tim Robbins) is a bad-tempered redneck, a motorbike policeman who hates dogs. He is lying to his wife Sheri (Madeleine Stowe), telling her hypocritical tales of late hours at work and secret investigations. The truth is that he has a lover, Betty Weathers (Frances McDormand), it's her birthday and she is waiting for him. Betty's husband Stormy (Peter Gallagher) promised to pick up their son, but instead he too is making a scene. Television anchorman Howard Finnigan (Bruce Davison) and his wife Ann (Andie MacDowell) are lying in bed watching his program. Cellist Zoe Trainer (Lori Singer) is giving a concert, while painter Marian Wyman (Julianne Moore) and her husband Ralph (Matthew Modine), a pediatric surgeon, are in the audience. They make friends with their neighbours and hold a barbecue together with

1   An American family (Madeleine Stowe and Tim Robbins: the only thing missing from this idyllic scene is a dog.

2   It's a strange world: the child needs oral satisfaction, and so do the clients on the other end of the phone (Jennifer Jason Leigh).

3   In Altman's films, only drink provides moments of happiness (Lily Tomlin and Tom Waits).

"One feels that the film can never end, that here we will stay in the company of these ten families that we have learnt to recognise on sight, who enact beneath our eyes their lives of petty frustrations and intimate betrayals." *Le Monde*

unemployed sales rep Stuart Kane (Fred Ward) and his wife Claire (Anne Archer) who works as a clown at children's birthday parties.

Lois Kaiser (Jennifer Jason Leigh) helps pay the family bills by working for a telephone sex line. While she fakes oral and anal intercourse for her client on the other end of the line, she changes her baby's nappy and makes obscene gestures to her husband Jerry (Chris Penn) which leave us in no doubt as to what she thinks of him. Doreen Piggott (Lily Tomlin) works as a waitress in a coffee shop. Stuart Kane and his friends start off from the coffee shop on a fishing expedition. When they find a naked woman's body in the river, they decide to tie it up so they can get on with their fishing undisturbed.

One episode follows another and the audience is permitted brief glances into the lives of the 22 figures. Altman never uses longer sequences to tell us more about the couples he introduces and very few of the scenes are directly connected. The various plot strands are all heading straight for some sort of crisis or disaster. Gene Shepard is trying to give up smoking, his nerves are raw and he secretly kidnaps his children's dog and abandons it in another part of town. The Finnigans' son is run over on his way to school by Doreen. Although she is very concerned and tries her hardest to take care of him, he simply won't let her as he has been told not to speak to strangers. Once home he passes out and his mother has to rush him to hospital.

Despite its fragmentary nature, *Short Cuts* is more genuine and more tragic than a conventional melodrama could ever be, as it transforms chance and banality, those two poles of human life, into an artistic form. The tragic dimension of the film comes not from its presentation of a number of tragic existences, but rather from the way the sum of its scenes illustrates humanity's lovelessness. The characters' lives seem to be ruled by blind chance. Altman nonetheless manages to avoid any exaggeration or misplaced sentimentality. In this plot without classic storylines or tension, seemingly without any dramatic structure, there can be no heroes and no surprising revelations: the audience may hope for a happy ending, but those hopes are

dashed when the Finnigans' son dies and Zoe Trainer commits suicide. The stories continue without interruption and we see a family picnic. Bill Bush (Robert Downey Jr.) and Jerry Kaiser leave the party to go behind the bushes with two women they have just met. Kaiser, in a moment of madness, beats one of them to death.

As so often in Los Angeles, there is an earthquake, but this is no catastrophe of Biblical proportions and afterwards everything is much as it was before. At the end of the film we're not looking into a brighter future with different conditions and better people. Instead these fragments from the lives of so many different characters show us the difficulties of life itself. SL

"Old Master Robert Altman appears to have no difficulty at all in giving us an understanding of the stories of twenty-two protagonists using a highly unusual narrative style." *Fischer Film Almanach*

EPISODIC FILMS Episodic narration means that many storylines can exist alongside each other, and only occasionally be brought together in a common plot. Cinema has always been fascinated with parallels and simultaneous plot strands. In the 70s, directors tried to represent simultaneous action by dividing the screen into four or more parts in a technique known as split screen. Robert Altman uses a different method. *Short Cuts* gives the audience only brief glimpses of the lives of his numerous protagonists, and when their paths coincidentally cross in hot, summery Los Angeles, these meetings have tragic or even fatal consequences. This screenplay technique has remained extremely influential right up to the present day. Well known examples are *Pulp Fiction* (1994), *Playing by Heart* (1998) and *Magnolia* (1999). Because episodic movies do without conventional dramatic development, they rely more heavily on the quality of their cast. They are actors' cinema in the best sense.

4   Does this baker (Lyle Lovett) look like a happy man?

5   That's all we needed: Daddy (Jack Lemmon).

6   Men and their habits (Fred Ward, centre): a study in headwear …

7   Gene lies every time he opens his mouth. But it matters little, as nobody (Betty, Frances McDormand) believes him anymore.

FORREST GUMP

1994 - USA - 142 MIN. - COMEDY

DIRECTOR ROBERT ZEMECKIS (*1952)

SCREENPLAY ERIC ROTH, based on the novel of the same name by WINSTON GROOM **DIRECTOR OF PHOTOGRAPHY** DON BURGESS

MUSIC ALAN SILVESTRI **PRODUCTION** WENDY FINERMAN, STEVE TISCH, STEVE STARKEY, CHARLES NEWIRTH for PARAMOUNT.

STARRING TOM HANKS (Forrest Gump), ROBIN WRIGHT (Jenny Curran), GARY SINISE (Lt. Dan Taylor), SALLY FIELD (Mrs Gump), MYKELTI WILLIAMSON (Benjamin Buford "Bubba" Blue), MICHAEL CONNER HUMPHREYS (Forrest as a boy), HANNA HALL (Jenny as a girl), TIFFANY SALERNO (Carla), MARLA SUCHARETZA (Lenore), HALEY JOEL OSMENT (Forrest Junior).

ACADEMY AWARDS 1995 OSCARS for BEST PICTURE, BEST ACTOR (Tom Hanks), BEST DIRECTOR (Robert Zemeckis), BEST VISUAL EFFECTS (Allen Hall, George Murphy, Ken Ralston, Stephen Rosenbaum), BEST FILM EDITING (Arthur Schmidt), and BEST ADAPTED SCREENPLAY (Eric Roth).

"Shit happens!"

A bus stop in Savannah, Georgia. A man with the facial expression of a child sits on the bench, a small suitcase next to him and a box of chocolates in his hand. While he is waiting for the bus, he tells the story of his life to the others sitting around him.

The story begins sometime in the 1950s in a place called Greenbow in Alabama. Here Forrest Gump (Michael Conner Humphreys), a young boy named after a hero from the Civil War, is growing up without a father. He is different from the other children: his IQ of 75 is way below average, and as his mother (Sally Field) says, his spine is as bent as a politician's morals. But his mother is a strong-willed woman, and she manages to balance out these defects. She makes her boy wear leg braces and although she's prepared to

use her body to convince the headmaster that Forrest doesn't need to go to a special school, she teaches her son morals: "Dumb folks are folks who act dumb", being one of the many pearls of wisdom from her rich repertoire.

Forrest, who is friendly and unsuspecting, doesn't have an easy life. No one wants to sit next to him on the school bus, apart from Jenny (Hanna Hall), who soon becomes his only friend. When Forrest is being teased by his school mates for the thousandth time, she tells him to run away. Forrest always does what people tell him, and suddenly he discovers hidden gifts like speed and endurance. The leg braces shatter, and with them the limitations of his simple mind fall away. Swifter than the wind, Forrest runs and runs and runs through his youth.

Years later, when he's almost an adult, Forrest is running away from his schoolmates again and by mistake ends up on a football field. Simple-minded Forrest is offered a college scholarship and a place on an All-American football team.

"Life is like a box of chocolates. You never know what you're gonna get" – another gem from Mrs Gump's treasury. There's a lot in this for Forrest. Thanks to his knack for being in the right place at the right time, his football career is followed by military service and the Vietnam War, where he becomes not only a war hero but also a first-class table tennis player. After the war he fulfils a promise he made to Bubba (Mykelti Williamson), his friend and comrade in arms, and he makes his fortune as the captain of a

shrimping boat. He becomes even richer when he invests his millions in what he believes to be a fruit firm by the name of "Apple".

Forrest Gump's life is a 40-year, long-distance run through American post-war history. He shakes hands with Presidents Kennedy and Nixon, shows Elvis Presley the hip thrust and inspires John Lennon's song "Imagine". He invents the Smiley as well as the "Shit happens" sticker. By pure chance his finger is always on the pulse of the times. He gets mixed up in a protest action for racial integration, in a demonstration against the Vietnam War and accidentally witnesses the Watergate Affair.

Just as Forrest's career and his experiences of American history are unintentional, his meetings with the love of his life, Jenny (Robin Wright), are

1 As simple as they come: Forrest Gump (Tom Hanks) fulfils the American dream in his own way.

2 A safe seat: one of his mother's sayings was "Dumb folks are folks who act dumb" and this stays with him all his life.

3 Jenny (Hanna Hall) is Forrest's (Michael Conner Humphreys) only friend. She sticks by him, even though everybody teases him because he is so slow physically and mentally.

4 A woman's wiles: Forrest's single mother (Sally Field) uses everything in her power, even her own body, to ensure that her son leads a normal life.

also unplanned. Instead of fulfilling her dream and becoming a folksinger she has ended up a junkie hanging round the hippie scene, singing in a third-rate night club. When his mother dies, Forrest moves back to Greenbow, where he has a short but unsuccessful affair with Jenny. Once more, Forrest tries to run away from his destiny and he runs through America for three years without a concrete destination, accompanied by a growing band of followers.

Director Robert Zemeckis is known for being a specialist in technically demanding entertainment movies. He literally turned Meryl Streep's head in *Death Becomes Her* (1992) and his *Back to the Future* trilogy suggests that he has a weakness for time travel (*Back to the Future I-III*, 1985, 1989,

1990). *Forrest Gump*, adapted by Eric Roth from the novel of the same name by Winston Groom, is also a strange journey into the past.

With the help of George Lucas' special effects firm Industrial Light & Magic (ILM), Zemeckis uses sophisticated visual tricks and original film footage to create the illusion that Forrest was actually present at various historical occasions. For the scene where Forrest shakes hands with President Kennedy in the Oval Office, the digital technicians of ILM used archive material with the real people cut out and a superimposed image of Forrest Gump. Tom Hanks was filmed in front of a blue screen and this was combined with the archive film by computer. Computer technology is present throughout *Forrest Gump*, though audiences are unlikely to notice it. With its help, a

5

"Throughout, Forrest carries a flame for Jenny, a childhood sweetheart who was raised by a sexually abusive father and is doomed to a troubled life. The character's a bit obvious: Jenny is clearly Forrest's shadow – darkness and self destruction played against his lightness and simplicity." *San Francisco Chronicle*

thousand real extras were transformed into a hundred thousand simulated demonstrators.

The naive boy-next-door image which Tom Hanks had developed elsewhere made him the ideal actor for this part, which one critic described as "Charlie Chaplin meets Lawrence of Arabia". His Forrest Gump is the counterpart of Josh Baskin, the twelve-year-old who grows into the body of a man overnight in Penny Marshall's comedy *Big* (1988).

Forrest Gump is not a direct reflection of contemporary history, but it does reflect a distinctly American mentality. History is personalised and shown as a series of coincidences. The moral of the movie is as simple as

BLUE/GREEN SCREEN Blue/green screen is a process by which moving silhouettes can be combined with a picture background. The actors, figures or objects are first filmed in front of a blue screen. Then two versions of the movie are made: in the first all the colours are filtered out of the background, in the second only the silhouettes of the actors remain on a white background. The second version is transferred onto an unexposed film reel and this is used to film the actual scene. Finally, both versions are combined onto a third piece of film either in a compositing machine or by using a film printer.

5 Love, Peace and Happiness? Jenny (Robin Wright) resorts to drugs while running away from herself.

6 An inspired move: *Forrest Gump* owes a large part of its authentic feel to the special effects of Industrial Light & Magic. These lead the viewer to think that Forrest really did meet President Nixon.

7 A promise with consequences: Forrest promises his dying friend Bubba (Mykelti Williamson) that he will fulfil their shared dream of going shrimp fishing.

the sayings of Forrest's mother. Everything is possible – you just have to want something to happen, or be at the right place at the right time, even if you hardly realise what is going on and don't take an active part in events. International movie-goers loved the unique and entertaining worldview of this simple soul from Alabama, underscored by a sound track which is a musical cross section of the whole century. The movie made 330 million dollars in the USA, and almost doubled that sum worldwide. It was awarded six Oscars in 1995, and suddenly Smileys were in fashion again and everyone went around saying "Shit happens!". Winston Groom's novel and Bubba's shrimp cookbook stood on many bookshelves. *Forrest Gump* is somewhat

reminiscent of Hal Ashby's comedy *Being there* (1979), where Peter Sellers plays a simple gardener who only knows the world from his television. Ashby's movie is an intelligent and sometimes highly comic satire, but *Forrest Gump* didn't take that opportunity, or didn't want it: it's pure entertainment which only pretends to reflect on modern history. That combination of historical reproduction and conventional Hollywood plot links *Forrest Gump* to Steven Spielberg's *Schindler's List* (1993): the audience flick through the movie like a photo album, reassure themselves about their own past and leave the movie theatre two hours later, satisfied and by no means unpleasantly moved.   APO

CHUNGKING EXPRESS
Chongqing Senlin

1994 - HONG KONG - 97 MIN. - DRAMA

DIRECTOR WONG KAR-WAI [WANG JIAWEI] (*1958)
SCREENPLAY WONG KAR-WAI **MUSIC** ROEL A. GARCIA, FRANKIE CHAN [CHEN SHUNQI] **DIRECTOR OF PHOTOGRAPHY** CHRISTOPHER DOYLE, ANDREW LAU [LIU WEIQIANG] **PRODUCTION** CHAN YI-KAN [CHEN YIJIN] for JET TONE PRODUCTIONS.

STARRING BRIGITTE LIN [Lin Qingxia] (woman with the blond wig), KANESHIRO TAKESHI [He Qiwu] (# 223), TONY LEUNG [Liang Chaowei] (# 663), FAYE WONG [Wang Jinwen] (Faye), VALERIE CHOW [Shou Jialing] (Stewardess), "PIGGY" CHAN [Chen Jinquan], GUAN LINA, HUANG ZHIMING, LIANG ZHEN, ZUO SONGSHEN.

"California Dreamin'"

To begin with, *Chungking Express* was just occupational therapy for Wong Kar-Wai: he had a couple of months' break in the middle of a big production called *Ashes of Time* (*Dung che sai duk*, 1992–94) and he wanted to fill it in by knocking out a short movie. He started out with little more than a couple of clearly defined characters and locations to go with them. The internal links and the plot, were all to be found in the process of filming.

April 30, 1994. A woman (Brigitte Lin) in a garish blond wig and enormous sunglasses has to pass on a packet of drugs, but she loses it and has to go and look for it. At the same time policeman He Qiwu – officer no. 223 – sits in a snack bar drowning his sorrows, as his girl friend left him exactly a month ago. Since then he has survived on cans of pineapple whose sell-by date is today, symbolising the end of his love. Gloomily he gets more and more drunk and empties his last can of pineapple. To cap it all, today is his 25th birthday. He decides to fall in love with the first woman who comes into the snack bar. Enter the blonde with the sunglasses, worn out from a chaotic day and looking for comfort.

Another policeman – officer no. 663 – has also split up with his girl friend, an air hostess. She has left her key to his apartment in his regular bar with Faye the waitress, who constantly listens to the promises of "California Dreamin'". Faye has secretly been in love with the policeman for a long time, and has absolutely no intention of passing on the keys. She starts creeping into his apartment everyday. Sometimes she simply cleans up, often she plays some kind of trick, swaps labels on tin cans, dissolves sleeping pills in drinks or puts new fish in his aquarium. One day she finds a message from the policeman: he wants to meet her and arranges a date in the Restaurant California.

The particular conditions of the movie's production, meant that Wong had to fight not only with his inspiration but also with the plans of his film team, who were booked up for months ahead. Apparently the set was the scene of the most extraordinary comings and goings as both the actors and the technicians were constantly disappearing off to other film sets. Wong improvised a lot and filmed lots of individual scenes that had to be self-con-

tained, as it was unclear how the scenes would fit together at the end. Despite the movie's transitory character, this gives every moment a high degree of concentration. Wong withdrew to the editing room with the piece-meal material and two months later, *Chungking Express* was finished.

The movie became Wong Kar-Wai's greatest international success, the blonde with the sunglasses the icon of a whole generation and Chris Doyle one of the most important cameramen of the 90s. Wong Kar-Wai became a style. Wong Kar-Wai came to mean loose plots structured like poems, eccentric voice-overs, bright colours, spectacular hand-held camera work and outlandish picture composition: an urbane cinema of memories, where romance is only possible in retrospect, set in a city which is constantly changing, which denies its past and which will soon cease to exist.   OM

"It's beautiful, simple, funny and smart. I wish more films were like it." *Le Monde*

CHRISTOPHER DOYLE   Christopher Doyle was born in Sydney in 1952. His work together with director Wong Kar-Wai, whose movies he filmed from *Days of Being Wild* (*A Fei zhengzhuan*, 1990) onwards, made him into one of the most-imitated cameramen of the 90s. His sensitive approach to colour combined with precise hand-held camera work came to express the melancholy of the period's *fin-de-siècle* school of international art films. As Doyle now lives in Hong Kong, he has taken a Cantonese name: Duk Ke-feng (= lord, master, like the wind). As well as his work as a cameraman, he also directs music videos and commercials – for the fashion designer Yoji Yamamoto, for example. After several years of somewhat chaotic work, Doyle presented his first feature-length movie *Away with Words* in 1999.

1   "[I'm the] DJ of my own films."
    Wong Kar-Wai

2   Self-reflection, Hong Kong style: Cantonese pop superstar Faye Wong [Wang Jinwen] as Faye in a typical Wong game with the identities of his actors.

3   Another icon of 1990s cinema: Oriental hit-woman Brigitte Lin [Lin Qingxia] in a blonde wig.

4   "There is so little space in Hong Kong that you would have no chance with a fixed camera. You have to work with a hand-held camera."
    Cameraman Christopher Doyle

5   "The scenes in *Chungking Express* […] are set in places that he [Wong Kar-Wai] himself frequents, such as the 'Midnight-Express' Fast-Food Stand in the Lan Kwai Fong district."
    Production Manager & Chief Editor William Chang

LÉON / THE PROFESSIONAL

1994 - FRANCE / USA - 110 MIN. - ACTION FILM, DRAMA

DIRECTOR LUC BESSON (*1959)
SCREENPLAY LUC BESSON **DIRECTOR OF PHOTOGRAPHY** THIERRY ARBOGAST **MUSIC** ERIC SERRA **PRODUCTION** CLAUDE BESSON, LUC BESSON
for GAUMONT, LES FILMS DU DAUPHIN.

STARRING JEAN RENO (Léon), GARY OLDMAN (Norman Stansfield), NATALIE PORTMAN (Mathilda), DANNY AIELLO (Tony),
PETER APPEL (Malky), MICHAEL BADALUCCO (Mathilda's father), ELLEN GREENE (Mathilda's mother), ELIZABETH REGEN
(Mathilda's sister), CARL J. MATUSOVICH (Mathilda's brother), LUCIUS WYATT "CHEROKEE" (Tonto).

"No women, no kids, that's the rule."

In the virtuoso opening scene to Luc Besson's movie *Léon/The Professional* the camera "swings" from a starry night sky to daylight. From a bird's-eye view, it glides over trees until the skyline of New York fills the viewfinder. It then dives into the valleys of the city's long streets and finally comes to a standstill in front of an Italian restaurant. Inside two men are sitting opposite each other. One of them is Tony (Danny Aiello), a respectable member of society, while the other, Léon (Jean Reno), lives outside of any community. Léon doesn't say much – he prefers his pistol to do the talking. He is a "cleaner", the best professional killer of his kind. Apart from the orders that he receives from Tony, which he invariably carries out with clockwork precision, Léon has nothing: he has no friends, no women, no hobbies, and no money. His only companion is a pot plant that he cares for with the same thoroughness he demonstrates in his work. Mathilda (Natalie Portman), a twelve-year-old child-woman, lives in the same house as Léon and often has to take refuge from her violent father on the stairs. One day when she comes home from shopping, she finds that a corrupt team of plain clothes from the drug squad under the command of psychopath Norman Stansfield (Gary Oldman) has murdered her entire family. The camera shows the seemingly endless hallway that Mathilda walks down, past the corpse of her father and his murderers, up to Léon who is watching everything through the peephole in his door. Only after hesitating for a long time does Léon open the door to his apartment and to his life. When the girl discovers that Léon is a killer, she wants to avenge her little brother, and she convinces Léon to teach her his profession.

Léon would like to get rid of the girl, but he doesn't know how – "no women, no kids" is his professional watchword. The two stay together and start to learn from each other. Léon shows Mathilda how to clean a gun, she teaches him to read and write; he teaches her about death, and she teaches him about life.

This French/American co-production unites many opposites. The introverted, principled professional killer, Léon is a good contrast to Stansfield, the lunatic drugs cop who kills in a haze of bloodlust and amphetamines, and Léon, a child in the body of a man is played off against Mathilda, a woman in the body of a child. Eric Serra's atmospheric music contrasts with Thierry Arbogast's cool and effective camera work and the impressive choreographed action scenes form a fine contrast to what is after all a moving love story.

The main characters in Luc Besson movies are often outsiders who find it difficult to fit into society, but they have strong moral integrity and live by their own rules.

Léon/The Professional is like a continuation by other means *Nikita* (1990), a previous Besson movie. In *Nikita*, Jean Reno also plays a "cleaner", and a taste for murderous women is common to both movies: Nikita has been sentenced to death and can only save her skin by agreeing to kill for the government.

In 1996 the "Version intégrale" (Director's Cut) of *Léon/The Professional* was re-released in France. This longer version contains 26 minutes cut after disastrous US screenings. Not only do those missing minutes allow viewers to form a clearer picture of the unusual relationship between Léon and Mathilda, they also transform the whole nature of the movie – and what appeared to be basically an action film became a drama with action elements.

APO

2

"What Léon does is kill people – cleanly, efficiently and without the slightest trace of remorse. From all appearances, there is nothing else in his life. No friends, no hobbies, no distractions."

The Washington Post

3

4

"She's something like the Jodie Foster character in *Taxi Driver*, old for her years. Yet her references are mostly to movies: 'Bonnie and Clyde didn't work alone,' she tells him. 'Thelma and Louise didn't work alone. And they were the best.'" *Chicago Sun-Times*

SCREENING	Unfinished versions of high-budget movies are often given trial theatre showings to an audience (target group) which has been selected according to particular criteria. After the showing, the audience is asked for its opinion, usually in the form of voting slips. The results of this survey are then used to produce the version of the movie to be released to movie theatres. After bad screenings, screenplays are often reworked, whole parts of the movie filmed again or edited differently to ensure as large an audience as possible upon release.

1   A killer with the heart of a child: Léon (Jean Reno), kept as a childlike protégé by a Mafia godfather, doesn't grow up until the young girl Mathilda puts her life in his hands.

2   To arms: Léon teaches his bright young pupil Mathilda (Natalie Portman) the basic principles of his deadly trade.

3   A man like a loaded gun: Gary Oldman takes his role as drug-addicted cop Norman Stansfield to the very limit. He acts as if drunk: his character is unnerving and teeters constantly on the edge of hysteria.

4   Reformed: once Léon has given up his life for Mathilda, thus atoning for the death of her brother, the girl realises that from now on she will have to find her own path.

ED WOOD

1994 - USA - 126 MIN. - COMEDY

DIRECTOR TIM BURTON (*1960)
SCREENPLAY SCOTT ALEXANDER, LARRY KARASZEWSKI, based on the biographical novel *NIGHTMARE OF ECSTASY: THE LIFE AND ART OF EDWARD D. WOOD JR. by* RUDOLPH GREY DIRECTOR OF PHOTOGRAPHY STEFAN CZAPSKY
MUSIC HOWARD SHORE PRODUCTION DENISE DINOVI, TIM BURTON for BURTON/DINOVI PRODUCTIONS (for TOUCHSTONE).

STARRING JOHNNY DEPP (Ed Wood), MARTIN LANDAU (Bela Lugosi), SARAH JESSICA PARKER (Dolores Fuller), PATRICIA ARQUETTE (Kathy O'Hara), JEFFREY JONES (Criswell), BILL MURRAY (Bunny Breckinridge), G. D. SPRADLIN (Reverend Lemon), VINCENT D'ONOFRIO (Orson Welles), LISA MARIE (Vampira), MIKE STARR (Georgie Weiss).

ACADEMY AWARDS 1995 OSCARS for BEST SUPPORTING ACTOR (Martin Landau), and FOR BEST MAKE-UP (Ve Neill, Rick Baker, Yolanda Toussieng).

"Cut!!! Perfect!!!"

Ed Wood enjoys the doubtful but wonderfully marketable reputation of being the worst director of all time. Tim Burton's movie is a monument to a colleague who more than deserves it. Burton may have immeasurably more talent as a filmmaker, but he still feels that there is a spiritual link between his work and that of Wood, who was a tireless maker of cheap movies in the 50s. Accordingly, his homage always maintains a certain level of respect: even at his funniest and most absurd moments, Ed Wood is never made to look ridiculous.

Hollywood has always perpetuated its own myth by celebrating its heroes and legends. This movie is something of an exception as it turns its attention to one of tinsel town's hopeless losers. To prevent Ed Wood (Johnny Depp) from appearing an amiable but hopelessly incompetent idiot, Burton almost overdoes the thematic links between his career and that of Orson Welles (Vincent D'Onofrio). Like Wood, Welles was the epitome of the all-American filmmaker, who tried to realise his cinematic vision by being a

writer, producer, director and leading actor all rolled into one. He is now considered to be the embodiment of the uncompromising artist doomed to failure by a refusal to bow to the production conditions of a capitalist film industry.

The dimensions of their failures may have been different, but in a key scene of the movie, Ed and Orson are shown drowning their sorrows together as victims of the same system. Ironically, Burton himself was not free from the constraints of the industry, despite enjoying a wunderkind reputation in the mid 90s: as he wanted to give the movie the flatness of a 50s B movie and make it in black and white, he had to do without Columbia's financial backing and make *Ed Wood* as an independent production.

What Wood as director lacked in artistic talent and financial resources, he made up for with boundless enthusiasm and the noble art of improvisation. His absolute lack of (self) irony gives his movies their unmistakable touch. Everything was meant absolutely seriously, and one of Wood's great-

est problems was that he was even more naïve than the audience he hoped to bring flooding to the movie theatres. Johnny Depp plays Wood like a child who, even with the most unlikely-looking toys, is able to simply ignore reality and disappear into the fairytale world of his own imagination.

Plots are so crude they seem out of this world, dialogue is unintentionally comic, a colour-blind cameraman uses the same light for every scene regardless of whether it is day or night, special effects look as if they were made in a kindergarten and staggeringly untalented actors, all friends of the director, are constantly falling over the scenery. As one of Wood's actresses said, "His carelessness in technical matters is only surpassed by his com-

plete lack of concern in showing his amateurism". But Wood was far too wrapped up in himself and his work to be bothered with such details. He wasn't careless out of disrespect for his audience, it was just that his thoughts were always way ahead of the scene he was working on.

His problem was that he always saw things as a whole, as a complete vision, just like his great colleague Orson Welles. After every first take, Depp shouts "Cut!!! That was perfect!!!!" and opens his eyes as wide as they'll go to demonstrate his absolute abandonment to his own crazy ideas: this is Burton biting back any suggestion of cynicism, and it is exactly the attitude that gives the movie its human integrity. UB

1 Look at me: Ed Wood (Johnny Depp) and Bela Lugosi (Martin Landau) try their hand at long-distance hypnosis.

2 Strange passion: is Wood in love with his wife Dolores (Sarah Jessica Parker) or just with her angora jumper?

3 The director in discussion with his hero. On the wall are posters of films he used as models.

4 Wood's *Plan 9 From Outer Space* is considered to be one of the worst films of all time.

5 Wood's working principle: the first take is always the best.

"A moving, dream-like homage to a monstrous, childish form, *Ed Wood* is also a paean to the way love of film gets passed down." *Cahiers du cinéma*

ED WOOD Edward D. Wood jr. (1924–1978) belonged to a long-gone age when Hollywood directors were not mass-produced in film schools, but came from all walks of life and based their work on their own experiences. He was both a veteran of the war in the Pacific and a self-confessed transvestite (something which took great courage at the time) with a particular weakness for cuddly angora pullovers. He exposed his personal obsessions to the outside world without any regard for their effect in his very first movie, *Glen or Glenda?* (1952), a pseudo-religious, superficial horror film about a sex change. Audiences were outraged, alienated and way out of their depth. Later he preferred to indulge himself primarily in the genres of horror and science fiction. *Plan 9 From Outer Space* (1959), his most infamous movie, was a tale of alien grave robbers. Around that time Wood met Bela Lugosi, the original movie Dracula, who had long been cast off by official Hollywood and left for dead. With his practically non-existent means, Wood tried to save the great actor from oblivion and give him the sort of send-off that he deserved. This touching act of humanity makes the quality of the movies they made together seem almost irrelevant. The fact that the only Oscar *Ed Wood* won was best supporting actor for Martin Landau as Lugosi speaks volumes about the treatment of men and myths in Hollywood.

THE SHAWSHANK REDEMPTION

1994 - USA - 142 MIN. - PRISON FILM, DRAMA

DIRECTOR FRANK DARABONT (*1959)
SCREENPLAY FRANK DARABONT, based on the short novel *RITA HAYWORTH AND THE SHAWSHANK REDEMPTION* by STEPHEN KING **DIRECTOR OF PHOTOGRAPHY** ROGER DEAKINS **MUSIC** THOMAS NEWMAN **PRODUCTION** NIKI MARVIN for CASTLE ROCK ENTERTAINMENT.

STARRING TIM ROBBINS (Andy Dufresne), MORGAN FREEMAN (Ellis Boyd "Red" Redding), BOB GUNTON (Prison Director Norton), WILLIAM SADLER (Heywood), JAMES WHITMORE (Brooks Hatlen), CLANCY BROWN (Captain Byron Hadley), GIL BELLOWS (Tommy), MARK ROLSTON (Bogs Diamond), LARRY BRANDENBURG (Skeet), NEIL GIUNTOLI (Jigger).

"Fear can make you prisoner. Hope can set you free."

In 1947 bank clerk Andy Dufresne (Tim Robbins) is given two life sentences for the murder of his wife and her lover. Although he insists he is innocent in court, all the evidence seems to point to his guilt.

When the prisoner transport van passes through the gates of the Shawshank prison, the inmates press their faces against their cell doors and yell "Fresh fish! fresh fish!" Not a lot happens in Shawshank, and the bets as to which of the newcomers will break down and cry during his first night in gaol make a pleasant change. Prisoner Red (Morgan Freeman) bets two packets of cigarettes, the prison's currency, on Andy Dufresne. He loses his bet.

Red is a lifer, like Andy Dufresne. He acts as a small business man inside the prison walls and he can get hold of everything from cigarettes to movie posters. He is the first to notice Andy's behaviour when he saunters around the yard during exercise like a man "without a care in the world, like he's wearing an invisible coat that protects him from this place." At first Andy stays aloof from his fellow inmates and they know nothing about him or about what keeps him going. All they see is that the warders' hassling doesn't get him down, and neither do the repeated brutal rapes by the other prisoners. As first-person narrator and observer, Red is the central figure in *The Shawshank Redemption*. In the course of the movie he befriends the new prisoner and through his eyes we can at least observe Andy Dufresne, even if we don't know what's going on in his head.

The endless time can't pass slowly enough for Andy; who carves chess pieces with immense composure, writes petitions and over the years builds up an amazing library. He uses his professional training to climb up the prison pecking order: he starts off as tax advisor for all of the prison staff,

> **"Exactly the same kind of enigmatic smile is written all over the face of Tim Robbins in his role of the lifer, that Stephen King must have had in mind: a kind of inner light, where otherwise there is only darkness and hopelessness."**
>
> *Frankfurter Allgemeine Zeitung*

1   Hope with its back to the wall: his friendship with Andy Dufresne (Tim Robbins, left) teaches Red (Morgan Freeman) that you can break free of your chains if you manage to preserve your inner freedom.

2   Initiation: when Andy is assigned to special work with other prisoners, this sets the course for his rise in the prison hierarchy.

3   Andy Dufresne plays things close to his chest. He wears a mask as impenetrable as the prison walls, behind which he conceals an indomitable character who knows that revenge is not only sweet, but tastes best when served cold.

later he gets a desk in the director's office and keeps the accounts of his illegal dealings. When Andy manages to escape without anyone noticing in 1975 after 30 years of careful planning, he has not just feathered his own nest but also exacted an extremely subtle revenge: not with hot blood and burning sword, but in the manner of an accountant who "redeems" a debt.

The Shawshank Redemption, based on Stephen King's short novel *Rita Hayworth and the Shawshank Redemption* is no conventional prison movie, even if it does include motifs typical of the genre. It nods to other prison movies by seeing the prison as a closed system with immutable, often illogical rules that turn people into numbers, and mean that opposition to the warders is the only means of self definition available to the inmates. Darabont has an economical touch, and cleverly emphasises only vital

things. The movie posters in Andy's cell for example (Rita Hayworth, Marilyn Monroe, Raquel Welch) are not just an indication of the passing of time, but also symbols for cinema as a window onto life. *The Shawshank Redemption* is a great movie about time, patience and above all, hope. "Hope can drive a man mad" Red says at the beginning of the film. But he doesn't allow that to happen. Every ten years he has to appear before the probation board who ask him if he is fit for life in society. Although he confirms this every time (with conviction that decreases with the passing of the years) he is never pardoned. But when Andy Dufresne finally regains his freedom because he never lost either hope or patience, Red also dares to hope again. Hope sets him free, at least inwardly.

APO

GOOFS   One of the great pleasures of many regular cinema goers is looking out for "goofs" or mistakes in the movies. These include anachronisms, like someone using a cell phone in the Middle Ages. They also include continuity mistakes, as when a actor wears a tie in a particular scene or shot, but no longer has it on in the next. Factual errors also count as goofs, as would be the case for a movie set in Los Angeles, where the audience could see the Statue of Liberty. Technical mistakes also count, like visible microphones or members of the crew who suddenly wander into shot.

4　Life sentence: Red also knows ways of preventing the never-changing prison routine from wearing him down.

5　The insignia of power: prison is an enclosed system where the guards represent the authority of the state.

6　Victim of circumstantial evidence: everything points to the fact that Andy Dufresne murdered his wife and her lover.

NATURAL BORN KILLERS

1994 - USA - 119 MIN. - ROAD MOVIE, SATIRE

DIRECTOR OLIVER STONE (*1946)
SCREENPLAY DAVID VELOZ, RICHARD RUTOWSKI, OLIVER STONE, based on a story by QUENTIN TARANTINO
DIRECTOR OF PHOTOGRAPHY ROBERT RICHARDSON MUSIC VARIOUS SONGS PRODUCTION JANE HAMSHER, DON MURPHY,
CLAYTON TOWNSEND for IXTLAN, NEW REGENCY, J. D. PRODUCTIONS.

STARRING WOODY HARRELSON (Mickey Knox), JULIETTE LEWIS (Mallory Knox), ROBERT DOWNEY JR. (Wayne Gale),
TOMMY LEE JONES (Dwight McCluskey), TOM SIZEMORE (Jack Scagnetti), EDIE MCCLURG (Mallory's mother),
RODNEY DANGERFIELD (Mallory's father), BALTHAZAR GETTY (gas station attendant), RICHARD LINEBACK (Sonny),
LANNY FLAHERTY (Earl).

IFF VENICE 1994 SPECIAL JURY PRIZE (Oliver Stone).

"We got the road to hell in front of us."

Natural Born Killers begins on a desert highway with a close up of a hissing snake, accompanied by Leonard Cohen singing "Waiting for a Miracle" – a hypnotic introduction, which makes the scenes that follow all the more shocking. Mickey and Mallory (Woody Harrelson and Juliette Lewis) are letting off steam in a diner. Whilst Mickey calmly finishes his piece of cake, his ethereal girlfriend brutally beats up a young redneck. A blues song floats out from the jukebox. Later, the pair of them kill almost all the other diners. Mickey and Mallory are a nightmare couple: they are Bonnie and Clyde or Sid and Nancy, but most of all they are the natural born killers of Oliver Stone's title. During their odyssey through South West America they randomly kill 52 people and only spare witnesses who will report deeds.

Mickey and Mallory are a gift for the TV nation which quickly styles the two serial killers as TV superstars. They are pursued not only by the police but by the media too, who hope to profit from their fame. In many of his films, from *Salvador* (1986) and *The Doors* (1991) to *Any Given Sunday* (1999), Oliver Stone has worked on the contradictions and myths of modern America. *Natural Born Killers*, based on a story written by Quentin Tarantino, combines Stone's favourite themes – violence, capitalism, the media, pop culture – in a dark, satirical tour-de-force about the obsessions of the American media. The movie breaks the bounds of classic narrative cinema, polarising and disturbing its audiences, disappointing their expectations before leaving them in a state of breathless astonishment. To do that Stone makes use of practi-

1

2

DIRECTOR'S CUT   Directors' contracts which are made according to the conditions of the Hollywood Directors' Guild contain a clause which gives the director a period of six weeks to edit and synchronise a film as he or she wishes without any studio interruption or involvement. Generally however, director's cut is used to describe a version of the film made after its release in cinemas according to the director's own artistic criteria.

cally all of the cinema's technical possibilities, changing the cameras and the film and video formats, using all the colour and effect filters imaginable, and blending in back projections and archive material. He underscores Robert Richardson's hyperactive camera work and the occasionally hysterical editing with an eclectic sound track including everything from Orff's "Carmina Burana", Bob Dylan and Patsy Cline to Nine Inch Nails and Dr. Dre. Stone claimed to have used over 100 different pieces of music in the movie. The music often acts as a counterpoint to the action on screen, as in "I love Mallory", a scene filmed in the style of an American sitcom, where instead of wholesome family life the opposite is shown. Stone adds canned laughter and applause to the verbal and physical beating which Mallory's vile father deals out to his wife and daughter.

Stone knows full well that he is throwing a stone at the media glass house where he himself lives. When Mickey and Mallory have sex in front of a hostage, the window of their motel shows some explosive archive material: in between the reptiles and insects and the images of Hitler and Mussolini are scenes from *The Wild Bunch* (1969) and *Midnight Express*, the movie whose screenplay won Stone his first Oscar in 1978.

Does art imitate life or life art? Can images cause real violence? Stone's fiction was certainly overtaken by reality. One of Mickey and Mallory's admirers in the movie remarks that if he were a mass murderer he'd want to be just like them. Years later, Stone was still answering charges that his movie had inspired countless copy-cat crimes.

APO

1   Totally cracked up: Mickey Knox (Woody Harrelson) doesn't let anything stand in his way on his deadly journey towards media stardom.

2   Director Oliver Stone uses unusual visual devices like super-imposition and colour effects to convey his message to the general public.

3   Corpses litter their path: the cute little scorpion that Mallory (Juliette Lewis) has symbolically tattooed on her belly inflicts a deadly sting. Mickey and Mallory are just as dangerous and unpredictable, a nightmare made flesh on a death-dealing trip through the USA.

4   Look back in anger: Mallory's past is like a soap opera of brutality where the laughter of the band drowned out her father's physical and verbal beatings.

4

"Visually, the film is a sensation, resembling a demonically clever light show at a late '60s rock concert. The narrative is related in color 35mm, black-and-white, 8mm and video, and at different speeds." *Variety*

5   Prison director Dwight McCluskey (Tommy Lee Jones) is as fanatical as he is hungry for media attention. He later falls victim to the hell that he himself has created.

6   Messianic: in prison Mickey provokes a riot when he tells his interviewer about the cleansing power of killing.

INTERVIEW WITH THE VAMPIRE: THE VAMPIRE CHRONICLES

1994 - USA - 122 MIN. - HORROR FILM, DRAMA

DIRECTOR NEIL JORDAN (*1950)
SCREENPLAY ANNE RICE, based on her novel of the same name **DIRECTOR OF PHOTOGRAPHY** PHILIPPE ROUSSELOT
MUSIC ELLIOT GOLDENTHAL **PRODUCTION** DAVID GEFFEN, STEPHEN WOOLEY for GEFFEN PICTURES (for WARNER BROS.).

STARRING BRAD PITT (Louis), TOM CRUISE (Lestat), KIRSTEN DUNST (Claudia), CHRISTIAN SLATER (Malloy), STEPHEN REA (Santiago), ANTONIO BANDERAS (Armand), VIRGINIA MCCOLLAM (Prostitute on the riverbank), MIKE SEELIG (Pimp), SARA STOCKBRIDGE (Estelle), THANDIE NEWTON (Yvette).

"The world changes, we do not, and there lies the irony that finally kills us."

San Francisco. Two men sit in a hotel room high over the gloomy streets. One of them, Malloy (Christian Slater), is a journalist and he is here to take down the life story of the other. It's a fascinating, incredible story that begins two hundred years previously in New Orleans in 1791, when Louis (Brad Pitt) first became a vampire. When his wife dies in childbirth, the young widower is beside himself with grief and no longer capable of looking after his plantation. Searching for oblivion and death he spends his nights in the town's dives, and his sorrow drives him into the arms of prostitutes and to the gambling table – and he is constantly on the lookout for a fatal fight to end his torment. But however much he longs for death, his wishes are never granted. One night Louis meets the vampire Lestat (Tom Cruise), who tells him of eternal youth and an existence without grief. Louis then makes a fateful decision that he will later regret.

Neil Jordan's vampires have very little to do with the traditional mythology presented in innumerable movies and books. Rather, they are descended in a direct line from Friedrich Wilhelm Murnau's *Nosferatu* (1921), although they are considerably better looking. Being a vampire is no fun, and there is no escape except through crucifixes or silver bullets. Vampires are people – but they are forced to live as outcasts.

After his transformation into a vampire, Louis' grief is replaced by melancholy and solitude when he learns about the less appetising sides of a vampire's existence. He doesn't want to kill anybody and instead feeds on rats and other small animals. Lestat on the other hand is a bloodsucker who goes by the book. In haunts of low repute and at intoxicating balls he searches for his victims, handsome young men and women mostly, killing them and drinking their blood with the same carelessness with which he indulges his passion for the hunt.

One night Louis kill a little girl called Claudia (Kirsten Dunst), and to bind Louis to himself, Lestat turns her into a vampire. At first, the relationship between Louis, Lestat and their adopted daughter seems a happy menage à trois, but before long things turn sour and it becomes a living hell for all three of them. Only Lestat seems to enjoy being undead. Louis longs for the life which Lestat has taken from him, and the child-woman Claudia dreams of a life which she will never know.

The movie is based on Anne Rice's best-selling novel *Interview With the Vampire* and is Neil Jordan's second adaptation of fantasy literature. In 1984 he made the Red Riding Hood story *The Company of Wolves* based on a book by Angela Carter. In both movies there is a similar mixture of sensuality and

1   A vampire with style: Lestat (Tom Cruise) lives off the blood of his victims.

2   The reporter Malloy (Christian Slater) listens to an incredible story ...

3   ... Louis (Brad Pitt) tells him about his life as a vampire.

4   Louis is being destroyed by the paradox of his blood-sucking existence. He has to kill in order to live.

"The initial meeting between Louis and Lestat takes the form of a seduction; the vampire seems to be courting the young man, and there is a strong element of homoeroticism in the way the neck is bared and the blood is engorged." *Chicago Sun-Times*

the supernatural, and hints of homoeroticism, incest and paedophilia, although these elements are mostly latent in *Interview With the Vampire*, where they are concealed in looks and fatal embraces.

The opulent images of the film and the emotions they inspire are far more impressive than with the coherency of the plot. Dante Ferretti, the set designer, creates a visually overwhelming and uncanny vampire world that reaches from the swamps of Louisiana all the way to the catacombs of Paris. Cameraman Philippe Rousselot (*Diva*, 1981) uses colours which seem overlain with black velvet, as though to illustrate what Louis has lost: Louis has to wait a hundred years before he can see a glorious dawn again like the one he saw before his transformation: and when he sees it, it's in a black and white movie, in Murnau's silent classic *Sunrise* from 1927.   APO

VAMPIRE FILMS	The first known vampire movie was called *Le Manoir du Diable* (*The Devil's Manor*) and was produced by Georges Méliès in 1896. Vampire films are all about the ways in which plants, aliens, or beings either living or dead rob victims of their vital juices, mostly blood. Many vampire films, including F. W. Murnau's classic *Nosferatu* (1921), take their themes from Bram Stoker's novel *Dracula*. Vampire movies have been made in a wide variety of genres, including comedies, thrillers and westerns.

5   The picture of haughtiness. Lestat relishes his life as a vampire, and he is completely devoid of scruples.

6   The vampire Armand (Antonio Banderas) satisfies his blood lust on the stage.

7   Neither wife nor daughter: Claudia (Kirsten Dunst) becomes Louis' companion.

PULP FICTION

1994 - USA - 154 MIN. - GANGSTER FILM

DIRECTOR QUENTIN TARANTINO (*1963)
SCREENPLAY QUENTIN TARANTINO, ROGER ROBERTS AVARY **DIRECTOR OF PHOTOGRAPHY** ANDRZEJ SEKULA **MUSIC** VARIOUS SONGS
PRODUCTION LAWRENCE BENDER for JERSEY FILMS, A BAND APART (for MIRAMAX).

STARRING JOHN TRAVOLTA (Vincent Vega), SAMUEL L. JACKSON (Jules Winnfield), UMA THURMAN (Mia Wallace), HARVEY KEITEL (Winston Wolf), VING RHAMES (Marsellus Wallace), ROSANNA ARQUETTE (Jody), ERIC STOLTZ (Lance), QUENTIN TARANTINO (Jimmie), BRUCE WILLIS (Butch Coolidge), MARIA DE MEDEIROS (Fabienne), CHRISTOPHER WALKEN (Koons), TIM ROTH (Ringo/Pumpkin), AMANDA PLUMMER (Yolanda/Honeybunny).

IFF CANNES 1994 GOLDEN PALM.

ACADEMY AWARDS 1995 OSCAR for BEST ORIGINAL SCREENPLAY (Quentin Tarantino, Roger Roberts Avary).

"Zed's dead, baby. Zed's dead."

After his amazing directorial debut *Reservoir Dogs* (1991), Quentin Tarantino had a lot to live up to. The bloody studio piece was essentially a purely cinematic challenge, and such an unusual movie seemed difficult to beat. But Tarantino surpassed himself with *Pulp Fiction*, a deeply black gangster comedy. Tarantino had previously written the screenplay for Tony Scott's uninspired gangster movie *True Romance* (1993) and the original script to Oliver Stone's *Natural Born Killers* (1994). At the beginning of his own movie, he presents us with another potential killer couple. Ringo and Yolanda (Tim Roth and Amanda Plummer), who lovingly call each other Pumpkin and Honeybunny, are sitting having breakfast in a diner and making plans for their future together. They are fed up of robbing whisky stores whose multi-cultural owners don't even understand simple orders like "Hand over the cash!" The next step in their career plan is to expand into diners – why not start straight away with this one? This sequence, which opens and con-cludes *Pulp Fiction* serves a framework for the movie's other three inter-woven stories, which overlap and move in and out of chronological sequence. One of the protagonists is killed in the middle of the movie, only to appear alive and well in the final scene, and we only understand how the stories hang together at the very end.

The first story is "Vincent Vega and Marsellus Wallace's Wife". Vincent and Jules (John Travolta and Samuel L. Jackson), are professional assassins on their way to carry out an order. Their boss Marsellus Wallace (Ving Rhames) wants them to bring him back a mysterious briefcase. A routine job, as we can tell from their nonchalant chit-chat. Their black suits make them look as if they have stepped out of a 40s *film noir*. Vince is not entirely happy, as he has been given the job of looking after Marsellus' wife Mia (Uma Thurman) when the boss is away. In gangster circles, rumour has it that Vincent's predecessor was thrown out of a window on the fourth floor – apparently for doing nothing more than massaging Mia's feet.

"The Golden Watch", the second story in the film, is the story of has-been boxer Butch Coolidge (Bruce Willis). He too is one of Marsellus' "niggers" as the gangster boss calls all those who depend on him. Butch has accepted a bribe and agreed to take a dive in after the fifth round in his next fight. At the last minute, he decides to win instead and to run away with the money and his French girlfriend Fabienne (Maria de Medeiros).

In the third story, "The Bonnie Situation", a couple of loose narrative strands are tied together. Jules and Vincent have done their job. However, on the way back, Vincent accidentally shoots his informer who is sitting in the

"Hoodlums Travolta and Jackson — like modern-day Beckett characters — discuss foot massages, cunnilingus and cheese-burgers on their way to a routine killing job.
The recently traveled Travolta informs Jackson that at the McDonald's in Paris, the Quarter Pounder is known as 'Le Royal'. However a Big Mac's a Big Mac, but they call it 'Le Big Mac'."

The Washington Post

back of the car. The bloody car and its occupants have to get off the street as soon as possible. The two killers hide at Jim's (Quentin Tarantino), although his wife Bonnie is about to get back from work at any moment, so they have to get rid of the evidence as quickly as possible. Luckily they can call upon the services of Mr Wolf (Harvey Keitel), the quickest and most efficient cleaner there is.

To like *Pulp Fiction*, you have to have a weakness for pop culture, which this film constantly uses and parodies, although it never simply ridicules the source of its inspiration. Quentin Tarantino must have seen enormous quantities of movies before he became a director. The inside of his head must be

like the restaurant where Vincent takes Mia: the tables are like 50s Cabrios, the waiters and waitresses are pop icon doubles: Marilyn Monroe, James Dean, Mamie van Doren and Buddy Holly (Steve Buscemi in a cameo appearance). Vincent and Mia take part in a Twist competition. The way the saggy-cheeked, ageing John Travolta dances is a brilliant homage to his early career and *Saturday Night Fever* (1977).

With his tongue-in-cheek allusions to pop and film culture, Tarantino often verges on bad taste: in one scene from "The Golden Watch", a former prisoner of war and Vietnam veteran (Christopher Walken) arrives at a children's home to give the little Butch his father's golden watch. The scene begins like a kitsch scene from any Vietnam movie, but quickly deteriorates into the scatological and absurd when Walken tells the boy in great detail about the dark place where his father hid the watch in the prison camp for so many years.

Tarantino has an excellent feel for dialogue. His protagonists' conversations are as banal as in real life, they talk about everything and nothing, about potbellies, embarrassing silences or piercings. He also lays great value on those little details which really make the stories, for example the toaster, which together with Vincent's habit of long sessions in the bathroom will cost him his life – as he prefers to take a detective story rather than a pistol into the lavatory.

Tarantino's treatment of violence is a theme unto itself. It is constantly present in the movie, but is seldomly explicitly shown. The weapon is more important than the victim. In a conventional action movie, the scene where Jules and Vincent go down a long corridor to the apartment where they will kill several people would have been used to build up the suspense, but in Tarantino's film Vincent and Jules talk about trivial things instead, like two office colleagues on the way to the canteen.

One of the movie's most brutal scenes comes after Vincent and Mia's restaurant visit. The pair of them are in Mia's apartment, Vincent as ever in the bathroom, where he is meditating on loyalty and his desire to massage Mia's feet. In the meantime Mia discovers his supply of heroin, thinks it is

cocaine and snorts an overdose. Vincent is then forced to get physical with her, but not in the way he imagined. To bring her back to life, he has to plant an enormous adrenaline jab in her heart.

Pulp Fiction also shows Tarantino to be a master of casting. All the roles are carried by their actors' larger-than-life presence. They are all "cool": Samuel L. Jackson as an Old-Testament-quoting killer, and Uma Thurman in a black wig as an enchanting, dippy gangster's moll. Bruce Willis drops his habitual grin and is totally convincing as an ageing boxer who refuses to give up. Craggy, jowly John Travolta plays the most harmless and good-natured assassin imaginable. If *Pulp Fiction* has a central theme running through it, then it's the "moral" which is present in each of the three stories. Butch doesn't run away when he has the opportunity but stays and saves his boss's life. Vincent and Jules live according to strict rules and principles and are very moral in their immoral actions. Vincent is so loyal that it finally costs him his life. Jule's moment of revelation comes when the bullets aimed at him miraculously miss. Coincidence or fate? Jules, who misquotes a Bible passage from Ezekiel before each of the murders he commits, decides that henceforth he will walk the path of righteousness. In the last scene when Ringo and Honeybunny rob the diner, Ringo tries to take the mysterious shiny briefcase. He fails to spot Jules draw his gun and under normal circumstances he would be a dead man. But Jules, who has decided to turn over a new leaf, has mercy on both of them –and that's not normal circumstances.   APO

"**Tarantino's guilty secret is that his films are cultural hybrids. The blood and gore, the cheeky patter, the taunting mise-en-scene are all very American — the old studios at their snazziest.**" *Time Magazine*

1 Do Mia's (Uma Thurman) foot massages turn into an erotic experience?

2 The Lord moves in mysterious ways: Jules (Samuel L. Jackson) is a killer who knows his Bible by heart.

3 Completely covered in blood: Vincent (John Travolta) after his little accident.

4 Everything's under control: as the "Cleaner" Mister Wolf (Harvey Keitel) takes care of any dirty work that comes up.

5 Echoes of *Saturday Night Fever*: Mia and Vincent risk a little dance.

6 In his role as Major Koons Christopher Walken plays an ex-Vietnam prisoner-of-war as he did in *The Deer Hunter*.

7

"Split into three distinct sections, the tale zips back and forth in time and space, meaning that the final shot is of a character we've seen being killed 50 minutes ago."

Empire

PULP   Cheap novels in magazine format, especially popular in the 30s and 40s, owing their name to the cheap, soft paper they were printed on. The themes and genres of these mostly illustrated serial novels and short stories ranged from comics to science fiction to detective stories. The first pulp stories appeared in the 1880s in the magazine *The Argosy*. In the 1930s there were several hundred pulp titles available, but by 1954 they had all disappeared – pulp was replaced by the cinema, the radio and above all, the new paperback book.

7 Will his pride desert him? Boxer Butch (Bruce Willis) gets paid every time he loses in the ring.

8 You gotta change your life! Jules and Vincent talk about chance and predestiny.

9 Hand over the cash! Yolanda (Amanda Plummer) carries out ...

10 ... the plan that she and Ringo (Tim Roth) hatched a few moments before.

8

QUEEN MARGOT
La Reine Margot

1994 - FRANCE / ITALY / GERMANY - 144 MIN. - HISTORICAL FILM, DRAMA

DIRECTOR PATRICE CHÉREAU (*1944)
SCREENPLAY DANIÈLE THOMPSON, PATRICE CHÉREAU, based on the novel of the same name by ALEXANDRE DUMAS THE ELDER DIRECTOR OF PHOTOGRAPHY PHILIPPE ROUSSELOT MUSIC GORAN BREGOVIC PRODUCTION CLAUDE BERRI for RENN PRODUCTIONS, FRANCE 2 CINÉMA, D. A. FILMS, RCS FILMS & TV, NEF FILMPRODUKTION, DEGETO.

STARRING ISABELLE ADJANI (Marguerite de Valois/Margot), DANIEL AUTEUIL (Henri de Navarre), JEAN-HUGUES ANGLADE (Charles IX), VINCENT PEREZ (La Môle), VIRNA LISI (Catherine de Medici), PASCAL GREGGORY (Henri III), CLAUDIO AMENDOLA (Coconnas), MIGUEL BOSÉ (Guise), ASIA ARGENTO (Charlotte de Sauve), JEAN-CLAUDE BRIALY (Coligny), ULRICH WILDGRUBER (René).

IFF CANNES 1994 BEST ACTRESS (Virna Lisi), JURY PRIZE (Patrice Chéreau).

"But what fortunes await me tonight? A knife in my stomach, a cup of poison ...?"

In 1572, thousands of Protestant Huguenots travel to Paris to celebrate the marriage of Marguerite de Valois (Isabelle Adjani), sister of the French king Charles IX (Jean-Hugues Anglade), to the Protestant Henri de Navarre (Daniel Auteuil). Charles is officially head of state, but he is a weak man, and in reality France is ruled by Catherine de Medici (Virna Lisi), the king's mother, who is an expert in diplomatic intrigue. The marriage was her idea, and it is taking place against her daughter's wishes, with the intention of putting an end to years of conflict between the Protestants and the ruling Catholics. To consolidate her own power and the future of her three sons, she also arranges the assassination of Coligny (Jean-Claude Brialy), her son's closest advisor. When the murder attempt fails and the Huguenots threaten revenge, she decides to rid France of them altogether. On the night of August 23–24, 1572, which went down in history as the "St Bartholomew's Day Massacre" she had thousands of Huguenots slaughtered in Paris and the surrounding provinces. Patrice Chéreau's movie is based on Alexandre Dumas' 1845 novel La Reine Margot, a tale first published in serial form. It was produced by Claude Berri, and between them, they created a cinematic opera with a cast which is excellent all the way down to the minor roles. Virna Lisi was pronounced best actress at the Cannes International Film Festival for her portrayal of the power-obsessed Queen Mother who rules her family like a Mafia godfather, and indeed Chéreau named Francis Ford Coppola's three-part epic The Godfather (1971, 1974, 1990) as an important model for his film. She remains cool and calculating even when her son Charles is on his deathbed sweating blood as the result of a bungled poisoning carried out on her orders. Instead of going into mourning, she has heads roll.

Patrice Chéreau comes from a theatrical background – among other things, he once directed Wagner's Ring in Bayreuth – and this is very evident in the movie. Henri de Navarre and Margot are held captives in the Louvre

4

5

"The seat of power is laid waste, and the people are desolate."

Frankfurter Allgemeine Zeitung

6

1 The king with his sister and lover: Isabelle Adjani and Vincent Perez in an intimate embrace.

2 A political marriage: Roman Catholic Margot has to marry Protestant Henri (Daniel Auteuil), in an effort to bring the Wars of Religion to an end.

3 The gaze of a passionate but disciplined woman.

4 Cornered: the Protestant La Môle fends off his attackers.

5 Director Patrice Chéreau shows the unbelievable cruelty of the Wars of Religion.

6 Decadence and life at court: a scene at the royal palace.

after the massacre and this becomes his stage. But he still uses all the conventional expressive means of the cinema. The camera is never still, and restlessly follows the corridors which are as twisted, cramped and dark as the protagonists' thoughts. Behind secret doors, on narrow stairs and in halls lit only by candles, Chéreau presents the customs and atmosphere of a courtly society where the wrong word at the wrong time could cost your head, and a kiss might be punished with death. Anyone who shows feelings here is lost. Henri de Navarre has to learn this – but the statuesquely beautiful Margot, played by Isabelle Adjani, seems to have absorbed that with her mother's milk. Outwardly she is a plaything, abused by her mother and brothers in various ways. But secretly she has a relationship with the Protestant La Môle (Vincent Perez), who she picked up on her wedding night and saves from the massacre only a few days later. Outwardly she support her husband right to the end when she follows Henri to Navarre. But in her lap lies the head of her lover.

Queen Margot is a bloody, brutal and naturalistic picture of another age. When the camera closes in on the faces and the long, unkempt hair of the men, when it registers the endless series of murdered Protestants, the audience doesn't just see the terrors of the Counterreformation, it has their stench in its nose. One unforgettable scene shows that Chéreau wanted to make more than a historical drama: when hundreds of lifeless bodies are shovelled into a mass grave, there is more than a premonition of the Holocaust – there is a distant echo of all the massacres in history.

APO

HISTORICAL FILMS   An umbrella term for various kinds of fictional movies that portray clearly defined periods of time or particular historical events. Filmmakers have been recreating the past with the camera and the help of costumes and dialogue since the silent era, in films like D. W. Griffith's *Birth of a Nation* (1915). Within the genre there are various subgenres, including adventure movies, where the historical elements serve above all as background settings. Costume dramas, movies about myths and legends, and big-budget spectaculars are other types of film often included within the genre.

DISCLOSURE

1994 - USA - 128 MIN. - EROTIC THRILLER

DIRECTOR BARRY LEVINSON (*1932)
SCREENPLAY PAUL ATTANASIO, based on the novel of the same name by MICHAEL CRICHTON DIRECTOR OF PHOTOGRAPHY ANTHONY PIERCE-ROBERTS MUSIC ENNIO MORRICONE PRODUCTION BARRY LEVINSON, MICHAEL CRICHTON for BALTIMORE PICTURES.

STARRING MICHAEL DOUGLAS (Tom Sanders), DEMI MOORE (Meredith Johnson), DONALD SUTHERLAND (Bob Garvin), CAROLINE GOODALL (Susan Hendler), ROMA MAFFIA (Catherine Alvarez), DYLAN BAKER (Philip Blackburn), ROSEMARY FORSYTH (Stephanie Kaplan), DENNIS MILLER (Marc Lewyn), ALLAN RICH (Ben Heller), NICHOLAS SADLER (Don Cherry).

"Sex is power."

Tom Sanders (Michael Douglas) is the proud owner of a dream house and the mild-mannered head of a picture-book family. His domestic paradise is on a small island just outside the booming metropolis of Seattle and every morning he leaves with the ferry to cross over into the real world. There a battle rages of which Sanders is as yet completely unaware, even though he himself is one of the combatants. He works at DigiCom, a computer technology firm which despite being a market leader lacks capital, and is on the verge of being taken over. Although he is one of the company's most creative executives, his lack of power instinct means he is not very high up in the pecking order.

On the day Sanders expects to be promoted to Vice President, the ill-omened toothpaste fleck on his tie is not the only shadow which falls over his paradise. Sanders is cheated out of his reward for the pioneer work he put into the company by an intrigue which has clearly been developing for some time. He is passed over in favour of Meredith Johnson (Demi Moore), an ex-lover from his wilder days, who becomes his new boss under his very nose. Johnson is a power-dressing career woman, and she enjoys the protection of the company's founder Garvin (Donald Sutherland). At their very first meeting, she tries to exercise her new power by lighting up the sparks of the old relationship and Sanders, whose knowledge of human nature isn't quite on a level with his expertise in bits and chips, falls blindly into the trap. However, the model father and family man is overcome by moral scruples half way. In the face of the full frontal erotic attack launched with brute force by Demi Moore, he flees in an shambolic retreat which naturally serves only to get him into deeper trouble.

After this rebuff, the new Vice President uses every means at her disposal to accuse Sanders of what amounts to attempted rape, to try and force him out of the company. Up to this point, Tom Sanders has fitted into conventional role clichés: in a conversation on bringing up children he asks what is wrong with Barbie dolls, he pats his secretary on the behind and laughs at his colleagues' sexist jokes without a second thought. Suddenly forced onto the defensive, he develops unsuspected insights and fighting capacities.

In other hands this would be enough material for a dialogue-based courtroom drama, and for a few scenes Disclosure becomes precisely that. But the movie has a second, more wide-ranging theme that turns it into an exciting thriller: the career woman overestimates her own influence and is eventually disposed of in her turn as part of the global players' treacherous intrigues.

The movie is highly successful in creating an atmosphere full of latent threat. Although the company's office block seems welcoming with its open stairwells, hanging walkways and expanses of glass, what it really represents is a climate of permanent surveillance. Disclosure questions the computer age utopia where it is claimed that race and sex fade into the background in the face of new technology, and that the human race is freed from its physical existence as though from an unnecessary evil. A key scene in this respect is the fight between Meredith and Tom in cyberspace. It may not be sensationally new to show how every means is permissible to get rid of the competition, especially in the computer industry, where company culture is so demonstratively casual, but Disclosure's sophisticated and rigorously logical exploration of its themes guarantees genuine suspense and perfect entertainment. JM

3

4

1   Sex at the office. Tom Sanders' (Michael Douglas) female boss starts making advances.

2   Rejected, Meredith Johnson (Demi Moore) plans revenge.

3   The network of conspirators draws ever tighter. Bob Garvin (Donald Sutherland) is another colleague who proves disloyal to Sanders.

4   The struggle continues in cyber-space. Sanders' opponent attempts to manipulate the truth in her favour.

5   The computer as instrument of power. Sanders receives mysterious e-mails.

"*Disclosure* seems a very calculated attempt to tap the *zeitgeist.*" Sight and Sound

MICHAEL DOUGLAS   Michael Douglas has always had a feel for quality. Even when he was still appearing in TV series, he produced one of the cult movies of the 70s, *One Flew Over the Cuckoo's Nest* (1975). Endowed with a chin almost as impressive as that of his famous father, Michael can play both brutal and reckless or dumb and servile. As a result he is just as convincing as a ruthless neo-liberal trader in *Wall Street* (1987) as he is as office slave who takes the law into his own hands in *Falling Down* (1993). Douglas excels in sounding out and expressing the limits of his character's capacity for suffering. His looks mean that he fits perfectly into the wealthy, upper-class settings that form the backdrop to so many of his movies, like *A Perfect Murder* (1997). In a lesser movie, *The Game* (1997), his upper-class character is given the appropriate hobby of human game hunting. But no role has illustrated Michael Douglas' talents as comprehensively as the role of Sanders in *Disclosure*. The result was that he became the superstar of the corporate thriller, a genre where Hollywood condensed the spirit of the 90s as a transitional phase from industrial age to information society.

MAYBE ... MAYBE NOT
Der bewegte Mann

1994 - GERMANY - 93 MIN. - COMEDY

DIRECTOR SÖNKE WORTMANN (*1959)
SCREENPLAY SÖNKE WORTMANN, based on the comics *DER BEWEGTE MANN and PRETTY BABY* by RALF KÖNIG
DIRECTOR OF PHOTOGRAPHY GERNOT ROLL **MUSIC** TORSTEN BREUER **PRODUCTION** BERND EICHINGER for NEUE CONSTANTIN FILM, OLGA FILM GMBH.

STARRING TIL SCHWEIGER (Axel Feldheim), KATJA RIEMANN (Doro Feldheim), JOACHIM KRÓL (Norbert Brommer), RUFUS BECK (Walter/"Waltraut"), ARMIN ROHDE (Butcher), NICO VAN DER KNAAP (Fränzchen), ANTONIA LANG (Elke Schmitt), MARTINA GEDECK (Jutta), JUDITH REINARTZ (Claudia), KAI WIESINGER (Gunnar).

"I think I'd better go now!"

The young waitress secretly puffs away at a cigarette in the bathroom during her break, hears groans of pleasure from next door and grins. The grin fades quickly however when she discovers that the man in the next cubicle enjoying himself with another woman is her boyfriend. Or rather, was: Axel (Til Schweiger) gets his marching orders. Although his address book is full of telephone numbers from his past affairs, none of his old flames want to take him in. Eventually he finds a place to stay with Norbert (Joachim Król) of all people, perhaps the saddest but most caring man in the world. The bourgeois gay worrier and the self-confident, high-powered golden boy make the strangest pair of housemates since Jack Lemmon and Walter Matthau in *The Odd Couple* (1967). They are not only divided by their differing opinions on cleanliness and housekeeping, but also by a purely one-sided attraction.

Norbert falls hopelessly in love with Axel, cooking for him and mothering him, and hoping against hope that one day the robust hetero will have a moment of weakness. But all his efforts are in vain. "After all", wrote one critic, "this is a German movie, not a French one." An erotic high point is reached when the two of them lie naked in bed looking through holiday slides, and a nude picture of Axel has got mixed up with the sandy beaches and palm trees. But with impeccable timing, Doro (Katja Riemann), Axel's ex, arrives. Norbert hides in a cupboard and when she finds him there, they are both horrified. Norbert, the shy little man with the big button eyes, collects his clothes and takes his leave with an unforgettable "I think I'd better go now", and suddenly the audience knows who will fall by the wayside in this ménage à trois. When Axel discovers that Doro is pregnant with his child, there is only one possible solution for him. It's the high road to bourgeois contentment – home to his sweetheart, and time to found a little family, even though there is still plenty of hormonal confusion before the final happy ending, including a hilarious scene where he is found crouching naked on a 50s style kidney-shaped table.

1

2

3

Sönke Wortmann took stories from *Der bewegte Mann* and *Pretty Baby,* two comics by Ralf König, to make this comedy about relationships. Unlike the hard-liners who criticised the cinema version a soft soap version that pandered to the masses, the cartoonist himself did not seem bothered that some of his characters' spicier or more provocative moments were lost on screen. For even if the movie tones down König's swollen-nosed fairies, queens, gays and dykes to loveable mainstream sinners, it does not become less amusing or sharp-witted. Axel, the hetero hunk, may never doubt his sexuality, in contrast to the comic hero, but Wortmann sticks to the quick, clever and dry dialogue of his model and resists the temptation to create a couple of model gays.

Wicked, pointed and filled with mockery, *Maybe … Maybe Not* is an ironic kaleidoscope of vanities. The only downside is the portrayal of women, who seem one-dimensional paper cut outs, so that the relationship between Axel and Doro is a damp squib. There was never any talk of a new German movie dream couple. It was clear that Riemann-Schweiger was never going to be the dream couple that saved German movie comedy, but the movie itself did herald something of a renaissance. The movie's success (over 6 million viewers, the Bambi prize, the Federal Film Prize and the Ernst Lubitsch Prize) was followed by a long-lasting boom in German comedies about relationships.   AK

"Germany's funniest film for years …" *Variety*

1 Into the wardrobe! Although the lovestruck Norbert (Joachim Król) never gets his way, he's still pushed into the classic hiding place.

2 A sight that most women would prefer not to see: their boyfriend being entertained by a strange woman in the ladies' toilet.

3 Axel (Til Schweiger) is less than pleased when Waltraut (Rufus Beck) and the other queens turn up unexpectedly at his wedding.

4 Bernd Eichinger's productions frequently owe part of their success to the excellent cast. In Til Schweiger and Katja Riemann he picked two stars of the new German cinema boom.

5 Til Schweiger, the sexiest man German cinema has produced in decades, as an object of lust. Straight guy Axel is thunderstruck when a gay man doesn't hesitate to show him his "prize exhibit" as a come-on.

SÖNKE WORTMANN   Sönke Wortmann was born in 1959 and his movies were the touch paper for an explosion in new German comedy. At the beginning of the 90s, he hit a nerve with *Allein unter Frauen* ("Alone amongst Women", 1991) and *Kleine Haie* ("Little Sharks", 1992) and played an important part in changing the image of German cinema, which had come to be associated with auteur films and academic introversion. Wortmann first drew attention to himself during his studies at the Munich Academy for Film and Television when his graduation work *Drei D* ("Three Ds", 1988) was nominated for a student movie Oscar. *Kleine Haie* is a sensitive comedy about three young men who want to go to acting school and meet up over and over again as they travel from audition to audition across the German Republic. It was awarded the Federal Film Prize as well as the prize for best first film at the Montreal Film Festival. "The film shows many things which I experienced as a student ", Wortmann once explained. The definitive breakthrough came with the comic adaptation *Der bewegte Mann* followed by films of the best-sellers *Das Superweib* ("Superwoman", 1996, based on Hera Lind's book), *Der Campus* ("Campus", 1998, on the book by Dietrich Schwanitz) and – Wortmann's first US production – Leon de Winter's *Der Himmel von Hollywood* under the title *The Hollywood Sign* (2000).

SPEED

1994 - USA - 116 MIN. - ACTION FILM

DIRECTOR JAN DE BONT (*1943)
SCREENPLAY GRAHAM YOST   DIRECTOR OF PHOTOGRAPHY ANDRZEJ BARTKOWIAK   MUSIC MARK MANCINA   PRODUCTION MARK GORDON
for 20TH CENTURY FOX.

STARRING KEANU REEVES (Jack Traven), DENNIS HOPPER (Howard Payne), SANDRA BULLOCK (Annie), JOE MORTON
(Captain McMahon), JEFF DANIELS (Harry Temple), ALAN RUCK (Stephens), GLENN PLUMMER (Jaguar driver),
RICHARD LINEBACK (Norwood), BETH GRANT (Helen), JAMES HAWTHORNE (Sam).

ACADEMY AWARDS 1995 OSCARS for BEST SOUND (Bob Beemer, Gregg Landaker, David MacMillan, Steve Maslow) and
BEST EFFECTS, SOUND EFFECTS EDITING (Stephen Hunter Flick).

"Miss, can you handle this bus?" – "Oh sure. It's just like driving a really big Pinto."

Jack Traven (Keanu Reeves) and his partner Harry Temple (Jeff Daniels) work in the Anti-Terrorist Unit of the Los Angeles Police Department. When the film opens, they are trying to free some hostages who are trapped in an elevator in one of the city's skyscrapers. The kidnapper is demanding a ransom of three million dollars, without which a bomb will explode killing all the hostages. In the last second, Jack and Harry manage to get the captives to safety. In a normal movie, a moment's relaxation would follow. But in Jan de Bont's action spectacle *Speed,* what would normally be enough material for a whole evening's entertainment is merely the curtain-raiser to a racing roller coaster ride in three acts which grips the audience from beginning to end.

The next morning, while Harry Temple is still sleeping off his hangover after the celebrations, Jack sets off for work. Suddenly a bus explodes a few metres away, and a public telephone rings at the same moment. It is Howard Payne (Dennis Hopper), the bomber they had believed dead. This time he wants 3.7 million dollars – but the personal revenge is more important than the money. He sets Jack the task of finding a bus which is driving through Los Angeles full of passengers. On board is a bomb that will explode as soon as

the bus goes faster than 50 miles an hour. However, the bomb will also explode should the bus drop its speed below 50 miles an hour. Jack manages to find the bus, and to clamber on board. While he feverishly attempts to defuse the bomb, the bus driver is shot by one of the passengers. Annie (Sandra Bullock), another passenger, takes the wheel – and isn't about to let go of it again in a hurry. During the hellish ride that follows she steers the heavy bus at break-neck speed along congested freeways and through red lights.

At the last moment Jack manages to get all the passengers out of the exploding bus, which they have driven onto the runway of a nearby airport. Jack and Annie fall into each other's arms. In a normal film, we might expect that to be the end of the story. But Jan de Bont has yet another surprise in store: in the third act he has Annie covered in dynamite like a gift-wrapped present, racing towards certain death in an out-of-control subway train accompanied by Payne and Jack.

Before his debut as a director with *Speed,* Dutchman Jan de Bont was a cameraman on many big-budget action films. He obviously paid great attention to the directing on the sets of movies like *Die Hard* (1987), *The Hunt*

3

4

for Red October (1990) or *Lethal Weapon 3* (1992). *Speed*, his first movie, is the condensed essence of all action films, freed from all unnecessary ballast: with one exception, there are no senselessly violent scenes or mindless destruction. Minor figures are kept in the background, and we learn nothing about their previous lives. The terse dialogue isn't used for reasoning or moralising, it simply advances the plot or gives the audience a split-second pause to draw breath. De Bont tells his story almost exclusively with pictures, and the racing images alone create an almost unbearable tension. The focal point of *Speed* really is speed; and like the bus, the movie maintains its tempo without flagging from the first to the last. Its timing is as precise as the clockwork mechanism of Payne's bomb. APO

5

TYPECASTING   If actors play several similar roles in quick succession, their future career is often determined by this stereotype. A particular type of character, like a villain, becomes identified with an actor's face, and thereafter they may only be offered roles that correspond to that image. One of the most famous examples is Edward G. Robinson who played many different roles, but will always be remembered as a gangster.

---

1   Fasten your seatbelts: police officer Jack (Keanu Reeves) next to reluctant bus driver Annie (Sandra Bullock).

2   Other directors make cars fly, with action specialist Jan de Bont it's buses.

3   Yet another psychopath: Dennis Hopper plays the part of terrorist bomber Howard Payne.

4   Mind the gap: a dangerous initiative to save lives.

5   The psychopath means business: the explosion at the start of the film shows how dangerous an opponent he is.

6   Like Annie, viewers are held captive right up to the very last minute.

6

THE LION KING

1994 - USA - 88 MIN. - ANIMATION

DIRECTOR ROGER ALLERS, ROB MINKOFF
SCREENPLAY JIM CAPOBIANCO, IRENE MECCHI **MUSIC** HANS ZIMMER **PRODUCTION** DON HAHN, SARAH MCARTHUR, THOMAS SCHUMACHER, CLAYTON TOWNSEND for WALT DISNEY PRODUCTIONS.

VOICES JAMES EARL JONES (Mufasa), MATTHEW BRODERICK (Simba) JEREMY IRONS (Scar), WHOOPI GOLDBERG (Shenzi), ROWAN ATKINSON (Zazu), MOIRA KELLY (Nala), CHEECH MARIN (Banzai).

ACADEMY AWARDS 1995 OSCARS for BEST MUSIC (Hans Zimmer), BEST SONG (Elton John, Tim Rice, "Can You Feel The Love Tonight").

"Remember who you are. You are my son and the one true king."

The story begins on Pride Rock, a cliff in the middle of the vast empire of Mufasa, the ruling king of the lions. Proudly he presents to his people the little prince Simba, his son and heir.

However, Mufasa's power-hungry brother Scar sees the baby prince as a threat to his chances of ruling and forges a deadly plan, and Mufasa dies saving his son's life. Simba is plagued by feelings of guilt and runs away into the jungle, where he grows up with his faithful companions Timon the monkey and Pumbaa the warthog. This carefree life comes to an end when Simba meets his old friend Nala again. She convinces him that if he really wants to grow up, he must face the demons of the past and take on his responsibilities.

Whereas Disney's previous movies *Aladdin* (1992), *Beauty and the Beast* (1991) and *The Little Mermaid* (1989) focused on love stories between unequal partners, the romance between Simba and Nala is not the main story line. Instead, Disney's 32nd animated movie *The Lion King* is like a jungle version of Shakespeare's *Hamlet*, although it is the first animated movie in Disney's history not to be based on a literary model or story. This tragic tale of guilt and atonement, of to be or not to be – or rather to eat or be eaten – tells of intrigues at court and the power of blood ties, but has a happy ending.

Naturally, *The Lion King* also has comic moments, mostly thanks to the repartees handed out by Timon and Pumbaa. But it remains a somewhat gloomy and moralising movie about growing up and how to deal with guilt

1   Group portrait in the savannah: the King of the Lions and his subjects.

2   The lion and his lioness gaze proudly at the heir to the throne, Simba.

3   Zebras form a guard of honour: Simba and Nala are as yet relatively untouched by the burden of kingship.

4   Simba listens reverently to his father's instruction.

5   Walt Disney's Africa is enchantingly beautiful.

6   Hounded out of his kingdom, Simba finds two loyal friends in exile: Timon the meerkat and Pumbaa the warthog.

WALT DISNEY   Walt Disney, creator of Mickey Mouse and king of the animated movie, was born in Chicago in 1901. He sold his first drawings at the age of 7, but his career did not begin in earnest until 1923, when he set off for Hollywood with $ 40 in his pocket. In 1932 he was awarded the first of a total of 32 personal Academy Awards for *Flowers and Trees*. In the following years he created such animated classics as *Pinocchio* (1940), *Dumbo* (1941) and *Bambi* (1942). In 1940 Disney opened his studio in Burbank, where he employed over 1000 artists and technicians. He planned the Disney theme park in Florida, but it was first opened by his brother Roy in 1971, 5 years after Walt Disney's death.

5

> **"Music can break hearts and make the Top 40. But a cartoon's narrative imagination is first and finally in the images. Animation is a supple form; it can be as free as free verse, as fanciful as a Bosch landscape."**
>
> *Time Magazine*

and fear. Death and violence are not taboo and the audience is not presented with a perfect world. These elements put the movie back in the tradition of earlier Disney movies, which were often based on moral fables. The first-class detailed animation of *The Lion King* was produced by hundreds of artists and is one of the main reasons why the movie is the most successful feature-length cartoon of all time to date. With glowing colours and fine brushstrokes Disney's cartoonists brought the African steppe and its inhabitants to life.

Since the film music to *The Little Mermaid* (1989) won two Oscars, the musical element of Disney movies has become just as important as their visual side. *The Lion King*'s symphonic soundtrack with its colourful African elements was written by Hans Zimmer and the successful Broadway team Alan Menken and Howard Ashcroft created the songs which are performed by Elton John and Tim Rice.

As in all cartoon movies, pictures and music are used to evoke strong emotions. But the movie also contains a political element. When the hyenas march to the dissonant song "Be prepared" we are forcibly reminded of Leni Riefenstahl's film *Triumph des Willens* (*The Triumph of the Will*, 1935). Rather than a historical quotation from film, the pictures of the hyenas marching in step are an implied critique of totalitarian rule. APO

6

TRUE LIES

1994 - USA - 141 MIN. - ACTION FILM, COMEDY

DIRECTOR JAMES CAMERON (*1954)

SCREENPLAY JAMES CAMERON DIRECTOR OF PHOTOGRAPHY RUSSELL CARPENTER MUSIC BRAD FIEDEL PRODUCTION JAMES CAMERON, STEPHANIE AUSTIN for LIGHTSTORM ENTERTAINMENT (for 20TH CENTURY FOX).

STARRING ARNOLD SCHWARZENEGGER (Harry Tasker), JAMIE LEE CURTIS (Helen Tasker), TOM ARNOLD (Gib), BILL PAXTON (Simon), TIA CARRERE (Juno Skinner), ELIZA DUSHKU (Dana), ART MALIK (Salim Abu Aziz), GRANT HESLOV (Faisil), MARSHALL MANESH (Jamal Khaled), JAMES ALLEN (Colonel).

"Ask me a question I would normally lie to."

"If I can't sleep, I simply ask Harry how his day was. After six seconds I'm fast asleep." Helen Tasker (Jamie Lee Curtis) really loves her husband (Arnold Schwarzenegger), but it's not a barrel of laughs being married to a computer salesman who can't even get home on time on his own birthday. It's not surprising then that she has secret meetings with a spy called Simon (Bill Paxton) who may not be the physical equal of her husband, but who has a definite advantage. He needs her – supposedly to be able to travel to Europe without arousing suspicion.

Helen doesn't realise that her husband's job is nothing but a (perfect) façade, behind which he really leads the kind of excitement-filled life that she constantly dreams of. Harry, in actual fact, is a secret agent for the government project "Omega", and is a kind of super James Bond who regularly saves the world – with the same blasé attitude others develop selling computers or insurance policies.

While Helen is sitting at home bored, Harry infiltrates a group of fanatical Arab terrorists who are planning a nuclear attack on the USA, speaks flu-

ent Arabic and French, and shows he can dance the tango as well as he can handle his huge arsenal of weapons. Machine guns and Dobermans can't hold him back but no matter how good he is as a top agent, he is a complete failure as a husband. When he realises his wife has gone, he sets off to find her, and he soon discovers that she is with Simon, who turns out to be a second-hand car salesman. But instead of confronting her and agreeing to stop neglecting his duties as a husband, he uses all the tricks of his spying profession instead. Harry Tasker is in his element when he humiliates Helen by interrogating her using voice distortion and one-way mirrors, and he even calls in a SWAT team to break up Helen and Simon's tête-à-tête in a caravan.

James Cameron's movie is based on ideas taken from Claude Zidi's French comedy movie La Totale! (1991) and it breaks all the rules of the genre. It was made with a budget of 100 million dollars, which was gigantic to the standards of the time. That said, Cameron's Titanic, filmed only six years later in 1997, cost twice that amount.

True Lies is a fantastic action movie with breathtaking stunts, innumerable dead bodies and terrific chase scenes like the police horse that gallops through a hotel lobby. It was Schwarzenegger's third movie together with Cameron, with whom he had previously made the two *Terminator* films, and to some extent Cameron is Frankenstein and Schwarzenegger the monster he has created. In the seven years between *Terminator* (1984) and *Terminator 2 –Judgment Day* (1991), Arnie was transformed from a cyborg to a machine with almost human features. In *True Lies* Cameron didn't simply content himself with putting any number of pyrotechnics into Schwarenegger's hands and having him rescue his teenage daughter Dana (Eliza Dushku) with a Harrier jump-jet, he also gave him a heart to go with

the muscles. Like his earlier movie *The Abyss* (1989), *True Lies* tells the story of a couple who grow apart but are brought back together again by exceptional circumstances. Of course, *True Lies* is also a comedy, and its punch lines are as well aimed as Harry Tasker's machine gun salvos: "You're fired!" he shouts at the terrorist Malik (Salim Abu Aziz) as he fires the rocket which Malik is clinging to for dear life under the wing of his Harrier jet. It's also a homage to James Bond, and it uses technical and thematic set pieces straight out of the 007 adventures, and there is no shortage of unlikely but imaginative episodes involving groups of international terrorists, elegant parties and a female villain who is as beautiful as she is evil.

APO

"Schwarzenegger tackles patching up his marriage with the same macho attitude as saving the world ...." *Frankfurter Allgemeine Zeitung*

1   At last Helen (Jamie Lee Curtis) realises that her
     husband Harry (Arnold Schwarzenegger) is no
     couch potato.

2   Firing on all cylinders as usual: Schwarzenegger
     has everything under control.

3   Like something out of a James Bond movie:
     resourceful, elegant and professional, just like
     Her Majesty's Secret Agent 007, Harry knows
     how to keep his head in any situation.

4   "You're fired!", was the line just before he fired
     the rocket on the terrorists.

5   This is perhaps a little more adventure than Helen
     might have wished for.

REMAKE   Remakes, which are new versions of movies that already exist, are produced to bring out new aspects of old stories. Sometimes they develop different elements of the original idea, while at other times they are simply an attempt to penetrate new markets. Remakes are common after technical advances, as when silent films became talkies and black and white became colour. Today most remakes are made in the USA, as foreign language movies are not dubbed in America, and subtitles are unpopular with US cinema audiences.

4

"There is one image in the midst of all the commotion, which gives an insight into the film's essence: the woman drops the machine gun, which somersaults down a flight of steps firing

5

shots that finish off at least as many opponents as Arnie himself. The out of control weapon, which can take the place of any person, is this film's true heart, a soulless pacemaker." *Süddeutsche Zeitung*

1995 - USA - 139 MIN. - ADVENTURE FILM

DIRECTOR RON HOWARD (*1954)
SCREENPLAY WILLIAM BROYLES JR., AL REINERT, based on the book *LOST MOON* by JIM LOVELL, JEFFREY KLUGER
DIRECTOR OF PHOTOGRAPHY DEAN CUNDEY MUSIC JAMES HORNER PRODUCTION BRIAN GRAZER, TODD HALLOWELL for IMAGINE
ENTERTAINMENT.

STARRING TOM HANKS (Jim Lovell), BILL PAXTON (Fred Haise), KEVIN BACON (Jack Swigert), GARY SINISE (Ken Mattingly),
ED HARRIS (Gene Kranz), KATHLEEN QUINLAN (Marilyn Lovell), MARY KATE SCHELLHARDT (Barbara Lovell), EMILY ANN
LLOYD (Susan Lovell), MIKO HUGHES (Jeffrey Lovell), MAX ELLIOTT SLADE (Jay Lovell).

ACADEMY AWARDS 1996 OSCARS for BEST SOUND (Rick Dior, Steve Pederson, Scott Millan, David MacMillan) and BEST FILM
EDITING (Daniel P. Hanley, Mike Hill).

"Houston, we have a problem."

In May 1961, President Kennedy promised that an American would land on the moon before the decade was out. This was his answer to Russia's head start in the space race, which had been an unpleasant surprise for America. The first spacecraft to orbit the earth was a Russian Sputnik and a Russian cosmonaut was the first man to travel in space. Although the official reason for the space race was scientific research, in actual fact it was a prestige duel between the super powers. The astronauts were old fashioned explorers rather than servants of science.

However, after only two successful moon landings, mankind's final heroic chapter came to a shuddering halt. The third lunar mission Apollo 13 started on 11 April 1970. It seemed routine until five words uttered by Commander Jim Lovell (Tom Hanks) instantly entered everyday speech and

tore the nation and the watching world out of its complacency: "Houston, we have a problem." What Lovell meant by this heroic understatement worthy of Hemingway was that the oxygen tank vital to the astronauts' survival had exploded. Apollo 13 then suffered a whole series of related problems and there followed dramatic, drawn-out rescue attempts to bring back the three astronauts adrift in space. Like every modern American fairytale, the crisis brought together the potent combination of highly developed technology and the tried and tested virtues of a pioneer nation: inventiveness, pragmatism and selfless teamwork.

Apollo 13's dramatic handicap is that virtually every viewer knows from the very beginning that the story has a happy ending. However, Ron Howard set out to write a simple heroic epic – and succeeded in being just

2

as cool, laconic and unsentimental as Lovell's report of the near fatal disaster from 200,000 miles away. All the characters are in the same boat, they all put their personal problems aside and do their bit for the happy ending. That goes for the three astronauts themselves as much as for the colleague dropped from the mission shortly before the start with suspected measles, who goes over and over the most incredible rescue manoeuvres in the flight simulator. It also includes national hero Neil Armstrong, who reassures Lovell's mother in a nursing home, and goes right down to the most insignificant employee of the Texas mission control centre.

Movies that exalt supposed national virtues and claim as American the capacity to make impossible things possible by sheer force of will may seem naive or even dangerous. Manned space travel also has its critics, and the genre ingredients used here to create emotional effect have all been seen once too often. Nevertheless, as Apollo 13 approaches splashdown at the end of the movie and the entire mission control centre breaks out in shouts and cheers, it's a hard-baked and cynical viewer who begrudges them some sort of approving remark.

UB

3

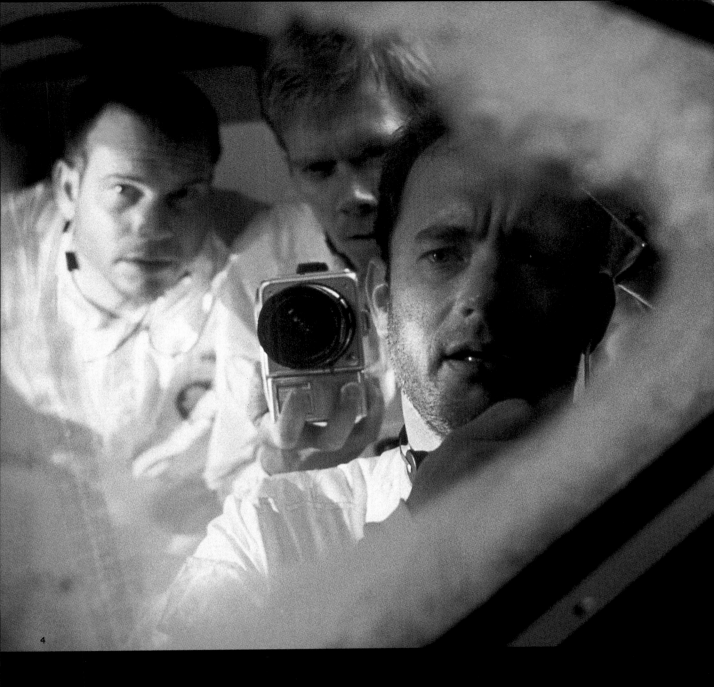

4

SPACE TRAVEL IN THE CINEMA

Manned space travel was promoted in the 60s as mankind's last great adventure. The crude fantasies of armies of SF authors aside, the real space race for the moon and stars features astonishingly seldom in Hollywood feature films. Strictly speaking, there are only two movies on the subject that can be considered anything like a masterpiece. The first is *The Right Stuff* (1983), Philip Kaufman's partly mythical, partly tongue-in-cheek adaptation of Tom Wolfe's reportage novel of the same name, describing the transition period when the first astronauts took over from the old test pilots and proclaimed themselves to be the true heroes of the modern-day Wild West. Clint Eastwood's late work *Space Cowboys* (2000), whose brilliant title says it all, would have to be the second: a laconic yet wry movie with a touch of melancholy, it tells the story of the forgotten pioneers of the first hour who are called upon to get Houston out of a tight spot. An old-fashioned satellite is out of control and the old-timers are the only ones who still know how it works. Their mission is a success and they finally receive the fame that is their due.

"In the summer *Apollo 13* shot like a rocket to the top of the US box office. President Clinton had it shown to him at the White House, and the Speaker of the House and science fiction writer Newt Gingrich declared the film quite simply 'brilliant'." *Frankfurter Rundschau*

5   Jim Lovell (Tom Hanks) during preparations for the flight.

6   Fred Haise (Bill Paxton) gives the other two astronauts a worried look.

7   Flight director Gene Kranz (Ed Harris) tries to keep a cool head.

8   Ken Mattingly (Gary Sinise), the astronaut who stayed behind, does everything he can to ensure his friends can come home.

9   Worrying images on TV: the Apollo 13 space module is just about to re-enter the earth's atmosphere.

7

8

9

HATE
La Haine

1995 - FRANCE - 98 MIN. - DRAMA, SOCIAL STUDY

DIRECTOR MATHIEU KASSOVITZ (*1967)
SCREENPLAY MATHIEU KASSOVITZ DIRECTOR OF PHOTOGRAPHY PIERRE AÏM MUSIC BOB MARLEY, ISAAC HAYES, ZAPP AND ROGER, etc.
PRODUCTION CHRISTOPHE ROSSIGNON for LES PRODUCTIONS LAZENNEC.

STARRING VINCENT CASSEL (Vinz), HUBERT KOUNDÉ (Hubert), SAÏD TAGHMAOUI (Saïd), KARIM BELKHADRA (Samir), EDOUARD MONTOUTÉ (Darty), FRANÇOIS LEVANTAL (Asterix), SOLO DIKKO (Santo), MARC DURET (Inspector "Notre Dame"), HÉLOÏSE RAUTH (Sarah), RYWKA WAJSBROT (Vinz's Grandmother).

IFF CANNES 1995 PRIZE for BEST DIRECTOR.

"Okay so far."

An Arab, a Black African and a Jew, all of them outsiders, underdogs, and socially disadvantaged. They're only twenty, but they're already used to staring into a bleak future and fighting for survival from one day to the next. The large families they come from have no fathers. They spent most of their school days as truants and their school burnt down in one of the riots that break out whenever the neighbourhood needs to work off its pent-up rage. The three of them are ready to take on the world, and they certainly won the hearts of cinema audiences, but with attitudes like that they had no hope of success in the world as portrayed in the film.

That world is a cheerless Paris suburb, where social dynamite seems to have become part of the architecture. In the opening sequence we see a single, fire-red lightning flash that is clearly meant to tell us that this world will soon be reduced to ruins and ashes – perhaps at the end of the movie, perhaps just a little later. The movie contents itself with telling the story of a 24-hour period in cold, high contrast black and white, a visual style totally appropriate for the subject of the film.

The title is also a clue to the movie's contents. Hate begins where other teen films leave off, and is a radical presentation of what in more enlightened times was known as structural violence. Despite the best hopes of starry-eyed film critics, director Mathieu Kassovitz is no genius ghetto kid, and neither is his film the result of a wish granted by a passing fairy godmother. It may look chaotic, but it's an integral part of the cultural scene. Kassovitz himself was clever enough to know that it was mostly chance that lit the touch paper to the dynamite keg. The plot of the movie is as tight as a straitjacket. – In the course of one of the many street battles with the police, a 16-year-old acquaintance of Saïd (Saïd Taghmaoui), Hubert (Hubert Koundé) and Vinz (Vincent Cassel) was arrested and beaten in the interrogation that followed. Now he lies in hospital fighting for his life. Vinz finds the duty weapon that the policeman lost in the heat of the fight, and swears revenge should the boy die. The audience realise from the very beginning that this is inevitable. What they don't know is where and how Vinz will unleash his rage, or whether one of the other two will beat him to it.

1
2

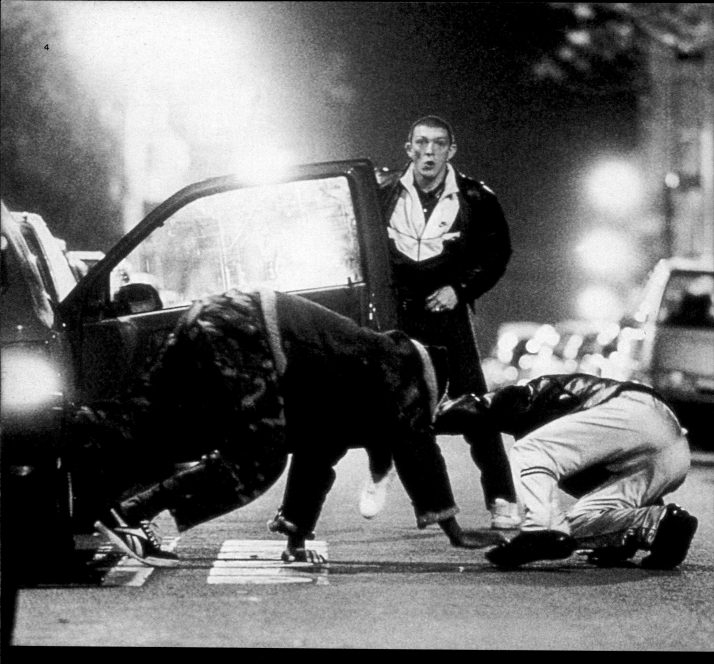

"This bloke falls from the fiftieth floor of a tower block.
As he falls, he says to himself as he passes each floor,
'Okay so far. Okay so far.
Okay so far. Okay so far.'
The moral of the story is:
It doesn't matter how you fall, but how you land."

The joke that is told at the beginning and end of the film.

Before the movie's violent climax Kassovitz uses the remaining 98 minutes to take a racy, sometimes hopeless, depressing but constantly witty and affectionate look at his characters and their milieu. He is well aware that realism is the audience's only yardstick for this kind of cinema, and that every look, word and gesture has to be right. The director sticks close to the protagonists and accompanies them everywhere with his restless hand-held camera. Sometimes they hang around bored, at other times they are driven by crazy energy, ricocheting off the walls of the concrete estates and trying their luck as touchingly amateurish petty criminals. Kassovitz draws us into an anonymous, senseless urban environment with straightforward natural-ism, neither preaching nor wallowing with the eyes of an outsider in ill-placed "ghetto chic". Here every stock phrase and every lie about why things are as they are has been heard at least once too often. The conventional explanations and solutions are no longer enough. Never for a moment does the director use the wedge of pop-psychology to divorce the characters from their awful world, and so we never really get to know them: Saïd constantly spouts verbal rubbish, Hubert dreams of a boxing career but is really just a child, and Vinz retreats ever further behind a protective shield of hate. We never get to know them very well, but we never really forget them once we've seen the film.   UB

CINÉMA BEUR

Beur is the slang term for French-born second-generation immigrants from the Maghreb in North Africa, predominantly from the former French colonies of Algeria and Morocco. *Cinéma Beur* discusses the problems of this ethnic minority, who are easily the largest minority in France. It portrays the day-to-day racism that the immigrants have to deal with, and shows the tricks of survival and the conformist strategies that the immigrants' children have been forced to adopt. In the mid 80s the growth of Jean-Marie Le Pen's Front National made it even more difficult to break down racist stereotypes and fight for a separate cultural identity.

Movies of many different genres are counted as part of the Cinéma Beur movement, from crime movies like Francis Girod's *The Big Brother* (*Le grand frère*, 1982) and *Tchao Pantin* (1983) by Claude Berri to comedies like *L'Œil au beur(re) noir* (1987) by Serge Maynard, which takes an ironic look at the social problems caused by housing deficits in big cities. This is as much part of Cinéma Beur as the touching, tongue-in-cheek youth drama *Le thé au harem d'Archimède* (1985) by Mehdi Charef, the best known filmmaker of this French minority group.

---

1   A sworn alliance: Saïd (Saïd Taghmaoui), Hubert (Hubert Koundé) and Vinz (Vincent Cassel) live in a bleak suburb of Paris.

2   Being cool: can the hero's actions be transferred from screen to real life?

3   Gun in hand. A deceptive moment of power.

4   A vicious circle: violence breeds violence.

5   Fit for the cold hard world: Hubert after boxing training.

BRAVEHEART

1995 - USA - 177 MIN. - HISTORICAL FILM

DIRECTOR MEL GIBSON (*1956)
SCREENPLAY RANDALL WALLACE DIRECTOR OF PHOTOGRAPHY JOHN TOLL MUSIC JAMES HORNER PRODUCTION MEL GIBSON, ALAN LADD JR., BRUCE DAVEY for ICON, LADD PRODUCTIONS.

STARRING MEL GIBSON (William Wallace), SOPHIE MARCEAU (Princess Isabelle), PATRICK MCGOOHAN (King Edward I), CATHERINE MCCORMACK (Murron), BRENDAN GLEESON (Hamish), JAMES COSMO (Campbell), DAVID O'HARA (Stephen), ANGUS MCFAYDEN (Robert the Bruce), PETER HANLY (Prince Edward), JAMES ROBINSON (William as a boy).

ACADEMY AWARDS 1996 OSCARS for BEST PICTURE, BEST DIRECTOR (Mel Gibson), BEST CINEMATOGRAPHY (John Toll), BEST SOUND EFFECTS EDITING (Lon Bender, Per Hallberg) and BEST MAKE-UP (Peter Frampton, Paul Pattison, Lois Burwell).

"Your heart is free. Have the courage to follow it."

"They fought like warrior bards. They fought like Scotsmen." After a long, but never dull 177 minutes, these two lines don't just bring the audience back from the Middle Ages to the present, but also from the sort of lavish, epic historical spectacle that most people assumed to have died out with *Lawrence of Arabia* (1962). Not least because of its return to a classic narrative style, *Braveheart* was a welcome and highly acclaimed exception at a time when most movies were non-committal, derivative and made only with reference to each other. As that medieval Scottish chronicler notes, *Braveheart* is a story of war, and as critics were quick to point out on its release, it brought a new dimension to the war movie genre. But it's also a movie filled with poetic moments and it tells us more about Scotland and its people than we would normally expect from a historical film. William Wallace is a mythical figure –Scotland's greatest folk hero, more popular than Rod Stewart, Sean Connery and Jock Stein put together. A simple man of the people who fought valiantly for the freedom of his fellow Scots against an arrogant, all-powerful enemy, who was prevented from achieving his aim by treachery from within his own ranks. He was a passionate patriot, a strate-

gic genius and a social revolutionary à la Robin Hood. He seems made for Hollywood, and it's surprising that there was no cinematic monument to him before El Gibson decided to try out his directorial skills.

Kevin Costner's sensational success with *Dances With Wolves* (1990) led to a host of other star actors taking over the director's chair, and that was the main reason why Gibson was able to attempt a 70 million dollar project after the flop of his previous effort, *The Man Without a Face* (1993). Australian by choice, Gibson is best known to the public for his action hero role in the *Lethal Weapon* movies (1986, 1988, 1992, 1997). He approached the risky business of *Braveheart* with admirable calm, trusting to his star qualities. The story unfolds with tantalising slowness. The first half-hour tells of the youth of William Wallace (James Robinson), and Gibson skilfully uses tried and tested genre conventions to introduce both sides of the coming conflict and to win the audience's sympathies for his hero.

From the very first frame, the leisurely pace seems to mirror the rhythm of life of a much slower age, making the later fight scenes even more impressive and dramatic. Gibson sketches in the social milieu with a few

3

"At last: a costume drama that wears its costumes with pride, a period drama that has the courage of its convictions." *Sunday Times*

muddy-coloured dimly lit sequences. The Scottish nobility want to maintain their material privileges and are prepared to compromise with the English whereas the peasants, who have been deprived of their rights, are spoiling for a fight and have literally nothing to lose but their lives.

The movie has its fair share of folklore clichés and features to tempt the modern palate. The hearty rough-and-tumble that leads to the firm friendship between William and his faithful vassal Hamish (Brendan Gleeson) is a little too reminiscent of Robin Hood and Little John. But, *Braveheart* is generally successful in transporting its audience back in time without too much visible effort.

A single ingenious but gruesome scene is all that is needed in the brilliant opening section to establish the perfidiousness of Edward I (played by that ever reliable "Prisoner" Patrick McGoohan), when dozens of good-natured and unarmed Scottish landowners are invited to negotiate with the English, only to be hung in a barn by the king's henchmen. William's father is one of the victims of this terror tactic, which does nothing to deter the freedom fighters: "The problem with Scotland is that it is full of Scots", comments the king. He then introduces the *jus primae noctis*, reasoning that if they can't throw the Scots out, they can at least outbreed them. This in turn leads to the murder of William's beautiful bride Murron (Catherine

1   The camera produces a hero. A low-angle shot
     sets off William Wallace (Mel Gibson), leader of
     the Scottish rebels.

2   The Scottish warriors try to defend themselves
     with powerful lances against the army of English
     knights.

3   "Warrior poets" in full war paint.

4   Caught between love and reasons of state: French
     princess Isabelle (Sophie Marceau) is married to
     the English heir to the throne.

5   English King Edward I (Patrick McGoohan) rules
     with a rod of iron and puts down the Scottish
     uprisings.

6   The French princess at the English court. The
     young woman manages to defy the king's
     demands repeatedly.

McCormack), adding personal vengeance to patriotic duty as his motives for the fight. At first, William resists the seemingly all-powerful enemy with just a handful of determined comrades, but following his first unexpected military successes, the local revolt soon becomes a rebellion which spreads through the whole of the North of Britain and even over to Ireland.

Braveheart's best moments are without a doubt the fight sequences. Seldom in the history of cinema has the horror of war been presented so grippingly, and the carefully planned attacks of cavalry, archers and infantry seem nothing more than random clashes between two huge masses of men, who hack and slash wildly. King Edward is forced onto the defensive despite his efforts to involve his daughter-in-law, the French Princess Isabelle (Sophie Marceau), and the crafty tricks he plays on the Scottish nobility. William Wallace becomes a legend in his own lifetime, the focus of all Scotland's dreams of national liberation. The beautiful Isabelle sides with the uncompromising rebel and the movie's second love story develops. However, Robert the Bruce (Angus McFayden), the best of the aristocrats, is a fickle ally who in the end cannot bring himself to go against the interests of his own class. His betrayal seals the rebels' fate. It only remains for Robert to fulfil the shameful task of recounting the heroic saga of William Wallace: "English historians will call me a liar. But history is written by those who hang the heroes".

UB

8

7   Forbidden love. The people's hero and the French princess.

8   Resolutely he rides off on a new mission. This is how the hero will be remembered.

MEL GIBSON   The first part of the *Mad Max* Trilogy (1979) was a new aesthetic departure in film and quickly became a cult movie. Mel Gibson, a complete unknown at the time, played the title role, and with his bright blue eyes and physical presence it was clear that he had what it took to become a star. At the beginning of his career, Gibson liked to remind people that his parents emigrated to Australia with their twelve children to spare his older brothers military service and Vietnam, but now that he is established as one of Hollywood's top stars, he has fewer qualms about appearing as an American patriot now and then. His two greatest successes were both filmed in the first half of the 80s: *Gallipoli* (1981), and *The Year of Living Dangerously* (1982). Their considerable success ought by rights to have led to more challenging roles, but these were slow in coming. Perhaps his best work has been done with the director Richard Donner, with whom he made the *Lethal Weapon* series (1986, 1988, 1992, 1997) and most recently *Conspiracy Theory* (1997). One of his most recent movies is *Payback* (1998), a remake of the classic gangster film *Point Blank* (1967).

BABE, THE GALLANT PIG (Australia)
BABE (USA)

1995 - AUSTRALIA - 92 MIN. - COMEDY

DIRECTOR CHRIS NOONAN (*1952)
SCREENPLAY CHRIS NOONAN, GEORGE MILLER, based on the book *THE SHEEP-PIG* by DICK KING-SMITH **DIRECTOR OF PHOTOGRAPHY** ANDREW LESNIE **MUSIC** NIGEL WESTLAKE **PRODUCTION** GEORGE MILLER, DOUG MITCHELL, BILL MILLER for KENNEDY MILLER PRODUCTIONS.

STARRING JAMES CROMWELL (Farmer Arthur Hoggett), MAGDA SZUBANSKI (Esme Hoggett), ZOE BURTON (Daughter) PAUL GODDARD (Son-in-law), WADE HAYWARD (Grandson), BRITTANY BYRNES (Granddaughter), MARY ACRES (Valda), DAVID WEBB (Vet), MARSHALL NAPIER (Presiding Judge).

ACADEMY AWARDS 1996 OSCAR for BEST VISUAL EFFECTS (Scott E. Anderson, Charles Gibson, Neal Scanlan, John Cox).

"Christmas? Christmas means dinner, dinner means death! Death means carnage; Christmas means carnage!"

From the very beginning of this movie, the images have a fairytale, unrealistic shimmer, making us fear one of those sugary celluloid feasts offered up as family entertainment in the run-up to Christmas. The only clue that this is a movie which will not gloss over the hard facts of life is the fact that its co-author is of all people George Miller, the man who gave us the *Mad Max* trilogy.

Babe, the Gallant Pig is as uncompromising as it is moving. Based on the popular Australian children's book *The Sheep Pig* by Dick King-Smith, this is a real movie in sheep's clothing, as it were. It tells the tale of a comical piglet who by chance (a chance almost as unlikely as winning the

national lottery and being struck by lightning on the same day) manages to escape being turbo-fattened and ends up in the idyllic farmyard of Farmer Hoggett (James Cromwell). Farmer Hoggett has all kinds of animals, but a strict pecking order is presided over by his fat wife, who is faced with the tricky task of deciding between duck or delicious roast pork for Christmas dinner. The movie's suspense comes from little Babe's efforts to escape the oven; he is of course incredibly plucky, has a heart of gold, and does everything in his power to avoid ending up as crackling and pork scratchings.

Two basic elements are used to ensure that his fight for survival tugs at the audience's heartstrings. All the animal figures are given human char-

Babe's most obvious model is the George Orwell novel *Animal Farm*, although not just because pigs and sheep are among its main protagonists. Orwell's text is a bitterly satirical critique of totalitarian government, a parable about the world during the Cold War and a subtle description of the powerful mechanisms of self-destruction inherent in all revolutions. *Babe* is a movie about individual self-fulfilment, and about the solidarity, friendship and courage we need to survive in a world which does not seem to have provided all its creatures with their own place or purpose.

acteristics and can talk to each other, although the humans in the movie don't realise this, and as in a fable, the animals' behaviour is a perfect reflection of the relations between human beings. As a strategy, that can be moving or comic, but it also runs the risk of being merely irritating.

The piglet's only hope is to prove that he is useful, or better still, indispensable, – an idea that he gets from the duck, his rival in the fight not to end up as the Christmas dinner. The duck decides to take over the job of the somewhat lazy rooster and gives bloodcurdling wake-up calls every morning, but his plan is foiled when Hoggett buys an alarm clock instead. For want of a better alternative, Babe dedicates himself to the long-term task of infil-

trating the domain of the sheepdogs, the animals who up until that point have been his only protectors. He tries to help looking after the herds of sheep that are the main source of income for the farm. And because movies of this kind always have a happy ending, not only does he manage to do this after various ups and downs, but he also manages to win the trophy his owner has long coveted, as an unusual competitor in the sheep dog trials.

As far as the film craft is concerned, the story is told in vivid images which skilfully combine the acting talents of real, meticulously trained animals with computer-animated models. This is a technique originally pioneered by Disney, and it is known as "animatronics". UB

1   A pig that thinks he's a dog. Babe and his "master" Arthur Hoggett (James Cromwell) at a sheep-dog competition.

2   The film depicts a rural idyll in picturesque images, but also brings across the hardships of living off the land.

3   At first the sheep are Babe the pig's opponents, but gradually he manages to win them over.

4   An unusual friendship. In the end the farmer considers Babe to be his best sheepdog.

5   Four watchful eyes: Babe learns from the dogs how to keep watch over a flock of sheep.

6   A hilarious trio: musical rats in concert.

2

3

SE7EN

1995 - USA - 125 MIN. - THRILLER

DIRECTOR DAVID FINCHER (*1964)
SCREENPLAY ANDREW KEVIN WALKER **DIRECTOR OF PHOTOGRAPHY** DARIUS KHONDJI **MUSIC** HOWARD SHORE **PRODUCTION** ARNOLD KOPELSON, PHYLLIS CARLYLE for ARNOLD KOPELSON PRODUCTIONS (for NEW LINE CINEMA).

STARRING MORGAN FREEMAN (William Somerset), BRAD PITT (David Mills), KEVIN SPACEY (John Doe), GWYNETH PALTROW (Tracy Mills), JOHN C. MCGINLEY (California), RICHARD ROUNDTREE (Talbot), R. LEE ERMEY (Chief of Police), JULIE ARASKOG (Mrs Gould), REGINALD E. CATHEY (Dr Santiago), JOHN CASSINI (Officer Davis).

"Detective, the only reason that I'm here right now is that I wanted to be."

One cop tries to pit his idea of order against the chaos of the world. After 34 years of service, disillusioned Detective William Somerset (Morgan Freeman) is about to retire but he is still not hardened to the job. He fights against decay and decadence with pedantry: the coffee jug is always rinsed out before he goes to work and his utensils for the endless grind in the urban jungle are tidily arrayed on the chest of drawers. The first ritual actions we see in this movie are Somerset carefully tying his tie and picking a piece of fluff off his jacket, but before long the movie is dominated by rituals of quite a different kind. When the first corpse of the day is found, Somerset registers the circumstances of the crime with a mixture of routine efficiency and mute fatalism.

Despite his outward appearance, Somerset's new colleague David Mills (Brad Pitt) is not made out of such stern stuff. The newcomer is shown the ropes as he is to be Somerset's successor. Pitt plays Mills with concentrated energy, giving us a character is an apparently confident go-getter. But Mills is soon forced to admit that both his older colleague and the murderer are his superiors. The audience also soon realises that the new arrival in this anonymous, permanently rainy city is not as clever as he makes out; the elevated railroad rumbles every quarter of an hour over the apartment he has been talked into taking. Tracy (Gwyneth Paltrow), is waiting for him there. She has been with him since high school.

This uneven pair, familiar from innumerable police films, the wise old veteran and the enthusiastic greenhorn, have to catch a serial killer who commits appalling crimes with missionary zeal, taking gluttony, greed, sloth, lust, pride, envy and anger – the seven deadly sins – as his pattern. The self-appointed avenger is also a familiar figure of the genre; he believes he has been chosen by a higher power to turn the sins of the world against the sinners. But there is more at stake in *Se7en* than simple character studies.

The killer (Kevin Spacey) works under the nom de guerre of John Doe – the name American authorities routinely give to unidentified male corpses. His readings in the great works of Western literature (Thomas Aquinas, Dante Alighieri, Geoffrey Chaucer) have inspired him to send a warning to the world. The first deadly sin he punishes is that of gluttony, when he forces a hugely fat man to literally eat himself to death. This extraordinary opening crime begins a series of murders which all feature sophisticated hidden hints left for the investigating cops. The indispensable minimum of shock effects and horrific images needed in a serial killer movie is delivered in an almost off-hand manner during the fat man's autopsy as if to fulfil an unavoidable obligation.

It soon becomes clear that director David Fincher is only marginally interested in the usual thrills and kicks, and that he is not concerned at all with any kind of guessing game as to who has committed the bizarre mur-

"If you want people to listen to you, tapping them on the shoulder isn't enough. You have to hit them with a sledge-hammer."

Quotation from film: John Doe

6

DAVID FINCHER   When the dark third part of the *Alien* series was released in 1991, it left both critics and audiences puzzled and it seemed that the Hollywood career of music video and commercials producer David Fincher had ended before it had properly begun. But *Se7en* marked quite a comeback. *The Game* (1997) is a similarly pessimistic film, showing Michael Douglas involved in strange happenings. Fincher's films are often extremely impressive visually; he uses apocalyptic settings to tell stories so dark they would have been unthinkable ten years ago. In retrospect *Alien 3* is now considered a fascinating conclusion to the SF horror saga of Officer Ripley. In *The Game* and *Fight Club* (1999) Fincher varies similar material in a memorably dark and sinister way. His main theme is always the decline of culture and civilization and he always finds the right, gripping story line for his sombre message.

...ders. Fincher has a message to proclaim, like his diabolically precise and brutal killer. It is delivered with shattering clarity and goes like this: the urban spaces of our civilisation are in dangerous decline. In this miserable setting, the murderer's crimes are merely the culmination of the general fear and alienation which creeps like a poison through the movie's stylised images from the very first moment. We see random pictures of a gloomy, dirty grey cityscape, where the constant rain can't wash away the filth, and people slink between the houses, bowed, anxious and filled with latent aggression that threatens to break out into violence at every moment.

Although the visual aspects of *Se7en* are often compared to Ridley Scott's *Blade Runner* (1982), Fincher's movie is a far cry from the overloaded metaphorical structure of that earlier movie with its visual symbols of a mythical past and a threatening future. Everything that happens here in the way of hidden codes and numbers serves almost exclusively to further the development of the plot.

The clues written in blood that the killer leaves at the second scene of crime leave the cops no doubt as to the serial nature of the murders. They are on the defensive and feel helpless, as all they know is that they can expect five further corpses in as many days. As the two detectives put together the first pieces of the fiendish mosaic and, in keeping with the rules of the genre, quickly become friends in the process, their methods and thoughts become inextricably intertwined with those of the killer. Early on, we begin to suspect that the finale will be a personal affair. However, when John Doe saunters into the police headquarters after the fifth murder has been discovered and gives himself up, the chase comes to an abrupt end thereby breaking all the conventions of the genre.

Se7en's main quality is its meditation on cultural pessimism. All three of the protagonists have failed in the face of modern civilisation, in the long tradition of archetypal American (anti-)heroes, and they all touch a raw nerve in our souls. Somerset is bowed with age and at odds with society, he wants to escape but he doesn't know where to, while his youthful partner barely hides his violent tendencies behind the rules of his job. The serial killer, that familiar institution in popular culture, escapes from his identity crisis and the perversion and madness of the world in a closed, cruelly logical system of thought and action but in the end wants only to die. *Se7en* is full of striking images. The opening sequence has become famous, and is visually so revolutionary that it is often copied in commercials.

UB

1   Cop David Mills (Brad Pitt) tries to uncover a system behind the murders. But common sense isn't enough to understand the psychopath's atrocities.

2   An end to terror: police officer William Somerset (Morgan Freeman) has the killer in his sights.

3   A gruesome discovery. The investigators catch their breath at the scene of the crime.

4   Seeking reassurance. Mills shortly before the final confrontation.

5   Nerve-racking police work. Somerset and Mills study photos of the crime scenes.

6   A rare moment of happiness. Mills and his wife (Gwyneth Paltrow) have invited his colleague to dinner.

DEAD MAN WALKING

1995 - USA - 122 MIN. - MELODRAMA

DIRECTOR TIM ROBBINS (*1958)
SCREENPLAY TIM ROBBINS, based on SISTER HELEN PREJEAN'S autobiography of the same name DIRECTOR OF PHOTOGRAPHY ROGER A. DEAKINS MUSIC DAVID ROBBINS PRODUCTION JON KILIK, TIM ROBBINS, RUDD SIMMONS for WORKING TITLE FILMS, HAVOC PRODUCTIONS.

STARRING SEAN PENN (Matthew Poncelet), SUSAN SARANDON (Sister Helen Prejean), ROBERT PROSKY (Hilton Barber), RAYMOND J. BARRY (Earl Delacroix), R. LEE ERMEY (Clyde Percy), CELIA WESTON (Mary Beth Percy), LOIS SMITH (Helen's mother), SCOTT WILSON (Farley), ROBERTA MAXWELL (Lucille Poncelet), MARGO MARTINDALE (Sister Colleen).

ACADEMY AWARDS 1996 OSCAR for BEST ACTRESS (Susan Sarandon).

IFF BERLIN 1996 SILVER BEAR for BEST ACTOR (Sean Penn).

"I want the last face you see in this world to be the face of love, so you look at me when they do this thing."

Never for a moment does this movie doubt the guilt of the condemned man, and the title makes it clear from the beginning that the execution will be carried out. Matthew Poncelet (Sean Penn), a vain, showy, shabby piece of white trash is to pay with his own messed-up life for the double murder of a pair of young lovers, symbol of America's hopes for a purer and better future.

Tim Robbins' second movie intentionally avoids the effects generally used in conventional prison thrillers to create suspense and win the audience's sympathy. There is no wrongly accused innocent saved at the last minute in a dramatic race against time, and no one pulls the condemned man's head out of the noose at the last moment. The movie does not set out to appeal against the death penalty, but rather to describe the grinding machinery of death row, with its strictly observed rituals and its wheels that turn with such agonising slowness.

Poncelet, the murderer in the film, has been waiting 6 years for his execution, while the national average is considerably more. He is not dragged to

the gallows the way he would be in a Western or forced into the electric chair like in a classic gangster film, as modern-day Louisiana takes a far more clinical approach when it comes to deciding over the life and death of its citizens. Nevertheless, shortly before the injection machine begins to pump poison into Poncelet's veins, the table he is tied to is set in an upright position. The impression that a diseased animal is being released from its suffering and put to sleep is replaced by an image of the crucifixion. Here the deeply-rooted religious symbolism of American society is plain to see: through his crucifixion, God is with the sinner. This is however combined with a fundamentalist idea of revenge and retaliation, anchored in the Manichaean view of many American churches that only absolute good and absolute evil exist.

That conviction, and the cliché of America as a nation eternally wedded to violence are arguments that are often trotted out to make capital punishment seem acceptable even today in "God's own country". But the thinking is that even though evil must be rooted out mercilessly, the condemned

3   4

"As ... in lighting and setdesign, the film discards prison movie cliché: this jail is no shadowy gothic hell hole but institutionally dull, almost cosy in its way. *Sight and Sound*

1   It takes Sister Helen Prejean (Susan Sarandon) some time to win the trust of condemned murderer Matthew Poncelet (Sean Penn).

2   A courageous woman. Sister Prejean does not desert the murderer on his final journey.

3   Love for her fellow man also means overcoming her own repulsion at the barbarity of the execution.

4   Even in the face of death there are happy moments. Laughter reaches across where words fail.

5   Poncelet only accepts responsibility for the crime at the very end.

5

should not be deprived of spiritual comfort. Poncelet writes to Helen Prejean (Susan Sarandon), a Catholic nun who is also a social worker in a ghetto, and asks her to visit him in prison. Helen takes up his invitation and gets her first insight into the grim workings of the prison system, which both upsets her and inspires her decision to accompany the murderer on his way to death. The offensive, boasting, dishonest side of Poncelet breaks through again and again, and Sean Penn is magnificent in the way he constantly alienates the audience and thereby creates a wholly convincing criminal. By a huge act of will, Helen eventually succeeds in building up relationship of trust with Poncelet, a closeness the limits of which are subtly emphasised by the director's constant use of grids and dividing walls. Although there are no explicit hints of forgiveness or redemption, Helen does nonetheless develop the beginnings of an understanding for this totally alien man.

According to her partner Robbins, Susan's character was intended to be the eyes of the audience. As we accompany this uncertain, doubt-ridden handmaid of the Lord, we see many other perspectives on Poncelet's case, all presented in an unsentimental and non-judgemental way. We see the victim's embittered families crying out for retribution, the self-sacrificing, dedicated but incompetent legal aid lawyer, the contemptuous prison officials who fulfil their duties so unwillingly, and the sympathy of hypocritical local politicians who are hopelessly constrained by the limitations of the system – and all of these figures are treated with the necessary respect. Like all good movies, *Dead Man Walking* takes its audience seriously and demands that it come to its own conclusions. The viewers themselves must decide whether, given the terrible conditions of the prisons, it is more humane to lock someone up for life without any prospect of early release (the only alternative to the death penalty in the USA), or to execute him straight away. It is no secret that the overwhelming majority of Americans are in favour of the latter, and *Dead Man Walking* is clever enough to avoid launching a direct attack on that conviction.   UB

MOVIES AND THE DEATH PENALTY

In real life we may never get to see an execution. But cinema allows us to examine the process at our leisure, and American cinema in particular has been fascinated by the theme since the early days of silent film. Two particularly memorable Hollywood movies have taken up the theme of capital punishment. In 1938, when hardly anyone doubted that the death penalty was an effective deterrent, James Cagney played a courageous game with his own image in Michael Curtiz's *Angels With Dirty Faces*. As a warning and example to other criminals and potential imitators, the toughest of all cinema gangsters is transformed into a trembling coward in the face of the electric chair under the influence of Pat O'Brien, his boyhood friend turned priest. Twenty years later Robert Wise produced a stirring appeal against capital punishment with his film biography of Barbara Graham, a murderess executed in the gas chamber. Susan Hayward won an Oscar for the role in *I Want to Live* (1958).

TOY STORY

1995 - USA - 81 MIN. - ANIMATION, COMEDY

DIRECTOR JOHN LASSETER (*1957)
SCREENPLAY JOSS WHEDON, ANDREW STANTON, JOEL COHEN, ALEC SOKOLOW DIRECTOR OF PHOTOGRAPHY JULIE M. MCDONALD, LOUIS RIVERA MUSIC RANDY NEWMAN PRODUCTION RALPH GUGGENHEIM, BONNIE ARNOLD for PIXAR ANIMATION STUDIOS (for WALT DISNEY PICTURES).

VOICES TOM HANKS (Woody), TIM ALLEN (Buzz Lightyear), DON RICKLES (Mr Potato Head), WALLACE SHAWN (Rex), JOHN RATZENBERGER (Hamm), JIM VARNEY (Slinky Dog), ANNIE POTTS (Bo Peep), JOHN MORRIS (Andy), LAURIE METCALF (Mrs Davis), R. LEE ERMEY (Sergeant).

"You've got a friend in me."

Day breaks in Andy's playroom. After the boy has gone to school, it's time for his toys to stretch and scratch and sometimes even to fit themselves back together. Rex the neurotic dinosaur broadcasts his problems to the whole world, Mr Potato Head gives a running sarcastic commentary, Slinky Dog slopes through the room in his friendly and melancholic way and Woody, the cowboy doll, calmly watches over his herd. The toys live, they have feelings, and above all they have a fine sense of irony about their function, although the humans know nothing of all that.

One day the fine social balance that has developed in the playroom over the years is destroyed by the arrival of a newcomer. His name is Buzz Lightyear, his vocation is to save the universe, and he takes his mission seriously. Woody and the others recognise this childish fresh-out-of-the-pack-

aging syndrome right away and try to explain to Buzz that he is only a toy. To no avail. The situation is not improved by the fact that in no time at all Buzz is Andy's favourite toy, and he begins to neglect all his other old play partners. Woody is depressed and tries to win back his place in Andy's heart. If anything should upset Buzz Lightyear's electronics in the process, then so much the better.

Soon however a tricky situation comes about, and Woody, Buzz and all the other toys have to pull together to solve it.

Even if the story weren't the little masterpiece that it is, this movie would still have a place in cinema history, for it was the first film ever to be made using only computer animation. Everything from the smallest blade of grass to the plastic army was developed inside a computer, from the earliest

1 Woody sees to it that communal life is harmonious in Andy's playroom. The voice of Tom Hanks
lends the wind-up cowboy a friendly, naïve soul.

2 Hamm, the piggybank, and Mr Potato Head, the
funny-face doll, are compulsive card-players. One
of many endearing pieces of fun in the world's
first full-length animated feature film produced
entirely using computer graphics.

3 Even a wind-up cowboy has feelings: Woody with
Bo Peep, his beloved shepherdess doll.

4 Cosmic warrior Buzz Lightyear has an identity crisis. His role as Messiah to a race of three-eyed
extra-terrestrials proves too much for him.

PIXAR STUDIOS   Pixar Studios originally belonged to George Lucas' "ILM – Industrial Light and Magic". Pixar was therefore responsible for the computer generated
pictures in Richard Marquand's *Return of the Jedi* (1982), as well as for Nicholas Meyer's *Star Trek – The Wrath of Khan* (1982) and Barry Levinson's
Young Sherlock Holmes (1985). In 1986 Pixar became an independent company under Steve Jobs, the founder of Apple. It began to concentrate on
the development of the software necessary for the creation of movies that were totally computer-animated. After the production of various short
films, Pixar finally succeeded in making *Toy Story*, which was the first movie in the world to have been produced entirely in a computer, under the
direction of the creative head of the studio, John Lasseter.

KIDS

1995 - USA - 91 MIN. - DRAMA

DIRECTOR LARRY CLARK (*1943)
SCREENPLAY LARRY CLARK, HARMONY KORINE DIRECTOR OF PHOTOGRAPHY ERIC ALAN EDWARDS MUSIC LOU BARLOW, JOHN DAVIS
PRODUCTION CARY WOODS for INDEPENDENT PICTURES, MIRAMAX.

STARRING CHLOË SEVIGNY (Jennie), LEO FITZPATRICK (Telly), JUSTIN PIERCE (Casper), YAKIRU PEGUERO (Darcy),
MICHELE LOCKWOOD (Kim), ROSARIO DAWSON (Ruby), BILLY VALDES (Stanly), BILLY WALDEMAN (Zack),
SARAH HENDERSON (Girl 1), SAJAN BHAGAT (Paul).

"When you are young not much matters. When you find something you like, that's all you got."

New York: teenage boys sit together and talk loud and long about sex, especially Telly (Leo Fitzpatrick), who "specialises" in virgins. New York: girls sit together and talk – with only slightly more reserve – about sex. Both groups soon start to talk about AIDS, and the boys are determined not to let it spoil their fun. Two of the girls have just had an AIDS test, although Jennie (Chloë Sevigny) really only went to make it less embarrassing for Ruby (Rosario Dawson). But when they go to collect the results, Jennie turns out to be HIV positive. Telly is the only person she has ever slept with, and alone, she sets off to find him. He's on the streets with his friend Casper (Justin Pierce) buying grass with money that he has stolen from his mother. In the park they meet another couple of teenagers. Together they beat up a passer-by who they suspect is gay, and all the while they talk uninterruptedly about sex. Telly keeps talking about how he going to "crack a virgin" that evening, as

he did in that morning. This time the lucky girl is 13-year-old Darcy (Yakiru Peguero). He picks her up with his friends, and after dark they all they break into swimming pool. While the others start playing games in the water, Telly begins to tell Darcy tenderly of his love – just like he did with another girl in the opening sequence of the movie.

As she trails him around the city, Jennie keeps arriving just after Telly has left. She has to listen to a taxi driver telling her that she should just forget about the test result because when she laughs, she looks like a prom queen. In a disco where she hopes to find Telly a friend persuades her to pop a few pills of the latest "stuff". When she finally catches up with Telly she finds him ensconced in the parents' bedroom at a friend's party, in the midst of deflowering Darcy. Jennie has come too late. Horrified and half numbed by the drugs, she watches through the doorway as they have sex.

1　When Jennie (Chloë Sevigny) goes for an AIDS test to support her friend, she's the one who turns out to be HIV positive …

2　… while her friend Ruby (Rosario Dawson) had been worrying for nothing.

3　When looking for a suitable image, nothing beats dramatising your sexuality and showing it off.

"I was trying to bring you into a reality that grownups just don't see. Think about what it's like to be a kid. How you're living for the moment. How you just want to have fun. How you're not thinking about tomorrow." *Larry Clarke, CNN*

4　The young boys emulate the older ones and experiment with their bodies and the topic of sex.

5　For they know not what they do: Telly (Leo Fitzpatrick) and Casper (Justin Pierce) aren't wicked or stupid, they just want to have fun.

6　For Telly this is just a kind of warm-up routine: he declares his love to any girl he likes, in order to be able to tell his mates about his sexual adventures afterwards.

AMATEUR ACTORS　　It is much easier to work with non-professional actors in a movie than it is on the stage. Camera work and editing both exercise a selection process which means that neither the overall effect of a performance nor its single elements are important, and that unclear articulation or an imperfect physique are much less of a problem than they would be on the stage. On the other hand, film sometimes uses non-professionals precisely because of some distinguishing physical feature, but that is mostly the case for supporting roles. Amateurs are sometimes used – although rarely – for an alienation effect, as in the movies of Straub/Huillet. Their clumsy performances are a deliberate effect to remind us that we are watching an artificial product. Amateur actors often appear in children's films and youth movies. Capturing their spontaneity requires extremely careful filming and directing however, and they cannot be simply put in front of the cameras. Some directors specialise in this, like the French director Jacques Doillon, who after years of working with children has developed his own special technique to avoid cuteness, which has the effect of making the kids in his movies appear as fully rounded characters.

Eventually, she sinks down onto a couch in the last free corner in the living room which is full of drunken and doped up kids who have all fallen asleep. Only Casper – the friendly ghost – is still wandering around, sipping all the half-empty bottles. He tries to wake Jennie but gives up, removes her pants and penetrates her on the creaking leather sofa. The following morning, the sun shines down on the parks of New York. Casper opens his eyes and mutters: "Sweet Jesus, what happened?"

The kids of the title curse, smoke and have continual sex with each other (or at least talk about it) and yet the movie still manages to avoid shock effects and cheap thrills. Photographer Larry Clark gives us an impressive portrait of the kids in what was only his first movie. Despite what critics said when the movie first appeared, the kids are by no means clichéd monsters.

The simple images tell the story of a single day and the audience are forced observe the chaotic search for satisfaction without any moral yardstick. The mitigating factors which customarily appear in similar movies to explain the kids' extreme behaviour are intentionally omitted here, and neither the social milieu nor ethnic conflicts have an important role to play. Clark dissects his kids with a surgeon's scalpel. The film succeeds partly because Clark worked with young amateurs, and the result was an enormous variety of faces and gestures the like of which is rarely seen in standardised Hollywood movies. He also resisted the temptation to make his kids into pop stars with music, clothes and other outward signs of coolness. Nevertheless, Chloë Sevigny – who takes the role of Jenny – has since been much in demand as an actress and has appeared in other films like *Boys Don't Cry*. 　MS

TWELVE MONKEYS

1995 - USA - 131 MIN. - SCIENCE FICTION

DIRECTOR TERRY GILLIAM (*1940)
SCREENPLAY DAVID PEOPLES, JANET PEOPLES, loosely based on CHRIS MARKER's movie *LA JETÉE*
DIRECTOR OF PHOTOGRAPHY ROGER PRATT **MUSIC** PAUL BUCKMASTER **PRODUCTION** CHARLES ROVEN for POLYGRAM, UNIVERSAL, CLASSICO, ATLAS.

STARRING BRUCE WILLIS (James Cole), MADELEINE STOWE (Dr Kathryn Railly), BRAD PITT (Jeffrey Goines), CHRISTOPHER PLUMMER (Dr Goines), JON SEDA (Jose), JOSEPH MELITO (Cole as a young man), MICHAEL CHANCE (Scarface), VERNON CAMPBELL (Tiny), FRED STROTHER (L. J. Washington), RICK WARNER (Dr Casey).

"You know what crazy is? Crazy is majority rules!"

In 1996 the world as we know it comes to an end, when a killer virus destroys almost all life on earth. A small number of people manage to survive by living in sewers and subway tunnels, where they start to build up a provisional culture. As the decades pass the survivors join together in a society based on mutual need, and they make it their aim to prevent the human race from dying out completely. Eventually scientists succeed in building a time travel machine, and it becomes possible to undo the apocalypse by preventing the unleashing of the virus. In 2035, a hardened criminal named James Cole (Bruce Willis) is sent on a journey back to the fateful year. He is chosen because society considers him dispensable and the journey is highly dangerous, but also because he is continually plagued by dreams of the virus catastrophe.

When he arrives in 1996 Cole is predictably put into a mental hospital, which is run by Dr Kathryn Railly (Madeleine Stowe). The symbol of the "Army of the 12 Monkeys" is all over the old world, and that is the symbol that Cole associates with his dreams and with the catastrophe. The leader of that secret association is a psychotic by the name of Jeffrey Goines (Brad Pitt) whose father is a virologist. Cole meets Goines in the mental hospital, and Goines helps him escape.

Terry Gilliam, visionary and iconoclast, uses Chris Marker's philosophical science fiction photo story *La Jetée* (1962) as inspiration for *Twelve Monkeys*. Gilliam claimed that he did not know *La Jetée* and that he only saw it after he had finished his own work, but given the many pictorial quotations which run through the movie's dense texture like distant memories this

seems a little unlikely. It might perhaps be fairer to say that *La Jetée* served as a model, as a short film can hardly be anything more than a point of departure. The journey in time is an idea of Marker's, as is the dramatic finale when Cole sees himself as a child and witnesses the catastrophe both as active participant and as passive spectator.

The biggest problem of *Twelve Monkeys* is that it adds little to the original. Both movies are ruled by the idea of the inevitability of death, and death is a force which both pursues the characters and which they rush towards in indefinable, semi-conscious fear. Gilliam's film is much less constrained in the means that it has at its disposal, whereas apart from a few animated moments, Marker's film consists entirely of static images given a narrative context by a combination of music and voiceover. There is a great simplicity

in the images and the content of the shots. *La Jetée* is hardly a movie at all in the traditional sense, but more a work made up of gaps or intervals. *Twelve Monkeys,* by contrast, overwhelms us with a flood of images. The audience is frequently left in the dark regarding the supposed reality of what is shown. We see sequences that we believe to be reality until the camera moves back and we discover we have been looking at a television screen all the while. Gilliam's film also borrows more than once from Hitchcock's *Vertigo* (1958), a film with which it shares a fundamentally elegiac mood.

Gilliam's film is about the paradox of the passage of time: its hero has his whole life in front of him but has already experienced everything. Like all travellers in time, James Cole pays a high price: he lives a life without a present, a life in which presentiment and memory destroy the moment.   OM

2

1   James Cole (Bruce Willis) has no idea that his
    assignment will turn out to be a metaphysical
    suicide mission.

2   A prime example of Terry Gilliam's unique fantasy
    world: a tense juxtaposition of early industrial
    architecture and a disturbingly realistic hospital
    interior.

3   Dr Kathryn Railly (Madeleine Stowe) is James
    Cole's only ally in his fight against the Army of
    the 12 Monkeys.

4   The end of the world in his eyes: Jeffrey Goines
    (Brad Pitt) reveals himself to be head of the Army
    of the 12 Monkeys.

CHRIS MARKER   The author and filmmaker Chris Marker is a particularly mysterious figure associated with the Nouvelle Vague movement. He was born in 1921 as Christian François Boche-Villeneuve in Neuilly-sur-Seine, or perhaps in Belleville or according to one telling in Ulan Bator. Like the American author Thomas Pynchon, he never appears in public. Marker is a master of the discursive film, and his movies switch effortlessly between fiction and documentation. Together with *La Jetée,* his most famous works include the movies *Le Joli Mai* (1962) and *Le Fond de l'air est rouge* (*The Air is Red*, 1977) which take political developments in France in the 60s and 70s as their theme. *Sans soleil* (*Sunless*, 1982) and its continuation *Level Five* (1995) are two studies of Japan, otherness and the search for the unfilmable self.

4

"It just seems that I have this German-Expressionistic-Destructivist-Russian-Constructivist view of the future."

Terry Gilliam in: Sight and Sound

CASINO

1995 - USA - 178 MIN. - GANGSTER FILM, DRAMA

DIRECTOR MARTIN SCORSESE (*1942)
SCREENPLAY NICHOLAS PILEGGI, MARTIN SCORSESE, based on the novel of the same name by NICHOLAS PILEGGI
MUSIC ADVISOR ROBBIE ROBERTSON DIRECTOR OF PHOTOGRAPHY ROBERT RICHARDSON PRODUCTION BARBARA DE FINA for SYALIS, LEGENDE, CAPPA (for UNIVERSAL).

STARRING ROBERT DE NIRO (Sam Rothstein), SHARON STONE (Ginger McKenna), JOE PESCI (Nicky Santoro), JAMES WOODS (Lester Diamonds), DON RICKLES (Billy Sherbert), ALAN KING (Andy Stone), KEVIN POLLAK (Phillip Green), L. Q. JONES (Pat Webb), DICK SMOTHERS (Senator), FRANK VINCENT (Frank Marino).

"Anywhere else I would be arrested for what I'm doing. Here they're giving me awards."

Sam "Ace" Rothstein (Robert De Niro) is a genius book-maker. All addicted gamblers wait until Sam has laid his bets so that they can copy him. His perfectionism is legendary. If a jockey has problems with his wife or if a horse is ill, Sam is the first to know. That's why the Mafia choose him to manage Tangiers, their Las Vegas casino. Sam makes it his life's work and keeps the Mafia bosses happy by constantly increasing their profit margins. Nothing escapes his tireless eye.

The casino Scorsese shows us is a perfect system where everyone spies on everyone else. Everything goes perfectly until two newcomers suddenly upset the workings of Sam's life. To protect him adequately and presumably also to keep an eye on him, the Mafia send Nicky Santoro (Joe Pesci) to Vegas. Santoro is a psychopath who will do any dirty work necessary, a little man with big ambitions, who is obsessed with power and devoid of scruples. Nicky immediately begins to build up his own gangster mob, and in no time at all they have won control of petty crime in Las Vegas.

Sam sees Ginger McKenna (Sharon Stone) for the first time through the peep-hole in the casino's false ceiling. A prostitute who is as hardened as

she is beautiful, she finds her clients among the ecstatic winners at the gambling tables. Sam falls in love with her. The only thing Ginger loves is her own self, but she is not adverse to Sam's money and power. To complicate matters, Lester, her former pimp, is still on the scene, and he still has a powerful hold on her. Scorsese retells a familiar tale of rise and fall, of powerful men who overreach themselves and end up losing everything, and he elevates his gangsters to the level of tragic heroes. Rothstein wants to rule the world by organising it perfectly and watching over it, and he ruthlessly uses everyone around him to his own immoral ends. But in the process, he unwittingly destroys his own happiness.

Nicky is intoxicated with Las Vegas, and he believes he can force his own rules on the city. He begins a brutal reign of terror at the bookmakers' and on the streets, only to fall victim of his own cycle of violence. Ginger, the third main figure, is unable to love and prefers to spend her life dependent on other people.

One of the great strengths of Scorsese's movies is they way they manage to present the Mafia and the underworld from constantly new and dif-

"I'm what's real out here. Not your country
clubs and your TV show. I'm what's real:
the dirt, the gutter, and the blood. That's
what it's all about." *Quotation from film: Nicky Santoro*

"What interested me was the idea of excess, no limits. People become successful like in no other city."

Martin Scorsese in: Sight and Sound

1 Expressions that speak volumes: the paths of Sam "Ace" Rothstein (Robert De Niro) and Nicky Santoro (Joe Pesci) are not leading in the same direction.

2 A ruler and his empire: Robert De Niro as Sam Rothstein in an inferno of light.

3 Heavy guys throw dark shadows (Frank Vincent as Frank Marino, left): Nicky Santoro already senses that further humiliation awaits him.

4 The artificial smile of the professional: Ginger McKenna (Sharon Stone) at her place of work. This is where Sam Rothstein sees her for the first time. Ginger's glittering appearance comes to embody what he imagines happiness to be.

ferent perspectives. *Goodfellas* (1991), for example, presents criminals in a casual, almost comic way, like the men next door. *Casino* takes a radically different track, as though Scorsese had resurrected figures from Shakespearean tragedy. The film forces us to feel sympathy for these heroes, and as soon as we fall into that trap, we are forced stand by and watch their downfall. Sam's megalomania gets him into trouble with local politicians and suddenly life gets much more complicated; Nicky thinks he can run the racket to his own advantage without the Mafia noticing, and even Ginger's brilliant beauty starts to fade when she agrees to marry Sam Rothstein, who buys her love with jewellery, money and furs.

Casino is a searingly beautiful movie. It presents the audience with the characters' innermost desires and fears through its off-screen narration. It does far more than tell one story, but is a complex weave of tales relating how love cannot be bought, and how friendship can be easily betrayed. Despite its tragic elements, the movie is witty in its depiction of the normal everyday life of the criminal fraternity. And Scorsese's special talent for allowing comedy tip over unexpectedly into violence makes the movie a real roller-coaster ride.

The story also reflects the rise and fall of Las Vegas itself. We see this from Sam and Nicky's perspective, reflected in the everyday routine of the casino, and the endless struggle against cheats and con-men, the constant search for new ways to evade taxation, and ever more effective means of controlling employees. The movie's discursive structure is mirrored in Robert Richardson's camera work; he swings and zooms, looking curiously here and there. Scorsese's Vegas is a hell of sound and fury. The world, as ever, is his stage.   OM

SAUL BASS   We have the graphic designer and filmmaker Saul Bass to thank for the fact that uninspiring opening credit sequences have now become art works in their own right. His work with Otto Preminger, for who he made the credits, promotional material and above all posters and adverts from the mid-50s onwards, played a major part in his development. Bass cultivated a minimalist style, using a small number of colours and motifs to emphasize the main theme of a movie. Although Saul Bass had officially retired, Martin Scorsese managed to persuade him to work on his movies. From *Goodfellas* (1991) to *Casino* (1995) Saul made all the credits for Scorsese's movies with the help of his wife Elaine. Bass has also directed music videos and many prize-winning short films as well as the feature film *Phase 4* (1973).

5   They've made it. Sam and Ginger blithely adopt the status symbols of the wealthy and the beautiful, unaware that nothing can protect them from a precipitous fall.

6   A fatal ménage à trois: the husband and his wife, the ex-callgirl and her pimp. Lester Diamonds (James Woods) has a greater hold over Ginger than Sam ever will.

6

"When you love someone, you've got to trust them. You've got to give them the keys to everything that's yours."

Quotation from film: Sam Rothstein

7　A dissolute icon of depravity: as Ginger McKenna Sharon Stone plays the most impressive role of her career.

8　A roll of the dice leads to deceptive success: Robert De Niro in his most complex Scorsese role to date.

9　Forbidden fruit: Nicky allows himself to be seduced by Ginger, in a relationship that will plunge him into oblivion.

DEAD MAN

1995 - USA / GERMANY - 120 MIN. - WESTERN

DIRECTOR JIM JARMUSCH (*1953)
SCREENPLAY JIM JARMUSCH **DIRECTOR OF PHOTOGRAPHY** ROBBY MÜLLER **MUSIC** NEIL YOUNG **PRODUCTION** DEMETRA J. MACBRIDE
for 12-GAUGE PRODUCTIONS, PANDORA FILM.

STARRING JOHNNY DEPP (William Blake), GARY FARMER (Nobody), JOHN HURT (John Scholfield), GABRIEL BYRNE (Charlie Dickinson), LANCE HENRIKSEN (Cole Wilson), MICHAEL WINCOTT (Conway Twill), EUGENE BYRD (Johnny Pickett), ROBERT MITCHUM (John Dickinson), ALFRED MOLINA (Missionary), IGGY POP (Salvatore "Sally" Jenko), BILLY BOB THORNTON (Big George Drakoulious), JARED HARRIS (Benmont Tench).

"That weapon will replace your tongue. You will learn to speak through it, and your poetry will now be written with blood."

After *Night on Earth* (1991) Jim Jarmusch realised that his filmmaking was in danger of getting stuck in a dead end, and that he had change as quickly as possible if he wanted to maintain his integrity as an artist. So it was that he made his greatest movie to date. In the guise of ramshackle western, *Dead Man* is a meditation on huge themes like the irony of all being and the idea of death as a final journey. In short: Jarmusch got serious.

America, somewhere in the west, sometime towards the end of the nineteenth century. With his few last dollars, William Blake (Johnny Depp) travels to Machine to take up a position at the metal company of the feared John Dickinson (Robert Mitchum). Machine turns out to be a desolate place bereft of morals, dignity and decency. Unsurprisingly, when he gets there, William learns that his job has already been given to someone else. When he tries to complain to Mr Dickinson in person, he is lucky to escape with his

life. He shoots Mr Dickinson's son in self-defence more or less by accident and is forced to flee Machine, getting wounded in the process.

He awakes to find himself being tended by a peculiar Indian by the name of Nobody (Gary Farmer). Nobody is pleased that William Blake has killed a white man, but he is also convinced that his patient is a reincarnation of the mystic poet of the same name, who he greatly admires. Nobody spent part of his youth in England studying the "white man's" civilisation, but when he returned and tried to tell his people about it, he was cast out and now wanders homeless through the forests. Mr Dickinson meanwhile has set a gang of three bounty hunters on William's trail, but they seem mostly concerned with killing each other. As the last of them gets closer and closer to William, he gradually finds his way to the eternal waters. The path to his redemption is purified with the blood of countless corpses.

1 William Blake (Johnny Depp) changes from a harmless employee into an unwilling killer.

2 William Blake makes friends with Native American Nobody (Gary Farmer), who thinks he is a reincarnation of the poet of the same name.

3 The capitalist and his portrait: John Dickinson (Robert Mitchum) emphatically demonstrates that the language of commerce matches that of war.

4 An American group portrait: cheerful psychopaths characterised by the attribute of the skull.

5 William Blake realises that his flight is in reality a metaphysical journey into the realm of transformation.

Jarmusch's usual audiences were left with a knowing laugh stuck in their throats. The eccentric characters, the actors who seem self-critical and distant, the delayed-timing dry humour were the same as ever, as was the poetic black and white. But there was also a spiritual depth that no one expected from the director of *Down by Law* (1986).

Seldom do cinema characters die as unspectacularly as in *Dead Man*. They stare at each other and shoot and then one, if not both, fall over, as casually as a branch cracks on a forest walk. Jarmusch was criticised in his turn for making killing a joke –worried critics were still dealing with the consequences of so-called "Tarantinoism". However, Jarmusch's abstract directing style counteracts any suggestion of pathos, and anyone who insists that *Dead Man* is in bad taste has completely failed to understand that killing and death here are part of a metaphysical joke called life. In this respect, although it is not thematized in the movie, *Dead Man* is spiritually close to a particular school of Buddhism, which believes that the souls of the murdered have a part to play in the redemption of their killers. *Dead Man* is a serene elegy, which glides along to Neil Young's hypnotic guitar phrases and blossoms in its glowing white and warm, intense black. OM

JIM JARMUSCH   Jim Jarmusch is the epitome of an 80s and 90s independent filmmaker in the US. He made his debut in 1980 with the New Wave-influenced *Permanent Vacation*, but international success only arrived with *Stranger than Paradise* (1984) and the television film *Down by Law* (1986). *Mystery Train* (1989) made it clear that his sense of the bizarre would always be his trademark, but unfortunately *Night on Earth* (1991) was a less than satisfactory follow up. However, in *Dead Man*, Jarmusch produced a masterpiece that lifted his work into a whole new dimension. As well as feature films he has also made several short films, including the *Coffee and Cigarettes* cycle. Jarmusch has made music videos and a remarkable tour and concert film for Neil Young entitled *Year of the Horse* (1997).

"Don't let the sun burn a hole in your ass: rise now, and drive your cart and your plow over the bones of the dead."

Nobody based on one of Blake's "Proverbs of Hell"

THE BRIDGES OF MADISON COUNTY

1995 - USA - 135 MIN. - MELODRAMA

DIRECTOR CLINT EASTWOOD (*1930)
SCREENPLAY RICHARD LAGRAVENESE, based on the novel of the same name by ROBERT JAMES WALLER
DIRECTOR OF PHOTOGRAPHY JACK N. GREEN MUSIC LENNIE NIEHAUS PRODUCTION CLINT EASTWOOD, KATHLEEN KENNEDY
for MALPASO PRODUCTIONS, AMBLIN ENTERTAINMENT.

STARRING CLINT EASTWOOD (Robert Kincaid), MERYL STREEP (Francesca Johnson), JIM HAYNIE (Richard Johnson),
ANNIE CORLEY (Carolyn Johnson), VICTOR SLEZAK (Michael Johnson), SARAH KATHRYN SCHMITT (Carolyn as a girl),
CHRISTOPHER KROON (Michael as a boy), PHYLLIS LYONS (Betty), DEBRA MONK (Madge), MICHELLE BENES
(Lucy Redfield).

"This kind of certainty comes but once in a lifetime."

Des Moines isn't Bari, which is why Italian war bride Francesca has never fulfilled the dreams of her youth. She earns a steady living at the side of her honest and upright husband, and lives a life of gentle boredom, until one day, when she is standing on the veranda of her farm house, a stranger appears in a cloud of dust on the horizon. Strangers are rare in this out-of-the-way corner of Iowa. The audience doesn't find out about Francesca's story until much later; as the movie has a gentle pace, but the fine nuances of Meryl Streep's acting make it clear from the start that she is torn between long suppressed hopes and the fear of losing the security of what she has. All the moral decisions in this melodrama have been taken before the movie begins and Francesca takes the first step; she offers to show the covered wooden bridge which is the area's only attraction to Robert Kincaid (Clint Eastwood), a widely-travelled photographer who works for the National Geographic Magazine. The lonely globetrotter with his laconic, decorous macho charm and the late flowering prairie rose slowly come together. A relationship begins, reserved and fragile at first, but soon becoming increasingly passionate. It's no coincidence that Robert J. Waller's successful novel, on which the movie is based, is set in Iowa, whose rigorous state motto proclaims "our liberties we prize, and our rights we will maintain".

Francesca's children Michael and Carolyn discover the story of her extraordinary sacrifice as they go through the things she has left after her death. This acts as a framework for the plot of the poignant love story, surrounding it like an iron cage. Another man has a previous claim on Francesca, and therefore the happiness that could have lasted for the rest of two lives is limited to four days in 1965 when Francesca's husband and her two teenage children are at the cattle show in Illinois. Husband Richard Johnson (Jim Haynie) hardly makes an appearance, but the way of life he stands for dominates the movie. Eastwood's movie may indulge overwhelming emotion, but in the final instance, it pays tribute to people who do not run away from their responsibilities.

Although the time the lovers spend together is limited, that only serves to make the affair more intense. The acting, camera work and music combine with the brief time span to make that rare thing in contemporary cinema: a believable adult love story in which every nuance rings true. The melodramatic figures that move us most are those who experience believable emotions and suffer in a way that we can understand. Doomed cinema romances enable audiences to enjoy the small victories and great defeats of the heart at one remove. This late work by Clint Eastwood is particularly effective because it manages to avoid that scourge of modern Hollywood melodramas – the self-righteous invocation of supposedly sacred values (family, faithfulness, etc) which are often nothing more than stifling Puritanism and naked possessiveness.

What remains are the girlish gestures of Meryl Streep and the uncertainty of the confirmed loner, played convincingly by Eastwood – the unlived life of two strong characters.

UB

1 Robert Kincaid is on the road to photograph the famous bridges of Madison County.

2 A symbolic moment. It's as if Kincaid and farmer's wife Francesca Johnson were meant for each other.

"Eastwood is unique among American film-makers today; no one else captures, with such concentrated intensity, a character's least breath, their least flicker of emotion."

Cahiers du cinéma

3 Her melancholy expression reveals that Francesca (Meryl Streep) won't be able to give up her previous life.

4 The performances of both principal actors make even naive actions both convincing and sincere.

5 Could Robert Kincaid (Clint Eastwood) have been the great love of Francesca's life?

CLINT EASTWOOD   No Hollywood star ever planned a career more intelligently than Clint Eastwood, although his early films meant that he was frequently underestimated. He quickly developed a disarming self-irony which prepared his fans for the day when the action-packed days of Dirty Harry would come to a close. The early 90s were something of a weak period for him (*White Hunter, Black Heart*, 1990 and *Rookie*, 1991) but he then resurrected the subgenre of the late Western, giving it an unexpected highlight with *Unforgiven* (1992). He followed that with a successful mixture of commercial fan fodder like *A Perfect World* (1993), ambitious attempts at art movies like *Midnight in the Garden of Good and Evil* (1997) and solid jobs for other directors, like *In the Line of Fire* (1993). However, what Clint was still missing was one of those roles which Clark Gable, Gary Cooper or Robert Taylor played in their later years and which Eastwood's biographer Richard Schickel describes as "classic, flat-out, leading-man romanticism". Robert Kincaid in *The Bridges of Madison County* is just such a figure. With unerring instinct Eastwood bought the film rights to the best-selling novel, outbidding Robert Redford who had also spotted its potential.

5

SENSE AND SENSIBILITY

1995 - USA - 140 MIN. - LITERATURE ADAPTATION, COSTUME FILM

DIRECTOR ANG LEE (*1954)

SCREENPLAY EMMA THOMPSON, based on the novel of the same name by JANE AUSTEN DIRECTOR OF PHOTOGRAPHY MICHAEL COULTER
MUSIC PATRICK DOYLE PRODUCTION LINDSAY DORAN for MIRAGE PRODUCTION, COLUMBIA PICTURES.

STARRING EMMA THOMPSON (Elinor Dashwood), KATE WINSLET (Marianne Dashwood), ALAN RICKMAN (Colonel Brandon),
HUGH GRANT (Edward Ferrars), HARRIET WALTER (Fanny Dashwood), EMILE FRANÇOIS (Margaret Dashwood),
JAMES FLEET (John Dashwood), TOM WILKINSON (Mr Dashwood), GREG WISE (John Willoughby), GEMMA JONES
(Mrs Dashwood), IMOGEN STUBBS (Lucy Steele).

IFF BERLIN 1996 GOLDEN BEAR.

ACADEMY AWARDS 1996 OSCAR for BEST ADAPTED SCREENPLAY (Emma Thompson).

"Please don't say anything important till I come back."

England in the late 18th century. Mr Dashwood, owner of Norland Park, has died suddenly. A son from his first marriage is declared his only heir, and he moves into the house with his wife. Mr Dashwood's second wife is left penniless and together with her daughters Elinor (Emma Thompson), Marianne (Kate Winslet) and Margaret (Emile François) is forced to move into a tiny cottage given to her by a distant relative, where she must henceforth survive on an insignificant allowance.

Ang Lee's Sense and Sensibility is one of several popular adaptations of Jane Austen novels that appeared in the second half of the 1990s. With its combination of light-hearted and sober stylistic elements – in keeping with the fashion of the times – director Ang Lee resurrected the Regency with great success. The emotional confusion of its characters is counterbalanced by the patiently observed, timelessly classic style of the production, which contains the sort of wisdom that the characters have to learn in the course of the movie.

Like all Jane Austen's novels, Sense and Sensibility focuses on a young woman whose intelligence and calm contradict the stereotype of her times and force her to go her own way in family matters, in society and above all in love in order to find true happiness.

In Ang Lee's literature adaption, Elinor is played by Emma Thompson, who fulfilled a long-held ambition with this intelligent and fresh interpretation of a classic novel. In life and love, Elinor corresponds exactly to the image of the clever, self-confident woman that Emma Thompson has cultivated throughout her acting career.

Before the second Dashwood family is forced to move to their new abode, Elinor happens to meet the clumsy yet loveable brother of the new

1   There is as much good sense as emotion in Elinor Dashwood's (Emma Thompson) polite smile.

2   Edward Ferrars (Hugh Grant) in a bitter moment of inner contemplation. Hugh Grant knows how to add dimension to the fairly one-sided character created by Jane Austin.

3   A typical example of the Flemish lighting that director Ang Lee and cameraman Michael Coulter were aiming for. The composition is based on a Vermeer.

4   The lightness and transparency of the Regency spirit are perfectly captured in the film's sets.

EMMA THOMPSON   Emma Thompson, daughter of the actress Phyllis Law and the director Eric Thompson, first became known outside England as wife of the British theatre and movie prodigy Kenneth Branagh. Although they are now divorced, while they were married, they ironised their situation in comedies like their Shakespeare adaptation *Much Ado About Nothing* (1993). Emma Thompson's first successes were in stage plays, television and finally in movies as a comedienne, for example in *The Tall Guy* (1989). She later delivered brilliant performances in serious roles like the housekeeper in James Ivory's *The Remains of the Day* (1993), *Sense and Sensibility* (1995) and as the artist Dora Carrington in Christopher Hampton's film biography *Carrington* (1995). However her best acting achievement to date is her performance as a terminally ill intellectual still full of the joys of life in Mike Nicholas television play *Wit* (2001).

mistress of Norland Park, Edward Ferrars (Hugh Grant) – and they fall in love at first sight. However, Edward's sister keeps a jealous eye on the proceedings, eager to ensure that her brother does not waste himself on a poor relative but looks for an advantageous match instead. She makes sure that he returns to London as quickly as possible. Elinor hides her unhappiness, and only later, she discovers that Edward has been secretly engaged for years.

There is no lack of amorous excitement in the life of Marianne (Kate Winslet), her younger sister. She is wooed by two suitors: the moody Colonel Brandon, whom life has not always treated well, and Willoughby (Greg Wise) a man of the world who is as dashing as he is fickle. After a stormy courtship, Marianne falls for the latter, who then suddenly disappears and leaves for London under mysterious circumstances.

For weeks, Marianne waits in vain for a message from her lover and then together with Elinor she is invited to London by a wealthy relative. Both Dashwood sisters set off with high hopes, one to fetch the love of her life, the other to find out who the love of her life really is.

At first glance, *Sense and Sensibility* seems a rather unlikely project for Ang Lee who had previously made a name for himself as a precise chronicler of contemporary Chinese family and love relationships with movies like *The Wedding Banquet* (*Hsi yen*, 1993) and *Eat Drink Man Woman* (*Yin shi nan nou*, 1994). But with the benefit of hindsight, *Sense and Sensibility* appears as a kind of liberating work where Lee freed himself from his cultural background for the first time without abandoning his interest in complex family and love relationships. OM

"Ang Lee (said that) he had Vermeer in mind, and indeed the creamily lit interiors and the close ups bursting with pensive longing do recall the Dutch master." *Film Comment*

5

6

7

5　Thrown on their own resources: three of the four Dashwood ladies (Emma Thompson, Kate Winslet, Gemma Jones).

6　Love in the time of quill pens. Another striking example of Michael Coulter's skill with a camera using Flemish lighting.

7　A moment of profound solitude, when reason struggles despairingly with emotion. Ang Lee is fond of filming his subjects discreetly from behind in moments of high drama.

8　The naturally spontaneous Marianne Dashwood has to learn to love not only with her heart but also with her head.

9　Marianne's zest for life is revealed during a country dance.

"*Sense and Sensibility* is a happy accident, the happy union of happy souls." *Film Comment*

8

9

LEAVING LAS VEGAS

1995 - USA - 112 MIN. - DRAMA

DIRECTOR MIKE FIGGIS (*1948)
SCREENPLAY MIKE FIGGIS, based on the novel of the same name by JOHN O'BRIEN **DIRECTOR OF PHOTOGRAPHY** DECLAN QUINN
MUSIC MIKE FIGGIS **PRODUCTION** ANNIE STEWART, LILA CAZES for INITIAL PRODUCTIONS.

STARRING ELISABETH SHUE (Sera), NICOLAS CAGE (Ben), JULIAN SANDS (Yuri), RICHARD LEWIS (Peter), STEVEN WEBER (Marc Nussbaum), KIM ADAMS (Sheila), EMILY PROCTOR (Debbie), VALERIA GOLINO (Terri), LAURIE METCALF (Landlady), DAVID BRISBIN (Landlord).

ACADEMY AWARDS 1996 OSCAR for BEST ACTOR (Nicolas Cage).

"I realised we didn't have much time, and I accepted him for what he was."

Ben (Nicolas Cage) is an alcoholic. He is so tired of life that he can't even bear it when he is completely drunk. When he loses his job, he takes it as a sign and decides to use his redundancy pay as a way of funding his alcohol consumption to the bitter end. As a failed scriptwriter, he feels that Las Vegas will be an appropriate setting for his intentions, as the bars in the city are open round the clock. On his way into town, he nearly runs over Sera (Elisabeth Shue), a young prostitute. She too is an addict, in her way: she is dependent on Yuri (Julian Sands), her Latvian pimp, who uses a knife on her whenever she disobeys. She has run away to Las Vegas in an attempt to regain control over her life, but Yuri has already tracked her down.

The next day, Ben and Sera meet again in a bar. Although Ben has been impotent for a long time, he takes her with him to his room. They get to know each other better. When Yuri finds out, he attacks Sera, as he has no patience with useless extras like emotional involvement. Luckily, it's for the last time:

a Mafia organisation from the former Soviet Union has a problem with Yuri and solves it by getting rid of him.

Sera likes Ben and decides to help him with his plan. She continues to earn on the streets and when she has time, she takes care of him.

One evening when Sera is at work, Ben goes to a casino, has an unexpected run of luck, and in a good mood hires a prostitute who happens to be free and takes her to Sera's apartment. When Sera returns home she finds them both there and, beside herself with jealousy and rage, she goes to the room of three college boys who rape her and beat her up. When she returns home completely distraught, Ben rings from a dosshouse. The end is near.

In the psychology of Ben and Sera's relationship there is no room for helper syndrome, so there is no need to fear sentimental last minute rescue scenes in the final act. Ben is serious, and that could have been a real dramatic problem: when the audience knows from the very beginning how the

movie will end, there is not much room left for suspense. Moreover, Yuri's forced exit from the scene removes the only unpredictable element from the constellation comparatively quickly. Mike Figgis uses this narrative stagnation to give his characters space to develop emotionally, and he gives his actors the chance to exercise their improvisation skills. This approach is emphasised by his much-discussed decision to film the movie on super 16, although in fact that was partly a budget decision. This method uses a compact, light camera and cheap, high sensitivity film. Although it had long been the material of choice for documentary filmmakers, it lost its place in the market when Digital Video appeared. As a material DV is even less expensive, and it quickly grabbed everyone's attention. It also inspired Figgis to make *Time Code* (2000), his most experimental film to date, a not entirely successful attempt at non-linear narration.

Technical aspects aside, *Leaving Las Vegas* is a movie truly remarkable for the honesty with which Figgis presents emotions it portrays. Occasionally he may be a little heavy on the Freud in the analysis of Ben and Sera – but it's their souls that remain his central concern.

OM

ALCOHOLISM IN CINEMA Drugs have always been an important theme in feature films. Alcohol especially is a central motif, whether as a necessary attribute of hard men or as a source of inspiration for writers and artists. The consumption of alcohol with fatal consequences has also often been thematised, as for example in Billy Wilder's masterpiece *The Lost Weekend* (1945), Blake Edwards' *Days of Wine and Roses* (1962) or John Huston's *Under the Volcano* (1984). Lives drowned in alcohol and memory loss through drinking are leitmotifs of "Film Noir". Memorable performances of alcoholics include James Stewart seeing a six-foot rabbit in *Harvey* (1950), Dean Martin as a drunken assistant sheriff in Howard Hawks' Western *Rio Bravo* (1959) and Mickey Rourke playing the title role in Barbet Schroeder's Bukowski homage *Barfly* (1987). Seldom was alcoholism so erotic.

---

1 Las Vegas: city of lights but no dreams, the collection of curios that is the American dream.

2 The alcoholic Ben (Nicolas Cage) realises that there is still love even for the lost and fallen. Even if it manifests itself in the form of the prostitute Sera (Elisabeth Shue).

3 Sera at work: here she is part of the false veneer of happiness of Las Vegas.

4 Elisabeth Shue made a breakthrough as a serious actress with this portrayal of a woman on the brink of spiritual self-realisation.

5 Mike Figgis' favourite supporting actor Julian Sands as Sera's pimp Yuri.

6 Ben and Sera find common ground in the weightless world of a motel swimming pool.

3

4

6

"Are you some sort of angel visiting me in one of my drunk fantasies?"

Quotation from film: Ben

5

HEAT

1995 - USA - 172 MIN. - GANGSTER FILM, POLICE FILM

DIRECTOR MICHAEL MANN (*1943)

SCREENPLAY MICHAEL MANN DIRECTOR OF PHOTOGRAPHY DANTE SPINOTTI MUSIC ELLIOT GOLDENTHAL PRODUCTION MICHAEL MANN, ART LINSON for FORWARD PASS PRODUCTION, REGENCY ENTERPRISES, LION BRAND FILM.

STARRING ROBERT DE NIRO (Neil McCauley), AMY BRENNEMAN (Eady), AL PACINO (Vincent Hanna), DIANE VENORA (Justine Hanna), VAL KILMER (Chris Shiherlis), ASHLEY JUDD (Charlene Shiherlis), JON VOIGHT (Nate), TOM SIZEMORE (Michael Cheritto), MYKELTI WILLIAMSON (Drucker), WES STUDI (Casals), KEVIN GAGE (Waingro).

"I'm alone, I'm not lonely."

Neil McCauley (Robert De Niro) and his team – Chris, Cheritto, and Trejo – are preparing their next strike. They need a fifth man to make sure it all goes smoothly. They take on a guy by the name of Waingro (Kevin Gage), who messes up the job. The team manages to escape with the loot but now they are wanted for robbery and murder, and the police are on their trails. Waingro shot one of the guards dead just for fun, and it's not too long till we realise that he is a psychopath and a serial killer too. When McCauley tries to get rid of him, he has vanished without trace.

Michael Mann depicts McCauley's gang as a close-knit group of conspirators who are absolute professionals at what they do. The armoured car robbery is carried out with the utmost precision, and they use extreme brutality whenever it's necessary.

A new detective, Vincent Hanna (Al Pacino), is assigned to the investigation of the case. One tiny detail and a seemingly crazy story told by an informer put Hanna on the trail of gang member Cheritto, and he unwittingly leads him to the others. As he has no proof, he has all of them shadowed.

During a break-in, McCauley realises he is being watched. He sets a trap for his pursuer to find out who he is up against. The team pretend to prepare a new heist and lead Hanna and his men to an abandoned part of the harbour where they make their escape and then observe their pursuers at their leisure.

In *Heat*, Michael Mann is concerned with much more than a simple game of cat and mouse. He shows us single combat between two equally matched opponents and does not shrink from drama and emotions in the depiction of his heroes.

Heat also tells the story of three relationships. McCauley falls in love with the shy graphic designer Eady, Vincent and Justine Hanna's marriage breaks down and almost destroys the life of their daughter Lauren, and Chris and Charlene Shiherlis' marriage is put to a test where there is no second chance. One of the most memorable and understated scenes is the McCauley team family dinner. It looks for all the world like a normal dinner party where couples enjoy sharing an evening with friends. This quiet moment forms a shocking contrast with the violence of the other side of their lives.

McCauley and his team want to carry out a last robbery with which they will make enough to be able to retire, even though they know that the police are hot on their heels.

Heat is great actors' cinema. McCauley and Hanna are outsiders. They live according to their own principles and follow their own code of honour. McCauley repeats over and over that he cannot afford to have any ties in his job, but his actions tell a different story. When he chooses to go back and

2

"We're sitting here like a coupla regular fellows. You do what you do. I do what I gotta do." *Quotation from film: Vincent Hanna*

1 Ready to take life as it comes: break-in specialist Neal McCauley (Robert De Niro) knows that plans can go wrong and that lives can be ruined.

2 A great moment in film history: Al Pacino as police officer Vincent Hanna …

3 … and Robert De Niro as burglar sit at the same table for the first time.

revenge his friends rather than escape to safety at the end of the movie, he is fully conscious of the danger he is in. His main motivation his loyalty.

One of the earliest mentions of the *Heat* project can be found in an interview with Michael Mann (*Film Comment*, 1983) which he gave shortly after the completion of his horror movie *The Keep* (1983). He talks about a screenplay called *Heat* that he wrote and loves, but doesn't want to direct himself. Clearly Mann decided that the project as too important to hand on to someone else and he eventually made two film versions of the same story.

The first work based on the *Heat* screenplay was a television film called *Showdown in L. A.* (1989) which was made as a pilot for *Made in L. A.,* a television series which was then never actually made. *Showdown in L. A.* is like an early sketch for the feature film as we know it. The basic structure of the

movie is already there and many key scenes are already well developed, including the famous cafe scene where Al Pacino meets Robert De Niro. But the earlier version doesn't have the emotional depth of the feature film, nor the uncomfortable feeling that we are watching extraordinary people caught up in an oppressively ordered world. Six years later work on the actual movie started. Spurred on by the world-wide success of his film of James Fenimore Cooper's *The Last of the Mohicans* (1992), Mann began work on his magnum opus.

Mann's production is emotional and dramatic without being exaggerated. The scene where the dying and the living reach out their hands to each other at the end of the movie is one of cinema's truly great moments.

OM

"A guy once told me, don't let yourself get attached to anything you're not willing to walk out on, if you feel the heat around the corner in 30 seconds flat." *Quotation from film: Neil McCauley*

EDWARD BUNKER Author and bit part actor Edward Bunker (*1933) first became known to a wider cinema audience with his role as Mr Blue in Quentin Tarantino's *Reservoir Dogs* (1994). A serious criminal with many convictions to his name, Bunker had been known to crime story fans since the publication of his extraordinary debut novel *No Beast so Fierce* (1973). Bunker was still in prison at the time. When this masterpiece of prison literature was filmed five years later by Ulu Grosbard under the title *Straight Time* (1978), Bunker not only made his acting debut but was also criminal advisor to the production. This is a role he has played for many prison films since then, including Andrej Kontschalowsky's *Runaway Train* (1985) – for which Bunker was nominated for an Oscar as screenplay writer. Edward Bunker also worked in an advisory function on Martin Bell's *American Heart* (1992), and Michael Mann's *Heat* (1995). The *Heat* character Nate is Michael Mann's homage to Bunker. Bunker's work on the screenplay of *Straight Time* was uncredited.

4 Jon Voight as Nate, the man in the background. The character was designed to pay homage to the writer Edward Bunker, who earned his living in the 1960s by planning break-ins.

5 One of the film's many mirror motifs: the searching look penetrates the inner person.

6 Wherever his gaze turns, it always lights upon himself: Val Kilmer as burglar Chris Shiherlis.

7 The street as battlefield. McCauley and Chris Shiherlis shoot their way to freedom after a holdup.

7

RUMBLE IN THE BRONX
Hung Fan Kui

1995 - HONG KONG - 90 MIN. - ACTION FILM, COMEDY, MARTIAL ARTS FILM

DIRECTOR STANLEY TONG (*1960)

SCREENPLAY EDWARD TANG, FIBE MA DIRECTOR OF PHOTOGRAPHY JINGLE MA MUSIC J. PETER ROBINSON, JONATHAN WONG PRODUCTION RAYMOND CHOW, LEONHARD HO, BARBIE TUNG for GOLDEN HARVEST.

STARRING JACKIE CHAN (Ah Keung), ANITA MUI (Elaine), FRANÇOISE YIP (Nancy), BILL TUNG (Uncle Bill), MARC AKERSTREAM (Tony), GARVIN CROSS (Angelo), MORGAN LAM (Danny), KRIS LORD (White Tiger), AILEN SIT (Gang Member), CHAN MAN SING (Gang Member).

"If you got the guts, drop the gun."

"Something's always happening here, that's New York for you." Keung (Jackie Chan) has just arrived from Hong Kong and he finds the American East Coast metropolis run-down and dangerous. At first his Uncle's words reassure him, but many adventures await him in the city and they're not all going to be fun,

Keung is a young man who has come over for the wedding of his Uncle Bill (Bill Tung), and on his very first night in America he has to defend the elegant white stretch limousine that Bill has borrowed for the occasion. Bill sells his supermarket in the Bronx and goes off on his honeymoon. Elaine (Anita Mui) buys the store, but still needs Bill's nephew's help and the very next day Keung discovers members of a biker gang raiding the place. He stops them and beats them up. After many chase scenes and fights between this gang, its leader Tony and Keung, the appearance of another gangster mob forces the rivals to pool their forces. Their new mutual enemies are unscrupulous diamond thieves with automatic rifles who make Tony's boys look like harmless school kids. In the meantime, Keung also makes friends in New York; he meets little Danny (Morgan Lam) who is in a wheelchair and his sister Nancy (Françoise Yip), the girlfriend of gangster leader Tony.

In most Jackie Chan films the story is of secondary importance, but in *Rumble in the Bronx* he gets down to the essentials even faster than normal. The economy of the movie is remarkable. In the space of three minutes Keung is established in New York, he is set up as a loveable character and skilled fighter, and we have also met his uncle and the boy in the wheelchair. Moments later his troubles with the rocker gang begins, they get down to business and the carefully choreographed fighting begins. Whether Jackie Chan runs, jumps, climbs over high fences or water skis on trainers, whether he fights using refrigerators, shopping trolleys or chairs as shields and weapons – his element is still the material world and he moves effortlessly

3

"I love action but I hate violence. For this reason, I think this choreographical solution is the best. In Asia I have become the children's idol and I do not want to set a bad example." *Jackie Chan in: Abendzeitung*

JACKIE CHAN – ASIA'S SUPERSTAR	He does all his stunts himself and during the closing credits shows what went wrong in the process. Unique superstar Jackie Chan was born in 1954. He learned his amazing physical skills at a Peking opera school in Hong Kong, where he was sent at the age of 7. Since his debut in 1971 he has made movie after movie, since 1980 he has also directed films, and the combination of martial arts and comedy is an idea he originally developed himself. Chan's role models are the cinema's great comedians to whom he regularly pays homage, like Harold Lloyd, whose famous clock tower scene he refers to in *Project A* (1983) and Buster Keaton, from whose *Steamboat Bill, Jr.* (1928) he borrows a scene in *Project A, Part 2* (1987). *Rumble in the Bronx* brought the Asian superstar fame and fortune in the USA, as well as an MTV Lifetime Achievement Award. On that occasion Quentin Tarantino said: "If I could choose which actor to be, I would choose Jackie Chan."

1 Keung (Jackie Chan) doesn't use guns, the most he ever uses as a weapon is a ski.

2 "As novelist Donald E. Westlake put it, 'Jackie Chan is Fred Astaire, and the world is Ginger Rogers'." *Time Magazine*

3 Keung dispatches the unscrupulous diamond robbers as promptly…

4 … as the louts from Tony's gangster mob.

5 In 1996 *Rumble in the Bronx* was awarded Best Film at the Hong Kong Film Awards, and Jackie Chan and Stanley Tong Best Action Choreography.

6 In with the wrong crowd: Nancy (Françoise Yip), little Danny's sister.

through it. Speed, flexibility and elegance dominate his films, but the fights are never really brutal and Chan's boyish charm and slapstick humour take away their violent edge. That said, *Rumble in the Bronx* is a movie of unusual extravagance. It rejoices in destructive orgies, like the complete destruction of a supermarket while its owner sits on the lavatory. It allows itself the liberty of showing things which have precious little to do with the plot but look good, such as the truck loaded with balls which topples from a multi-storey car park. And it is full of breathtaking chase scenes, like the one where a hovercraft races through busy streets and over a golf course until the baddie is finally run over. He survives, if a little shaken.

As in all his films, Jackie Chan does the stunts himself. He broke his ankle jumping on to the moving hovercraft, but then hid the plaster with his trouser leg and carried on. *Rumble in the Bronx* was his breakthrough in America. The movie was made in Vancouver in English, as US audiences don't like dubbed films. The American distributor New Line Cinema shortened the original 105 minute version to 90 minutes by shedding scenes like a wedding duet and a moralising speech by Chan, and launched the film with a massive advertising campaign. It made $ 10,000,000 in its first week.

HJK

MISSION: IMPOSSIBLE

1996 - USA - 110 MIN. - ACTION FILM, THRILLER

DIRECTOR BRIAN DE PALMA (*1940)
SCREENPLAY ROBERT TOWNE, DAVID KOEPP, based on characters from BRUCE GELLER'S TV series of the same name
DIRECTOR OF PHOTOGRAPHY STEPHEN H. BURUM **MUSIC** DANNY ELFMAN, LALO SCHIFRIN (theme tune) **PRODUCTION** TOM CRUISE,
PAULA WAGNER for PARAMOUNT PICTURES.

STARRING TOM CRUISE (Ethan Hunt), JON VOIGHT (Jim Phelps), EMMANUELLE BÉART (Claire), KRISTIN SCOTT THOMAS
(Sarah Davies), VANESSA REDGRAVE (Max), JEAN RENO (Krieger), VING RHAMES (Luther), HENRY CZERNY (Kittrigde),
EMILIO ESTEVEZ (Electronics Expert), DALE DYE (Frank Barnes).

"Dear boy, you are a sport."

Jim Phelps (Jon Voight) of the IMF (Impossible Mission Force) is supposed to be neutralising an enemy agent in Kiev. He succeeds thanks to the help of his wife Claire (Emmanuelle Béart) and his colleague Ethan Hunt (Tom Cruise),who specialises in disguise. He gets home to find the next assignment waiting for him – a traitor called Golitsyn must be found and stopped. Phelps sets a trap for him at the American embassy in Prague: during a reception he gives Golitsyn the opportunity to steal a list of names of double agents. Claire and Ethan also take part along with several other younger agents.

At the beginning it seems as if everything is going to plan and Golitsyn is soon unmasked, but gradually, successive members of the team are put out of action. At first we think only Ethan survives the trap that has been set for him, but later we realise that Claire has also survived. The failed trap means that Ethan becomes the CIA's prime suspect, and he is accused of being a double agent, especially as the actual aim of the operation was to unmask the traitors in their own ranks.

Ethan is able to escape but knows he will only be able to prove his innocence by finding the real culprit. He searches Jim Phelps' apartment and finds clues to a mysterious contact person called Max. Ethan meets up with Claire again who wants to join in his investigations and find out who murdered her husband. Max turns out to be an elderly lady who deals in top security information and is ready to pay a large sum of money for the real list of double agents' names. That list however only exists in the central CIA computer, and to get the data Ethan has to break in. He is helped by Luther (Ving Rhames), a technical genius and former CIA employee and Krieger (Jean Reno), an enigmatic killer.

1

2

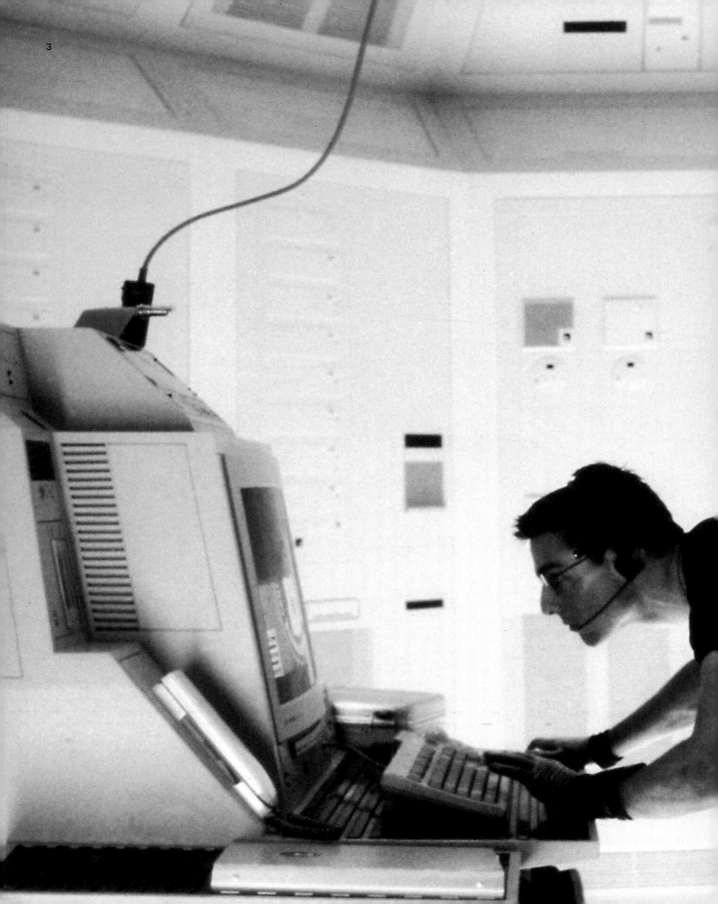

The break-in and data theft are successful. Ethan, Claire, Luther and Krieger hide in London where Ethan sees his parents being arrested on the television news. To protect them, he leaves his hiding place and turns himself in to the CIA. Jim Phelps, who everyone thought was dead, unexpectedly reappears.

Mission: Impossible is basically typically 90s high-concept cinema, with Tom Cruise in some breathtaking action scenes. The opening scene is typical: Cruise blows up a restaurant that has massive aquariums built into its walls. He hangs on a thin line over a floor alarmed with a hypersensitive movement detector. Finally he clings to the roof of a high-speed train which is being followed by a helicopter into a tunnel.

But Brian de Palma's movie is also open to a second interpretation, and the breathless action sequences can also be seen as a meditation on the nature of images and the idea of deception as cinema's main inspiration. Spectators of *Mission: Impossible* are constantly forced to ask themselves what they are really watching, and wonder whether it is simply another trick. De Palma is brilliant at directing scenes where at first we believe what we see and then have to admit that we have been deceived. The central scene of the movie and its decisive moment is the meeting between Ethan Hunt and Jim Phelps – the only two figures who were taken from the TV series. Ethan and Jim discuss the things that have gone wrong, and we see individual moments again in flashback. At first the consequences and events seem clear, but the longer the discussion continues, the more the actual truth emerges: in fact, none of the images are to be trusted. They are all part of a cunningly conceived plot, which is uncovered step by step before our very eyes.

OM

JEAN RENO Jean Reno made his cinema debut in 1978 in Raul Ruiz's *L'Hypothèse du tableau volé* (*The Hypothesis of The Stolen Painting*) after which he appeared in masterpieces such as Bertrand Blier's *Notre histoire* (*Our Rooms and Separate Rooms*, 1984) and Marco Ferreri's *I Love You* (1986). His big breakthrough came in 1987 with Luc Besson's successful movie *Le Grand Bleu* (*The Big Blue*, 1987). Reno's work with the director Jean-Marie Poiret was also very significant for his career. The three comedies *Operation Corned Beef* (1991), *Les Visiteurs* (*The Visitors*, 1993) and *Les Couloirs du temps: Les Visiteurs II* (*The Corridors of Time: The Visitors II*, 1998) made Reno a superstar in his native country. His role as a melancholy hired assassin in Luc Besson's *Léon/The Professional* (1994) made him known to a wider international audience.

4

5

"*Mission: Impossible* makes of Brian de Palma the key analyst of the transformation of our society into a civilisation of image and technology."

Cahiers du cinéma

6

1   Tom Cruise is Ethan Hunt: a man of many masks, whose true character can't be read in his face.

2   A key scene in the movie: Ethan Hunt blows up the aquariums in a restaurant and saves himself with an almighty leap. The reality behind the reflective surfaces is as misleading as it is hard to grasp – a perfect metaphor for Brian de Palma's amoral universe of betrayal.

3   One of the film's most striking images: Ethan Hunt gains access to the CIA's central computer.

4   Jean Reno plays mercenary agent Krieger.

5   Face to face: it doesn't take long for Hunt and Krieger to stop trusting each other.

6   Emmanuelle Béart plays Claire, wife of Hunt's boss Jim Phelps (Jon Voight).

7   The computer specialist Luther played by Ving Rhames proved to be a key figure in the film: he also plays a decisive role in John Woo's sequel.

7

SHALL WE DANCE?

Shall we Dansu?

1996 - JAPAN - 119 MIN. - COMEDY

DIRECTOR MASAYUKI SUO (*1956)
SCREENPLAY MASAYUKI SUO DIRECTOR OF PHOTOGRAPHY NAOKI KAYANO MUSIC YOSHIKAZU SUO PRODUCTION SHOJI MASUI, YASUYOSHI TOKUMA, YUJI OGATA for DAIEI, NIPPON TELEVISION NETWORK.

STARRING KOJI YAKUSHO (Shohei Sugiyama), TAMIYO KUSAKARI (Mai Kishikawa), NAOTO TAKENAKA (Tomio Aoki), ERIKO WATANABE (Toyoko Takahashi), AKIRA EMOTO (Toru Miwa), YU TOKUI (Tokichi Hattori), HIROMASA TAGUCHI (Masahiro Tanaka), REIKO KUSAMURA (Tamako Tamura), HIDEKO HARA (Masako Sugiyama), SHUCHIRO MORIYAMA (Ryo Kishikawa).

"Slow, slow, quick quick slow"

Shohei Sugiyama (Koji Yakusho) leads the sober life of an average Japanese citizen. He is married with a daughter, owns his own home in the suburbs and has an office job in the city. But he still feels unfulfilled. One day on his way home in the train, he happens to see a woman standing at the window in the upper storey of a dance studio. The next day he sees her again. and soon he is waiting impatiently every day for the moment when his train will pass her building. One evening he can resist the temptation no longer and he gets out and goes to the studio. The beautiful stranger – whose name is Mai (Tamiyo Kusakari) – is a teacher there. Social dancing is not the done thing in Japan, but Shohei steels himself and puts his name down for a beginners' course. All he really wants is to get to know Mai. However, although his efforts in this direction fail, he begins to make real progress as a dancer after his first clumsy attempts. Gradually he is gripped by dance fever and his whole outlook on life begins to change, so much so that his wife becomes suspicious and engages a private detective to investigate the source of her husband's renewed vigour.

Back in 1937, Mark Sandrich directed *Shall We Dance?*, one of Hollywood's greatest musical successes. Fred Astaire and Ginger Rogers danced their way into the public's heart in the main roles, and for a few moments America could forget that its daily life was still overshadowed by the consequences of the Depression. Masayuki Suo's film of the same name was a smash hit in Japan in 1996 when economic recession hit the country. Decades of economic euphoria had come to an end, and more and more people began to question Japan's legendary work ethos and look instead for ways of satisfying their individual needs. This social change is reflected in Suo's charming comedy. Unlike the Astaire film, Suo's movie does not use professional dancers to distract his audiences from their daily cares. Instead it shows how an ordinary family man in mid-life crisis discovers a love of dance that lifts him out of his depression. Shohei Sugiyama is a figure familiar primarily from European and American movies, but with whom many Japanese were able to identify.

The shape and narrative form of Suo's pictures are strongly influenced by the conventions of the Western. His references however are often ironic as he plays on the Americanisation of Japanese culture. Shohei is attracted by a woman in a window, a motif which has a long tradition in European and American film and has become something of a stale cliché. The mysterious beauty usually turns out to be a femme fatale, who threatens the man with sexual obsession and almost always with existential ruin, whereas in Suo's comedy, she turns out to be a comparatively harmless dancer who teaches the hero the simple lesson that there is pleasure in life outside work. Shohei's marriage still seems to be in danger, but only because he has to keep his dance course secret from his wife and work colleagues.

The drama and comedy of *Shall We Dance?* come above all from the heightened absurdity of daily routine at a time of national crisis. Despite his frequent ironic asides, Suo never fails to take his characters and their longing seriously – although their lives often seem banal, he gives them a heroic aspect. This opens the way for wonderful things at the movie's end.

JH

FRED ASTAIRE   Fred Astaire was born in 1899 in Omaha and died in 1987 in Los Angeles. He appeared on the stage as an actor, dancer and singer from his earliest youth. His film career began in 1933 during the most glamorous period of the Hollywood musical. Despite his skinny build and unusual looks Fred Astaire became one of Hollywood's most popular stars over the years that followed, with the help of his partner Ginger Rogers. He was famous above all for his extraordinary and incomparable dancing talent, which was a combination of precision, versatility and elegance. He was also very popular as a singer. Astaire made his last appearance as a singer and dancer in Francis Ford Coppola's *Finian's Rainbow* (1968) but continued acting to a ripe old age. His most famous musicals include *Top Hat* (1935), *Shall We Dance?* (1937), *Easter Parade* (1948) and *Daddy Long Legs* (1955).

1   And all your dreams will come true: Shohei and Mai (Koji Yakusho and Tamiyo Kusakari) find common ground in dancing.

2   The beautiful dance teacher shows the way.

3   Carried away by the music: at Mai's side Shohei really flies across the dance floor.

4   Beautiful and unattainable: the mysterious Mai arouses Shohei's passion.

5   Shohei is transformed from a run-of-the-mill penpusher into an elegant dancer.

6   Laborious first steps: at the beginners' course Shohei and his fellows are treading on unfamiliar ground.

> **"The movie has a great deal of zest and charm, and Yakusho gets so exactly that crest of melancholy that is a man's early 40s, until he decides to go for another kind of life, that the movie is infinitely touching."** *The Washington Post*

7 Gripped by dance fever, Shohei adds unexpected élan to a normal day at the office.

8 The Japanese reveal their individual needs: spell-bound, Shohei watches the dance teacher's demonstration with his comrades-in-arms.

WHEN WE WERE KINGS

1974/1996 - USA - 87 MIN. - DOCUMENTARY

DIRECTOR LEON GAST (*1936)
SCREENPLAY LEON GAST **DIRECTOR OF PHOTOGRAPHY** MARYSE ALBERTI, PAUL GOLDSMITH, KEVIN KEATIN, ALBERT MAYSLES, RODERICK YOUNG **MUSIC** WAYNE HENDERSON, TABU LEY **PRODUCTION** DAVID SONNENBERG, LEON GAST, TAYLOR HACKFORD, VIKRAM JAYANTI, KEITH ROBINSON for UFA NON FICTION.

STARRING MUHAMMAD ALI, GEORGE FOREMAN, DON KING, JAMES BROWN, B. B. KING, MIRIAM MAKEBA, MOBUTU SESE SEKO, SPIKE LEE, NORMAN MAILER, GEORGE PLIMPTON.

ACADEMY AWARDS 1997 OSCAR for BEST DOCUMENTARY.

"Say it loud, I'm Black and proud."

Muhammad Ali was a rapper. His speech is poetic, melodic, full of images and rhymes. He insulted his opponents, humiliated them and predicted their downfall in the ring ("dissing" as this is known among rappers today). His charisma attracted people who went away inspired – that would be enough for any rap musician.

Documentary maker Leon Gast shows Ali as a rapper, he lets him do the talking and puts a drum beat under his words at the beginning of the movie; he also shows sport and the music of artists like James Brown and B. B. King as part of the Black Consciousness Movement. Gast documents the legendary fight between Ali and the then world champion George Foreman in Kinshasa, Zaire, today's Congo.

As a result of his refusal to fight in the Vietnam War, Ali received a five-year prison term in 1967 and lost the world champion title of the "World Boxing Association" (WBA). In 1970 his sentence was lifted and Ali set about trying to win back the title. The decisive fight between the 32-year-old and Foreman, who was six years younger, was a huge event, not just because Foreman had a unique record to defend (37 K. O. victories and no defeats since he turned professional) and Ali was considered an ageing sportsman in comparison. The circumstances were also spectacular: the boxing promoter Don King offered both Ali and Foreman five million dollars. He cast around for the total of ten million that he needed and finally received it from Mobutu Sese Seko, military dictator of Zaire. The great fight, which quickly became known as "the rumble in the jungle", was supposed to take place on 25 September 1974 in the capital Kinshasa. The three days preceding the fight were reserved for a big music festival with James Brown, B. B. King, Miriam Makeba and The Spinners. The festival took place but the fight had to be postponed by six weeks as Foreman injured his eye during training and had to wait until it healed. In this six weeks, most of the documentary recordings that Gast filmed with Muhammad Ali were made.

Gast's Ali is a fascinating figure, and the director gives him plenty of opportunity to play up to the camera. What jumps out to the eye is Ali's tremendous musicality, which is made all the clearer by the way Gast sandwiches the Ali scenes between montages of the music festival. His speech, his movements and his fighting are filled with rhythm, and as Ali keeps repeating himself he's going to dance, dance, dance, so that Foreman won't even be able to find him in the ring. That was pure bluff, as the pictures of the fight prove. In interviews with the writer Norman Mailer and George Plimpton, who were there at the time, the situation before and during the fight is analysed over and over, and Ali's obvious fear of the giant Foreman is compared to his fighting strategy.

Gast finds wonderful rhythm for his images and the film is just as musical as its protagonist. Eyewitness statements, interviews from the time

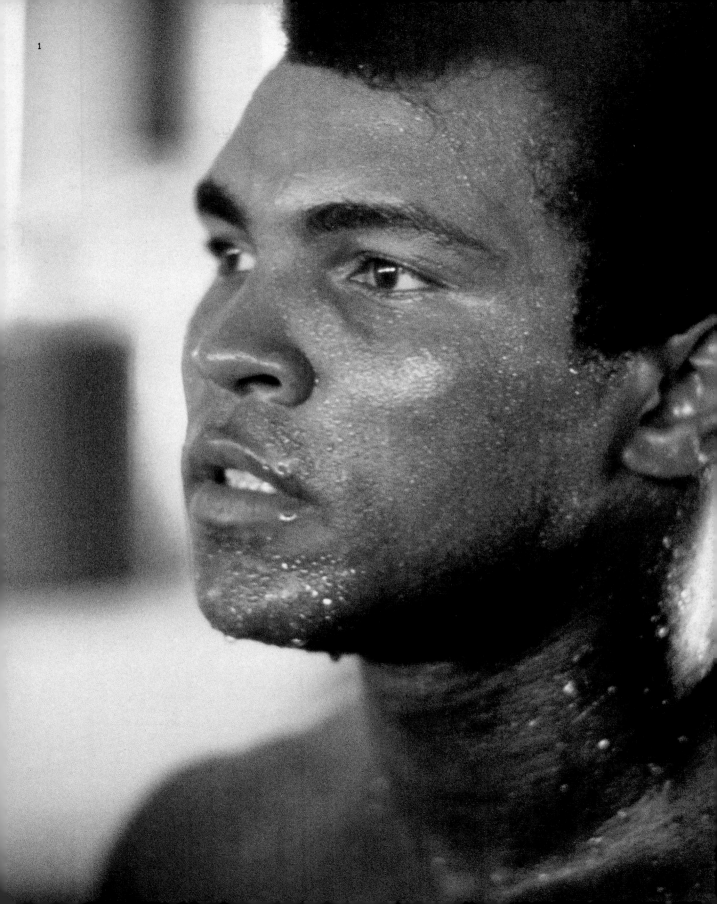

"This film is more besides being a successful movie about Muhammad Ali – it is a film about Ali's skill at combining sport and politics and in so doing becoming the epitome of a people's hero." Frankfurter Allgemeine Zeitung

2

3

BOXING AT THE MOVIES Boxing has often been used as a film subject over the years, both in documentaries and feature films. At the beginning of cinema history, boxing was ideal for the static cameras used as it offered lots of movement in an enclosed space, and it is a subject that has remained popular with cinema audiences. It gives excellent scope for rags to riches stories about people who box their way to the top, like John Garfield as the Jewish boy in *Body and Soul* (1947) and Sylvester Stallone as the small fry hired fighter paid by gangsters in *Rocky* (1977). Rocky has remained the prototype of the boxer who loses in the ring but wins in life – he finds himself instead. Many biographies have made idols of the ring into film heroes, for example the American middle weight champion Jake La Motta played by Robert De Niro in *Raging Bull* 1980 and the IRA pugilist Danny Boy Flynn played by Daniel Day Lewis in *The Boxer* (1997). There is also another documentary film about Ali, a feature-length French documentary entitled *Muhammad Ali, The Greatest* (1964–1974).

1 Did he always believe he would win? In the ring, Ali seemed to have occasional doubts about himself.

2 Two icons of black culture: Muhammad Ali and soul star James Brown.

3 Ali won the Zairians' hearts with elaborate descriptions of his preparations, loud-mouthed threats against Foreman – and by kissing babies, just like a politician.

4 "Ali Bomaye!" – "Ali, kill him!" A thousand voices spur Muhammad Ali on.

5 Advance announcements that he would dance in the ring were a ruse – Ali let Foreman box himself into exhaustion.

archive material and music scenes are bound together in a harmonious whole – and the result is a gripping portrait of a genuine idol.

The film took decades to take on its finished form. Gast had already made several music movies (including *The Dead*, 1977, on The Grateful Dead) and originally was only supposed to document the music festival. When the fight was cancelled, he decided to stay on in Zaire and film. He used 100,000 metres of film, and needed nearly 15 years to get the money together to develop it all. The editing took another couple of years. His film-maker friend Taylor Hackford filmed the additional interviews with Mailer, Plimpton and the Black Cinema director Spike Lee, to complete Gast's material. Almost 22 years after the filming began, *When We Were Kings* was given its first showing at the Sundance film festival. HJK

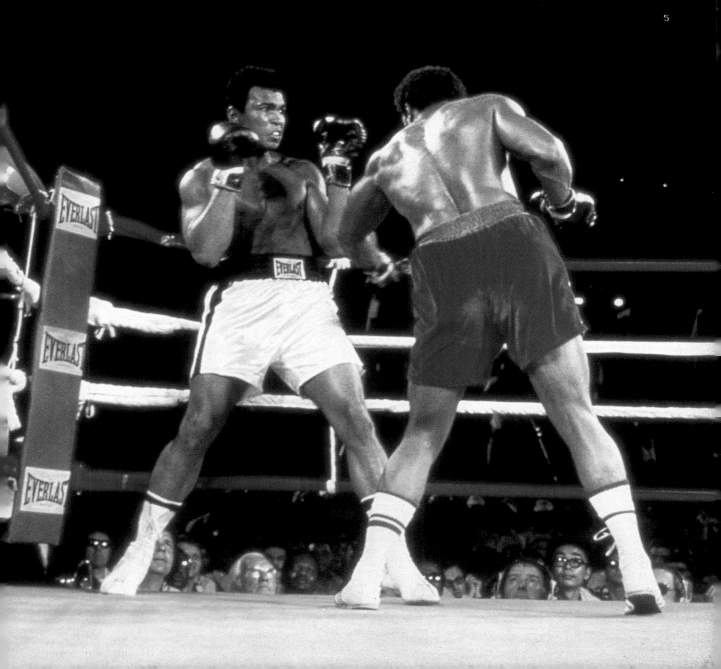

FARGO

1996 - USA - 98 MIN. - CRIME FILM

DIRECTOR JOEL COEN (*1954)
SCREENPLAY JOEL COEN, ETHAN COEN **DIRECTOR OF PHOTOGRAPHY** ROGER DEAKINS **MUSIC** CARTER BURWELL **PRODUCTION** ETHAN COEN for WORKING TITLE FILMS.

STARRING FRANCES MCDORMAND (Marge Gunderson), STEVE BUSCEMI (Carl Showalter), PETER STORMARE (Gaear Grimsrud), WILLIAM H. MACY (Jerry Lundegaard), HARVE PRESNELL (Wade Gustafson), KRISTIN RUDRÜD (Jean Lundegaard), JOHN CARROLL LYNCH (Norm Gunderson), TONY DENMAN (Scotty Lundegaard), LARRY BRANDENBURG (Stan Grossman), BRUCE BOHNE (Lou).

IFF CANNES 1996 BEST DIRECTOR (Joel Coen).

ACADEMY AWARDS 1997 OSCARS for BEST ACTRESS (Frances McDormand) and BEST ORIGINAL SCREENPLAY (Joel Coen, Ethan Coen).

"Jean and Scotty never have to worry about money."

Minnesota, 1987. Two tiny lights appear in the distance, vanish suddenly, and return somewhat larger. They are the headlights of a car in a hilly landscape. Winter, the movie seems to suggest, is the only possible season in Minnesota. The Coen brothers have a nasty story to tell. Car salesman Jerry Lundegaard (William H. Macy) is heavily in debt and has come up with a cunning plan to solve his problem: he's going to have his wife Jean (Kristin Rudrüd) kidnapped and demand a ransom from his father-in-law. Carl Showalter (Steve Buscemi) and Gaear Grimsrud (Peter Stormare) are to do the dirty work for him, and he'll pocket the one million dollars ransom money that he wants his rich father-in-law Wade Gustafson (Harve Presnell) to pay. He tells his accomplices that it's only a matter of 80,000 dollars, of which they'll get half for their pains. The two henchmen are total caricatures, Gaear in particular coming across as a complete fool. Their stupidity means that the abduction scene, where they snatch Jean from the shower, is a combination of the comic and the macabre, and cinema connoisseurs can hardly fail to recognise a parody of Hitchcock's *Psycho* (1960). Subsequently however the plan goes badly awry and the story becomes both brutal and grisly. When Carl and Gaear try to take Jean to the hiding place in one of Jerry's cars and are held up close to Brainerd by a police patrol, they kill a policeman and two tourists. Gaear seems devoid of any feeling, first killing Jean and then disposing of Carl.

Since it's one of her officers who has been murdered, the heavily pregnant police chief of Brainerd Marge Gunderson (Frances McDormand) decides to get personally involved in the hunt for the killers. Her husband Norm meanwhile paints nature pictures for a postage stamp picture competition. When Marge finds the remaining killer he is busy stuffing the corpse of his partner in crime through a woodchip shredder. He tries to run away and Marge shoots him dead. One of Norm's pictures is selected to go on a

postage stamp, the three cent stamp which is only needed for higher postage rates.

Fargo is a hard movie to categorise. It is grotesque and definitely absurd, but above all it is eerie. Cruelty and brutality become forces in their own right, and the story ends in an unexpected bloodbath because the protagonists have so little control over the situation. In *Fargo* everything moves a little more slowly. Not just because the world is deep in snow and each movement requires three times the usual effort, but also because the people of Minnesota, largely descendants of Scandinavian immigrants, are generally slower. Slow in the sense of speaking in a strange provincial drawl, and slow on the uptake. All of which has a role to play in this story about the real-

ity of crime and the ability of evil to assert itself. It is a movie which aim infallibly for the worst-case scenario with pessimistic Protestant determin ism. The criminals are greedy, stupid and nervous, the police are powerles to do anything but trudge after them and pick up the pieces, counting th corpses and finally making a useless arrest criminals.

Fargo is the Coen brothers' coolest, most reserved movie to date, part ly because it is so unspectacular optically. The colours are simple, almos monochrome, the music is practically minimalist and the dialogues ar uncommunicative poetry intensified by the grinding singsong of the loca dialect. The Coen brothers were born in Minnesota and *Fargo* is a grotesqu and gruesome homage to their homeland.   ON

WILLIAM H. MACY Character and ensemble actor par excellence and one of the most interesting faces of the 90s, Macy first became famous as part of David Mamet's team of actors. He is particularly convincing when he plays a small town characters whose livelihood is in danger. Above all, it was his brilliant interpretation of the desperate car salesman who becomes a criminal in *Fargo* that imprinted his face on audiences' memories. His convincing performance as the clinically precise family man who discovers the Nazi in himself (*Pleasantville*, 1998), is equally as striking as his role in *Magnolia* (1999) as a former quiz show child prodigy who feels unloved. Macy's brilliance shows above all in his capacity to give the most ridiculous figures their own dignity.

1 Dim petty criminals with a tendency to overreact: Steve Buscemi as Carl Showalter and Peter Stormare as Gaear Grimsrud.

2 Trudging along single-mindedly in pursuit of the criminals. Frances McDormand in the role of a lifetime as pregnant polices Officer Marge Gunderson.

3 A man with an enormous problem: William H. Macy as car salesman Jerry Lundegaard.

5

6

"*Fargo* is undoubtedly our most traditional film. It's also the first time that we've used a news story."

Ethan Coen in: Cahiers du cinéma

4   The facial expression of the film: grim determination bordering on the grotesque.

5   After a meal like that the day can only turn out
well: one of the many Minnesota-cum-
Scandinavian idiosyncrasies that turn the film into
a parody of a sentimental regional film.

6   A sticky end: stupidity and greed cause events to
escalate.

FROM DUSK TILL DAWN

1996 - USA - 108 MIN. - HORROR FILM, COMEDY

DIRECTOR ROBERT RODRIGUEZ (*1968)
SCREENPLAY QUENTIN TARANTINO, based on an idea by ROBERT KURTZMAN DIRECTOR OF PHOTOGRAPHY GUILLERMO NAVARRO
MUSIC GRAEME REVELL PRODUCTION GIANNI NUNNARI, MEIR TEPER for A BAND APART, MIRAMAX, LOS HOOLIGANS PRODUCTIONS.

STARRING HARVEY KEITEL (Jacob Fuller), GEORGE CLOONEY (Seth Gecko), QUENTIN TARANTINO (Richard Gecko), JULIETTE LEWIS (Kate Fuller), ERNEST LIU (Scott Fuller), SALMA HAYEK (Santanico Pandemonium), CHEECH MARIN (Border Guard/ Chet Pussy/Carlos), DANNY TREJO (Razor Charlie), TOM SAVINI (Sex Machine), FRED WILLIAMSON (Frost).

"All right, vampire killers – let's kill some fucking vampires!"

Mexico is so near and yet so far… The Gecko brothers are on the run, and Mexico is their only hope. The border is swarming with Texan policemen who close off every possible route into the promised land, but cool gangsters like the Geckos (George Clooney and Quentin Tarantino) shoot first and ask questions later: they currently have 16 dead men, a bank robbery and a bombed-out store on their conscience. Jacob (Harvey Keitel), a former priest, happens to cross their path, on holiday with his kids in a camper van. With his unwilling help the brothers smuggle themselves over the border by hiding inside the bodywork of the camper. The Geckos promise that they will set their hostages free as soon as they find Carlos, their Mexican contact man. They drink to their freedom with the family in an exotic, eccentric trucker bar called "Titty Twister". Too late, they realise that all five of them have landed in the pit of hell: the barman and the snake dancers suddenly turn into bloodthirsty vampires before their very eyes.

From Dusk Till Dawn is a double feature, a double whammy combining two completely different movies in one show. It begins like a gangster film and then completely out of the blue is transformed into a comic-like splatter

film where blood hits the screen in bucketfuls and all kinds of limbs fly through the air. Whilst director Robert Rodriguez (Desperado, 1995) is allowed to spread gore to his heart's content in the fight scene in the "Titty Twister" bar, the first half of the movie is clearly the work of Quentin Tarantino. Screenwriter and main actor, Mr "Pulp Fiction" himself clearly had a strong influence on the look and the tone of the movie, from the gangsters' laid-back remarks ("Fight now, cry later") to insane dialogue like "Where are we going?" – "Mexico." – "What's in Mexico?" – "Mexicans."

Both Rodriguez and Tarantino love quotations and constantly refer to their cinematic models, so the characters eat "Kahuna Burger" and smoke the "Red Apple" cigarettes that we already know from Pulp Fiction (1994). "Precinct 13", written on a T-shirt, refers to John Carpenter's film Assault on Precinct 13 (1976), from which the directors also steal one dialogue word for word. They play this self-reflexive game so comprehensively that From Dusk Till Dawn is like a patchwork movie cobbled together from bits of other films.

It takes an especially bizarre twist when the figures begin to question their own roles. In a short break in the action, everyone who hasn't been

5

6

1 Wherever the Gecko brothers show up, there's sure to be blood. To prepare themselves for their roles as brothers, George Clooney and Quentin Tarantino spent whole nights wandering the clubs of Los Angeles.

2 The "Titty Twister", the wildest dive this side of the Rio Grande. What the Gecko brothers do not know is that the truckers' and bikers' bar is located right on top of an enormous vampires' grave.

3 Bar customer Sex Machine shows what's hiding in his trousers. Tom Savini is an expert in blood-thirsty films: he has written books on the art of make-up in horror movies, and even produced a few such films himself, as well as taking part now and then as an actor. He can be found, for instance, in *Martin* (1977) by George A. Romero.

QUENTIN TARANTINO Tarantino was only just 31 years old when he was awarded the most important trophies in the movie business. He won the Golden Palm at Cannes for *Pulp Fiction* (1994) and an Oscar for the screenplay. The movie where killers shoot people as casually as they eat hamburgers caused a veritable outbreak of "Tarantinomania", and several directors tried to copy that special Tarantino touch. There was a sudden rash of gangsters dropping cool wisecracks against a backdrop of as much bloodshed as possible and a shameless parade of quotations from other films. Tarantino's enormous knowledge of films didn't come from any university, but from his job in a video shop in Los Angeles. To pass the time, he wrote film scripts. After the unexpected success of his first movie *Reservoir Dogs* (1991), a gangster story about a bungled bank robbery, the scripts he had in his bottom drawer suddenly became very desirable: Oliver Stone bought the rights to *Natural Born Killers* (1994) and Tony Scott filmed *True Romance* (1993). After *Pulp Fiction* Tarantino filmed an episode for the hotel film *Four Rooms* (1995) and made the comic-like horror comedy *From Dusk Till Dawn* (1996) together with Robert Rodriguez. Tarantino's last movie in the 90s was *Jackie Brown* (1997). This was a departure from the self-indulgent brutality of his early works and proved that he can also produce exciting narrative cinema without playing violent games.

chomped gets together to consider how to defend themselves against the monstrous vampires. Someone suggests crossing two sticks, as that was how Peter Cushing always defeated Dracula alias Christopher Lee. Jacob the ex-priest doesn't think much of this idea: "Has anybody here read a real book about vampires, or are we just remembering what some movie said?" What makes this scene so comical is that the film figures find themselves in a grotesque nightmare situation and yet they consider their options and come up with rational arguments. Jacob talks with contempt about "some movie" – and is himself part of one.

Unfortunately most critics didn't think this far, however. They weren't happy with *From Dusk Till Dawn* at all, and it was almost universally written off as too bloody and too self-satisfied. They only thing about the movie was George Clooney. The role of the gangster Seth, who has to deal not only with the vampires but also with his sex-obsessed younger brother Richard (Quentin Tarantino) liberated Clooney from the operating theatre of the TV series *Emergency Room* and smoothed his path to stardom on the silver screen.

NM

7

4   Santanico Pandemonium (Salma Hayek) bewitch-
es the Titty Twister clientele with her erotic snake
dance. To the horror of the Gecko brothers, she
too turns into a bloodthirsty monster when the
first drops of blood appear.

5   The vampires in the "Titty Twister" have little in
common with Dracula-style bloodsuckers. Roberto
Rodriguez based them on models from the mythological culture of the Aztecs.

"Those who think that *From Dusk Till Dawn* is a fake horror movie, be warned. Rodriguez gives the viewer *the real thing*: the high art of tastelessness, pure unadulterated Punch and Judy." *epd Film*

6   George Clooney's screen career began with the
role of Seth Gecko. Juliette Lewis plays Kate,
daughter of Jacob the priest, who is taken
hostage by the Geckos along with her brother and
father.

7   The monsters in the "Titty Twister" come straight
from the underworld. Tarantino originally wrote
the screenplay for a special effects company, who
give ample demonstration of their talents in the
second half of the movie.

8   Seth pleads with the priest Jacob Fuller (Harvey
Keitel) to find his faith again, since the preacher
had turned his back on God after the agonising
death of his wife. Now he is the final weapon in
the battle against evil.

8

KOLYA

1996 - CZECH REPUBLIC / GREAT BRITAIN - 105 MIN. - TRAGICOMEDY

DIRECTOR JAN SVERAK (*1965)
SCREENPLAY ZDENEK SVERAK, based on an idea by PAVEL TAUSSIG; DIRECTOR OF PHOTOGRAPHY; VLADIMIR SMUTNY
MUSIC ONDREJ SOUKUP **PRODUCTION** ERIC ABRAHAM, JAN SVERAK for PORTOBELLO PICTURES, BIOGRAF JAN SVERAK, PANDORA CINEMA, CESKA TELEVIZE, CINEMART.

STARRING ZDENEK SVERAK (Frantisek Louka), ANDREJ CHALIMON (Kolya), LIBUSE SAFRANKOVA (Klara), STELLA ZAZVORKOVA (Frantisek's Mother), ONDREJ VETCHY (Mr Broz), LADISLAV SMOLJAK (Mr Houdek), IRENA LIVANOVA (Nadeshda), LILIYA MALKINA (Tamara), PETRA SPALKOVA (Pasa), NELLA BOUDOVA (Brozova).

ACADEMY AWARDS 1997 OSCAR for BEST FOREIGN LANGUAGE FILM.

"You filthy little rascal, when are you going to grow up?"

A reverent string quartet fills the chapel, and the camera swings up over the musicians. Now we see a foot tapping in time to the beat, a sock full of holes, a beer bottle standing on the floor and a kettle that starts to boil. Louka (Zdenek Sverak), a cellist from Prague, and his three musician colleagues play funerals with singer Klara (Libuse Safrankova) to make ends meet. Louka once played in the Philharmonic Orchestra, but he was fired after he wrote obscenities in a survey conducted by the state security forces. Now he has given up any idea of political protest and as far as he's concerned, the country can go to the dogs in its own sweet time.

Louka lives from day to day, plays the occasional gig between funerals and works as a mason restoring inscriptions on gravestones. He is 55 years old, single, flirts with virtually every woman he meets, and is in debt to the funeral director Broz (Ondrej Vetchy). One day, Broz suggests an unusual

deal: Louka should marry his Russian niece Nadeshda (Irena Livanova) – in a marriage of convenience so that she gets a Czech passport. His reward: 40,000 Krone. Marriage, family and above all children terrify the philanderer Louka, and he refuses in horror. But slowly the idea starts to grow on him. With 40,000 Krone, he could finally buy himself a car, replace the drainpipes at his mother's house and still pay off most of his debts. Louka, the inveterate bachelor, finally gets hitched, and so begin the developments that plunge him into a series of catastrophes. Nadeshda immediately disappears to West Germany, leaving her son Kolya (Andrej Chalimon) with his grandmother who lives in Prague. The grandmother has a stroke and then dies in hospital, and suddenly Louka has to take care of his "stepson". The combination of the ageing womaniser who only speaks Czech and the shy lonely five-year-old who only speaks Russian, both under the same roof looks like a recipe for

"Kolya and Louka. Two lonely souls, from two different generations, two races in a love-hate relationship, with two languages that refuse to understand one another despite being related, are suddenly forced to share life." *Zoom*

4

CZECH FILM AND THE WEST If Klara's face seems familiar to some viewers, that may be because Libuse Safrankova appeared in the classical fairytale movie *Three Nuts for Cinderella* (*Tri orisky pro popelku*) way back in 1973. The West often thinks of Czech film primarily in terms of children's movies. Pan Tau, the innumerable fairytale adaptations, are well known all over the world but Czech cinema has a lot more than that to offer. *Kolya* was not the first Czech movie to win the foreign-language Oscar: in 1967, Jiri Menzel carried off the prize with *Closely Observed Trains* (*Ostre sledované vlaky*). Together with directors such as Vera Chytilova, Menzel symbolises a Nouvelle Vague in Czech cinema. Milos Forman can also be included in this group – he is still the most famous Czech director, although he emigrated to Hollywood after making his first three films in his native land.

1 It's a long hard road before philandering bachelor Louka (Zdenek Sverak) and timid Kolya (Andrej Chalimon) finally come to trust each other.

2 "It's not hard to become a father: the only woman with whom Louka spends the night without their sleeping together leaves him a son."
Frankfurter Allgemeine Zeitung

3 The age of Communism is over: Louka and Kolya at a demonstration during the Velvet Revolution.

4 Zdenek Sverak, who plays Louka, has been appearing on stage since the 1960s; he has acted in various films and written plays and filmscripts.

5 "Children rank among the oldest tricks in the book. They transform embittered loners into warm-hearted family types, and even convicted atheists start to hope that something like mercy exists."
Süddeutsche Zeitung

5

disaster. The boy cries and won't eat, and Louka has to give up many a pleasurable hour with his young female cello pupils. But eventually an unusual friendship develops out of the strange relationship between the two of them, and as their own little revolution takes shape, outside on the streets the Velvet Revolution of the autumn of 1989 also begins.

The red carpet in the church is punctured through and through on the right-hand side where innumerable brides have walked up and down in stiletto heels. A man sinks his tired head down onto the table in a bar, only to be reminded that he's not at work. Louka takes off the shoes of his little Russian and lectures him: "You Russians can't go anywhere without it becoming an invasion." It is delightful, precisely observed miniatures like that which make the charm and magic of this movie. Some are fond but iron-

ic commentaries on life in Czechoslovakia in the lead-up to the 1989 revolution; others are an entire story in themselves. Louka's transformation from Casanova to adoptive father is demonstrated in simple but effective gestures: the Louka of old used his cello bow to lift the skirt of Klara the singer as she performed in the church, whereas the new model Louka uses it to warn Kolya to be careful as he clambers around the organ loft. Director Jan Sverak continues in the Czech tradition of Jiri Menzel or Milos Forman with his attention to the small things in life and simple people. Big issues like politics only appear implicitly, in people's living conditions, or an upset in the life of the ordinary man in the street. *Kolya* is not just about a family; it was also made by a family. The screenplay was written by director Jan Sverak's father Zdenek Sverak, who also plays the role of Louka.

H.JK

TRAINSPOTTING

1996 - GREAT BRITAIN - 93 MIN. - DRAMA

DIRECTOR DANNY BOYLE (*1956)
SCREENPLAY JOHN HODGE, based on the novel of the same name by IRVINE WELSH   DIRECTOR OF PHOTOGRAPHY BRIAN TUFANO
MUSIC VARIOUS, including IGGY POP, LOU REED, LEFTFIELD, NEW ORDER, BRIAN ENO, BLUR, UNDERWORLD
PRODUCTION ANDREW MACDONALD for FIGMENT FILM.

STARRING EWAN MCGREGOR (Renton), EWEN BREMNER (Spud), JONNY LEE MILLER (Sick Boy), ROBERT CARLYLE (Begbie), PETER MULLAN (Swanney), KELLY MACDONALD (Diane), SUSAN VIDLER (Alison), KEVIN MCKIDD (Tommy), PAULINE LYNCH (Lizzy), IRVINE WELSH (Mikey).

"And the reasons? There are no reasons, who needs reasons when you've got heroin."

Two youths run through the streets, the police hot on their heels. Off-screen, the voice of the protagonist debates the consequences of saying yes to "normal" life and concludes that heroin is a way of escaping from convention and banality. Danny Boyle's *Trainspotting* is one of the fastest-moving films of the 90s. To the sound of Iggy Pop's "Lust for Life", we see a rapid overview of the highlights of the lives of a group of youngsters. Mark Renton (Ewan McGregor), "Sick Boy" Simon (Jonny Lee Miller), "Spud" Daniel (Ewen Bremner) and Alison (Susan Vidler) – together with Dawn, the baby she has from one of the other three – all live together in a filthy, dilapidated apartment in a shabby neighbourhood of Edinburgh. The main thing they have in common is their drug addiction. The course of their daily lives revolves solely around the quickest possible way of getting a fix of drugs, preferably without ever having to take on gainful employment.

From time to time almost all of them try to kick the habit and begin a normal life. Their other interests are not so different from those of other young people: football, the pub, sex. "Sick Boy" is a snobby James Bond fan who holds forth about Ursula Andress and considers her to be the definitive Bond girl. Robert Carlyle gives an astonishing performance as the universally feared psychopath Begbie and Ewan McGregor appears in one of his best roles to date.

The movie may be gruesome, but above all, it is funny. At its best, *Trainspotting* is reminiscent of the British films of Swinging London, where social reality was dosed with a generous dollop of surrealism. Renton, for example, dives into the lavatory in search of his drugs and finds them at the bottom of the sea. Instead of moralising about the dangers of drug abuse we are shown pictures of the joys of drug taking – and the price that has to be paid.

The friends' situation escalates when Dawn's baby dies as a result of drug-induced neglect. Renton and Spud are caught shoplifting and Spud goes to prison; Renton is allowed out on parole, takes one of his many guar-

1

"Mainly due to the ambivalence in McGregor's face, you get the feeling that Mark wouldn't say no to a bit of feeling. But he's numb – he can't say yes and he can't say no." *Sight and Sound*

anteed "last ever" shots and overdoses. At the hospital they just manage to save him, but his parents have had enough and they lock him up in his bedroom and force him to go cold turkey. Once he is clean he moves down to London and reinvents himself as an estate agent. But his past catches up with him when "Sick Boy" and Begbie turn up. To get away from his friends for good, Renton eventually has to betray them.

Irvine Welsh's novel *Trainspotting* came out in 1992 and quickly became a runaway cult success. The English edition quoted the self-confident comment "Deserves to sell more copies than the Bible; Rebel Inc.".

The novel was crying out to be made into a movie – and that cry was heard by a team with a sure instinct for works with cult status: Danny Boyle (director), John Hodge (screenplay), Andrew Macdonald (production) and Brian Tufano (director of photography), who had had a global success with their black comedy *Shallow Grave* (1994) and were able to go one better with *Trainspotting*. The movie became the cinema event of 1996, the first Britpop film with a promotion campaign using posters designed to look like concert publicity.

OM

1   An antihero for the 1990s: The only thing Renton (Ewan McGregor) cares about is where his next fix is coming from.

2   The working classes run amok: Begbie (Robert Carlyle) is the psychopath of the group. He embodies everything that goes wrong in all the pubs on the island every Friday and Saturday night.

3   Renton is swallowed up by the primeval sludge of his fears and dreams. This is one of the most frequently referred to scenes in the film, and became a commonplace among cinema images of the 1990s.

2

"(Sick Boy is) the chief trainspotter, with his encyclopedic riffs on the career and charisma of Sean Connery. Connery being Scotland's only super-star, what more apt than a Glasgow junkie high on movie junk to get off on earnest comparisons between Dr No and Thunderball. This is siege-warfare iconolatry." *Film Comment*

4

"The book is exciting, funny and dangerous in a way that a severe heroin addict's life isn't. The book has the vibrancy which connects with why people take drugs. It blazes away with this sense of experiment and risk." *Danny Boyle in: Sight and Sound*

DANNY BOYLE Danny Boyle is head and director of a typical 1990s movie team. Alongside the director the team includes scriptwriter John Hodge and producer Andrew Macdonald. Their debut *Shallow Grave* (1994) was an immediate success. A thriller, it tells the story of the increasing paranoia that takes root in a group of young people who almost accidentally make money through an illegal drug deal. *Trainspotting* (1996) was without doubt their greatest success to date. *A Life Less Ordinary* (1998) was another elegant black comedy, but it didn't quite match their previous successes. Their movie of the best seller *The Beach* (2000) starring Leonardo DiCaprio, was also something of a disappointment.

4 Renton at work: rarely has drug use been so casually portrayed as by Danny Boyle, who briefly became a superstar of European cinema thanks to this film.

5 Air of defiance: Renton is not only sickened by consumer society, but also by the status of his native country as a supposed colony of England.

6 Time for a change: Renton and his mates (Jonny Lee Miller, Kevin McKidd) take a trip to the country.

MARS ATTACKS!

1996 - USA - 106 MIN. - SCIENCE FICTION, COMEDY

DIRECTOR TIM BURTON (*1958)

SCREENPLAY JONATHAN GEMS based on the TOPPS COMIC COLLECTOR'S CARDS "MARS ATTACKS!" DIRECTOR OF PHOTOGRAPHY PETER SUSCHITZKY MUSIC DANNY ELFMAN PRODUCTION TIM BURTON, LARRY FRANCO for WARNER BROS.

STARRING JACK NICHOLSON (President James Dale/Art Land), GLENN CLOSE (Marsha Dale), ANNETTE BENING (Barbara Land), PIERCE BROSNAN (Donald Kessler), DANNY DEVITO (Gambler), MARTIN SHORT (Jerry Ross), NATALIE PORTMAN (Taffy), ROD STEIGER (General Decker), SARAH JESSICA PARKER (Nathalie West), MICHAEL J. FOX (Jason Stone), LUKAS HAAS (Richie Norris), SYLVIA SIDNEY (Grandmother).

"Nice Planet. We'll take it!"

A white dove of peace flies up into the air and is accidentally roasted by a stray shot from a laser gun. The Martians have landed! Unfortunately, things don't quite go the way earthlings had imagined. An enormous military contingent has travelled to the desert of Nevada, accompanied by hordes of media people, curious spectators, New Age disciples and alien fans. It's a warm welcome from the blue planet to the little green men, who must have come peace as they come from more highly-developed culture. But things don't quite work out as planned. The huge-brained creatures babble "dagg dagg dagg", open fire, and shoot wildly all around them. They take the reporter Nathalie (Sarah Jessica Parker) on board their space ship and subject her to useless medical experiments. They then leave a path of destruction in their wake as they rampage through the world – Big Ben is reduced to rubble, the faces of the presidents on Mount Rushmore are shot off and the sculptures on the Easter Islands tipped over.

For generations it was automatically assumed that beings from outer space would be belligerent warriors. At some point however, doubtless inspired by the television series *Star Trek – The Next Generation* and its message of tolerance, we moved away from such one-sided images, and started believing that aliens would have peaceful intentions. Director Tim Burton laughs openly in the face of such intergalactic political correctness. His aliens were moved to undertake the long journey from Mars by their most base instincts. For them the Earth is just one big galactic fairground shooting range, they fire at everything that moves and have a great time in the process. At the same time, they cunningly stress their peaceful intentions.

The people they meet are however not necessarily loveable and well meaning either. The powerless President James Dale (Jack Nicholson) is desperate for some kind of success in foreign affairs and wants to take up diplomatic relations with the Martians – even after their first attacks. Dodgy property speculator Art Land (Nicholson again) scents new – green! – clients for his casinos. A white trash family who live in a trailerpark only have one thought when the Martian invaders arrive: "They're not getting the TV!" Journalists want a sensation to sell, and the mad scientist Kessler (Pierce

ARTIAN ANATOMY

1 "Lisa Marie as a seven-foot-tall, blankly gum-chewing bubble-coiffed, hip-swivelling, torpedo-breasted, alien-designed sex doll."
Sight and Sound

2 With true British style and without the faintest idea of what he's talking about, Dr Kessler (Pierce Brosnan) explains all there is to know about the Martians.

3 "I'm not allowing that thing in my house." – The world is coming to an end, and the First Lady (Glenn Close, second from right) is worried about the carpet.

"The Martians gabble like geese, and the President is a lame duck, yet they still fail to find a common language."

Frankfurter Allgemeine Zeitung

"*Mars Attacks!* in particular arose from the certainty that it is itself an alien."

Tim Burton in: Süddeutsche Zeitung

4   In keeping with the trash aesthetic of *Mars Attacks!* the Martians weapons look like toys. They're deadly all the same.

Brosnan) wants to show off his knowledge and skill although he hasn't a clue about the Martians or their motives. Ross (Martin Short), the President's spokesman is overcome by his animal instincts, and he allows a big-bosomed beauty into the White House (Lisa Marie, Vampira from *Ed Wood*) out of sheer lust, and thus opens the door for the invaders to the centre of American power.

Burton only permits a tiny number of earthlings to come out of it with any credit: soul legend Tom Jones plays himself, a cool and stylish singer who directly after the end of the Martian invasion is allowed to sing "It's Not Unusual". Jim Brown plays the black boxer Byron Williams, who works in Las Vegas in a pharaoh costume. And last but not least, there is the deaf grand-mother (Sylvia Sidney), who saves the world with appalling folk music, the yodel blues by Slim Whitman.

Once again, Burton gives us a loving adaptation of popular culture: *Mars Attacks!* is based on collector's cards from the chewing gum brand Topps. The original cards numbered 55 and went on the market in 1962 although they were withdrawn soon afterwards. Card titles such as "Crushed to Death" or "Destroying a Dog" make it easy to understand why.   HJK

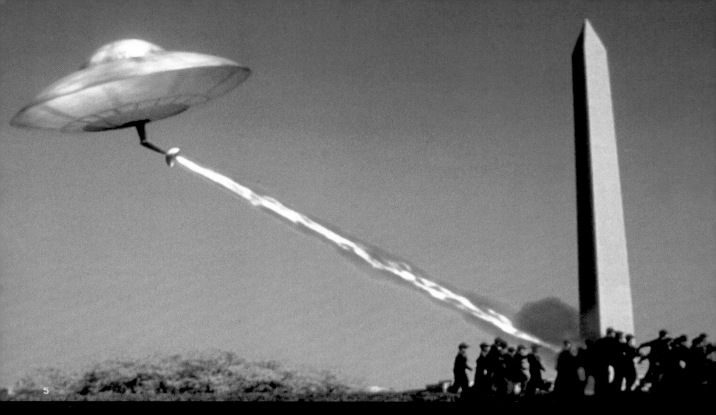

"**Burton tells of a world that it no longer sure of itself and that therefore looks for meaning in the most stupid of things. However, 'daggdagg dag' simply means 'daggdagg dag'.**" *Süddeutsche Zeitung*

5 "Although *Mars Attacks!* often seems to parody *Independence Day*, it was actually longer in the production pipeline." *Sight and Sound*

6 The Martians not only use X-ray weapons, they can also see right through people's selfishness and delusions of grandeur (Danny DeVito).

7

TIM BURTON: FILMMAKER AND FILM CONNOISSEUR

The head of the journalist Nathalie, which has been transplanted onto the body of her own Chihuahua, and the free floating head of the scientist Kessler declare their undying love for each other – a moment which is pure Tim Burton. His films – from *Beetlejuice* (1988) to *Batman* (1989), from *Edward Scissorhands* (1990) and *Ed Wood* (1994) to *Sleepy Hollow* (1999) – are fairytales, fantasy stories which show his love of fantastic genres (science fiction, classic horror movies) and of the B-Movies of the 50s. This can be seen most clearly in his film biography of the trash filmmaker *Ed Wood*. Tim Burton worked for a short time as a cartoonist for Disney, and among his role models he includes the cartoonist Ray Harryhausen, who awakes fencing skeletons and mythological creatures to life in single image animation. This is known as Stop-Motion technique and was actually what Burton wanted to use for the little green men in *Mars Attacks!* However, the process was too lengthy and expensive and Burton decided on computer animation instead.

7 Highly advanced, particularly in the military domain: no terrestrial tank can withstand the Martians' "plastic weapons".

8 Voyeurs, hooligans, murderers – it was the Martians' baser instincts that brought them to Earth.

8

ROMEO & JULIET

1996 - USA - 120 MIN. - LOVE FILM, LITERATURE ADAPTATION

DIRECTOR BAZ LUHRMANN (*1962)
SCREENPLAY CRAIG PEARCE, BAZ LUHRMANN, based on the drama of the same name by WILLIAM SHAKESPEARE
DIRECTOR OF PHOTOGRAPHY DONALD M. MACALPINE **MUSIC** NELLEE COOPER **PRODUCTION** GABRIELLA MARTINELLI, BAZ LUHRMANN
for MAZMARK PRODUCTIONS, 20TH CENTURY FOX.

STARRING LEONARDO DICAPRIO (Romeo), CLAIRE DANES (Julia), BRIAN DENNEHY (Ted Montague), JOHN LEGUIZAMO (Tybalt), PETE POSTLETHWAITE (Father Laurence), PAUL SORVINO (Fulgencio Capulet), HAROLD PERRINEAU (Mercutio), M. EMMET WALSH (Apothecary), CARLOS MARTÍN MANZO (Petruchio), CHRISTINA PICKLES (Caroline Montague).

IFF BERLIN 1997 SILVER BEAR for BEST ACTOR (Leonardo DiCaprio).

"Did my heart love 'till now? For swear at sight, I never saw true beauty 'till this night."

"Two households, both alike in dignity (in fair Verona, where we lay our scene) from ancient grudge break to new mutiny, where civil blood makes civil hands unclean." The prologue of Shakespeare's *Romeo and Juliet* resounds from the television. Boys from the two rival gangs meet at a petrol station. One insult leads to another, guns are drawn and the petrol station goes up in smoke. The war between the Montague and Capulet families makes the whole city hold its breath and keeps the police on their toes. Romeo (Leonardo DiCaprio), old Montague's only son moons around in his unrequited love for Rosalinde and keeps out of the fighting. He lets his friend Mercutio (Harold Perrineau) persuade him to go to a fancy-dress party at the Capulet's where his beloved is also expected to appear. Instead however Romeo finds his true love: Juliet (Claire Danes), the daughter of his archenemy Capulet.

The works of William Shakespeare (1564–1616) have inspired movie adaptations since the beginning of cinema history, but it may well be the case that no other director has set an adaptation of a Shakespeare play so radically in his own times as the Australian Baz Luhrmann (*Strictly Ballroom*, 1991) did with *Romeo and Juliet*. The prologue is delivered by the most important news medium of the late 20th century: the television. "Fair Verona" is Verona Beach (although most of the film was made in Mexico City), a multicultural mega-city with a sunny beach, smog, skyscrapers, police helicopters and an enormous Jesus statue like the one in Rio de Janeiro. The offices of the Capulets' businesses are on one side of a wide street, those of the Montagues on the other. The rival families have been transformed into gangster dynasties. The Capulets are Hispanic Americans and the Montagues white Americans (as in *West Side Story*, another *Romeo and Juliet* adaptation). The Capulets wear black, the Montagues Hawaii shirts; one family drives cars with CAP numberplates, the other with MON. Their weapons are 9mm pistols made by the firm "Sword" (and can still therefore be referred to as "sword" in the script). The gangsters are like action movie heroes, their

iduals reminiscent of black gangster films like *New Jack City* (1990) or *Menace II Society* (1993). The fancy-dress ball at the Capulets' is a loud, trashy party featuring an appearance by a drag queen.

It's not just lovingly devised, creative details like those which transpose the play into the present (and that includes today's self-referential cinema and its world of quotations) but the production as a whole. Luhrmann permits himself a playfulness that goes far beyond the formal idiom of narrative cinema and does more than nod in the direction of the aesthetic of the video clip, with techniques like quick takes, high speed panning shots, slow motion and fast forward, extreme camera perspectives (shots from great heights, shots through an aquarium or a wash basin), and a wide ranging use of music and uneven acting styles (from serious to hammy overacting). The movie is a self-confident piece of pop culture and wallows in the superficial thrill of images that have become kitsch symbols in their own right: white doves, burning hearts, a priest with a tattoo of the Cross, and Juliet going to the fancy-dress party as an angel with Romeo as her knight. Amazingly, all of this combines to make a homogenous, seductively beautiful movie that miraculously maintains the magical rhythm of Shakespeare's language and verse.

HJK

3

"His works had to compete with bear fights and prostitutes. He was an entertainer, mixing comedy, song, violence and tragedy. Just like MTV today." *Baz Luhrmann in: Abendzeitung*

Three other Shakespeare films were made in 1997 as well as *Romeo & Juliet*, including Kenneth Branagh's 4-hour version of *Hamlet*. Cinema history is full of Shakespeare adaptations, and a scene from *King John* was seen on the silver screen as early as 1899. Branagh has made a considerable contribution to the number of adaptations. His *Henry V* started off a new Shakespeare boom in 1989 and in *Love's Labours Lost* (1999) he combined Shakespeare with more modern classics when he used the melodies of George Gershwin, Cole Porter and others. Alongside direct adaptations there are also films with looser links to the works of the bard, for example *West Side Story* (1960, based on *Romeo and Juliet*) and the science fiction classic *Forbidden Planet* (1956), which is a film version of *The Tempest*.

"The language of Shakespeare, the acting of Quentin Tarantino." *Zoom*

5

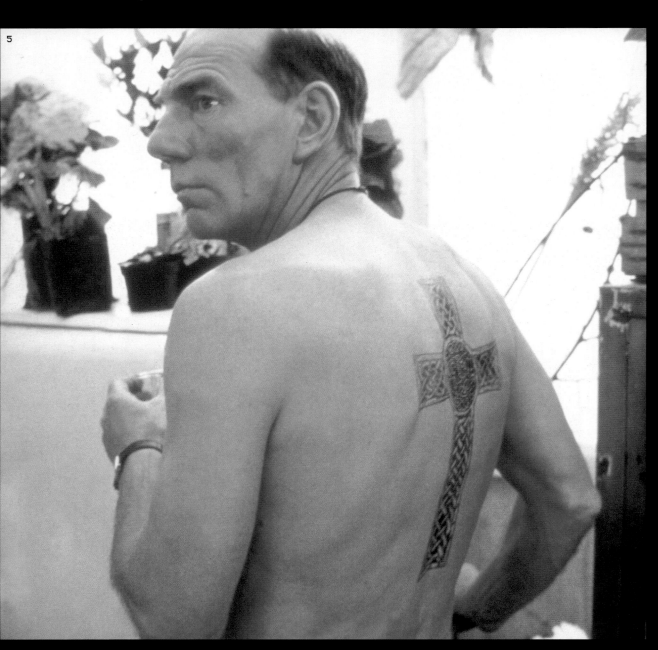

6

"All-consuming youth culture opens its greedy mouth and with great relish polishes off the classics hook, line and sinker." *Süddeutsche Zeitung*

1   Star-crossed lovers: a whole world separates Romeo (Leonardo DiCaprio) …

2   … and Juliet (Claire Danes) – but the lovers are unaware of this.

3   Grief at the death of his beloved – Baz Luhrmann sticks close to the Shakespeare original.

4   Objects "speak" in this film: Juliet floats into Romeo's life as if on wings; the fact that he is the "great enemy's only son" weighs him down like armour.

5   The priest is no longer wearing the Crucifix around his neck: Father Laurence (Pete Postlethwaite).

6   The quarrel between the Montagues and the Capulets – gangster warfare.

LOST HIGHWAY

1996/1997 - FRANCE / USA - 135 MIN. - THRILLER, NEO FILM NOIR

DIRECTOR DAVID LYNCH (*1946)
SCREENPLAY DAVID LYNCH, BARRY GIFFORD DIRECTOR OF PHOTOGRAPHY PETER DEMING MUSIC ANGELO BADALAMENTI PRODUCTION DEEPAK NAYAR, TOM STERNBERG, MARY SWEENEY for ASYMMETRICAL, CIBY 2000.

STARRING BILL PULLMAN (Fred Madison), PATRICIA ARQUETTE (Renee Madison/Alice Wakefield), BALTHAZAR GETTY (Pete Dayton), ROBERT LOGGIA (Dick Laurent/Mr. Eddy), ROBERT BLAKE (Mystery Man), MICHAEL MASSEE (Andy), GARY BUSEY (Bill Dayton), NATASHA GREGSON WAGNER (Sheila), LUCY BUTLER (Candace Dayton), GIOVANNI RIBISI (Steve "V"), HENRY ROLLINS (Henry).

"I'd like to remember things my own way. Not necessarily the way they happened."

At the beginning and at the end of *Lost Highway* we hear the same statement: "Dick Laurent is dead." Initially Fred Madison (Bill Pullman) hears it through his intercom, and at the end we realise that he is saying it at the same time as well. Lynch presents us with a paradox. Between those two events the movie switches characters and changes its mood, so much so that it can almost be considered to be made up of two separate films. The first tells the story of Fred, a saxophonist who lives with his wife Renee (Patricia Arquette with brown hair) in a villa as elegant as it is cold. He suspects that his wife is unfaithful to him and only leaves the house to go to work. He works off his angst and aggression in his playing, in free jazz solo riffs bursting with energy. The couple are sent anonymous video tapes which seem to confirm Fred's suspicions, but also cast doubt on his capacity to understand reality. The video begins with a take of their house, the camera slides in from a high angle into the house and up to their bed, and then

shows Fred, steeped in the blood of his murdered wife. Fred is condemned to death for murder.

In the "second" film, instead of Fred, we meet a young car mechanic called Pete (Balthazar Getty), who is in prison. As nothing can be proved against him, he is released, and his parents come to collect him and take him home. Somehow, Pete has changed, and he has lost interest in his former girlfriend. Instead he falls in love with Alice (Patricia Arquette, now blonde), the lover of one of his regular customers, underworld porno king Mr Eddy (Robert Loggia). Pete and Alice begin an affair and soon it becomes clear that they will have to run away from the unprincipled Eddy. They try to get the money for their escape by robbing one of his business partners, but the plan fails.

In both movies a naïve man falls victim to a *femme fatale*. The first movie is slow, dark and has a threatening, echoing soundtrack, while the

"*Lost Highway* isn't a journey into a man's convoluted mind; from the very beginning we are right there at the centre of it." *steady cam*

1 A truly magical moment: Alice (Patricia Arquette) turns up at Pete's garage while Lou Reed sings "This Magic Moment".

2 Pete experiences worrying things on breaking into the villa – and all the while Rammstein roars: "You can see him slinking round the church".

3 "The highway leads on endlessly into the night. Leading to nowhere and back to the beginning." *Filmbulletin*

4

5

"Remote telescopy and virtual coitus: David Lynch goes to the heart of present-day cinema with a violent poetry that places us in the forefront of the spectator's condition." *Cahiers du cinéma*

second is lighter and more dynamic. Superficially it is clear how the two hang together: the male protagonist of the first movie is transformed in an incomprehensible fashion into that of the second. The female protagonists are played by the same actress.

But in fact nothing is clear. Lynch dovetails the two stories in many ways. A policeman gives Fred a bloody nose, and Pete's nose begins to bleed when he sees the photo of Alice and Renee. In his workshop, Pete hears the saxophone solo that Fred played in the club. Is the Pete story just a fantasy that Fred creates in his cell on death row, or are the arrest and Pete story a fantasy which the escaped murderer Fred dreams up? Is Lo*st Highway* the story of Fred's schizophrenia? That possibility is alluded to by the pale Mystery Man (Robert Blake) who speaks to Fred at a party, and explains to him that he is both here and at Fred's house at the same time. There are various clues that point towards and away from each of these interpretations.

Lynch lays trails only to backtrack on them – and then start off on them once again. Alice seems to be a reincarnation of Renee, until we see them together on a photo. They might be sisters, but when we see the photo again, only one of them is in it.

The movie resists any one interpretation, and Lynch invites multiple interpretations by stuffing it full of quotations, from *Alice in Wonderland* and Edvard Munch's "The Scream" (in the final take) to *The Wizard of Oz* (1939). Arquette's transformation from brunette to blonde is a reference to Hollywood stereotypes of ideal female beauty, but the more individual elements we pick out, the less we succeed in forming a complete final picture of the movie. David Lynch refuses to narrate in a conventional cinematic manner and *Lost Highway* maintains its mysterious character to the very end. As Lynch said in an interview: "Many things in life are incomprehensible, but when movies are like that, people get upset."   HJK

6

DAVID LYNCH – CHAMPION OF MYSTERY From his underground debut *Eraserhead* (1974) to the movies *Blue Velvet* (1986) and *Wild at Heart* (1990) and the television series *Twin Peaks* (1989–1991), David Lynch has always made disturbing films about the dark side of the human soul – visually striking films with sombre, distressing sound montages that maintain an element of mystery which is never really resolved. The Mystery Man in *Lost Highway* appears as a symbol of this hidden meaning and as a herald of the key word "schizophrenia". Here however Lynch goes further than in any of his previous works, and mystery and enigma become the structural principles of the movie. In his work, audiences have no choice but to confront the great unsolved secrets …

4 Pete falls under Alice's spell at first sight, and after one night he is ready to do anything for her.

5 Mystery Man (Robert Blake): does he live in a house on the seafront – or in Fred's head?

6 Renee (Patricia Arquette in a double role): her house is as barren as a tomb, and her love for Fred has died.

7 "Pete (Balthazar Getty) meets gangster's wife Alice – a classic film noir siren."
Süddeutsche Zeitung

"A kind of horror movie, a kind of thriller, but essentially a mystery. That's what it is. A mystery."

David Lynch in: Lynch on Lynch

SCREAM

1996 - USA - 111 MIN. - HORROR FILM

DIRECTOR WES CRAVEN (*1939)
SCREENPLAY KEVIN WILLIAMSON DIRECTOR OF PHOTOGRAPHY MARK IRWIN MUSIC MARCO BELTRAMI PRODUCTION CARY WOODS, CATHY KONRAD for WOODS ENTERTAINMENT, DIMENSION FILMS, MIRAMAX.

STARRING DREW BARRYMORE (Casey Becker), NEVE CAMPBELL (Sidney Prescott), DAVID ARQUETTE (Deputy Dewey Riley), COURTENEY COX (Gale Weathers), JAMIE KENNEDY (Randy), MATTHEW LILLARD (Stewart), SKEET ULRICH (Billy Loomis), ROSE MCGOWAN (Tatum Riley), W. EARL BROWN (Cameraman Kenny), LIEV SCHREIBER (Cotton Weary).

"What's your favourite scary movie?"

It was supposed to be a cosy video evening with popcorn, boyfriend and a scary movie. It turns into pure horror. Casey (Drew Barrymore) gets an anonymous call. It starts off like a silly boys' trick and ends fatally. The caller draws her into a horror film quiz. What's the name of the killer in *Halloween*? Who's the bloodthirsty murderer in *Friday 13th*? It turns out that if you get the answer right, you get to stay alive: wrong answers are punishable by death. Casey gets the answer wrong.

The killer's next victim is Sidney Prescott (Neve Campbell), a classmate of the dead girl at Woodsboro High School. Ever since her mother's gruesome murder exactly a year ago, Sidney has been living alone with her father. He goes away on a business trip, and she's left on her own for a few days. The killer calls first, as before, then he stands there in a mask with a knife glinting in his hand. Sidney manages to escape, as her boyfriend Billy (Skeet Ulrich) appears and frightens the psychopath away. But then a hand falls out of Billy's pocket – is he the killer? He is arrested and kept in the local jail

overnight. He is released again in the morning: the night the killer struck again during the night, so it can't be him.

In the meantime all of Woodsboro is in uproar. Camera teams from all over the country have arrived, including the journalist Gale Weathers (Courteney Cox) who reported the death of Sidney's mother a year ago, starting off a media mud fight in the process. The thrill seekers find plenty of trophies as the killer leaves a bloody trail through the town. His next victims are the school director and some more teenagers.

The horror movie genre was dead until Wes Craven awoke it to brilliant new life with *Scream*. "Until now the murderers always acted as if they had just invented killing. Mine knows his predecessors." In *Scream* the killer acts with self-reflective irony, fully conscious of the conventions of the horror movie, and the result is an effective combination of horror and humour. The humour is that of a connoisseur who knows that the dead killer will get up one last time at the end; the humour of Wes Craven who in his short appear-

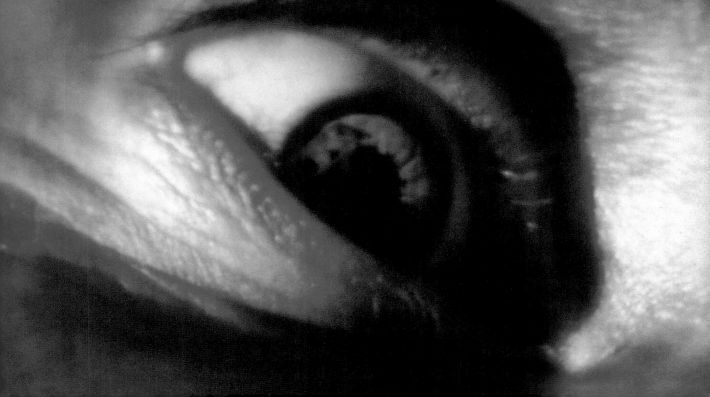

3

ance as a caretaker wears Freddy Krueger's striped pullover (from his masterpiece *Nightmare on Elm Street*) and even that of the bourgeois art connoisseur: the makeup is based on Edvard Munch's "The Scream". The recognition factor is satisfying. The laughter provides brief pauses in each tense scene – the fundamental suspense, the thrill, the feverish identification with the protagonists still remain. The shock remains too: the resurrection of the killer is not just taken for granted here, it is even announced. And yet we are still shocked when it actually happens. Despite all the quotations and the games with genre conventions *Scream* never becomes a simple parody.

The protagonists are horror movie fans just like normal people, acted by youngsters already familiar from television series, like Neve Campbell from *Party Of Five* (1994–1998) and Courteney Cox from *Friends* (1994–). The only established film actress is Drew Barrymore, but she disappears from the scene within a few minutes – like Janet Leigh in *Psycho* (1960). The characters know what is going on. They know the rules of the teenage horror movie: no sex, no drugs, no booze, and never say you'll be back in a minute. But they don't stick to them – they have sex, they smoke and they pass round the joints– and they have to pay the consequences.   HJK

THE SCREAM TRILOGY   "Don't kill me, I want to be in the sequel", one girl says, trying to talk the killer out of his bloody intention. He kills her all the same, but *Scream* has had two sequels. Craven continues the insider jokes: in *Scream 2* (1997) Sidney leaves her hometown and goes to study at a film academy – giving plenty of opportunity to reflect on horror movies and their sequels. The students begin a macabre game – anyone who doesn't die must be the killer. Sidney survives and goes back to Woodsboro in *Scream 3* (2000) – not to the real town, but to a film set where her experiences are being filmed under the title *Stab 3*. That way the number of potential victims is doubled, as each of the protagonists also has an actor playing their part in the movie.

---

1   A "slasher" like *Halloween*, with the mask of Edvard Munch: Wes Craven draws on a wide range of cultural references.

2   "I don't believe in motives. Did Hannibal Lecter have a reason for wanting to eat people?" *Quotation from film*

3   Victim number one: Drew Barrymore starts chatting to a stranger on the phone about horror films, before discovering that she's talking to a lunatic.

4   For reporter Gale Weathers (Courteney Cox) all this is just part of the job – until the killer turns his knife on her.

5   Has Sidney (Neve Campbell) survived everything? Not yet: there are two sequels still to go.

4

5

"People like dying in my films. Even my lawyer asks me when he'll finally get to play a corpse."

Wes Craven in: Zeit-Magazin

BREAKING THE WAVES

1996 - DENMARK / SWEDEN / NORWAY / NETHERLANDS / FRANCE - 159 MIN. - MELODRAMA

DIRECTOR LARS VON TRIER (*1956)
SCREENPLAY LARS VON TRIER, PETER ASMUSSEN **DIRECTOR OF PHOTOGRAPHY** ROBBY MÜLLER **MUSIC** JOACHIM HOLBEK
PRODUCTION PETER AALBAECK-JENSEN, VIBEKE WINDELØW for ZENTROPA.

STARRING EMILY WATSON (Bess), STELLAN SKARSGÅRD (Jan), KATRIN CARTLIDGE (Dodo), JEAN-MARC BARR (Terry), ADRIAN RAWLINS (Dr Richardson), UDO KIER (Sadistic Sailor), JONATHAN HACKETT (Priest), SANDRA VOE (Bess's mother), MIKKEL GAUP (Pits), ROEF RAGAS (Pim).

IFF CANNES 1996 GRAND JURY PRIZE.

"We do not need bells in our church to worship God."

The scene is a remote coastal village in Scotland in the 70s. Bess (Emily Watson), a good-natured girl who some say has visions of God and others term mentally ill falls in love with Jan (Stellan Skarsgård), an oil rig worker, and incurs the wrath of the elders of her strict Presbyterian community. Only Dodo, her brother's widow, stands by her. As if to remind her once again of the power of the church, she is forced to watch a funeral where the elders damn the deceased for all eternity. Despite this, Bess and Jan get married and everything goes well in the first few days they spend together, particularly where their sex life is concerned.

When Jan has to return to the oil rig, Bess is overcome with yearning and desire. Once again she retreats to the church to speak to God: everything else is unimportant if only she can have Jan back with her again. In a terrible way, her wish becomes true: Jan breaks his back in an accident and is paralysed from the neck down. Bess's mental state deteriorates so badly

that Dodo calls in the doctor. He proclaims her sane, and as Jan gets better, Bess recovers her equilibrium. One day, under the influence of the painkillers he is forced to take, Jan makes a suggestion to his wife. As he can no longer fulfil his marital duties, and as she enjoyed sex so much and he doesn't want her love for him to be dependent on what he can no longer do, she should take a lover, for his sake as well as her own. Bess takes up his suggestion and this is the beginning of her fall in the eyes of the community. Only God knows her passion, the depths of her love and her suffering. It's a monstrous story, often bordering on the edge of madness. A bare summary of the facts makes them appear to border on the ridiculous, but Lars von Trier has exactly the right touch for the material. He develops a radical closeness to his characters and a strongly improvised, almost careless way of directing reminiscent of the Dogme films. In his TV series *The Kingdom* (*Riget*, 1994) von Trier developed a method of working in which he allows his actors to move

3

freely and play the scenes through in their entirety. The scenes are only loose structures until they have been through the AVID, a computerised editing program.

This method, with its wildly swinging cameras, syncopated montage and grainy, washed-out picture quality is a return to the kind of realism that began in documentary films of the 50s as "direct cinema" or "cinéma vérité". It both distances the audience from the movie's characters and emphasises the gap between the material and the immaterial, between body and soul, the ever-widening abyss which tears Bess apart and features in songs such as Procol Harum's "A Whiter Shade of Pale" or Leonard Cohen's "Suzanne".

Von Trier emphasises the physicality of his figures, most memorably in the beautifully frank sex scenes between Jan and Bess, and the selflessness with which Bess gives her body to other men, until it is lacerated first by a sadistic sailor then by a psychotherapist. It's impossible to say whether *Breaking the Waves* is a Catholic movie or not, as has so often been claimed. What's more important is that it's a movie about the range and spiritual depth of emotion.   OM

LARS VON TRIER   Lars von Trier shot to immediate international fame with his debut film *The Element of Crime* (1984). Along with the following two movies *Epidemic* (1987) and *Europa* (1990), it forms a loose trilogy held together as much by von Trier's formal experiments as by thematic links. The television series *The Kingdom* (*Riget*, 1994) marked a turning point in his work. Instead of the cool clarity of his earlier movies, he began to use an aesthetic familiar from documentary films. From then on he only used a mobile hand camera and structured his movies with jump cuts. These techniques also dominate the trilogy known as the "Golden Heart Trilogy", which includes *Breaking the Waves* (1996), *The Idiots* (*Idioterne*, 1998) and *Dancer in the Dark* (2000), all movies which examine the relationship between passion and sexuality. Lars von Trier was one of the initiators of the Dogme 95 Manifesto.

---

1   Everything is still fine in Jan's world… Stellan Skarsgård, probably Sweden's best-known international actor, in one of his most extrovert roles.

2   Bess in a rare moment of calm: Emily Watson ranks among the great discoveries of the 1990s.

3   Jan and Bess get married against the advice of their parents and the parish elders.

4   Heart of gold: Bess as a naturally self-sacrificing lover.

5   Sex as an existential experience: Bess recognises divine beauty in physical love, while a satisfied Jan dreams of all the days together to come.

6   Ungodly happiness: Terry (Jean-Marc Barr) really paints the town red at his best friend's wedding.

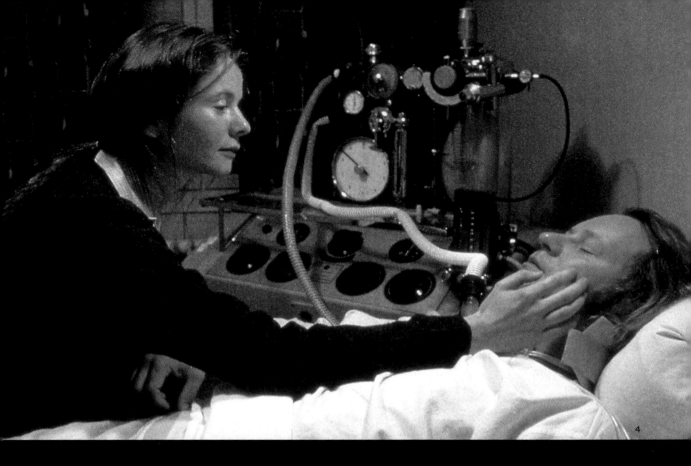

"I (...) remember that Emily was the only one who came to the casting barefoot and with no make-up at all! There was something Jesus-like about her which attracted me." *Lars von Trier in: Sight and Sound*

THE ENGLISH PATIENT

↑↑↑↑↑↑↑↑↑

996 - USA - 162 MIN. - MELODRAMA, LITERATURE ADAPTATION

DIRECTOR ANTHONY MINGHELLA (*1954)

SCREENPLAY ANTHONY MINGHELLA, based on the novel of the same name by MICHAEL ONDAATJE   DIRECTOR OF PHOTOGRAPHY JOHN SEALE MUSIC GABRIEL YARED PRODUCTION SAUL ZAENTZ, HARVEY WEINSTEIN, SCOTT GREENSTEIN, BOB WEINSTEIN for SAUL ZAENTZ PRODUCTIONS, MIRAMAX.

STARRING RALPH FIENNES (Graf Laszlo Almásy), KRISTIN SCOTT THOMAS (Katharine Clifton), JULIETTE BINOCHE (Hana), WILLEM DAFOE (Caravaggio), NAVEEN ANDREWS (Kip), COLIN FIRTH (Geoffrey Clifton), JULIAN WADHAM (Madox), JÜRGEN PROCHNOW (Major Müller), KEVIN WHATELY (Hardy), CLIVE MERRISON (Fenalon Barnes).

ACADEMY AWARDS 1997 OSCARS for BEST PICTURE, BEST DIRECTOR (Anthony Minghella), BEST SUPPORTING ACTRESS (Juliette Binoche), BEST CINEMATOGRAPHY (John Seale), BEST ART DIRECTION-SET DECORATION (Stuart Craig, Stepheny McMillan), BEST FILM EDITING (Walter Murch), BEST MUSIC, category DRAMA (Gabriel Yared), BEST SOUND (Chris Newman, Ivan Sharrock) and BEST COSTUMES (Ann Roth).

IFF BERLIN 1997 SILVER BEAR for BEST ACTRESS (Juliette Binoche).

"The heart is an organ of fire."

The camera glides over an undulating yellow-brown surface. It looks like a desert, but in fact it's paper, and a brush starts to paint stylised human forms that swim about. We cut to a different yellow-brown surface that undulates more strongly – this time it is the desert. An aeroplane flies by, its shadows racing over the hillocks and valleys of the desert plain. Shots ring out, and we see that the biplane is being fired at from the ground. Dark flecks of flak dot the sky, getting ever closer, until suddenly they hit the plane. The aeroplane dives and bursts into flames.

The English Patient tells the story of the pilot and his great love – in an unhurried, old-fashioned way. The film unfolds gradually, slowly accumulating additional information and perspectives, and only at the end is the entire story revealed. The pilot is dubbed the "English patient" when he is delivered to an Allied hospital in Italy shortly before the end of the Second World War – he was in an English plane that was shot down by the Germans. He is deformed by hideous burns, and the flames have destroyed his face, his skin and his lungs. He doesn't have long to live, has lost his memory, and does not even seem to know his name or nationality. The only clue is the book he carries with him – Herodotus' *History*, a Greek tale from the 5th century BC with maps, photos and letters tucked in between the pages. He is too badly

injured to be transported any further and so Franco-Canadian nurse Hana (Juliette Binoche) stays behind with him in a half-ruined monastery in Tuscany. Here he spends his remaining days in peace, and gradually he recovers the memory of his great love.

The story begins in 1937. The "English patient" is Count Laszlo Almásy (Ralph Fiennes), a Hungarian aristocrat who has devoted himself to the study of the desert and joined a group of English cartographers in the Sahara. One day an English couple come to join them: Geoffrey and Katharine Clifton (Colin Firth, Kristin Scott Thomas). He is an enthusiastic pilot and she is a painter. To begin with, Katharine is dismissive and almost hostile towards the silent, introverted Laszlo. But after their car breaks down and they are forced to sit out a sandstorm together in the desert, their relationship changes. While exploring the interior of the Sahara, the group discovers a cave filled with unusual wall paintings of people swimming. The explorers are dispersed when war breaks out, but they meet again in Cairo. Love blossoms out of the friendship between Laszlo and Katharine, and they begin a passionate affair. Eventually, her husband realises, and reacts with an act of jealous rage: he flies into the desert with Katharine to find Laszlo and tries to kill all three of them in a plane crash.

As these memories and visions return to the "English patient", life continues around him. Hana treats him lovingly, not least because she believes that she is cursed. Everyone close to her – her lover, her friend, even a fellow nurse – have all died. She has no reason not to be fond of her patient as he is going to die anyway. She wants to make his last days bearable and give him an easy death. Their solitude is short-lived however, and they are soon joined in the ruined monastery by the devious Caravaggio (Willem Dafoe), a Canadian trader of Italian descent. He was also in North Africa when the war broke out, and in contrast to Hana, he asks critical questions when the English patient's memory begins to return. Caravaggio was tortured by the Germans in the Libyan town of Tobruk, where they cut off his thumbs. Two bomb disposal experts from the British Army also take up quarters in the monastery, the Sikh Kip (Naveen Andrews) and his colleague Hardy (Kevin Whately). A fragile love affair develops between Kip and Hana, although Hana will not let herself become too involved because she still believes that she is cursed. In the meantime Laszlo lives out his love for Katharine in his memories, and images return to him with ever greater power.

English director Anthony Minghella (*Mr. Wonderful*, 1993) films Michael Ondaatje's novel as a melodramatic epic, with grandiose images of desert adventure. The movie unfolds on two narrative planes that dove-tail elegantly and constantly mirror each other. The outbreak of war dovetails with its end, the burning yellow-brown of the desert is played off against the cool green of Tuscany, the great love between Katharine and Laszlo is set off against the fragile relationship between Hana and Kip, Katharine lies fatally wounded in a cave in the desert, and Laszlo faces death in the ruined monastery. The two narrative planes are not only separated by the war, but also seem to take place in entirely different eras. The cartographic exploration of the desert by the English is part of colonial history. Katharine is an aristocratic lady of the British Empire whereas practical, energetic Hana is a woman of the 20th century.

Ondaatje's 1992 novel, winner of the English Booker Prize, also works with flashbacks and dovetailing and spans the length of the Second World War. Minghella maintains the chronological framework but thins out the cast and the plot strands of what is an extensive novel. In the novel for instance

| THE RETURN OF THE MELODRAMA | Love in a time of war. *The English Patient* tells the story of strong emotions in a tone of complete seriousness devoid of irony. This makes it part of the long cinema tradition of melodrama that began in the silent era. Its artistic highpoint came in the 50s with the movies of Douglas Sirk, and it reached a commercial peak with the tearjerker *Love Story* in 1969. Melodramas went out of fashion in the 80s and 90s, when emotions could only be shown mixed with irony, when they weren't being ridiculed altogether. Two films at the end of the 90s brought melodrama back into cinemas: *Titanic* (1997) and *The English Patient*. The latter was perhaps the most typical of the genre, as *Titanic* is a disaster movie as well as a love story and an adaptation of a historical event. *The English Patient* on the other hand is simply the simple story of a great love that can only be fulfilled in death. |

"Of course David Lean's *Lawrence of Arabia* comes to mind. But the comprehensive way in which Minghella tells the story, leaving nothing in his film open to doubt, is something David Lean did not permit himself." *Frankfurter Allgemeine Zeitung*

1 Count Laszlo Almásy – he finds his great love in the desert.

2 "It is principally the actors, Ralph Fiennes as the dying, ironically broken Almásy…

3 … and Kristin Scott Thomas, who up until now had only appeared as a wallflower, who lift this film above the average." *Zoom*

5

4   Almásy flees from the aeroplane flown by his lover's jealous husband.

5   In the novel Caravaggio (Willem Dafoe) and Hana knew each other during peacetime. The film dispenses with this prehistory.

6   Everyone that she loves dies. Understandably, Hana doesn't want to be drawn into a relationship with Kip (Naveen Andrews).

7   An award winner at the Berlin Film Festival and Oscars ceremonies: Juliette Binoche as the nurse Hana.

the love story between Hana and Kip plays a much more important role. The movie never denies its literary origins, however, and literature and books feature throughout, and whatever happens, Laszlo also manages to save his copy of Herodotus – Hana reads it to him, and it eventually outlives him. Hana uses books to stop the gaps in the stairs, and the Sahara itself appears in the first scene as paper, on which the love story is written.

Production of the film was an adventure story in itself. Minghella had long cherished the idea of adapting the book for the screen. After eleven producers had refused it, *The English Patient* was eventually accepted by independent producer Saul Zaentz, winner of a total of 13 Oscars and maker of seven great films over the last twenty years, including *One Flew Over the Cuckoo's Nest* (1975) and *Amadeus* (1984). All seemed well at first but a funding crisis developed when 20th Century Fox pulled out of the project. Fox's casting preferences hadn't been taken into consideration: it wanted Hollywood stars whereas Zaentz and Minghella insisted on Ralph Fiennes, Kristin Scott Thomas and Juliette Binoche. Salvation finally arrived in the shape of Harvey Weinstein, head of Miramax. He contributed 26 of the movie's total budget of 32 million dollars and filming could go ahead. His courage was rewarded with nine Oscars.

HJK

6

THE PEOPLE VS. LARRY FLYNT

1996 - USA - 130 MIN. - DRAMA

DIRECTOR MILOS FORMAN (*1932)
SCREENPLAY SCOTT ALEXANDER, LARRY KARASZEWSKI **DIRECTOR OF PHOTOGRAPHY** PHILIPPE ROUSSELOT **MUSIC** THOMAS NEWMAN
PRODUCTION OLIVER STONE, JANET YANG, MICHAEL HAUSMAN for IXTLAN PRODUCTIONS, PHOENIX PICTURES.

STARRING WOODY HARRELSON (Larry Flynt), COURTNEY LOVE (Althea Leasure), EDWARD NORTON (Alan Isaacman), JAMES CROMWELL (Charles Keating), CRISPIN GLOVER (Arlo), JAMES CARVILLE (Simon Leis), BRETT HARRELSON (Jimmy Flynt), DONNA HANOVER (Ruth Carter-Stapleton), VINCENT SCHIAVELLI (Chester), LARRY FLYNT (Judge).

IFF BERLIN 1997 GOLDEN BEAR.

"What is more obscene: Sex or War?"

Even as a child, Larry Flynt had a good nose for business. He distilled spirits with his brother and sold them to the local farmers. And when their father drank it all himself, Larry lost his temper and threw the jug at his head. Later he became a millionaire by selling sex magazines. And when someone got in his way, he broke china in the courtroom. *Entertainment Weekly* described *Hustler* editor Larry Flynt as a "pioneer of gynaecological photojournalism". Milos Forman is somewhat free with the truth in his account of the story, but Flynt himself worked on the movie as consultant and actually appears briefly as a judge in the first court case.

In 1972 Flynt (Woody Harrelson) was running strip-tease joints in Ohio with his brother Jimmy (Harrelson's brother Brett). To improve business he started publishing a magazine where the ladies can be "surveyed" in advance, and so *Hustler* was born. Circulation figures soared when he published naked pictures of Jackie Onassis, the first lady. Flynt became rich, married his girlfriend Althea (Courtney Love) and moved into a villa that had

exactly the same number of rooms as the mansion owned by *Playboy* editor Hugh Hefner. The first of a series of court cases then began where Flynt had to appear before the judge, and where time and again the core issues were the conflict between decency and freedom of speech. He lost his first case but won the appeal, and subsequently he began to style himself a guardian of the freedom of speech. He then formed an organisation for the freedom of the press at whose meetings he alternately showed pictures of naked women and of the destruction of war and concentration camps. Bizarrely, he found an ally in the evangelist Ruth Carter-Stapleton, sister of president Jimmy Carter (played by Donna Hanover, wife of squeaky-clean New York mayor Rudolph Giuliani).

In Forman's film, Flynt appears in court with an American flag wrapped round his hips. He throws oranges at a judge. He has a card on his desk that reads "Jesus H. Christ, Publisher". He has an epiphany in the shape of the American national symbol, the eagle, and he makes Santa Claus and the

1   Anyone can do it! – As the embodiment of the
    American Dream Flynt (Woody Harrelson) is a true
    patriot.

2   "Courtney Love lets all the raw, untamed,
    provocative impetus of her musical career and the
    echoes of her marriage to Kurt Cobain pour into her
    role as Flynt's lover Althea." *epd Film*

characters from the *Wizard of Oz* into sex figures. He likes to have sex six times a day but after an assassination attempt is stuck in a wheel chair and impotent. Doubtless it is hard to narrate the story of a figure so colourful figure with utter seriousness, but Forman finds a fine balance between irony, coarseness and a touch of mockery to describe his protagonist. Two things remain sacrosanct: Flynt's love for his wife, and his right to freedom of speech. The film makes no effort to turn Flynt into an aesthete, who makes pretty pictures of naked women (which would be far from the truth). Forman

presents him honestly as a pornographer, a tasteless horror, even a mean old devil – but he still supports his right to publish his magazines. Flynt is typical of Forman's film protagonists. Forman had previously given us figures like the rebel McMurphy, played by Jack Nicholson, who ends up in a psychiatric ward in *One Flew Over the Cuckoo's Nest* (1975), and the childishly sniggering Mozart who says obscenities backwards in *Amadeus* (1984). Flynt is a fool and rogue in that tradition, – a contrary spirit who questions the status quo with extraordinary nerve.

HJK

> **"Larry Flynt, pornographer and lowest of the low, has achieved what he never dared to hope for – a place in American history."** *Frankfurter Allgemeine Zeitung*

3 "Woody Harrelson's broad smile contains a hint of the "natural born killer" that he played for Oliver Stone." *epd Film*

4 25 years imprisonment! Charles Keating's (James Cromwell) first court action against Larry Flynt is successful.

"What distinguishes Larry Flynt from Hugh Hefner is his almost messianic obsession with pursuing sex photography to the furthest limits permitted by law." *film-dienst*

6

MILOS FORMAN Forman was born in 1932 in a small town near Prague and studied at the Prague Film Academy. In 1963 he made his debut with *Cerný Petr* (*Black Peter*), an autobiographical story about a teenager in a small Czech town, and he went on to become one of the foremost protagonists of the Czech Nouvelle Vague. He shot three films in his native land and then emigrated via France to America when the Soviets arrived in 1968. His big break in America was *One Flew Over the Cuckoo's Nest* (1975) which became the cult film of an entire generation and won five Oscars, including one for Forman as best director. His adaptation of the musical *Hair* was less successful, as his version of the hippie idyll simply arrived too late (1977). Nine years later, he won a second Oscar for best director with *Amadeus*. The movie of the theatre play of the same name by Peter Shaffer was filmed in Prague, and that gave Milos Forman his first opportunity to return to his native country.

5 His own lawyer (Edward Norton), a private jet: Flynt is almost a normal entrepreneur.

6 Flynt appears in court wearing battle dress like a freedom fighter.

7 Scantily clad girls empty out bags of dollar bills: this is how Larry Flynt pays his cash fine.

7

CRASH

1996 - GREAT BRITAIN / CANADA - 100 MIN. - DRAMA, THRILLER

DIRECTOR DAVID CRONENBERG (*1943)
SCREENPLAY DAVID CRONENBERG, based on the novel of the same name by JAMES GRAHAM BALLARD   DIRECTOR OF PHOTOGRAPHY
PETER SUSCHITZKY MUSIC HOWARD SHORE PRODUCTION JEREMY THOMAS, ROBERT LANTOS, DAVID CRONENBERG for
ALLIANCE COMMUNICATIONS, CORPORATION IN TRUST.

STARRING JAMES SPADER (James G. Ballard), HOLLY HUNTER (Dr Helen Remington), ELIAS KOTEAS (Vaughan), DEBORAH
KARA UNGER (Catherine Ballard), ROSANNA ARQUETTE (Gabrielle), PETER MACNEILL (Colin Seagrave), YOLANDE JULIAN
(Prostitute), CHERYL SWARTS (Vera Seagrave), JUDAH KATZ (Car Salesman), ALICE POON (Chamber Maid).

IFF CANNES 1996 JURY PRIZE.

"Maybe next time ... Maybe next time."

James Ballard (James Spader) and his wife Catherine (Deborah Kara Unger) are completely open to each other about their extramarital affairs. Sex with strangers stimulates their relationship. One day James has a serious car accident – a head-on collision, in which the driver of the other car is killed. James and the wife of the dead man, Dr Helen Remington (Holly Hunter), are both badly injured. After his release from the hospital, James goes to inspect his wrecked automobile, and by chance meets Helen. He gives her a lift, and they narrowly escape being involved in a second accident. They both find this highly arousing, and so they drive to a car park and make love in the front seat. Helen introduces James to Vaughan (Elias Koteas), a man whose entire body is covered with scars, and who performs reconstructions of famous car crashes at illegal car shows. But for Vaughan, car accidents are

a passion in the fullest sense – as the head of a group of like-minded crash survivors, he seeks sexual fulfilment in them. James and Catherine become more and more deeply involved in this bizarre obsession. It also becomes progressively more dangerous as Vaughan loses control of his sexual urges, and searches for satisfaction outside of the stunt shows.

David Cronenberg has always been a master of provocation. As was to be expected, his film version of the novel by J. G. Ballard brought forth a storm of protest, culminating in the accusation that the film's perverse theme would inspire imitation – a curious claim, given the gloominess of the vision that Cronenberg conjures up.

Crash is far more than a quick look at a strange obsession. Cronenberg's deeper aim is to portray an essential form of human desire

"It's like a porno movie made by a computer: It downloads gigabytes of information about sex, it discovers our love affair with cars, and it combines them in a mistaken algorithm."

Chicago Sun-Times

3

where the erotic and the morbid meet. This is accompanied by transformation of the human body – a central theme in all of Cronenberg's films – manifested in *Crash* in the scarring, the prosthetics, and the bizarre orthopaedic accessories of its central figures. The characters in the film are searching for total sexual fulfilment, for the most extreme experience they can possibly have. They find this in the sado-masochistic destruction of their own bodies, and in the fusion of the human body with technical apparatus. This aspect is already taken up in the title sequence, where metallic lettering advances forwards as though drilling into the spectators' eyes, an impression that is reinforced by the piercingly cold sounds of Howard Shore's brilliant film music. The music emphasises the film's trance-like atmosphere. This impression is reinforced further by the futuristic sets, which are bathed in blue-grey light-

ing. They surround the human figures in the movie, making them appear driven souls whose speech is reduced to mere panting and gasping.

Cronenberg does not in any way attempt to rationalise the behaviour of his figures, which is reduced to the level of pure sexual desire. And yet the behaviour appears perfectly plausible, the natural consequence of our hi-tech environment dominated by cars and traffic. Once, mankind dreamt of unity with nature: in Cronenberg's world, that yearning has been transformed into a sexual desire for total fusion with ubiquitous technology. The recurring image of James watching the streams of traffic through a telescope from his balcony is a symbol of that perverse longing – a longing perhaps that can only be stilled by a final crash.

JH

1 Crash-crazy: wrecked cars as the violent fusion of man and machine.

2 In his quest for sexual fulfilment James Ballard (James Spader) succumbs to the fascination of the smash.

3 Metal and leather: Helen (Holly Hunter) and James seek out the close confines of the car for sex.

4

5

4 As though in a trance: the minds of the characters in Cronenberg's film are occupied only by the search for satisfaction: Catherine Ballard (Deborah Kara Unger).

5 Traffic is meaningless until there's a crash.

DAVID CRONENBERG The director David Cronenberg, born in Toronto in 1943 as the son of a journalist and a pianist, began writing science fiction stories as a child. He began making his first short movies on 16mm film during his university studies in Natural Science and Literature. His subsequent career began in 1974 with the Canadian television production *Shivers*, a film following in the tradition of Don Siegel's *Invasion of the Body Snatchers* (1956) and George A. Romero's *Night of the Living Dead* (1968). Over the years, Cronenberg has developed an unmistakable horror style, famous for its graphic representation of bizarre transformations of the human body, which often leads to heated reactions from the public. He scored a particular success with his version of *The Fly* (1986), a remake of the horror classic by Kurt Neumann (1958). The films *Scanners* (1980), *Videodrome* (1982), *Dead Zone* (1983), *Naked Lunch* (1991) and *Crash* (1996) enjoy cult status among his numerous fans.

L. A. CONFIDENTIAL

1997 - USA - 138 MIN. - POLICE FILM, DRAMA, NEO FILM NOIR

DIRECTOR CURTIS HANSON (*1945)
SCREENPLAY CURTIS HANSON, BRIAN HELGELAND based on the novel *L. A. CONFIDENTIAL* by JAMES ELLROY
DIRECTOR OF PHOTOGRAPHY DANTE SPINOTTI **MUSIC** JERRY GOLDSMITH **PRODUCTION** CURTIS HANSON, ARNON MILCHAN, MICHAEL G. NATHANSON for REGENCY ENTERPRISES.

STARRING RUSSELL CROWE (Bud White), KEVIN SPACEY (Jack Vincennes), GUY PEARCE (Ed Exley), KIM BASINGER (Lynn Bracken), DANNY DEVITO (Sid Hudgeons), JAMES CROMWELL (Dudley Smith), DAVID STRATHAIRN (Pierce Patchett), RON RIFKIN (D. A. Ellis Loew), MATT MCCOY (Brett Chase), PAUL GUILFOYLE (Mickey Cohen).

ACADEMY AWARDS 1998 OSCARS for BEST SUPPORTING ACTRESS (Kim Basinger), AND BEST ADAPTED SCREENPLAY (Curtis Hanson, Brian Helgeland).

"Why did you become a cop? – I don't remember."

Sun, swimming pools, beautiful people: "Life is good in L.A., it's a paradise ..." That Los Angeles only exists in commercials. In *L. A. Confidential* – set in the early 50s – the city looks quite different, and is a morass of crime and corruption. Three policemen try to combat this with varying dedication and varying motives. Ambitious young police academy graduate Ed Exley (Guy Pearce) is a champion of law and order, and his testimony against his colleagues in an internal police trial catapults him straight to the top of the station house hierarchy. Bud White (Russell Crowe) is a hardened cynic who is prepared to extract confessions with force, but cannot stand violence against women and Jack Vincennes (Kevin Spacey) is nothing more than a corrupt phoney who uses his police job to get in with the entertainment industry. He is advisor to the television series "Badge Of Honor" and sets up stories for Sid Hudgeons (Danny DeVito), slimy reporter on the gossip magazine "Hush-Hush".

Exley's first case is a spectacular bloodbath in the Nite Owl bar. Five lie dead in the bathroom, killed with a shotgun. Three back youths seen near the scene of the crime are swiftly arrested, and with his brilliant interrogation technique, Exley gets them to admit to having kidnapped and raped a Mexican girl. While White frees the victim and shoots her captor, the three blacks escape from police custody. Exley hunts them down and shoots them dead. He is hailed as a hero and awarded a medal, and it would seem that that is the end of the case. But it doesn't seem to quite add up, and Exley,

1

2

3

> # "It's striking to see how the elegance and lightness of touch in the atmosphere of *L.A. Confidential* seem both to derive from and influence the actors."
> *Cahiers du cinéma*

4

1   He may have deserved it much more for this film, but Russell Crowe didn't win an Oscar until 2001 for *Gladiator*.

2   Bud White (Russell Crowe) doesn't waste any time with the kidnapper of the Mexican girl.

3   Kim Basinger's Oscar for the part of Lynn Bracken brought her long-overdue universal acclaim.

4   A Christmas angel: Lynn out on business until late in the evening with her employer.

5   A few moments of melancholy apart, Bud White doesn't let the corruptness of the world get to him.

6   Brief moments of happiness: is there a future for Bud and Lynn's love?

7   Lynn the prostitute's little trick: she does herself up to look like 1940s glamour star Veronica Lake.

White and Vincennes continue their investigations until they discover a conspiracy which reaches up into the highest echelons of police and city administration, involving drugs, blackmail, and a ring of porn traders.

L.A. Confidential is a reference to the first and perhaps most brazen American gossip magazine "Confidential" (1952–1957), and Hudgeons, the reporter played by Danny DeVito (who is also the off-screen narrator) is an alter ego of Robert Harrison, its infamous editor. Hudgeons gets his kicks from filth and sensationalism, and typifies the moral decadence that seems to have infected the entire city. The police make deals with criminals, the cops who uncover the conspiracy are far from blameless and even the naive greenhorn Exley looses his innocence in the course of the film.

Director Curtis Hanson conjures up the brooding atmosphere of the film noir crime movies of the 40s and 50s, but *L.A. Confidential* is far more than a throwback of a simple nostalgia trip. Cameraman Dante Spinotti shoots clear images free from any patina of age and avoids typical genre references like long shadows. The crime and the corruption seem even more devastating when told in pictures of a sunny, crisp Los Angeles winter. The plot is complex and difficult to follow on first viewing, but Hanson does not emphasise this so much as individual scenes which condense the city's amorality into striking images, like Vincennes saying he can no longer remember why he became a cop. Above all, the director focuses on his brilliant ensemble. Australians Russell Crowe and Guy Pearce, who were virtually unknown before the movie was made, make a great team with the amazing Kevin Spacey. Kim Basinger is a worthy Oscar winner as prostitute and Veronica Lake look-alike Lynn.

HJK

5

6

"When I gave Kevin Spacey the script, I said I think of two words: Dean Martin."

Curtis Hanson in: Sight and Sound

8

JAMES ELLROY: L.A.'S INDEFATIGABLE CHRONICLER

His own life sounds like a crime story. James Ellroy was born in Los Angeles in 1948. When he was ten, his mother fell victim to a sex killer, a crime he works through in his 1996 novel *My Dark Places*. The shock threw Ellroy completely off the rails: drugs, petty crime and 50 arrests followed, and he came to writing relatively late. His first novel *Brown's Requiem* was published in 1981 and made into a movie with the same name in 1998. He then wrote a novel trilogy on the figure of the policeman Lloyd Hopkins. The first of this series *Blood on the Moon* (1984) was filmed in 1988 as *Cop* starring James Woods in the title role. Ellroy's masterpiece is the L.A. tetralogy, novels on historical crimes from the period 1947 to 1960. *L.A. Confidential* is the extensive third volume of the series; it took Hanson and co-author Brian Helgeland a whole year and seven different versions to adapt it as a screenplay.

8 Tabloid reporter Sid Hudgeons (Danny DeVito) loves digging up other people's dirt.

9 Officer Vincennes (right) likes to take Hudgeons and a photographer along to his arrests.

1O Vincennes (Kevin Spacey) makes sure that first and foremost he's looking after number one.

11 Officer Ed Exley (Guy Pearce) earns praise from the press and from his boss Dudley Smith (James Cromwell, right).

9

10

11

MY BEST FRIEND'S WEDDING

1997 - USA - 105 MIN. - ROMANTIC COMEDY

DIRECTOR P. J. HOGAN (*1962)
SCREENPLAY RONALD BASS DIRECTOR OF PHOTOGRAPHY LASZLO KOVACS MUSIC JAMES NEWTON HOWARD PRODUCTION JERRY ZUCKER, RONALD BASS for PREDAWN, TRISTAR PICTURES, COLUMBIA PICTURES.

STARRING JULIA ROBERTS (Julianne Potter), DERMOT MULRONEY (Michael O'Neal), CAMERON DIAZ (Kimberley "Kimmy" Wallace), RUPERT EVERETT (George Downes), PHILIP BOSCO (Walter Wallace), M. EMMET WALSH (Joe O'Neal), RACHEL GRIFFITHS (Samantha Newhouse), CARRIE PRESTON (Amanda Newhouse), SUSAN SULLIVAN (Isabelle Wallace), CHRISTOPHER MASTERSON (Scott O'Neal).

"I am a busy girl. I've got exactly four days to break up a wedding, steal the bride's fella and I haven't one clue how to do it."

Beautiful women can be amazingly devious. They can also sing amazingly out of tune. *My Best Friend's Wedding* is the story of a duel between two beautiful women. They fight over – a man, of course. Julianne (Julia Roberts), a New York restaurant critic, is one of the two. She may be devious but she is also clueless when it comes to matters of the heart. In her high school days she dated Michael (Dermot Mulroney) and since then they have been the best of friends. She never realised that she was in love with him all along until he rings to say he has found the woman of his dreams and is going to marry her – in four days' time.

Kimmy (Cameron Diaz) is the name of the perfect creature who has come into his life, and her disastrous singing voice is her only blemish: winsome and beautiful, she even gives up her studies for Michael, who is now a sports reporter. She's rich too – her father is a Chicago businessman who owns the local baseball club and the sports channel on TV. Julianne travels to Chicago, officially as a bridesmaid, but unofficially to break up the party. The would-be wedding wrecker realises right away how difficult her task will be when a radiant Kimmy greets her at the airport as the sister she never had and always wanted.

In his debut movie *Muriel's Wedding* (1994), the Australian director P. J. Hogan told the story of a plump young lady who aspires to social acceptance through marriage. *My Best Friend's Wedding* also plays with female stereotypes, but whereas *Muriel's Wedding* was sensitive and serious, the later movie is boisterous and full of very direct humour. Kimmy is blonde, young and naïve, but her charm and spontaneity captivate everyone she meets. Julianne is a brunette, a little older, successful in her career and has both feet firmly on the ground. After several romantic disappointments, she claims

1　"In the classics of this subgenre like *It Happened One Night*, it was the man who caused the rumpus. But different tropes for different folks." *Time Magazine*

2　Confounding expectations: doe-eyed Julia Roberts as the plotting and scheming Julianne Potter.

3　The embodiment of kindness: how could anyone want to harm Kimmy (Cameron Diaz)?

4　George (Rupert Everett) gives it plenty in Julianne's ridiculous game of make-believe .

5　"The film wallows enthusiastically in the brightly coloured hues of the Hollywood musical and the magnificent luxury of Hollywood-style weddings." *Süddeutsche Zeitung*

6　Sports reporter Michael (Dermot Mulroney) would be made if he married into Kimberley's father's business empire.

"Maybe there won't be marriage, maybe there won't be sex, but God there'll be dancing."

Quotation from film: George

BURT BACHARACH　Next to wedding dresses, the thing the protagonist in *Muriel's Wedding* (1994) loves most is Abba. The movie was completely saturated with the music of the Swedish quartet, and in *My Best Friend's Wedding* it's that genius composer of catchy melodies Burt Bacharach who takes up the baton. The opening credits feature a quartet of girls singing "Wishin' and Hopin'", a hint at the movie's plot: only wishing and hoping can help to win someone's love. Other Bacharach songs that comment on the plot include Kimmy's catastrophic karaoke song "I Just Don't Know What to Do With Myself" and "What the World Needs Now is Love", which js playing on the radio of the delivery van that Julianne rents. Burt Bacharach wrote hundreds of songs, many of which were performed by the singer Dionne Warwick. He also composed film music, including the Oscar-nominated title song to *What's New, Pussycat?* (1965). He won Oscars for "Raindrops Keep Fallin' on My Head", "Two Bandits" (from *Butch Cassidy and the Sundance Kid*, 1969) and the title song to *Arthur* (1981). Bacharach himself made a brief appearance in *Austin Powers* (1997).

to be in control of her feelings. She devises a battle campaign against Kimmy, of which the most harmless element is the forced singing in a karaoke bar. But even after the truly dreadful singing, Kimmy emerges from every encounter stronger than before. Her charm seems invincible, and Michael's love is not to be shaken. The plot is in the best tradition of old screwball comedies like *The Philadelphia Story* (1940), and is cleverly constructed, with excellent acting and original dialogues. The movie also contains some delightful smaller episodes at the edge of the main action which sometimes hold up the plot, as when one of the bridesmaids at the wedding party gets stuck to a David statue made of ice – with her tongue in a promi-

nent place. Three boys breathe in helium instead of using it to fill balloons and sing John Denver's "Annie's Song" with Mickey Mouse voices. There is one scene of complete madness: Julianne's gay friend and boss George (Rupert Everett) comes for a day from New York, and she introduces him as her fiancé and he plays along. The party are in a lobster restaurant when he tells the hair-raising story of their first meeting, in which he manages somehow to involve the singer Dionne Warwick and promptly strikes up her song "I Say a Little Prayer". Soon the other guests join in and the waiters wave their lobster claw-shaped gloves in time.

HJK

BOOGIE NIGHTS

1997 - USA - 152 MIN. - DRAMA

DIRECTOR PAUL THOMAS ANDERSON (*1970)
SCREENPLAY PAUL THOMAS ANDERSON DIRECTOR OF PHOTOGRAPHY ROBERT ELSWIT MUSIC MICHAEL PENN PRODUCTION JOHN LYONS, LLOYD LEVIN, PAUL THOMAS ANDERSON, JOANNE SELLAR for GHOULARDI (for NEW LINE CINEMA).

STARRING MARK WAHLBERG (Eddie Adams/Dirk Diggler), JULIANNE MOORE (Amber Waves), BURT REYNOLDS (Jack Horner), DON CHEADLE (Buck Swope), PHILIP SEYMOUR HOFFMAN (Scotty), JOHN C. REILLY (Reed Rotchild), HEATHER GRAHAM (Rollergirl), WILLIAM H. MACY (Little Bill), NICOLE PARKER (Becky Barnett), ALFRED MOLINA (Rahad Jackson).

"Everyone's blessed with one special thing."

His fans waited in vain: for years, Abel Ferrara (*Driller Killer*, 1979; *Bad Lieutenant*, 1992), iconoclast and untiring rebel of the US movie scene, invited the wildest speculations by declaring that he was going to make a film about the life of pornstar legend John C. Holmes. In the end Paul Thomas Anderson got there before him. His effervescent, epic portrayal of the rise and fall of a pornstar and his clique in San Fernando Valley, California is however only loosely based on the biography of the world's most famous male pornstar. Anderson was only 27 when *Boogie Nights* was made, but he succeeded in producing what is perhaps the definitive movie about the American sex film industry of the 70s and 80s, despite – or perhaps because – of conscious omissions. In *Boogie Nights* we see nothing of its Mafia structure or the organised exploitation of women that is endemic in the business. Instead, Anderson depicts a tender, sympathetic, almost romanticised portrait of a surrogate family. In *Hard Eight* (1996), the melodrama that marked his debut as a director, Anderson's solitary gambling figures sought comfort by bonding together as a replacement family, and *Magnolia* (1999), his Berlin Festival winner, also underlines the strength and uniqueness of family ties.

Boogie Nights was not just a breakthrough for its young director, but also for its main actor. Previously known as a model for Calvin Klein under-

wear and as white bad boy rapper Marky Mark, Mark Wahlberg had already found a measure of success in small supporting roles, but here he conclusively proved his potential as a character actor. His character Eddie Adams is the focal point of the movie: a boy from the 'burbs who works as a bouncer in a disco, convinced that he was born both for and with greater things. His impressive penis length of 32 centimetres gets him noticed by porno producer Jack Horner, who takes him under his fatherly wing. Burt Reynolds, who made a great comeback with this role, plays Horner with wonderful coolness; he is a man with a vision. He wants to make porn films that are so entertaining and gripping that people will stay in the cinema even after they have been sexually satisfied to find out what happens next. He works on this with his new superstar Eddie under the name Dirk Diggler, with his porn muse Amber (Julianne Moore) and with the many other crew members who hang around his fashionable villa. The porn star Dirk Diggler quickly learns to take for granted all the luxurious idols of the 'American way of life' which as high school drop-out Eddie he could only worship on posters in his room: fast cars, hot dates, cool clothes, endless pool parties, cocktails and coke brought to him on a tray. But in the early 80s the idyll races to a crash as the classic porn movie is replaced by videos made quickly and cheaply with

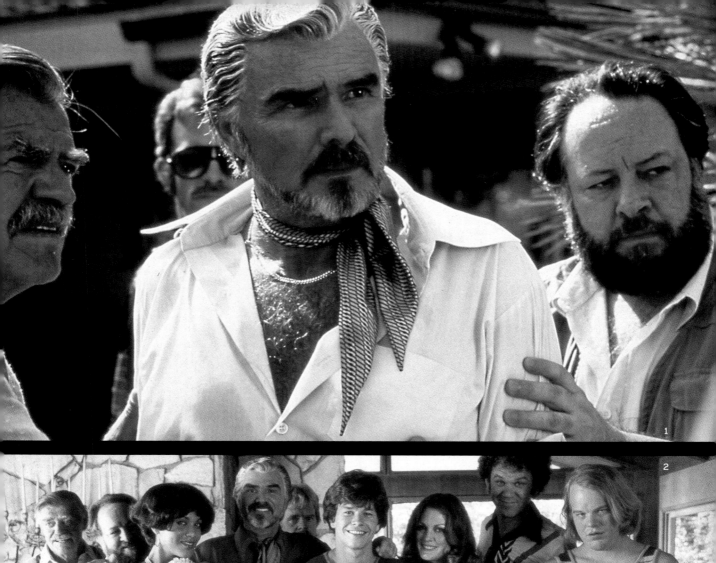

3

| 1 | Sex sells: porn film director Jack Horner (Burt Reynolds) gambles with the secret fantasies of his viewers. | 2 | Group portrait with porn star: his colleagues come to be a substitute family for high school drop-out and runaway Eddie Adams (Mark Wahlberg). | 3 | In the porn industry people have seen just about everything. But Eddie's natural talent surprises even the oldest hands. |

anonymous amateurs lolling about in front of the cameras. The big stars' careers are over and the porn cinemas close. Dirk's drug consumption spirals out of control, and he is even involved in an armed robbery on a millionaire – this is one of the episodes taken from the true story of John Holmes.

Boogie Nights is a hedonistic film. It revels in the sounds of the 70s and the well-proportioned California bodies. It is provocative and politically incor-

rect, but as a movie it exploits neither its actors nor its theme for cheap thrills. Dirk Diggler's greatest asset is only seen once in the final shot. This seriousness made the tragicomic melodrama a hit even in prudish America. In its wake, the cable channel HBO produced *Rated X* (2000) a mainstream film on the brothers Jim and Artie Mitchell, who began a porn revolution in the 70s with the classic movies *Behind the Green Door* (1972) and *Inside Marilyn Chambers* (1975).   AK

"It kind of got me down, watching six hours of solid fucking. You really don't have any desire to go home and kiss your girlfriend."

Paul Thomas Anderson in: Sight and Sound

4   A star is born! With his multifaceted and sensitive portrayal ex-rapper Mark Wahlberg finally achieved his transformation into actor.

5   Horner's girlfriend Amber (Julianne Moore) leads a double life. Fascinated and tempted by luxury, drugs and sex, she is fighting a losing battle for custody of her child …

4

5

6

6   With its disco soundtrack and garish costumes, *Boogie Nights* celebrates the hedonistic lifestyle of the 1970s.

7   Heather Graham as Rollergirl, an artificial figure she created herself. We don't find out her real name, which she disowns as she does her past, until the end of the film.

"Razor-sharp dialogue, interlocking destinies splendidly contrived, and a blend of humour and melancholy: this film might have turned out uniform grey. In fact, it's wonderful. You emerge with the conviction that a glimpse of paradise, a moment of grace has been vouchsafed." *Le nouvel observateur*

PHILIP SEYMOUR HOFFMAN

Although he claims to have become a professional actor only to impress a girl, Philip Seymour Hoffman, born in 1967 in Fairport, New York, seldom gets the leading roles. With his massive build, dull complexion and unmanageable red-blond hair, he doesn't fit into the part of typical film beau at all – which is probably what gets him the perhaps more exciting roles such as the drag queen in *Flawless* (1999) cursed with a homophobic neighbour played by Robert De Niro or the snob Freddy in the movie of Patricia Highsmith's novel *The Talented Mr. Ripley* (1999). Not that Hoffman's characters are devoid of romantic impulses: it's hard to think of any movie moment in recent years as touching as the scene in *Boogie Nights* when, in a badly-fitting tank top, he asks Mark Wahlberg if he can kiss him on the mouth. The magazine *Talk* hit the nail on the head when it claimed that Hoffman is "a new sort of Hollywood handsome: real." Hoffman has played leading roles in all of Anderson's movies. The director first noticed him in *Scent of a Woman* (1992) and in the Broadway play *True West* where he appeared with his friend John C. Reilly, another actor who often works with Anderson.

LIFE IS BEAUTIFUL
La vita è bella

1997/1998 - ITALY - 122 (124) MIN. - TRAGICOMEDY

DIRECTOR ROBERTO BENIGNI (*1952)
SCREENPLAY VINCENZO CERAMI, ROBERTO BENIGNI **DIRECTOR OF PHOTOGRAPHY** TONINO DELLI COLLI **MUSIC** NICOLA PIOVANI
PRODUCTION ELDA FERRI, GIANLUIGI BRASCHI for MELAMPO CINEMATOGRAFICA, CECCHI GORI GROUP.

STARRING ROBERTO BENIGNI (Guido), NICOLETTA BRASCHI (Dora), GIORGIO CANTARINI (Giosuè), GIUSTINO DURANO (uncle), SERGIO BUSTRIC (Ferruccio), MARISA PAREDES (Dora's mother), HORST BUCHHOLZ (Dr Lessing), LYDIA ALFONSI (Guicciardini), LIULIANA LOJODICE (school teacher), AMERIGO FONTANI (Rodolfo).

ACADEMY AWARDS 1999 OSCARS for BEST FOREIGN LANGUAGE FILM, BEST ACTOR (Roberto Benigni), BEST MUSIC (Nicola Piovani).

IFF CANNES 1998 GRAND JURY PRIZE (Roberto Benigni).

"Buongiorno, Principessa!"

Telling stories about the indescribable without trivialising is a tall order. So is defending defend the right to liberating laughter in the face of utter inhumanity without being guilty of cynicism. Roberto Benigni got round the issue by telling a fairytale, in the form of the story of a father who lands in the hell of a German concentration camp with his son.

Fairytale circumstances bring the happy-go-lucky Italian Jew Guido (Roberto Benigni) to Arezzo in the 30s to open a bookshop. On his way he meets Dora (Nicoletta Braschi) his "Princess", who literally falls into his arms from the sky. As Dora is already promised to another, whom she does not love, Guido feels obliged to abduct her from her own engagement party – a further fairytale motif.

Up to this point, the film has been dominated by the tricks and clowning of its hero, but all at once the amusing, bubbly style of the story becomes pointed for the first time: Guido and his Princess ride out of the hall on a horse under the astonished eyes of the guests, but their steed has been painted green by an unknown hand. The skull and crossbones painted on its flanks are accompanied by anti-Semitic slogans.

Undeterred by these first ominous signs, the two settle down and start a family. In the next scene their son Giosuè (Giorgio Cantarini) is already five years old and he is helping his father in the bookshop. All the books are half price, and the shop is obviously about to close. The town has changed, there are soldiers everywhere and little Giosuè, who can barely read, makes out the words "Out of bounds to dogs and Jews" on a sign. As usual his father saves the situation with a joke: after all, no one can stop people refusing entry to kangaroos and Frenchmen and tomorrow the shop will be closed even to spiders and Visigoths. The following day is Giosuè's birthday, but Dora comes home to find her family gone. Giosuè and his father are already on their way to a concentration camp. Dora hurries to the station and demands to be put in the train too, only to be separated from her husband and child again on arrival.

To protect the boy from the cruel reality surrounding them, Guido pretends that all the people are there to take part in a competition, whose winner will get a real tank to take home. In this way he helps his son to survive both the psychological and physical brutality of life in the camp.

In Italy *La vita è bella* was a smash hit, but hotly debated by critics of all political persuasions. Many people outside Italy were also uncertain as to whether it was right to laugh at a concentration camp story, and wondered whether Benigni was toning down the historical facts too much. This question arises from a fundamental misunderstanding. Whatever critics said, the movie can by no means be divided into a funny first part and a tragic second part. Benigni subtly prepares us from the very beginning for the points he plans to make in the course of the plot. His aim is not to give an accurate presentation of the Holocaust as a historical event, and so he tells us nothing about the motives of the perpetrators, who are presented either as com-

1 Lies in times of need: to protect him from the horror of the Nazis, bookseller Guido (Roberto Benigni) invents imaginative stories for his son Giosuè (Giorgio Cantarini).

2 Pitting humour and *joie de vivre* against the stupidity of inhuman brutes: Guido abducts his Principessa from her own wedding. Fascists have daubed his uncle's horse with anti-Semitic slogans.

3 Little Giosuè thinks that life in the concentration camp is a game.

4 The young family's happiness will soon be overshadowed by the first signs of war. Many shops in Arezzo are now "closed to Jews".

5 Torn between fear and hope: Dora (Nicoletta Braschi) voluntarily followed her husband and child to the concentration camp.

pletely ordinary German citizens or as ridiculous figures who can do nothing but shout. There is only one scene where we can vaguely make out a mountain of corpses in the morning mist and that brief glance into hell shows us dimensions of cruelty that the movie doesn't even attempt to sound out. Its theme instead is the use of the imagination as a survival strategy in the midst of inhumanity. Benigni was well aware that he was treading a knife-edge in addressing that issue. Guido befriends the German Dr Lessing (Horst Buchholz, who gives the best performance next to Benigni) whom he meets again in his post as camp medic. Lessing has gone insane in the face of the Nazis' incomprehensible cruelty; his madness is a protective wall against brutal reality and his own responsibility. *Life is Beautiful* is a fairytale that goes beyond tragedy and comedy – it also goes beyond good and evil.   SH

4

5

Actor, comedian, director and scriptwriter Roberto Benigni was born in 1952 in the Tuscan village of Misericordia. The son of a railway worker, he grew up in poor surroundings. In the early 70s Benigni started out on his career with alternative theatre and one-man shows. After appearances in a TV series, his first film job came in 1977 with Giuseppe Bertolucci. Two roles in the films of the American Independent director Jim Jarmusch brought him international recognition: he speaks pigeon English as a wheeler-dealer jail breaker in the comedy *Down by Law* (1986 with Tom Waits and John Lurie) and plays a taxi driver making his confession to a priest he is carrying as a passenger who promptly suffers a heart attack and dies in *Night On Earth* (1990). In 1990, Benigni also acted in the last film made by the Italian director Federico Fellini, *The Voice of the Moon* (*La voce della luna*). As well as his own movies – *Johnny Stecchino* ("Johnny toothpick", 1991) or *The Monster* (*Il Monstro*, 1994) – Benigni is a masterly self-publicist, a talent much to the fore in his spectacular appearance at the 1999 Oscar ceremony. Benigni married the actress Nicoletta Braschi in 1991.

"*Life is Beautiful* relates a dream, while at the same time warning us of the danger of dreaming."

epd Film

6   Laughter in the face of terror: even in moments of the most extreme danger Guido plays the part of the joker and in doing so ultimately saves his son's life.

7   Director and leading man Roberto Benigni plays the role of his career in his own film, for which he won the most prestigious awards at Hollywood and Cannes.

6

7

GATTACA

1997 - USA - 112 MIN. - SCIENCE FICTION

DIRECTOR ANDREW NICCOL (*1964)
SCREENPLAY ANDREW NICCOL DIRECTOR OF PHOTOGRAPHY SLAWOMIR IDZIAK MUSIC MICHAEL NYMAN PRODUCTION DANNY DEVITO, MICHAEL SHAMBERG, STACEY SHER for JERSEY FILMS.

STARRING ETHAN HAWKE (Vincent/Jerome), UMA THURMAN (Irene Cassini), ALAN ARKIN (Det. Hugo), JUDE LAW (Jerome Eugene Morrow), LOREN DEAN (Anton), GORE VIDAL (Director Joseph), ERNEST BORGNINE (Caesar), BLAIR UNDERWOOD (Geneticist), XANDER BERKELEY (Lamar), ELIAS KOTEAS (Antonio).

"I not only think that we will temper Mother Nature. I think Mother wants us to."

A brave new world? Perhaps. *Gattaca*'s director, New Zealander Andrew Niccol, made television commercials for ten years before turning to full-length movies, and the vision he gives of the future is a world where expectant parents no longer have to worry about their off-spring's health. Thanks to the genetic testing of every fertilised egg, they know not only the sex, eye and hair colour of their baby, but also its present and future state of health, and even its likely life expectancy. Death is thus a factor before the baby's birth and the selection of a genetic elite has become part of everyday life. No system is perfect however, and alongside the designer babies there are still those who were not conceived in a test-tube but quite conventionally on the backseat of a Cadillac. Babies like Vincent (Ethan Hawke). Seconds after his birth, a DNA test showed with 99% certainty that he had a weak heart and was unlikely to survive beyond the age of 32. With genes like his, the state decides not to invest in his education, his health or his life. The likes of Vincent are never allowed to become an astronaut, no matter how much they dream of conquering outer space. Vincent ends up cleaning the bathrooms in the AIDS and cancer-free futuristic paradise of the space travel company Gattaca.

Like most science fiction movies, *Gattaca* tells of mankind's urge to push back the frontiers of space exploration and conquer far-away planets. But rather than vast expanses of space, the opening sequence shows us microscopic particles like treacherous beard stubble, skin cells, and eyelashes. Every morning Vincent scrubs and washes his body until it hurts. Despite all the obstacles and discrimination, he has managed to become a top engineer at Gattaca. To continue to do this he has to destroy all traces of his identity every day, and use borrowed blood, urine and hair samples to pretend he has the genetic make-up of Jerome (Jude Law), an Olympic swimmer who was paralysed in an accident and suffers from depression. Their identity swap seems to work and Vincent is eventually chosen for a mission to outer space. His dreams are about to be fulfilled and the spacecraft is on the point of departure when a murder interrupts Gattaca's customary calm and suddenly the company is swarming with police.

The movie is an appeal for chance instead of planning and for open-mindedness rather than clinical diagnoses. When Vincent's girlfriend Irene (Uma Thurman) and the company's doctor decide not to betray his secret, emotions win over sterility and individuality triumphs over conformity. The

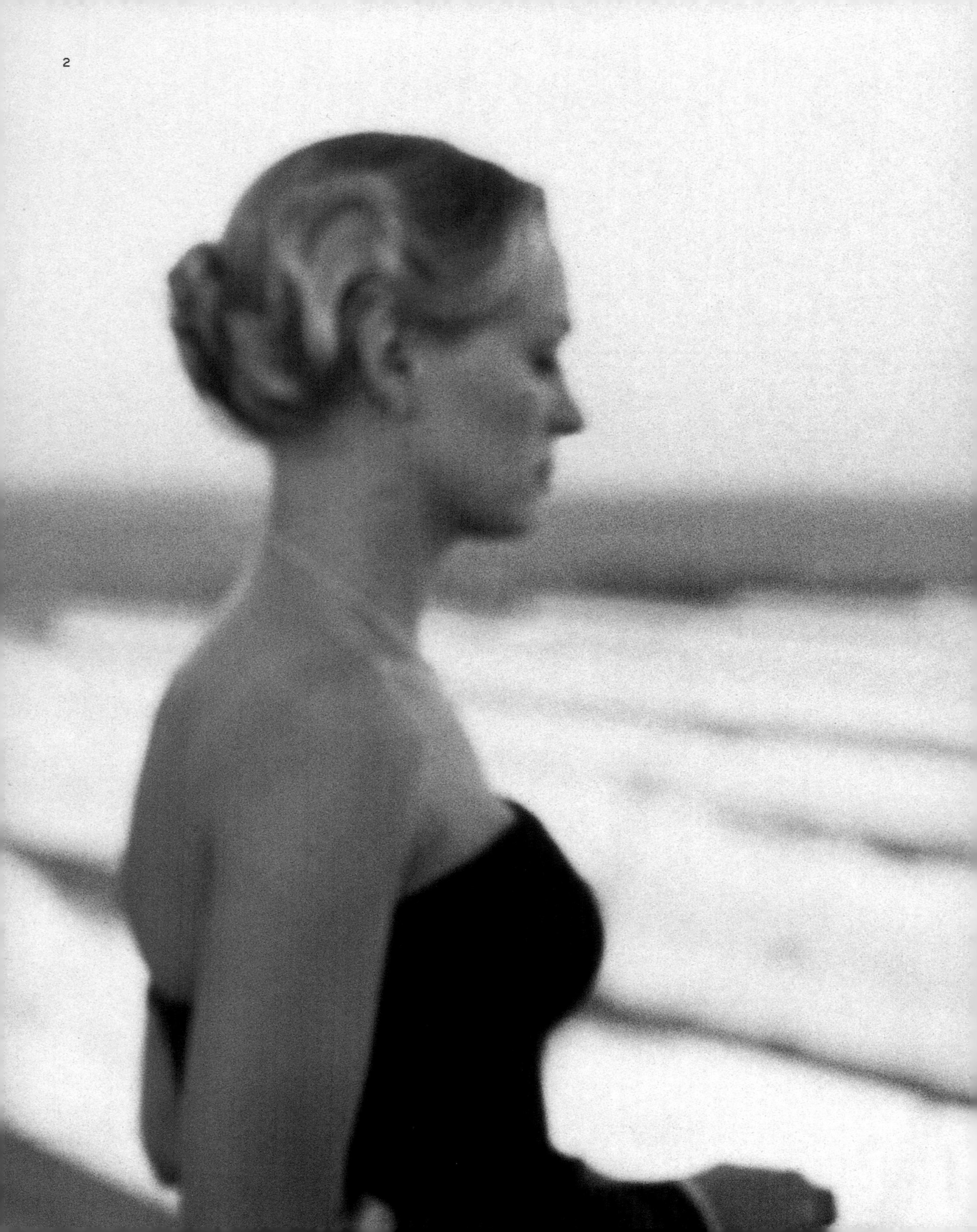

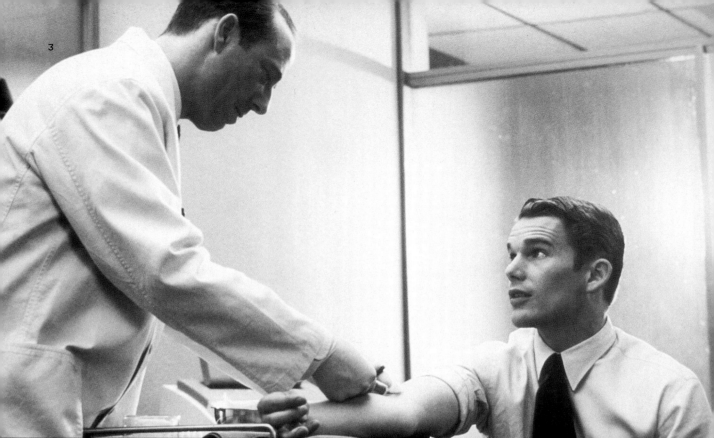

3

4

"Niccol provides us with the one thing sci-fi films are almost always lacking: interesting characters."

Libération

5

warning tone of the film is reminiscent of other futuristic detective classics such as *1984* (1956) and *Fahrenheit 451* (1966), from whose super-cool optics it also takes its aesthetic reference points. The plot unfolds, as a sub-title tells us, in "the not-too-distant-future", but the dark suits and closely tailored outfits are very much in the style of the 40s and the minimalist archi-tecture is 60s. *Gattaca* has a retro charm whose rigorous restraint is com-pletely at odds with typical 90s action movies and their ever bigger, ever brighter and ever louder special effects that minimise plot and maximise spectacular computer-generated pictures. In contrast to all of that, *Gattaca*

depends entirely on calculated coolness and tells its story with such under-statement that many allusions and hints, like the significance of the charac-ters' names, are easily missed. Vincent is a subversive rebel who beats state surveillance with his own resources: his surname is Freeman. Jerome's mid-dle name is Eugene, which comes from the Greek word *Eugenik* meaning the science of selective breeding, which is the main theme of the movie; and Irene's surname is Cassini, like the Franco-Italian astronomer Jean Dominique Cassini, who had a life-long fascination with Saturn – just like Vincent. AK

UMA THURMAN Anyone who grows up with the name of a Hindu goddess is unlikely to lead an uneventful life. Uma Thurman does not stand out among America's actresses solely on account of her willowy height of over 1.80 metres or her elegant, almost transparent beauty reminiscent of screen goddesses Greta Garbo and Lauren Bacall. She is also one of the most intelligent actresses currently on the scene. In 1988 she made her screen breakthrough with Stephen Frears' film of the Choderlos de Laclos novel *Dangerous Liaisons*, and John Malkovich, her partner in the movie, described her as having "Jayne Mansfield's body and a horrifying great brain". Her roles – as a human present in *Mad Dog and Glory* (1993), dance-mad gangster's wife in *Pulp Fiction* (1994) or Poison Ivy in *Batman & Robin* (1996) – are just as scintillating as her life. She was born in 1970, and her father is a professor of religion who is a close friend of the Dalai Lama and was also the first American national to become a Buddhist monk. Her mother is a Swedish ex-model who was previously married to Timothy Leary. Thurman left school at the age of 15, was married to British bad guy Gary Oldman and is now Mrs Ethan Hawke and the face of Lancôme.

1 The irony of casting: it just had to be ladies' heart-throb and cinema pin-up Ethan Hawke who acted the part of Vincent, branded an outsider because of his genetic make-up.

2 Irene (Uma Thurman) doesn't know what to make of her colleague Jerome – but she suspects that she will fall in love with him.

3 The brave new world of genetic design is in reality a surveillance state, where blood tests are the order of the day.

4 Her intelligence, loyalty and not least her super-cool self-controlled elegance make Irene the per-fect employee for the Gattaca group.

5 Vincent tries to beat the system with a fake heart-beat recording. Only those who are fit are select-ed for missions in outer space.

GOOD WILL HUNTING

1997 - USA - 126 MIN. - DRAMA

DIRECTOR GUS VAN SANT (*1952)
SCREENPLAY MATT DAMON, BEN AFFLECK DIRECTOR OF PHOTOGRAPHY JEAN-YVES ESCOFFIER MUSIC DANNY ELFMAN, JEFFREY KIMBALL
PRODUCTION LAWRENCE BENDER, KEVIN SMITH, SCOTT MOSIER for BE GENTLEMEN, A BAND APART (for MIRAMAX).

STARRING ROBIN WILLIAMS (Sean Maguire), MATT DAMON (Will Hunting), BEN AFFLECK (Chuckie), MINNIE DRIVER (Skylar), STELLAN SKARSGÅRD (Gerald Lambeau), COLE HAUSER (Billy), CASEY AFFLECK (Morgan), JOHN MIGHTON (Tom), RACHEL MAJOROWSKI (Krystyn), COLLEEN MCCAULEY (Cathy).

ACADEMY AWARDS 1998 OSCARS for BEST ORIGINAL SCREENPLAY (Matt Damon, Ben Affleck) and BEST SUPPORTING ACTOR (Robin Williams).

"Real loss is only possible when you love something more than you love yourself."

Matt Damon and Ben Affleck love throwing red herrings to journalists when asked in interviews for the secret of their successful collaboration: "we're lovers" is the invariable reply. The two boyhood friends, who grew up just a few houses away from each other, have every reason to joke about things. *Good Will Hunting* was received enthusiastically by critics and fans alike. Robin Williams was by far the movie's biggest star, but it was still basically their movie, despite the controlling hand of cult director Gus Van Sant (*Drugstore Cowboy, My Own Private Idaho*) and the fact that cinema tycoons Bob and Harvey Weinstein saved the movie by buying the rights for their company Miramax. The two young shooting stars do more than play main parts, they also wrote the screenplay – and it took Bob and Harvey Weinstein to recognise the potential of this atmospherically intense drama about a rebellious but emotionally isolated genius.

Matt Damon, who himself studied at Harvard and left the elite university shortly before graduating, plays Will Hunting, a cleaner at MIT. The cleaning job is one of his probation orders, for Will can't keep out of trouble.

Whenever the opportunity for a fight or a quick buck presents itself, he's there. He spends almost as much time in the young offenders' centre as he does in his run-down apartment in the centre of Boston.

But Will is a many-sided character. When Professor Lambeau (Stellan Skarsgård) discovers the answer to a difficult maths problem on the board and none of his students will own up to having solved it, he sets out to find the mysterious mathematical genius – and finds him of all places in the boy who cleans the institute's floors. Lambeau saves Will from another stay in prison by taking him under his wing and making sure he goes to the therapy sessions the court has decreed with an old friend from his student days, psychologist Sean Maguire (Robin Williams). While Will and Lambeau work together in euphoric harmony on complicated mathematical equations, Maguire has his work cut breaking through Will's emotional defences. Williams plays the widowed Maguire without pathos, and shows him to be an affectionate yet saddened man with the smallest of gestures. Befriending his stubborn patient is a lengthy process, but Maguire quickly realises that

behind Will's rebellious and angry façade an unhappy and vulnerable boy is hiding …

As so often in Hollywood, success didn't arrive over night, not just in the movie but in real life as well. Damon and Affleck wrote the screenplay years previously on a scriptwriting course and several Hollywood studios had even shown an interest in it. Damon and Affleck's condition however was that they should both star in the movie, and as they were completely unknown at the time, none of the studios accepted. That changed instantly with Damon's great success in the main role of Francis Ford Coppola's film of the Grisham novel *The Rainmaker* (1997).

Miramax finally bought the rights to *Good Will Hunting* after its authors took the advice of their experienced colleagues Rob Reiner, Terrence Malick and William Goldman, cutting the suspense element and adding love interest to the plot. In the revised version, Will, the social outsider, falls in love with Skylar (Minnie Driver) a British medical student who is the daughter of a respectable family. The emotional conflict which dominates Will's life is intensified by the love Skylar offers him and which he finds almost impossible to accept. Maguire gives him the courage to let his cynical, smart alec mask fall and face his feelings – even if this means that the world will have to do without the next Albert Einstein …

AK

"A heart-warming, credible piece of cinema full of human impressions and sparkling wordplay."

Neue Zürcher Zeitung

MATT DAMON Hollywood's latest golden boy was born in Cambridge, Massachusetts in 1970. His breakthrough was the starring role in Francis Ford Coppola's adaptation of John Grisham's legal bestseller *The Rainmaker* (1997), where he played a young, inexperienced but indomitable lawyer who fights against a dishonest multimillion dollar insurance company and its star defence lawyers. Everything he has done since has been a success. With his boyish charm and understated good looks he seems predestined to play the sensitive heroes of American film. He received enthusiastic reviews for the title role in Steven Spielberg's *Saving Private Ryan* (1998) and fascinated critics with the contrast between his innocent boyish face and cynical indifference as the cold-blooded murderer in the film of Patricia Highsmith's novel *The Talented Mr. Ripley* (1999). Together with his boyhood friend Ben Affleck, Damon has also written successful screenplays, and the script for *Good Will Hunting* won a Golden Globe and an Oscar. They went on to found a production company together aimed at giving young hopefuls like themselves a chance.

1 Hollywood clown Robin Williams is brilliant in his role as psychologist Sean Maguire, acting with an earnestness that is not merely by chance reminiscent of Peter Weir's *Dead Poets' Society* (1988).

2 Knowledge as power? All the knowledge he has picked up from books has given Will (Matt Damon) a feeling of superiority – but hasn't brought him happiness.

3 Medical student Skylar (Minnie Driver) embodies the complete opposite of social underdog Will, who doesn't dare to love her.

4 Professor Lambeau (Stellan Skarsgård) discovered Will's genius. But how honourable are his motives?

5 Shortly before a brawl: Will is still sitting peacefully with his mates (Ben Affleck, right) watching a baseball game.

MEN IN BLACK

1997 - USA - 98 MIN. - SCIENCE FICTION, COMEDY

DIRECTOR BARRY SONNENFELD (*1953)
SCREENPLAY ED SOLOMON, based on a MALIBU comic by LOWELL CUNNINGHAM DIRECTOR OF PHOTOGRAPHY DON PETERMAN
MUSIC DANNY ELFMAN PRODUCTION WALTER F. PARKES, LAURIE MACDONALD for AMBLIN ENTERTAINMENT, COLUMBIA PICTURES.

STARRING TOMMY LEE JONES (K), WILL SMITH (J), LINDA FIORENTINO (Laurel), VINCENT D'ONOFRIO (Edgar), RIP TORN (Zed), TONY SHALHOUB (Jeebs), SIOBHAN FALLON (Beatrice), MIKE NUSSBAUM (Gentle Rosenberg), JON GRIES (Van Driver), SERGIO CALDERÓN (José).

ACADEMY AWARDS 1998 OSCAR for BEST MAKE-UP (David LeRoy Anderson, Rick Baker).

"There are approximately 1500 aliens in Manhattan."

Sylvester Stallone is an alien. Elvis isn't dead, he's just gone home. And every word you read in the *National Enquirer* is true. – If you've ever had the feeling that you have to deal with aliens in your terrestrial life, this movie is the confirmation you've long been waiting for: "Sometimes there are up to 1500 aliens on earth, most of them here in Manhattan." Two things are necessary to ensure that humans and aliens can coexist peacefully: cover-up jobs and ceaseless vigilance. The "Men in Black" are responsible for both of these, black-clad agents from the department six, the immigration board. They do everything to stop the humans from realising that they are not alone on their blue planet, and make sure that the guests from outer space don't step out of line. At an interstellar airport the MiB supervise the arrival of creatures from far-off planets. They inspect their luggage and grant them entry permits to limited areas of New York and the world. If they try to travel in other parts, the agents fetch them back or shoot them dead. Alien civil rights are fairly low down on the agenda.

We see an example of this on the Mexican border. Police hold up a dilapidated truck full of illegal immigrants from the neighbouring Latin American country. State officials muscle in on their local colleagues; "Man in Black" K (Tommy Lee Jones) and a colleague take over and release all the refugees except one – he comes from further afield than Mexico. Under his poncho he is hiding a slimy body and tentacles, and the blue ooze in his veins sprays out all over one of the sheriffs when K summarily blows the creature up with a "De-atomiser". With a gadget know as a "Neuralyzer" which looks like a pen with a light instead of a nib, the agent then wipes all trace of the incident from the sheriff's memory.

In New York another policeman is chasing someone right through Manhattan, without realising of course that he is an alien. Cop James Darrel Edwards (Will Smith) stays hot on the criminal's heels even when he runs up the wall of the Guggenheim museum like a fly. James stops him on the roof, but the runaway avoids capture by throwing himself to his death. This attracts K's attention to James. And since the cheeky cop often clashes with the authorities, he's a good candidate to be K's new partner. Edwards passes an absurd test in which he is the only competitor and is taken on. The ends of his fingers are cauterized to stop him leaving any fingerprints. He is

3

"Mind you, the best thing is the two stars Will Smith and Tommy Lee Jones, whose humour is so bone-dry that they can deliver lines and keep their cool, where others would let the lines die on their lips." *Süddeutsche Zeitung*

fitted up with the black uniform and given dark glasses and a new name. Henceforth he is J, reduced like his colleagues to a single letter of the alphabet. Anonymity is their name, silence their language.

J and K's very first assignment is big. An alien bug has landed secretly on earth, a dangerous species that would never have been given an entry permit in the first place. The bug has killed Farmer Edgar (Vincent D'Onofrio), sucked out his entrails and put on his skin. He manages – more or less – to pass himself off as a human and is looking for the Galaxis, a valuable jewel worn by the son of the Aquilians' ruler who is living unobtrusively on earth

disguised as a jeweller. K and J's assignment becomes really difficult when the Aquilians decide they want the jewel back. If they don't get it, they're going to destroy the world. The time limit is a stellar week – a mere sixty earth minutes!

Men in Black is an almighty parody. Goggle-eyed, slimy aliens like the monsters in 50s movies, secret government organisations reminiscent of the television series *The Man From U.N.C.L.E.,* (1964–1968) and the uncanny modern mystery series *The X Files* (1993–), the *Blues Brothers'* black gear (1980) and *Casablanca's* escape scenario (1942) – it's all there. Director

1 They have to make sure they keep their shades on, otherwise the neutraliser would wipe the memories of the "Men in Black" as well.

2 Edwards (Will Smith, left) wins through in the aptitude test, against candidates who follow the regulations.

3 "Here come the Men in Black" – the song performed by Will Smith in the film also became a hit.

4 Perfectly disguised among humankind: son of the ruler of the Aquilians.

5 Dry humour and futuristic mega-weapons were the secret of *Men in Black's* success.

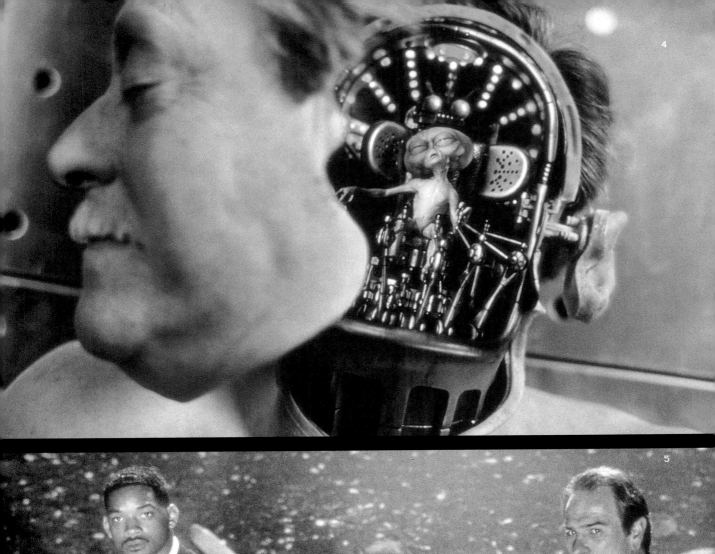

4

5

6   Useful aliens: at "M.I.B." headquarters they dish out coffee along with cheeky comments.

7   Disguised as a Mexican: an extraterrestrial immigrant tries to get into the USA, but he can't fool K.

8   Aliens bring some strange luggage with them on their trip to Earth.

Barry Sonnenfeld creates a funny, exciting mix from these quotations, and then goes a step further and adds historical dates and real events: the steel remains of the 1964 world exhibition in Queens are nothing less than the remnants of a space ship. The New York powercuts of 1977 were caused by … aliens. Microwaves, zips and silicon implants were all invented somewhere in another galaxy, and confiscated from alien tourists when they arrived on earth. Elvis lives. We learn that we are surrounded by aliens – not only Sylvester Stallone and the Republican politician Newt Gingrich, but singer Dionne Warwick too are all aliens. Sonnenfeld and his scriptwriter Ed Solomon take the game with facts and outrageous UFO fantasies to the extreme when the headlines of a gossip magazine read: "Aliens stole my husband's skin!" – scandal sheets are an important source of information for the MiB.

   Men in Black is also a buddy movie. Rapper Will Smith – best known as an actor for the television series *The Fresh Prince of Bel-Air* (1990–96) – is seen here in his first main role as an energetic, go-getting action character. Tommy Lee Jones is the wise old timer experienced in the alien business, and the two of them make an irresistible team. With stoicism and laconic humour, they go about their daily alien work; their immaculate black suits are spattered with one burst of slime after another. K is eaten alive by an alien and J helps deliver an alien baby. Although it often conjures up the charm of old B features, *Men in Black* is actually a huge modern production with a 100 million dollar budget and effects by George Lucas' Industrial Light and Magic company. Rick Baker (*Gremlins*), perhaps Hollywood's most brilliant monster creator, made the aliens. His creativity was allowed free rein: one bug-eyed alien in human form grows a new head every time it is shot off; a quartet of curious beings – naked pipsqueaks on two legs – live by the coffee machine in the MiB headquarters and make sarcastic wisecracks; a tiny creature with enormous eyes operates a huge machine from a control tower – the machine is a human body and the control tower is its head. Baker won a well-deserved Oscar for the make-up effects.

   The efforts were well rewarded, as the production was by far the most successful movie of 1997. It had millions of viewers in Europe and was a box-office smash in the USA where it earned over 250 million dollars. In the same year a television series started with the alien hunters as cartoon figures. A sequel to the movie *Men in Black* is planned for 2002.   HJK

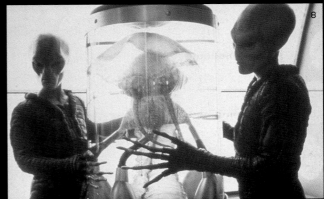

7

"In the best sci-fi movie tradition, *Men in Black* gets straight to the point in the very first scene." *epd Film*

BARRY SONNENFELD With the comic adaptations *Addams Family* (1991) and *Men in Black*, the Hollywood novel *Get Shorty* (1995) and the television series *Wild Wild West* (1998) Barry Sonnenfeld has made a name for himself as specialist in pop culture. He studied politics and then film and began his career as a cameraman, first of all for documentary films. He made his first feature film *Blood Simple* (1983) for his former classmates, the Coen brothers. He worked with them two more times, on *Raising Arizona* (1987) and *Miller's Crossing* (1990). The first *Addams Family* film was Sonnenfeld's debut as a director. He was asked to direct *Forrest Gump* and refused; Robert Zemeckis took over and the film won six Oscars. Sonnenfeld's disappointment didn't last long. He filmed the Elmore Leonard Adaptation *Get Shorty* which was a huge hit, and it became Sonnenfeld's ticket to the upper echelons of Hollywood.

CONSPIRACY THEORY

1997 - USA - 135 MIN. - THRILLER

DIRECTOR RICHARD DONNER (*1939)
SCREENPLAY BRIAN HELGELAND DIRECTOR OF PHOTOGRAPHY JOHN SCHWARTZMAN MUSIC CARTER BURWELL PRODUCTION JOEL SILVER, RICHARD DONNER for SILVER PICTURES, SHULER-DONNER PRODUCTIONS.

STARRING MEL GIBSON (Jerry Fletcher), JULIA ROBERTS (Alice Sutton), PATRICK STEWART (Dr Jonas), CYLK COZART (Agent Lowry), STEVE KAHAN (Wilson), TERRY ALEXANDER (Flip), ALEX MCARTHUR (Cynic), BRIAN J. WILLIAMS (Clarke), ROD MCLACHLAN (Guard), GEORGE AGUILAR (Piper).

"A good conspiracy is unprovable"

Jerry Fletcher (Mel Gibson) is a man on a mission – he's got to let people know. Fluoride is added to the water to rob them of their willpower. The Vietnam war happened because Howard Hughes lost a bet against Aristotle Onassis. Earthquakes are triggered from space and one will soon kill the President of the US. Fletcher, a New York cab driver, shares discoveries like these with his passengers. He also publishes them in his newspaper "Conspiracy Theory", which only has five subscribers. He has uncovered a gigantic conspiracy, and "they" are behind it all. He doesn't know exactly who "they" are, but he does know that they are out to get him. That's why he lives in a fortress and places an empty beer bottle on the door handle as an early warning system against intruders.

Fletcher feels misunderstood and lonely. Like the hero of JD Salinger's *Catcher in the Rye*, a book he compulsively buys wherever he sees it, he can't find anyone who understands him. He trusts no one, with the sole exception of Alice Sutton (Julia Roberts), who is an employee of the Justice Department. Jerry regularly tells her his latest revelations. He secretly watches her in her apartment, and he is in love with her. Jerry is crazy alright.

America loves conspiracy theories like "Elvis is alive" or "the Mafia had John F. Kennedy killed". Director Richard Donner, of *Lethal Weapon* fame (1986,1988,1992,1997) and scriptwriter Brian Helgeland (*L.A. Confidential*, 1997) spin a tale about such theories in a deliberately deceptive way. Fletcher, their protagonist, wins the audience's sympathy and tugs at their heartstrings, but he is undeniably mad. He suffers from full-blown paranoia, and we can only shake our head at its more extreme manifestations. And then, suddenly, Fletcher is right. The conspiracies really do exist, although they are not quite as widespread as Fletcher imagines, nor are they motivated by the same reasons. Nonetheless, "they" do exist, and they want to kill him.

Together with Alice, who initially thinks it's all nonsense, we are drawn into Fletcher's world. We observe his insanity, but gradually we start to notice that some of his claims seem to be true, at least in part. Helgeland's deftly-

"Madness and reality are two sides of the same coin in this film."

Süddeutsche Zeitung

constructed story shows how Alice slowly begins to believe Jerry, to the point where she too trusts no one and ends up putting an empty beer bottle on her door handle. The President's narrow escape from an earthquake finally convinces her that it's not all mere coincidence.

Director Richard Donner evokes a number of previous movies. Travis Bickle, the taxi driver from Martin Scorsese's film of the same name, is present – he was no conspiracy theorist, but a paranoid schizophrenic of the first order. Oliver Stone, who gives us his own personal Kennedy theory in *JFK* (1991), is one of the "greats" in Fletcher's pantheon: "Stone practises disin-

formation for 'them'". Finally, John Frankenheimer's *Ambassador of Fear* (*The Manchurian Candidate*, 1962) is used in *Conspiracy Theory* to explain what is really happening. Donner even includes his own fantasy film *Ladyhawk* (1985), which is playing in the cinema where Fletcher hides from his pursuers. The film, however, can be enjoyed independently of all these in-jokes. Mel Gibson's brilliant one-man-show, together with Julia Roberts' wide-eyed charm and cameraman John Schwartzman's wonderful pictures of New York are pleasure enough on their own.

HJK

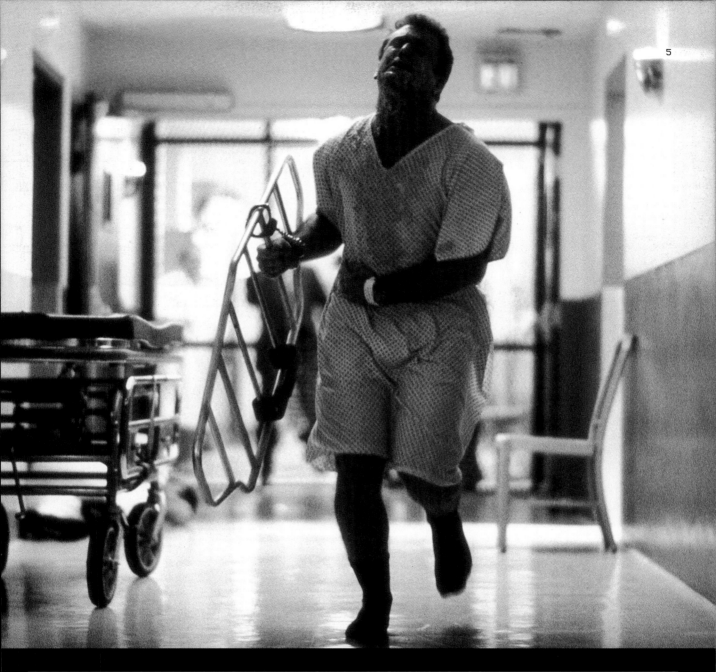

PARANOID CINEMA   "MC Ultra" is the name of the secret government program that has made Fletcher what he is. MC stands for *The Manchurian Candidate* – a masterpiece of Paranoid Cinema made by John Frankenheimer in 1962.
Films of this genre, made mostly in the 60s and 70s, rely heavily on threat scenarios: global conspiracies, society infiltrated by aliens, or better still communists. Frankenheimer's movie manages to unite the seemingly contradictory themes of "Anti-communism" and "Anti-McCarthyism" and virtually predicts the assassination of John F. Kennedy (1963). A soldier returns from a prisoner-of-war camp in Korea and is treated as a war hero. In reality he is a killing machine, programmed by the North Koreans, i. e. the communists, to kill the most promising US presidential candidate. This will clear the way for the election of the rival candidate, who in his turn is the puppet of his own wife – a communist agent.

1 Can he be trusted? Fletcher (Mel Gibson) sometimes behaves rather oddly.

2 The streets of New York: meeting place for criminals, loners and lunatics.

3 Fletcher doesn't understand what Dr Jonas (Patrick Stewart) wants from him.

4 Step by step Alice (Julia Roberts) finds her way into the world of Fletcher's madness.

5 Saved at the very last minute: Fletcher manages to escape from Dr Jonas' power.

THE FULL MONTY

1997 - USA / GREAT BRITAIN - 91 MIN. - COMEDY

DIRECTOR PETER CATTANEO (*1964)
SCREENPLAY SIMON BEAUFOY DIRECTOR OF PHOTOGRAPHY JOHN DE BORMAN MUSIC ANNE DUDLEY PRODUCTION UBERTO PASOLINI, POLLY LEYS for REDWAVE FILMS, CHANNEL FOUR, FOX.

STARRING ROBERT CARLYLE (Gaz), TOM WILKINSON (Gerald), MARK ADDY (Dave), LESLEY SHARP (Jean), STEVE HUISON (Lomper), PAUL BARBER (Horse), EMILY WOOF (Mandy), HUGO SPEER (Guy), DEIRDRE COSTELLO (Linda), BRUCE JONES (Reg), WILLIAM SNAPE (Nathan).

ACADEMY AWARDS 1998 OSCAR for BEST MUSIC, category COMEDY/MUSICAL (Anne Dudley).

"We dare to bare!"

Labouring steelworkers, shopping malls full of people, a lively swimming pool – urban paradise? According to a 70s promotional film, "thanks to steel Sheffield really is a city on the move" (*City on the Move*, 1971). 25 years on, the boom is well and truly over and South Yorkshire is deep in crisis. The steel works have closed down, and Gaz (Robert Carlyle) and his friend Dave (Mark Addy) are unemployed. Their attempt to earn some money with a rusty steel beam leaves them out of pocket and dripping wet from an unintentional swim in the river.

The queue is always long at the unemployment benefit counter. One particular day however there is an even longer queue outside the local club, as women wait for a performance by a troupe of male strippers. Dozens of shrieking women have turned up to be entertained. As the club is temporarily closed to men, Gaz climbs through the club toilet window to take a look at the "Dream Boys" with the help of his son Nathan (William Snape). Whatever they can do, he can do better. The crazy idea ripens into a plan: a couple of lads will have to be found, dance steps practised. And to make up for the fact that the professionals are better looking, they'll go one step further. The "Dream Boys" always keep something on; they'll take off the lot, even their tanga briefs, and go the "Full Monty".

After weeks of effort Gaz finally gets a stripper troupe together. His mate Dave joins in even though he isn't exactly happy with his body and can't perform in bed anymore. Gerald, their former boss (Tom Wilkinson), who goes to dance classes with his wife, agrees to do the choreography. The Black Horse (Paul Barber) might be getting on a bit, but he has rhythm in his blood. Lomper (Steve Huison) was on the verge of committing suicide and so he has nothing more to lose. Guy (Hugo Speer) can't dance, but he has a definite advantage over the others when it comes to the final act of the striptease show. The six dancers – and Gaz's son Nathan who works the cassette recorder – practise together in the deserted steel works. But there are still plenty of difficulties to be overcome before they appear on the stage of the local that they have hired: self-doubt, stage fright, and a police raid.

Time and time again, English movies to transform difficult social conditions with dance. *The Full Monty* is the first movie that does this with a striptease, and here, taking your clothes off in front of other people is anything but humiliating. On the contrary, the men regain their self-esteem and take control of their lives, in the way that they desperately need to do. The financial situation portrayed in Peter Cattaneo's cinematic debut is not utterly hopeless: it is possible to survive on the dole, and nobody starves. But the movie shows how men have lost their place as the breadwinner and are unclear about what their new role should be. Gaz is not allowed to see his son as he cannot afford to pay maintenance. Gerald still pretends to his wife that he goes to work every morning. When she discovers the truth, she leaves him. The men do not need the money – they need something to do, some way of winning respect. And the way in which they do this is hugely engaging, delightfully comic and full of unforgettable scenes: as the future strippers stand in the queue for their unemployment benefit, Donna Summer's disco classic "Hot Stuff" comes on the radio and they cannot help but move to the music. In perfect unison, they perform a quick dance in front of the counter.

HJK

"When the men strip, showing their scrawny chests, their aging bodies or their fat bellies, it says just as much, just as eloquently, about the humiliation of being unemployed and permanently hard-up." *Süddeutsche Zeitung*

KITCHEN SINK CINEMA

The mine has shut, but the miners' band still practises valiantly: they may have lost their jobs, but they're not going to let that spoil their music. *Brassed Off* – also released in 1997 – tells a story of the struggle against hopeless circumstances that it not dissimilar to *The Full Monty*. Once again, as in the era of the socialist realist "Kitchen Sink" dramas of the 60s, English cinema is dealing with themes like poverty and unemployment. Ken Loach, a "working class" director who is still active today, began his career in the 60s – as Peter Cattaneo did 20 years later – with the BBC. Loach found soulmates in directors such as Mike Leigh (*Secrets and Lies*, 1995) and Stephen Frears (*The Van*, 1996) – but also in filmmakers like Cattaneo and the director of *Brassed Off* Mark Herman, who spice up their commitment to social issues with a generous dash of humour.

1 There is seriousness behind the dancing: Gaz (Robert Carlyle) dances to win back his self-respect and the right to see his son again.

2 "Suddenly, these guys were forced to look at themselves the way they had always looked at women." *Robert Carlyle in: New York Times*

3 Playing football all day brings little satisfaction to the unemployed men.

4 Practice makes perfect: a disused steelworks can be used for anything.

5 "The entire film was shot in original locations in Sheffield. The strip club was a real strip club and the women in the audience were women from Sheffield."
Peter Cattaneo in: Zoom

3

FACE/OFF

1997 - USA - 138 MIN. - ACTION FILM

DIRECTOR JOHN WOO (*1946)
SCREENPLAY MIKE WERB, MICHAEL COLLEARY DIRECTOR OF PHOTOGRAPHY OLIVER WOOD MUSIC JOHN POWELL PRODUCTION DAVID PERMUT, BARRIE M. OSBORNE, TERENCE CHANG, CHRISTOPHER GODSICK for DOUGLAS-REUTHER PRODUCTION, WCG ENTERTAINMENT.

STARRING JOHN TRAVOLTA (Sean Archer), NICOLAS CAGE (Castor Troy), JOAN ALLEN (Eve Archer), ALESSANDRO NIVOLA (Pollux Troy), GINA GERSHON (Sasha Hassler), DOMINIQUE SWAIN (Jamie Archer), NICK CASSAVETES (Dietrich Hassler), HARVE PRESNELL (Victor Lazarro), COLM FEORE (Dr Malcolm Walsh), CCH POUNDER (Dr Hollis Miller).

"In order to catch him, he must become him."

Sepia pictures, images in someone's memory. A father rides with his son on a carousel horse. A shot rings out. The father is wounded and the son is killed. Six years later L. A. cop Sean Archer (John Travolta) still hasn't caught up with Castor Troy (Nicolas Cage), the psychopathic sharp shooter who killed his son. He gets another chance at a private airfield. Castor and his brother Pollux (Alessandro Nivolla) are about to take off, and Archer tries to stop them.

A shoot-out ensues where Pollux is arrested and Castor is injured and falls into a coma. But Archer still hasn't shaken off Castor Troy's evil legacy. His brother is carrying a disc that contains information on a gigantic bomb attack in Los Angeles, but the whereabouts of the bomb is a mystery. Pollux insists that he will only speak to his brother. To find out the truth about the bomb, a team of scientists from a secret project make Archer an unbelievable offer.

The parallel between hunter and hunted is a well-worn theme: the cop has to empathise with the criminal in order to predict his next move. Many movies have used this device, perhaps none so systematically as *Heat* (1995), where cop Al Pacino and gangster Robert De Niro meet for a tête-à-tête. *Face/Off*'s director John Woo takes the motif to new heights when he turns the cop into the gangster. With the help of the latest medical technology, Archer is given the face, stature and voice of the gangster Troy. He already knows more than enough about Troy's story, deeds and accomplices as he has been chasing him for years. To get the information out of him, Archer is admitted to the high security prison where Pollux is being kept. The mission remains a secret, and not even Archer's boss or his wife know anything about it. At any time, with the help of the same techniques, he can be given back his own body. But suddenly that escape route is suddenly blocked. Troy wakes out of his coma and appears in the prison – as Archer.

490

3

4

1   A shock: police officer Archer (John Travolta) wearing the face of the villain he has been pursuing like a man possessed for the last six years.

2   "Ridiculous chin", says Castor (Nicolas Cage) when Archer's face is fixed onto his.

3   The parallel between the hunter and the hunted is a well-known film motif, but nobody has ever taken it as far as John Woo.

4   It's not easy for Archer: locked up in the body of Castor in a high-tech jail.

5   The moment of truth: Archer (as Castor) runs his arch-enemy to ground.

6   Sean and Eve Archer (Joan Allen) have lost their son. Their grief lends a dark mood to the whole film.

JOHN TRAVOLTA   John Travolta's career began in 1975 with the role of Vinnie Barbarino in the popular television series *Welcome Back, Kotter*. His enormous success in the dance movies *Saturday Night Fever* (1977) and *Grease* (1978) was based on his clichéd roles as attractive lady's man, and as a result Travolta practically disappeared from the screen in the 1980s. He wasn't able to return to Hollywood's premiere league until Quentin Tarantino cast him as the off-beat killer Vincent Vega in *Pulp Fiction* (1994). Since then, Travolta has established himself as a versatile character actor who is just as at home in comedy roles as in action films (for example, *Operation: Broken Arrow*, 1995) or in existential dramas such as *Mad City* (1996). Travolta has become one of Hollywood's biggest earners in the 1990s: following *Pulp Fiction*, which made him 140,000 dollars, his fee per movie has risen to 20,000,000 dollars.

He has had the cop's face put on and shot the scientists and the people who witnessed the "swap". Archer manages to escape from the prison and has to make his way as an outlaw while Troy lives in his comfortable home with his wife and daughter.

Two movies gave new life to the Hollywood Action Film genre in the 90s: *Speed* (1994) and *Face/Off*. *Speed* is a fast-paced, light-footed celebration of pure movement, whereas *Face/Off* – despite its virtuoso action scenes – has dark, elegiac undertones and a much more complex plot. Archer is a tragic figure from the outset, first losing his son and then his life. The idea of changing bodies might seem far-fetched, but it offers the director plenty of opportunities to play with the hunter/hunted motif. John Woo goes through all of them one by one. Troy in Archer's body becomes a more subtle kind of gangster: he defuses his own bomb, becomes a hero and decides he wants to run the whole police department. Archer in Troy's body holds Troy's son in his arms as he used to hold his own. And Archer's wife Eve is delighted with the reawakened passion of her husband, who seems like a new man.

The doppelgänger motif reaches a visual highpoint in the scene where Archer and Troy stand on two sides of a mirror and aim their pistols at their own reflections, each of them wearing the face of their archenemy. The visual stylisation typical of Woo is everywhere in the movie – like the white doves in a church, or the slow motion billowing overcoat.   HJK

"Woo is such an action wizard that he can make planes or speed boats kick box, but his surprising strength this time is more on a human level." *New York Times*

THE ICE STORM

1997 - USA - 113 MIN. - DRAMA

DIRECTOR ANG LEE (*1954)
SCREENPLAY JAMES SCHAMUS, based on the novel of the same name by RICK MOODY **DIRECTOR OF PHOTOGRAPHY** FREDERICK ELMES
MUSIC MYCHAEL DANNA **PRODUCTION** TED HOPE, JAMES SCHAMUS, ANG LEE for GOOD MACHINE.

STARRING KEVIN KLINE (Ben Hood), SIGOURNEY WEAVER (Janey Carver), JOAN ALLEN (Elena Hood), TOBEY MAGUIRE (Paul Hood), CHRISTINA RICCI (Wendy Hood), HENRY CZERNY (George Clair), COURTNEY PELDON (Billie), ADAM HANN-BYRD (Sandy Carver), ELIJAH WOOD (Mikey Carver), KATIE HOLMES (Libbets Casey).

IFF CANNES 1997 SILVER PALM for BEST SCREENPLAY (James Schamus).

"The only big fight we've had in years is about whether to go back into couples therapy."

November 1973. Paul Hood (Tobey Maguire) travels home to his family in New Canaan, Connecticut for Thanksgiving Day. But home is no family idyll. His parents have grown apart, and his Father Ben (Kevin Kline) comforts himself with vodka or with his neighbour's wife Janey Carver (Sigourney Weaver), while his mother Elena (Joan Allen, who plays the President's wife in Stone's *Nixon*) has withdrawn completely into herself. Paul's fourteen-year-old sister Wendy (Christina Ricci) seems to be suffering as much from Vietnam and Watergate as she is from puberty. The parents may have lost interest in sex, but the children are just beginning to discover it. Wendy and the Carvers' two sons, fourteen-year-old Mikey (Elijah Wood) and his younger brother Sandy (Adam Hann-Byrd), explore each other's bodies. Paul is often interested in the girls in his class, but his room-mate Francis is always one step ahead. Paul's latest love interest is Libbets, the daughter of a rich family, and one evening he goes to New York to see Libbets, while Wendy meanwhile is over at the Carvers' and the parents are at a partner-swapping party. That night, an ice storm sweeps over the country, making the roads treach-

erous and covering high-voltage cables with icicles, and the morning after, nothing is ever quite the same again …

The Ice Storm tells a tale of puberty, of the period between the childhood and adulthood of its young protagonists. It also describes an interim period in American history. In November 1973 a cease-fire treaty was signed in the Vietnam War, ten years to the month after the shooting of President Kennedy, but the fighting still continued. The Watergate story had just broken, and although Richard Nixon had resigned as President, the affair was far from over. This "interim" feeling also extends to the life of the Hood family: the parents are still married but inwardly divorced, and the children are in puberty. They live "in between" even in a geographical sense: they are not in the flatlands, but New York is still a train ride away.

Taiwanese director Ang Lee has always shown himself to be a clear-sighted analyst of social relationships and family ties. Whether his subject is the world of Chinese immigrants in New York (*The Wedding Banquet*, 1992), England at the end of the 18th century (*Sense and Sensibility*, 1995), America

at the beginning of the Civil War (*Ride With the Devil*, 1999) or China shortly before its opening to the West (*Crouching Tiger, Hidden Dragon*, 2000), Lee always manages to show the social order through his protagonists without reducing them to mere symbolic ciphers. In that sense, *The Ice Storm* is typical of his other work: adults hold "key parties" (women choose car keys at random, and go home with the men whose keys they have chosen), and they discuss the porn film *Deep Throat* over canapés but they are incapable of real passion.

Paralysis, stagnation, and weariness — America's middle classes are deeply disturbed by the domestic turmoil of Watergate and the chaos of Vietnam abroad, but at the same time they believe they must live up to the sexual revolution of the none-too-distant 60s.

When Wendy puts on a Nixon mask to fool around with Mikey, the connection between sex and politics is made quite clear, and the film is full of such symbols and metaphors. The ice storm of the title is the most obvious example, but another is the characters' names: father Hood doesn't have a definitive identity, and everyone calls him something different (Ben, Benji, Benjamin). By turns bitter and grotesque, *The Ice Storm* never deteriorates into stereotypes or facile theories despite its wealth of symbols, and that is perhaps the real strength of what is a virtuoso drama.   HJK

CHRISTINA RICCI   Rumour has it that Natalie Portman was originally intended to play Wendy, but her parents found the role too sexy. That said, the part of a fourteen-year-old desperate to experiment with her sexuality seems tailor-made for Christina Ricci. With her large, expressive eyes and mysterious air, Ricci often plays girls who don't fit into the traditional Hollywood image of the carefree teenager. One of her first successes was at the age of eleven when she played the daughter of the horror clan the *Addams Family* (1991). After that film, much was made of her looks, her full figure leading people to claim that she was "too healthy" to make it in a city where a waif-like is the norm. Despite that, the "slightly different" roles keep coming, and she has excelled as the bleached blonde floozy in *The Opposite of Sex* (1999), the ghost hunter's brooding companion in *Sleepy Hollow* (1999) and the mysterious child-woman Layla in *Buffalo '66* (1997), who, incidentally, the male protagonist introduces to his parents as Wendy.

1   As Wendy Hood, Christina Ricci knows how to bring across the dark, unsettling aspects of puberty.

2   Exciting and terrifying: Mikey (Elijah Wood) and Wendy carry out their first experiments with the opposite sex.

3   Ben Hood (Kevin Kline) and Janey Carver (Sigourney Weaver): double-quick sex without the small-talk.

4   A partner-swapping party — as unsettling for parents as the first sexual experiments are for their children.

5   "The story takes place during a period of crisis in the USA, the early Seventies. The whole thing is like a kind of hangover from the Sixties: there is no real passion any more, a kind of weariness prevails — like a transition into what America is today." *Ang Lee in: the Süddeutsche Zeitung*

4

5

"The family is the antithesis of the self. The family is the void from which you came, and also the place to which you return when you die."

Quotation from film: Paul

TITANIC

1997 - USA -194 MIN. - MELODRAMA, DISASTER FILM

DIRECTOR JAMES CAMERON (*1954)
SCREENPLAY JAMES CAMERON **DIRECTOR OF PHOTOGRAPHY** RUSSELL CARPENTER **MUSIC** JAMES HORNER **PRODUCTION** JAMES CAMERON, JON LANDAU for 20TH CENTURY FOX, LIGHTSTORM ENTERTAINMENT, PARAMOUNT PICTURES.

STARRING LEONARDO DICAPRIO (Jack Dawson), KATE WINSLET (Rose DeWitt Bukater), BILLY ZANE (Cal Hockley), KATHY BATES (Molly Brown), GLORIA STUART (Rose as an old woman), BILL PAXTON (Brock Lovett), BERNARD HILL (Captain Smith), DAVID WARNER (Spicer Lovejoy), VICTOR GARBER (Thomas Andrews), JONATHAN HYDE (Bruce Ismay).

ACADEMY AWARDS 1998 OSCARS for BEST PICTURE, BEST DIRECTOR (James Cameron), BEST CINEMATOGRAPHY (Russell Carpenter), BEST FILM EDITING (Conrad Buff, James Cameron, Richard A. Harris), BEST MUSIC, category DRAMA (James Horner), BEST SONG ("My Heart Will Go On"; Melody: James Horner, Text: Will Jennings, Performed by Céline Dion), BEST ART DIRECTION – SET DECORATION (Peter Lamont, Michael Ford), BEST COSTUMES (Deborah Lynn Scott), BEST VISUAL EFFECTS (Robert Legato, Mark Lasoff, Thomas L. Fisher, Michael Kanfer), BEST SOUND (Gary Rydstrom, Tom Johnson, Gary Summers, Mark Ulano), BEST SOUND EFFECTS EDITING (Tom Bellfort, Christopher Boyes).

"So this is the ship they say is unsinkable."

The sinking of the passenger ship Titanic is usually interpreted as a warning of the catastrophic end of the modern belief in progress, which was confirmed in the trenches of World War One only a few years later. The numerous film versions of the event demonstrate the fascination that the luxury liner's fate has always held. The movies themselves have had an influence on the Titanic myth, which in turn has become an integral part of our cultural memory. The story never varies: technology clashes with nature, human inventiveness with destructive natural power, arrogant presumption with impassive creation. Film versions were made almost immediately after the accident, like the long-forgotten *Saved From the Titanic* (by Etienne Arnaud, 1912) and Pier Angelo Mazzolotti's *Titanic* (1915).

Subsequently many vast and expensive films were made in which private unhappiness and technical disaster developed side by side only to fuse together in an infernal catastrophe at the end. Jean Negulesco's film version of the event was awarded an Oscar for best original screenplay in 1953. Cameron's *Titanic* cost 200 million dollars and was awarded a total of eleven Oscars – the time any film had matched the previously unbeatable *Ben Hur* (1959).

Cameron's interpretation of the Titanic myth is more proof of his talent for telling melodramatic love stories. The proletarian prince almost accidentally rescues the world-weary princess while "polite society" postures and poses to conceal its spiritual and moral decay. The megalomania that inspired the construction of a gigantic luxury liner like the Titanic is part of that modern decadence.

The film's recipe for success could be summed up as strong emotion reflected by huge disaster. And it works. The penniless painter Jack Dawson

"The scene where a lifeboat is carefully edging its way between frozen corpses floating in the water as it searches for survivors is as horrific as it is unforgettable."

Frankfurter Allgemeine Zeitung

...eets beautiful, of noble birth but unhappy Rose DeWitt Bukater. She tries to ...ill herself, he saves her and they fall in love. A passionate romance devel-...ps between this young man from the lower decks and the upper class lady ...om the top echelons of society. The love story becomes a social drama ...here class differences become apparent not just in location and decor but ...lso in everyday life. Upstairs there is distinguished, arrogant small talk ...bout money accompanied by pleasant string music, downstairs there is ...ild dancing to fast and furious Irish folk music. The class barrier becomes ...xtremely real. Rose's fiancé Cal Hockley (Billy Zane) wants to put an end to ...e subversive relationship and eventually manages to have Jack forbidden ...om coming up to the top deck, but this is not enough to drive the two apart

Jack makes a secret drawing of Rose wearing nothing but a diamond on a chain around her neck and the social barriers to their love seem to dissolve in the magic of art. When Cal discovers this drawing in the safe, he sends out servants to track the couple down, but Rose and Jack escape into the enormous underbelly of the ship. At the same time, the captain gets the first iceberg warnings, which he ignores. Both plot strands reach a critical phase and destiny takes its course: the lovers' high spirits and the captain's arrogance combine in a tragic conclusion.

The story is told in a long flashback by the now elderly Rose after she has seen on television that a diving team has found Jack's drawing in a safe lying on the bottom of the sea. The movie takes great care to adopt a light

---

LEONARDO DICAPRIO DiCaprio was born in Hollywood in 1974 and stood in front of the camera for the first time when he was only five years old. The boyish star began his career with publicity spots and television series before getting his first big movie breakthrough with *This Boy's Life* (1993) alongside Robert De Niro and Ellen Barkin. He was nominated for an Oscar for his performance as the mentally retarded Arnie Grape in *What's Eating Gilbert Grape* (1993). Similarly difficult roles followed, for example as drug-addict and sports scholarship holder in *The Basketball Diaries* (1993) or as the homosexual poet Rimbaud in *Total Eclipse* (1995). DiCaprio also shone in his role as a youthful Romeo in Baz Luhrmann's contemporary adaptation of *Romeo & Juliet*. After *Titanic* (1997), the most successful box office hit of all time, DiCaprio played the lead role in the dark adventure film *The Beach* (1999).

---

1 Impending disaster reflected in the lovers' eyes (Leonardo DiCaprio as Jack and Kate Winslet as Rose).

2 Tenderness in a time of decadence.

3 Humanity's presumptuousness embodied as a machine on her journey into the abyss.

4 The betrayed fiancé (Billy Zane) loses his appetite.

5 Fashion photography on film: the young lover as rebel...

6 ... and the super-cool eroticism of buttoned-up beauty.

"The outside shots of the stern breaking up, the tidal waves inside, the drama around and in the lifeboats rank among the best special effects Hollywood has ever produced." *Frankfurter Allgemeine Zeitung*

7 An arrogant society falls from a great height.

8 Classical grandeur in a watery grave. Any hope of being saved is ebbing away.

9 Fireworks and music bid them farewell: the cruel irony of fate.

touch with just a hint of melancholy when passing from this fairytale beginning to an atmospheric portrayal of the early years of the 20th century.

This was the first Titanic movie to use pictures of the actual wreck after it had been located and explored, giving an added note of authenticity. *Titanic* fuses the two time dimensions of its tale in many poetic pictures: like Kubrick's famous "match cut" in *2001: A Space Odyssey* (1968) where a bone is thrown into the air and the editing turns it into a space ship, past and present are combined with blend-ins and morphing effects. All of which of course is enhanced by the movie's impressively atmospheric soundtrack

When the inevitable finally happens and the Titanic sinks after colliding with the iceberg, Jack drowns in the icy water. But their love survives. When Rose, now an old woman, returns to her lover's watery grave for the last time at the end of the film, she throws the blue diamond that she saved from the wreck into the sea as a symbol of her eternal love. The ship may not have been unsinkable, but the myth of the Titanic is. Watching the movie is like looking at an old photograph. We can only discover its secrets by looking at it many times from different angles, like a sparkling diamond that always has new facets to be discovered.

RR

BUFFALO '66

1997/1998 - USA - 110 MIN. - DRAMA, ROMANCE

DIRECTOR VINCENT GALLO (*1962)
SCREENPLAY VINCENT GALLO, ALISON BAGNALL DIRECTOR OF PHOTOGRAPHY LANCE ACORD MUSIC VINCENT GALLO PRODUCTION CHRIS HANLEY for MUSE, LIONS GATE FILMS.

STARRING VINCENT GALLO (Billy Brown), CHRISTINA RICCI (Layla), ANJELICA HUSTON (Janet Brown), BEN GAZZARA (Jimmy Brown), KEVIN CORRIGAN (Goon), MICKEY ROURKE (Bookie), ROSANNA ARQUETTE (Wendy), JAN-MICHAEL VINCENT (Sonny), JOHN RUMMEL (Don Shanks), BOB WAHL (Scott Woods).

"Just don't touch me!"

Billy Brown (Vincent Gallo), an innocent man, has spent five years in Buffalo jail because of a gambling debt. When he gets out, he wants to revenge himself on Scott Woods (Bob Wahl), the man who caused his misery. Once a football star with the Buffalo Bills, Woods' poor performance in a game on which Billy bet 10,000 dollars made the Bills lose. After his release, Billy needs a good excuse for his parents (Anjelica Huston and Ben Gazzara) who have no idea where their son has spent the last five years. Billy makes a snap decision and kidnaps a young woman called Layla (Christina Ricci) and forces her to pretend to the Browns that she is his wife. "Your job is to make me look good", he instructs her. Layla throws herself into the role whole-heartedly, but we realise that Billy's parents have never really cared about him. His mother is a devoted fan of the Buffalo Bills and his father has a paranoid mistrust of his own son. It becomes increasingly clear that behind Billy's tough façade is a lonely, vulnerable young man. Layla, who soon sees through him, feels herself more and more drawn to him, although he keeps her at a distance. They leave the Browns' house together, go to a bowling centre and a fast food restaurant and finally, in a motel room that evening,

Billy seems to thaw. Everything could turn out well, but Billy still has a score to pay.

Buffalo '66 is one of that rare kind of American movies which could only have been made as the debut film of an independent filmmaker. The movie is badly proportioned, overloaded with the ideas of its director, over-dramatic, autobiographical and unrelentingly egocentric – and for exactly those reasons it has its own kind of magic. Vincent Gallo is the director, scriptwriter and leading actor of Buffalo '66. Always a gifted self-publicist as an actor, artist and Calvin Klein model, he never misses an opportunity to draw attention to the autobiographical nature of his directorial first-born. Buffalo is Gallo's native town, and the Browns are based on his parents, or so he claims. On first viewing, the movie appears to be the self-portrait of a selfish outsider. But its fairy-tale quality is at least as important as its autobiographical aspects and its often rough and ready realism. The artificial colours, the overemphasis on narrative and cinematic effects and above all the almost parodic characterisation make Buffalo '66 a surprisingly tender tale of existential loneliness and the indispensable nature of love. From being

"Gallo, who also wrote, directed and scored *Buffalo '66*, is a smart young filmmaker, not least in his casting. Gazzara, angrily mourning his lost career as a local lounge singer, and Huston, obsessing on the Bills' football frustrations, are glorious eccentrics. And Christina Ricci, as the tap dancer Billy forces to play his faux fiancée, is just lovely." *Time Magazine*

3

1 Suburban blues: Layla (Christina Ricci) on a search for love.

2 It takes some time for Billy (Vincent Gallo) to overcome his fear and open up to Layla.

3 A blond suburban angel: Christina Ricci lends a fairytale quality to Layla.

4 Buffalo can be very cold: Vincent Gallo directs himself as a tragi-romantic loner.

GUEST APPEARANCE   In contrast to the cameo appearance, where famous people – often to comic effect – appear as themselves for a short moment to disturb the fictional plot of a film, a guest appearance is a small role that fits into the plot. Both were already popular in the era of silent movies. Charlie Chaplin for instance had a cameo role in King Vidor's *Show People* (1928), and he is to be found in his own film *A Woman of Paris* (1923) in a guest appearance as a porter. The difference between guest and cameo roles is sometimes rather artificial. In Robert Altman's *The Player* (1992), a satire about the film industry, various Hollywood stars can be seen in guest or cameo roles. A more restrictive definition of the term limits guest appearances to appearances by directors in movies made by their colleagues.

5 Two icons of independent US cinema: Christina Ricci and Vincent Gallo as distant lovers.

6 A sideways glance: Jimmy Brown (Ben Gazzara) harbours a paranoid distrust of his son Billy.

7 Her world revolves around football and nothing else: Billy's mother (Anjelica Huston) is an obsessive fan of the Buffalo Bills.

the autistic son of unfeeling average Americans, Billy, with his lanky figure and his heavily shadowed, light blue eyes in an unusually pale face, becomes the ideal embodiment of a tragic-romantic loner and plump, big-eyed Layla is his blonde suburban angel.

Buffalo '66 is a movie full of wonderful moments and witty cinematic magic tricks. Gallo demonstrates both his artistic originality and his admiration of other creative talents from the Independent scene. Ben Gazzara gets

a melancholy singing scene, Christina Ricci an introverted tap-dance number and Anjelica Huston is stunning in the role of football-obsessed bad mother. Mickey Rourke, one of the most eccentric cult figures of US cinema in the 80s, also turns up with a guest appearance as a criminal bookie. These moments are lovingly set up and if they don't make Buffalo '66 a masterpiece, they do make it at least a high point of American independent cinema in the 90s.   JH

"Buffalo '66 is an American response to the European autobiographical film."

Neue Zürcher Zeitung

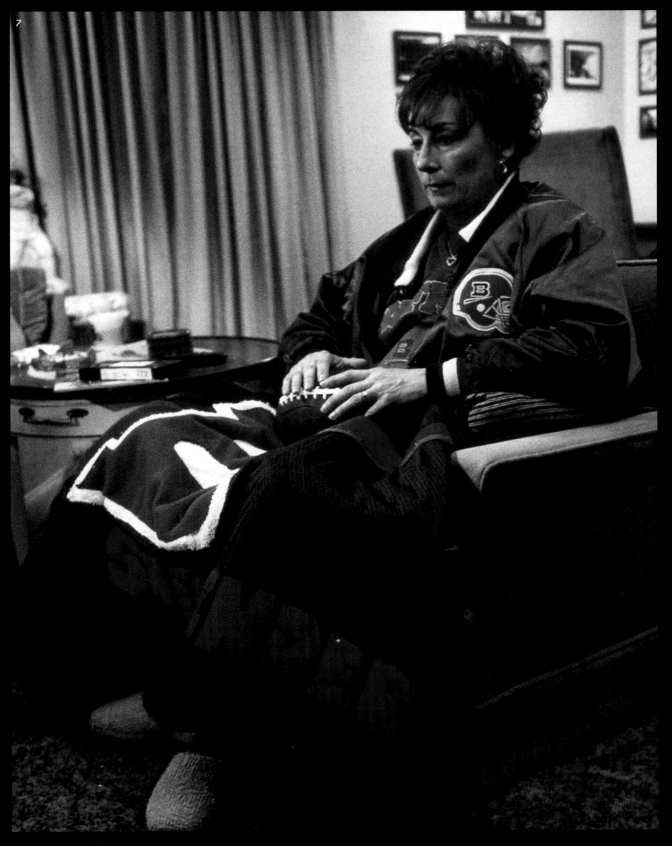

JACKIE BROWN

1997 - USA - 154 MIN. - GANGSTER FILM

DIRECTOR QUENTIN TARANTINO (*1963)
SCREENPLAY QUENTIN TARANTINO, based on the novel *RUM PUNCH* by ELMORE LEONARD **DIRECTOR OF PHOTOGRAPHY** GUILLERMO NAVARRO **MUSIC** Various Soul and Hip-Hop songs **PRODUCTION** LAWRENCE BENDER for A BAND APART, MIGHTY MIGHTY AFRODITE PRODUCTIONS, MIRAMAX FILMS.

STARRING PAM GRIER (Jackie Brown), SAMUEL L. JACKSON (Ordell Robbie), ROBERT FORSTER (Max Cherry), BRIDGET FONDA (Melanie Ralston), MICHAEL KEATON (Ray Nicolette), ROBERT DE NIRO (Louis Gara), MICHAEL BOWEN (Mark Dargus), CHRIS TUCKER (Beaumont Livingston), TOMMY "TINY" LISTER JR. (Winston).

IFF BERLIN 1998 SILVER BEAR for BEST ACTOR (Samuel L. Jackson).

"You're not old, you look great."

Pam Grier is an icon of the "Blaxploitation" cinema of the 70s and, since *Foxy Brown* (1974), a black sex symbol. Quentin Tarantino tailored the role of Jackie Brown especially for her. Although the plot of the film is based on Elmore Leonard's novel *Rum Punch*, Tarantino completely ignored the fact that the book's main figure is a white woman, creating a true homage to Grier. He also featured another star of the 70s cinema, Robert Forster. The whole movie is retro, the sets, decor and music are all taken from the 70s and once again Tarantino does a lot of quoting from other movies. Ordell and Jackie remind us of figures like Joe Cabot (*Reservoir Dogs*, 1991) or Winston Wolf (*Pulp Fiction*, 1994) who try to manage other people's lives as though they had a script. In *Jackie Brown* there is also a shot from the inside the boot of a car, video films play an important role, and killings are filmed with the same gruesome nonchalance. Such things are fixed co-ordinates in the Tarantino universe.

His recreation of the 70s is colourful and atmospheric. It's there from the very first shot: a woman appears at the left of the scene, the camera lingers on her whilst she is carried along on a moving walkway in front of a multicoloured tile mosaic to the music of Bobby Womack. Psychedelic colours and forms combine with Pop Art textures and Soul Music to build an imaginary framework. The woman's steady gaze is fixed straight ahead, her posture suggests determination and self-confidence – we know that Jackie Brown has arrived. She is a stewardess with a small airline and improves her slim earnings by carrying money for arms dealer Ordell Robbie. When she is caught the police find a plastic bag of cocaine together with the 50,000 dol-

1

"This thriller isn't dominated by the pressure of rising tempo, nor is the escalation of events heralded by any frantic facial expressions. Instead, it is the law of inertia that rules; everything moves as slowly as possible, and faces change expression slowest of all." *Frankfurter Allgemeine Zeitung*

1 Mature sex appeal and cool charm: Pam Grier in
the role of Jackie Brown. All those beautiful young
Hollywood actresses were left out in the cold …

2 Whose side is cold-blooded Ordell (Samuel L.
Jackson) on?

3 Solid eroticism within touching distance.

4 Filled with love beyond sexual desire: Max Cherry
(Robert Forster).

lars in the wallet she is carrying. Jackie ends up in prison. Ordell Robbie
sends a bail broker named Max Cherry (Robert Forster) to visit her, and a
touching affair begins. Their meetings in the prison courtyard, in a bar and in
Jackie's apartment, the almost blind trust and mutual esteem are unexpected examples of a new kind of empathy from Tarantino, the supposed master
of cinematic brutality. Once again, he proves that his gangsters are nothing
more than caricatures and that his criminals are merely comic figures –
especially when they are "being serious". Ordell jabbers on in a macho and
hypocritical manner about street credibility and then shoots his black "brother" Beaumont in cold blood. Ordell's weak right-hand-man Louis (Robert De

Niro) kills Ordell's girlfriend Melanie (Bridget Fonda) without thinking twice
when she nags him. The trio are played by Samuel L. Jackson, Bridget Fonda
and gangster icon Robert De Niro, as though to illustrate the Tarantino philosophy of deconstructing film stereotypes through grotesque exaggeration.
The interpersonal relationships between them are reduced to watching
videos, smoking joints, showing off, having sex and having fun. They form a
striking contrast to the real love story in the film, the relationship between
Jackie and Max.

The turning point comes when Jackie arranges to hand over some
money and then plays a trick with Max's help on the police. The police want

> ## "Where the formal rage of *Reservoir Dogs* and *Pulp Fiction* is reminiscent of Godard, Jackie Brown's leisureliness shows an unexpected affinity on Tarantino's part with the stylistic devices of Rohmer and – even more so – Rivette."

epd Film

5   Echoes of *Pulp Fiction*: gangsters (Robert De Niro)
   are also only human.

6   Good-looking blonde Melanie (Bridget Fonda) isn't
   as dumb as she seems.

Ordell, and Ordell wants his money. She strikes a deal with both parties in advance but makes sure that she will be the only winner. The movie shows the handing over of the bag from the three different perspectives of Jackie, Melanie and Max – and each one of the chronologically overlapping sequences reveals a further element of the transaction. Panning shots and circular camera movements mark the story's climax: we know that this is the decisive moment, but we don't know if Jackie's sophisticated plan will succeed or fail. All does go according to plan: Max picks up the money unnoticed, and only Ordell realises that he has been cheated. He is then lured to Max's office where the police are already waiting, and they shoot Ordell when Jackie shouts that he has a gun. Jackie wins; the police know nothing about the rest of the money which Jackie and Max have already hidden.

The film spins this gangster story around Jackie Brown with humour and sophistication. Once again Tarantino revolutionises the linear narrative structure typical of mainstream cinema by delaying the handing over of the money and effortlessly juxtaposing lots of seemingly unconnected story lines. Much of the charm of *Jackie Brown* comes from its 70s retro look. Part of this is the almost forgotten "split screen" technique where the screen is divided into two halves so that action taking place in different places at the same time can be shown in the same picture.

At the end of the movie, Jackie leaves with her loot – and we feel she really deserves it. Max, sad and lonely, is left behind. Pam Grier alias Jackie Brown looks thoughtful and moves her lips to the music which shows her the way "Across 110th Street".   BR

BLAXPLOITATION Following the civil rights movement at the end of the 60s the film industry began to work on a market segment which previously had been neglected; movies with coloured people both in front of and behind the cameras, dealing with things that concerned the Afro-American population. To exploit the market potential of frustrated coloured employees, many low budget productions were made with tough, sexually potent heroes set in a milieu dominated by drug dealings, prostitution and Mafia organisations, underpinned by bombastic, sentimental soundtracks. Like most "exploitation films", these crime and gangster movies, mostly set in run-down coloured neighbourhoods, have little claim to artistic merit. Quick market success was the aim, so the films break down easily into readily identifiable sensational elements. Classics of the Black Exploitation movie include *Cotton Comes to Harlem* (1969), Melvin Van Peebles' angry, experimental *Sweet Sweetback's Baadasssss Song* (1971) and glamorous Hollywood productions like the extraordinarily popular *Shaft* series (1970–1975). In the final instance however, the stereotyped superficiality of these movies and their rigid separation from white culture served above all to drive coloured pop culture further into the ghetto.

6

THE SWEET HEREAFTER

1997 - CANADA - 112 MIN. - DRAMA

DIRECTOR ATOM EGOYAN (*1960)
SCREENPLAY ATOM EGOYAN, based on the novel of the same name by RUSSELL BANKS   DIRECTOR OF PHOTOGRAPHY PAUL SAROSSY
MUSIC MYCHAEL DANNA   PRODUCTION ATOM EGOYAN, CAMELA FRIEBERG for ALLICANE FILMS, TELEFILM CANADA,
THE HAROLD GREENBERG FUND.

STARRING IAN HOLM (Mitchell Stephens), SARAH POLLEY (Nicole Burnell), BRUCE GREENWOOD (Billy Ansell), TOM MCCAMUS
(Sam Burnell), GABRIELLE ROSE (Dolores Driscoll), ALBERTA WATSON (Risa Walker), ARSINÉE KHANJIAN (Wanda Otto),
STEPHANIE MORGENSTERN (Alison), MAURY CHAYKIN (Wendell Walker), CAERTHAN BANKS (Zoe Stephens).

IFF CANNES 1997 JURY PRIZE.

"Something terrible is happening. It's taken our children away."

The car wash has gone crazy. It holds the strange car prisoner with its brushes and water sprinklers as if it were the gatekeeper of the small Canadian settlement. Inside the car sits the lawyer Stephens (Ian Holm), who has come to the wintry mountains from the city far away because he scents an opportunity to make capital out of a tragedy. 14 children have just died in an accident where a school bus skidded off a slippery road and sank in an icy lake. The only survivors were the driver and the oldest schoolgirl, 13-year-old Nicole (Sarah Polley), and the lawyer wants to persuade the parents of the victims to claim compensation. In the 90s nothing happens without a reason, so someone must be legally responsible for the catastrophe: even if it's just a mechanic who failed to tighten a bolt the last time the bus was serviced, Stephens is convinced that he will find someone to pay for the children's lives. He's not the type to spend much time wondering if he is welcome or not. He breaks out of the car wash with the help of his umbrella, and then forces his way into the houses of the mourning community.

Everything is ambivalent in *The Sweet Hereafter,* nothing is clear at first sight. By day, Nicole seems like a normal teenager who looks after the neighbours' baby, but at night she fondles her father in a haystack. Even the determined lawyer turns out to be a broken man who has never got over the loss of his daughter. An HIV-positive drug addict, she vegetates in a state of living death in a strange city. Instead of dealing with his pain, he feels only bitter anger. With the words "Let me direct your rage" he gains the support of the drowned children's parents, and convinces them that he will be able to find an explanation for the tragic events. Under his influence however, that rage begins to drown out the memories of the children that they have lost.

The Sweet Hereafter is a disturbing movie about grief and loss. It's disturbing because Atom Egoyan doesn't tell his story chronologically but jumps instead back and forth between various time periods. Sometimes we see the time before the bus accident, sometimes the direct aftermath. There is also an epilogue that takes place two years later, and this fragmentary narrative

1

2

"Egoyan's films are complex and eccentric, inwardly torn and full of longing, just like people are. Although with *The Sweet Hereafter* Egoyan has for the first time adapted foreign material following a novel by Russell Banks, he has never made a richer or more profound film." *epd Film*

style makes the film resemble a fascinating mosaic. Spectators are constantly made aware that they are seeing only one of many possible truths, as Egoyan could just as easily have assembled the pieces of the mosaic in quite a different way.

The movie is beautiful to watch, with fantastic tableaux and pictures of great depth. It avoids being overly weepy despite the emotional theme. It ends with the optimistic hope of a sweet hereafter, where people will live together in peace. That place is where the Pied Piper of Hamelin led the children of the town. As it says in the Robert Browning poem which runs through the movie like a leitmotif: "a wondrous portal opened wide, as if a cavern was suddenly hollowed / And the Piper advanced and the children followed / And when all were in at the very last / The door in the mountain-side shut fast." *The Sweet Hereafter* is a modern version of the old tale, but there is more than one piper: the bus driver, who collects children like berries, Nicole's father, who abuses his daughter, and the lawyer who lures the parents with sweet promises of money and divides the community in two. They are all part of a society where the space available for children to be children seems to get smaller and smaller.

Egoyan's film gives no answers but it raises questions long after the curtain in the cinema has fallen. NM

ATOM EGOYAN Atom Egoyan makes movies about pictures: about the pictures from his characters' memories and about pictures from the media, made by video or film cameras. Above all he works with the pictures we have of ourselves, which we use to form our identities. Atom's Armenian parents chose his unusual name as he was born in 1960, the year in which the first Egyptian nuclear power station became operational. Soon the family of artists moved to Canada, where Egoyan studied politics and classical guitar. He became one of Canada's most important filmmakers after *Speaking Parts* (1989). His subsequent movies *The Adjuster* (1991), *Calendar* (1993) and *Exotica* (1994) were well received by the critics but didn't necessarily reach a wide public. This changed with *The Sweet Hereafter* (1997) and the thriller *Felicia's Journey* (1999), where Egoyan turned away from purely intellectual cinema to psychological narrative cinema. He is married to the actress Arsinée Khanjian who appears in most of his films.

---

1 Ian Holm is outstanding in the role of angry attorney Mitchell Stephens. He stepped in at the last minute for Donald Sutherland, who was originally intended for the main part.

2 The school bus never reaches its destination: it skids off the road at the next bend and drags 14 children down to their death.

3 Nicole (Sarah Polley) survives the accident. The decision to bring charges or not all rests on her testimony.

4 A movie image like a painting. The idyll of the sleeping family represents peace and harmony, but also denotes the transitory nature of things.

5 By day Nicole's father (Tom McCamus) supports his daughter's appearances as a folk singer. By night he forces his affections upon her in the hay.

6 In Egoyan's film, the hereafter is the Promised Land, a place of transcendence. To reach the light, Nicole has only one option: to tell a lie.

AS GOOD AS IT GETS

1997 - USA - 138 MIN. - ROMANTIC COMEDY

DIRECTOR JAMES L. BROOKS (*1940)

SCREENPLAY JAMES L. BROOKS, MARK ANDRUS based on a story by MARK ANDRUS **DIRECTOR OF PHOTOGRAPHY** JOHN BAILEY

MUSIC HANS ZIMMER **PRODUCTION** JAMES L. BROOKS, BRIDGET JOHNSON, KRISTI ZEA for GRACIE FILM, TRISTAR.

STARRING JACK NICHOLSON (Melvin Udall), HELEN HUNT (Carol Connelly), GREG KINNEAR (Simon Bishop), CUBA GOODING JR. (Frank Sachs), SHIRLEY KNIGHT (Beverly), SKEET ULRICH (Vincent), JESSE JAMES (Spencer), HAROLD RAMIS (Dr Martin Bettes), LAWRENCE KASDAN (Dr Green), TODD SOLONDZ (man in bus).

ACADEMY AWARDS 1998 OSCARS for BEST ACTRESS (Helen Hunt) and BEST ACTOR (Jack Nicholson).

"You don't love anything, Mr. Udall!"

Melvin Udall (Jack Nicholson) is eccentric, selfish, and irritating- an embittered misanthrope who tyrannises and terrorises those around him. It's hard to believe that he made his fortune writing syrupy romantic novels. When an enthusiastic fan asks him how he manages to describe women so well, he hesitates for a second and answers, "I think of a man. Then I take away reason and accountability."

We make his acquaintance as he sends the dwarf pinscher owned by his gay neighbour Simon (Greg Kinnear) out into the world by shoving it down the garbage chute. His heartfelt farewell is a piece of cynical advice: "This is New York. If you can make it here you can make it anywhere." When Melvin is at home, he barricades himself behind a battery of door locks. When he goes out, he makes sure never to step on the cracks between the paving stones. And when he eats in his favourite café, he brings his own plastic cutlery. The waitress Carol (Helen Hunt) is the only person at all willing to serve the quarrelsome guest and to put up with his abuse. When Simon is beaten up by a gang of burglars so badly that he has to go into hospital, it falls to Melvin of all people to take care of Verdell, his beloved dog. At first the little beast drives hygiene-obsessed Melvin to distraction, but slowly it manages to conquer his lonely heart. With astonishing results: Melvin, whose knowledge of love until now was purely theoretical, actually starts to fall in love with single mother Carol …

No, it really doesn't get any better than this!

Jack Nicholson, the man with the diabolical grin and Hollywood's most arched eyebrows, delivers the insults with such bravura and self-irony that his portrayal of the grumbling anti-hero made its way not only into the hearts of the public, it also earned him an Oscar and a Golden Globe. As did the performance of his partner Helen Hunt, who as the snappy waitress matches his bitchy quips blow for blow. She counters Melvin's insults with the speed and accuracy of a machine gun: "When I saw you when you first came into breakfast, I thought you were handsome", she explains, and then pauses in barely perceptible melodramatic fashion before sending a sharp look in his direction. She delivers the punch line with dryness and charm: "Then, of course, you spoke." That hits home! Hunt had to struggle to secure the role in this feel-good Beauty and the Beast movie, which, after the sit-com *Mad About You* and the disaster Blockbuster *Twister* (1996) gave her her big breakthrough. Veteran director James L. Brooks (*Terms of Endearment* 1983) initially had the charmingly pert Holly Hunter in mind, as she had already shone in his media satire *Broadcast News* (1987). But that plan broke down over her salary demands. Clearly it wasn't quite so hard for Brooks to persuade other prominent personalities to step in front of the camera: cameo appearances by cult directors Harold Ramis, Lawrence Kasdan and Todd Solondz put the finishing touches to this enchanting mixture of romantic comedy and biting social satire.

AK

1 She has the potential to play the blonde bomb-
shell, but Helen Hunt generally feels more at
home in the role of the homely girl-next-door.
Here she plays waitress and single mum Carol
Connelly.

2 Misanthrope Melvin Udall, grimly fighting his way
through the jungle of the metropolis: a showpiece
role for Hollywood veteran Jack Nicholson.

3 With his hatred of dogs, Udall proves a worthy fol-
lower of W. C. Fields, who once declared: "Anyone
who hates small dogs and children can't be all
bad."

"The cascades of words and succinct punch-lines of this film make you realise the amount of impoverished dialogue that contemporary comedy usually fobs you off with."

Abendzeitung

4   Enemies can become friends – in spite of the age difference there is a real spark between Carol and Melvin.

5   Greg Kinnear as Simon, the gay painter who is beaten up by a gang and forced to rely on his horrible neighbour for help.

6   When health is a matter of money: Carol's son Spencer (Jesse James) can only get the best medical care with Udall's financial support.

HELEN HUNT   From the age of six, Oscar award winner Helen Hunt only ever wanted to be an actress. The daughter of director Gordon Hunt was born in California in 1963, and already at the age of nine had her first role in a television film (*Pioneer Woman*). In 1986, she came to the attention of a broader public playing the daughter of Kathleen Turner and Nicolas Cage in *Peggy Sue Got Married*. In the successful sitcom *Mad About You*, Hunt was not only brilliant as the newly wed wife, but also acted as producer, and occasionally took on the direction. Her first international breakthrough came with Jan de Bont's disaster film *Twister* (1996). Since then "the hardest working girl in show biz" (according to fellow actor Eric Stoltz) has celebrated one hit film after another, playing alongside the likes of Kevin Spacey (*Pay it Forward*), Mel Gibson (*What Women Want*, 2000), and Tom Hanks (*Castaway*, 2000).

THE CELEBRATION
Festen (Dogme 1)

1998 - DENMARK - 106 MIN. - DRAMA

DIRECTOR THOMAS VINTERBERG (*1969)
SCREENPLAY THOMAS VINTERBERG, MOGENS RUKOV DIRECTOR OF PHOTOGRAPHY ANTHONY DOD MANTLE MUSIC MORTEN HOLM
PRODUCTION BRIGITTE HALD, MORTEN KAUFMANN for NIMBUS FILM.

STARRING ULRICH THOMSEN (Christian), THOMAS BO LARSEN (Michael), PAPRIKA STEEN (Helene), HENNING MORITZEN (Helge), BIRTHE NEUMANN (the mother), TRINE DYRHOLM (Pia), HELLE DOLLERIS (Mette), BJARNE HENRIKSEN (Chef), GBATOKAI DAKINAH (Gbatokai), KLAUS BONDAM (Master of Ceremonies), THOMAS VINTERBERG (Taxi Driver), JOHN BOAS (Grandfather).

IFF CANNES 1998 SPECIAL JURY PRIZE.

"Here's to the man who killed my sister, a toast to a murderer."

A dogma is a religious teaching or a doctrine of belief. When four Danes got together to draw up ten commandments in 1995, baptised them "Dogme 95" and described them as a cinematic vow of chastity, it seemed a bizarre act of self-chastisement in a post-ideological age. Perhaps, critics suggested, the whole thing was a bid for freedom at a time of computer animation and post-modern indifference. They wanted to do away with all the trappings of technology and to get back to the basics: strict classical form following crazy, ornate Baroque. Perhaps, the sceptics replied, it was nothing more than a publicity stunt: Tarantino meets *It's A Wonderful Life*.

Nobody could have guessed at that point that the same four Danes would go on to open an agency that watches over the keeping of the commandments and distributes certificates. By the beginning of 2001 a dozen films had been adjudged worthy to promote themselves as "produced in accordance with the rules of the Dogme Manifesto". Both the manifesto and the certification process are inspired by deadly seriousness tempered with a certain dose of ironic humour, and certificates can cost anything from nothing at all to 2000 dollars, according to the budget of the film in question. One of the signatories, Thomas Vinterberg, director of the first brilliant Dogme film *The Celebration*, admitted in an interview that the whole thing oscillates between being "a game and in deadly earnest".

That is also a good description of *The Celebration*'s relationship to its subject matter: whenever viewers attempt to look at it purely as a comedy or solely as drama, it is guaranteed to topple over into the opposite. Drama and comedy are most likely to meet at their extremes. *The Celebration* is not exactly a black comedy, more a bitter reckoning with the deceptive façade of the institution of family life. The best ideas often come from a new look at traditional models and the movie's departure point is very simple: patriarch Helge (Henning Moritzen) is celebrating his 60th birthday with his family at a country mansion. The party turns into a night of grim revelations and innumerable skeletons are dragged out of the family closet.

Basically, the film is about the accusations of the oldest son Christian (Ulrich Thomsen). He claims that he and his twin sister were abused by their father, and that this was the reason for his sister's recent suicide. After a shocked pause, the guests return to the festivities as if nothing had happened. At first, Christian's repeated accusations are received with the same equanimity as the table speeches of Grandfather (John Boas) who always tells the same anecdote. Later his mother (Birthe Neumann) attempts to smooth over the situation and finally his hot-tempered youngest brother Michael (Thomas Bo Larsen) explodes. It takes a message from the next world to convince those present of Christian's story.

The Discreet Charm of the Dogme Commandments

Some critics consider the Dogme commandments to be a self-important waste of time, but the rules for the use of natural sound and hand-held cameras result in films that look like home movies, giving a picture and sound quality which contributes greatly to the believability of their story lines. At first sight, high-resolution video shot without artificial light and transferred onto 35mm looks like an amateur recording of a private birthday party. The unusual, often underexposed or unfocused pictures force the audience to concentrate. Like a source of purity and liberation, they contrast with the family's repression of the party's shocking revelations. The Dogme films' rejection of skilfully produced, artificial images gives them a feeling of undiluted directness and a whole new pallet of expressive means. This is the attack of the documentary hand-held camera on the bastion of the feature film – direct cinema as a presentation of the truth in fiction.

Once spectators get used to the grainy, wobbly pictures, which have quite a different beauty from polished Hollywood pictures, the movie itself is highly coherent both visually and dramatically. The camera angles have been chosen with extreme care: there is a bird's eye view from the corner of the room, a jump shot over a fence and a camera hidden behind the banisters. Furniture or objects often obstruct the camera's viewfinder. There are two possible interpretations of this: firstly, a blocked viewpoint implies that the place of filming is treated spontaneously and that potential obstacles are dealt with as they arise. Secondly, obscured viewpoints give the movie a documentary feel, as if the camera were a hidden witness or a passer-by.

1   The patriarch Helge shortly before his fall from power: Henning Moritzen, Birthe Neumann.

2   Michael (Thomas Bo Larsen) lets himself be waited on by his ex-lover (Birgitte Simonsen).

3   "When my sister died a couple of months ago, it became clear to me that with all the baths he took, Helge was a very clean man." Christian (Ulrich Thomsen) accuses his father.

4   Chopped-off heads, blurred images and natural lighting – camera technique applying the Dogme 95 resolutions.

5   Two brothers still fighting for their father's favour: Christian is thrown out of the house at the instigation of his younger brother Michael.

he plot follows the classic division in three acts with Christian as the hero and focal point overcoming opposition and obstacles. At the beginning he only has the support of the hotel staff who have known him since he was little, like the chef Kim, who spirits away the guests' keys so that they are isolated in the country house like the guests in Buñuel's *The Exterminating Angel* (*El angel exterminador*, 1962). But Mexico or Denmark, 1962 or 1998, bourgeois charm is revealed to be nothing but a veneer of civilisation that peels away all too easily.

With great intensity and directness, Vinterberg and his actors show how the respectable bourgeois atmosphere is rapidly transformed into hate-filled racism, how finally the aggressive brother Michael changes sides and erupts against his father instead of shouting at his wife and children, his sister's black boyfriend and his brother. The abyss in *The Celebration* lurks just below the surface: the official face of the family only just manages to con-

cear the grimace behind it. Vinterberg is so committed and uncompromising he almost seems like a descendent of the iconoclasts of the '68 generation

Vinterberg grew up in a hippy commune. In interviews, he often point out that the Catholic terminology of the Dogme Manifesto came from co-signatory Lars von Trier and has nothing to do with him. He prefers the communist component implicit in the word "Manifesto". To him, this artistic manifesto is also a compelling call to revolt, a return to the basics of collective filmmaking and an appeal for the rejection of production hierarchies, so as a protest against the cult of the auteur, the director's name is not allowed to appear on the film. The aim above all is to reclaim film from the spirit of postmodernism. Dogma means nothing less than forgetting everything you've already seen and done, beginning again from the beginning, and reinventing cinema. Vinterberg is still filled with awe and wonder in the face of "living pictures" and he shares this with his audience.　　　MI

DOGME 95

1. Shooting must be done on location. Props and sets must not be brought in. **2.** The sound must never be produced apart from the images or vice versa. **3.** The camera must be hand-held. **4.** The film must be in colour. Special lighting is not acceptable. (If there is too little light for exposure the scene must be cut or a single lamp be attached to the camera) **5.** Optical work and filters are forbidden. **6.** The film must not contain superficial action. (Murders, weapons, etc. must not occur.) **7.** Temporal and geographical alienation are forbidden. (That is to say that the film takes place here and now.) **8.** Genre movies are not acceptable. **9.** The film format must be Academy 35mm. **10.** The director must not be credited.

"Something terrible happens and everyone says, 'Let's have another cup of coffee, let's sing a song and have a dance'. That is typical of the Danes."

Thomas Vinterberg in: Zoom

RUN LOLA RUN
Lola rennt

1998 - GERMANY - 79 MIN. - LOVE FILM, ACTION FILM

DIRECTOR TOM TYKWER (*1965)
SCREENPLAY TOM TYKWER **DIRECTOR OF PHOTOGRAPHY** FRANK GRIEBE **MUSIC** TOM TYKWER, JOHNNY KLIMEK, REINHOLD HEIL
PRODUCTION STEFAN ARNDT for X FILME CREATIVE POOL, ARTE, WDR.

STARRING FRANKA POTENTE (Lola), MORITZ BLEIBTREU (Manni), HERBERT KNAUP (Lola's father), ARMIN ROHDE (Mr Schuster), JOACHIM KRÓL (Norbert von Au – Bum), HEINO FERCH (Ronnie), NINA PETRI (Jutta Hansen), SUZANNE VON BORSODY (Mrs Jäger), LARS RUDOLPH (Kassierer Kruse), SEBASTIAN SCHIPPER (Mike).

"Ball's round. Game lasts 90 minutes. I can follow that much. All the rest is just theory."

Tom Tykwer's first films caused a stir – his elegiac debut *Deadly Maria* (*Die tödliche Maria*, 1993) and the prize-winning *Wintersleepers* (*Winterschläfer*, 1997), although naturally the interest came more from critics and impassioned art house fans than it did from the general public. *Run Lola Run* came as a surprise in every respect. Its content is as complex as his previous film, the mournful, difficult melodrama *Wintersleepers*, but formally it is exactly the opposite with its hip, contemporary look. It combines classic means of expression such as split screen, slow motion, time lapse and animated sequences with a modern pop video aesthetic resulting in some impressive visual fireworks. Those visuals are complimented by Franka Potente and Moritz Bleibtreu, its fresh, cool, attractive young stars, but above all by its speed. *Run Lola Run* is a throwback to the childish enthusiasm inspired by the earliest cinema pictures, the simplest of all film images: a person in motion.

It's high-speed cinema. Tykwer's movie is literally a running film, and spectators are carried along with it through the streets of Berlin, where Lola (Franka Potente) races panting over the asphalt and cobblestones, over bridges, building sites and squares, puffing and gasping but determined, driven on by the pumping techno soundtrack. The movie was also a welcome surprise where the image of German films abroad was concerned. Humour is difficult to translate, and while domestic German cinema had turned out some excellent relationship comedies like *Maybe … Maybe Not* (1994) in the 90s, they had never really made it abroad. *Lola* on the other hand ran not only all over German cinema screens but was also invited to international festivals such as Venice and Sundance.

Hers is a race against time, for love: Lola has 20 minutes to find 100,000 marks. That's the amount of money that her boyfriend Manni (Moritz Bleibtreu) has lost in the subway – money which actually belonged to the gangster boss Ronnie (Heino Ferch), and if Manni doesn't deliver the sum on the dot of 12, he's a dead man – "it's as simple as that". And so Lola runs through Berlin, first to her father, who is a bank director, then to meet Manni, who is threatening to rob a supermarket.

Run Lola Run is physical, dynamic, speed-dominated action cinema. With her fire-red shock of hair, Lola runs like the Pippi Longstocking of the ecstasy generation. "I make the world how I like it …" she seems to say, and Lola's streets are empty and wide. Anyone who knows Berlin soon realises

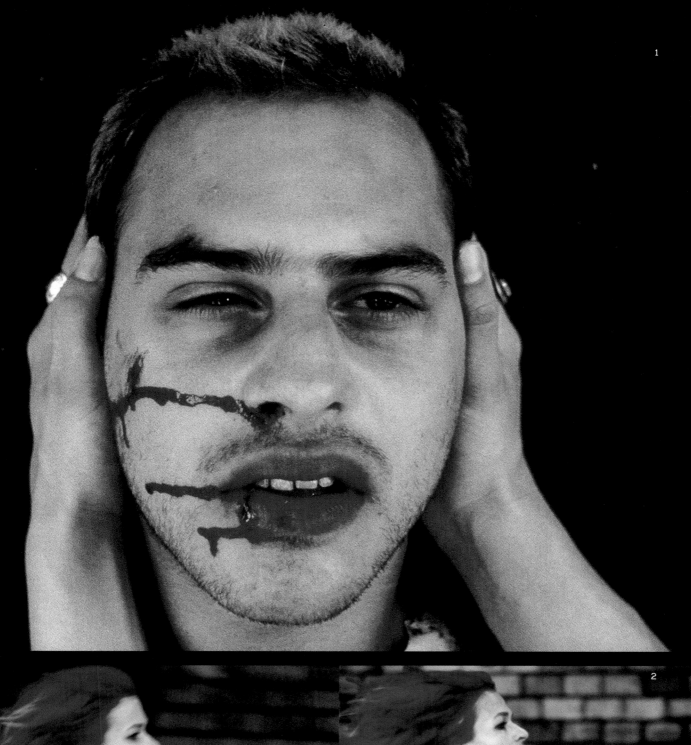

1

2

3

4

1 After *Knockin' on Heaven's Door* Moritz Bleibtreu's role as Manni in *Run Lola Run* finally made him a star.

2 79 minutes of speed, 79 minutes of life in the fast lane: Franka Potente as Lola.

3 On a narrative and visual level, *Run Lola Run* is a sophisticated play of displacements, duplications, about-turns and mirror-images.

4 The film slackens its pace for a few moments during conversations about love.

5 German heart-throb Heino Ferch, barely recognisable as shaven-headed gang leader Ronnie.

6 Lola's costume, a city brat outfit representing something near permanence in the metropolitan jungle with boots, combat trousers and vest quickly found a place in the Berlin Film Museum.

DIGITAL PICTURES   With the development of the computer, a completely new realm of possibilities opened up for Special Effects experts. Pictures scanned into the computer can be changed at will – whether it is to delete a price label left on a coffee cup by mistake, or to integrate actors with pictures of historical personalities as in Robert Zemeckis' *Forrest Gump* (1994) or to save an army of extras by copying digital pictures as in Wolfgang Petersen's *In the Line of Fire* (1993) and Ridley Scott's *Gladiator* (2000). CGI (Computer Generated Images) open up an entire new dimension of trick techniques. Pictures can now be created completely in the computer without needing initial photographs or drawings, and can then be combined with live action pictures. This is how the dinosaurs were created for Steven Spielberg's *Jurassic Park* (1993).

---

that the routes she runs have nothing to do with the real geography of the city. But that's not just an error, for *Run Lola Run* is also a philosophical film, an illustration of chaos theory, a hypothetical game of "what if …". Lola sets off three times to save Manni, in three lots of twenty minutes. Her way across town is different every time, according to how she reacts to the dog that snarls at her in the stairwell of her apartment building. Does she jump over it? Is she momentarily frightened? Or does the child with the dog stick a leg out and trip her up? Every second won or lost in leaving the house changes her own fate and that of many others. The first time Lola bursts into her father's office to discover him embracing his lover, the second time he has just discovered that she is pregnant, and a third time it becomes clear that the child is not his. One time Lola dies, another time Manni dies and there is one happy ending. This game with destiny, with possibilities, options and their effects on time and space is also played on an emotional level in the few quiet moments of the movie. Manni and Lola lie in bed together and talk like Valentine's Day cards, asking "Well, do you love me or not?". Spectators immediately identify with the dialogues – Manni wants to find out whether Lola would still love him if he were dead, or if she met someone else or if she didn't even know that he existed.

AK

"This image of the running woman contains everything: despair, emotion, dynamism — all the reasons why you actually wanted to make films ..."

Tom Tykwer in: Süddeutsche Zeitung

THE TRUMAN SHOW

1998 - USA - 103 MIN. - SCIENCE FICTION, DRAMA

DIRECTOR PETER WEIR (*1944)
SCREENPLAY ANDREW NICCOL DIRECTOR OF PHOTOGRAPHY PETER BIZIOU MUSIC PHILIP GLASS, BURKHART DALLWITZ PRODUCTION EDWARD S. FELDMAN, ANDREW NICCOL, SCOTT RUDIN, ADAM SCHROEDER for PARAMOUNT PICTURES.

STARRING JIM CARREY (Truman Burbank), ED HARRIS (Christof), LAURA LINNEY (Meryl Burbank/Hanna Gill), NOAH EMMERICH (Marlon/Louis Coltrane), NATASCHA MCELHONE (Lauren Garland/Sylvia), HOLLAND TAYLOR (Angela Burbank, Truman's mother), BRIAN DELATE (Kirk Burbank, Truman's father).

"We accept the reality of the world with which we are presented."

During our childhood, we often have the impression that world around us was made solely for our benefit. This makes it all the more depressing when things happen to make us realise that this is not the case. Film and television have made it their task over the last hundred years to try and console us for the loss of this naive notion. It sounds like an absurd idea, but what if the world really did revolve around us? What would happen if we found out? George Orwell's fictional Big Brother in his futuristic novel *1984* was the first to make us suspicious, but now reality TV shows like "Big Brother" have confirmed that we are both observing and observed, guinea pigs in an experimental labyrinth watching other animals try to find their way around. When Truman Burbank (Jim Carrey) finds that a spotlight has fallen out of the sky and landed at his feet, that amusing yet horrifying process of realisation begins for him.

In Peter Weir's media parable *The Truman Show*, the life of Truman Bank, the main character, has been organised like an enormous soap opera that has millions glued to their screens every day – and Truman is the only person who knows nothing about it. Since his birth 30 years ago his life has taken place in a kind of TV test-tube, in a huge production hall where no expense is spared to create the realistic effects that make up his world. What appears outside on the screen as fiction is grotesque reality inside, the result of the production crew's hard work. Outside nobody needs to worry about that, as they make their money out of Truman's life and his emotions. Truman

is totally financed by advertising. He is a merchandising concept, exposed without mercy, available round the clock, a genuine 24-hours a day, seven days a week star. The idea is the life's work of Christof (Ed Harris), the genius producer of the "Truman Show".

Without Jim Carrey in the role of Truman Burbank, it might have been a much more cynical movie. Truman's smooth and superficial world is beginning to crack under the strain of too much product placement and over-perfection. Carrey's comic genius saves us – luckily, some might say – from too many worrying insights. In the synthetic television world of his own show Truman is a charmingly innocent insurance agent, who wants nothing more than to relax after a stressful day at the office, and one day, to travel to the far-away Fiji islands. But that is absolutely impossible, for reasons of which he is unaware – in reality he is the prisoner of a mass media spectacle. The entire production team spends all its time trying to distract him from this thought, either with faked traffic jams or posters which warn against long journeys or discouraging travel agents.

The production team of the "Truman Show" tends to Truman's every need, every second of the day. But as the system gets bigger it becomes increasingly difficult to control. Then Truman sees a homeless bum, and he suddenly recognises his father. A flashback explains that Truman had always believed his father to have died in a tragic accident at sea when he was still a child, and this new revelation brings his world crashing down around him.

2

1 Friendly, cheerful and a bit backward: Truman Burbank (Jim Carrey) is half Forrest Gump, half Jerry Lewis.

2 The real world as a real whirl of merchandise: attractively packaged promises of happiness, shown off by a friendly nurse (Laura Linney).

3 Can Truman really trust his friend Marlon (Noah Emmerich)?

"Truman Burbank, the 'true man' from Burbank, the place in California where all the big studios are based, is completely normal, authentic down to the smallest detail, and famous the world over." *Frankfurter Allgemeine Zeitung*

JIM CARREY His performances are reminiscent of another great comedian and clown of American cinema: Jerry Lewis. Like Lewis, Carrey, who was born in Canada in 1962, favours a crazy, exaggerated physical style of comedy. The distinguishing features of Carrey's appearances are an enormous grin and his penchant for bizarre characters and zany pranks. After appearing in the television comedy *In Living Color* (1990), Carrey became famous as the title character in the surprise hit *Ace Ventura, Pet Detective* (1993) which made over 100 million dollars. His next two movies were the equally successful *Dumb & Dumber* (1994) and *The Mask* (1994). Extrovert and multitalented, he has conquered American mainstream cinema over recent years like no other. In *The Truman Show* he turned his hand to serious acting – without of course completely suppressing his comic talent – and proved his dramatic abilities. Carrey's most recent movie is Ron Howard's *The Grinch* (2000).

4

5

"In an age where the mass media of television and film are exploiting their very own simulation strategies and how these relate to 'reality' with wavering quality, we were crying out for a satire on these media." *epd Film*

ON AIR

TRUMAN HOUSE

4 A god of artifice: director Christof (Ed Harris) as creator and supreme father of the world.

5 Television-style TLC.

6 The view in the mirror: who is watching whom?

He is the main character in a perfect illusion that is shattered by one of its own elementary principles, repetition. The same actor is hired to play the homeless man as played by his father in his fake yet traumatic childhood memories. Additional goofs mount up: spotlights repeatedly fall from the sky, it only rains where Truman happens to be, stage directions are broadcast on the radio by mistake and passers-by and cars move at implausibly regular intervals along the same trajectories. The movie cleverly combines ironic humour and important truths. The pictures of Truman's life are framed by iris patterns that constantly remind us of the secret observers, the voyeuristic gaze of the hidden camera which registers Truman's every move with no less than 5000 lenses.

Luckily, however, there is a limit to this entertaining yet deeply disturbing scenario. When Truman tries to escape from his home on Seahaven Island in a sailing dinghy, he crashes into the painted horizon on the scenery wall and both audiences breathe a sigh of relief. Life as a cliché in a cliché comes to a – happy – end here in the literal sense of the word. BR

THE THIN RED LINE

1998 - USA - 170 MIN. - WAR FILM

DIRECTOR TERRENCE MALICK (*1943)
SCREENPLAY TERRENCE MALICK, based on the novel of the same name by JAMES JONES DIRECTOR OF PHOTOGRAPHY JOHN TOLL
MUSIC HANS ZIMMER PRODUCTION ROBERT MICHAEL GEISLER, GRANT HILL, JOHN ROBERDEAU for PHOENIX, GEISLER-ROBERDEAU-PRODUCTIONS.

STARRING SEAN PENN (First Sgt. Edward Welsh), ADRIEN BRODY (Corp. Fife), JIM CAVIEZEL (Priv. Witt), BEN CHAPLIN (Priv. Jack Bell), GEORGE CLOONEY (Capt. Charles Bosche), JOHN CUSACK (Capt. John Gaff), WOODY HARRELSON (Sgt. Keck), ELIAS KOTEAS (Capt. James Staros), NICK NOLTE (Col. Gordon Tall), JOHN TRAVOLTA (Brig. Gen. Quintard).

IFF BERLIN 1999 GOLDEN BEAR, SPECIAL COMMENDATION for CINEMATOGRAPHY (John Toll).

"Is there an avenging power in nature?"

War movies are characterised by much more than their own iconography, and aren't limited to uniforms and aeroplanes, gaping wounds and amputated limbs, or helmets and weapons. They differ from other action films as they tend not to have an individual hero with a private adventure, but usually concentrate instead on a group of soldiers who have to overcome internal tensions in order to carry out a difficult mission together. This team is either played by lesser-known actors or is cast with a whole ensemble of stars, as both possibilities guarantee equality inside the team. When Hollywood outsider Terrence Malick decided to come out of a self-imposed 20-year period of seclusion by making a war movie, few expected him to stick to the established rules of the genre. The Thin Red Line did not disappoint these expectations. The movie tells the story of a group of soldiers on an island in the Pacific during the Second World War who are ordered to storm a hill held by the Japanese. The task seems simple and clearly defined, but the wider strategic importance of the battle is never really explained. At times, war doesn't seem to be the real theme of Malick's movie at all, and the many stars who grace the film seem to be tactically deployed, mere commercial calculations without whose presence no producer would have agree to finance the film.

The movie doesn't suffer from the typical dilemma of anti-war films that portray the horrors of war so brutally and graphically that it is impossible for them not to hold a certain fascination. Malick's recipe is anti-dramatisation, and a clear division into three parts which are as different as possible. It is almost as if The Thin Red Line falls apart, so different are the sections in tempo and in mood: in the first three-quarters of an hour, atmosphere is created, the characters and settings are introduced, and not one shot is fired. The main part of the film narrating the attack on the hill lasts about 75 minutes and is the part that comes closest to obeying the classic rules of plot development. The last 45 minutes are an epilogue that brings together a number of the plot strands and contains one last action sequence.

Some movies demand utter trust and self-abandonment from their audiences. They are not easy for viewers used to the standards of the typical Hollywood film, but the rewards are accordingly much higher. The Thin Red Line is one such movie. The perspective changes constantly and we are never sure who the actual main figures are – stars like Nick Nolte and Sean Penn or newcomers like Jim Caviezel and Ben Chaplin. The movie is more interested in the personal experiences of the recruits than it is in the actual fighting. Numerous narrative voices distract us from the action with philosophical thoughts that cause our mind to wander from the plot. The result is a clear refusal to conform to the conventional rules of drama, but what the movie loses in form, it wins in its freedom to illuminate different aspects of war.

"As a visual spectacle, *The Thin Red Line* meets the expectations raised by *Badlands* and *Days of Heaven*. There's no question that Malick's ability to lend depth and texture to his images is without rival in Hollywood at the moment."

Sight and Sound

War and Creation

The main part of the movie shows how the American soldiers try to conquer a hill occupied by the Japanese. The soldiers lose themselves in the waving grass of the hill: bent double, the scouts sneak forward through waist-high vegetation, half-crawling, half-running. The other soldiers watch anxiously and tensely. Shots ring out like whip-cracks in the silence. The fallen soldiers disappear into the hill like stones dropped in a pond; the hill remains as still and seemingly untouched as before. When the weapons fall silent for a moment, nothing can be heard but the soft rustling of the wind as it blows through the blades of grass, forming a constant acoustic accompaniment to the attack. Then all hell breaks loose in a maelstrom of rockets, machine guns, grenades, shots, explosions and shouts. In the midst of this commotion, a solider trips over a snake in the grass. For a split second the battle fades into the background and nature penetrates our consciousness with all her power. Again and again the movie turns away from the immediate threat in moments of danger or tension and shows colourful exotic birds, gnarled logs or the tropical tree tops with the sun shining brightly through them.

Malick contrasts the majesty of nature with the corruption of war and its culture of destruction. These diversions are not self-indulgently picturesque or irrelevant animal images, they serve to sharpen our eyes for the contrast between nature and culture and therefore also for war. There are unforgettable images, the like of which is rarely seen in other war movies, like a dying bird hit by a bullet, writhing in agony, or a native striding past a jungle patrol, who shows no sign of having seen the soldiers. Another soldier stares fascinated at a bizarrely-shaped leaf in the midst of the battle while his comrades die around him.

Unlike Steven Spielberg's *Saving Private Ryan* (1998), which was made at more or less the same time, the viewer is never told exactly why or for what the soldiers are fighting. The actors go through the movie seemingly without an aim or motivation. They retreat into the background for half an hour or so or leave the picture completely, then unexpectedly reappear. This makes them a symbol of the expendability of soldiers in war. It is therefore

1 Battle plans during a temporary lull: First Sergeant Welsh (Sean Penn), Colonel Tall (Nick Nolte) and Captain Staros (Elias Koteas).

2 Mail from home: Bell (Ben Chaplin) misses his wife, who eventually leaves him for an Air Force Captain.

3 Captain Staros, of Greek origin, refuses to send his men into a battle they have no hope of winning, bringing great trouble upon himself.

4 Staring the high casualty rate in eye. The natural surroundings so prominent in the film remain unmoved by the war.

5 An innocent paradise? Two blueprints for civilisation collide on a Pacific island (Jim Caviezel, right).

6

TERRENCE MALICK When Terrence Malick finished *Days of Heaven* in 1978, two years had passed since the end of filming. Through endless fights with the producers and Richard Gere, the movie's leading actor, the stubborn and self-willed Malick stuck to his vision. *Days* was a jealousy drama among harvesters in Texas set during World War One, and it followed his debut movie *Badlands* (1973) in which a young criminal couple flees through the deserted landscapes of Dakota and Montana. Terrence Malick, the son of an oil magnate from the south of the US, studied at Harvard and worked as a journalist for the *New Yorker* and other papers. After his first two movies, Malick moved to Paris in the 80s and 90s and made his living as an uncredited scriptwriter, before returning to the Hollywood limelight after an absence of 20 years.

"Death appears in the endless sea of green like an episode in Nature's never-ending drama."

Die Zeit

6   Facing death: Keck (Woody Harrelson) has acci-
    dentally pulled the pin from a hand grenade.

7   Commander Tall wants to capture the hill at any
    price.

8   Keck and Welsh still find something to laugh
    about.

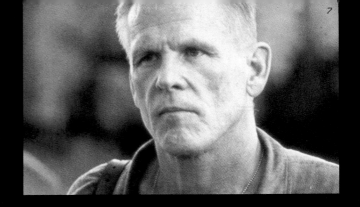

all the more surprising that famous stars agreed to be treated this way; how-ever, as with Woody Allen or Stanley Kubrick, working with Malick is a distinction for which many actors are prepared to waive their usual conditions.

John Travolta appears at the beginning of the movie for three brief minutes as a brigadier general who does little other than cast meaningful glances out to sea, and George Clooney appears in an even shorter scene at the end of the movie in a pastiche of the patriarchal "family man" who talks down to his soldiers as though they were children. Scenes filmed with Lukas Haas and Bill Pullman were later cut and the role planned for Gary Oldman never materialised.

At the end of the movie the survivors return on a battleship and we see new recruits arrive on the island. The movie may be over, but the war goes on.

Malick once again confirmed his place as a leading outsider in Hollywood with *The Thin Red Line*. By mixing chaotic images of war with sublime pictures of the natural world, he shows the ambivalence of human nature. The movie claims the right to ask questions which go beyond visible reality. Who are we, if we are capable of such utter madness, while still being able to appreciate and experience the beauties of nature?

MH

THE BIG LEBOWSKI

1998 - USA - 113 MIN. - COMEDY

DIRECTOR JOEL COEN (*1954)
SCREENPLAY JOEL COEN, ETHAN COEN DIRECTOR OF PHOTOGRAPHY ROGER DEAKINS MUSIC CARTER BURWELL, T-BONE BURNETT
PRODUCTION ETHAN COEN for WORKING TITLE PRODUCTIONS.

STARRING JEFF BRIDGES (Jeffrey "The Dude" Lebowski), JOHN GOODMAN (Walter Sobchak), JULIANNE MOORE
(Maude Lebowski), STEVE BUSCEMI (Donny), DAVID HUDDLESTON (The Big Lebowski), PETER STORMARE (Nihilist no.1),
FLEA (Nihilist no. 2), TORSTEN VOGES (Nihilist no. 3), PHILIP SEYMOUR HOFFMAN (Brandt), JOHN TURTURRO (Jesus
Quintana), SAM ELLIOTT (The Stranger), BEN GAZZARA (Jackie Treehorn).

"Quite possibly the laziest man in Los Angeles County ... which would place him high in the runnin' for laziest worldwide."

Woe betide anyone who calls him Mr Lebowski. "I'm the Dude", he insists, "so that's what you call me. That, or Duder. His Dudeness. Or El Duderino." A hairy old hippy whose nourishment consists entirely of White Russian cocktails, likes to smoke his joints in the bathtub and listens to whale calls at great length.

It's 1991. The Gulf War rages at the other end of the world, but the Dude (Jeff Bridges) is still floating in the serene intoxication of the psychedelic 70s. The centre of his life is the bowling alley where he meets his friends Walter (John Goodman) and Donny (Steve Buscemi) to prepare for the next tournament, although even there his main aim is to move as little as possible. However, these leisurely days come to an abrupt halt when some debt collectors confuse the Dude with a millionaire of the same name from Pasadena and pee on his beautiful Persian carpet as a warning. The Big Lebowski is Joel and Ethan Coen's third movie about kidnapping, following Raising Arizona (1987) and Fargo (1996); their weakness for this particular plot mechanism is because "everything can go so very wrong". Accordingly,

the Dude's life runs completely out of control when Bunny, the wife of the other Lebowski, is kidnapped. After the Dude and his bad-tempered friend, Vietnam veteran Walter, have messed up handing over the money, they suddenly find themselves involved in an absolutely impenetrable tangle of interests and are threatened by a legendary porn producer, the police and a trio of German nihilists.

Unmistakably a Coen movie, this hash-fuelled comedy is filled with quotations, hints and post-modern mannerisms. The Big Lebowski begins like a parody of the standard Western and develops into a gloriously laconic and ironic homage to the classics of hard-boiled literature. It may be a disinterested day dreamer who lopes through Los Angeles instead of a cool, hardened private detective, but the plot is just as confused as Raymond Chandler's The Big Sleep where even Philip Marlowe's creator couldn't say for sure who shot the chauffeur. At the end of The Big Lebowski nobody knows exactly what's going on, nor how the events hang together – least of all the Dude himself. The Coens are only superficially interested in estab-

lishing the logical reconstruction of a crime, they are much more interested in indulging their weakness for bizarre characters, crazy situations and sophisticated bluffs. Aspects of the movie are even reminiscent of the great musicals of the 30s, and one of its highlights is a flashy musical sequence that seems to have been choreographed by Busby Berkeley on acid. Under pressure from all sides, the happy hash dreams of the Dude give way to fearful fantasies where he ends up in a porn film being made by one of his enemies. With its characteristic top shots, the long legs of the glamour girls and its symmetrical choreography, his dream production (called "Gutterballs") looks like a down-market version of a famous Warner Bros musical from the 30s. But fear creeps into the glittering arrangement of paste jewels and feathers, Saddam Hussein grins slyly in front of a shelf of bowling shoes and the German nihilists in flaming red catsuits brandish enormous scissors and threaten to remove Lebowski's "Johnson". Apparently, according to the Coen brothers, the figure of the Dude is based on an uncle of theirs – although who knows if they're to be trusted!   AK

"The Coens have an incredible sense for the crazy spirit of the contemporary age. They can't fall short of their surreal standard, and *The Big Lebowski* casts a glimmer of nightmare comedy on life." *Neue Zürcher Zeitung*

1 "The Dude" Lebowski (Jeff Bridges): one man and his drink. A White Russian is a mixture of vodka, kahlua and cream.

2 "You said it, man. Nobody fucks with the Jesús!" – The most uptight challenger of the threesome is Jesús Quintana (John Turturro), a macho Latino dressed head to toe in purple.

3 "Losers like the Dude like hanging out at bowling alleys best. Bowling is a comfortable sport where you don't have to worry about keeping fit. We were also attracted by the design with the retro fifties and sixties feel to it." *Joel Coen*

4   When Jesús makes fun of him yet again, Walter (John Goodman) flips and pulls a gun on him. The Dude tries to calm him down, *"This is not Nam. This is bowling."*

5   Julianne Moore as the devious Maude Lebowski.

6   After his exaggerated role as the *kinda funny looking* kidnapper in *Fargo* (1996), Coen regular Steve Buscemi played Lebowski's withdrawn, almost melancholy buddy Donny.

OUT OF SIGHT

1998 - USA - 123 MIN. - GANGSTER FILM, ROMANCE

DIRECTOR STEVEN SODERBERGH (*1963)
SCREENPLAY SCOTT FRANK, based on the novel of the same name by ELMORE LEONARD DIRECTOR OF PHOTOGRAPHY ELLIOT DAVIS
MUSIC DAVID HOLMES PRODUCTION DANNY DEVITO, MICHAEL SHAMBERG, STACEY SHER for JERSEY FILMS (for UNIVERSAL).

STARRING GEORGE CLOONEY (Jack Foley), JENNIFER LOPEZ (Karen Sisco), VING RHAMES (Buddy Bragg), DON CHEADLE (Maurice "Snoopy" Miller), DENNIS FARINA (Marshal Sisco), ALBERT BROOKS (Richard Ripley), STEVE ZAHN (Glenn Michaels), LUIS GUZMÁN (Chino).

"It's like seeing someone for the first time, and you look at each other for a few seconds, and there's this kind of recognition like you both know something."

Jack Foley (George Clooney) is a smart bank robber. He doesn't need a mask or a gun. His only weapons are his intelligence, his eloquence, and above all his irresistible charm. He's just finished relieving a bank of its earnings for the day, while still managing to give the insecure teller the feeling that she's doing a great job. There's only one thing missing from his life – luck. The getaway car fails to start up, the police are closing in, and it looks like another spell in the big house for our gentleman-gangster.

U.S. Marshal Karen Sisco (Jennifer Lopez) is a smart policewoman. She's clever, pretty, stylishly dressed, and has a soft spot for cold steel weapons. No birthday present could make her happier than the Sig-Sauer 380 that her father gives her, wrapped up in an elegantly worked box, polished and glittering like a piece of expensive jewellery.

Clearly, two such contrasting types are destined to be adversaries. Except that in Hollywood, the conventions teach us that opposites attract and that the protagonists, particularly when they are cast so ostentatiously, are bound to end up in each other's arms. When Karen and Jack meet for the first time, they are not only on opposing sides of the Law, but are also quite literally separated by the trench and security fence of a prison. Jack attempts his tunnel escape from prison at the very moment that Karen is parking her car in the prison parking lot. With iron determination Karen Sisco, in a low-cut Chanel suit, loads her pump-gun, sets her sights on the escapee, and walks toward him with steady pace, tough and sexy like no

other film star of the past few years. But that irresistible appeal is of little use to Karen here, and seconds later she finds herself overpowered, tied up in the trunk of the getaway car, and face to face with Foley, her kidnapper. Their politely distanced conversation illuminated by the red-hot brake lights crackles with submerged tension and passion. And so it continues. Officially Karen trails the escaped criminal in order to arrest him, but in reality she just wants to be near him – to protect, to watch, to cherish, and to touch him. In this film, in an unusual reversal of the traditional gender clichés, it's the woman's fantasies that we watch on screen, and the man we are forced to see as a sex object. But Jack also longs to be with Karen. The nervous tension between attraction and separation, between intimacy and distance reminds us of classical stories of love between enemies like Achilles and Penthesilea. It is a drama of revelation and self-deception.

Steven Soderbergh's adaptation of Elmore Leonard's novel is an elegantly filmed and cleverly constructed collage. It doesn't tell a strictly linear story, but permanently shifts perspective by means of numerous jumps back and forth in time. The editing that results and the unsteady hand-held camera work make *Out of Sight* a cool and stylish film that doesn't make a show of its coolness. It doesn't celebrate coolness with self-conscious pomp, like Barry Sonnenfeld's *Get Shorty* (1995) or Quentin Tarantino's *Jackie Brown* (1997, based on Leonard's novel *Rum Punch*), both of which helped bring about a Leonard renaissance. Compared with their calculated precision, the

3

1   Not even a spell in jail can dim George Clooney's
    image as the "sexiest man alive".

2   Soderbergh stages the love scenes between
    police officer Karen (Jennifer Lopez) and runaway
    Jack (George Clooney) with clever chronological
    leaps.

3   As a charming womanizer Clooney is reminiscent
    of classic Hollywood's great heroes.

4   From background dancer in musicals to highly-
    paid Latin star: Jennifer Lopez has forged her
    path with determination.

5   They wanted to bring off the major coup together,
    but from the start the two gangs distrusted each
    other. Nonetheless, Jack Foley agrees to take part
    in the deal – with disastrous results …

JENNIFER LOPEZ   Jennifer Lopez is one of the few female entertainers who enjoy an equal measure of international success both as a singer and as an actress. Her
albums "On the 6" and "J.Lo." both reached the top of the U.S. Charts. She was the first Latino in cinema to break the salary barrier of a million
dollars in the title role in *Selena*, a biography of an almost mythically revered Tejano singer who was brutally murdered. Lopez was born in the Bronx
in 1970, and in her screen debut as young mother in Nava's *Mi Familia* (1995) she played a role that corresponded to her ethnic background.
Following her successes in *Anaconda* (1996), *U-Turn* (1997), *Out of Sight* and *The Cell* (2000) she joined the Hollywood mainstream with the romantic comedy *Wedding Planner* (2001). At present she commands a salary of nine million dollars, and she has well and truly "arrived".

> **"As the suavest-looking thief since Cary Grant played a cat burglar on the Riviera, Clooney stares at her meaningfully, half-smiling, as he sweet-talks his way through the crime."** *New York Times*

mannerisms of *Out of Sight* seem lighter, more playful, and almost improvised. And yet it is the more carefully staged movie as far as its overall effect is concerned.

This passionate hormone-filled thriller was a brilliant come-back for Steven Soderbergh. With *Sex, Lies and Videotape* (1989) director and scriptwriter Soderbergh became the youngest ever award winner in Cannes. The films that followed however fell below critical and market expectations. With *Out of Sight* he seemed to find his touch again, and his next two movies, *Erin Brockovich* (2000) and *Traffic* (2000) were nominated in 2001 for an Oscar in the best film category – an honour last enjoyed by Michael Curtiz in 1939. AK

4

5

HAPPINESS

1998 - USA - 134 MIN. - DRAMA

DIRECTOR TODD SOLONDZ (*1960)
SCREENPLAY TODD SOLONDZ **DIRECTOR OF PHOTOGRAPHY** MARYSE ALBERTI **MUSIC** ROBBIE KONDOR **PRODUCTION** TED HOPE, CHRISTINE VACHON for GOOD MACHINE.

STARRING JANE ADAMS (Joy Jordan), LOUISE LASSER (Mona Jordan), LARA FLYNN BOYLE (Helen Jordan), BEN GAZZARA (Lenny Jordan), DYLAN BAKER (Bill Maplewood), JARED HARRIS (Vlad), PHILIP SEYMOUR HOFFMAN (Allen), JON LOVITZ (Andy Kornbluth), JUSTIN ELVIN (Timmy Maplewood), CYNTHIA STEVENSON (Trish Maplewood), EVAN SILVERBERG (Johnny Grasso).

"I want kids that love me as much as I hated my mother."

The "pursuit of happiness" is a central element in American culture. The right of the individual to seek happiness after his own fashion is enshrined in the American Constitution. In his film, which is sarcastically entitled *Happiness*, Todd Solondz shows that this basic right does not always lead to success, and can easily end in its opposite. The film focuses on a disturbed relationship between three sisters. We are introduced to their crazy parents, who live in a kind of pensioners' theme-park, and to a host of other eccentric characters – all of whom are engaged in the pursuit of that most elusive commodity, happiness itself. What initially sounds like a cheerful social comedy ultimately reveals itself to be a cynical and nightmarish treatment of the American Dream in all its facets. The park is filled with serial killers instead of canoodling lovers, golf courses mean heart-attacks rather than relaxed recreation, and sexual delinquency replaces the suburban family idyll.

The first person we meet is Joy (Jane Adams), a lonely woman who writes songs about happiness that nobody wants to hear until her guitar is stolen by one of her lovers. She telephones her sister Helen (Lara Flynn

Boyle), who cuts her short because she's busy in bed with her body-builder boyfriend. Yet when Helen visits her other sister Trish (Cynthia Stevenson), whose model family seems – on the surface at least – to uphold the middle-class ideal, they have a venomous debate about which of the two their unloved sister Joy trusts the most. Their parent's relationship has long been a war-zone. Life is a daily battle, and normal human relations are the exception rather than the rule.

When Solondz shows us his long and carefully composed images of housing and external walls, he does this not only to characterise the lifestyles of his protagonists, but also to signal that the film is taking a look behind the scenes of this bogus bourgeois prosperity. When we peer behind the façade, things seem to be much less rosy for the middle-class people at the centre of this film.

Happiness shows a nation that is threatening to suffocate under its own neuroses. The difficult theme of child abuse, which is also treated in the film, caused huge problems for its producers and distributors, and at one

"Yes, Solondz's film is no less amusing than the best Woody Allen comedies. But it's more ambitious than that, too: it's the grave of American family values."

Le nouvel observateur

6

point *Happiness* was in danger of being boycotted throughout the United States. The sympathetic portrayal of the father who sexually abuses the friend of his eleven-year-old son had the conservative majority of Americans up in arms. What the film mercilessly reveals is the almost hysterical tendency to bring everything sexual out into the open, the disappearance of any last vestiges of shame or decency. Helen writes poems about an imaginary rape that she never suffered as a young girl. The greatest concern of Trish's son is whether he has reached sexual maturity or not, and Joy's frantic search for a boyfriend is just as pathological as Helen's promiscuity.

Whereas Solondz's first film *Welcome to the Dollhouse* (1996) shows how the pretensions of a single family are dismantled from the perspective of an eleven-year-old child, *Happiness* deconstructs the entire lifestyle of middle-class suburban America. It is no accident that Trish and Allen's son is also eleven years old. Solondz portrays childhood as a kind of anteroom to hell, where we don't yet understand what's tormenting us. Things can only get worse with sexual maturity.

MH

BEN GAZZARA   Ben Gazzara is one of those actors who has still to reach the level of fame that his talents would seem to merit. He has, however, consistently attracted the sort of directors who have never entirely capitulated to the Hollywood system. The son of Sicilian immigrants, he originally studied engineering before going on to learn acting under Erwin Piscator and at the Actors Studio. He played the suspect in Otto Preminger's *Anatomy of a Murder* (1959) and the leading roles in John Cassavetes' *Husbands* (1970) and *The Killing of a Chinese Bookie* (1976). He has always been well regarded inside the industry, but his career cooled off somewhat in the eighties. Since then he has since been rediscovered by a generation of innovative young directors including the Coen brothers (*The Big Lebowski*, 1998), Vincent Gallo (*Buffalo '66*, 1997/1998), Spike Lee (*Summer of Sam*, 1999) and Todd Solondz.

1   Three sisters: Trish (Cynthia Stevenson), her husband Bill (Dylan Baker), who has a dark secret…

2   … Joy (Jane Adams), who sings along to her guitar to cheer herself up, until she loses the instrument on a one-night-stand…

3   … and Helen (Lara Flynn Boyle), who is the successful author of allegedly autobiographical sensational fiction.

4   Imprisoned by his obsession: the paedophile psychiatrist Bill watches children playing baseball.

5   Allen (Philip Seymour Hoffman) pesters his neighbour Helen with obscene phone calls.

6   Hell comes early in Solondz's world: Johnny Grasso (Evan Silverberg) and the toilet.

BUENA VISTA SOCIAL CLUB

1998/1999 - GERMANY / USA / FRANCE / CUBA - 105 MIN. - MUSIC FILM, DOCUMENTARY

DIRECTOR WIM WENDERS (*1945)
SCREENPLAY WIM WENDERS DIRECTOR OF PHOTOGRAPHY ROBBY MÜLLER, JÖRG WIDMER, LISA RINZLER MUSIC RY COODER, BUENA VISTA SOCIAL CLUB PRODUCTION ULRICH FELSBERG, DEEPAK NAYAR for ROAD MOVIES, KINTOP PICTURES, ARTE, ICAIC.

STARRING IBRAHIM FERRER, RUBÉN GONZÁLES, ELIADES OCHOA, OMARA PORTUONDO, COMPAY SEGUNDO, PIO LEYVA, MANUEL "PUNTILLITA" LICEA, ORLANDO "CACHAÍTO" LÓPEZ, RY COODER, JOACHIM COODER.

"It's good not to have to pass the hat round anymore, but you don't forget."

Right at the beginning of the movie, we see pictures of Castro in front of the Lincoln Memorial in Washington. "David and Goliath" is the photographer's dry comment. It would be wrong however to expect *Buena Vista Social Club*, the film version of the album recorded by Ry Cooder with legendary Cuban Son musicians, to be a political movie. If the musicians portrayed are not at all concerned with material possessions, that is not because of their socialist convictions, but rather because there is only one meaning to their lives: music.

The movie came about through a series of coincidences. Producer Nick Gold and guitarist Ry Cooder had planned to record an album with African and Cuban musicians in the mid-90s, but when they arrived in Havana for the recording they found that the Africans were stuck in Paris. Since they were already in Cuba, they looked round for alternatives and got hold of numerous old Son legends. Cooder named the demo tape of this session

after the legendary "Buena Vista" dance club of the 40s and 50s, and gave it to his old friend Wim Wenders. Cooder had previously written the music for two Wenders movies, *Paris, Texas* (1984) and *The End of Violence* (1997). Before the actual boom took off, Wenders accompanied Cooder to Cuba on a trip to record Ibrahim Ferrer's solo album and also filmed the only concerts the Buena Vista Social Club performed together, in the Carré Theatre in Amsterdam and New York's Carnegie Hall.

The Buena Vista Social Club ensemble did not exist before its one and only album and after these concerts, it will in all probability cease to exist. The musicians of the all-star project of popular Cuban music of past decades already knew each other well, but it was the first time they had played together in this combination. Most of them already had successful solo careers. We get to know and love many of them in the movie: the die-hard philanderer Compay Segundo, who at 90 has fathered five children and, as

1   Ry Cooder and his son Joachim (in the back-
    ground) got the Buena Vista Social Club musicians
    together and set the ball rolling for one of the
    most astounding success stories in all Cuban
    music.

2   A line-up of old men: the Buena Vista Social Club
    takes the audience's applause.

3   Guitarist Eliades Ochoa accompanies Omara
    Portuondo singing "Dos Gardenias para ti", her
    duet with Ibrahim Ferrer.

4   A triumphal reception in the heart of the USA:
    standing ovations from the New York audience in
    Carnegie Hall.

5   Director Wim Wenders described the dilapidated
    charm of Havanna as a "submerged city of the
    future".

CONCERT MOVIES   The US film maker D. A. Pennebaker is a veteran of music documentary films, having begun with the movie *Don't Look Back* about Bob Dylan's
1965 England tour. Two years later, he filmed a predecessor of the legendary Woodstock concert, *Monterey Pop*, for posterity. The years that followed saw what are perhaps still the best-know "rockumentaries" ever: *Woodstock* (1969, Michael Wadleigh), which branded the event onto the
collective memory and *Gimme Shelter* (1971, David & Albert Maysles) about a Rolling Stones concert where Hell's Angels acting as stewards kill a
black man right in front of the stage. Various other film auteurs have also tried their hand at the genre, for example Jean-Luc Godard in *One Plus
One* (1968), also about the Rolling Stones, and Martin Scorsese's *The Band* (1978), while projects such as *U2 – Rattle and Hum* (1988) or *In Bed
with Madonna* (1991) show the music industry's increasing commercialisation.

he says with a grin, is currently working on the sixth; the gifted pianist Rubén Gonzáles who for ten years did not even possess a piano and claimed he could no longer play, the amazing Ibrahim Ferrer, who had promised himself never to sing again, and the *grande dame* Omara Portuondo. Almost completely forgotten, most of the one-time music stars of Son and Bolero of the 40s, 50s and 60s were eking out a miserable existence in Havana.

Many little things remain unforgettable – Ferrer surreptitiously wiping tears of emotion from Portuondo's eyes during their concert duet; Portuondo striding through the streets of Havana, shot by Wenders in nostalgic pastel tones and filmed with all the charm of decay. She waves to some women who join in her song. The Cubans give a triumphant concert at the Carnegie Hall, stronghold of US music, and then wander through New York wondering at many things that we have long taken for granted. Gonzáles accompanies children's gymnastics and exercises in an old dance hall, and gradually draws them around his piano in a clumsy dance.

House walls display slogans like "The revolution will last for ever", but the musicians seem to have little interest in that. The audience in New York presents them with a Cuban flag at the end of their concert and they gather around it. However, even in the anti-Cuban United States, this doesn't resemble a political gesture so much as a symbol of belated recognition for these captivating performers and their beautiful music.

MH

"I came to Havana, because I wanted to let these musicians speak for themselves, since their music speaks so powerfully for itself."

Wim Wenders in: Sight and Sound

YOU'VE GOT MAIL

1998 - USA - 119 MIN. - ROMANTIC COMEDY

DIRECTOR NORA EPHRON (*1941)
SCREENPLAY NORA EPHRON, DELIA EPHRON, based on the theatre play *PARFUMERIE* by MIKLOS LASZLO and the screenplay *THE SHOP AROUND THE CORNER* by SAMSON RAPHAELSON DIRECTOR OF PHOTOGRAPHY JOHN LINDLEY MUSIC GEORGE FENTON PRODUCTION LAUREN SHULER DONNER, NORA EPHRON for LAUREN SHULER DONNER PRODUCTIONS.

STARRING TOM HANKS (Joe Fox), MEG RYAN (Kathleen Kelly), PARKER POSEY (Patricia Eden), GREG KINNEAR (Frank Navasky), JEAN STAPLETON (Birdie), DAVID CHAPPELLE (Kevin), STEVE ZAHN (George Pappas), DABNEY COLEMAN (Nelson Fox), HEATHER BURNS (Christina), JOHN RANDOLPH (Schuyler Fox).

"So much of what I see reminds me of something I read in a book, when shouldn't it be the other way around?"

It's clear from the beginning: such complete opposites just have to attract. She wears hand-knitted clothes and puts home-made ornaments on her Christmas tree, he buys designer suits and has someone else decorate his tree; she pours out human warmth, he cappuccino. But they both want to sell books. Her shop is old-fashioned and wittily named "Shop Around the Corner" after Ernst Lubitsch's clever 1940s comedy, which served as a model for *You've Got Mail*. His chain of shops on the other hand, the baddie of the piece, is called Fox – the name of the main competitors of Warner Studios who made this movie.

At the outset, none of this is important. When Joe Fox (Tom Hanks) and Kathleen Kelly (Meg Ryan) get home in the evenings, they grab their laptops and write mails to each other. For a long time they don't know that behind the pseudonyms under which they exchange poetic comments on the changing seasons and life in New York their main competitor is hiding. Conflict between them is unavoidable as Joe wants to open a book superstore right next door to Kathleen's little shop, and that is a move that is bound to ruin her. The Internet and the anonymity of e-mail as a means of communication facilitate the unprejudiced exchange of ideas, although it's hard to transfer that into everyday life, as the movie is careful to point out.

Internet pioneers believed that its revolutionary power lay in its ability to bridge gaps of nationality, colour or social status. Hollywood chooses pure love, untouched by external factors such as looks or profession. Accordingly, the movie brought the Internet into contemporary American mainstream cinema for once and for all – previously it had only ever provided material for science fiction movies such as *Johnny Mnemonic* (1995) and *The Matrix* (1999) or pessimistic global conspiracy thrillers like *Disclosure* (1994) and

1 Sleepless in New York: Joe Fox (Tom Hanks) sends e-mails under a pen-name to …

2 … Kathleen Kelly (Meg Ryan), who thinks her unknown e-mail correspondent is a romantic.

3 However, in the tough business world of Manhattan the couple are competitors, and cannot stand each other.

4 Kathleen's intellectual technophobe of a boyfriend Frank (Greg Kinnear) still writes his texts on a mechanical typewriter.

5 The romantic dream couple of the 1990s: Meg Ryan's girlish charm meets Tom Hanks' mischievous pragmatism.

ROMANTIC COMEDY From the days of Shakespeare and earlier, love has been used both to deliver material for drama and for comedies. Hollywood is also keen to exploit its commercial potential and offers us both sides of the coin in movies such as *Love Story* (1969) and *Pretty Woman* (1989). In the latter, the comedy is mostly a product of the situations in which the characters find themselves and the misunderstandings that result. *You've Got Mail* on the other hand takes a humorous look at the battle of the sexes. Often it simply is a matter of one character knowing more than the other and letting the audience in on this knowledge. In *You've Got Mail* Tom Hanks is mostly one step ahead of Meg Ryan – he knows who she is, but she doesn't know who he is. The movie's comedy and excitement is generated by this discrepancy.

> **"The star couple of the Nineties is Ryan und Hanks, and they sell the well-seasoned comedy material in attractive, contemporary e-mail packaging."** *Zoom*

The Net (1995). The internet becomes part of the plot of this romantic comedy because people type away on their keyboards, not because of events that are taking place inside the computer. Text on the monitor is shown for its content, not for its graphics. When Kathleen checks her e-mail at night in bed or Joe fails even to register the spectacular view from his office after a meeting because he is waiting for a message from her, the result is a picture of intimacy in the 90s.

Even if Hollywood is putting in a sentimental word here for the little shop round the corner, we shouldn't forget that as businesses, the big studios are much more like the Fox chain in the movie. Hollywood in the 90s is not a cosy family firm, but a profit-oriented multinational. The movie also seems a little contrived as Meg Ryan and Tom Hanks had already played a couple who find each other through modern communication methods in the extremely popular *Sleepless in Seattle* (1993). In that film it was telephones and the radio, but the name of the director and the author of the screenplay was also Nora Ephron. This latter film depends quite heavily on the practised interaction of Ryan and Hanks. She is dreamy and nervy, romantic and a little girlish, a mermaid in the shark tank of turbo capitalism; he is a successful businessman who has stayed a boy at heart. It's loving courtship as hostile takeover. The kisses come right at the very end – and bed is only for checking your e-mail.

MH

LOCK, STOCK AND TWO SMOKING BARRELS

1998 - GREAT BRITAIN - 107 MIN. - THRILLER, COMEDY

DIRECTOR GUY RITCHIE (*1968)
SCREENPLAY GUY RITCHIE DIRECTOR OF PHOTOGRAPHY TIM MAURICE-JONES MUSIC DAVID A. HUGHES, JOHN MURPHY PRODUCTION MATTHEW VAUGHN for HANDMADE FILMS LTD., STEVE TISCH CO., SKA FILMS.

STARRING JASON FLEMYNG (Tom), DEXTER FLETCHER (Soap), NICK MORAN (Eddie), JASON STATHAM (Bacon), STEVEN MACKINTOSH (Winston), VINNIE JONES (Big Chris), STING (J. D.), LENNY MCLEAN (Barry the Bapist), P. H. MORIARTY (Hatchet Harry), STEVE SWEENEY (Plank), FRANK HARPER (Dog), STEPHEN MARCUS (Nick the Greek), PETER MCNICHOLL (Little Chris), VAS BLACKWOOD (Rory Breaker), JAKE ABRAHAM (Dean), STEPHEN CALLENDER-FERRIER (Lenny), SUZY RATNER (Gloria).

"It's as kosher ... as Christmas"

Eddie (Nick Moran) is unbeatable at poker. Or at least that's what his friends think. Tom (Jason Flemyng), Bacon (Jason Statham) and Soap (Dexter Fletcher), all young crooks from London's East End, put their money together to get Eddie into Hatchet Harry's (P. H. Moriarty) poker game. The infamous gangster boss demands a minimum stake of 100,000 pounds, but a correspondingly juicy win beckons. Eddie, however, doesn't have a hope, because the game is rigged. At the end, all four players are in debt to Harry to the tune of half a million pounds. They have one week to get hold of the money, otherwise they'll lose fingers and worse. The friends come up with a crafty plan to save their skin. They set a trap for the gang of the brutal killer Dog (Frank Harper) after they have made rich pickings at a robbery. The hold-up goes off without a hitch, but for Eddie, Tom, Bacon and Soap the problems are just beginning. From now on, all the gangs in the East End are after them.

It's difficult to reduce Lock, Stock and Two Smoking Barrels to one story. Five or six plot strands weave around the actions of the four friends. Director Guy Ritchie burns them off at an absurd tempo in his debut movie only to bring them back again in an equally bravura manner. The question of

who will be the last man standing when the smoke clears at the end is not really important, for Ritchie is more concerned with madcap fun, with pouring comedy into a bloody-thirsty crime movie until it overflows. London's East End is not so much a convincing setting for a feverish gangster story as a font of ideas for a whole slew of gags, opened up by a collection of scurrilous types, outrageous plot twists and merciless repartee. Despite its local colour, the film has little in common with the traditions of typical British situation cinema, and Ritchie shows himself to be very much a director of the 90s. His characters, the aggressive humour of the dialogue and above all the complex narrative techniques of Lock, Stock and Two Smoking Barrels are clear references to the movies of Quentin Tarantino. The film's anarchic style would be equally unthinkable without Danny Boyle's pioneering Trainspotting (1996). That said, Lock, Stock and Two Smoking Barrels has its own form, influenced by Ritchie's background in music and commercials, where extreme speed, both visually and as far as the plot is concerned, is absolutely key. Long stretches of the movie closely resemble pop videos, characters are sketched in a split second, action is subordinated to the film music, and

2   3

"The movie is frolicsome but pushy, the triumph of flash over style." *Time Magazine*

classic movie mechanisms are deconstructed. The movie is characterised by an originality of form that seems to have been forced upon it by the outrageous behaviour of its protagonists.

Despite all its emphasis of the fun factor, *Lock, Stock and Two Smoking Barrels* is also a tongue-in-cheek look at the British zeitgeist of the late 90s. Eddie, Tom, Bacon and Soap are ideal heroes of Tony Blair's "New Labour" – creative working-class lads who pool their talents to further their careers.

Unfortunately, the free market soon turns out to be a shark-infested swamp where they have to swim desperately for their lives. When at the end the friends frantically reach for their mobile phones to try for their last chance, someone else has got there long before them. The only "professional" in the whole film is a merciless money collector (Vinnie Jones) who retires to become a banker.

JH

4

1 Cards on the table: Guy Ritchie's production is pure cinematic pleasure.

2 Gang leader Hatchet Harry (P. H. Moriarty) enjoys manipulating people, and plays by his own rules.

3 Classic cinema set-piece: the inevitable poker game.

4 Echoes of Tarantino: Ritchie's film is unabashed in its imitation.

5 New heroes: Soap, Eddie and Tom embody the entrepreneurial spirit of the late 1990s (Dexter Fletcher, Nick Moran, Jason Flemyng).

GANGSTER FILM Originally an American genre, the classic gangster movie tells the tale of the rise and fall of a member of a criminal organisation. The hero usually comes from a poor family, and therefore realises an illegal version of the American dream for which he must pay in the end. There were already gangster movies in the era of silent film, although their golden age really began after the introduction of sound at the beginning of the 30s in America, when the gangster became a movie hero for a public suffering under the Great Depression. The gangster movie then developed into a full-blown genre with its own conventions. Famous movies from that time include Mervin LeRoy's *Little Caesar* (1930), William Wellman's *The Public Enemy* (1931) and finally Howard Hawks' *Scarface* (1931).

THERE'S SOMETHING ABOUT MARY

1998 - USA - 119 MIN. - COMEDY

DIRECTOR PETER FARRELLY (*1957), BOBBY FARRELLY (*1958)
SCREENPLAY ED DECTER, JOHN J. STRAUSS, PETER FARRELLY, BOBBY FARRELLY DIRECTOR OF PHOTOGRAPHY MARK IRWIN
MUSIC JONATHAN RICHMAN PRODUCTION FRANK BEDDOR, MICHAEL STEINBERG, CHARLES B. WESSLER, BRADLEY THOMAS for 20TH CENTURY FOX.

STARRING CAMERON DIAZ (Mary Jensen Matthews), MATT DILLON (Pat Healy), BEN STILLER (Ted Stroehman), LEE EVANS (Tucker), CHRIS ELLIOTT (Dom Woganowski), LIN SHAYE (Magda), JEFFREY TAMBOR (Sully), MARKIE POST (Mary's mother), KEITH DAVID (Mary's father), W. EARL BROWN (Warren Jensen).

"Husband ... negative.
Children and a Labrador ... negative.
Tight little package ... affirmative."

How about this for a nightmare experience: you pick up your dream girl for the school prom, first you get beaten up by her little brother and then you get a body part so sensitive caught in your zip in her family bathroom that half of the town arrives to witness the rescue attempts by the police and the fire brigade. Perhaps this hasn't actually happened to many people, but generations have dreaded of this or similar disasters on their first date.

The Farrelly brothers have a passion for everyday visions of horror. They take the underside of the everyday life of moderately intelligent small town inhabitants with an average number of complexes, and then take them to extremes. They don't really care much whether their assortment of coarse, dirty jokes and grotesquely embarrassing situations is bearable for less hardened viewers or not.

Dumb & Dumber (1994) sounded the depths of absolute stupidity and *King Pin* (1996) dared to investigate the seedy world of American professional bowling, a world of sweaty feet and damp hotel beds. In *There's Something About Mary* the Farrellys decided to try their hand at a love story. With inevitable results: painful fishing accidents, spunk as hair gel, burning dogs, gross jokes about gynaecology and the disabled – let's face it, not

everyone will share the Farrellys' view of romance. But in the end, and this is what *Something About Mary* brings home with a vengeance, they do make us aware that the confused, impoverished and disadvantaged of this world have a love life too.

Ever since the memorable bathroom fiasco, Ted (Ben Stiller) hasn't been able to get Mary (Cameron Diaz) out of his head. Years later, his monstrous braces and bowl cut have gone, but he still has a despairing conviction that a woman like Mary could never be interested in a loser like him. Dom (Chris Elliott), his best friend, is full of useful advice, and he sends Ted off to see shady private detective Pat Healy (Matt Dillon), who sets off to find Mary and promptly falls in love with her himself.

When Ted discovers that Mary is by no means the wheelchair-bound enormously overweight woman with four children that Healy describes to put him off the scent, he screws up his courage and goes to Miami to the scene of the action to try and conquer Mary's heart. He soon comes to the unwelcome realization that her hordes of admirers are larger than he thought. Before the key issue of whether he gets the girl or not is resolved, the heavy hand of fate deals Ted some mighty blows, to the delight of sadistic viewers.

"Peter and Bobby Farrelly are Hollywood's 'bad boys' of the moment: two cunning confidence tricksters who have found their place in mainstream cinema with a mixture of catchy material and provocative disregard for taboos."

film-dienst

3

4

1. A hair-style to the taste of the Farrelly brothers: Mary (Cameron Diaz) tries out a very unusual hair gel made from purely natural ingredients.

2. Asking for trouble: the loathsome Pat Healy (Matt Dillon) thinks he knows how to win women over and see off any annoying competition.

3. With a winning smile Ted (Ben Stiller) demonstrates his stylish but passion-killing dental adornment.

4. A little kiss for mummikins: fans of the Farrellys have to have a strong stomach.

5. Terrier in plaster: the battle over Mary leaves its mark on people and animals alike.

6. Who could resist this smile? To win the beautiful Mary as their girl, her admirers will stoop to any nastiness.

CAMERON DIAZ Born in San Diego, California in 1972 as the daughter of a Cuban and a German American, Cameron Diaz left home at the age of 16 to travel the world. She spent the following five years in Japan, Australia, Mexico, Morocco and Paris. When she returned to the USA she worked as a model until she was given her first role in *The Mask* (1994) with Jim Carrey. Her natural, open way of acting instantly made her famous. Subsequent important movies are *Head Above Water* (1996) and *My Best Friend's Wedding* (1997).

There is no kind of silly joke or disgusting substance that the transparent plot is not prepared to feature, and it is mostly saved from banality by the unscrupulous womanisers Matt Dillon and the English stand-up comedian Lee Evans. That tricky task was carried out with great panache by Jim Carrey and Jeff Daniels in *Dumb & Dumber* and Woody Harrelson and Randy Quaid in *King Pin*. Part of the Farrellys' success is that high quality actors are always more than ready to work with them, even Cameron Diaz, who is as breathtakingly beautiful as ever. The music for the movie was composed by independent cinema icon Jonathan Richman. One rule seems to do for the production team and audience alike where the Farrelly brothers' movies are concerned: put aside your political correctness, good taste and common sense, and you will have loads of fun. SH

SHAKESPEARE IN LOVE

1998 - USA - 123 MIN. - LOVE FILM, COSTUME FILM

DIRECTOR JOHN MADDEN (*1949)
SCREENPLAY MARC NORMAN, TOM STOPPARD **DIRECTOR OF PHOTOGRAPHY** RICHARD GREATEX **MUSIC** STEPHEN WARBECK **PRODUCTION** DAVIT PARFIT, DONNA GIGLIOTTI, HARVEY WEINSTEIN, EDWARD ZWICK, MARC NORMAN for BEDFORD FALLS PRODUCTIONS.

STARRING JOSEPH FIENNES (William Shakespeare), GWYNETH PALTROW (Viola de Lesseps), GEOFFREY RUSH (Philip Henslowe), JUDI DENCH (Queen Elizabeth), SIMON CALLOW (Tilney), BEN AFFLECK (Ned Alleyn), COLIN FIRTH (Lord Wessex), JOE ROBERTS (John Webster), TOM WILKINSON (Hugh Fennyman), RUPERT EVERETT (Christopher Marlowe).

ACADEMY AWARDS 1999 OSCARS for BEST PICTURE, BEST ACTRESS (Gwyneth Paltrow), BEST SUPPORTING ACTRESS (Judi Dench), BEST ART DIRECTION-SET DECORATION (Martin Childs, Jill Quertier), BEST ORIGINAL SCREENPLAY (Marc Norman, Tom Stoppard), BEST COSTUMES (Sandy Powell), BEST MUSIC, category COMEDY (Stephen Warbeck).

IFF BERLIN 1999 SILVER BEAR for BEST SCREENPLAY (Marc Norman, Tom Stoppard).

"I know something of a woman in a man's profession."

Viola (Gwyneth Paltrow) loves William (Joseph Fiennes), and William loves Viola. This becomes clear relatively quickly and seems to be a good thing, but it's also where all the problems begin. For William's surname is Shakespeare, and being a writer in Elizabethan England is not a particularly respectable profession. Viola on the other hand is a member of the respectable de Lesseps family and is promised in marriage to the aristocrat Lord Wessex (Colin Firth), who may be in dire financial straits but can at least offer her a title. We understand immediately that there is going to be a conflict of interests as far as matters of the heart are concerned: but what we don't suspect are the questions of money and art.

Unfortunately, theatre owner Philip Henslowe (Geoffrey Rush) is also in dire financial straits. He is desperate for Shakespeare to finish the play he has promised Henslowe's Rose Theatre, *Romeo and Ethel – The Pirate's Daughter*, but Shakespeare is suffering from writer's block. He only overcomes it when he meets Viola, who turns up disguised as a boy – women

were not allowed to act in Shakespeare's day – to audition for the main part of Romeo. However, Lord Wessex soon gets wind of the unbecoming plans of his future wife and decides to get rid of the inconvenient and disreputable writer.

These events are mirrored in the plot of the play that Shakespeare writes during the rehearsals in the theatre. The movie's two levels are closely connected and intelligently dovetailed but never become incomprehensible, and their interaction is the driving force of the film. Art neither imitates life nor life art – the two feed off each other instead.

Against a well-researched backdrop of Elizabethan theatrical life, the plot speculates about Shakespeare's private life, which in fact remains a mystery to experts even today. The screenplay skilfully combines elements from his plays with historical fact and pure fantasy. But there's nothing dry or dusty about it, it's not only about English theatre in the 16th century but is also a radical modernisation of Shakespeare. Its authors were inspired by the

1 Writer's block, Renaissance-style: when Shakespeare (Joseph Fiennes) isn't in love, he can't write a single line.

2 All the world's a stage and we are merely players: a stage battle becomes a real skirmish.

3 Shakespeare's enigmatic object of desire: Lady Viola (Gwyneth Paltrow).

4 "Shall I compare thee to a summer's day…"

5 Always on his guard against creditors: Henslowe (Geoffrey Rush), the notorious bankrupt theatre director.

6 Gwyneth Paltrow disguised as Thomas Kent on the way to her first Oscar.

"We had 25 million dollars, not that much for a project of this size. The set was hugely expensive. We had to build not only two theatres, but also a whole district of the city from a brothel to Shakespeare's digs, behind Shepperton Studios in London." *John Madden in: Abendzeitung*

idea that if Shakespeare lived today he would be a screenplay writer and a Hollywood star, so they fill the film with comic anachronisms and quotes from other movies: Shakespeare goes to confess on the psychoanalyst's couch, Philip Henslowe is introduced in the opening sequences as a businessman with cash flow problems, and with a sharp "Follow that boat!" Shakespeare directly quotes innumerable crime movies.

Rather than allowing the movie to be dominated by opulent costumes and imagery, director John Madden gathered a first-class ensemble whose talent shines in every scene. Judi Dench may only appear in a few scenes as Queen Elizabeth, but she is all the more impressive for that. Joseph Fiennes is convincing as the bard and Gwyneth Paltrow as his muse, particularly in her breeches role. The rest of the ensemble, from Geoffrey Rush and Ben Affleck to a brief but memorable appearance from Rupert Everett as Christopher Marlowe, lend great naturalness and texture to the wonderful recreation of 1590s London.

Shakespeare in Love is intelligent and well-made entertainment cinema. It was rewarded with a shower of Oscars, not least because Hollywood was flattered to see the US film industry portrayed as the legitimate heir to Shakespeare's theatre.

MH

6

7　A queen with a natural wit: Judi Dench as Queen
　　Elizabeth, with scowling villain Lord Wessex (Colin
　　Firth).

8　Their world is the Globe Theatre, as the ill-fated
　　love of William and Viola can only exist on stage.

GWYNETH PALTROW　Some found her enchanting, others insufferable: when Gwyneth Paltrow accepted an Oscar for her performance as Viola in *Shakespeare in Love*, her voice was choked with tears. Born in Los Angeles in 1972, she quickly became famous for her roles in costume movies and literature adaptations. She earned early recognition in the historical biographies *Jefferson in Paris* (1995) and *Mrs Parker and her Vicious Circle* (1994). She played the title role in the film version of Jane Austen's *Emma* (1996) which brought her to the attention of a wider public even before she won an Oscar as Shakespeare's muse. Her penchant for literary material is also apparent in the 1997 version of Charles Dickens' *Great Expectations* and in the Patricia Highsmith adaptation *The Talented Mr Ripley* (1999).

586

"**The heterogenous mixture, a rich and satisfying pudding, works really well, (...) and changes from one mood to another with hardly any effort.**"
Sight and Sound

BLADE

1998 - USA - 120 MIN. - HORROR FILM, ACTION FILM

DIRECTOR STEPHEN NORRINGTON (*1965)
SCREENPLAY DAVID S. GOYER, based on the comics of the same name **DIRECTOR OF PHOTOGRAPHY** THEO VAN DE SANDE **MUSIC** MARK ISHAM **PRODUCTION** PETER FRANKFURT, WESLEY SNIPES, ROBERT ENGELMANN for AMEN RA FILM, IMAGINARY FORCES (for NEW LINE CINEMA).

STARRING WESLEY SNIPES (Blade), STEPHEN DORFF (Deacon Frost), KRIS KRISTOFFERSON (Whistler), N'BUSHE WRIGHT (Karen), DONAL LOGUE (Quinn), UDO KIER (Dragonetti), TRACI LORDS (Racquel), ARLY JOVER (Mercury), KEVIN PATRICK WALLS (Krieger), TIM GUINEE (Dr Curtis Webb).

"There are worse things out there than vampires."

As parents have always known, discos are dangerous places. A young man lets himself be lured by a seductive young blonde (cameo appearance by ex porn queen Traci Lords) into a secret dancing temple in the cold room at a local slaughterhouse. But this young techno party animal is in for a rude awakening: before he has a chance to wonder at the sombre expressions of his fellow dancers, the sprinkler system turns the dance-floor into a blood-bath. Our friend is surrounded by vampires. And things would get a lot worse were it not for the sudden appearance of a figure clad in black leather and a vampire-slayer's cap, who disperses the evil bloodsuckers with the help of a silver machete.

In fact, Blade (Wesley Snipes) is himself a Vampire, but only just: his mother was bitten by a vampire shortly before he was born, and therefore her son became a "Daywalker". He is gifted with supernatural powers, but doesn't have to shun the light of day. And so, with the help of the ageing vampire-hunter Whistler (Kris Kristofferson), Blade has declared war on his stepbrothers and sisters. Whistler supplies Blade with the serum that suppresses his inborn thirst for blood, but which is gradually losing its effect. During a battle in a hospital, Blade saves the life of a young haematologist

called Karen (N'Bushe Wright), who shows her gratitude by trying to develop a more effective serum.

Stephen Norrington is only marginally interested in the tragic dimension of the Blade figure from the 70s comic-strip original. Instead, the director stages his film version as a battle of the generations: Blade's arch-enemy Deacon Frost (Stephen Dorff), who is a transformed mortal himself, and therefore not a full-fledged member of the honourable batty brotherhood, rebels against the aristocracy of the hereditary bloodsuckers. These Vampire elders, with their leader Dragonetti ruling from a long conference table, are like the board of directors of a large company. Referring to principles like rank and tradition, they close their eyes to the fact that their day is over. Frost is a revolutionary who has nothing less than the globalisation of vampirism in mind, and with the help of an archaic demon he plans to transform the community of the undead into a kind of religious sect, to which human blood donors will convert of their own free will.

A generation conflict also lies at the root of the confrontation between Blade and Frost. Frost is a mixture between smart laptop-yuppie and a kind of horror-figure Robbie Williams, aptly described by one critic as a

WESLEY SNIPES

Born in 1962, Wesley Snipes grew up in the South Bronx, and is now a genuine heavyweight in the film industry. Like Arnold Schwarzenegger, though lacking Arnie's touch of self-irony, he shot and fought his way stony-faced through numerous action films like *New Jack City* (1991), *Passenger 57* (1992) and *Demolition Man* (1993). These days, it's hard to believe that he made his first appearance in the musical *Fame,* and that he originally planned a career as a dancer. It explains, however, the precision and accuracy with which he moves through even the most complicated martial arts choreography.

1 Crossing the line between life and death: Daywalker Blade (Wesley Snipes) struggles against his vampire legacy.

2 Army of darkness: although he is not born a vampire himself, Deacon Frost (Stephen Dorff, centre) wants to destroy the rule of the vampire nobility with the help of his gang.

3 Lonely warrior: because his mother was killed by a vampire, Blade has dedicated his life to the fight against the Undead.

4 After thousands of years of rule in the Underworld, the power of vampire supremo Dragonetti (Udo Kier) is under serious threat.

5 Ageing hippy on a vampire hunt: Whistler (Kris Kristofferson) stands by Blade as a fatherly friend and medicine man.

6 Pretty playmate: Frost's girlfriend Racquel (Traci Lords) is in thrall to her lord and master.

4

"*Blade* is a vagrant between worlds, an avenging angel between day and night, van Helsing as an Afro-American superhero." *epd Film*

"Generation X Dracula". Above all, the conflict between the two outcast vampires is a cultural struggle between old-school rocker and pop star – between old-fashioned righteous anger and the cool calculations of a (blood-) hungry, charismatic climber. Wesley Snipes' biker getup is in tune with this contrast, as is the Blues and Country look of bard Kris Kristofferson, who appears as a kind of ex-hippie in his supporting role as Blade's father-

ly friend and advisor, tripping out on bizarre designer drugs. The corrupt policeman who is a servant of the bloodsuckers and pays a visit to Karen in her apartment is drawn along similarly ironic lines. If we follow this line of interpretation, it is only natural to see the techno disco at the beginning of the movie as a kind of modern entrance to Hell, a sarcastic reference to the spirit of the times. SH

5

6

BLACK CAT, WHITE CAT

Chat noir, chat blanc / Crna macka, beli macor

1998 - GERMANY / FRANCE / YUGOSLAVIA - 130 MIN. - COMEDY

DIRECTOR EMIR KUSTURICA (*1955)

SCREENPLAY GORDAN MIHIC **DIRECTOR OF PHOTOGRAPHY** THIERRY ARBOGAST **MUSIC** NELLE KARAJLIC, VOGISLAV ARALICA, DEJAN SPARAVALO **PRODUCTION** KARL BAUMGARTNER for CIBY 2000, PANDORA FILM, KOMUNA, FRANCE 2 CINÉMA.

STARRING BAJRAM SEVERDZAN (Matko Destanov), SRDAN TODOROVIC (Dadan), BRANKA KATIC (Ida), FORIJAN AJDINI (Zare Destanov), LJUBICA ADZOVIC (Sujka,the grandmother), ZABIT MEMEDOV (Zarije Destanov), SABRI SULEJMANI (Grga Pitic), JASAR DESTANI (Grga Veliki), ADNAN BEKIR (Grga Mali), STOJAN SOTIROV (customs official), PREDRAG PEPI LAKOVIC (priest).

IFF VENICE 1998 SILVER LION for BEST DIRECTOR (Emir Kusturica).

"Love is still the most important thing!"

A Sinti settlement somewhere on the banks of the Danube. Matko (Bajram Severdzan) and his 17-year-old son Zare (Forijan Ajdini) bear up as best they can by trading on the black market. One day Matko decides to hold up a goods train that is loaded with petrol. He borrows the money to bribe the Bulgarian customs officer from an old godfather, whose gold teeth glitter as brightly as his mirror shades. When he lets Dadan (Srdan Todorovic) in on the raid, the gangster tricks him and Matko doesn't just lose the train, he loses the money too. Deep in the gangster's debt he has no other choice but to accept the suggestion that his son Zare marry Dadan's stunted sister, despite the fact that he is already in love with someone else. At the end however love triumphs and the unhappy wedding becomes an uproarious, joyful party where two grandfathers thought dead are resurrected, the bad guy winds up literally up to his neck in shit and two cats are the witnesses to the marriage.

Fairytales, says Emir Kusturica, are the only way to express reality today. Politicians influence our day-to-day lives so much that reality seems to have become nothing more than a power game for the people in charge. "Real" reality, on the other hand, lies beyond our daily lives, in the realm of dreams and fairytales. *Black Cat, White Cat* gives a visionary picture of this world, and it is anarchic, tough and intensely physical, a world full of absurd situations and bizarre characters. We can't believe our Hollywood-trained eyes when a white goose is used to wipe a dirty body. But once we enter the world of the film there is no escape, and it draws us in like a vortex: we meet a hefty singer who can pull nails out of a beam with her behind, a pig that eats a small car bit by bit, a gangster who juggles with hand grenades and a brass band who carry on playing even after they have all been tied to a tree.

After the controversy surrounding *Underground* (1995), it looked as Emir Kusturica would never make another movie. French and German critics made such polemical attacks on his parable about the Yugoslavian civil war that he announced he was retiring from the film business for good. Luckily, his team were able to talk him into making a portrait of the musicians from *Underground* and this gradually developed into the idea for *Black Cat, White Cat*. Filming began in late summer 1996 in Slovenia and was finished two years later, due to permanently bad weather. This patience paid off; the light that floods the pictures glows as warmly as if the Danube were the Mediterranean.

The movie's energy comes from its vital creativity and its seemingly inexhaustible flow of ideas, but also from the optimism and love of the people that it demonstrates. However much Kusturica exaggerates his characters, he never makes them ridiculous but treats them with respect and affection. The director already made an earlier declaration of love for the Sinti and their way of life, also filmed mostly with amateur actors. But the melancholy that characterized *Time of the Gypsies* (*Dom za vesanje*, 1988) is blown away by the brass band. *Black Cat, White Cat* is a vibrant comedy on the joys of life and the power of love.

NM

> "It's a mad scramble though the Felliniesque realm of Kusturica's imagination, and it proves nothing if not this much: give this man the Danube, Gypsy musicians and a camera, and you've got a party." *New York Times*

1 The wild music, a combination of traditional Balkan sounds and modern beats, originates from Emir Kusturica's band "The No Smoking Orchestra".

2 Branka Katic fizzes with pure energy as Ida. Wherever she whirls, the feathers fly.

3 The eternally broke Matko (Bajram Severdzan) borrows money from his godfather Grga (Jasar Destani).

4 Ida and Zare (Forijan Ajdini) are paired up and sold off by the old people. But they won't stand for that.

5 "Kiss me, stupid": Emir Kusturica quotes Billy Wilder and *Casablanca*.

6 Jasar Destani in his first cinema role. In real life, he works as a smelter in an iron factory.

EMIR KUSTURICA The director Emir Kusturica loves being provocative. His movies are loud and carnivalesque, populated by uncouth figures and eccentric images. He's no clown however, he's a poet of the cinema. His magical dream worlds have their roots in the history and myths of his homeland. He was born in Sarajevo in 1955 and studied at the Film Academy in Prague. Since his debut *Do You Remember Dolly Bell?* (*Sjecas li se Doli Bell?*, 1981) he has won all of Europe's important film prizes. He was awarded the Golden Palm for *When Father Was Away on Business* (*Otac na sluzbenom putu*, 1985) and *Underground* (1995), and the director's prize at Cannes for his great gypsy epic *Time of the Gypsies* (*Dom za vesanje*, 1988). His one and only American production to date, *Arizona Dream* (1992), was awarded a Berlin Bear and the Venice Film Festival gave *Black Cat, White Cat* a Silver Lion.

SAVING PRIVATE RYAN

1998 - USA - 170 MIN. - WAR FILM

DIRECTOR STEVEN SPIELBERG (*1947)

SCREENPLAY ROBERT RODAT DIRECTOR OF PHOTOGRAPHY JANUSZ KAMINSKI MUSIC JOHN WILLIAMS PRODUCTION STEVEN SPIELBERG, IAN BRUCE, MARK GORDON, GARY LEVINSOHN for AMBLIN ENTERTAINMENT, DREAMWORKS SKG, MUTUAL FILM COMPANY (for PARAMOUNT).

STARRING TOM HANKS (Captain Miller), TOM SIZEMORE (Sergeant Horvath), EDWARD BURNS (Private Reiben), BARRY PEPPER (Private Jackson), ADAM GOLDBERG (Private Mellish), VIN DIESEL (Private Caparzo), GIOVANNI RIBISI (Wade), JEREMY DAVIES (Corporal Upham), MATT DAMON (Private Ryan), TED DANSON (Captain Hamill).

ACADEMY AWARDS 1999 OSCARS for BEST DIRECTOR (Steven Spielberg), BEST CINEMATOGRAPHY (Janusz Kaminski), BEST FILM EDITING (Michael Kahn), BEST SOUND (Gary Rydstrom, Gary Summers, Andy Nelson, Ronald Judkins), BEST SOUND EFFECTS EDITING (Gary Rydstrom, Richard Hymns).

"What's the use in risking the life of the eight of us to save one guy?"

With an abrupt, muffled crack, a bullet pierces a steel helmet. Boats landing on the beach are met by salvos of machine gun fire, soldiers run into a hail of bullets. Death and blood are everywhere. One soldier is hurled into the air, his thigh is blown off, another searches for his left hand. Steven Spielberg shows D Day, the landing of the allied forces on the French Atlantic coast 6 June 1944, like something out of a horror movie that grabs the viewer with physical force. It lasts 25 almost unbearable minutes, before we cut to America, where military bureaucracy is dealing with the administration of the dead. Secretaries sit at desks and compose telegrams of condolence like a production line. Here people type, while in Europe they die. From afar the invasion is a strategic necessity, while on the beaches of Normandy, as one critic wrote, the participants experience it as a meaningless "chaos of noise, filth, blood, vomit and death". Immediately after this shocking opening, Spielberg establishes the contrast between military tactics and their practicalities, which result in nothing but undignified death.

A decision by the military leadership then introduces the actual theme of the film. During the Normandy landing three sons of the Ryan family in Iowa have died, while a fourth, James Ryan (Matt Damon), has been para-

chuted into France behind the German lines. To save mother Ryan from losing him as well, he must be sent home. The task of finding Ryan is given to Captain Miller (Tom Hanks), an experienced and reliable soldier, but a man badly affected by the burdens of the war as we see from his trembling hands. Together with a small group of soldiers – Mellish, a sniper (Adam Goldberg), Wade, a first aider (Giovanni Ribisi), and Upham, an interpreter who has no experience of war (Jeremy Davies) – he sets off to find Ryan. He finds him, and he and his troops take part in a battle over a strategically important bridge. Only one of them survives, the solider who we see in the framework of the movie, set in our times.

War movies are fraught with problems. Should the horrors be presented realistically or metaphorically? Should a director show the action on the battlefield or should he describe its consequences for the survivors? Spielberg chose a realistic mode for the opening and final sequences of this movie. They mirror each other, although the final sequence is not quite as ferocious. He filmed the opening sequence with 3000 extras in 30 days on the Irish coast, and the intensity that resulted may not be unique in modern cinema, but is certainly a rare thing. The camera mingles with the soldiers,

2

1   He hardly talks about his life back home, and his
men are not supposed to see his shaking hands.
Captain Miller (Tom Hanks) doesn't doubt the
sense of the war, but he does doubt whether he can
survive it.

2   Miller and Sergeant Horvath (Tom Sizemore, left)
have to lead their men straight towards the
German positions.

blood and filth spurt onto the lens, and the sound cuts out when we see underwater pictures of sinking corpses. The viewer is directly involved in the events and there is no option to retreat into the position of an observer.

The middle part of the movie has a more distanced narrative perspective. During his search for Ryan, Miller is busy with the arithmetic of death. He has lost 94 men, he reckons, but has saved ten or twenty times as many. A gruesome sum, but one way for the soldiers to make their daily work of death more bearable. However, another calculation seems to contradict this

logic: risking the life of eight soldiers and Miller to save one life, that of Ryan. Is that morally justifiable? Aren't they just as human as he is? Is he worth more than they are?

The movie doesn't have an answer to that question, but it does raise the issue and the characters repeatedly turn it over in their minds. And the resulting tension shows us the grisly absurdity of war perhaps more effectively than any of the realistic action scenes can.

HJK

> ## "I asked myself throughout, is this a mission of mercy or a mission of murder? But I can't answer the question. I don't think anyone can."
>
> Steven Spielberg in: *Time Magazine*

3 The American military cemetery where the film begins.

4 "Since the end of World War II and the virtual death of the western, the combat film has disintegrated into a showcase for swagger, cynicism, obscenely overblown violence and hollow, self-serving victories. Now, with stunning efficacy, Spielberg turns back the clock." *New York Times*

TOM HANKS The *New York Times* claimed that Hanks had never put his everyman qualities to better effect than in *Saving Private Ryan*. Born in 1956, Hanks is the James Stewart of the 90s, the boy next door. Hardly any other American actor invites such a high level of audience identification, whether he plays a burned out ex-baseball player who trains a women's team, as in *A League Of Their Own* (1992) or a widowed single father in *Sleepless in Seattle* (1993). He won the hearts of many with his portrayal of AIDS suffer and lawyer in *Philadelphia* (1993) and became a prototypical American in the title role of *Forrest Gump* (1994) which takes us through three decades of American history. He played another historical role in *Apollo 13* (1995), appearing as the astronaut Jim Lovell. After Spencer Tracy in 1937 and 1938, Hanks was the first person to receive an Oscar for best actor two years running: in 1994 for *Philadelphia,* and in 1995 for *Forrest Gump.* 1996 saw his debut as a director with *That Thing You Do*, a nostalgic musical comedy.

5 "The film's persuasive power lies in the camera-work of Janusz Kaminski, which is reminiscent of the weekly news reports from that time." *epd Film*

6 Master of death: sniper Jackson (Barry Pepper) on the lookout.

7 An allusion to the German film *Die Brücke* (*The Bridge*, 1959): after they have found Ryan, Miller and his men have to defend a bridge.

"It has its place in cinema history, due to the first 25 minutes. The picture it gives of this war is already as mythically transfigured as the violent event in its entirety, just as *Gone with the Wind* showed the numbers of wounded in the ruins of Atlanta."

Süddeutsche Zeitung

THE MATRIX

1999 - USA - 136 MIN. - SCIENCE FICTION

DIRECTOR ANDY WACHOWSKI (*1967), LARRY WACHOWSKI (*1965)
SCREENPLAY ANDY WACHOWSKI, LARRY WACHOWSKI DIRECTOR OF PHOTOGRAPHY BILL POPE MUSIC DON DAVIS PRODUCTION JOEL SILVER, DAN CRACHIOLO for SILVER PRODUCTIONS.

STARRING KEANU REEVES (Neo), LAURENCE FISHBURNE (Morpheus), CARRIE ANNE MOSS (Trinity), HUGO WEAVING (Agent Smith), GLORIA FOSTER (Oracle), JOE PANTOLIANO (Cypher), MARCUS CHONG (Tank), JULIAN ARAHANGA (Apoc), MATT DORAN (Mouse), BELINDA MCCLORY (Switch).

ACADEMY AWARDS 2000 OSCARS for BEST FILM EDITING (Zach Staenberg), BEST SOUND EFFECTS EDITING (Dane A. Davis), BEST VISUAL EFFECTS (Steve Courtley, John Gaeta, Janek Sirrs, Jon Thum), BEST SOUND (David E. Campbell, David Lee, John T. Reitz, Gregg Rudloff).

"The Matrix is the world that has been pulled over your eyes to blind you from the truth."

A Cinderella story in a technological Wonderland: Thomas Anderson (Keanu Reeves) spends his days in a tiny office at a computer firm, doing his best to avoid working. At night, using the pseudonym "Neo", he hacks his way through the international data network. His boss's threats to kick him out are as much a part of the daily routine as dealing in illegal diskettes, which he keeps hidden inside a book titled *Simulacra and Simulation* – an early reference to the central theme of the film, which is the rift between reality and perception. Somewhere out in cyberspace Morpheus (Laurence Fishburne) is waiting for him, believing him to be the Saviour, but Neo has not yet heard his call.

That call is a call to revolution, and for liberation from the machines. Morpheus is the leader of a rebellion whose sole aim is to free mankind from its undeserved bondage. In *The Matrix*, the human race has been enslaved by the artificial intelligence of its electronic apparatus, which derives its energy from human cells. People are lined up in endless rows, like units in a power station, and while their bodies are trapped in this giant battery, their minds roam free in a computer-generated parallel universe. This prison that gives the illusion of freedom is the matrix of the title, and it has all the appearance of reality.

The movie initially inspired controversy on account of its cross-cultural plundering, but critics were united in the opinion that *The Matrix* would set stylistic trends. Techno discos, crumbling Victorian houses, abandoned subway stations, and wastelands of social housing – images of global turbo-capitalism alternating with pictures of post-industrial decay present a portrait of the post-modern world. *The Matrix* marks the spot where late capitalism tips over into the new economy, where the oversized production grounds of mono-industry make way for the revolutionary cells of the new market. In that new economy questions like the limits of our knowledge become increasingly pressing, and it is questions like those that are raised by *The Matrix*, with giddy twists and disorienting turns. Our world is revealed to be a façade and the real world looks more like the hippest and coolest music videos of the nineties. The monopoly on the interpretation of reality no longer belongs to the person who has the strongest arguments or the best evidence, it belongs instead to the person who's most good-looking. Style is

"Our main aim in *The Matrix* was to shoot an intellectual action movie. We like action movies, guns and Kung Fu, so we'd had enough of watching mass-produced action movies that didn't have any kind of intellectual content. We were determined to put as many ideas as possible into the film." *Larry Wachowski in: American Cinematographer*

1 Trinity (Carrie Anne Moss) and the other rebels can only escape the illusory world of the Matrix using telephone lines.

2 Neo (Keanu Reeves) is the chosen one, who will inform the world about all the computer-generated scenery, that at least is the claim made by…

3 … Morpheus (Laurence Fishburne), leader of the rebels in the fight against the Agents.

reality and truth says the film, its greenish tint an imitation of the screen colour of early computer monitors.

In Ovid's *Metamorphoses*, Morpheus is the son of Sleep, and the god of dreams. "Neo" is the Greek prefix for "new". Trinity (Carrie Ann Moss), the third protagonist, completes this pop-culture three-in-one as the Holy Spirit. In practically every scene and dialogue, *The Matrix* delights in pointing out parallels between ancient mythology and modern pop culture, piling up quotations from other films on top of references to philosophical disputes before pulling them apart in the scenes that follow. Accusing this movie of not being serious is like expecting pop music to follow the rules of mathematical logic. The scene with the Oracle is especially brilliant: the Oracle is an old woman who bakes cookies and spouts platitudes, but her prophecies turn out to be true in the end. *The Matrix* makes ingenious use of anything that can serve as a stone in its mosaic: the world is a mine of these stones for our imagination.

MH

"On the visual front, it's been such a success that most subsequent action films include a passing genuflection to *The Matrix*. Which probably defines the genius of the Wachowski brothers: by sheer ingenuity in making new from old, they've become a point of reference." *Télérama*

610

4   In skin-tight black leather, angel of death Trinity
    fights an Agent.

5   Computer batteries generate the illusion of the
    world that we live in.

6   Next summer's fashion: *The Matrix* not only set
    standards in the domain of special effects, but
    even created a "look" which was taken up by
    films and music videos.

7   The rebel base is located on a neo-noir version of
    the legendary Nautilus submarine, which cruises
    through the interior of the Matrix.

> ## "The Wachowskis clearly designed *The Matrix* as a comic-book, before it became a screenplay, and many decisions taken 'because it's cooler' disregard the discipline that you would expect of a literary film."
>
> *Sight and Sound*

ANIMATION TECHNOLOGY The Wachowski Brothers are great fans of Anime (Japanese comics and animated films) and of action films from Hong Kong, both of which left their mark on the special effects in *The Matrix*, elevating it above run-of-the-mill Hollywood films where effects are confined to rapid cutting and a small number of explosions. The brothers managed to persuade Hong Kong kung-fu film veteran Yuen Woo-Ping to design the elaborate choreography, before Yuen went on to give a further demonstration of his talents in Ang Lee's *Crouching Tiger, Hidden Dragon* (2000). Specialist John Gaeta was brought in for the computer-animation. Rather than fast editing and simulation, dozens of cameras were placed in a circle around Keanu Reeves and the film was shot simultaneously by all of them in extreme slow motion. This meant that the actor could then be frozen in one position and a camera shot simulated all the way around him.

8 Burn, baby, burn: mutiny on the rebels' ship.

9 Mind triumphing over matter: Neo and Smith (Hugo Weaving) defy the laws of gravity with perfect balance.

10 Morpheus and Agent Smith both await sequels, which have already been shot and are scheduled to reach cinemas in 2002

ALL ABOUT MY MOTHER

Todo sobre mi madre

1999 - SPAIN / FRANCE - 101 MIN. - MELODRAMA

DIRECTOR PEDRO ALMODÓVAR (*1951)

SCREENPLAY PEDRO ALMODÓVAR **DIRECTOR OF PHOTOGRAPHY** AFFONSO BEATO **MUSIC** ALBERTO IGLESIAS **PRODUCTION** AGUSTIN ALMODÓVAR, CLAUDE BERRI for EL DESEO, RENN PRODUCTIONS, FRANCE 2 CINÉMA.

STARRING CECILIA ROTH (Manuela), ELOY AZORÍN (Estéban), MARISA PAREDES (Huma Rojo), PENÉLOPE CRUZ (Sister Rosa), ANTONIA SAN JUAN (Agrado), CANDELA PEÑA (Nina), ROSA MARÍA SARDÀ (Rosa's mother), FERNANDO FERNÁN GÓMEZ (Rosa's father), TONI CANTÓ (Lola), CARLOS LOZANO (Mario).

IFF CANNES 1999 SILVER PALM for BEST DIRECTOR (Pedro Almodóvar).

ACADEMY AWARDS 2000 OSCAR for BEST FOREIGN LANGUAGE FILM.

"The only genuine thing about me is my feelings."

The loss of a child is the worst thing that can happen to a mother. Manuela (Cecilia Roth) never mentioned the child's father, even when asked, but now that she is completely on her own she continues her son's search for his other parent. Bowed by suffering and yet filled with strength she is driven back deep into her own past, and she travels from Madrid to Barcelona, from her present existence back to an earlier one. The people she meets on this journey to the end of the night generally only appear on our screens as the bad crowd in television crime series, as pathetic informers or more likely as corpses. Here, transsexuals and junkie prostitutes, pregnant nuns and touchy divas are not only the main characters, but with all their failings and weaknesses, they also win our sympathy.

In her search for comfort, Manuela eventually finds the father of her dead son Estéban (Eloy Azorín), and he has now become a dark angel of death, a terminally ill transsexual who earns his living as a prostitute. Eighteen years ago when they were a couple he was also called Estéban, but now (s)he calls herself Lola (Toni Cantó). Although (s)he was once attractive, those days are long gone: Estéban the First no longer exists and Lola is not long for this world either. Nevertheless, at the end of the movie a third Estéban is born, giving us a utopian hope against all the odds.

The audience shares Manuela's perspective and the Spanish director guides us skilfully through the glittering microcosm of Barcelona's transsex-ual scene. Almodóvar however has no intention of giving us a documentary; he does not claim to portray objective reality in an authentic manner, and neither is it his intention to teach us a lesson in pity. Instead he takes all the expressive means at the disposal of a melodrama to their extreme: tears, blood, blows, violence, fucking, birth, love, hate, life and death. The plot may sound unlikely, but nothing seems artificial or false and that is the true miracle of this movie, an effect due in no small part to its fantastic actresses.

They all play actresses in the movie as well: Manuela does role plays with hospital employees to teach them how to deal with the families of deceased patients, and when Nina (Candela Peña), partner of the theatre diva Huma (Marisa Paredes) can't go on stage because she's too doped up, Manuela takes her place. The faithful companion Agrado (Antonia San Juan) is perhaps the greatest actress in the true sense of the word; her body has been operated on innumerable times until it is nothing but artificial illusion. One of the best scenes is where she has to announce the cancellation of a play but manages to whip up the disappointed audience into storms of enthusiasm with an autobiographic monologue. This movie about mothers is also dedicated to all actresses who have ever played actresses.

At their best Almodóvar's men are senile like the father (Fernando Fernán Gómez) of AIDS sufferer Rosa (Penélope Cruz), but for the most part men are conspicuous by their absence. However, even in his short appear-

1 Women in the mirror: Marisa Paredes (with lip-pencil) and Cecilia Roth.

2 Three women, three different stories: Manuela (Cecilia Roth, left), whose son died, and Rosa (Penélope Cruz, right), whose son provides a glim-mer of hope at the end of the film, on either side of Rosa's mother (Rosa María Sardà).

3 The actress Huma Rojo (Marisa Paredes), larger than life, looks through the railings at her fan Estéban (Eloy Azorín), who is soon to die.

4 Penélope Cruz, *shooting star* of Spanish cinema, finds herself on the road to Hollywood.

5 It's the "End of the line for desire" not only for the dreams of Almodóvar's heroines, but also as a play in the film.

ances the double father Estéban/Lola – who is in theory the villain of the piece – is given a dignity which no other character acquires in the course of the whole movie. Almodóvar respects every single human emotion, however bizarre his characters might appear. "The only genuine thing about me is my feelings," says Agrado, the faithful transsexual girlfriend in *All About My Mother*. This also applies to Almodóvar's movie, where feelings always remain genuine despite the visual artistry. And that's more than can be said of most films.   MH

"*All About My Mother* is all about art, women, people, life, and death, and must be one of the most intense films I've ever made." *Pedro Almodóvar in: Cahiers du cinéma*

PEDRO ALMODÓVAR   In the 1980s Almodóvar was hailed as an icon of Spain's gay subculture and was a welcome guest at international festivals. His biting satire ensured that midnight showings of his films were invariably sold out and eventually he became a great figure of European art cinema. In the 90s he was awarded all of cinema's most important prizes and came to be considered one of the most important contemporary filmmakers. He started off being provocative for the sake of it, but gradually he has given his figures depth and complexity whilst still taking a critical look at conventional bourgeois family life and sexual morals. Nowadays Almodóvar is seen as part of the great tragicomic tradition alongside directors such as Fassbinder or Buñuel.

EYES WIDE SHUT

1999 - USA - 159 MIN. - DRAMA, LITERATURE ADAPTATION

DIRECTOR STANLEY KUBRICK (*1928, † 1999)
SCREENPLAY STANLEY KUBRICK, FREDERIC RAPHAEL, based on Arthur Schnitzler's *Dream Story* (*Traumnovelle*)
DIRECTOR OF PHOTOGRAPHY LARRY SMITH **MUSIC** JOCELYN POOK, GYÖRGY LIGETI, DMITRI SHOSTAKOVICH, CHRIS ISAAK
PRODUCTION STANLEY KUBRICK, JAN HARLAN for POLE STAR, HOBBY FILMS (for WARNER BROS.).

STARRING TOM CRUISE (Dr William Harford), NICOLE KIDMAN (Alice Harford), MADISON EGINTON (Helena Harford), JACKIE SAWIRIS (Roz), SYDNEY POLLACK (Viktor Ziegler), SKY DUMONT (Sandor Szavost), MARIE RICHARDSON (Marion), TODD FIELD (Nick Nightingale), RADE SERBEDZIJA (Milich), LEELEE SOBIESKI (Milich's daughter).

"May I ask why a beautiful woman who could have any man in this room wants to be married?"

Traditionally, Hollywood is only interested in marriage insofar as the customary kiss at the end of the movie provides the obligatory happy ending and hints at a future wedding, whose preparation has filled the preceding two hours. The marriage takes place during and after the credits and Hollywood remains in a state of infantile bachelordom. In mainstream films, married couples seldom appear in prominent roles, in Stanley Kubrick's *Eyes Wide Shut* by contrast, sexuality, faithfulness and desire inside marriage are the main themes.

Eyes Wide Shut is admittedly not a Hollywood film in any conventional sense. It was made in England, but as Tom Cruise and Nicole Kidman played the main roles, the film qualified automatically for the premiere multiplex league. They play what they were real life, at least at the time the movie was made a married couple. Bill Harford is a doctor, his wife Alice paints Unambiguous advances are made to both of them - separately - at a party they go to together. Although they reject them, the possibility of unfaithfulness sparks off a crisis in their marriage.

Driven by his wife's confessions of her sexual fantasies about another man, Bill sets off aimlessly into the night and into the abyss of his subconscious. His wanderings are punctuated by black and white images of Alice's imagined night of passion with a naval officer – or are we seeing her memories? Bill's sexual odyssey spins him around in a whirl of desirable women who for one reason or another are all forbidden the daughter of a patient who has just died, a prostitute, the underage daughter of the owner of a costume shop and the masked, naked beauty he met at an orgy that he should not have attended

The model for *Eyes Wide Shut* is Arthur Schnitzler's *Dream Story*, which is set in Vienna at the turn of the 19th century. The movie is set in contemporary New York It isn't a literature adaptation in the conventional sense, but an experiment that follows Schnitzler's model for long stretches and then deviates at important points There was much critical debate about whether enough of the bourgeois ideal of marriage has survived the last hundred years to make Schnitzler's Freudian investigation of married morals still relevant today Kubrick's opponents accused him of having an antiquated concept of society and morality, whereas others considered his movie a successful modernisation, particularly as today's sexual behaviour is still relatively conservative in spite of the sexual revolution

2

1 In spite of the length of time taken to shoot *Eyes Wide Shut* Nicole Kidman and Tom Cruise were prepared to accept pay cheques way below their usual income.

2 The portrayal of marital sexuality is a rarity in Hollywood.

3 The Harfords' marital crisis forces William, a successful doctor working on the Upper East Side, to take a long painful look inside himself.

4 Nicole Kidman was highly regarded as an actress well before her marriage to Cruise.

STANLEY KUBRICK Many English have moved to America and live and work in Hollywood, but there are very few American filmmakers who have settled in England. Stanley Kubrick was an exception. Following his experiences of the Hollywood system (*Spartacus*, 1959/1960) this doctor's son from New York moved to England. His largely independent productions in England showed his mastery of various genres and won him complete freedom and control over all the aspects of his movies, for example *Dr Strangelove* (1964), *2001: A Space Odyssey* (1968) and *A Clockwork Orange* (1971). Kubrick became a living legend, and withdrew from the public eye whilst continuing to make films at longer and longer intervals: *Barry Lyndon* (1975), *The Shining* (1980), *Full Metal Jacket* (1987) and his legacy *Eyes Wide Shut*.

Many legends surround the story of the movie's production: instead of the nine months originally planned, Kubrick filmed in complete secrecy for 19 months in a studio near London. Stars such as Harvey Keitel and Jennifer Jason Leigh were swapped around and edited out, during or even after the filming. In the orgy scene, which is a cross between a Venetian carnival and a Baroque inquisition in Moorish halls, digital figures and objects were added in the US to obscure the audience's view of the proceedings to prevent the movie from ending up on the porn shelves in video shops. When Kubrick, control freak and grand master of PR, died a week after the film was finished, it was even claimed that his death was his ultimate, best-ever publicity stunt.

Even if Bill defends monogamy with rational arguments in his discussions with Alice, his behaviour betrays his forbidden desires. At what point does secret sexual desire break the vow of married faithfulness and where do reality and dreams converge? Paradoxically, the marriage partner is both beloved subject and desired object: Alice's self-confidence and freely admitted desire is as much a witness to the insufficiency of language as Bill's weak attempts to justify his behaviour. Both are attracted to outsiders, but in the final instance, they remain faithful to each other.

MH

"If a scene basically consists of acting, and the feelings of the actors show ninety percent of what you want to say, then you have to do everything you can so that the actors achieve this result." *Stanley Kubrick in: Positif*

3

4

5   William Harford roams through Manhattan by
    night, a driven man – and "lucky", as the newspa-
    per proclaims, he certainly is not.

6   Not long after *Eyes Wide Shut* was completed the
    press announced the separation of Cruise and
    Kidman after more than ten years – half an eterni-
    ty for Hollywood.

7   For a long while Cruise, born in New York state in
    1962, was considered to be a good-looking boy
    with no acting talent – but roles in *Eyes Wide Shut*
    and *Magnolia* (1999) won many critics over to his
    side.

8   Director Sydney Pollack played the part of roué
    Viktor Ziegler for his colleague and friend Kubrick.

"There are many questions left unanswered in *Eyes Wide Shut*. However, these are questions that viewers themselves can answer. Everything is there."

Kubrick's brother-in-law Jan Harlan in:
Stanley Kubrick. The Director as Architect

FIGHT CLUB

1999 - USA - 139 MIN. - THRILLER

DIRECTOR DAVID FINCHER (*1963)
SCREENPLAY JIM UHLS, based on the novel of the same name by CHUCK PALAHNIUK DIRECTOR OF PHOTOGRAPHY JEFF CRONENWETH
MUSIC DUST BROTHERS PRODUCTION ART LINSON, CEAN CHAFFIN, ROSS GRAYSON BELL for LINSON FILMS (for FOX 2000 PICTURES, REGENCY ENTERPRISES, TAURUS FILM).

STARRING BRAD PITT (Tyler Durden), EDWARD NORTON (Narrator), HELENA BONHAM-CARTER (Marla Singer), MEAT LOAF ADAY (Robert Paulsen), JARED LETO (Angel Face), ZACH GRENIER (Richard Chesler), RACHEL SINGER (Chloe), THOM GOSSOM JR. (Detective Stern), GEORGE MAGUIRE (Leader "Remaining Men Together"), PAT MCNAMARA (Jacobs).

> "Our generation has had no Great Depression, no Great War. Our war is a spiritual war. Our depression is our lives."

Hollywood producers like to say of good scripts that they begin like an earthquake then slowly build up to a climax. *Fight Club* comes very close to that: in a furious opening sequence the camera races through the nerve system of a human body accompanied by the music of the Dust Brothers. It captures the tiny hairs and drops of sweat on the surface of the skin before finally focusing on a pistol between the teeth of the man whose body we have just seen, whose voice will guide us through the movie. The movie changes time and place many times at a furious speed, winding backwards and forwards until the story finally begins from the beginning.

He can't sleep. His doctor won't prescribe him anything for it. When you can't sleep, everything looks like the copy of a copy of a copy. The young narrator can only find peace by infiltrating self-help groups under false pretences, so he fakes testicular cancer, tuberculosis, and incest. Only in the face of the pain and fears of others can the anonymous narrator (Edward Norton) find himself – he can cry and sleep. An ambitious young yuppie, he starts doubting his career and lifestyle and ends up convinced that he is deeply dissatisfied. The catalyst he needs to help him to this realisation and the trigger of the action of the movie is Tyler Durden. When his Ikea apartment is burnt out, he goes to stay with Tyler and so begins one of the most unusual male friendships in recent film history, and their relationship becomes the driving force behind the rest of the movie. With ostentatious coolness and almost pretentious nonchalance, Brad Pitt plays Durden as a demonic, seductive alternative to the narrator's permanently insecurity.

What do men do when they don't know what to do? They fight until they bleed. *Fight Club* doesn't actually offer any concrete solutions to society's ills, but it draws a precise, comprehensive picture of social disaffection. It's

a rebellion against advanced capitalist consumerism. Individuals are no longer worth anything as individuals, they only have value as consumers, and elf-expression has come to mean choosing something to buy. Advertisements and television decide how we should look or behave. *Fight Club* sets itself up as an alternative, a mental and physical regeneration programme which replaces the consumerist "I shop therefore I am", with "I bleed, therefore I am". Brutal physicality and the threat of violence, pain and injury offer new possibilities for finding an individual personality.

In no time at all the Fight Club spreads throughout the land as a successful franchise business, but when Tyler begins to form an underground army, the narrator's doubts begin all over again. A conflict flares up between the two protagonists, who follow each other coast to coast across the United States of America before returning to their point of departure – although by then their circumstances have changed beyond recognition. Only men are to be seen fighting each other, however: as Durden explains: "Our generation was brought up by women. I ask myself if another woman is really the answer we need."

With *Fight Club*, David Fincher made one of the most cryptic movies of the 90s which – on first viewing at least – blows the audience away.

MH

2

3

"If the spirit has gone to sleep, the body has to take care of feeling alive. A fight is just the right atavistic ritual to remedy post-modern damage to civilization." *Der Spiegel*

BRAD PITT
From pretty boy to leading man on the Hollywood market with earnings in the millions. A Levi's advertisement (20th Century Boy) first introduced Brad Pitt's face to the public. Pitt was born in Oklahoma in 1963 and began his rapid rise to stardom with a short but impressive appearance as the hitchhiker in *Thelma & Louise* (1991), where he gave Thelma an unforgettable sexual experience before running off with her savings. Pitt quickly emancipated himself from his image as the good-looking guy with the washboard stomach and learned the craft of serious acting in melodramas like *Legends of the Fall* (1994) and *A River Runs Through It* (1992), although he continued to appear in more predictable roles like the Bonnie and Clyde adaptation *Kalifornia* (1993). He really got into his stride when he began to work with the director David Fincher, for whom he played the over-ambitious Detective Mills in the serial killer thriller *Se7en* (1995) as well as Tyler Durden in *Fight Club* (1999) – a portrayal of male fantasies of violence. Other movies which feature him as a broken hero include *Twelve Monkeys* (1995), where he plays an underground fighter pitted against his own father and Guy Ritchie's *Snatch* (2000), where he appears as a mumbling incomprehensible gypsy.

1   Masculinity in crisis: the anonymous narrator (Edward Norton) unexpectedly finds himself in the arms of Robert Paulsen (Meat Loaf Aday) again.

2   Who wouldn't want to be like Tyler Durden (Brad Pitt)? – Good-looking, charming, quick-witted and uncompromising.

3   America's urban guerillas of the future? Brad Pitt's casual nonchalance meets Edward Norton's broken office worker existence.

"Fincher's film worlds are always cold, angry places, in which you wouldn't want to live." *epd Film*

4   "The internal monologue gives a kind of context and also humour. In the absence of this voice, the story is simply sad and ridiculous." *David Fincher*

5   With the role of Marla Singer, Helena Bonham-Carter, who was born in England in 1966 and until now had usually favoured harmless costume parts, opened up a whole new sphere of activity.

6   The narrator (Edward Norton) meets enigmatic *femme fatale* Marla Singer for the first time at a self-help group.

5

6

629

THE MESSENGER: THE STORY OF JOAN OF ARC

1999 - FRANCE / USA - 158 MIN. - HISTORICAL FILM, DRAMA

DIRECTOR LUC BESSON (*1959)
SCREENPLAY ANDREW BIRKIN, LUC BESSON DIRECTOR OF PHOTOGRAPHY THIERRY ARBOGAST MUSIC ERIC SERRA PRODUCTION PATRICE LEDOUX
for GAUMONT, LEELOO PRODUCTIONS.

STARRING MILLA JOVOVICH (Joan of Arc), JOHN MALKOVICH (Charles VII), FAYE DUNAWAY (Yolande d'Aragon), DUSTIN
HOFFMAN (Conscience), PASCAL GREGGORY (Duke of Alençon), VINCENT CASSEL (Gilles de Rais), TCHEKY KARYO
(Dunois), RICHARD RIDINGS (La Hire), DESMOND HARRINGTON (Aulon), TIMOTHY WEST (Cauchon), JANE VALENTINE
(Joan as a child).

"Follow me!"

France in 1420. War has raged for decades and large stretches of the country are occupied by the English, but Jeanne (Jane Valentine) has a happy childhood in her home village of Domrémy. The devout girl goes to confession several times a day and tells the priest that God speaks to her. One day when Jeanne is playing in the fields she has a vision. When she comes to her senses, she finds a sword lying next to her in the grass. Excited, she runs home only to witness how the English burn the village down and rape and murder her sisters. We then skip forward nine years. The war is still raging, and Jeanne (Milla Jovovich), who is now a young woman, believes that she has discovered the meaning of her vision: God has chosen her to lead the French to victory against the English and help the Dauphin (John Malkovich) onto the throne of France. She is received at court and manages to convince the Dauphin of the truth of her mission. She rides to Orléans at the head of the army.

Luc Besson has always been a master of the big-budget spectacular, and his vision of Joan of Arc is very much a continuation of the style he used in *The Fifth Element* (1996), his previous film. There are few stories that have been filmed as often as the life of this French national heroine. Besson however is probably the first to concentrate almost exclusively on the fight at Orléans and on the action. The fighting takes up almost half of the movie, while her childhood, trial and sentencing are shown almost in passing. His Joan above all is a warrior, an amazon-like figure. Accordingly, the movie's most beautiful moments are when Milla Jovovich rides into battle with short hair and shining armour. Besson is in his element here.

However, when we compare this movie with earlier versions it becomes clear how unusual and even unsuitable all this action is in a story that is motivated above all by spiritual processes and by religious and moral issues. Jacques Rivette's *Jeanne la pucelle* (1994) for instance develops Joan's personality and story with incredible calm and power, but as a supporter of anti-intellectual cinema, Besson aims to do the exact opposite. He wants to grab spectators from the opening frame. His film has no time for development and progression, but merely shows events. The camera is in permanent move-

2

3

4

1   Sent by God to rid France of the English: top-model Milla Jovovich is a Joan of Arc for the masses in the 1990s.

2   Spectacular cinema: Faye Dunaway in the role of Yolande d'Aragon in period costume with shaved brow.

3   As in classic adventure films, the old warhorses get the sympathy vote in the film (in the centre: Tcheky Karyo).

4   Luc Besson in his element: almost half the film is dominated by tumultuous battle scenes.

5   Power-crazy and cynical: Charles VII (John Malkovich) concocts his plots surrounded by his advisers.

"Is Joan a servant of God or a pill-popping freak who watches too much MTV?" *The Washington Post*

ment looking for brilliant images, while the elliptical narrative style means that there are no slow moments in the story. Besson externalises everything, and we see both Joan's vision and her conscience. When she is plagued by doubt in prison, a dark man appears to her in a monk's habit (Dustin Hoffman) and confronts her with the contradictions of her existence. Joan's psychological make-up is also overly obvious and her behaviour is reductively explained as a consequence of her traumatic childhood experience. Her story is simplified until it becomes little more than an artificial pictorial intoxication. Besson's attempt to create a contemporary Joan of Arc for the mass audiences of the 90s fails because the complexity of his chosen material contradicts the aesthetic of his film.

JH

5

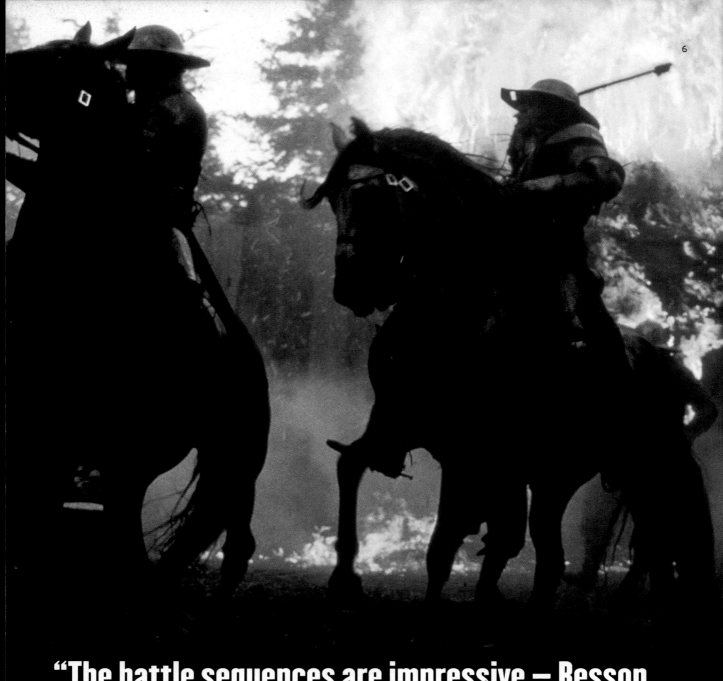

"The battle sequences are impressive – Besson (*The Fifth Element*) has a thunderclap visual style. But too much of the rest is the adventures of a flighty action heroine." *San Francisco Examiner*

7

6 Pillaging demons: Joan's transformation is triggered by a traumatic childhood experience.

7 Joan of Arc as an Amazon: Luc Besson turns the French national heroine into the champion of a jousting tournament. Whereas earlier films tried to

explore the spiritual, moral and religious dimension of the figure, Besson's version is above a visually dazzling spectacular showpiece.

JOAN OF ARC MOVIES — Joan of Arc is a historical figure who was born in Domrémy in 1412 and died in Rouen in 1431. The story of France's liberator was first filmed in the earliest days of cinema history, and since then numerous great directors have tried their hand at the story. Carl Theodor Dreyer's famous silent film *La passion de Jeanne d'Arc* (1928) concentrated on her trial, as did Robert Bresson's *Le procès de Jeanne d'Arc* (*The Trial of Joan of Arc*, 1962). Victor Fleming's *Joan of Arc* (1948) by contrast was nothing more than a star vehicle for Ingrid Bergman. In *Saint Joan* (1957), Otto Preminger investigated the story's moral dimensions. Finally, Jacques Rivette staged the life of *Jeanne la pucelle*, (*Joan the Maid*, 1994) using medieval books of hours before Luc Besson turned the devout virgin into an action heroine in *The Messenger: The Story of Joan of Arc*.

AMERICAN BEAUTY

1999 - USA - 121 MIN. - DRAMA

DIRECTOR SAM MENDES (*1965)

SCREENPLAY ALAN BALL DIRECTOR OF PHOTOGRAPHY CONRAD L. HALL MUSIC THOMAS NEWMAN PRODUCTION BRUCE COHEN, DAN JINKS for DREAMWORKS SKG, JINKS/COHEN COMPANY.

STARRING KEVIN SPACEY (Lester Burnham), ANNETTE BENING (Carolyn Burnham), THORA BIRCH (Jane Burnham), WES BENTLEY (Ricky Fitts), MENA SUVARI (Angela Hayes), PETER GALLAGHER (Buddy Kane), CHRIS COOPER (Colonel Frank Fitts), ALLISON JANNEY (Barbara Fitts), SCOTT BAKULA (Jim Olmeyer), SAM ROBARDS (Jim "JB" Berkley).

ACADEMY AWARDS 2000 OSCARS for BEST PICTURE, BEST ACTOR (Kevin Spacey), BEST CINEMATOGRAPHY (Conrad L. Hall), BEST DIRECTOR (Sam Mendes), and BEST ORIGINAL SCREENPLAY (Alan Ball).

"You have no idea what I'm talking about, I'm sure. But don't worry, you will someday."

In one year's time Lester Burnham (Kevin Spacey) will be dead: that much we learn right at the beginning of the movie. And he already knows this himself, for he's the one who tells his own story. A dead man speaks to us from off screen, and the strangest thing about it is his amused detachment. With a sweeping movement making the off-screen narration seem like a message of salvation, the camera moves down on the world from above and closes in on the dismal suburban street where Lester lives. We are introduced to the situation in which he finds himself: his marriage to Carolyn (Annette Bening) is over, and she considers him a failure, while his daughter Jane (Thora Birch) hates him for not being a role model. The only highpoint of Lester's sad daily routine is masturbating under the shower in the morning while his wife gathers roses in the garden to decorate the dinner table where they conduct their daily fights.

Family happiness, or whatever passed for it, only ever existed in the photos that Lester often looks at to remind himself of his past, and of the interest in life which he once had but which is now buried under the pressure of conformity. It is only when he falls in love with Angela (Mena Suvari), his daughter's Lolita-like friend, that he rediscovers his zest for life. This second spring changes Lester, but his wife Carolyn meanwhile is doing worse and worse as a property dealer. He reassesses his position and discovers old and forgotten strengths. She by contrast becomes inextricably entwined in the fatal cycle of routine and self-sacrifice. As Lester puts it, trying to live as though their life were a commercial nearly destroys them both. Outward

conformity and prosperity results in inner impoverishment. The business mantras that Carolyn repeats over and over to herself to bolster her self-confidence sound increasingly ridiculous under the circumstances.

At this point, it becomes abundantly clear what we are intended to understand by "American Beauty". The title is not a reference to the seductive child-woman who helps Lester break out of the family prison – that would be too superficial. The subject of *American Beauty* is the question of the beauty of life itself. Mendes' movie is about whether or not it is possible to live a fulfilling life in a society where superficiality has become the norm. To put it in more philosophical terms, *American Beauty* uses the expressive means of drama and satire to go through all the possibilities for leading an honest life in a dishonest environment. Sadly this turns out to be impossible, or at least Lester's attempt ends in death.

It's a gem of a movie, thanks to Sam Mendes' careful use of film techniques. He never exposes his characters to ridicule and he protects them from cheap laughs by giving them time to develop. He also gives depth to their relationships and arranges them in dramatic constellations. Mendes' experience as a theatre director shows in a number of carefully staged scenes whose strict form is well suited to the Burnham's oppressive and limited family life. Many scenes put us in mind of plays by Samuel Beckett, like the backyard sequence where Rick teaches Lester not to give in to circumstance. The symmetrical arrangements of characters around the table or the television are further reminders of family dramas on the stage.

1 A seductively beautiful image.

3 … and sensitive Jane (Thora Birch).

5 Liberation from the familial cage brings happiness to Lester Burnham (Kevin Spacey).

2 Hollywood's new bright young things: saucy Angela (Mena Suvari) …

4 Carolyn Burnham (Annette Bening) on the brink of madness.

"At first the film judges its characters harshly; then it goes to every effort to make them win back their rights." *Frankfurter Allgemeine Zeitung*

In an important subplot, Lester's daughter Jane falls in love with Rick, the boy next door, who is never seen without his video camera and films constantly, to "remind himself", as he says. He documents the world and discovers its beauty in grainy video pictures of dead animals and people. It is his father, the fascist ex-marine Colonel Frank Fitts – brilliantly acted by Chris Cooper – who in a moment of emotional turmoil shoots Lester Burnham and thereby fulfils the prophecy made at the beginning of the film. The hopeless struggle between internal and external beauty comes to a bloody end, but the issue remains open. The movie points to a vague possibility for reconciling these two opposites, but at the end this seems to have been an illusion. Despite our right to the "pursuit of happiness", material and spiritual wealth seem to be mutually exclusive, and the good life remains a promise of happiness which is yet to be fulfilled. With irony and humour, *American Beauty* shows that modern American society's mental state is by no means as rosy as the initiators of the Declaration of Independence would have hoped.   BR

KEVIN SPACEY   What would the cinema of the 90s have been without Kevin Spacey? Born in 1959, this friendly looking actor with his ordinary face portrayed some of the most complex and disturbing characters of the decade with impressive depth. Nobody demonstrated so clearly the difference between being and appearance, between a deceptive façade and the brutal reality behind it as drastically as Kevin Spacey playing John Doe, "The Man Without Qualities" in *Se7en* (1995), or the sinister Keyser Soze who pulls the strings in *The Usual Suspects* (1995). Spacey is an enigmatic minimalist who needs only a few striking gestures, and with cool irony can play great emotional cinema as he shows in the role of Lester Burnham in *American Beauty*. When he dies at the turning point of a story – as he does in *L. A. Confidential* – it's a great loss, both for us and for the movie.

"When I made *American Beauty*, I wanted the film's vision to offer every spectator a very intimate experience. I hope it's a universal work, which helps one understand life that little bit better." *Sam Mendes in: Le Figaro*

6   Grotesque victim of his own ideology: sinister neighbour Colonel Fitts (Chris Cooper) shortly before his surprise coming out.

7   Scenes from a marriage in ruins.

8   Wes Bentley is very convincing as Ricky Fitts, the introverted young man from next door.

9   Jane is fascinated by Ricky's puzzling hobby.

10 Life's true beauty can only be appreciated in a video image.

10

THE BLAIR WITCH PROJECT

999 - USA - 87 MIN. - HORROR FILM

DIRECTOR DANIEL MYRICK (*1964), EDUARDO SANCHEZ (*1969)
SCREENPLAY DANIEL MYRICK, EDUARDO SANCHEZ **DIRECTOR OF PHOTOGRAPHY** NEAL FREDERICKS **MUSIC** TONY CORA **PRODUCTION** GREGG HALE, ROBIN COWIE, MICHAEL MONELLO for HAXAN FILMS, ARTISAN ENTERTAINMENT.
STARRING HEATHER DONAHUE (Heather), MICHAEL WILLIAMS (Michael), JOSHUA LEONARD (Joshua), BOB GRIFFIN (Angler), JIM KING (Interview partner), SANDRA SANCHEZ (Waitress), ED SWANSON (Angler with glasses), PATRICIA DECOU (Mary Brown), MARK MASON (Man with the yellow hat), JACKIE HALLEX.

"It's very hard to get lost in America these days and even harder to stay lost."

We know the story from the brothers Grimm: young people get lost in a wood and struggle with a witch. In the contemporary adaptation *The Blair Witch Project* there is however no tempting gingerbread and the witch doesn't get pushed into the oven – instead film students Heather (Heather Donahue), Michael (Michael Williams) and Joshua (Joshua Leonard) set off into the woods in Maryland with their camera to investigate stories of a witch, and they come to a sticky end. First the three youngsters ask people in the village of Blair about the stories, then they go off into the woods to look. It soon becomes ominously clear that they are being watched and they realise too late that they are lost.

The Blair Witch Project cost only a fraction of the cost of a normal Hollywood production. The plot is driven by the movie's own frugal production conditions. A horror movie disguised as a documentary, it begins with a text insert saying that in October 1994 three film students disappeared in the woods near Burkittsville, Maryland while making a documentary film and that their film material was found a year later. This material is what we are about to see. Unlike Danish Dogme films such as *The Celebration* (*Festen*, 1998), which base their stark simplicity on a pseudo-religious creed and a wish to take cinema back to its basics, in this case the movie's lack of technical sophistication is an integral part of its storyline.

Physical movement always has a psychological dimension in cinema: as the three students move further and further away from a normal investigative outing, they penetrate deeper and deeper into the woods and become more and more convinced that they are hopelessly lost. The nearer they get to the witch's house, the closer they are to the darkness within themselves. The would-be filmmakers become increasingly tense. They neither look nor act like future stars, but more like we would imagine ordinary film students: they are not particularly attractive, they're not necessarily very nice and they're ultimately a bit nerdy. This makes it all the more believable that we are seeing the material from their filming expedition: wobbly and unfocused images of a journey with no return, to which the pictures are the only witnesses. Their journey through the woods of Maryland is also an excursion into American history. This wild countryside on the East Coast was where the first settlers arrived, and it was here that James Fenimore Cooper's last Mohican roamed and hunted. It is a sad reflection on today's civilisation that the descendants of this pioneering generation are destroyed by their forefathers' legends. City-dwellers in the wilderness are mostly their own worst enemies, and they fall victim to their own fears rather than to the hostile environment. Trapped in a situation that seems increasingly hopeless, the three students mercilessly document each other's despair and psychic disintegration.

Its innovative marketing aside, the movie still basically functions as a relatively old-fashioned horror film. The three students tramp up hill and down dale, and live in terror of what they might find in front of their tent in the morning. But there is actually nothing to be seen – we can't make out anything for sure in the partly blackened pictures and the fear only exists where it is at its worst: in our own heads.

1

2

"The *Blair Witch Project* basically isn't about spooky witches and horrific murderers, but about the primeval fear you feel when you are lost in the woods, alone, hungry and freezing cold." *Focus*

"*Blair* is the clearest example of a new phenomenon: the film's success was driven not by a conventional publicity campaign, but by a web site combined with word of mouth." *Süddeutsche Zeitung*

MARKETING The Blair Witch Project cost 35,000 dollars and in the USA alone the movie made 140 million – profit margins which most investors can only dream of. The movie first attracted attention in January 1999 at the Sundance Festival, which is the El Dorado for US independent film. Artisan, a small distribution company, secured the distribution rights to *BWP* and began an unrivalled marketing campaign. Week after week the Internet site www.blairwitch.com published new titbits on the background to the mythology of the Blair Witch. When the movie was released in June 1999 only 27 copies were made, although this number was gradually increased. As copies were kept short, cinema screenings sold out in a few places and the word on the street spread. This is quite unlike the usual Hollywood practice where the market is flooded with as many copies as possible

1 Face to face with terror – the observer is stuck there with his own fear

2 Always aim for the other camera

3 Heather (Heather Donahue) alone in the woods

4 Michael (Michael Williams) and Joshua (Joshua Leonard) in the face of horror which is always located somewhere near the camera

5 Securing evidence of an expedition into the heart of darkness

6 Seemingly realistic images of a fictional story

THE INSIDER

1999 - USA - 157 MIN. - THRILLER

DIRECTOR MICHAEL MANN (*1943)
SCREENPLAY ERIC ROTH, MICHAEL MANN, based on the article "THE MAN WHO KNEW TOO MUCH" by MARIE BRENNER in
VANITY FAIR, MAY 1996 DIRECTOR OF PHOTOGRAPHY DANTE SPINOTTI MUSIC PIETER BOURKE, LISA GERRARD, GRAEME REVELL
PRODUCTION PIETER JAN BRUGGE, MICHAEL MANN, MICHAEL WAXMAN for BLUE LIGHT PRODUCTIONS, FORWARD PASS,
KAITZ PRODUCTIONS, MANN/ROTH PRODUCTIONS, TOUCHSTONE PICTURES.

STARRING AL PACINO (Lowell Bergman), RUSSELL CROWE (Jeffrey Wigand), CHRISTOPHER PLUMMER (Mike Wallace),
DIANE VENORA (Liane Wigand), PHILIP BAKER HALL (Don Hewitt), LINDSAY CROUSE (Sharon Tiller), DEBI MAZAR
(Debbie De Luca), STEPHEN TOBOLOWSKY (Eric Kluster), COLM FEORE (Richard Scruggs), GINA GERSHON (Helen
Caperelli), MICHAEL GAMBON (Thomas Sandefur), RIP TORN (John Scanlon).

"What the hell do you expect? Grace and consistency?"

Jeffrey Wigand (Russell Crowe) is what is known as an insider: as a former employee of the cigarette manufacturer Brown & Williamson, he has information about the dangerous additives in tobacco, which increase addiction and cause cancer. This should be enough to finish off the tobacco lobby, who stand accused of endangering public health. But things turn out a little differently. When this loyal and conscientious scientist tells his boss that he is worried about the possible dangers of a flavour enhancer, he is immediately fired. His redundancy money is at stake and with it his family's hard-earned prosperity. The firm tries to force him to sign a contract promising to say nothing about his work, but Jeffrey refuses and then the psychological terror against him and his family begins. Threatening, stony-faced muscle-men in big white limousines observe his every movement, nocturnal visitors to the back garden disturb the children, and his wife receives terrifying death threats by e-mail. With breathtaking speed and drastic changes of perspective, Dante Spinotti's camera shows how Jeffrey Wigand's world breaks down practically over night. There are unfocused close-ups, hectic swings, daring camera angles and quick cuts combined with slow motion as the camera captures Jeffrey's persecution complex and his psychological collapse. The pictures seem to fall apart, just like Jeffrey's life. His wife can't

take it any longer and leaves him. In desperation, Jeffrey finally turns to Lowell Bergman (Al Pacino), who is the producer of "60 Minutes", a famous television news show. The movie changes its narrative perspective at this point. *The Insider* shows Bergman as a forthright, persuasive man from the very beginning. His negotiating skills even get him an interview with the Islamic Hezbollah leader. This episode foreshadows Wigand's case, showing the tobacco industry to be a criminal organisation and its bosses and leaders to be shameless criminals who think nothing of presenting their appalling deeds as promises of happiness. This is where *The Insider* comes to its real theme, which is the difficulty of being successful, upright and truthful as an individual in a land where every aspect of life is ruled by a conglomerate of industrial, legal and media cartels. The insider Jeffrey Wigand becomes an outsider. The tobacco industry puts private detectives on his trail, the media are only interested in him as a headline that increases circulation, the legal system uses the "Wigand case" to increase its own importance, and all of them profit from him financially. Even the influence of the few upright people in the corrupt system disappears before our very eyes. Lowell Bergman is sent on holiday when the managers of CBS stop the broadcast of an interview with Wigand because it might endanger the channel's lucrative sale to

3

"You have to speak Pacino's language. Before and after the take. 'Cos he always comes up and asks what I thought of the take, what we might do differently. Then it's really important to find the right words. Anyone who thinks Pacino is a 'method actor' will realise that's all nonsense. Pacino is a graduate of the Pacino School of Acting."

Michael Mann in: Süddeutsche Zeitung

1 Humiliated but not completely crushed, in the end Jeffrey Wigand (Russell Crowe) loses everything – except his beliefs.

2 Al Pacino is outstanding as crafty media action man Lowell Bergman.

3 Lowell Bergman is unflinching in the battle against the tobacco industry's machinations.

4 The revelations in the media catapult Jeffrey Wigand and the tobacco mafia into an existential crisis.

a subsidiary company of the tobacco firm. But Bergman doesn't let them pull the wool over his eyes and his morals are not for sale. He knows only too well that truth is what the public think is true. He goes to work incognito to find out the truth about the machinations of the tobacco companies and bring them to the public's attention, while also hoping to find some kind of justice for Jeffrey. But in the end even he fails, and he gets out of the whole dishonest business.

Michael Mann and Dante Spinotti had worked together since *Red Dragon* (1986, video title *Manhunter*). The distinguishing characteristics of their work, as they demonstrated most perfectly in *Heat* (1995), are super-cool sets and highly mobile camera techniques. *Heat* has an extraordinary lyrical quality in the poetic sheen of its wild shoot-outs, and every shot and cut in *The Insider* is saturated with the same style. The cinemascope format means that the movie takes the audience to the very limits of what cinema can offer. The flood of pictures however never overwhelms the plot and characters, and *The Insider* takes time to develop various different plot strands and believable psychological profiles for its main characters. Although the movie is dominated by an atmosphere of permanent menace, this is a thriller without a single death. And when it stops being a psychological thriller and becomes a media and legal drama, it still doesn't break step. Two and a half hours fly by. *The Insider* only comes to a halt when Bergman Lowell is finally forced to give up.   BR

MICHAEL MANN With his TV series *Miami Vice*, Michael Mann had a lasting influence the aesthetics of television and cinema. A student at the London International Film School, Mann began to make a name for himself in the mid-60s as a director of commercials and documentaries. Back in the USA he wrote for the TV Police series *Starsky & Hutch* before making an impressive cinema debut with *Thief* (1981). Six years before Jonathan Demme revolutionised the thriller genre in 1991 with *The Silence of the Lambs*, Mann filmed the same material under the title *Red Dragon* (video title *Manhunter*), leaving an indelible mark on the story of the psychopathic genius Hannibal Lecter. Mann was a pioneer of the supercool visuals that became such a characteristic of 90s cinema. His greatest box office hit was in 1992 with *The Last of the Mohicans*, and he later brought together superstars Al Pacino and Robert De Niro in *Heat* (1995), an impressive gangster story.

5   In the end even alcohol is no help anymore.

6   News makers are powerful but isolated: anchorman Mike Wallace (Christopher Plummer).

7   The news is always a compromise between quota
requirements and the truth.

"Since *Miami Vice* Mann has loved great turbulent drama beneath a flat, cool surface." *epd Film*

THE STRAIGHT STORY

1999 - USA / FRANCE - 112 MIN. - ROAD MOVIE

DIRECTOR DAVID LYNCH (*1946)
SCREENPLAY JOHN ROACH, MARY SWEENEY DIRECTOR OF PHOTOGRAPHY FREDDIE FRANCIS MUSIC ANGELO BADALAMENTI PRODUCTION NEAL EDELSTEIN, ALAIN SARDE, MARY SWEENEY for ASYMMETRICAL PRODUCTIONS, CIBY 2000, LE STUDIO CANAL+, LES FILMS ALAIN SARDE, THE PICTURE FACTORY, THE STRAIGHT STORY INC.

STARRING RICHARD FARNSWORTH (Alvin Straight), SISSY SPACEK (Rose Straight), EVERETT MCGILL (Tom), JOHN FARLEY (Thorvald Olsen), KEVIN P. FARLEY (Harold Olsen), HARRY DEAN STANTON (Lyle Straight), JANE GALLOWAY HEITZ (Dorothy), JENNIFER EDWARDS-HUGHES (Brenda), JOSEPH A. CARPENTER (Bud), DONALD WIEGGERT (Sig).

"I've got to make this trip on my own."

Alvin Straight (Richard Farnsworth) is an ageing patriarch. He lives in the American outback together with his seemingly retarded daughter, who has lost the custody of her children. Alvin is a good man, honest and polite, full of good advice, and ready to help wherever he can. Alvin has a brother living at the other end of the Midwest. He hasn't spoken to his brother for quite a while, as their relationship went sour after an old argument. When his brother Lyle suffers a stroke, Alvin decides that he wants to see Lyle one more time. And so he climbs onto the uncomfortable seat of his mini tractor (complete with trailer) and heads for Mt. Zion, Wisconsin. He is a penitent on a pilgrimage, at the end of which lies forgiveness.

The Straight Story forms a kind of counterpart to Lynch's previous film Lost Highway (1996). While the first film delved alarmingly into the spiritual depths of its central figure, making the images themselves into expressions of psychological disturbance, The Straight Story, at least when viewed superficially, seems to be a parable of loneliness and slowness. The Straight Story is told in extended passages of sparse dialogue, and bright, quiet pictures. Cameraman Freddie Francis' opulent landscape shots evoke a peaceful atmosphere tinged with pathos – an atmosphere that spills over into the lives of the human figures in it. Alvin meets only humane and helpful people along his torturous route. When he finally arrives at his destination, Lyle is already doing much better, as though Alvin Straight's bone-headed determination had miraculously healed the rift between the two brothers. And even though they exchange very few words, their brotherhood is re-established. This at least is the story on the surface – a story based on a true incident, which Lynch retells with the appropriate directness and simplicity. Yet from another point of view, the thoughtful, sentimental "straight story" is a front for another story which is part of the theme that Lynch has been exploring since Blue Velvet (1986): the secret torments that people harbour, and the

"With a minimum of external effects Lynch has achieved a maximum of human emotion. The simple story that he tells is ultimately about the dignity of the protagonists." *Frankfurter Allgemeine Zeitung*

1 The journey on the highway to happiness is long and arduous.

2 Daring to make a fresh start at the end of his life: Alvin Straight (Richard Farnsworth) blazes a trail.

3 Life has left visible traces of its passage.

4 Comical family idyll in the countryside: father and daughter (Sissy Spacek as Rose Straight).

5 Alvin Straight: never wavering and keeping straight on ahead …

6 … even in the face of dangerous competition out on the road.

7 Imperturbable and out in front: the slowest sets the pace.

abyss that lies just below the surface of human existence. From that perspective *The Straight Story* shows itself in a more malevolent light. The second story, which is not quite so "straightforward" as the first, is filled of fatal twists tinged with the tragedy of undisclosed mistakes and omissions. It is a tale of drunkenness, of a comrade killed during the war, of carelessness in dealing with others – and of the inescapable tyranny of memory. When we pick up on that background, we suddenly detect a multitude of references and thematic borrowings from Lynch's other films. Individual episodes develop their own existence, independently of the simple travelogue. The tractor pilgrimage serves as a way of extending time and place, with the purpose of freeing up Alvin's memories and those of the spectators too. In this sense, the film plays a double game. The rural neighbourhood is transformed into a fateful warning. We see the whitewashed fence, the dog playing in the yard, the lawn chairs, just as in *Blue Velvet*. We hear a crash, and look for the terrible accident and are relieved to see Alvin picking himself up after a fall in the kitchen. Or the woman who has run over a deer on the open highway: her shocked reaction evokes the worst memories of the nocturnal car accident and the motorcycle accident in *Wild at Heart* (1990). Like *Wild at Heart* and, most recently, *Lost Highway*, *The Straight Story* is a radical new take on the road movie genre. Not only does it treat the central transportation motif ironically, with the almost laughable garden tractor, but the insufferable slowness of Alvin's progress turns the trip itself into an endless Calvary in an infinite wilderness. Lynch obsessively repeats and develops his own motifs and themes, going over them time and again, and constantly revealing fresh facets.

Alvin is oppressed by his memories, and the passage of time is not enough to heal his wounded soul. It is as impossible to erase the ugly truths of his memories as it is to portray them adequately. They lie beyond the beauty of the landscape, the grace of old age, or the monumental calm of the rural idyll. Ultimately it is the restrained acting of the main character that draws our attention to the story below the surface. Richard Farnsworth, unforgettable as Alvin, once worked as a stunt man with the Marx Brothers. He was terminally ill with cancer when making this film, and he put an end to his own life a few weeks after his eightieth birthday. BR

FILM QUOTATION Quotation actually means the word for word transposition of one text passage into another text for purposes of reference. Filmmakers too have always made frequent use of quotation or cross-reference from other films. The golden age of film quotation arrived with the French Nouvelle Vague of the 60s, when quotation established itself as an art form in cinema historiography. There has been a renewed interest in the technique since the 80s. The current high-point in the use of film quotation is unquestionably Quentin Tarantino's *Pulp Fiction* (1994) which consists almost exclusively of references to other films and genres. David Lynch is one of the subtlest masters of the quotation technique.

NOTTING HILL

1999 - GREAT BRITAIN - 124 MIN. - ROMANTIC COMEDY
DIRECTOR ROGER MICHELL
SCREENPLAY RICHARD CURTIS DIRECTOR OF PHOTOGRAPHY MICHAEL COULTER MUSIC TREVOR JONES PRODUCTION DUNCAN KENWORTHY
for NOTTING HILL PRODUCTIONS, WORKING TITLE.

STARRING JULIA ROBERTS (Anna Scott), HUGH GRANT (William Thacker), RHYS IFANS (Spike), GINA MCKEE (Bella), HUGH BONNEVILLE (Bernie), EMMA CHAMBERS (Honey), TIM MCINNERNY (Max), JAMES DREYFUS (Martin).

"Rita Hayworth used to say: 'They go to bed with Gilda; they wake up with me'."

What happens when you fall in love with a well-known actress without even realising that she is famous? Right! You're just as clumsy as you would be trying to approach any other woman. William Thacker (Hugh Grant), a bookshop owner who is as nice as he is unsuccessful, plays this part with bravura.

Movie star Anna Scott (Julia Roberts) comes to London for the premiere of her new film and spends some free time incognito in the picturesque district of Notting Hill. Here, seemingly miles away from the influence of the gossiping press, she is not immediately recognised. An amorous adventure begins when she comes into William Thacker's bookshop looking for travel books, and William promptly spills orange juice all over her.

The main character in this romantic comedy gets his name from the English writer William Thackeray, whose panoramic society novels investigated human weakness with sympathy and understanding. He deconstructed the idea of the hero and criticised bourgeois values like property and status. Like Thackeray's works, *Notting Hill* is based around an impossible love story between the rich and the poor, between the unsuccessful Willliam and the successful Anna, between the stiff Englishman and the beautiful, vibrant American. They keep in touch and Anna sees a chance to break out of her

golden cage. For her, taking part in the life of ordinary people means winning back a part of her own life that she badly misses. William loves Anna's carefree beauty. The world of success and riches means nothing to him.

They flirt one moonlit night, climbing over the fence into a park to sit on an ancient bench. However, when Anna's boyfriend arrives in London from the US, their relationship comes to a swift, if temporary end.

When Anna has to flee from her own past – naked photos of her have turned up in the press – she turns up unexpectedly at William's flat to hide. The next morning, hordes of paparazzi besiege the house, and she is furious and leaves him. William's flatmate Spike let the cat out of the bag in the pub the night before after a couple of beers. The two are separated once more and this time it no longer looks like things will end happily. The efforts of William's friends to introduce him to other women can't make him forget his unhappiness. The passing of time is shown in poetic pictures: whilst William strolls through Notting Hill market, the four seasons leave their mark on the setting within one single shot. His longing for Anna is finally fulfilled when she comes back to London for another film premiere.

Notting Hill is an old-fashioned movie in the best sense of the word. Alongside the two successful stars of the genre who act perfectly and with-

"Of course, the character of Anna Scott is drawn up so that she remains a fairy-tale princess until the very end. Otherwise, the film would have got too complicated and wouldn't have been a romantic love story." *Frankfurter Allgemeine Zeitung*

HUGH GRANT Elected one of the "100 Sexiest Stars in Film History" in 1995 by *Empire Magazine*, Hugh Grant is a multitalented actor who has had considerable success on the stage, on television and above all, in the movies. Born in London in 1962, the Oxford graduate's distinguishing characteristics are his boyish, sensitive, intelligent good looks. His extremely well kept, gentlemanly appearance makes him an ideal candidate to play romantic heroes in film adaptations of literary classics. He first became well known in the film of E. M. Forster's novel *Maurice* (1987). The surprise smash hit *Four Weddings and a Funeral* (1993) made him an international star.

1 Two people who were made for each other: book-seller William Thacker and Hollywood actress Anna Scott (Hugh Grant and Julia Roberts).

2 Bookworm as lady-killer: William Thacker in his shop.

3 Incognito: media star Anna Scott is always on the run.

4 Spike (Rhys Ifans), William's flatmate, throws a temporary spanner in the works.

3

4

out affectation are some offbeat figures who could only exist in England. Spike, William's flatmate, counterbalances the two main figures in an amusing manner with his advice and his pithy comments, his lanky figure and his scruffy hippie appearance. But *Notting Hill* has some critical undertones too. It takes more than one sideswipe at the mass media, contrasting Anna's terrible treatment in the papers with the respectful admiration of the people on the street. Yet it's thanks to the media that the two lovers find each other again: at the last moment William manages to get into a press conference and mix with the reporters. He asks Anna in an understated, charming manner whether she intends to return to the USA. The ruse succeeds, and Anna promises to stay "for ever".

BR

THE SIXTH SENSE

999 - USA - 106 MIN. - THRILLER, DRAMA, HORROR FILM

DIRECTOR M. NIGHT SHYAMALAN (Manoj Nelliyattu Shyamalan) (*1970)
SCREENPLAY M. NIGHT SHYAMALAN DIRECTOR OF PHOTOGRAPHY TAK FUJIMOTO MUSIC JAMES NEWTON HOWARD PRODUCTION KATHLEEN
KENNEDY, FRANK MARSHALL, BARRY MENDEL for HOLLYWOOD PICTURES, SPYGLASS ENTERTAINMENT.

STARRING BRUCE WILLIS (Dr Malcolm Crowe), HALEY JOEL OSMENT (Cole Sear), TONI COLLETTE (Lynn Sear), OLIVIA
WILLIAMS (Anna Crowe), TREVOR MORGAN (Tommy Tammisimo), DONNIE WAHLBERG (Vincent Grey), MISCHA BARTON
(Kyra Collins), PETER ANTHONY TAMBAKIS (Darren), JEFFREY ZUBERNIS (Bobby), BRUCE NORRIS (Stanley Cunningham).

"I don't want to be scared anymore."

Although death waits for us all, its nature is beyond our knowledge. No film of the 90s brings this closer to home than *The Sixth Sense*. Little Cole (Haley Joel Osment) has a secret: he has a sixth sense, and he can see the dead. They have chosen him to be their medium. They want to tell him of their torment and reveal the mysterious circumstances of their deaths. Dr Malcolm Crowe (Bruce Willis) is a child psychologist. He is also dead, shot by a former patient whose treatment failed. The unusual thriller that results from this situation strikes a subtle and moving balance between psychological drama, horror film, buddy movie, and melodrama. In it Bruce Willis, who alongside Stallone and Schwarzenegger is an action star par excellence, demonstrates an unexpected mastery of restrained feeling. The exceptional performance of Haley Joel Osment provides the perfect counterpart as the little boy whose daily encounters with the dead leave painful traces on his body.

Willis portrays the dead psychologist with a combination of melancholy and loneliness, making his vague sense of loss perceptible in every gesture and expression. He's quite unaware that he has joined the ranks of the dead. Only Cole can see him. They meet for the first time in a church near the home that Cole shares with his mother. Cole is tormented by his sixth sense and

Crowe offers assistance, not knowing that in fact it is Cole who will be of greater help to him in coming to grips with his past. The exchange between these two characters gives the film emotional plausibility, in spite of its being a ghost story which is not without horrifying moments of subtle terror. *The Sixth Sense* brings a new dimension to the mystery / ghost story horror genre. The nightmarish tale, with its surprise ending, is staged with remarkable creativity and assurance by Night Shyamalan. The plot plays with our expectations, exploiting the viewer's assumption that all that is seen is real and that time, place and causality all correspond to his everyday experience. After Malcolm Crowe is shot in the stomach, the film fades into darkness. It fades in again to the figure of Crowe, who is sitting on a bench and observing a child in the distance. Further deception is provided by a subtitle, fixing the event in space and time. Nothing recalls the previous injury, and the world seems to be back in order. From this position of security, the viewer scarcely notices that Crowe no longer has any contact with his fellow humans, with the exception of Cole. Scenes showing Crowe together with other people are staged so cunningly that the audience takes it for granted that he is alive and is still treating Cole's case. In fact, the reverse is true and

> **"The film is so well plotted and the ending so unforeseen that the surprise is complete. This is a film worth seeing several times over to grasp all its nuances."** *M. Night Shyamalan in: Le Figaro*

the film is treating the case of Crowe, but to make the twist at the end of the movie work, the audience must believe that he is still in the world of the living.

In Tak Fujimoto, Shyamalan had one of Hollywood's most distinguished cameramen at his disposal, and it is his artistic mastery that is responsible to a large extent for the great visual power of the film. The calm camerawork together with the subdued colouring of the individual scenes blend to create an atmosphere of morbid foreboding. There is also plenty of visual quotation from other films, like the winding staircase from Hitchcock's *Vertigo*. Shyamalan also follows Hitchcock's lead in making a cameo appearance as hospital doctor.

Hitchcock's unusual habit of self-portrayal and his subversive brand of psycho-terror are not the only sources of inspiration for this movie. A number of visual shock effects, and the motif of the child's hallucinatory abilities are reminiscent of Stanley Kubrick's horror classic *The Shining* (1980), and the sudden inexplicable opening of kitchen cupboards remind us of Tobe Hooper's *Poltergeist* (1982). *The Sixth Sense* is an illustrious example of the

way filmmakers of the 90s are often masters of the art of quotation. By playing with repetition, ironic refraction, parody and reversal of meaning, directors open up new perspectives for themselves while at the same time offering audiences a fresh source of entertainment in finding points of comparison with their own knowledge of film. The name of the young protagonist "Cole" for example is a direct reference to the figure played by Bruce Willis in *Twelve Monkeys* (1995) by Terry Gilliam. The characters do much more than share a name – in both films their extraordinary stories are so implausible that they are held to be sane. Both figures find themselves in the same predicament, that they can both see dead people.

The childhood nightmares that make a nightmare of Cole's childhood are dispelled when he accepts his role as go-between and offers the dead his services. When realisation of his own death finally catches up with the shocked Crowe, he recalls Cole's words: "I see people – they don't know they're dead". This is the real moment of death for Crowe. The scene is consumed in brilliant white light, and our last visual impression is a short excerpt from his wedding video.

4

1 Young Cole (Haley Joel Osment) knows what Dr Malcolm Crowe (Bruce Willis) doesn't know yet.

2 Enough to take your breath away: horrific visions from the realm of the dead.

3 The descent into hell is never-ending: the boy sees one frightening image after the other.

4 Childish fears and crippling fantasies of death: horror lurks behind the door at the top of the stairs.

CAMERAMAN TAK FUJIMOTO

The visual power of Tak Fujimoto's images had a lasting influence on the cinema of the 90s. He trained at the International Film School in London and has left his mark on the style of a generation of cameramen. His impressive debut in 1973 with *Badlands* (director: Terrence Malick) was an early demonstration of his virtuosity and sense of style.
Caged Heat (1974) was the first of several collaborations with director Jonathan Demme. The originality of this director's American images is large-ly due to Fujimoto's rich colouring and judicious lighting. Above all, in *The Silence of the Lambs* (1991) Fujimoto developed his virtuoso games with space, with nearness and distance, and with the visible and the invisible to unique perfection.

THE LIMEY

1999 - USA - 90 MIN. - GANGSTER FILM, NEO FILM NOIR

DIRECTOR STEVEN SODERBERGH (*1963)
SCREENPLAY LEM DOBBS DIRECTOR OF PHOTOGRAPHY EDWARD LACHMAN MUSIC CLIFF MARTINEZ PRODUCTION JOHN HARDY, SCOTT KRAMER for ARTISAN ENTERTAINMENT.

STARRING TERENCE STAMP (Wilson), LESLEY ANN WARREN (Elaine), LUIS GUZMÁN (Ed), BARRY NEWMAN (Avery), JOE DALLESANDRO (Uncle John), NICKY KATT (Stacy), PETER FONDA (Terry Valentine), AMELIA HEINLE (Adhara), MELISSA GEORGE (Jennifer), MATTHEW KIMBROUGH (Tom).

"Do you understand half the shit he says? – No, but I know what he means."

The English are not fond of talking. Americans, on the other hand, most definitely are. In his film *The Limey*, American cinema prodigy Steven Soderbergh concentrates on showing rather than saying. A newspaper clipping with the information that a woman has been killed on the Mulholland Highway, a photograph of the young woman, a man sitting pensively in an aeroplane: images take the place of words in setting up the story. The name of the man in the aeroplane is Wilson (Terence Stamp), and he is investigating the mysterious circumstances surrounding the car accident in which his daughter Jenny died. As in the best examples of film noir, Wilson has already reached a kind of ending as the story begins. The aeroplane scene takes place after the mystery has been solved and Wilson has finished his savage vendetta against his daughter's killers. He is on his way home, returning to his private life in England. He didn't kill media promoter Terry Valentine (Peter Fonda) who had been having an affair with his daughter. Instead, he forced him to talk, and, in a strange sense, saw his own mirror image. Jenny, he learnt, was killed accidentally in a fistfight. She loved Valentine and she was trying to stop him committing more crimes by betraying him to the police. When she was a child, she had once threatened to do the same to her criminal father. Now, all Wilson has left are his memories. Silent, blue-toned images of his daughter playing on the beach are shown again and again. A flash of light dances over her features. There is poetry in this repose, a stillness that contrasts with the other hectic and agitated images of the film. Wilson starts to be extremely depressed in the face of his failure and his loss. In casting Terence Stamp, Soderbergh made a first-class choice. The British actor's stony-faced style seems the perfect medium for expressing both the brutal and the tragic sides of Wilson's character. The director plays with this interaction between emotion and cold detachment: in one scene, Wilson enters a warehouse, and a hand-held camera follows him in. His questions are followed by a fistfight, and Wilson is brutally beaten and thrown out. He picks himself up and goes back in, but this time the camera stays outside. Shots are fired. The camera films calmly from a safe distance. There are flashes of light and screams, and one man escapes from the warehouse and

1 With stony features and iron determination Wilson (Terence Stamp) tracks down his daughter's murderers.

2 Organised crime lives high above the roofs of the metropolis: Peter Fonda plays music producer Terry Valentine.

runs past the camera. Wilson returns. Agitated, the camera picks up and closes in on him. He calls: "Tell him, I'm coming." Soderbergh's sequencing of shots disrupts the chronology of events and their chain of causality. The spectators only discover the plot connections bit by bit, as they gradually piece together the story. Often they have to rely on assumptions. This process of mystification is intensified by the separation of action and sound: a figure is shown, we hear him talking, but his lips are not moving. Image and tone are not synchronised again until the next shot. In addition, Soderbergh integrates images from a totally different film. Scenes from Ken Loach's debut movie *Poor Cow* (1967) – also starring Terence Stamp – are incorporated as flashbacks into Wilson's happier past. In fact *The Limey* is also a homage. Parts of it look exactly like Jean-Luc Godard's first film *À bout de souffle* (*Breathless*, 1960), thanks to the hand-held cameras, the jump cuts, and the seemingly improvised gangster story. But Wilson is quite different to Michel Poiccard, the small-time crook played by Jean-Paul Belmondo in the Godard film. Wilson is a professional, an expert criminal who is taking care of business, and nothing can stand in his way. Terry Valentine in his white suit and Wilson in black are like two sides of the same coin, each the embodying a different lifestyle, one American and the other English. And yet they have much more in common than they would care to admit. For that reason, although Terry has Wilson's daughter quite literally on his conscience, Wilson lets him live. BR

"Soderbergh's style evokes the memory of John Boorman's *Point Blank*, which in its time was misunderstood because of its similarly complex narrative style and which also dealt with revenge taken by a determined loner."

epd Film

JUMP CUT

A jump cut is an abrupt transition between shots. It may involve continuous motion being interrupted by the removal of certain film material, or a static scene being disrupted by rapidly shifting points of focus. By fragmenting temporal and spatial continuity the director can actively steer the viewer's attention. Jump cutting is used extensively by Jean-Luc Godard in *À bout de souffle* (*Breathless*, 1960) as a move away from conventional "continuity editing" and a way of drawing the attention of the spectators to the structural aspect of film. It can also be used as a technical means of placing the viewer at the centre of the dramatic action, as for example, in Steven Spielberg's *Jaws* (1975).

---

3   The smart ruler of the underworld.

4   Beauty, elegance and crime make an unholy trinity.

5   Gangsters together: the showdown leads to self-knowledge.

5

BEING JOHN MALKOVICH

1999 - USA - 112 MIN. - COMEDY

DIRECTOR SPIKE JONZE (*1969)
SCREENPLAY CHARLIE KAUFMAN **DIRECTOR OF PHOTOGRAPHY** LANCE ACORD **MUSIC** CARTER BURWELL, BÉLA BARTÓK **PRODUCTION** STEVE GOLIN, VINCENT LANDAY, SANDY STERN, MICHAEL STIPE for GRAMERCY PICTURES, PROPAGANDA FILMS, SINGLE CELL PICTURES.

STARRING JOHN MALKOVICH (John Horatio Malkovich), JOHN CUSACK (Craig Schwartz), CAMERON DIAZ (Lotte Schwartz), NED BELLAMY (Derek Mantini), ORSON BEAN (Dr Lester), CATHERINE KEENER (Maxine), MARY KAY PLACE (Floris), K. K. DODDS (Wendy), REGINALD C. HAYES (Don), BYRNE PIVEN (Captain Mertin).

"I think, I feel, I suffer."

To be famous and desired. To be inside someone else, to see what he sees, to feel what he feels. To be a star, to enjoy his privileges and to bathe in his success, and yet remain incognito – that would be the perfect material for a fairytale, a play or a movie. Well clear the stage and raise the curtain, because the play's called *Being John Malkovich*.

Struggling puppeteer Craig Schwartz (John Cusack) could use more public and financial success for his virtuoso marionette theatre. The lonely "Dance of Despair" of his wooden hero, an expression of Craig's own mental state, is performed with astonishing perfection and intensity, but the public prefers something bigger. To get into television and become famous you need gigantic puppets, the sort that you would have to manipulate from the side of a bridge. This is the starting point for newcomer Spike Jonze's bizarre film comedy. The frustrated Craig is forced to work as a filing clerk for the Lester Corporation, where he meets and falls for the fetching Maxine. She, for her part, is more interested in Craig's wife Lotte (Cameron Diaz). The

vehicle for the self-centred preoccupations of all three becomes John Malkovich, who plays himself. This trick allows for a side-story about the identity of actors and the problems they have giving expression, face and body to countless different characters without losing themselves in the process.

The main story is dedicated to the kafkaesque idea that by crawling through a dwarf-sized door in the wall of the seven-and-a-halfth storey of an office building, it is possible to enter into the head of John Malkovich and take part in his life. Based on this unusual and arresting idea, *Being John Malkovich* becomes an ironic illustration of the theory that we only see ourselves through the eyes of others. A convoluted amorous quadrangle develops. John Cusack and Cameron Diaz play the young couple whose relationship falls apart after Craig's discovery. At first they take turns sliding through the dark corridor beyond the small door that leads into the skull of John Malkovich. He is seduced by Maxine. Maxine actually has her sights on Lotte,

2

1　The anguish of not being master in your own house: John Malkovich.

2　The light at the end of the tunnel is called John Malkovich.

3　Queue here for bliss.

"Hollywood hasn't dared to entrust itself so casually to an absurd initial idea for many years." *Frankfurter Allgemeine Zeitung*

who for her part is not averse to Maxine's advances. Together, they stage their sexual adventure with the help of John Malkovich's body, cuckolding Craig at the same time. In contrast to her character in Tom DeCillo's media satire *Living in Oblivion* (1995, a film whose high spirits are shared by *Being John Malkovich*) Catherine Keener's portrayal of the clever Maxine is coldly erotic. Thanks to her business sense the hole in the wall leading to John Malkovich's brain becomes a source of income, and the secret passage becomes an insider attraction for anyone willing to pay money to have a prominent identity for a change, even if it's only for fifteen minutes. That's the length of the visits, and afterwards visitors find themselves miles away lying in the dirt beside the New Jersey turnpike. When Malkovich finally discovers the unscrupulous business, it's already too late. His ego is no longer

master in its own abode. Craig has taken possession of his mind, and Maxine changes her loyalties to Craig alias Malkovich, from whom she is expecting a child. Craig has finally made it: he's transformed Malkovich into a living puppet and he basks in the brilliance of his success. As if the story were not already full of supernatural situations, it then transforms into a tale of migrating souls like *Cocoon* (1985) where the undead are forced to change their host bodies from time to time. After Maxine's outrageous kidnap attempt, Craig leaves the body of John Malkovich to make room for the spirit of Captain Merten, the builder of the office building with the seventh-and-a-half floor. Craig's attempt to achieve happiness by exploiting John Malkovich's fame turns out to be an illusion of the mind.

BR

"It is precisely the vanity, which Malkovich portrays with remarkable self-irony and without exaggeration so that it always seems authentic, that makes many scenes so funny." *Frankfurter Allgemeine Zeitung*

FILMS ABOUT FILMMAKING The medium of film has always been preoccupied with different aspects of its own make-up,: from scriptwriting (*Sunset Boulevard*, Billy Wilder, 1950) to camerawork (*The Camera Man*, Buster Keaton, 1928), from directing (*Otto e Mezzo*, Federico Fellini, 1963) to acting (*Chaplin*, Richard Attenborough, 1992) and on-location shooting (*Living in Oblivion*, Tom DiCillo, 1995). But the movie business does more than examine aspects of its own creative process. In remakes and film quotations, directors consistently return to imagery created by other filmmakers, and thus construct their own history. The cinema of the 90s is particularly characterised by such self-reflective films, from *Cape Fear* (1991) to *Pulp Fiction* (1994).

4 Puppeteer Craig Schwartz (John Cusack) as a fake Mephistopheles.

5 Cameron Diaz in the role of the wife Lotte Schwartz discovers that she is in love with Maxine.

6 The shock of realisation: I am not myself.

7 Unscrupulous *femme fatale* Maxine (Catherine Keener) turns everybody's head.

6

7

MAGNOLIA

1999 - USA - 188 MIN. - DRAMA, EPISODIC FILM

DIRECTOR PAUL THOMAS ANDERSON (*1970)

SCREENPLAY PAUL THOMAS ANDERSON DIRECTOR OF PHOTOGRAPHY ROBERT ELSWIT MUSIC JON BRION, AIMEE MANN PRODUCTION PAUL THOMAS ANDERSON, JOANNE SELLAR for GHOULARDI FILM COMPANY, NEW LINE CINEMA, THE MAGNOLIA PROJECT.

STARRING JOHN C. REILLY (Jim Kurring), TOM CRUISE (Frank T. J. Mackey), JULIANNE MOORE (Linda Partridge), PHILIP BAKER HALL (Jimmy Gator), JEREMY BLACKMAN (Stanley Spector), PHILIP SEYMOUR HOFFMAN (Phil Parma), WILLIAM H. MACY (Quiz Kid Donnie Smith), MELORA WALTERS (Claudia Wilson Gator), JASON ROBARDS (Earl Partridge).

IFF BERLIN 2000 GOLDEN BEAR.

"It would seem that we're through with the past, but it's not through with us."

According to Quentin Tarantino, the plot of *Pulp Fiction* (1994) is three stories about a story. Shortly before that, the film virtuoso Robert Altman gave the episodic movie new elegance with *Shorts Cuts* (1993), where many short stories revolve around a centre, overlap, move away from each other again and form new combinations. Although director Paul Thomas Anderson originally tried to play down the link, *Magnolia* can definitely be seen in relation to these earlier movies. The denial was probably just the reaction of a promising young filmmaker who wanted audiences to take a second look at his *Boogie Nights* (1997).

At the centre of the tragicomedy *Magnolia* is Big Earl Partridge (Jason Robards), a TV tycoon of the worst kind. He lies dying, a wilting magnolia. Earl is the key figure, the man behind the scenes and the origin of all evils. His name alone is a programme for the movie ... Earl is the only figure who always stays in the same place, unable to move from his deathbed. When the camera looks down on him from above and the mighty fanfare from Richard Strauss's *Also sprach Zarathustra* sounds, it's not just an ironic reference to

his once all-powerful influence, but also to the end of Stanley Kubrick's *2001 – A Space Odyssey* (1968). There we see the astronaut David Bowman as an old man alone on a big bed, shortly before the next evolutionary leap transforms him into the famous foetus from the final shot of 2001 and the cycle of human development moves onto a higher plane. Earl's end also signifies new beginnings, but before that can come about all the suffering that he has brought into the world must be dealt with. And that is no easy task.

With great humour and sympathy, *Magnolia* tells the stories of all the people on whose lives he has had such a lasting influence. First of all comes Earl's son Frank (Tom Cruise) who trains frustrated men to become supermacho in his "Seduce and Destroy" seminars. He got this motto from his father, who destroyed his wife with his complete lack of consideration. Now, shortly before his death, the shallow patriarch searches for his lost son, who he had abandoned as a teenager when his mother fell ill with cancer. When the two come together at the end, their broken relationship is shown in all its misery. Earl's young wife Linda (Julianne Moore) only married him for his

"Almost exactly in the middle is *Magnolia* – which lasts for three hours and isn't a second too long – so close to its characters that we can almost feel their breath."

Frankfurter Allgemeine Zeitung

1 Prodigal son (Tom Cruise) and hated father (Jason Robards).

2 Relationship at an end: scenes from a marriage on its deathbed. Julianne Moore in the role of Linda Partridge.

3 The incarnation of law and order: good-natured police officer Jim Kurring (John C. Reilly).

4 Claudia (Melora Walters), abused by her own father and addicted to drugs, provides an optimistic ending to the film.

5 Phil (Philip Seymour Hoffman), the carer of ailing patriarch Earl, demonstrates patience and sensitivity.

6 Confessions under duress: homosexual Donnie (William H. Macy) becomes the victim of his inferiority complex.

money. She realises the shallowness of her own character and starts to go through a crisis of identity. Quiz master Jimmy Gator (Philip Baker Hall) presents the bizarre show "What Do Kids Know?" for Big Earl Partridge TV Productions, where three children compete against three adults answering general knowledge questions. Jimmy has absorbed his boss's way of thinking to such a degree that his extramarital affairs even include his daughter Claudia, who is now a cocaine addict and funds her habit with occasional prostitution. When the neighbours complain about her loud music, she gets a visit from a policeman who promptly falls in love with her, and even greater confusion ensues. Finally, there are the two child prodigies who have become famous through the quiz show. Former child star Donny now tries vainly to chat up a good looking barman and Stanley wets his pants at the show's decisive moment, as the production team's strict rules don't allow him to go to the lavatory before the broadcast.

The movie's interpersonal conflicts run along the fault lines between parents and children and men and women. All these relationships have been ruined by an inability to build up and maintain friendships, and by the impossibility of any real communication. *Magnolia* is an affectionate but cynical critique of the medium of television, and all the people in the movie seem to be trying to emulate its clichés. Behind everything is the television magnate Earl. The characters' lives are nothing more than television made flesh, absurd TV drama on the wrong side of the screen.

The movie begins with a macabre, satirical undertone and it becomes increasingly sarcastic and even cynical. An amused, concise voice-over at the beginning talks about the absurdity of life and denies the existence of coincidence, and the film goes on to prove that thesis. Although at first the episodes appear to be a transitory collection of unconnected events, a dense network of links gradually appears. The movie draws the audience into a

PAUL THOMAS ANDERSON Paul Thomas Anderson first worked as a production assistant on television films, video productions and game shows in Los Angeles and New York, before leaving the New York University Film School after only two days to get back to the practical side of things again. He developed his short film *Cigarettes and Coffee* (1993) into his first feature film *Hard Eight,* which was presented at the 1996 Cannes Film Festival. *Boogie Nights* (1997) was nominated for three Oscars. His innovative directing style doesn't balk at confusing plots or complex characters, and he is not afraid to break taboos. Paul Thomas Anderson is considered one of the most promising young directors around today.

7   The strain of the TV quiz is written all over the face of young genius Stanley (Jeremy Blackman).

8   Donnie runs into more and more trouble.

9   Learning from children: a hard task even for compère Jimmy Gator (Philip Baker Hall)

whirl of failed relationships and unfulfilled yearnings for freedom, love and mutual respect. This descent influences the movie's images, and their rhythm becomes slower and their colours darker, and spectators start to feel that the downward spiral could go on forever. But *Magnolia* is anything but a pessimistic movie: shortly before the final catastrophe, all the figures suddenly begin to sing the same song wherever they happen to be. After the initial surprise, this absurd directorial idea turns out to be a wonderful trick, which counteracts the seemingly inevitable end with off-beat humour in a manner not dissimilar to the song at the end of *Monty Python's Life of Brian* (1979). When it rains frogs at the very end, spectators heave a sigh of relief along with the characters in the movie. This surreal event makes it clear that anything is possible in this movie. We may not be able to believe our eyes, but "it did happen" as the text under the pictures tells us. The event shakes the characters out of their lethargy and reminds them of the incredible opportunities that life can offer. And a small smile into the camera in the final shot holds the key to the way out of this crisis whose name is life.   BR

"*Magnolia* takes a long run-up, then jumps and lands in the middle of our present. It is the first film of the new millennium." *Frankfurter Allgemeine Zeitung*

"The film pauses for a moment: suicides forget to press the trigger, addicts forget their fix, and those in pain their pain. Then the play is over, the world appears fresh once more, the dead are buried and the living are given a second chance." *Süddeutsche Zeitung*

10 ◊ Tom Cruise in the unusual role of a repulsive advocate of machismo.

11 Victim of self-delusion: Julianne Moore is a convincing Beauty and the Beast.

SLEEPY HOLLOW

1999 - USA - 105 MIN. - HORROR FILM, CRIME FILM, LITERATURE ADAPTATION

DIRECTOR TIM BURTON (*1958)
SCREENPLAY ANDREW KEVIN WALKER, based on the novel *THE LEGEND OF SLEEPY HOLLOW* by WASHINGTON IRVING
DIRECTOR OF PHOTOGRAPHY EMMANUEL LUBEZKI **MUSIC** DANNY ELFMAN **PRODUCTION** SCOTT RUDIN, ADAM SCHROEDER, FRANCIS FORD COPPOLA for PARAMOUNT PICTURES, MANDALAY PICTURES.

STARRING JOHNNY DEPP (Constable Ichabod Crane), CHRISTINA RICCI (Katrina Anne Van Tassel), MIRANDA RICHARDSON (Lady Mary Van Tassel), MICHAEL GAMBON (Baltus Van Tassel), CASPER VAN DIEN (Brom Van Brunt), JEFFREY JONES (Reverend Steenwyck), CHRISTOPHER LEE (Magistrate), MARC PICKERING (Masbath), CHRISTOPHER WALKEN (The Hessian Horseman).

ACADEMY AWARDS 2000 OSCAR for BEST ART DIRECTION-SET DECORATION (Rick Heinrichs, Peter Young).

"Truth is appearance, but appearance isn't always truth."

This truism, first expressed by Jean-Luc Godard, is exploited by filmmakers every second. And it is only because audiences know the principle so well that they are entertained by the film industry's more ghastly and peculiar offerings. Even if it means watching a film in which eighteen people are beheaded by a headless, black-clad and merciless horseman. For that's what we get in the cheerful grisliness that is Tim Burton's *Sleepy Hollow*. The fact that Washington Irving's short story *The Legend of Sleepy Hollow* (1820) is widely known and has served as the basis for a number of films, might also play a role, and it makes some, if not all of the story, a lot easier to swallow.

Luckily, spectators have an ally in Ichabod Crane, the main character in this gothic mystery-horror. The year is 1799. Armed with the scientific instruments of the Enlightenment, Constable Crane (Johnny Depp) is sent to Sleepy Hollow, a small Dutch settlement not far from New York City, to investigate a series of mysterious murders. All of the victims have been beheaded. The villagers don't take to Crane's modern methods, and in fact his outlandish instruments and feeble attempts at logical argumentation are of little use. Things take a new turn when he has a personal encounter with the feared horseman, who is the ghost of a soldier punished for his bloody involvement in the American War of Independence by being beheaded with his own sword. This terrifying meeting leaves a deep mark on Crane and his enlightenment world-view threatens to crumble, and for a while it seems that age-old superstitions and the archaic powers of a bygone age have caught up with him. But the Enlightenment is not so easily defeated, and he

"*Sleepy Hollow* is a masterpiece of visual and emotional atmosphere, Burton's best film to date." *epd Film*

takes up the challenge of understanding the strange phenomena. Following this salutary shock to his system, the fearless criminologist Crane becomes a perfect Sherlock Holmes figure. His Dr Watson is the young Masbath (Marc Pickering), who lost his own father in the battle with the horseman. Unearthing some hidden facts, Masbath helps Crane find his way back onto the right track. What he finds is a web of intrigue and conspiracy woven by the two most influential families in town, the Van Tassels and the Van Garretts, together with the Mayor, Brom Van Brunt, and the Reverend Steenwyck. It all revolves around property and inheritance. It seems that the horseman is operating at the behest of one of these parties, and his victims are not chosen at random at all. Yet in the end, it turns out that it is not

Crane's prime suspect Baltus Van Tassel (Michael Gambon) who is at the bottom of the uncanny attacks, but his second wife (Miranda Richardson), stepmother to the beautiful Katrina Van Tassel (Christina Ricci). Using the skull of the dead soldier, she conjures up his ghost to carry out her revenge for past injustices.

With consummate visual precision, this story about the conflict between the Enlightenment values and Romantic beliefs leads us to a blackened windmill. In fact, as well as reminding us of *Frankenstein* (1931) it's also a replica of a windmill from a 1937 Disney animation entitled *The Old Mill* (Burton worked for quite a while as an animation artist with Disney. He also has a weakness for the horror films produced by the British Hammer Studios,

688

5

"Fairy tales are overwhelming. And in any case there is no safer medium than the cinema." *Tim Burton in: steady cam*

1 Echoes of Caspar David Friedrich: gothic romanticism to die for. Johnny Depp in the part of Constable Ichabod Crane.

2 Seductress or witch? Katrina (Christina Ricci) hides a dark secret.

3 It's not just superstition: love too makes you blind.

4 The tools of the Enlightenment are powerless in Sleepy Hollow.

5 Demonic eroticism and deadly passion: stepmother Lady Mary (Miranda Richardson).

6 Fearless and determined, Ichabod gets to the mill.

as well as B-Movies, which are low-budget features made in the 1950s. These two film traditions combine in the windmill scene and in the carriage chase that follows it. *Sleepy Hollow* has sets rich in detail and looks quite unreal, filmed as it is in dark, blue-tinted images that are a suitably threatening realisation of Andrew Kevin Walker's script. Walker previously wrote the script for the sinister thriller *Se7en* (1995), but it is the uncredited influence of Tom Stoppard, screenplay writer of *Brazil* (1985), that gives the film its ironic perspective, adding a strangely humorous tone to what would otherwise be a straightforward tale of terror. Gothic horror and enlightened laughter combine – and the truth lies somewhere in between.

BR

"Burton, who never willingly speaks about his models, for the set and costumes unmistakably took a look at the work of one of America's most unusual painters, Albert Pinkham Ryder (1847–1917), who was known as the 'Painter of Dreams'." *steady cam*

7   Raging Christopher Walken shines in the support-
    ing role of the death-dealing rider from Hesse.

8   Johnny Depp is ideally cast as romantic lover and
    bringer of rational Enlightenment Ichabod Crane.

9   The ghostly rider is not nearly as headless as he
    appears.

HAMMER FILM STUDIOS   Founded in 1948 by Will Hammer and Sir John Carreras, Hammer Studios was the biggest financial success in the history of British film studios.
Their first hits came in 1956 with a series of low-budget horror film productions. Later, they also made costume dramas, science fiction and psychological thrillers, but the horror genre remained at the centre of their output. The films served to make the graphic portrayal of violence acceptable, and, thanks to Technicolor and morally unhampered depictions, breathed new life into classic horror figures like Dracula, Frankenstein and
the Werewolf. Major stars who worked there include Peter Cushing and Christopher Lee, and directors like Joseph Losey also worked for a time at
Hammer Studios.

STAR WARS: EPISODE 1 – THE PHANTOM MENACE

1999 - USA - 133 MIN. - SCIENCE FICTION, ADVENTURE FILM

DIRECTOR GEORGE LUCAS (*1944)
SCREENPLAY GEORGE LUCAS DIRECTOR OF PHOTOGRAPHY DAVID TATTERSALL MUSIC JOHN WILLIAMS PRODUCTION RICK MCCALLUM for LUCASFILM LTD.

STARRING LIAM NEESON (Qui-Gon Jinn), EWAN MCGREGOR (Obi-Wan Kenobi), NATALIE PORTMAN (Queen Amidala/Padmé Naberrie), JAKE LLOYD (Anakin Skywalker), SAMUEL L. JACKSON (Mace Windu), TERENCE STAMP (Chancellor Finis Valorum), PERNILLA AUGUST (Shmi Skywalker), FRANK OZ (Yoda), IAN MCDIARMID (Senator Palpatine), OLIVER FORD DAVIES (Sio Bibble).

"There's always a bigger fish."

The empire strikes back: for many years now, computers have had dramatic authority and even acted as narrators in movies. The *Star Wars* trilogy changed the design of computer games in the 70s and 80s, and now computers influence contemporary film. Technology freak George Lucas made sure of that by founding his own special effects company. Smash hits at the box office like the *Toy Story* films (1995 and 1999) are impressive examples of the potential that still waits to be released. Lucas himself prophesised in an interview that there would soon be a boom in monumental films, thanks to the virtually unlimited visual potential of computer technology and its comparatively low-budget costs.

For the time being, however, Lucas himself is concentrating on old stories, and filling in the background to the phenomenally successful *Star Wars* trilogy (1977, 1980 and 1983). *Episode 1 –The Phantom Menace* predates the adventures of the Skywalkers – Darth Vader and Luke, Obi-Wan Kenobi,

the Jedi knights, the Princess, R2D2, C3PO and all the popular figures that populate the fairytale world. Jedi knight Qui-Gon (Liam Neeson) and his pupil Obi-Wan Kenobi (Ewan McGregor) are fighting against a double-dealing trading empire that has taken over the small planet of Naboo and is trying to get rid of its occupants. Good struggles against evil, and light sabres battle against droids, fighting robots and the dark side of the Force, which is plotting to do away with the good Queen Amidala (Natalie Portman). During their crusade, the knights land on the planet Tatooine, where they find little Anakin Skywalker (Jake Lloyd), who is living with his mother in serfdom to a scrap metal merchant called Watto. The boy has extraordinary powers and this is how the story of Anakin Skywalker, later Darth Vader, begins. George Lucas enriches his movie with references to the most famous monumental action films in the history of the cinema, the *Ben Hur* movies (1907, 1925 and 1959). In the Pod Racing sequences, which won an MTV Movie Award, *Stars*

1   The powers of darkness are fiendishly good fighters.

2   The monks of the future spread the light by the sword: Ewan McGregor as Obi-Wan Kenobi.

3   Striking similarities: reality and make-believe become indistinguishable thanks to lavish special effects. Natalie Portman as Queen Amidala.

"The flawlessness with which these figures are put next to real actors is supremely impressive, in fact the technical flawlessness is possibly the most impressive thing about *Episode 1*." *epd Film*

Wars brings together the historical film model and computer-generated pictures of the digital age as the ancient charioteers are transformed into joystick acrobats on two huge turbines. But the technology does have its pitfalls: the excellent cast of the movie demonstrate the downside to computerised realism, and how difficult it is for actors to work in a totally digitalised environment. *Star Wars* is an indication that technological changes will require the same kind of quantum leap for acting as the transition from silent film to the talkies.

Star Wars however is not just a computerised fairytale for game-addicted console freaks, it's also a nostalgia trip for all those grown up fans of the original trilogy. The result is perfect family cinema with great entertainment value. The sets effortlessly combine the architecture of ancient temples with futuristic touches from *Metropolis*, old-fashioned blend-ins with modern morphing effects and battle scenes in the open field with Asiatic martial arts sword fighting. In keeping with the rules of the genre good wins at the end in spite of the death of the Jedi Qui-Gon, and the evil trading empire finally bows down to the good queen. The evil that has been sown will not grow until later. Episodes 2 and 3 will continue the story, and fans are curious to find out how the innocent Anakin Skywalker becomes – or rather is turned into – the evil Darth Vader.   BR

"The film is a riot of signs and symbols that you can put together and interpret as you will." *epd Film*

4 Holy Family iconography: fatherly Jedi knight Qui-Gon Jinn (Liam Neeson) takes the child with special powers away from his Marian mother.

5 Wisdom is helpless in the face of evil: Samuel L. Jackson as Mace Windu.

6 The computer game is harsh reality here: Anakin Skywalker (Jake Lloyd) on the starting-line of the pod race.

GEORGE LUCAS AND "INDUSTRIAL LIGHT AND MAGIC"

"Industrial Light and Magic" (ILM) is the name of the special effects firm that George Lucas founded in 1975 for his *Star Wars* production. The aim was to work with young artists and develop revolutionary and innovative methods to simulate by computer the movement of space ships in fight scenes and make them look as realistic as possible. The overwhelming success of *Star Wars* rewarded all of Lucas' innovative work. Later ILM became part of Lucas' production company Lucasfilm Ltd. and went on to become the number one company for computer-generated film trick techniques. As well as visual effects, ILM also developed the cinema sound standard THX to perfect our experience at the movies even further. THX regulates the acoustics according to the structure of the individual cinema (size of screen, angle, air conditioning noises, apparatus available etc). Today's special effects would be unthinkable without Lucas' pioneering work.

7   Stunning animation ensures that the artificial   8   Computer-generated warrior ballet.   9   This is how rulers of the future look: the corpulent
figure of JarJar Binks looks as if he's organic.   King Jabba.

"Digital realism is an American speciality; they invest huge sums of money in the design of complete film illusions such as *Toy Story 2* or *Star Wars: Episode 1*."

epd Film

CROUCHING TIGER, HIDDEN DRAGON ⭡⭡⭡⭡
Wo hu zang long

2000 - CHINA / HONG KONG / TAIWAN / USA - 120 MIN. - MARTIAL ARTS FILM, FANTASY

DIRECTOR ANG LEE (*1954)
SCREENPLAY JAMES SCHAMUS, WANG HUI LING, TSAI KUO JUNG, based on a novel by WANG DU LU **DIRECTOR OF PHOTOGRAPHY** PETER PAU **MUSIC** TAN DUN **PRODUCTION** BILL KONG, HSU LI KONG, ANG LEE for UNITED CHINA VISION, SONY, COLUMBIA, GOOD MACHINE, EDKO FILMS.

STARRING CHOW YUN-FAT (Li Mu Bai), MICHELLE YEOH (Yu Shu Lien), ZHANG ZIYI (Jiao Long Yu/Jen), CHANG CHEN (Xiao Hu Luo/Lo), LUNG SIHUNG (Sir Te), CHENG PEI-PEI (Jade Fox), LI FAZENG (Yu), GAO XIAN (Bo), HAI YAN (Madam Yu), WANG DEMING (Tsai).

ACADEMY AWARDS 2001 OSCARS for BEST FOREIGN LANGUAGE FILM, BEST CINEMATOGRAPHY (Peter Pau), BEST MUSIC (Tan Dun), BEST ART DIRECTION (Tim Yip).

"Sharpness is a state of mind"

Crouching Tiger, Hidden Dragon is in every sense a fairy tale, while still remaining a classic martial arts film. This is no contradiction, the martial arts film genre is a perfect medium for telling fairy tales and has never been afraid of the extreme exaggeration that is necessary to film the fantastic. In *Crouching Tiger, Hidden Dragon*, the world of the fairytale is already evoked by the setting: the synthesised studio shots, the fantastic landscapes shot on location in the People's Republic of China, and the original costumes and architecture. The historic reconstruction of an idyllic past goes hand in hand with its stylisation. Into this opulent scenario steps Wu-dan master Li Mu Bai (Chow Yun-Fat). Wu-Dan is a style of swordsmanship that teaches self-negation and internal strength. Sharp wits become the practitioner's greatest weapon. Li Mu Bai wishes to turn his back on his earlier life as a swordsman, in search of greater enlightenment, and therefore entrusts his fabled sword "Green Destiny" to the keeping of the State Administrator in Peking. The sword is delivered by his female colleague Yu Shu Lien (Michelle Yeoh), who is bound to him in a sort of Platonic imprisonment through a secret bond of unspoken love. Jen (Zhang Ziyi), the daughter of an aristocratic family,

also lives in the city but is trapped in the gilded cage of her social circumstances. She is being forced into an arranged marriage. Jen has a servant and companion who is interested in far more than her socially appropriate upbringing. She is in fact the witch Jade Fox, wanted by the police for the murder of Li Mu Bai's teacher. Not only does she assist the beautiful Jen in maintaining her flawless looks and behaviour, she also secretly trains her in various martial arts. Jen much prefers adventure to the dreariness of her sheltered life in the city. A lengthy flashback relates how she fell in love with the desert bandit Lo following his assault on her caravan. In spite of his wild appearance, Lo is a warm-hearted person. As a pair, they counterbalance Li Mu Bai and Yu Shu Lien. Although their youth makes it easier for them to ignore social constraints, their love is also destined for an unhappy end.

But before the film leads us into this web of relationships, a crime occurs: the priceless sword is stolen. A furious chase ensues, but the masked thief just manages to escape. The film's repeated chase-scenes, where the participants follow each other over rooftops, through alleyways, and even over treetops may at first appear absurd, but are in fact an integral

1

part of Chinese folk mythology. By collaborating with the same team that choreographed the fight-scenes in *The Matrix* (1999), Ang Lee reaches new heights of intercultural film style in *Crouching Tiger, Hidden Dragon*. The stolen sword acts as a kind of "McGuffin", carrying the story forward without playing an important role in its outcome. Even before all the relationships in the film are clearly established, transformations begin. During the chase and fight-scenes they are literally set in motion. At times, the camera work reduces the action into dancing graphic patterns. Where the human eye can only discern lines of motion – in the rapid oscillation between long and short-range shots – the fight-scenes nonetheless remain carefully controlled. They are a reflection of the same ethic of discipline and self-control that governs social behaviour in the film. The art of fighting is also a social art.

"A faithful heart makes wishes come true"

Ang Lee's *Crouching Tiger, Hidden Dragon* is a remarkable martial arts film. While respecting the conventions of the genre, it is also a fascinating vehicle for the portrayal of tragic-romantic love stories in a poetic setting. The movie owes its persuasiveness to the manner in which Ang Lee extends the boundaries of the genre without betraying its innate virtues. As in his other films – especially *Eat, Drink, Man, Woman* (1994), *The Wedding Banquet* (1993), *Sense and Sensibility* (1995), *The Ice Storm* (1997), and *Ride with the*

1   Fairylike grace and unbridled energy are not mutually exclusive: beautiful and wilful Jen (Zhang Ziyi) casts her spell over the film.

2   The sword of power is reason, and nobody knows this better than the monk Li Mu Bai (Chow Yun-Fat).

3   Love beyond death: earthly barriers are no obstacle. Michelle Yeoh in the role of Hu Shu Lien.

"Sword and sabre shiver and redound like lovers in this portrait of contrasted temperaments locked in battle. This is a whirligig of literal revenges, slings and arrows ... Ang Lee enters the ranks of his past masters." *Libération*

Devil (1999), the film whose production practically coincided with *Crouching Tiger, Hidden Dragon,* Lee's strength lies in the careful balance between the powerful visual images and the mastery of epic storytelling. This reflects Lee's equal experience of western and eastern culture. *Crouching Tiger, Hidden Dragon* has reflective moments where it devotes itself to its protagonists' personal concerns, but then it erupts into phases of extreme action, before settling effortlessly back into contemplative situations. The film never loses its rhythm, and great attention is paid to every detail.

Crouching Tiger, Hidden Dragon combines images of the director's youth in Taiwan with a story from the fourth book of a pentology by Du Lu Wang. The novel is a product of East Asian popular literature comparable with the penny-romance, featuring stereotyped heroes and predictable love stories. Ang Lee adapts this cultural tradition with great skill. In his version,

virtues like bravery, friendship, and honour turn out to be impossible ideals. He does not reject them, but takes leave of them with melancholy regret and not before he has pointed a way out of the resulting emptiness.

In contrast to the value system of a male-dominated society, the film emphasises womanly virtues. In an irony typical of Ang Lee's films, the fate of the male protagonist lies in the hands of three women who are all struggling for independence from the patriarchal norm. Finally, *Crouching Tiger, Hidden Dragon* is an ideal film realisation of the principle of Yin and Yang: contemplative stillness and furious action, peaceful dialogue and sword battles, the cramped city and the wide-open Chinese landscapes. The balanced harmony of its composition makes *Crouching Tiger, Hidden Dragon* a fairy tale constructed on an epic scale.

BR

"The choreography was new to me. It had its roots in the Peking Opera, and they are completely different from the Western method of producing action scenes." *Ang Lee in: epd Film*

4 At the moment of maximum concentration, body and soul fuse together.

5 Jen's desire for a life full of adventure and love is being fulfilled, but not quite as she imagines.

6   In the fantasy world of *Crouching Tiger, Hidden Dragon* the normal laws of physics don't apply.

7   During the fight, the rival women's bodies hover and fly through space with no apparent efforts.

8   Brigand Lo (Chang Chen) makes a good haul.

MARTIAL ARTS FILMS   Generally, martial arts films are films featuring oriental combat sports and their accompanying philosophical traditions. The plots normally revolve around a hero figure whose sense of loyalty and justice free him from moral scruples in meting out vengeance to evil-doers. The martial arts film developed into a mass product in Hong Kong and gradually shifted its focus away from psychological complexity towards the representation of spiritual states through choreographed motion, and dynamic movement therefore takes on a metaphorical perspective. In the 70s martial arts found their way into American action movies via Hong Kong cinema. Martial arts movies had an increasing influence in the 80s on the related genres of gangster movies, historical epics and even comedy. Alongside Bruce Lee and the no less popular Jackie Chan, directors like John Woo or Tsui Hark have made martial arts acceptable within the action movie genre, giving it a whole new dimension.

BEFORE NIGHT FALLS

2000 - USA - 133 MIN. - DRAMA, BIOPIC

DIRECTOR JULIAN SCHNABEL (*1951)
SCREENPLAY CUNNINGHAM O'KEEFE, LÁZARO GÓMEZ CARRILES, JULIAN SCHNABEL based on the autobiography by REINALDO ARENAS DIRECTOR OF PHOTOGRAPHY XAVIER PÉREZ GROBET MUSIC CARTER BURWELL, LAURIE ANDERSON, LOU REED PRODUCTION JON KILIK for EL MAR PICTURES/GRANDVIEW PICTURES.

STARRING JAVIER BARDEM (Reinaldo Arenas), OLIVIER MARTINEZ (Lázaro Gómez Carriles), ANDREA DI STEFANO (Pepe Malas), JOHNNY DEPP (Bon Bon/Lieutenant Victor), MICHAEL WINCOTT (Herberto Zorilla Ochoa), OLATZ LOPEZ GARMENDIA (Reinaldo's mother), SEBASTIAN SILVA (Reinaldo's father), GIOVANNI FLORIDO (young Reinaldo), PEDRO ARMENDÁRIZ JR. (Reinaldo's grandfather), LOLÓ NAVARRO (Reinaldo's grandmother).

IFF VENICE 2000 SPECIAL GRAND JURY PRIZE (Julian Schnabel), BEST ACTOR (Javier Bardem).

"Beauty is the enemy. Artists are escapists, artists are counterrevolutionary."

Cuba, before the Revolution, somewhere in the countryside. Reinaldo, a boy without a father, grows up in poverty. At an early age, he carves poems into the bark of trees. When his poetic talent comes to the attention of a school teacher, his reward is a slap on the head from his grandfather. When the Revolution breaks out, Reinaldo, now a teenager, joins the rebel forces. He marches victoriously into Havana alongside Fidel Castro and Che Guevara. The years that follow are full of new liberties. As an adult, Reinaldo (Javier Bardem) discovers his homosexuality and lives it openly with his friends and lovers. He also makes a literary breakthrough and has his first book published. Before long however times change, and Castro's regime becomes increasingly mistrustful of independent artists and gays. Persecution begins and show trials are held. Reinaldo's years of suffering begin when he is arrested and imprisoned on flimsy evidence.

Before Night Falls is New York painter Julian Schnabel's second film, and like his debut film Basquiat (1996), this too, is a portrait of an artist. And in both cases the movies tell the deeply tragic life story of an outsider. Schnabel unrolls the pattern of an artist's life for whom truth, art and beauty are inseparably linked and for whom failure is almost inevitable, given his unwillingness to compromise. The film is based on the autobiography of Cuban writer Reinaldo Arenas, which he wrote in exile in New York before committing suicide in 1990 while suffering from AIDS. Schnabel keeps the subjective perspective of the literary model without allowing the spoken word to intrude into the foreground of the movie. Even when Javier Bardem declaims some of Arenas' texts off camera, the real emphasis of the film remains on the images. Schnabel uses them to follow the emotions and imaginative leaps of the writer.

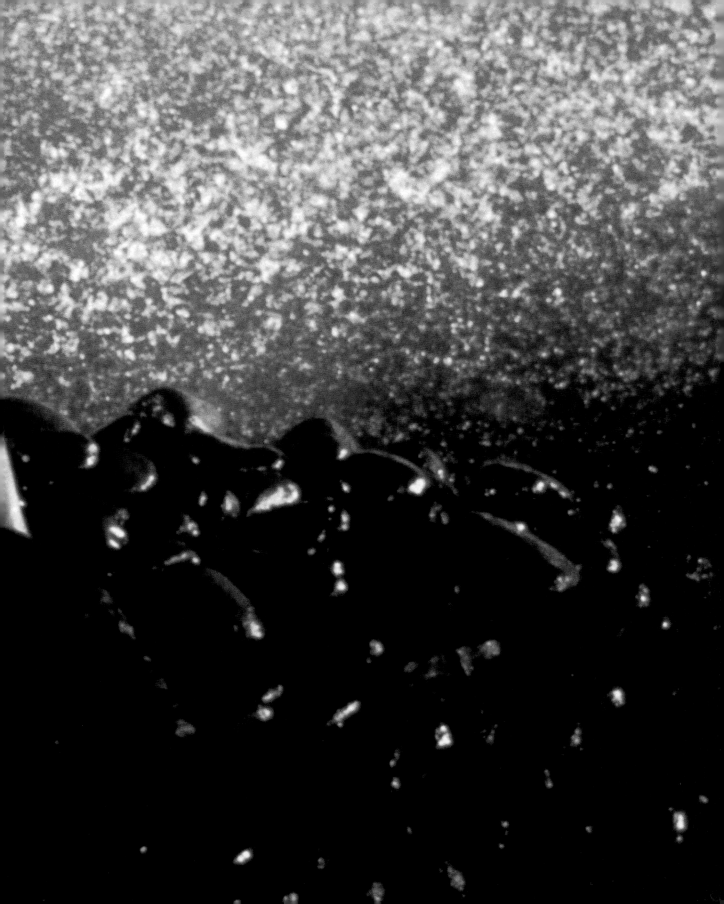

3

"This is a film which makes you want to know everything about its subject, to hear his voice again from a printed page. Extraordinary." *The Observer*

1 The sadistic prison governor: Johnny Depp proves twice over his preference for unusual roles in Julian Schnabel's movie.

2 The Revolution devours its children: gay free-thinker Reinaldo Arenas (Javier Bardem) is soon an outcast in Castro's Cuba.

3 Javier Bardem (right), who usually takes macho roles, shows his feminine side as Reinaldo Arenas.

4 Reinaldo (Javier Bardem, front left) enjoys unheard-of liberties in the immediate aftermath of the Revolution.

5 A blond angel: Johnny Depp (right) in his second brief part as Bon Bon, the beautiful transvestite.

6 Barely recognisable: an offbeat cameo appearance by Sean Penn (left) as a Cuban farmer.

4

5

6

The virtuoso camera movements and the slow rhythm of the images, perfectly harmonized with Carter Burwell's music, make *Before Night Falls* a poetic masterpiece in which Arenas' life and work seem to flow into each other. Although depicted with a certain reserve, Arenas' homosexuality is all-pervasive in Schnabel's extremely sensual movie.

But above all, *Before Night Falls* is Javier Bardem's film. He won the "Best Actor" award at the Venice Film Festival for his brilliant achievement and was nominated for both an Oscar and a Golden Globe. Bardem had long been a star in his native Spain and became known internationally for his part in Pedro Almodóvar's *Live Flesh* (*Carne trémula*, 1997). His previous roles had all been emphatically masculine, but in *Before Night Falls* he gives a finely nuanced performance of the homosexual writer, which is far removed from any of the usual gay clichés. He shows all the facets of Reinaldo's character, his initial timidity, his curiosity and joie de vivre, but also his toughness and his suffering. Johnny Depp's short but spectacular double appear-ance seems like an incarnation of the homosexual writer's feverish imagination: as the beautiful transvestite Bon Bon and the sadistic prison guard he plays two extremes of gay fantasy.

Schnabel's movie is also a statement about the widespread Cuba euphoria of today. Although it is in no way to be understood as a political pamphlet against the socialist state, *Before Night Falls* clearly shows the shadowy sides of Castro's regime, which some fail to see behind the whirl of music and folklore. The movie also reveals that it was equally impossible for Arenas to find a home in the USA of the 80s.

The movie's colours are never so stunning as in the sequences which show the writer's childhood, and never so grey and bleak as in the pictures of New York where Arenas, without health insurance and suffering from AIDS, puts a bitter end to his life with the help of sleeping tablets and a plastic bag printed "I love NY".

JH

OFF CAMERA   "Off camera" is the area outside the picture that the audience is aware of but remains hidden to their view. Through noises or movements out of the picture or into the picture or through the gestures of the actors, off camera can play an important part in the action of a movie. For example, the dangers lurking for the hero off camera in thrillers are a simple, effective and frequently used way of creating tension.

ERIN BROCKOVICH

2000 - USA - 131 MIN. - DRAMA

DIRECTOR STEVEN SODERBERGH (*1963)

SCREENPLAY SUSANNAH GRANT DIRECTOR OF PHOTOGRAPHY EDWARD LACHMAN MUSIC THOMAS NEWMAN PRODUCTION DANNY DEVITO, MICHAEL SHAMBERG, STACEY SHER, GAIL LYON for JERSEY FILMS, COLUMBIA PICTURES, UNIVERSAL PICTURES.

STARRING JULIA ROBERTS (Erin Brockovich), ALBERT FINNEY (Ed Masry), AARON ECKHART (George), MARG HELGENBERGER (Donna Jensen), CHERRY JONES (Pamela Duncan), DAWN DIDAWICK (Rosalind), DAVID BRISBIN (Dr Jaffe), VALENTE RODRIGUEZ (Donald), CONCHATA FERRELL (Brenda), ERIN BROCKOVICH-ELLIS (waitress).

ACADEMY AWARDS 2001 OSCAR for BEST ACTRESS (Julia Roberts).

"For the first time in my life, I got people respecting me ..."

A failed job interview, a car accident, an orthopaedic cushion round the pretty neck, high heels and short skirts, broke, unemployed, and a single mother – Erin Brockovich (Julia Roberts) is a modern woman alright.

Steven Soderbergh's movie tells a real-life incident from the life of lawyer's assistant Erin Brockovich. He comes to the point swiftly and directly. No false sentiment, no glamorous super-woman, but an emancipated, self-confident and attractive woman who understands how to assert herself – not with her elbows, rather with her powers of persuasion and by having the better argument. This is how she gets her job at the firm of defence lawyer Ed Masry (Albert Finney), who wasn't able to get her the compensation she desperately needed following her car accident. The overwhelmed lawyer can't resist and employs Erin on the spot out of sympathy, admiration and a vestige of social conscience.

More or less by chance Erin ends up working on the Jensens case, representing a family who have received an offer from a company that own a nearby factory and want to buy up their house and land. There seems to be an ulterior motive however, for the Jensens are seriously ill. What makes Erin suspicious is that for years the doctor who treats the Jensens has been in the pay of Pacific Gas & Electric, the company who also want to buy their house. During her research she finds documents from the local water works which record a high concentration of deadly poisonous hexavalent chromium that has never been officially monitored. She stumbles on an environmental scandal of enormous proportions. More and more people who live or lived near the factory and have become ill start to get in touch with her. A factory employee finally admits that the poisonous substance contaminates the water due to slipshod factory standards. A magistrate rules that the

plaintiffs are right to sue the company and a first partial success is scored. However, Erin's own family suffer because of her commitment to helping other people. George (Aaron Eckhart), the biker from next door, who under his macho exterior and initial difficulties turns out to be a highly sensitive replacement father for Erin's kids, eventually gives up and leaves the family.

But Erin is not to be stopped. When the case becomes too big and risky for the little lawyer's office, Ed Masry turns to a bigger legal firm. Erin feels she has been passed over, and things become critical. She knows and sympathises with the affected families and their problems and this clashes with the new partner's cool, academic approach. However, only after Erin manages to get incriminating material from an informer is there a swift and financially lucrative compromise in favour of the injured parties.

"... please, don't ask me to give it up."

A plot summary alone cannot convey how unconventional Soderbergh's use of the real-life material is in comparison with other recent disclosure movies. *Erin Brockovich* contains echoes of Soderbergh's highly successful debut movie, *Sex, Lies and Videotape* (1989), without losing the benefits of later film experiments like *Out of Sight* (1998). Light, hand-camera sequences show how Erin's world falls apart and lend emotional depth to the pictures.

Some of them have an improvised feel that reminds us of French cinema. Picture montages that work like jump cuts and the light narrative touch are inevitable reminders of Godard's Nouvelle Vague classic *Breathless* (*À bout de souffle*, 1960). These moments alternate with more conventional, straight shots in which the movie takes time for the characters and their relationships to develop. The unobtrusive yet dramatic use of colours plays an important role. The camera accompanies the characters and empathises with them, and the result is a movie that reveals small-scale, hidden human dramas and tragedies. Sensationalism never gets the upper hand over the precise observation of human life endangered by big industry and corporate law. If there is such a thing as a humanistic narrative style, then Soderbergh is one of its current masters and *Erin Brockovich* is a prototype.

The movie owes much to Julia Roberts' acting. Although she is cast against her usual image, she performs magnificently. Seldom in contemporary cinema has an actress embodied emancipation so simply and yet so convincingly. In full knowledge of her social position, Erin always tries to get the best for her family in every situation. There is an almost comic side to her attempts to make society do what she wants rather than vice versa. In spite of what she knows of her own value on the merciless American job market, Erin winds up neither victim nor heroine, which makes her all the more sympathetic. Her separation from George is presented unpretentiously and realistically, and is one of the things which makes the movie so believable. There is no sentimental tragedy; Erin and George realise that their ways of life are too different when Erin begins to prioritise her job, and their sep-

"*Erin Brockovich* is the first of Soderbergh's films to draw its being from the rousing description of a person rather than from the build-up of a conflict."

epd Film

1 We love her like this: Julia Roberts in the role of the punchy Erin Brockovich.

2 Erin's main concern is for her children.

3 Happy family beyond any clichés.

4 Erin becomes right-hand man to lawyer Ed Masry (Albert Finney).

5 An unusual role for Harley-Davidson afficionado George (Aaron Eckhart).

6 The difficulties of her objective force Erin to adopt extreme measures.

7 George rises to the task of being a substitute father with style.

8 Committed information-seeker and family woman: Erin makes it her job to ensure a better future for small defenceless citizens.

"Erin may be a hero, but she's definitely no angel." *Sight and Sound*

JULIA ROBERTS Julia Roberts was born in 1967 and became world famous overnight in 1990 with *Pretty Woman*. Her performance as a prostitute and rich businessman's lover brought her an Oscar nomination. The downside of this great success was however that she was typecast as an all-American beauty in romantic comedies. With *Erin Brockovich* (2000) and thanks to Steven Soderbergh's support, Julia Roberts was able to fundamentally change her image. She won an Oscar in 2001 for her convincing portrayal of the self-confident lawyer's assistant. She is currently Hollywood's most popular and most successful actress.

aration is a rational solution to the crisis. This realistic, honest, calm presentation isn't scandalous, but it is sensational; it causes the deep grief that inspires Erin to carry on. Instead of being followed by rage and aggression, as in by mainstream cinema, in Soderbergh grief is followed by optimism in a synergetic process. Humour, which forms a link between the two, makes Erin and her boss an extraordinarily successful team. Cheekiness and wit are the best weapons against the adversities of every day life. Erin's recipe for success is to show her teeth, smiling and undaunted. That gives us hope, and gives hope to the families that she is trying to help. In the end, truth lies in compromise, not in a drastic head to head. Simplicity instead of exaggeration, and a sense of proportion rather than heroism. This is the difference between *Erin Brockovich* and other films with similar themes like *Silkwood* (1983) with Meryl Streep in the leading female role. *The Insider* (1999), made shortly before Erin Brockovich, is a hint that a new trend in disclosure dramas is developing – although *The Insider* depends more on highly developed aesthetics than on sensitive understatement.

BR

8

WHAT LIES BENEATH

2000 - USA -129 MIN. - THRILLER

DIRECTOR ROBERT ZEMECKIS (* 1952)
SCREENPLAY CLARK GREGG, based on a story by CLARK GREGG, SARAH KERNOCHAN **DIRECTOR OF PHOTOGRAPHY** DON BURGESS
MUSIC ALAN SILVESTRI **PRODUCTION** JOAN BRADSHAW, MARK JOHNSON, CHERYLANNE MARTIN for 20TH CENTURY FOX, DREAMWORKS SKG, IMAGE MOVERS.

STARRING HARRISON FORD (Norman Spencer), MICHELLE PFEIFFER (Claire Spencer), DIANA SCARWID (Jody), MIRANDA OTTO (Mary Feur), JAMES REMAR (Warren Feur), JOE MORTON (Dr Drayton), AMBER VALLETTA (Madison Elizabeth Frank), VICTORIA BIDEWELL (Beatrice), KATHARINE TOWNE (Caitlin Spencer), ELLIOTT GORETSKY (Teddy).

"Well, I'm seeing ghosts in the bathtub, aren't I?"

Claire and Norman Spencer (Michelle Pfeiffer, Harrison Ford) have a happy marriage. Actually it's a bit too happy for a couple "in the prime of life". It's only when daughter Caitlin (Katharine Towne) moves out to go to college that the situation changes. Like a good mother Claire misses her daughter and cries over the family photo album. Strange things start to happen in the neighbourhood. Like L. B. Jeffries in Hitchcock's *Rear Window* (1954), Claire begins to suspect that the neighbour has murdered his wife – until suddenly the woman unexpectedly reappears. This part of the film seems to be a red herring, but in fact it's a hint at what is to come.

Robert Zemeckis' film not only borrows from Hitchcock, but also from horror classics like Roman Polanski's *Rosemary's Baby* (1968) and Stanley Kubrick's *The Shining* (1980). It gives us other clues apart from this first plot strand: doors open by themselves, a computer is switched on by a ghostly hand and mysterious messages appear on the monitor, the bathtub con-

stantly fills with water, a picture showing Claire together with her husband falls off the wall again and again, and a mysterious key is found in a hole in the ground. The movements of these inanimate objects turn *What Lies Beneath* from family romance to melodrama, with aspects of the thriller and the ghost film thrown in for good measure. Clearly, a sinister secret is waiting to be discovered. Claire seems to lose her powers of perception and logic and begins to see paranoid hallucinations.

What she sees may or may not be real: the movie leaves that open. A short report on the back of the picture which falls down so many times tells of the disappearance of a young student. The ghost continues its determined efforts along conventional lines that still however have the power to shock. Claire sees a face in the reflective surface of the lake in front of the house, in the water in the bathtub or in the bathroom mirror. The face gets clearer every time. Finally Claire is sure that it is Madison Elizabeth Frank, a student

"This film is like a belated gift in honour of Alfred Hitchcock's 100th birthday, giving the viewer a constant impression of déjà-vu."

epd Film

from the newspaper article who disappeared without trace. The ghost is real and calling on a psychiatrist won't solve the problem. Things really get going after a spiritualist meeting, and Claire discovers the truth about her own past. A year previously she lost her memory in a car accident, and in a souvenir shop called "The Sleeping Dog" she discovers the key to the student's fate which is closely connected to her own.

Suddenly we realise that under the surface of the Spencers' wholesome world there is a hidden abyss very much in the Hitchcock tradition. Claire is neither the caring, attractive mother she seems, nor is Norman Spencer merely a charming and successful scientist. In fact their marriage is on the rocks, Claire is a selfish monster and Norman is the cynical killer of the vanished student whose ghost is now seeking revenge. Moreover, the

5

1 Claire (Michelle Pfeiffer) shortly before the bleak-
   est moments in her marriage …

2 … to shady scientist Norman Spencer (Harrison
   Ford).

3 The view from the window onto the yard turns the
   neighbour into a monster.

4 Insight is a weak and treacherous light.

5 Risen from the watery grave of her own amnesia.

RED HERRING   A red herring is a distraction or deviation built into a storyline to lead the main figure and the audience to particular conclusions that then turn out
to be completely irrelevant to the rest of the plot. A red herring is a way of creating tension by giving the audience the chance to form false hypothe-
ses and therefore a false sense of security. According to how much attention the movie gives the red herring motif, the audience are surprised,
shaken and annoyed by the early resolution and unexpected development. At the same time this shock or thrill intensifies the audience's emotional involvement. The art of playing with audience expectations was developed to perfection by Alfred Hitchcock, particularly in *Psycho* (1960).

---

final shot of the seemingly never ending showdown shows that Claire and
Madison Elizabeth Frank are sisters "in spirit" in their relationship with
Norman.

As well as the virtuoso music and film quotations (from the bathtub
scene in *Fatal Attraction* (1987) and from Henri-Georges Clouzot's classic
Les Diaboliques (*Diabolique*, 1955), the film's central motif is the idea of the
surface, under which nothing is quite as it seems. From the very beginning
we can't quite trust our eyes, as the whole situation seems too perfect.
Reflective surfaces then bring the truth to light.

Robert Zemeckis set out to make a perfect Hitchcock thriller, and he
brought it off with incredible precision. But the movie does far more than rely
on Hitch. Claire's paranoia reminds us of Rosemary Woodhouse in

Rosemary's Baby, and the transformation of Claire's face in the bath water
is a quotation from the bathroom sequence with the young/old woman in *The
Shining*. Claire's desperate escape from her bloodthirsty husband Norman at
the end of the movie is also a quotation from that same film. Last, but not
least, the underwater scenes remind us of Charles Laughton's *The Night of
the Hunter* (1955). *What Lies Beneath* unmasks people as completely
voyeuristic creatures in a Hitchcockian manner and is also a brilliant social
satire as well as a thriller. Like his great role model, Zemeckis lays great
emphasis on elegant visuals. In the course of the film the pictures become
darker and darker and the camera follows the development of the story. To
show "what lies beneath", it starts at eye level and moves gradually down-
wards.   BR

GLADIATOR

2000 - USA - 155 MIN. - MONUMENTAL FILM, HISTORICAL FILM, ACTION FILM

DIRECTOR RIDLEY SCOTT (*1937)
SCREENPLAY DAVID FRANZONI, JOHN LOGAN, WILLIAM NICHOLSON DIRECTOR OF PHOTOGRAPHY JOHN MATHIESON MUSIC HANS ZIMMER, LISA GERRARD, KLAUS BADELT PRODUCTION DOUGLAS WICK, DAVID FRANZONI, BRANKO LUSTIG, STEVEN SPIELBERG for UNIVERSAL, DREAMWORKS SKG.

STARRING RUSSELL CROWE (Maximus), JOAQUIN PHOENIX (Commodus), CONNIE NIELSEN (Lucilla), RICHARD HARRIS (Marcus Aurelius), OLIVER REED (Proximo), DEREK JACOBI (Gracchus), RALF MOELLER (Hagen), SPENCER TREAT CLARK (Lucius Verus), DAVID HEMMINGS (Cassius), TOMMY FLANAGAN (Cicero).

ACADEMY AWARDS 2001 OSCARS for BEST FILM, BEST ACTOR (Russell Crowe), BEST VISUAL EFFECTS (John Nelson, Neil Cotbould, Tim Burke, Rob Harvey), BEST SOUND (Ken Weston, Scott Millan, Bob Beemer), BEST COSTUMES (Janty Yates).

"In the end, we're all dead men."

Germania, Anno Domini 180. A hand sweeps through a golden yellow corn-field and gently touches the ears of the waving sheaves of corn – a dream-like image, a premonition of death. The dreamer is a general: Maximus (Russell Crowe), the greatest, undefeated in battle, beloved of the Roman people and by his mentor Marcus Aurelius (Richard Harris), Caesar of the Roman Empire. The movie contrasts this peaceful mental image with the bloody reality of battle that the warrior Maximus conducts with cold preci-sion. The portrayal of battle at the beginning of the movie reminds us of the fighting scenes in John Boorman's *Excalibur* (1981).

Maximus' strategic intelligence, modesty and unconditional loyalty make him Marcus Aurelius' favourite candidate to be his successor. With Maximus' help, he wants to purify the political centre of his global empire of corruption, return to the virtues of old and give the senate in Rome more democratic powers. However, his jealous and power-hungry son Commodus (Joaquin Phoenix) is standing in his way. He realises what his father is plan-

ning to do, so he murders him and becomes heir to the throne, and has Maximus thrown out of the army. To eliminate the popular hero for once and for all, Commodus orders that he be executed. However, Maximus manages to escape and he returns to the Roman province of Spain that is his native land, where he finds his family dead, murdered on Commodus' orders. His will to live sapped, Maximus is captured by a slave trader and sold to a glad-iator school.

His strategic intelligence and his experience of fighting mean that he soon becomes a successful gladiator. His new profession eventually takes him back to Rome, where he quickly becomes popular for his spectacular fighting, and eventually he attracts the attention of Commodus himself. In the meantime, Commodus' sister Lucilla (Connie Nielsen) and the democratical-ly minded Senator Gracchus (Derek Jacobi) plan an intrigue against the emperor in which Maximus also becomes involved. Maximus' popularity forces Commodus to descend into the public arena to fight him in single

1

2

3

"*Gladiator* takes up the bâton for this genre where, 35 years ago, Anthony Mann's masterpiece *The Fall of the Roman Empire*, had let it fall." *Le Monde*

combat. To be sure he will win, Commodus inflicts a serious wound on his opponent Maximus before the fight in the corridors of the Colosseum. In the final single combat both are killed and Commodus' sister Lucilla charges Gracchus with the running of the Empire. The film moves into almost monochrome, bluish dream pictures that take up the motifs of the opening sequence and provide a frame. They tell of the end of Maximus' dream, the fulfilment of his longing for peaceful family life. A hand reaches for a gate, strokes through the ears of a cornfield, and wife and son welcome the warrior home.

Gladiator is a typical example of Ridley Scott's preference for imperfect heroes and huge extravagant sets, as in *Blade Runner* (1982) and *Alien* (1979). *Gladiator* marks the arrival of the computer-generated image in

Scott's films. His approach to the venerable genre of the historical epic is surprisingly varied: he uses genre patterns from the Western for the revenge motif and from martial arts films for the gladiators' fights. He also uses dramatic methods from the action movie, and finally gives us a melodramatic ending that adds variety adds to the entertainment. Although many of the movie's conflicts are not actually resolved, *Gladiator* is visually overwhelming. Scott isn't always too particular with historical truth, but his dizzyingly sensual compositions, the fantastic editing, the excellent music of Hollywood's star composer Hans Zimmer and the brilliant acting – particularly from Joaquin Phoenix as the incestuous, evil Commodus – make *Gladiator* an exciting and impressive historical movie.

BR

5

1 Nothing is impossible in Ancient Rome: virtuous tribune Maximus (Russell Crowe) is forced to become a gladiator …

2 … if the capricious Emperor Commodus (Joaquin Phoenix) so dictates.

3 Losers become heroes in the magnificent battle scenes in the Colosseum.

4 Life and death decisions are made without reflection in the Emperor's box.

5 Quo vadis Commodus? The emperor and his sister Lucilla (Connie Nielsen).

6 Folk hero Maximus shortly before the fatal climax to his gladiatorial career.

RUSSELL CROWE Russell Crowe was born in New Zealand in 1964. His role as the violent, gruff policeman Bud White in Curtis Hanson's *L. A. Confidential* (1997) introduced him to a wider audience in America and beyond. A one-time child star from TV productions, he had stopped acting for a long time, but returned to the scene with great success in 1992 with a role in the Australian skinhead drama *Romper Stomper*. Having proved that he could also act character roles convincingly in Michael Mann's sensational drama *The Insider* (1999), where he plays a tobacco industry maverick, he was awarded an Oscar two years later for his performance as Maximus in Ridley Scott's *Gladiator*.

O BROTHER, WHERE ART THOU?

2000 - GREAT BRITAIN / USA / FRANCE - 106 MIN. - COMEDY

DIRECTOR JOEL COEN (*1954)
SCREENPLAY ETHAN COEN, JOEL COEN DIRECTOR OF PHOTOGRAPHY ROGER DEAKINS MUSIC T-BONE BURNETT PRODUCTION ETHAN COEN for BUENA VISTA PICTURES, STUDIO CANAL, TOUCHSTONE PICTURES, UNIVERSAL, WORKING TITLE FILMS.

STARRING GEORGE CLOONEY (Ulysses Everett McGill), JOHN TURTURRO (Pete), TIM BLAKE NELSON (Delmar), JOHN GOODMAN (Big Dan Teague), HOLLY HUNTER (Penny Wharvey), CHRIS THOMAS KING (Tommy Johnson), MICHAEL BADALUCCO (George "Babyface" Nelson), WAYNE DUVALL (Homer Stokes), RAY MCKINNON (Vernon T. Waldrip), DANIEL VON BARGEN (Sheriff Cooley).

"We're in a tight spot!"

Joel and Ethan Coen have perfected the art of lovingly disembowelling well-known stories and stereotypes of cinema history. From the cinema in their heads they make wonderful movies about the things that they love, like the cinema itself and the stories to which it owes its existence. It was therefore only to be expected that sooner or later they would use the one story that is considered to be the root of all others – Homer's *Odyssey*. It is equally unsurprising that their adaptation is not a film of the epic but their own unique translation of the tale into cinematic pop culture. That said, it's still a remarkable achievement in the way it blends the ancient material with film myths of the 30s and contemporary country and pop music to form a densely textured fabric of quotation and allusion.

The story is a variation on its classical model. The vain and arrogant Ulysses (George Clooney) is stuck in prison, and he hints at a hidden sum of 1.2 million dollars to persuade his fellow prisoners Pete (John Turturro) and Delmar (Tim Blake Nelson) to escape with him. They're in a bit of a hurry as within three days the loot from a bank raid has to be dug up before the area where it is hidden is flooded. However, the real truth of the matter is that Ulysses wants to hit the road home as quickly as possible for the simple reason that his wife (Holly Hunter) is threatening to marry another man. A wonderfully funny odyssey through the south of the US ensues, along the banks of the Mississippi.

The three convicts are chained to each other and, as in the individual episodes of Homer's epic, they meet a hybrid figure from Greek mythology at every station of their escape or characters from the early era of the talkies. The borders between the two become blurred: first they meet a venerable soothsayer by the name of Homer who predicts that they will find treasure, then the one-eyed, Cyclops figure Big Dan Teague who sells Bibles but turns out to be a no-good Ku Klux Klan member, then three seductive and cunning sirens washing their laundry, who whisk Pete back into prison, and finally Ulysses' unfaithful wife, who even has the same as the wife in Homer's epic, Penelope (alias Penny). During their escape they also make the acquaintance of a Blues guitar player who has sold his soul to the devil, record a country song at a radio station with a blind manager under the band name "The Soggy Bottom Boys" (which then becomes a smash hit) and involuntarily become accomplices of the gangster George "Babyface" Nelson who gives them the loot from his bank raid. They have serious problems with slimy provincial politicians and a series of other bizarre companions.

As well as the typically caricatured and exaggerated characters, *O Brother, Where Art Thou?* includes the Coen brothers' characteristic stylised postcard pictures of idyllic, almost kitsch landscapes. The backdrop of the southern states is made up of an abundance of clichéd motifs such as enormous cornfields, never-ending railroads, boggy swamps and old-timer cars.

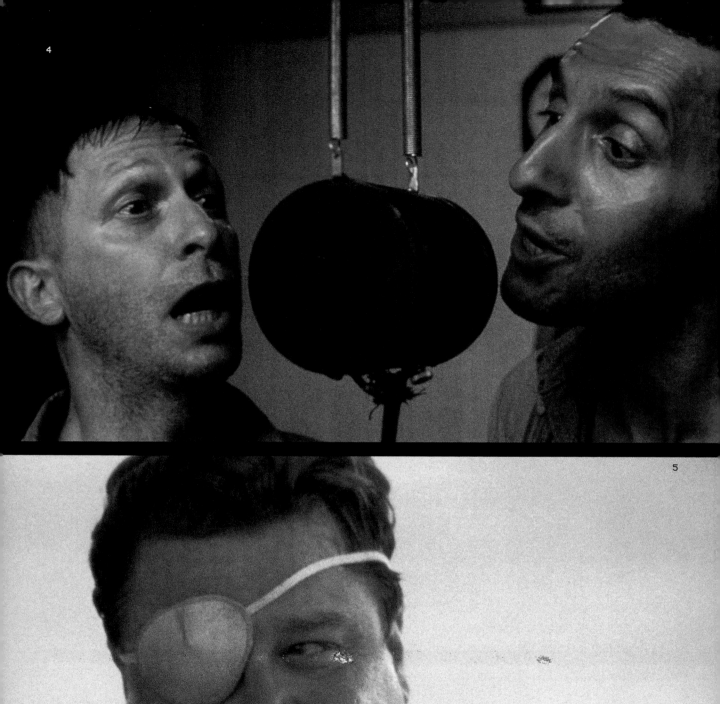

4

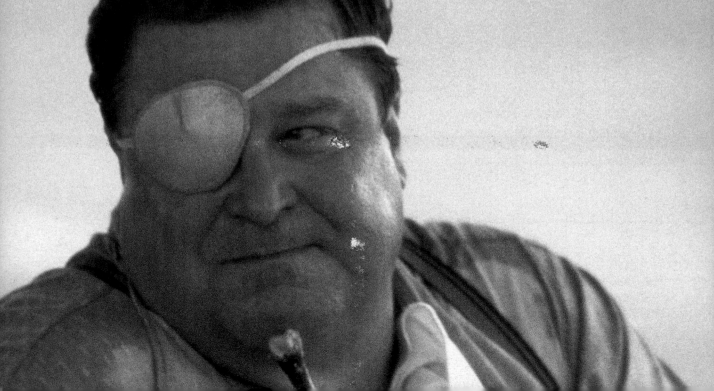

5

1 Ulysses, Pete and Delmar: George Clooney, John Turturro and Tim Blake Nelson (right to left) provide impressive evidence of their comic talent in *O Brother, Where Art Thou?*.

2 In classic Laurel and Hardy style the three jailbirds are overpowered by a child.

3 Just like a sentimental painting: the exaggerated pose of a saved man.

4 Popular melodies by mistake: while on the run they produce songs that go straight to people's hearts.

5 The one-eyed Bible-seller reveals himself to be an unholy patron: John Goodman as Big Dan Teague.

6 Taking a roundabout route to their goal: the three jailbirds are linked by more than just their treasure hunt.

"The Coen brothers seem to have understood. In their films they help stupidity to improve its reputation. In *O Brother, Where Art Thou?* for example, there is nothing at all between the ears of the three jail-breakers Ulysses, Pete and Delmar. And it is only because they never stop to think that they survive their long voyage across Mississippi." *Süddeutsche Zeitung*

The synthetic atmosphere comes from the computer process used to digitally adapt the colours of the movie. Its soundtrack was completed before the film itself and is an irresistible compendium of American folk music. Inspired by Blues, Gospel and Country, the movie is also part of a musical tradition where the music is always "on scene". There are references and allusions aplenty. In *Miller's Crossing* (1990), *Barton Fink* (1991), *The Hudsucker Proxy* (1994) and all their other productions, the Coen brothers have always found inspiration inside the tradition of the movies. *O Brother, Where Art Thou?* is a homage to the director Preston Sturges, from whose comedy *Sullivan's Travels* (1941) it takes its curious title. Tired of the monotony of shallow

entertainment movies, the director John L. Sullivan sets out in Sturges' film to let society's underdogs, those at whom the entertainment movies are aimed, have their say. The title of the movie he plans to make is *O Brother, Where Art Thou?*

Because of the Coen brothers' love of parody there is always the danger that they might pull away the ground from under their own feet at some point, and there's a hint of the self-portrait about the ending, when the three convicts are about to be hanged and their absurd journey seems to have come to a close. But a flood wave saves them from that gruesome fate, and we are rewarded with a happy ending after all.   BB

7 She has no sympathy for the way her husband's life is going: Ulysses' wife Penny (Holly Hunter) is already looking elsewhere.

8 The song of the sirens: undreamed-of prospects open up in the middle of the forest.

9 Ulysses the vain: George Clooney uses a hairnet and pomade for his role.

"The Coens love to butter up the screen with beautiful images, but when they have to they use dynamite." *Frankfurter Allgemeine Zeitung*

GEORGE CLOONEY Born in 1961, George Clooney began his career as the heart-throb Dr Doug Ross in the successful television hospital series *Emergency Room*. His progression from television popularity to feature films is a typical one for the 90s. Like Bruce Willis, whose image as an action star was revitalised in 1994 with *Pulp Fiction* (1994), movies helped Clooney get away from his typecasting as a loveable and good looking TV doctor in the 90s. Alternating between irony and action, he has given proof of his acting talent in his brilliant performances in *O Brother, Where Art Thou?* and in other movies such as *From Dusk Till Dawn* (1996), *Out of Sight* (1998), and *Three Kings* (1999).

MISSION: IMPOSSIBLE 2

2000 - USA - 123 MIN. - ACTION FILM, THRILLER

DIRECTOR JOHN WOO (*1946)
SCREENPLAY RONALD D. MOORE DIRECTOR OF PHOTOGRAPHY JEFFREY L. KIMBALL MUSIC TORI AMOS (title song), LALO SCHIFRIN
(theme tune), HANS ZIMMER PRODUCTION TERENCE CHANG, TOM CRUISE, MICHAEL DOVEN, PAUL HITCHCOCK, AMY
STEVENS, PAULA WAGNER NAME for CRUISE-WAGNER PRODUCTIONS, PARAMOUNT PICTURES.

STARRING TOM CRUISE (Ethan Hunt), DOUGRAY SCOTT (Sean Ambrose), THANDIE NEWTON (Nyah Nordoff-Hall), VING
RHAMES (Luther Stickell), BRENDAN GLEESON (John McCloy), DOMINIC PURCELL (Ulrich), RADE SERBEDZIJA
(Dr Nekhorvich), RICHARD ROXBURGH (Hugh Stamp), JOHN POLSON (Billy Baird), WILLIAM MAPOTHER (Wallis).

"Every search for a hero must begin with something which every hero requires, a villain."

Chimera is a deadly disease. It is caused by an extremely dangerous virus created in a high-tech geneticists' laboratory belonging to McCloy, a pharmaceutics tycoon who wants to earn lots of money with the antidote. What would happen if it fell into the hands of unscrupulous criminals doesn't bear thinking about. At the very beginning of the movie, professional gangsters steal the briefcase containing the antidote Bellerophon in a spectacular aeroplane hijack. Using an astonishingly convincing disguise, they manage to surprise both passengers and crew, but they don't manage to steal the virus itself. The scientist Dr Nekhorvich who dies in the plane crash was carrying it in his own body. When the kidnappers discover this, they try to sell the stolen antidote back to McCloy.

Ethan Hunt (Tom Cruise) is the hero who is assigned the recovery of the virus and its antidote by the head of the Secret Service – an impossible mission. Hunt is a James Bond figure who like his role model is given an enchanting female companion, Nyah (Thandie Newton). She is to play the decoy, but after a passionate affair under the Spanish sun they fall in love. The baddie, Sean Ambrose (Dougray Scott), is not just a former Secret Service colleague turned terrorist, but also happens to be

2

Nyah's ex-boyfriend. The impossible mission is complicated by a love triangle.

Mission: Impossible 2 is the sequel to Mission: Impossible (1996) by Brian de Palma, and both are a continuation of the 60s TV series of the same name. Typically for its genre, Mission: Impossible 2 is not concerned with plausibility, logic or seriousness but is ready to use any kind of movement which furthers its plot. In John Woo, the producers found a master choreographer for the action scenes. Woo had previously given a new lease of life to Hong Kong action films with classics like A Better Tomorrow (1985), The Killer (1989), Bullet in the Head (1990) and Hard-Boiled (1992). Woo's camera and montage techniques lend an incomparable lightness to the movie's action sequences.

Woo found his creative inspiration for MI-2 in the Spanish Flamenco tradition. In the car duel between Ethan and Nyah the partners circle and woo each other, and the flamenco motif becomes a matter of passion and death. It is also mirrored in the structure of the plot; the two sides circle each other, and the aim of the dance is not only to carry out the assignment but also to win the heroine's favour. The circling helicopter, the continual video surveillance, the mutual deception, the waiting, the faked attack, the hesitation and the furious finale all add up to a deadly flamenco dance which is passionate and precise, and inscribed in the cinematic structure of the movie itself. The movie is characterised by distinctive Woo features like slow motion, shootouts slowed to deadly ballets, ascending white doves, masquerades and games of identity. In Face/Off (1997), Woo gave this combination of images

1   For Ethan Hunt (Tom Cruise) no mission is impossible.

2   A razor-sharp scrape past death and it's straight back into the fray: Hunt won't be intimidated.

3   Echoes of the Terminator: the agent once again just manages to escape a blazing inferno.

4   Good mates: superstars Tom Cruise and Ving Rhames playing Luther Stickell.

"Like all Woo films, *Mission: Impossible 2* concludes with an extended action sequence of almost hallucinatory intensity." *Sight and Sound*

an almost mystical dimension. But *Mission: Impossible 2* is much more than a martial arts movie, and the motorbike duel in the showdown at the end of the film turns into a joust where two knights aim their steeds at one another.

Woo also permits himself a few ironic asides where his producers and the main character Tom Cruise are concerned. Sean Ambrose, who used to double for Ethan when they still worked together, says "You know, the hardest part about playing you is grinning like an idiot every fifteen bloody minutes!" At the very end, order is restored in the manner of the best Westerns in a man to man shoot-out. After all the martial furore, Woo once again uses contemplative slow motion pictures – a welcome moment of calm.

4

BR

5

"Dougray Scott meets her with a purposeful gleaming in his eye, and as the scarf around her neck is about to slip away, he reaches out and catches it. You can argue that this is clichéd symbolism – Beauty captured by the Beast – but at least it's wonderfully executed." *Sight and Sound*

6

5   Hunt's attention is fixed not only on his
     mission …

6   … but also on the enigmatic Nyah (Thandie
     Newton), who has to act as bait.

JOHN WOO   One of the main characteristics of cinema in the 90s was the use of the human body as a narrative object. Asiatic cinema has always used the body as the weapon of the spirit, and its directors pioneered this in Western movies. In 1992 the body cinema virtuoso John Woo moved to Hollywood and breathed new life into the action movie, beginning with *Hard Target* (1993). In gripping gangster ballads like *A Better Tomorrow* (1986), Woo experimented with the cinematic possibilities of breaking down fast movements into their component parts with the help of editing and slow motion effects. The abstract nature of movement is the distinguishing feature of his body cinema philosophy such as it developed in the 90s. In the most intense moments of his films, which are often ballet-like shoot-outs, Woo's broken heroes float through the air as if totally divorced from their surroundings. His stereotypical characters and melancholic story lines constantly circle themes of loyalty and betrayal, and have their roots in Asiatic martial arts and karate films.

DANCER IN THE DARK

2000 - DENMARK / GERMANY / NETHERLANDS / USA / GREAT BRITAIN / FRANCE / SWEDEN / FINLAND / ICELAND / NORWAY - 140 MIN. - MUSICAL, MELODRAMA

DIRECTOR LARS VON TRIER (*1956)
SCREENPLAY LARS VON TRIER DIRECTOR OF PHOTOGRAPHY ROBBY MÜLLER MUSIC BJÖRK PRODUCTION VIBEKE WINDELØV for ARTE FRANCE CINÉMA, BLIND SPOT PICTURES, CINEMATOGRAPH, DANISH FILM INSTITUTE, DINOVI PICTURES, FILM I VÄST, FRANCE 3 CINÉMA, GOOD MACHINE, ICELANDIC FILM CORPORATION, LIBERATOR PRODUCTIONS, PAIN UNLIMITED, SWEDISH FILM INSTITUTE, TRUST FILM, WHAT ELSE?, ZENTROPA ENTERTAINMENTS.

STARRING BJÖRK (Selma Yeskova), CATHERINE DENEUVE (Kathy), DAVID MORSE (Bill), PETER STORMARE (Jeff), UDO KIER (Dr Porkorny), JOEL GREY (Oldrich Novy), CARA SEYMOUR (Linda Houston), VLADICA KOSTIC (Gene Yeskova), JEAN-MARC BARR (Norman).

IFF CANNES 2000 GOLDEN PALM, BEST ACTRESS (Björk).

"Because in a musical nothing dreadful ever happens."

A musical that ends with an execution – that could only work in European cinema. In Hollywood musicals, like those the main character Selma dreams about in *Dancer in the Dark*, nothing like that ever happens. In the tragedy by Danish director Lars von Trier two very different stories of music and violence collide with unrelenting narrative rigour and forceful images. Robby Müller's hand-camera pictures are uncompromising: they are faded and pale and seem improvised, like the life of the protagonist. Selma is a Czech immigrant who lives with her son Gene in a small trailer. She works in a factory at a metal press to earn the money she needs for an eye operation for her son. She tells the others however that she sends the money to her father in the Czech Republic.

Icelandic pop icon Björk plays the naive Selma, whose day dreams are integrated into the movie as musical sequences. The wan colours of every-day life are transformed into multicoloured pictures, and there is dancing, laughter and singing. The rhythm of Selma's surroundings sets the beat for the songs and Selma stars in the dance sequences. Björk's singing is the same as it always is; her energetic voice booms out, only to sound fragile and childish a moment after. Selma's fantasies are illusions of a better life like in the film models from Hollywood's dream factories, perfect illusions to which she clings. The truth however is that Selma is an ordinary worker, who struggles to bring up her own son and dedicates the little free time she has to an amateur theatre group. Selma's sight however is gradually failing as well, and when she is no longer capable of working the metal press she is fired. Then her landlord and neighbour Bill steals her savings when she refuses to lend him money to finance his wife's extravagant life style. Selma goes to see him to demand her money back. There is fighting, a shot is fired

1 An unusual pair: Icelandic pop star Björk as Selma
 Yeskova, and French *grande dame* of the cinema
 Catherine Deneuve as factory worker Kathy.

2 The gift of a bicycle makes poverty more bearable.

3 Innocent, child-like and doomed: Selma is going
 incurably blind.

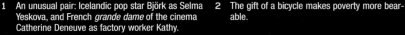

"'Björk cannot act, she can only feel', Lars von Trier is supposed to have said after shooting the film. That may well be true, and it makes this film quite unique. The intense dedication and dedicated intensity with which she throws herself into her part — these are things she will not be able to give to another director a second time." *Süddeutsche Zeitung*

and hits Bill. This is followed by a longing for atonement completely in keeping with the Christian tradition of sacrifice. Bill becomes a penitent sinner, who can't however get the confession over his lips. To avoid being exposed in front of his wife, he begs Selma to solve his money and debts problems by killing him.

    Lars von Trier's film constantly return to motifs of guilt and atonement, for which sight is the main metaphor. Bill's forbidden, greedy gaze makes him guilty while Selma's loss of sight by contrast calls forth her innocent musical fantasies. At the same time the movie thematises sight on a visual level. It is difficult to watch because the pictures wander restlessly from one motif to another, although they are deprived of life, of colour. Only in Selma's

dreams do the pictures become colourful and lively, and only when she sings does the improvised feel of the hand camera give way to the glossy look of the musical montage as we know it from Busby Berkeley musicals like *42nd Street* (1933), *Gold Diggers of 1935* (1935) or *Broadway Serenade* (1939). As in Berkeley's films, the choreography in *Dancer in the Dark* is enhanced with careful editing, which replaces the camera as narrative authority during the musical scenes. The contrast between the rough pictures of miserable reality in which Selma fights for her life and the life of her son and the detailed musical dream sequences make the drama of Selma's life seem even more disastrous. When Selma is finally caught after she has killed Bill, the tragedy of her real life begins to seep into her fantasies as well. She is sentenced to

4   For Jeff (Peter Stormare), Selma remains unattainable.
    5   Music dispels the worries of everyday life.
    6   Choreography as a study of movement: Von Trier uses phase sequence photography of the dancing in a visual experiment.

MUSICAL   The triumphal progress of the talkie or sound movie produced the musical genre in the late 20s. The success of *The Broadway Melody* (1929) marked the beginning of a boom. Early musicals were more like filmed dance performances with stories from the theatre world, but then directors such as Rouben Mamoulian and Ernst Lubitsch began to use moving cameras to create witty and zesty stories about love and marriage. In the 30s former army drill office Busby Berkeley had a lasting influence on the genre by replacing individual dances with technically and formally perfect dance routines. At the same time the genre began to produce its own stars, and dancers like Ginger Rogers and Fred Astaire became icons of figured choreography. From the 40s onwards, all the style elements began to coalesce to form the modern musical in which both dreams and reality suspend the rules of everyday life. The end of the studio system in Hollywood meant the decline of the musical. In the mid-60s was there a revival with films such as *West Side Story* (1961) and *The Sound of Music* (1965).

---

death. She doesn't want new investigations that might lead to a pardon when she discovers that they would use up all the money she has saved for her son. She chooses death to give her son sight, which means life. And just as her musical fantasies become more and more a part of the real events, the film itself becomes a melodramatic vortex. It drags viewers irresistibly into the shattering scene at the end of the movie when Selma is hanged, but continues singing. She falls through a trapdoor in the floor into a kind of stage room where the spectators see her swinging dead from the end of the rope. The curtain falls swiftly, the movie has reached its tragic climax at the moment where musical and drama meet. Selma's last song is interrupted by violent death.   BR

SPACE COWBOYS

2000 - USA - 130 MIN. - DRAMA

DIRECTOR CLINT EASTWOOD (*1930)
SCREENPLAY KEN KAUFMAN, HOWARD KLAUSNER DIRECTOR OF PHOTOGRAPHY JACK N. GREEN MUSIC CLINT EASTWOOD, LENNIE NIEHAUS
PRODUCTION CLINT EASTWOOD, ANDREW LAZAR for CLIPSAL FILMS, MAD CHANCE, THE MALPASO COMPANY, VILLAGE
ROADSHOW PRODUCTIONS.

STARRING CLINT EASTWOOD (Frank Corvin), TOMMY LEE JONES (Hawk Hawkins), DONALD SUTHERLAND (Jerry O'Neill),
JAMES GARNER (Tank Sullivan), JAMES CROMWELL (Bob Gerson), MARCIA GAY HARDEN (Sara Holland), WILLIAM
DEVANE (Eugene Davis), LOREN DEAN (Ethan Glance), COURTNEY B. VANCE (Roger Hines), RADE SERBEDZIJA (General
Vostow).

"Boys will be boys."

Clint Eastwood's space comedy *Space Cowboys* begins like the early careers of its now greying main characters: in black and white. In a flashback to the year 1958 we see young airforce hotshots from the Dedalus team. They break all the existing height and speed records, crash prototype aeroplanes worth millions of dollars into the desert sand and dream of burning their wings as they all want to be the first person to fly to the moon. They are all heartbroken when NASA is founded and sends a chimpanzee to the moon instead of one of them.

Forty years later, the Cold War is long over. A Russian communication satellite has become defective and as its failure is likely to cause a civil war in the former Soviet states, NASA manager Bob Gerson (James Cromwell) offers to help the Russians. Oddly enough the Russian satellite was made according to the same specifications as the American Skylab model, which

Frank Corvin (Clint Eastwood), a former member of the Dedalus team, designed in 1969. No one else knows now how to deal with the old-fashioned Skylab technology, so the Dedalus team is reactivated to repair this Russian hulk from the satellite Stone Age.

The team meet up again for the first time in decades. Tank Sullivan (James Garner) has swapped his officer's bars for the pulpit of a Baptist church; the engineer Jerry O'Neill (Donald Sutherland) designs roller coasters and pursues young women; Hawk Hawkins (Tommy Lee Jones) shows amateur pilots what a double loop-the-loop is.

Clint Eastwood, 1930 vintage, has aged gracefully as an actor, and as a director he gives his characters the same dignity. Even during the NASA aptitude tests, when they have to let their trousers down, they cut as dashing a figure as their age will allow. For 30 days they struggle with modern

"No actor, with the possible exception of Paul Newman, has aged better on film than Eastwood, who turned 70 in May and whose lined and weathered face makes Mt. Rushmore look like the Pillsbury Doughboy."

Los Angeles Times

3

4

5

JAMES GARNER   The American actor James Garner was born in 1928 as James Bumgarner in Oklahoma, and came to the cinema by chance. After the Korean War, a producer friend got him a role in a Broadway version of the play *The Caine Mutiny Court Martial*. There he was discovered by Warner Bros. who offered him a contract in 1955. Garner will always be associated with two TV series produced by Roy Huggins, where he played the main role, and which today have cult status: from 1957 to 1960 he played the pokerfaced Maverick in 55 episodes of the Western series of the same name, and from 1974 to 1980 he played the humorous and charming private detective Jim Rockford in *The Rockford Files* – a role which won him an Emmy, the coveted television prize, and many new fans. Between those two series he turned his back on television for over a decade and went into film. James Garner has appeared in innumerable feature films and TV movies to date, the most recent of which was Clint Eastwood's *Space Cowboys*.

technology and their failing physical strength, until at last they are sent up into space to repair the satellite, which turns out to be a deadly relic of the Cold War.

Ken Kaufman and Howard Klausner wrote the screenplay to *Space Cowboys* inspired by John Glenn, who carried out his last space shuttle mission at the age of 77. The predictable story with its conventional conflicts – the ancient rivalry between the pilots Corvin and Hawkins, the tension between the young and the old astronauts, the way the old confront death and disease – is enlivened with some witty dialogue. It's a screenplay that is

caught between comedy and drama, but above it's a showpiece for its loveable and charismatic ageing actors.

Clint Eastwood allows plenty of time for the plot to develop. The reunion of the old comrades and their preparations for take-off take up two thirds of the film. Only then are the dreams of the four men realised.

Eastwood was almost certainly attracted to this movie by the idea of letting four old war horses fight one last battle. *Space Cowboys* is a space age Western, and Westerns were the genre that made Clint Eastwood a Hollywood icon.   APO

1   A fine view: astronaut Frank Corvin (Clint Eastwood) looks at the blue planet.

2   A task that only experienced hands can do: Corvin and his team are in outer space to repair a Russian satellite.

3   Tank Sullivan (James Garner) is a member of the team of astronauts.

4   Jogging for their trip into space. As well as Frank and Tank, Hawk Hawkins (Tommy Lee Jones) and Jerry O'Neill (Donald Sutherland) are also part of the team.

5   The flight into space requires highly specific preparation. The team in training

HIGH FIDELITY

2000 - USA - 113 MIN. - COMEDY, MUSIC FILM

DIRECTOR STEPHEN FREARS (*1941)
SCREENPLAY D. V. DEVINCENTIS, STEVE PINK, SCOTT ROSENBERG, JOHN CUSACK, based on the novel of the same name by NICK HORNBY **DIRECTOR OF PHOTOGRAPHY** SEAMUS MCGARVEY **MUSIC** HOWARD SHORE **PRODUCTION** TIM BEVAN, RUDD SIMMONS for DOGSTAR FILMS, NEW CRIME PRODUCTIONS, TOUCHSTONE PICTURES, WORKING TITLE FILMS.

STARRING JOHN CUSACK (Rob Gordon), IBEN HJEJLE (Laura), TODD LOUISO (Dick), JACK BLACK (Barry), LISA BONET (Marie DeSalle), CATHERINE ZETA-JONES (Charlie Nicholson), JOAN CUSACK (Liz), TIM ROBBINS (Ian Raymond), LILI TAYLOR (Sarah), NATASHA GREGSON WAGNER (Caroline).

"Do I listen to pop music because I'm miserable? Or am I miserable because I listen to pop music?"

Life is like an LP record: one groove sums up all its aspects, however various they may be. On average it only contains one hit – but precisely because of this it is worth buying, at least for the connoisseur. Rob (John Cusack) is a connoisseur, as well as a music fetishist and a failed Casanova. Together with his friends Barry (Jack Black) and Dick (Todd Louiso) he runs a record shop where time seems to stand still. A niche that is also a hideaway, they gather there to indulge their little quirks and judge the rest of the world by their own taste in music. They are stuck in a phase sometime at the end of the 80s when choosing between the analogue vinyl of the good old LP record and the digitally reworked plastic of the unfeeling CD was still a matter of faith … From a distance, that sort of passion now seems comic and absurd, but watching the film, we are all reminded of a phase in our own lives despite ourselves. Unobtrusive colours and sparing furniture makes this

pseudo-existentialism visible to outsiders and are as necessary as printed T-shirts which express the wearer's current mental state.

Following the logic of the music market, unhappy Rob, hyperactive Barry and shy Dick put their faith in a ranking system by which all human experience can be evaluated: the universal principle of the "Top 5". It simplifies many things but also makes others more difficult. The "Top 5" is the lowest common denominator in the specialist discussions of these three students of pop, but it is also the basis for Rob's monologue on his failed relationships. Apart from his mother, up till now five women have influenced his life. *High Fidelity* tells us in flashbacks how they managed to get onto Rob's personal "Top 5" relationship list. Each one has their own good and bad points but, like on an LP, only one turns out to be a top hit: Laura, convincingly played by Iben Hjejle. Rob is the movie's all knowing, repressed macho

1 Good vibrations: music makes it possible to get close to someone. Rob Gordon (John Cusack) and his girlfriend Laura (Iben Hjejle).

2 Experts together: Rob and his friend Dick (Todd Louiso).

3 Embarrassing confessions: Rob and Liz (Joan Cusack).

4 Barry (Jack Black) isn't the sharpest tool in the box.

5 Sparkling eyes and a smile to die for: only Laura can save Rob.

"With Rob, Frears manages to create the Woody Allen effect to a certain extent: he's annoying from time to time, but we like him." *epd Film*

narrator, and he comments with intensely black smugness on the qualities of his exes. Like Jeff Daniels in Woody Allen's *The Purple Rose of Cairo* (1985), Rob steps out of the fictive story, looks straight into the camera and directs his monologue at the audience. This involuntary conspiracy has some extremely funny moments. John Cusack's combination of innocence and mischief remind us of the unnerving and pleading eyes of comedian Oliver Hardy, pushed into "another fine mess" thanks to his partner Stan Laurel. Like his model Hardy, Rob takes on the role of victim, although he sometimes ignores the fact that he is not entirely innocent in the calamities that befall him. We learn for instance from a conversation between Laura and her friend Liz that Rob has been unfaithful, that she had an abortion because he was having an affair, and that he hasn't paid back the money that he owes her.

Fortunately, Rob is able to escape from this largely self-induced misery in music. Stephen Frears' movie follows Nick Hornby's novel with black humour and gentle irony. Hornby describes that time in the life of growing men when the divide between pop culture and philosophy seems to be bridged. Pop songs become vessels of almost supernatural wisdom which can help with the trials and tribulations of life. This vinyl philosophising however is incomprehensible to Rob's potential partners. His escape into music isn't just a way of escaping from his failures, but also an activity that turns him into an extremely lonely man, and soon Laura has had enough and leaves him. He tries his luck with the singer Marie DeSalle (Lisa Bonet) but the brief affair only salves his battered ego and is little more than a one-night stand. He wants more. In desperation, he follows some advice from Bruce Springsteen and visits all his past girlfriends, whose attraction, like an outdated hit, has greatly worn off. They are all now either ill or married. Inevitably, Rob returns to Laura. In the meantime his friends have been successful: Dick falls in love with a customer and Barry finally finds a band.

In the end music brings everything together again, and the relationships between women and men take on the form of a musical composition, an idea last used in the poetic images of Alain Resnais' wonderful *Same Old Song* (*On connaît la chanson*, 1997). Three single (people) who only find harmony when they play together: the LP turns out to be a good metaphor for life after all.   BR

VOICE OVER The voice of a narrator who is not visible in the movie is known as a "voice over". In documentary films, the voice over mostly comments on the pictures whilst voices in a feature film take on the narrative of the movie's plot. Here the voice over comments on actions or explains the context, it prepares future events or explains connections to events which are not shown in the movie. As opposed to continual editing, the voice over emphasises the narrative structure of a feature film. Both documentary films and film noir make frequent use of this technique, but comedies often also use it as well.

TRAFFIC

2000 - USA / GERMANY - 143 MIN. - CRIME FILM, POLITICAL THRILLER

DIRECTOR STEVEN SODERBERGH (*1963)

SCREENPLAY STEPHEN GAGHAN, based on the TV series *TRAFFIC* by SIMON MOORE DIRECTOR OF PHOTOGRAPHY PETER ANDREWS (= Steven Soderbergh) MUSIC CLIFF MARTINEZ PRODUCTION LAURA BICKFORD, MARSHALL HERSKOVITZ, EDWARD ZWICK for INITIAL ENTERTAINMENT GROUP, BEDFORD FALLS PRODUCTIONS, SPLENDID MEDIEN AG, USA FILMS.

STARRING MICHAEL DOUGLAS (Robert Wakefield), DON CHEADLE (Montel Gordon), BENICIO DEL TORO (Javier Rodriguez), LUIS GUZMÁN (Ray Castro), DENNIS QUAID (Arnie Metzger), CATHERINE ZETA-JONES (Helena Ayala), ERIKA CHRISTENSEN (Caroline Wakefield), STEVEN BAUER (Carlos Ayala), MIGUEL FERRER (Eduardo Ruiz).

ACADEMY AWARDS 2001 OSCARS for BEST SUPPORTING ACTOR (Benicio Del Toro), BEST DIRECTOR (Steven Soderbergh), BEST FILM EDITING (Stephen Mirrione), BEST ADAPTED SCREENPLAY (Stephen Gaghan).

IFF BERLIN 2001 SILVER BEAR for BEST ACTOR (Benicio Del Toro).

"How can one fight a war when the enemy is your own family?"

The sun shines mercilessly on Mexico. The heat is so terrible that on the American border even the landscape itself seems tanned. Mexico, land of the lawless and refuge of so many movie villains is more a metaphor than a real place, and here, it's the home of drug dealing. The USA has great difficulty controlling the southern border, and the Mexican and the American police forces are powerless to stem the tide of drugs which floods through the border into the country. The borderlands are as unwelcoming as they are unreal, and yet it is here that a great crime is taking place. Javier Rodriguez (Benicio Del Toro) is from the Mexican drugs squad and he has contacts who give him information about illegal drug deals. Unfortunately his hands are tied, because his boss, General Salazar, is himself a member of the rival drugs cartel in the border town Tijuana. All that Rodriguez dreams of are floodlights for the stadium so that the town's children can play baseball there after dark.

On the other side of the border in the USA a judge named Robert Hudson Wakefield (Michael Douglas) is made America's drugs commissioner, whilst his daughter Caroline (Erika Christensen) is taking the first steps towards drug addiction.

Carlos Ayala (Steven Bauer) is the subject of ongoing investigations on both sides of the border. He gets drugs into America and organises their distribution. Carlos is arrested, but his wife Helena (Catherine Zeta-Jones) takes his place and carries on the business with a firm hand – for the good of her children, as she says. All she wants is to never have to go back to the gutter that she came from.

These three interwoven stories all deal with the same themes: the tense relationship between the private and public spheres and the difficult relationship between family and politics. They are also about the responsibility of one generation for the next. The problem is that the drug business

2

1   Concerned for her own family: Helena Ayala (Catherine Zeta-Jones) as mother-to-be and syndicate boss.

2   Embarrassing questions: attorney Arnie Metzger (Dennis Quaid) and the drug dealer's wife. Should you ply an illegal trade in order to be able to support your own family? Helena knows her answer.

3   Drugs commissioner Robert Wakefield (Michael Douglas) is having trouble explaining: what good are the law and justice, if their weapons aren't up to the job?

"One of the main themes is certainly greed. That's a human emotion that I don't understand. I have experienced it often enough, but I don't understand it."

Steven Soderbergh in: Frankfurter Allgemeine Zeitung

has long since conquered private spheres that cannot be controlled by politics, whilst politicians are still trying to mechanically control the country's borders.

Traffic tells of a lack of responsibility, of a lack of perspective and of a problem that could destroy the foundations of society. *Traffic* isn't about illegal border crossings between Mexico and the USA, nor is it about the hopelessness of fighting against drugs in just one place. The border is merely an image and a surface, for the real transgressions and catastrophes are happening elsewhere. They take place in the private sphere, in the family, and in the lives of children who are sacrificed for profit margins. Behind the official façade of pretty promises and efforts, the root of the problem lies in broken families.

Steven Soderbergh, who manages the camera himself under a pseudonym, dissects this surface with cinematic means, and penetrates to the core of the problem with great care and intensity. Places are marked out with exaggerated colour and light, with Mexico overexposed with a yellow filter and the USA shown in a cold blue light. Smooth surfaces are destroyed by the use of grainy film and the hand camera sometimes gets unbearably close to the action, leaving the audience nowhere left to hide. The various plot strands separate and then combine, breaking up the chronology with abrupt changes of theme and scene. Single episodes are often only linked by very small details and it is impossible to identify who the main characters are or to unravel the various story lines. What remains is a disturbing picture of ruined youth, exemplified in the story of the addict Caroline. Eventually the

> "Soderbergh places before our eyes a scourge that imperils the entire human race ... And since the work is, in purely cinematic terms, a miracle of imagination and variety, this production marks an epoch in both the seventh art and the history of our time." *Le Figaro*

problem rises to the surface and returns to its origin. The perfect surface of the Wakefield's family life is corroded and its certainties begin to crumble. Wakefield holds his first press conference as drugs commissioner, and, searching desperately for the right words, he admits that he can't support the government's official policies. Meanwhile, on the other side of the border, Javier Rodriguez has worked wonders: the children of Tijuana are finally able to play baseball in the floodlights. Seeing the family as part of the public sphere and behaving responsibly in small matters is the answer that *Traffic* offers, which may not sound original but is extremely convincing in the context of the film. Thanks to Soderbergh's cinematic vision, the movie is not sensationalist but quietly self-confident and artistic. As Jean-Luc Godard said, it's not enough to make political films – films must also be made political. Steven Soderbergh manages to do that in *Traffic*.

BR

| BENICIO DEL TORO | Benicio Del Toro was born in 1967. After Peter Weir's *Fearless* (1993), his next, more prominent role was as the gangster Fred Fenster in *The Usual Suspects* (1995) by Bryan Singer. As well as roles in Abel Ferrara's *The Funeral* (1996) and Julian Schnabel's *Basquiat* (1996), he was recently extremely successful in Terry Gilliam's comedy *Fear and Loathing in Las Vegas* (1998). A short period of calm followed that, but he went on to win an Oscar and a Silver Bear for his role as a Mexican policeman in *Traffic* in 2001. Del Toro's distinguishing features are his slurred, throaty voice and his cold, reserved minimalism punctuated by explosive emotional breakouts. |

4   Children on the road to ruin: Caroline Wakefield (Erika Christensen) and her boyfriend.

5   His dejection knows no bounds: police officer Javier Rodriguez (Benicio Del Toro) in his almost hopeless mission against drug dealing.

ALMOST FAMOUS

2000 - USA - 123 MIN.- MUSIC FILM, DRAMA

DIRECTOR CAMERON CROWE (*1957)

SCREENPLAY CAMERON CROWE DIRECTOR OF PHOTOGRAPHY JOHN TOLL MUSIC NANCY WILSON, DIVERSE ROCKSONGS PRODUCTION CAMERON CROWE, IAN BRYCE, LISA STEWART for VINYL FILMS.

STARRING PATRICK FUGIT (William Miller), BILLY CRUDUP (Russell Hammond), FRANCES MCDORMAND (Elaine Miller), KATE HUDSON (Penny Lane), JASON LEE (Jeff Bebe), PHILIP SEYMOUR HOFFMAN (Lester Bangs), ANNA PAQUIN (Polexia), FAIRUZA BALK (Sapphire), NOAH TAYLOR (Dick Roswell), ZOOEY DESCHANEL (Anita Miller).

ACADEMY AWARDS 2001 OSCAR for BEST ORIGINAL SCREENPLAY (Cameron Crowe).

"I am a golden God."

San Diego, 1973. 15-year-old William Miller (Patrick Fugit) dreams of becoming a music critic – much against the wishes of his single mother Elaine (Frances McDormand), who believes rock music to be nothing more than the glorification of drugs and sexual dissipation. Against the odds, William's dream comes true when he meets his idol Lester Bangs (Philip Seymour Hoffman), the legendary editor of the music magazine *Creem*. Bangs is impressed by the boy's enthusiasm and commissions him to write a portrait of Black Sabbath, who are about to play in the town. At the concert William meets a pretty groupie called Penny Lane (Kate Hudson) and the musicians of the newcomer band Stillwater, who take him backstage. Before William realises what is happening, he is accompanying the band on a tour bus through the USA for *Rolling Stone* magazine. He experiences the musicians' free and easy lifestyle at first hand, with its seductive mix of rock euphoria, habitual drug consumption and casual sex.

As the band become more and more successful, internal tensions grow and William finds himself increasingly torn between private loyalties and the critical distance his job demands. He becomes friends with the guitarist Russell (Billy Crudup) and falls in love with Penny Lane.

In the movies of the 90s, the 70s underwent a great revival. Like Todd Haynes' glittering glamrock film *Velvet Goldmine* (1998), many works have a nostalgic feel despite the fact that the 70s are not yet that distant in time. It is almost as if they had been submerged in some mysterious way. Such movies tend to emphasise the freedom and decadence of the decade with 70s music and fashion as a superficial acoustic and visual accompaniment. Only occasionally does a movie really communicate something of the spirit of those years, and *Almost Famous* is one of these exceptions.

Much of the movie is autobiographical. Author and director Cameron Crowe wrote for *Creem* and *Rolling Stone* as a youngster in the 70s before he turned to film, but there is never any danger that the movie will become an uncritical glorification of those times. Although he had a generous budget, *Almost Famous* is unusually simple and straightforward for its genre. Crowe makes it into an initiation story, which is told from the protagonist's

1 Almost famous: Kate Hudson was awarded the Golden Globe for her portrayal of elfin groupie Penny Lane.

2 Loss of innocence: the road to fame leads the band Stillwater to sell out their ideals.

3 Rock stars without glamour: compromise and middle-class limitations seep into the band's sex and drugs lifestyle (Billy Crudup and Kate Hudson).

4 The journalist and the groupie: in their naïve enthusiasm William (Patrick Fugit) and Penny embody the ideals of rock music.

5 Filmed at eye-level: in contrast to other films about the music of the 1970s Crowe's film is characterised by being true-to-life.

6 Rock music as collective ecstasy: Crowe manages to bring the unifying power of rock back to life.

"A bitter-sweet, moving and intelligent film and we love first of all the precise and loving way the various characters are presented." *Süddeutsche Zeitung*

"*Almost Famous* is about the world of rock, but it's not a rock film, it's a coming-of-age film, about an idealistic kid who sees the real world, witnesses its cruelties and heartbreaks, and yet finds much room for hope." *Chicago Sun-Times*

point of view. William's experiences are especially meaningful because everything is new for him – love, friendship, life with the band and the American landscape. Although Crowe cannot resist some comic exaggeration, using William's perspective means he can create a lifelike portrait of scenery and figures from his intimate knowledge of the material.

In fact the musicians are presented as anything other than larger than life. Their wild lifestyle often looks like compensation and their petty jealousies and career worries reveal them to be limited and bourgeois in their outlook. The movie also tells of a time when rock music had already lost its utopian force and was threatening to become an entirely commercial venture. Like Crowe's earlier film *Jerry Maguire* (1996), *Almost Famous* is about the loss of innocence and personal integrity. William and Penny Lane embody these values, and the movie uses the two outsiders to formulate its belief in the unbroken spirit of rock'n'roll despite everything. The people who manage to retain their initial innocent enthusiasm for rock not only find themselves through the music, they also find friends for life. The movie's energetic, vital soundtrack provides a persuasive back up for this conclusion.

JH

KATE HUDSON Kate Hudson was born in Los Angeles in 1979; her mother is Goldie Hawn. She made her movie debut in Risa Bramon Garcia's ensemble comedy *200 Cigarettes* (1998). After several smaller appearances, Hudson's breakthrough came with Cameron Crowe's *Almost Famous*, a movie about musicians. Her performance as the elfin groupie Penny Lane won her a Golden Globe, although the role was originally intended for Sarah Polley. With her ethereal beauty, she is now considered one of the upcoming stars of the US movie world. Hudson showed that she is able to hold her own against the greats of the industry in Robert Altman's comedy *Dr T. and the Women* (2000), where she appeared alongside Richard Gere and Helen Hunt.

ACADEMY AWARDS *1991–2000*

1991 OSCARS

Here we follow the convention of giving the year of the US launch
instead of giving the year of the award as in the other texts.

BEST PICTURE	THE SILENCE OF THE LAMBS
BEST DIRECTOR	JONATHAN DEMME for *The Silence of the Lambs*
BEST LEADING ACTRESS	JODIE FOSTER in *The Silence of the Lambs*
BEST LEADING ACTOR	ANTHONY HOPKINS in *The Silence of the Lambs*
BEST SUPPORTING ACTRESS	MERCEDES RUEHL in *The Fisher King*
BEST SUPPORTING ACTOR	JACK PALANCE in *City Slickers*
BEST ORIGINAL SCREENPLAY	CALLIE KHOURI for *Thelma & Louise*
BEST ADAPTED SCREENPLAY	TED TALLY for *The Silence of the Lambs*
BEST FOREIGN LANGUAGE FILM	*Mediterraneo* by GABRIELE SALVATORES (Italy)
BEST CINEMATOGRAPHY	ROBERT RICHARDSON for *JFK*
BEST ART DIRECTION / SET DECORATION	DENNIS GASSNER, NANCY HAIGH for *Bugsy*
BEST FILM EDITING	JOE HUTSHING, PIETRO SCALIA for *JFK*
BEST MUSIC	ALAN MENKEN for *Beauty and the Beast*
BEST SONG	ALAN MENKEN, HOWARD ASHMAN for "BEAUTY AND THE BEAST" in *Beauty and the Beast*
BEST MAKE-UP	STAN WINSTON, JEFF DAWN for *Terminator 2*
BEST COSTUMES	ALBERT WOLSKY for *Bugsy*
BEST VISUAL EFFECTS	DENNIS MUREN, STAN WINSTON, GENE WARREN JR., ROBERT SKOTAK for *Terminator 2*
BEST SOUND	TOM JOHNSON, GARY RYDSTROM, GARY SUMMERS, LEE ORLOFF for *Terminator 2*
BEST SOUND EFFECTS EDITING	GARY RYDSTROM and GLORIA S. BORDERS for *Terminator 2*

3 1991 James Cameron and his creation, which he dispatches to save humanity.
4 1992 No less convincing behind the camera than in front: Clint Eastwood.

1992 OSCARS

BEST PICTURE	UNFORGIVEN
BEST DIRECTOR	CLINT EASTWOOD for *Unforgiven*
BEST LEADING ACTRESS	EMMA THOMPSON in *Howards End*
BEST LEADING ACTOR	AL PACINO in *Scent of a Woman*
BEST SUPPORTING ACTRESS	MARISA TOMEI in *My Cousin Vinny*
BEST SUPPORTING ACTOR	GENE HACKMAN in *Unforgiven*
BEST ORIGINAL SCREENPLAY	NEIL JORDAN for *The Crying Game*
BEST ADAPTED SCREENPLAY	RUTH PRAWER JHABVALA for *Howards End*
BEST FOREIGN LANGUAGE FILM	*Indochine* by RÉGIS WARGNIER (France)
BEST CINEMATOGRAPHY	PHILIPPE ROUSSELOT for *A River Runs Through It*
BEST ART DIRECTION / SET DECORATION	LUCIANA ARRIGHI, IAN WHITTAKER for *Howards End*
BEST FILM EDITING	JOEL COX for *Unforgiven*
BEST MUSIC	ALAN MENKEN for *Aladdin*
BEST SONG	ALAN MENKEN, TIM RICE for "A WHOLE NEW WORLD" in *Aladdin*
BEST MAKE-UP	GREG CANNOM, MICHÈLE BURKE, MATTHEW W. MUNGLE for *Bram Stoker's Dracula*
BEST COSTUMES	EIKO ISHIOKA for *Bram Stoker's Dracula*
BEST VISUAL EFFECTS	KEN RALSTON, DOUG CHIANG, DOUGLAS SMYTHE, TOM WOODRUFF, JR. for *Death Becomes Her*
BEST SOUND	CHRIS JENKINS, DOUG HEMPHILL, MARK SMITH, SIMON KAYE for *The Last of the Mohicans*
BEST SOUND EFFECTS EDITING	TOM C. MCCARTHY, DAVID E. STONE for *Bram Stoker's Dracula*

1993 OSCARS

BEST PICTURE	SCHINDLER'S LIST
BEST DIRECTOR	STEVEN SPIELBERG for *Schindler's List*
BEST LEADING ACTRESS	HOLLY HUNTER in *The Piano*
BEST LEADING ACTOR	TOM HANKS in *Philadelphia*
BEST SUPPORTING ACTRESS	ANNA PAQUIN in *The Piano*
BEST SUPPORTING ACTOR	TOMMY LEE JONES in *The Fugitive*
BEST ORIGINAL SCREENPLAY	JANE CAMPION for *The Piano*
BEST ADAPTED SCREENPLAY	STEVEN ZAILLIAN for *Schindler's List*
BEST FOREIGN LANGUAGE FILM	*Belle Epoque* by FERNANDO TRUEBA (Spain)
BEST CINEMATOGRAPHY	JANUSZ KAMINSKI for *Schindler's List*
BEST ART DIRECTION / SET DECORATION	ALLAN STARSKI, EWA BRAUN for *Schindler's List*
BEST FILM EDITING	MICHAEL KAHN for *Schindler's List*
BEST MUSIC	JOHN WILLIAMS for *Schindler's List*
BEST SONG	BRUCE SPRINGSTEEN for "STREETS OF PHILADELPHIA" in *Philadelphia*
BEST MAKE-UP	GREG CANNOM, VE NEILL, YOLANDA TOUSSIENG for *Mrs Doubtfire*
BEST COSTUMES	GABRIELLA PESCUCCI for *The Age of Innocence*
BEST VISUAL EFFECTS	DENNIS MUREN, STAN WINSTON, PHIL TIPPETT, MICHAEL LANTIERI for *Jurassic Park*
BEST SOUND	GARY SUMMERS, GARY RYDSTROM, SHAWN MURPHY, RON JUDKINS for *Jurassic Park*
BEST SOUND EFFECTS EDITING	GARY RYDSTROM, RICHARD HYMNS for *Jurassic Park*

1994 OSCARS

BEST PICTURE	FORREST GUMP
BEST DIRECTOR	ROBERT ZEMECKIS for *Forrest Gump*
BEST LEADING ACTRESS	JESSICA LANGE in *Blue Sky*
BEST LEADING ACTOR	TOM HANKS in *Forrest Gump*
BEST SUPPORTING ACTRESS	DIANNE WIEST in *Bullets Over Broadway*
BEST SUPPORTING ACTOR	MARTIN LANDAU in *Ed Wood*
BEST ORIGINAL SCREENPLAY	QUENTIN TARANTINO, ROGER AVARY for *Pulp Fiction*
BEST ADAPTED SCREENPLAY	ERIC ROTH for *Forrest Gump*
BEST FOREIGN LANGUAGE FILM	*Burnt by the Sun* by NIKITA MICHALKOV (Russia)
BEST CINEMATOGRAPHY	JOHN TOLL for *Legends of the Fall*
BEST ART DIRECTION / SET DECORATION	KEN ADAM, CAROLYN SCOTT for *The Madness of King George*
BEST FILM EDITING	ARTHUR SCHMIDT for *Forrest Gump*
BEST MUSIC	HANS ZIMMER for *The Lion King*
BEST SONG	ELTON JOHN, TIM RICE for "CAN YOU FEEL THE LOVE TONIGHT" in *The Lion King*
BEST MAKE-UP	VE NEILL, RICK BAKER, YOLANDA TOUSSIENG for *Ed Wood*
BEST COSTUMES	LIZZY GARDINER, TIM CHAPPELL for *The Adventures of Priscilla – Queen of the Desert*
BEST VISUAL EFFECTS	KEN RALSTON, GEORGE MURPHY, STEPHEN ROSENBAUM, ALLEN HALL for *Forrest Gump*
BEST SOUND	BOB BEEMER, GREGG LANDAKER, DAVID MACMILLAN, STEVE MASLOW for *Speed*
BEST SOUND EFFECTS EDITING	STEPHEN HUNTER FLICK for *Speed*

1995 OSCARS

BEST PICTURE	BRAVEHEART
BEST DIRECTOR	MEL GIBSON for *Braveheart*
BEST LEADING ACTRESS	SUSAN SARANDON in *Dead Man Walking*
BEST LEADING ACTOR	NICOLAS CAGE in *Leaving Las Vegas*
BEST SUPPORTING ACTRESS	MIRA SORVINO in *Mighty Aphrodite*
BEST SUPPORTING ACTOR	KEVIN SPACEY in *The Usual Suspects*
BEST ORIGINAL SCREENPLAY	CHRISTOPHER MCQUARRIE for *The Usual Suspects*
BEST ADAPTED SCREENPLAY	EMMA THOMPSON for *Sense and Sensibility*
BEST FOREIGN LANGUAGE FILM	*Antonia's Line* by MARLEEN GORRIS (Netherlands)
BEST CINEMATOGRAPHY	JOHN TOLL for *Braveheart*
BEST ART DIRECTION	EUGENIO ZANETTI for *Restoration*
BEST FILM EDITING	MIKE HILL, DAN HANLEY for *Apollo 13*
BEST MUSIC	DRAMA – LUIS ENRIQUE BACALOV for *The Postman*
	MUSICAL, COMEDY – ALAN MENKEN, STEPHEN SCHWARTZ for *Pocahontas*
BEST SONG	ALAN MENKEN, STEPHEN SCHWARTZ for "COLORS OF THE WIND" in *Pocahontas*
BEST MAKE-UP	PETER FRAMPTON, PAUL PATTISON, LOIS BURWELL for *Braveheart*
BEST COSTUMES	JAMES ACHESON for *Restoration*
BEST VISUAL EFFECTS	SCOTT E. ANDERSON, CHARLES GIBSON, NEAL SCANLAN, JOHN COX for *Babe*
BEST SOUND	RICK DIOR, STEVE PEDERSON, SCOTT MILLAN, DAVID MACMILLAN for *Apollo 13*
BEST SOUND EFFECTS EDITING	LON BENDER, PER HALLBERG for *Braveheart*

3 *1996 The return of the melodrama: Anthony Minghella and Ralph Fiennes.*
4 *1996 Sceptical looks from the Coen Brothers.*

1996 OSCARS

BEST PICTURE	THE ENGLISH PATIENT
BEST DIRECTOR	ANTHONY MINGHELLA for *The English Patient*
BEST LEADING ACTRESS	FRANCES MCDORMAND in *Fargo*
BEST LEADING ACTOR	GEOFFREY RUSH in *Shine*
BEST SUPPORTING ACTRESS	JULIETTE BINOCHE in *The English Patient*
BEST SUPPORTING ACTOR	CUBA GOODING JR. in *Jerry Maguire*
BEST ORIGINAL SCREENPLAY	JOEL COEN, ETHAN COEN for *Fargo*
BEST ADAPTED SCREENPLAY	BILLY BOB THORNTON for *Sling Blade*
BEST FOREIGN LANGUAGE FILM	*Kolya* by JAN SVERAK (The Czech Republic)
BEST CINEMATOGRAPHY	JOHN SEALE for *The English Patient*
BEST ART DIRECTION / SET DECORATION	STUART CRAIG, STEPHENIE MCMILLAN for *The English Patient*
BEST FILM EDITING	WALTER MURCH for *The English Patient*
BEST MUSIC	DRAMA – GABRIEL YARED for *The English Patient*
	MUSICAL, COMEDY – RACHEL PORTMAN for *Emma*
BEST SONG	ANDREW LLOYD WEBBER, TIM RICE for "YOU MUST LOVE ME" in *Evita*
BEST MAKE-UP	RICK BAKER, DAVID LEROY ANDERSON for *The Nutty Professor*
BEST COSTUMES	ANN ROTH for *The English Patient*
BEST VISUAL EFFECTS	VOLKER ENGEL, DOUGLAS SMITH, CLAY PINNEY, JOSEPH VISKOCIL for *Independence Day*
BEST SOUND	CHRIS NEWMAN, WALTER MURCH, MARK BERGER, DAVID PARKER for *The English Patient*
BEST SOUND EFFECTS EDITING	BRUCE STAMBLER for *The Ghost and the Darkness*

1   *1997 The final instructions before the big scene: James Cameron and his two leads.*
2   *1997 James L. Brooks and the third star of the film.*

1997 OSCARS

BEST PICTURE	TITANIC
BEST DIRECTOR	JAMES CAMERON for *Titanic*
BEST LEADING ACTRESS	HELEN HUNT in *As Good As It Gets*
BEST LEADING ACTOR	JACK NICHOLSON in *As Good As It Gets*
BEST SUPPORTING ACTRESS	KIM BASINGER in *L. A. Confidential*
BEST SUPPORTING ACTOR	ROBIN WILLIAMS in *Good Will Hunting*
BEST ORIGINAL SCREENPLAY	MATT DAMON, BEN AFFLECK for *Good Will Hunting*
BEST ADAPTED SCREENPLAY	BRIAN HELGELAND, CURTIS HANSON for *L. A. Confidential*
BEST FOREIGN LANGUAGE FILM	*Karakter* by MIKE VAN DIEM (The Netherlands)
BEST CINEMATOGRAPHY	RUSSELL CARPENTER for *Titanic*
BEST ART DIRECTION / SET DECORATION	PETER LAMONT, MICHAEL FORD for *Titanic*
BEST FILM EDITING	CONRAD BUFF, JAMES CAMERON, RICHARD A. HARRIS for *Titanic*
BEST MUSIC	DRAMA – JAMES HORNER FOR *Titanic*
	MUSICAL, COMEDY – ANNE DUDLEY for *The Full Monty*
BEST SONG	JAMES HORNER, WILL JENNINGS for "MY HEART WILL GO ON" in *Titanic*
BEST MAKE-UP	RICK BAKER, DAVID LEROY ANDERSON for *Men in Black*
BEST COSTUMES	DEBORAH L. SCOTT for *Titanic*
BEST VISUAL EFFECTS	ROBERT LEGATO, MARK LASOFF, THOMAS L. FISHER, MICHAEL KANFER for *Titanic*
BEST SOUND	GARY RYDSTROM, TOM JOHNSON, GARY SUMMERS, MARK ULANO for *Titanic*
BEST SOUND EFFECTS EDITING	TOM BELLFORT, CHRISTOPHER BOYES for *Titanic*

3   1998 All the world is a stage: John Madden giving instructions to the actors.
4   1998 Nothing makes him lose his cool: Spielberg while shooting.

1998 OSCARS

BEST PICTURE	SHAKESPEARE IN LOVE
BEST DIRECTOR	STEVEN SPIELBERG for *Saving Private Ryan*
BEST LEADING ACTRESS	GWYNETH PALTROW in *Shakespeare in Love*
BEST LEADING ACTOR	ROBERTO BENIGNI in *Life is Beautiful*
BEST SUPPORTING ACTRESS	JUDI DENCH in *Shakespeare in Love*
BEST SUPPORTING ACTOR	JAMES COBURN in *Affliction*
BEST ORIGINAL SCREENPLAY	MARC NORMAN, TOM STOPPARD for *Shakespeare in Love*
BEST ADAPTED SCREENPLAY	BILL CONDON for *Gods and Monsters*
BEST FOREIGN LANGUAGE FILM	*Life is Beautiful* by ROBERTO BENIGNI (Italy)
BEST CINEMATOGRAPHY	JANUSZ KAMINSKI for *Saving Private Ryan*
BEST ART DIRECTION / SET DECORATION	MARTIN CHILDS, JILL QUERTIER for *Shakespeare in Love*
BEST FILM EDITING	MICHAEL KAHN for *Saving Private Ryan*
BEST MUSIC	DRAMA – NICOLA PIOVANI for *Life is Beautiful*
	MUSICAL, COMEDY – STEPHEN WARBECK for *Shakespeare in Love*
BEST SONG	STEPHEN SCHWARTZ for "WHEN YOU BELIEVE" in *The Prince of Egypt*
BEST MAKE-UP	JENNY SHIRCORE for *Elizabeth*
BEST COSTUMES	SANDY POWELL for *Shakespeare in Love*
BEST VISUAL EFFECTS	JOEL HYNEK, NICHOLAS BROOKS, STUART ROBERTSON, KEVIN MACK for *What Dreams May Come*
BEST SOUND	GARY RYDSTROM, GARY SUMMERS, ANDY NELSON, RONALD JUDKINS for *Saving Private Ryan*
BEST SOUND EFFECTS EDITING	GARY RYDSTROM, RICHARD HYMNS for *Saving Private Ryan*

1   *1999 Sam Mendes casts his unerring gaze on our life-long lies.*
2   *1999 Spectacular images: Andy and Larry Wachowski.*

1999 OSCARS

BEST PICTURE	AMERICAN BEAUTY
BEST DIRECTOR	SAM MENDES for *American Beauty*
BEST LEADING ACTRESS	HILARY SWANK in *Boys Don't Cry*
BEST LEADING ACTOR	KEVIN SPACEY in *American Beauty*
BEST SUPPORTING ACTRESS	ANGELINA JOLIE in *Girl Interrupted*
BEST SUPPORTING ACTOR	MICHAEL CAINE in *The Cider House Rules*
BEST ORIGINAL SCREENPLAY	ALAN BALL for *American Beauty*
BEST ADAPTED SCREENPLAY	JOHN IRVING for *The Cider House Rules*
BEST FOREIGN LANGUAGE FILM	*All About My Mother* by PEDRO ALMODÓVAR (Spain)
BEST CINEMATOGRAPHY	CONRAD L. HALL for *American Beauty*
BEST ART DIRECTION / SET DECORATION	RICK HEINRICHS, PETER YOUNG for *Sleepy Hollow*
BEST FILM EDITING	ZACH STAENBERG for *The Matrix*
BEST MUSIC	JOHN CORIGLIANO for *The Red Violin*
BEST SONG	PHIL COLLINS for "YOU'LL BE IN MY HEART" in *Tarzan*
BEST MAKE-UP	CHRISTINE BLUNDELL, TREFOR PROUD for *Topsy-Turvy*
BEST COSTUMES	LINDY HEMMING for *Topsy-Turvy*
BEST VISUAL EFFECTS	STEVE COURTLEY, JOHN GAETA, JANEK SIRRS, JON THUM for *The Matrix*
BEST SOUND	DAVID E. CAMPBELL, DAVID LEE, JOHN T. REITZ, GREGG RUDLOFF for *The Matrix*
BEST SOUND EFFECTS EDITING	DANE A. DAVIS for *The Matrix*

3   2000 Steven Soderbergh.
4   2000 Ang Lee maintains his bird's-eye view.

2000 OSCARS

BEST PICTURE	GLADIATOR
BEST DIRECTOR	STEVEN SODERBERGH for *Traffic*
BEST LEADING ACTRESS	JULIA ROBERTS in *Erin Brockovich*
BEST LEADING ACTOR	RUSSELL CROWE in *Gladiator*
BEST SUPPORTING ACTRESS	MARCIA GAY HARDEN in *Pollock*
BEST SUPPORTING ACTOR	BENICIO DEL TORO in *Traffic*
BEST ORIGINAL SCREENPLAY	CAMERON CROWE for *Almost Famous*
BEST ADAPTED SCREENPLAY	STEPHEN GAGHAN for *Traffic*
BEST FOREIGN LANGUAGE FILM	*Crouching Tiger, Hidden Dragon* by ANG LEE (Taiwan)
BEST CINEMATOGRAPHY	PETER PAU for *Crouching Tiger, Hidden Dragon*
BEST ART DIRECTION	TIM YIP for *Crouching Tiger, Hidden Dragon*
BEST FILM EDITING	STEPHEN MIRRIONE for *Traffic*
BEST MUSIC	TAN DUN for *Crouching Tiger, Hidden Dragon*
BEST SONG	BOB DYLAN for "THINGS HAVE CHANGED" in *Wonder Boys*
BEST MAKE-UP	RICK BAKER, GAIL RYAN for *Dr Seuss' How the Grinch Stole Christmas*
BEST COSTUMES	JANTY YATES for *Gladiator*
BEST VISUAL EFFECTS	JOHN NELSON, NEIL CORBOULD, TIM BURKE, ROB HARVEY for *Gladiator*
BEST SOUND	SCOTT MILLAN, BOB BEEMER, KEN WESTON for *Gladiator*
BEST SOUND EFFECTS EDITING	JON JOHNSON for *U-571*

INDEX OF FILMS

English Title *Original Title*

A

All About My Mother *Todo sobre mi madre* 614
Almost Famous 762
Les Amants du Pont-Neuf
    The Lovers on the Bridge 72
American Beauty 636
Apollo 13 272
Arizona Dream 112
As Good As It Gets 526

B

Babe 290
Bad Lieutenant 116
Basic Instinct 80
Batman Returns 120
Bawang Bie Ji **Farewell My Concubine** 176
The Beautiful Troublemaker *La Belle Noiseuse* 52
Before Night Falls 708
Being John Malkovich 672
La Belle Noiseuse **The Beautiful Troublemaker** 52
Der bewegte Mann **Maybe ... Maybe Not** 252
The Big Lebowski 552
Black Cat, White Cat *Chat noir, Chat blanc* 592
Blade 588
The Blair Witch Project 642
Boogie Nights 452
Boyz N the Hood 42
Braveheart 284
Breaking the Waves 416
The Bridges of Madison County 330
Buena Vista Social Club 566
Buffalo '66 510

C

Cape Fear 18
Casino 316
The Celebration *Festen (Dogme 1)* 530
Chat noir, Chat blanc **Black Cat, White Cat** 592
Chongqing Senlin **Chungking Express** 204
Chungking Express *Chongqing Senlin* 204
The Commitments 76
Conspiracy Theory 480
Crash 434
Crouching Tiger, Hidden Dragon / *Wo hu zang long* 700

D

Dahong Denglong Gaogao Gua 26
    Raise the Red Lantern
Dancer in the Dark 742
Dead Man 324
Dead Man Walking 300
Delicatessen 62
Disclosure 248

E

Ed Wood 214
The English Patient 420
Erin Brockovich 714
Eyes Wide Shut 618

F

Face/Off 490
Farewell My Concubine *Bawang Bie Ji* 176
Fargo 372
Festen (Dogme 1) **The Celebration** 530
A Few Good Men 106
Fight Club 624
The Firm 172

Forrest Gump 198
Four Weddings and a Funeral 136
From Dusk Till Dawn 378
The Fugitive 188
The Full Monty 484

G
Gattaca 464
Gladiator 724
Good Will Hunting 470
Groundhog Day 148

H
La Haine **Hate** 278
Happiness 562
Hate La Haine 278
Heat 346
High Fidelity 752
Hung Fan Kui **Rumble in the Bronx** 352
Husbands and Wives 126

I
The Ice Storm 496
In the Line of Fire 152
The Insider 648
Interview With the Vampire 228

J
Jackie Brown 516
JFK 22
Jurassic Park 130

K
Kids 308
Kolya 384

L
L. A. Confidential 440
The Lawnmower Man 98
Leaving Las Vegas 342
Léon / The Professional 210
Life is Beautiful La vita è bella 458
The Limey 668
The Lion King 260
Lock, Stock and Two Smoking Barrels 574
Lola rennt **Run Lola Run** 534
Lost Highway 406
The Lovers on the Bridge
      Les Amants du Pont-Neuf 72

M
Magnolia 678
Mars Attacks! 394
The Matrix 606
Maybe ... Maybe Not Der bewegte Mann 252
Men in Black 474
The Messenger: The Story of Joan of Arc 630
Mission: Impossible 358
Mission: Impossible 2 736
My Best Friend's Wedding 448
My Own Private Idaho 30

N
Natural Born Killers 222
Notting Hill 658

O
O Brother, Where Art Thou? 730
Out of Sight 556

INDEX OF FILMS

P

The People vs. Larry Flynt 428
A Perfect World 168
Philadelphia 144
The Piano 182
The Player 102
Point Break 46
Pulp Fiction 234

Q

Queen Margot *La Reine Margot* 242

R

Raining Stones 140
Raise the Red Lantern 26
    Dahong Denglong Gaogao Gua
La Reine Margot Queen Margot 242
Romeo & Juliet 400
Rumble in the Bronx *Hung Fan Kui* 352
Run Lola Run *Lola rennt* 534

S

Saving Private Ryan 598
Schindler's List 162
Scream 412
Sense and Sensibility 336
Se7en 294
Shakespeare in Love 582
Shall We Dance? *Shall we Dansu?* 364
Shall we Dansu? Shall We Dance? 364
The Shawshank Redemption 218
Short Cuts 192
The Silence of the Lambs 34
The Sixth Sense 662

Speed 256
Star Wars: Episode 1 – The Phantom Menace 692
The Straight Story 654
The Sweet Hereafter 522

T

Terminator 2: Judgment Day 66
Thelma & Louise 56
There's Something About Mary 578
The Thin Red Line 546
Three Colours: Blue *Trois Couleurs: Bleu* 156
Titanic 500
Todo sobre mi madre All About My Mother 614
Toy Story 304
Traffic 756
Trainspotting 388
Trois Couleurs: Bleu Three Colours: Blue 156
True Lies 266
The Truman Show 540
Twelve Monkeys 312
Twin Peaks: Fire Walk With Me 94

U

Unforgiven 86

V

La vita è bella Life is Beautiful 458

W

What Lies Beneath 720
When We Were Kings 368

Y

You've Got Mail 570

GENERAL INDEX

This list contains the names of the people involved in the production of a film.
Production companies are in italics and film categories are preceded by a dash.
Numbers in bold refer to a glossary text.

A

Aalbaeck-Jensen, Peter *416*
Abraham, Jake *574*
Abrams, Peter *46*
Ackroyd, Barry *140*
Acord, Lance *510, 672*
Acres, Mary *290*
– Action film *46, 66, 130, 210, 256, 266, 352, 358, 490, 534, 588, 724, 736*
Adams, Jane *562*
Adams, Kim *342*
Aday, Meat Loaf *624*
Addy, Mark *484*
Adjani, Isabelle *242*
Adrien, Gilles *62*
– Adventure film *272, 692*
Adzovic, Ljubica *592*
Affleck, Ben *470, 582*
Affleck, Casey *470*
Aguilar, George *480*
Aherne, Michael *76*
Aiello, Danny *210*
Aïm, Pierre *278*
Ajdini, Forijan *592*
Akerstream, Marc *352*
Alan-Williams, Greg *152*
Albert, Trevor *148*
Alberti, Maryse *368, 562*
Alcoholism in cinema **344**
Alexander, Scott *214, 428*
Alexander, Terry *480*
Alfonsi, Lydia *458*
Ali, Muhammad *368*
Allen, James *266*
Allen, Jim *140*
Allen, Joan *490, 496*
Allen, Tim *304*
Allen, Woody *126,* **128**
Allers, Roger *260*
Alliance Communications 434
Allicane Films 522
Allied Vision 98

Almodóvar, Agustin *614*
Almodóvar, Pedro *614,* **616**
Altman, Robert *102, 192*
Amateur actors **311**
Amblin Entertainment 18, 130, 162, 474, 598
Amen Ra Film 596
Amendola, Claudio *242*
Amos, Tori *736*
Anderson, David LeRoy *474*
Anderson, Laurie *708*
Anderson, Paul Thomas *452, 678,* **681**
Anderson, Scott E. *290*
Andrews, Naveen *420*
Andrews, Peter [= Steven Soderbergh] *756*
Andrus, Mark *526*
Anglade, Jean-Hugues *242*
Animals as people **292**
– Animation *260, 304*
Animation technology **612**
Anthony, Lysette *126*
The anti-hero **92**
Appel, Peter *210*
Apple, Jeff *152*
Arahanga, Julian *606*
Aralica, Vogislav *592*
Araskog, Julie *294*
Arbogast, Thierry *210, 592, 630*
Arbona, Gilles *52*
Archer, Anne *192*
Arenas, Reinaldo *708*
Argento, Asia *242*
Argo, Victor *116*
Arkin, Alan *464*
Arkins, Robert *76*
Armandáriz Jr., Pedro *708*
Arndt, Denis *80*
Arndt, Stefan *534*
Arnold Kopelson Productions 294
Arnold, Bonnie *304*
Arnold, Tom *266*

Arquette, David *412*
Arquette, Patricia *214, 406*
Arquette, Rosanna *234, 434, 510*
Arte 534, 566
Arte France Cinéma 742
Artisan Entertainment 642, 668
Ashbrook, Dana *94*
Asmussen, Peter *416*
Astaire, Fred **366**
Asymmetrical 406, 654
Atkins, David *112*
Atkinson, Rowan *260*
Atlas 312
Attanasio, Paul *248*
Attenborough, Richard *130*
August, Pernilla *692*
Austen, Jane *336*
Austin, Stephanie *266*
Auteuil, Daniel *242*
Avary, Roger Roberts *234*
Avenue 102, 192
Azorín, Eloy *614*

B

Bacharach, Burt **450**
Bacon, Kevin *106, 272*
Bad Lt. Productions 116
Badalamenti, Angelo *94, 406, 654*
Badalucco, Michael *210, 730*
Badelt, Klaus *724*
BAFTA Award **139**
Bagnall, Alison *510*
Bailey, John *148, 152, 526*
Baker, Diane *34*
Baker, Dylan *248, 562*
Baker, Joe Don *18*
Baker, Rick *214, 474*
Baker, Tungia *182*
Bakula, Scott *636*
Balk, Fairuza *762*
Ball, Alan *636*
Ball, Angeline *76*

Ballard, James Graham *434*
Balsam, Martin *18*
Baltimore Pictures 248
Balzac, Honoré de *52*
A Band Apart 234, 378, 470, 516
Banderas, Antonio *144, 228*
Banks, Caerthan *522*
Banks, Russell *522*
Barber, Paul *484*
Bardem, Javier *708*
Barhydt, Frank *192*
Barlow, Lou *308*
Barr, Jean-Marc *416, 742*
Barry, Raymond J. *300*
Barrymore, Drew *412*
Bartkowiak, Andrzej *256*
Bartók, Béla *672*
Barton, Mischa *662*
Basinger, Kim *440*
Bass, Ronald *448*
Bass, Saul **321**
Bassett, Angela *42*
Bastel, Victoria *116*
Bates, Kathy *500*
Bauer, Steven *756*
Baumgartner, Karl *592*
Be Gentlemen 470
Beacon Communications 76
Bean, Orson *672*
Béart, Emmanuelle *52, 358*
Beato, Affonso *614*
Beaufoy, Simon *484*
Beck, Rufus *252*
Beddor, Frank *578*
Bedford Falls Productions 582, 756
Beemer, Bob *256, 724*
Beer, Daniel *46*
Beijing Film Studios 176
Bekir, Adnan *592*
Belkhadra, Karim *278*
Bell, Ross Grayson *624*
Bellamy, Ned *672*

Bellfort, Tom *500*
Bellows, Gil *218*
Belluc, Marie *52*
Beltrami, Marco *412*
Bender, Lawrence *234, 470, 516*
Bender, Lon *284*
Benes, Michelle *330*
Benigni, Roberto *458*
Bening, Annette *394, 636*
Bennett, Richard Rodney *136*
Bentley, Wes *636*
Berkeley, Xander *464*
Bernstein, Elmer *18*
Berri, Claude *242, 614*
Besson, Claude *210, 630*
Besson, Luc *210*
Bevan, Tim *752*
Bhagat, Sajan *308*
Bickford, Laura *756*
Biddle, Adrian *56*
Bidewell, Victoria *720*
Bigelow, Kathryn *46*
Binoche, Juliette *72, **75**, 156, 420*
Biograf Jan Svěrák 384
– Biopic *708*
Birch, Thora *636*
Birkin, Andrew *630*
Birkin, Jane *52*
Biziou, Peter *540*
Björk *742*
– Black comedy *62*
Blackjack *752*
Blackman, Jeremy *678*
Blackwood, Vas *574*
Blake, Robert *406*
Blaxploitation ***521***
Bleibtreu, Moritz *534*
Blind Spot Pictures 742
Blue Light Productions 648
Blue/Green screen ***203***
Blur *388*
Boen, Earl *66*

Bohne, Bruce *372*
Bondam, Klaus *530*
Bonet, Lisa *752*
Bonham-Carter, Helena *624*
Bonitzer, Pascal *52*
Bonneville, Hugh *658*
Borders, Gloria S. *66*
Borgnine, Ernest *464*
Bosco, Philip *448*
Bosé, Miguel *242*
Boudová, Nella *384*
Bourke, Pieter *648*
Bowen, Michael *516*
Bower, Charles *136*
Bowie, David *72, 94*
Boxing at the movies ***370***
Boyes, Christopher *500*
Boyle, Danny *388, **392***
Boyle, Lara Flynn *562*
Boyle, Sharon *46*
Bozman, Ron *34*
Bradshaw, Joan *720*
Brandenburg, Larry *218, 372*
Braschi, Gianluigi *458*
Braschi, Nicoletta *458*
Bregovic, Goran *112, 242*
Bremner, Ewen *388*
Brennan, Lee *140*
Brenneman, Amy *346*
Brenner, Marie *648*
Breuer, Torsten *252*
Brialy, Jean-Claude *242*
Bridges, Jeff *552*
Brimley, Wilford *172*
Bringelson, Mark *98*
Brion, Jon *68*
Brisbin, David *342, 714*
Brockovich-Ellis, Erin *714*
Broderick, Matthew *260*
Brody, Adrien *546*
Brokaw, Cary *192*
Brooks, Albert *556*
Brooks, James L. *526*

Brosnan, Pierce *98, 394*
Brown, Clancy *218*
Brown, David *102, 106*
Brown, James *368*
Brown, Julie *140*
Brown, W. Earl *412, 578*
Broyles Jr., William *272*
Bruce, Ian *598*
Brugge, Pieter Jan *648*
Bryce, Ian *762*
Bryniarski, Andrew *120*
Buain, Daniel *72*
Buchholz, Horst *458*
Buckmaster, Paul *312*
Buena Vista Pictures 730
Buena Vista Social Club 566
Buff, Conrad *500*
Bullock, Sandra *256*
Bunker, Edward ***351***
Burgess, Don *198, 720*
Burke, Tim *724*
Burmester, Leo *168*
Burnett, T-Bone *552, 730*
Burns, Edward *598*
Burns, Heather *570*
Burrows, Robin *116*
Bursztein, David *52*
Burton, Tim *120, 214, 394, **399**, 686*
Burton, Zoe *290*
Burton/DiNovi Productions 214
Burum, Stephen H. *358*
Burwell, Carter *372, 480, 552, 672, 708*
Burwell, Lois *284*
Buscemi, Steve *372, 552*
Busey, Gary *46, 172, 406*
Bushnell, Paul *76*
Bustric, Sergio *458*
Butler, Lucy *406*
Byrd, Eugene *324*
Byrne, Gabriel *324*
Byrnes, Brittany *290*

C

CAB Productions 156
Cage, Nicolas *342, 490*
Caifei, He *26*
Calderon, Paul *116*
Calderón, Sergio *474*
Caldwell, L. Scott *188*
Callender-Ferrier, Stephen *574*
Callow, Simon *136, 582*
Cameron, James *66, 266, 500*
Campbell, David E. *606*
Campbell, John *30*
Campbell, Neve *412*
Campbell, Rob *86*
Campbell, Vernon *312*
Campion, Jane *182*
Canal+ 112
Candy, John *22*
Cantarini, Giorgio *458*
Cantó, Toni *614*
Capobianco, Jim *260*
Cappa 18, 316
Carax, Léos *72*
Carhart, Timothy *56*
Carlyle, Phyllis *294*
Carlyle, Robert *388, 484*
Caro, Marc *62*
Carolco 66, 80
Carpenter, Joseph A. *654*
Carpenter, Russell *98, 266, 500*
Carrere, Tia *266*
Carrey, Jim *540, **543***
Carrilles, Lázaro Gómez *708*
Cartlidge, Katrin *416*
Carver, Raymond *192*
Carville, James *428*
Caselli, Chiara *30*
Cassavetes, Nick *490*
Cassel, Vincent *278, 630*
Cassini, John *294*
Castle Rock Entertainment 106, 152, 218
Cathey, Reginald E. *294*

GENERAL INDEX

Cattaneo, Peter 484
Caviezel, Jim 546
Cazes, Lila 342
Cecchi Gori Group 458
CED Productions 156
Cerami, Vincenzo 458
Ceska Televize 384
Chaffin, Cean 624
Chalimon, Andrej 384
Chambers, Emma 658
Chan, "Piggy" 204
Chan, Frankie 204
Chan, Jackie 352, **356**
Chance, Michael 312
Chancellor, Anna 136
Chang, Terence 490, 736
Changwai, Gu 176
Channel Four 136, 484
Chaplin, Ben 546
Chapman, Jan 182
Chapman, Michael 188
Chappelle, David 570
Chaykin, Maury 522
Cheadle, Don 452, 556, 756
Chen, Chang 700
Chéreau, Patrice 242
Chestnut, Morris 42
Cheung, Leslie 176
Child stars **171**
Childs, Martin 582
China Film 26, 176
Chong, Marcus 606
Chow, Raymond 352
Chow, Valerie 204
Christensen, Erika 756
Christopher, Bojesse 46
Chun, Li 176
Ciby 2000 182, 406, 592, 654
Ciby Pictures 94
Cinéma beur **283**
CinemArt 384
Cinematic architecture **28**
Cinematograph 742

Clark, Larry 308
Clark, Spencer Treat 724
Clarke, Stanley 42
Classico 312
Clement, Dick 76
Clinica Estetico 144
Clipsal Films 748
Clooney, George 378, 546, 556, 730, **735**
Close, Glenn 394
Coen, Ethan 372, 552, 730
Coen, Joel 372, 552, 730
Coffey, Colleen 98
Cohen, Bruce 636
Cohen, Joel 304
Cole, Gary 152
Coleman, Charlotte 136
Coleman, Dabney 570
Colleary, Michael 490
Collette, Toni 662
Columbia 42, 144, 148, 152, 106, 700, 714, 336, 448, 474
– Comedy 76, 126, 136, 148, 198, 214, 252, 266, 290, 304, 352, 364, 378, 394, 474, 484, 552, 574, 578, 592, 672, 730, 752
– Comic 120
Comics and movies **125**
Conaway, Christi 120
Concert movies **568**
Constellation 62, 112
Cooder, Joachim 566
Cooder, Ry 566
Cooksey, Danny 66
Cooper, Chris 636
Cooper, Nellee 400
Copeland, Stewart 140
Coppola, Francis Ford 686
Co-production **142**
Cora, Tony 642
Corley, Annie 330
Corman, Roger 34

Corporation In Trust 434
Corrigan, Kevin 510
Cosmo, James 284
Costello, Deirdre 484
Costner, Kevin 22, 168
– Costume film 176, 336, 582
Cotbould, Neil 724
Coulter, Michael 336, 658
Courtley, Steve 606
– Courtroom drama 106, 144
Cowie, Robin 642
Cox, Courteney 412
Cox, Joel 86
Cox, John 290
Cozart, Cylk 480
Crachiolo, Dan 606
Craig, Stuart 420
Craven, Wes 412
Crichton, Michael 130, 248
– Crime film 116, 168, 372, 686, 756
Cromwell, James 290, 428, 440, 748
Cronenberg, David 434, **439**
Cronenweth, Jeff 624
Cross, Garvin 352
Crouse, Lindsay 648
Crowe, Cameron 762
Crowe, Russell 440, 648, 724, **729**
Crowe, Sara 136
Crudup, Billy 762
Cruise, Tom 106, **111**, 172, 228, 358, 618, 678, 736
Cruise-Wagner Productions 736
Cruz, Penélope 614
Cube, Ice 42
Cuifeng, Cao 26
Cundey, Dean 130, 272
Cunningham, Lowell 474
Curley, Jim 152
Curtis, Jamie Lee 266
Curtis, Richard 136, 658

Cusack, Joan 752
Cusack, John 546, 672, 752
Cyber thriller **101**
Czapsky, Stefan 120, 214
Czech film and the West **386**
Czerny, Henry 358, 496

D
D.A. Films 242
d'Alessio, Carlos 62
D'Onofrio, Vincent 102, 214, 474
Da, Ying 176
Dafoe, Willem 420
Dahan, Alain 72
Daiei 364
Dakinah, Gbatokai 530
Dallesandro, Joe 668
Dallwitz, Burkhart 540
Damon, Matt 470, **473**, 598
Dan, Li 176
Danes, Claire 400
Dangerfield, Rodney 222
Daniels, Jeff 256
Danish Film Institute 742
Danna, Mychael 496, 522
Danner, Blythe 126
Danson, Ted 598
Darabont, Frank 218
Davey, Bruce 284
David Brown-Addis Wechsler Productions 102
David, Keith 578
Davidtz, Embeth 162
Davies, Jeremy 598
Davies, Oliver Ford 692
Davis, Andrew 188
Davis, Dane A. 606
Davis, Elliot 556
Davis, Geena 56
Davis, John 172
Davis, John 308, 606
Davis, Judy 126

Davison, Bruce *192*
Dawn, Jeff *66*
Dawson, Rosario *308*
de Bont, Jan *80, 256*
De Borman, John *484*
de Fina, Barbara *18, 316*
de Medeiros, Maria *234*
de Niro, Robert *18, 316, 346, 516* de Palma, Brian *358*
Deakins, Roger A. *218, 300, 372, 552, 730*
Dean, Loren *464, 748*
DeCou, Patricia *642*
Decter, Ed *578*
Degeto 242
Del Toro, Benicio *756*, **760**
Delate, Brian *540*
Delia, Joe *116*
Delli Colli, Tonino *458*
Deming, Peter *406*
Deming, Wang *700*
Demme, Jonathan *34, 144*
Dench, Judi *582*
Deneuve, Catherine *742*
Denicourt, Marianne *52*
Denman, Tony *372*
Dennehy, Brian *400*
Dennett, Peter *182*
Depp, Johnny *112*, **115**, *214, 324, 686, 708*
Dern, Laura *130, 168*
Deschanel, Zooey *762*
Destani, Jasar *592*
Devane, William *748*
DeVincentis, D.V. *752*
DeVito, Danny *120, 394, 440, 464, 556, 714*
Di Palma, Carlo *126*
Di Stefano, Andrea *708*
Di, Tong *176*
Diaz, Cameron *448, 578*, **581**, *672*
DiCaprio, Leonardo *400, 500*, **503**

Didawick, Dawn *714*
Diesel, Vin *598*
Digital pictures **538**
Dikko, Solo *278*
Dillon, Matt *578*
Dimension Films 412
DiNovi Pictures 742
DiNovi, Denise *120, 214*
Dion, Celine *500*
Dior, Rick *272*
Director's cut **226**
– Disaster film *500*
Disney, Walt **264**
Dobbs, Lem *668*
– Documentary *368, 566*
Dodds, K.K. *672*
Dogme 95 **533**
Dogstar Films 752
Dolleris, Helle *530*
Donahue, Heather *642*
Donner, Lauren Shuler *570*
Donner, Richard *480*
Doran, Lindsay *336*
Doran, Matt *606*
Dorff, Stephen *588*
Douglas, Illeana *18*
Douglas, Michael *80, 248*, **251**, *756*
Douglas-Reuther Productions 490
Dougnac, Marie-Laure *62*
Downey Jr., Robert *192, 222*
Doyle, Christopher *204*, **209**
Doyle, Maria *76*
Doyle, Patrick *336*
Doyle, Roddy *76*
Doyle-Murray, Brian *148*
– Drama *22, 26, 30, 42, 46, 52, 56, 72, 116, 126, 140, 144, 162, 168, 176, 182, 192, 204, 210, 218, 228, 242, 278, 308, 316, 342, 388, 428, 434, 440, 452, 470, 496, 510, 522, 530,*

540, 562, 618, 630, 636, 678, 708, 714, 748, 762
DreamWorks SKG 598, 636, 720, 724
Dreyfus, James *658*
Dreyfus, Jean-Claude *62*
Driver, Minnie *470*
Dryburgh, Stuart *182*
Ducommun, Rick *148*
Dudley, Anne *484*
Dufour, Bernard *52*
Duke, Robin *148*
Dumas d.Ä., Alexandre *242*
Dumont, Sky *618*
Dun, Tan *700*
Dunaway, Faye *112, 630*
Duneton, Claude *156*
Dunst, Kirsten *228*
Durano, Giustino *458*
Duret, Marc *278*
Dushku, Eliza *266*
Dust Brothers *624*
Duvall, Wayne *730B*
Dye, Dale *358*
Dyrholm, Trine *530*
Dzundza, George *80*

E
Eastwood, Clint *86, 152, 168, 330*, **335**, *748*
Eckhart, Aaron *714*
Edelstein, Neal *654*
Edko Films 700
Edwards, Eric Alan *30, 308*
Edwards-Hughes, Jennifer *654*
Eginton, Madison *618*
Egoyan, Atom *522*, **525**
Eichinger, Bernd *252*
El Deseo 614
El Mar Pictures *708*
Elfman, Danny *120, 358, 394, 470, 474, 686*
Elliott, Chris *148, 578*

Elliott, Sam *552*
Ellroy, James *440*, **446**
Elmes, Frederick *496*
Elswit, Robert *452, 678*
Elvin, Justin *562*
Emmerich, Noah *540*
Emoto, Akira *364*
Engelmann, Robert *588*
Engels, Robert *94*
Eno, Brian *388*
Ephron, Delia *570*
Ephron, Nora *570*
– Episodic film *192*, **197**, *678*
ERA International 26
Ermey, R. Lee *294, 300, 304*
– Erotic thriller *80, 248*
Escoffier, Jean-Yves *72, 470*
Estevez, Emilio *358*
Eszterhas, Joe *80*
Evans, Lee *578*
Everett, Gimel *98*
Everett, Rupert *448, 582*

F
Faction **24**
Fahey, Jeff *98*
Fallon, Mike *140*
Fallon, Siobhan *474*
– Fantasy *700*
Farina, Dennis *556*
Farley, John *654*
Farley, Kevin P. *654*
Farmer, Gary *324*
Farnsworth, Richard *654*
Farrelly, Bobby *578*
Farrelly, Peter *578*
Farrow, Mia *126*
Fazeng, Li *700*
Fechner, Christian *72*
Fei, Zhao *26*
Feldman, Edward S. *540*
Felsberg, Ulrich *566*
Feng, Hsu *176*

GENERAL INDEX

Fengyi, Zhang *176*
Fenton, George *148, 570*
Feore, Colm *490, 648*
Ferch, Heino *534*
Ferrara, Abel *116*
Ferrell, Conchata *714*
Ferrell, Tyra *42*
Ferrer, Ibrahim *566*
Ferrer, Miguel *756*
Ferrero, Martin *130*
Ferri, Elda *458*
Fiedel, Brad *66, 266*
Field, Sally *198*
Field, Todd *618*
Fienberg, Gregg *94*
Fiennes, Joseph *582*
Fiennes, Ralph *162, 420*
Figgis, Mike *342*
Figment Film 388
Filac, Vilko *112*
Film A 272
Film adaptations of literature
55
Les Films Alain Sarde 654
Film and TV **96**
Les Films du Dauphin 210
Film Four 140
Film i Väst 742
Film quotation **657**
Films about filmmaking **676**
Films Christian Fechner 72
Fincher, David *294,* **299,** *624*
Fine Line Features 192
Finerman, Wendy *198*
Finnegan, Dave *76*
Finney, Albert *714*
Fiorentino, Linda *474*
Firth, Colin *420, 582*
Fishburne, Laurence *42, 606*
Fisher, Frances *86*
Fisher, Thomas L. *500*
Fitzpatrick, Leo *308*
Flaherty, Lanny *222*

Flanagan, Tommy *726*
Flea *30, 552*
Fleet, James *136, 336*
Flemyng, Jason *574*
Fletcher, Dexter *574*
Flick, Stephen Hunter *256*
Florido, Giovanni *708*
Flowers, Leslie *168*
Flynt, Larry *428*
Fonda, Bridget *516*
Fonda, Peter *668*
Fontani, Amerigo *458*
Ford, Harrison *188,* **191,** *720*
Ford, Michael *500*
Foreman, George *368*
Forman, Miloš *428,* **433**
Forster, Robert *516*
Forsyth, Rosemary *248*
Forward Pass 346, 648
Foster, Gloria *606*
Foster, Jodie *34*
Fox 2000 Pictures 624
Fox 484
Fox, Michael J. *394*
FR3 Films 52
Frampton, Peter *284*
France 2 Cinéma 242, 592,
614
France 3 Cinéma 742
Francis, Freddie *18, 654*
Franco, Larry *394*
François, Emile *336*
Frank, Scott *556*
Frankfurt, Peter *588*
Franzoni, David *724*
Frears, Stephen *752*
Fredericks, Neal *642*
Freeman, Morgan *86, 218, 294*
Frieberg, Camela *522*
Fritsch, Thomas *260*
Fugit, Patrick *762*
Fujimoto, Tak *34, 144, 662,*
667

Furlong, Edward *66*
Fu-Sheng, Chiu *26*

G
Gaeta, John *606*
Gage, Kevin *346*
Gaghan, Stephen *756*
Gallagher, Bronagh *76*
Gallagher, Peter *102, 192, 636*
Gallo, Vincent *112, 510*
Gambon, Michael *648, 686*
– Gangster film *234, 316, 346,*
516, 556, **577,** *668*
Garber, Victor *500*
Garcia, Roel A. *204*
Garcia, Ron *94*
Garner, James *748,* **751**
Garrison, Jim *22*
Gast, Leon *368*
Gaumont 210, 630
Gaup, Mikkel *416*
Gazzara, Ben *510, 552, 562,* **565**
Gebel, Malgoscha *162*
Gedeck, Martina *252*
Geffen 18, 228
Geffen, David *228*
Geisler, Robert Michael *546*
Geisler-Roberdeau-Productions
546
Geller, Bruce *358*
Gems, Jonathan *394*
George Reinhart Productions 52
George, Melissa *668*
Geraghty, Marita *148*
Gerrard, Lisa *648, 724*
Gershon, Gina *490, 648*
Getty, Balthazar *222, 406*
Ghoulardi 452, 678
Gibson, Charles *290*
Gibson, Mel *284,* **289,** *480*
Gifford, Barry *406*
Gigliotti, Donna *582*
Gilliam, Terry *312*

Giuntoli, Neil *218*
Glass, Philip *540*
Gleeson, Brendan *284, 7386*
Glenn, Scott *34*
Glover, Crispin *428*
Goddard, Paul *290*
Godsick, Christopher *490*
Goetzman, Gary *34*
Goldberg, Adam *598*
Goldberg, Whoopi *102, 260*
Goldblum, Jeff *130*
Golden Harvest 352
Goldenthal, Elliot *228, 346*
Goldsmith, Jerry *80, 440*
Goldsmith, Paul *368*
Goldstein, Jenette *66*
Golin, Steve *672*
Golino, Valeria *342*
Gómez, Fernando Fernán *614*
Gonzáles, Rubén *566*
Good Machine 496, 562, 700, 742
Goodall, Caroline *162, 248*
Gooding jr., Cuba *42, 526*
Goodman, John *552, 730*
Goofs **220**
Gordon, Mark *256, 598*
Goretsky, Elliott *720*
Gormley, Félim *76*
Gormley, Peggy *116*
Gossom Jr., Thom *624*
Gough, Michael *120*
Goyer, David S. *588*
Gracie Film 526
Graham, Heather *452*
Gramercy Pictures 672
Grandview Pictures 708
Grant, Beth *256*
Grant, Hugh *136, 336, 658,* **660**
Grant, Richard E. *102*
Grant, Susannah *714*
Grazer, Brian *272*
Greatex, Richard *582*
Green, Jack N. *86, 168, 330, 748*

Greenberg, Adam 66
Greene, Ellen 210
Greenhut, Robert 126
Greenstein, Scott 420
Greenwood, Bruce 522
Gregg, Clark 720
Greggory, Pascal 242, 630
Grenier, Zach 624
Grey, Joel 742
Grey, Rudolph 214
Griebe, Frank 534
Grier, Pam 516
Gries, Jon 474
Griffin, Bob 642
Griffin, Jennifer 168
Griffiths, Rachel 448
Grise, Pierre 52
Grisham, John 172, **174**
Grobet, Xavier Pérez 708
Groom, Winston 198
Grüber, Klaus-Michael 72
Grusin, Dave 172
Guerra, Castulo 66
Guest appearance **513**
Guest, Christopher 106
Guggenheim, Ralph 304
Guilfoyle, Paul 440
Guinee, Tim 588
Gunton, Bob 218
Guzmán, Luis 556, 668, 756

H
Haas, Lukas 394
Hachette Premiere 62, 112
Hackett, Jonathan 416
Hackford, Taylor 368
Hackman, Gene 86, 172
Hahn, Don 260
Hald, Brigitte 530
Hale, Gregg 642
Hall, Allen 198
Hall, Conrad L. 636
Hall, Hanna 198

Hall, Philip Baker 648, 678
Hallberg, Per 284
Hallex, Jackie 642
Hallowell, Todd 282
Hamilton, Linda 66
Hamm, Sam 120
Hammer film studios **691**
Hamsher, Jane 222
Han, Lei 176
Hancock, John Lee 168
Handmade Films Ltd. 576
Hanks, Tom 144, 198, 272, 304,
   570, 598, **601**
Hanley, Chris 510
Hanley, Dan 272
Hanly, Peter 284
Hann-Byrd, Adam 496
Hanover, Donna 428
Hansard, Glen 76
Hanson, Curtis 440
Hara, Hideko 364
Harden, Marcia Gay 748
Hardy, John 668
Harlan, Jan 618
The Harold Greenberg Fund 522
Harper, Frank 574
Harrelson, Brett 428
Harrelson, Woody 222, 428, 546
Harrington, Desmond 630
Harris, Ed 172, 272, 540
Harris, Jared 324, 562
Harris, Richard 86, 724
Harris, Richard A. 500
Harris, Thomas 34
Harvey, Rob 724
Hauser, Cole 470
Hausman, Michael 428
Havoc Productions 300
Hawke, Ethan 464
Hawthorne, James 256
Haxan Films 642
Hayek, Salma 378
Hayes, Isaac 278

Hayes, Reginald C. 672
Haynie, Jim 330
Hayward, Wade 290
Heald, Anthony 34
Heil, Reinhold 534
Heinle, Amelia 668
Heinrichs, Rick 686
Heitz, Jane Galloway 654
Helgeland, Brian 440, 480
Helgenberger, Marg 714
Hemmings, David 724
Henderson, Sarah 308
Henderson, Wayne 368
Henriksen, Bjarne 530
Henriksen, Lance 324
Herrmann, Bernard 18
Herskovitz, Marshall 756
Heslov, Grant 266
Hibbin, Sally 140
Hickey, Tom 140
Hill, Bernard 500
Hill, Grant 546
Hill, Mike 272
Hines, Desi Arnez 42
Hingle, Pat 120
Hipp, Paul 116
– Historical film 162, 182, 242,
   247, 284, 630, 724
Hitchcock, Alfred **21**
Hjejle, Iben 752
Ho, A. Kitman 22
Ho, Leonhard 352
Hobby Films 618
Hodge, John 388
Hoffman, Dustin 630
Hoffman, Philip Seymour 452,
   456, 552, 562, 678, 762
Hogan, P.J. 448
Holbek, Joachim 416
Holbrook, Hal 172
Holgado, Ticky 62
Hollywood on Hollywood **105**
Hollywood Pictures 662

Holm, Ian 522
Holm, Morten 530
Holmes, David 556
Holmes, Katie 496
Homosexuality in the movies **147**
Hope, Ted 496, 562
Hopkins, Anthony 34
Hopper, Dennis 256
Hornby, Nick 752
Horner, James 272, 284, 500
– Horror film 228, 378, 412, 588,
   642, 662, 686
Howard, James Newton 188, 448,
   662
Howard, Ron 272
Huddleston, David 552
Hudson, Kate 762, **766**
Huggins, Roy 188
Hughes, David A. 574
Hughes, Miko 272
Hughes, Sally 152
Huison, Steve 484
Humphreys, Michael Conner 198
Hunt, Helen **529**
Hunter, Holly 172, 182, **187**, 434,
   730
Hurd, Gale Anne 66
Hurt, John 324
Huston, Anjelica 510
Hutshing, Joe 22
Hyde, Jonathan 500
Hymns, Richard 130, 598

I
ICAIC 566
Icelandic Film Corporation 742
Icon 284
Idziak, Slawomir 156, 464
Ifans, Rhys 658
Iglesias, Alberto 614
Iliff, W. Peter 46
Image Movers 720
Imaginary Forces 588

GENERAL INDEX

Imagine Entertainment 272
Independent Pictures 308
Independents **32**
Industrial Light and Magic **697**
Initial Entertainment Group 756
Initial productions 342
Irons, Jeremy *260*
Irving, Washington *686*
Irwin, Mark *412, 578*
Isaak, Chris *94, 618*
Isham, Mark *46, 192, 588*
Ivanir, Mark *162*
Ixtlan 22, 222, 428

J

J.D. Productions 222
Jackson, Samuel L. *130, 234, 516, 692*
Jacobi, Derek *724*
James, Jesse *526*
James, Jonathan *140*
Janevski, Boban *62*
Janney, Allison *636*
Jarmusch, Jim *324*, **328**
Jayanti, Vikram *368*
Jennings, Will *500*
Jenny, Lucinda *56*
Jersey Films 234, 464, 556, 714
Jet Tone Productions 204
Jeunet, Jean-Pierre *62*
Jingwu, Ma *26*
Jinks, Dan *636*
Jinks/Cohen Company 636
Jiping, Zhao *26, 176*
Joan of Arc movies **635**
John, Elton *260*
Johnson, Bridget *526*
Johnson, Mark *168, 720*
Johnson, Tom *66, 500*
Jones, Bruce *140, 484*
Jones, Cherry *714*
Jones, Gemma *336*
Jones, James *546*

Jones, James Earl *260*
Jones, Jeffrey *214, 686*
Jones, L.Q. *316*
Jones, Tommy Lee *22, 188, 222, 474, 748*
Jones, Trevor *658*
Jones, Vinnie *574*
Jonze, Spike *672*
Jordan, Neil *228*
Jover, Arly *588*
Jovovich, Milla *630*
Judd, Ashley *346*
Judkins, Ronald *130, 598*
Julian, Yolande *434*
Jump cut **671**
Jung, Tsai Kuo *700*

K

Kahan, Steve *480*
Kahn, Michael *162, 598*
Kaige, Chen *176*
Kaitz Productions 648
Kaminski, Janusz *162, 598*
Kane, Bob *120*
Kanfer, Michael *500*
Karajlic, Nelle *592*
Karaszewski, Larry *214, 428*
Karmitz, Marin *156*
Kar-Wai, Wong *204*
Karyo, Tcheky *630*
Kasdan, Lawrence *526*
Kassar, Mario *80*
Kassovitz, Mathieu *278*
Katic, Branka *592*
Katsulas, Andreas *188*
Katt, Nicky *668*
Katz, Judah *434*
Kaufman, Charlie *672*
Kaufman, Ken *748*
Kaufmann, Morten *530*
Kayano, Naoki *364*
Keatin, Kevin *368*
Keaton, Michael *120, 516*

Keener, Catherine *672*
Keitel, Harvey *56, 116,* **118***, 182, 234, 378*
Kelly, Moira *94, 260*
Kelsch, Ken *116*
Keneally, Thomas *162*
Kennedy Miller Productions 290
Kennedy, Jamie *412*
Kennedy, Kathleen *130, 330, 662*
Kenworthy, Duncan *136, 658*
Ker, Edith *62*
Kernochan, Sarah *720*
Khanjian, Arsinée *522*
Khondji, Darius *62, 294*
Khouri, Callie *56*
Kidman, Nicole *618*
Kier, Udo *30, 416, 588, 742*
Kieslowski, Krzysztof *156,* **160**
Kilik, Jon *300, 708*
Kilmer, Val *346*
Kimball, Jeffrey *470*
Kimball, Jeffrey L. *736*
Kimbrough, Matthew *668*
King, Alan *316*
King, B. B. *368*
King, Chris Thomas *730*
King, Don *368*
King, Jim *642*
King, Meta *42*
King, Rick *46*
King, Stephen *98, 218*
Kingsley, Ben *162*
King-Smith, Dick *290*
Kinnear, Greg *526, 570*
Kinney, Terry *172*
Kintop Pictures 566
Kitchen Sink cinema **488**
Kitman Ho Productions 22
Klausner, Howard *748*
Klimek, Johnny *534*
Kline, Kevin *496*
Kluger, Jeffrey *272*
Knaup, Herbert *534*

Knight, Shirley *526*
Knight, Wayne *80*
Koepp, David *130, 358*
Komuna 592
Kondor, Robbie *562*
Kong, Bill *700*
Kong, Hsu Li *700*
König, Ralf *252*
Konrad, Cathy *412*
Kopelson, Arnold *188, 294*
Korine, Harmony *308*
Kostic, Vladica *742*
Koteas, Elias *434, 464, 546*
Koundé, Hubert *278*
Kovacs, Laszlo *448*
Krabbé, Jeroen *188*
Kramer, Scott *668*
Kristofferson, Kris *588*
Król, Joachim *252, 534*
Kroon, Christopher *330*
Kubrick, Stanley *618,* **620**
Kühne, Wolfgang *260*
Kurtzman, Robert *378*
Kusakari, Tamiyo *364*
Kusamura, Reiko *364*
Kusturica, Emir *112, 592,* **597**

L

La Frenais, Ian *76*
Lachman, Edward *714*
Ladd Jr., Alan *284*
Ladd Productions 284
LaGravenese, Richard *330*
Lakovic, Predrag Pepi *592*
Lam, Morgan *352*
Lamont, Peter *500*
Landaker, Gregg *256*
Landau, Jon *500*
Landau, Martin *214*
Landay, Vincent *672*
Lang Pringle 98
Lang, Antonia *252*
Lange, Jessica *18*

Lantieri, Michael *130*
Lantos, Robert *434*
Larsen, Thomas Bo *530*
Larsson, Chrichan *72*
Lasoff, Mark *500*
Lasser, Louise *562*
Lasseter, John *304*
Laszlo, Miklos *570*
Lau, Andrew *204*
Laughlin, John *98*
Laurent, Christine *52*
Lavant, Denis *72*
Law, Jude *464*
Lazar, Andrew *748*
Ledoux, Patrice *630*
Lee, Ang *336, 496, 700*
Lee, Christopher *686*
Lee, David *606*
Lee, Jason *762*
Lee, Lilian *176*
Lee, Sheryl *94*
Lee, Spike *368*
Leeloo Productions 630
Leftfield 388
Legato, Robert *500*
Legend 16
LeGros, James *46*
Leguizamo, John *400*
Leigh, Jennifer Jason *192*
Lemmon, Jack *192*
Lemmons, Kasi *34*
Lemon, Geneviève *182*
Leonard, Brett *98*
Leonard, Elmore *516, 556*
Leonard, Joshua *642*
Lepine, Jean *102*
Lesnie, Andrew *290*
Leto, Jared *624*
Leung, Tony *204*
Levantal, François *278*
Levin, Lloyd *452*
Levine, Ted *34*
Levinsohn, Gary *598*

Levinson, Barry *248*
Levy, Robert L. *46*
Levy, Shmulik *162*
Lewis, Geoffrey *98*
Lewis, Huey *192*
Lewis, Jerry *112*
Lewis, Juliette *18, 126, 222, 378*
Lewis, Richard *342*
Ley, Tabu *368*
Leys, Polly *484*
Leyva, Pio *566*
Li, Gong *26, 176,* **180**
Liberator Productions *742*
Licea, Manuel "Puntillita" *566*
Ligeti, György *618*
Lightstorm Entertainment 66, 266, 500
Lillard, Matthew *412*
Lin, Brigitte *204*
Lin, Kong *26*
Lina, Guan *204*
Lindley, John *570*
Lineback, Richard *222, 256*
Ling, Wang Hui *700*
Linney, Laura *540*
Linson Films 624
Linson, Art *346, 624*
Lion Brand Film 346
Lions Gate Films 510
Lipton, Peggy *94*
Lisi, Virna *242*
Lister Jr., Tommy "Tiny" *516*
– Literature adaptation *26, 52, 102, 336, 400, 420, 618, 686*
Liu, Ernest *378*
Livanova, Irena *384*
Lloyd, Emily Ann *272*
Lloyd, Jake *692*
Lloyd, Walt *192*
Loach, Ken *140*
Lockwood, Michele *308*
Logan, John *724*
Loggia, Robert *406*

Logue, Donal *588*
Lojodice, Liuliana *458*
Long, Nia *42*
Lopez Garmandia, Olatz *708*
Lopez, Jennifer *556,* **560**
López, Orlando "Cachaíto" *566*
Lord, Kris *352*
Lords, Traci *588*
Lorenzengel, Frank *260*
Los Hooligans Productions 378
Louiso, Todd *752*
– Love film *400, 534, 582*
Love, Courtney *428*
Lovell, Jim *272*
Lovett, Lyle *192*
Lovitz, Jon *562*
Lowther, T.J. *168*
Lozano, Carlos *614*
Lu, Wei *176*
Lubezki, Emmanuel *686*
Lubtchansky, William *52*
Lucas, George *692*
Lucasfilm Ltd. 692
Luhrmann, Baz *400*
Lund, Zoë *116*
Lustig, Branko *162, 724*
Lynch, David *94, 406,* **411,** *654*
Lynch, John Carroll *372*
Lynch, Pauline *388*
Lynch-Frost Productions 94
Lyon, Gail *714*
Lyons, John *452*
Lyons, Phyllis *330*

M
Ma, Fibe *352*
Ma, Jingle *352*
MacAlpine, Donald M. *400*
MacBride, Demetra J. *324*
Macdonald, Andrew *388*
MacDonald, John D. *18*
Macdonald, Kelly *388*
MacDonald, Laurie *474*

MacDowell, Andie *136, 148, 192*
Mackintosh, Steven *574*
MacLachlan, Kyle *94*
MacMillan, David *256, 272*
MacNeill, Peter *434*
Macy, William H. *372,* **376,** *452, 678*
Mad Chance 748
Madden, John *582*
Madsen, Michael *56*
Maffia, Roma *248*
The Magnolia Project 678
Maguire, George *624*
Maguire, Jeff *152*
Maguire, Tobey *496*
Mahler, Gustav *126*
Mahoney, John *152*
Mailer, Norman *368*
Main, Percy *56*
Majorowski, Rachel *470*
Makeba, Miriam *368*
Malick, Terrence *546,* **550**
Malik, Art *266*
Malkina, Liliya *384*
Malkovich, John *152, 630, 672*
Malone, Dorothy *80*
Malpaso 85, 168, 330, 748
Mancina, Mark *256*
Mandalay Pictures 686
Manesh, Marshall *266*
Mann, Aimee *678*
Mann, Michael *346, 648,* **651**
Mann/Roth Productions 648
Mantle, Anthony Dod *530*
Manzo, Carlos Martín *400*
Mapother, William *736*
Marceau, Sophie *284*
Marcus, Stephen *574*
Marie, Lisa *214*
Marignac, Martine *52*
Marin, Cheech *260, 378*
Marker, Chris *312,* **315**
Marketing **647**

GENERAL INDEX

Marley, Bob 278
Mars, Jim 22
Marshall, Frank 662
Marshall, James 106
– Martial arts film 352, 700, **707**
Martin, Cherylanne 720
Martindale, Margo 300
Martinelli, Gabriella 400
Martinez, Cliff 668, 756
Martinez, Olivier 708
Marvin, Niki 218
Maslow, Steve 256
Mason, Candyce 112
Mason, Mark 642
Massee, Michael 406
Massey, Dick 76
Masterson, Christopher 448
Masui, Shoji 364
Mathieson, John 724
Mathou, Jacques 62
Matthau, Walter 22
Matusovich, Carl J. 210
Maurice-Jones, Tim 574
Maxwell, Roberta 300
Mayeux, Rosalee 98
Mayo, Whitman 42
Maysles, Albert 368
Mazar, Debi 648
Mazmark Productions 400
Mazzello, Joseph 130
McArthur, Alex 480
McArthur, Sarah 260
McCallum, Rick 692
McCamus, Tom 522
McCauley, Colleen 470
McClory, Belinda 606
McClurg, Edie 222
McCollam, Virginia 228
McCormack, Catherine 284
McCoy, Matt 440
McDermott, Dylan 152
McDiarmid, Ian 692
McDonald, Christopher 56

McDonald, Julie M. 304
McDormand, Frances 192, 372, 762
McElhone, Natascha 540
McFayden, Angus 284
McGarvey, Seamus 752
McGill, Everett 654
McGinley, John C. 46, 294
McGoohan, Patrick 284
McGowan, Rose 412
McGregor, Ewan 388, 692
McInnerny, Tim 658
McKee, Gina 658
McKidd, Kevin 388
McKinnon, Ray 168, 732
McLachlan, Rod 480
McLean, Lenny 574
McNamara, Pat 624
McNicholl, Peter 574
Mecchi, Irene 260
Melampo Cinematografica 458
Melito, Joseph 312
– Melodrama 156, 300, 330, 416, 420, 500, 614, 742
Memedov, Zabit 592
Mendel, Barry 662
Mendes, Sam 636
Merkerson, S. Epatha 66
Merrill, Dina 102
Merrison, Clive 420
Metcalf, Laurie 22, 304, 342
Michell, Roger 658
Mighton, John 470
Mighty Mighty Afrodite Productions 516
Mihic, Gordan 592
Milchan, Arnon 440
Millan, Scott 272, 724
Miller, Bill 290
Miller, Dennis 248
Miller, George 290
Miller, Jonny Lee 388
Mills, Charles 42

Minghella, Anthony 420
Minkoff, Rob 260
Mirage 172, 336
Miramax 182, 234, 308, 378, 412, 420, 516
Mirrione, Stephen 756
Mitchell, Doug 290
Mitchum, Robert 18, 324
MK2 Productions 156
Modine, Matthew 192
Moeller, Ralf 726
Molen, Gerald R. 130, 162
Molina, Alfred 324, 452
Monello, Michael 642
Monk, Debra 330
Montero, Zully 18
Montouté, Edouard 278
– Monumental film 724
Moody, Rick 496
Moore, Demi 106, 248
Moore, Julianne 188, 192, 452, 552, 678
Moore, Ronald D. 736
Moore, Simon 756
Moran, Nick 574
Morgan, Trevor 662
Morgenstern, Stephanie 522
Moriarty, P. H. 574
Moritzen, Henning 530
Moriyama, Shuchiro 364
Morphing **68**
Morricone, Ennio 152, 248
Morris, John 304
Morse, David 742
Morton, Joe 66, 256, 720
Mosier, Scott 470
Moss, Carrie Anne 606
Movies and the death penalty **303**
Mucci, David 86
Mui, Anita 352
Mullan, Peter 388
Müller, Robby 324, 416, 566, 742

Mulroney, Dermot 448
Mune, Ian 182
Murch, Walter 420
Muren, Dennis 66, 130
Murphy, Don 222
Murphy, George 198
Murphy, John 574
Murphy, Johnny 76
Murphy, Michael 120
Murphy, Shawn 130
Murray, Bill 148, **151**, 214
Muse 510
– Music film 76, 566, 752, 762
Music movies **79**
– Musical 742, **747**
Mutual Film Company 598
Myles, Lynda 76
Myrick, Daniel 642
– Mystery drama 94

N

Napier, Charles 144
Napier, Marshall 290
Nathanson, Michael G. 440
Navarro, Guillermo 378, 516
Navarro, Loló 708
Nayar, Deepak 406, 566
Neeson, Liam 126, 162, 692
NEF Filmproduktion 242
Neill, Sam 130, 182
Neill, Ve 214
Nelson, Andy 598
Nelson, John 724
Nelson, Tim Blake 730
– Neo film noir 406, 440, 668
Neue Constantin Film 252
Neumann, Birthe 530
New Black Cinema **44**
New Crime Productions 752
New Deal 42
New Line Cinema 30, 294, 452, 588, 678
New Order 388

New Regency *222*
Newell, Mike *136*
Newirth, Charles *198*
Newman, Barry *668*
Newman, Chris *420*
Newman, Randy *304*
Newman, Thomas *102, 218, 428, 630, 714*
Newton, Thandie *228, 736*
Niccol, Andrew *464, 540*
Nicholson, Jack *106, 394, 526*
Nicholson, William *724*
Nicolaides, Steve *42*
Niehaus, Lennie *86, 168, 330, 748*
Nielsen, Connie *724*
Nimbus Film 530
Nippon Television Network 364
Nivola, Alessandro *490*
Nolte, Nick *18, 546*
Noonan, Chris *290*
Noonan, Polly *112*
Norman, Marc *582*
Norrington, Stephen *588*
Norris, Bruce *662*
Norton, Edward *428, 624*
Notting Hill Productions 658
Nunnari, Gianni *378*
Nussbaum, Mike *474*
Nyman, Michael *182, 464*
Nyswaner, Ron *144*

O
O'Brien, Austin *98*
O'Brien, John *342*
O'Hara, David *284*
O'Keefe, Cunningham *708*
Ochoa, Eliades *566*
Off camera **713**
Ogata, Yuji *364*
Oldman, Gary *22, 210*
Olga Film GmbH 252
Ondaatje, Michael *420*

Orion 34
Orloff, Lee *66*
Osborne, Barrie M. *490*
Osment, Haley Joel *198, 662*
Ossard, Claudie *62, 112*
Otto, Miranda *720*
Overton, Rick *148*
Oz, Frank *692*

P
Pacific Western 66
Pacino, Al *346, 648*
Pain Unlimited 742
Palahniuk, Chuck *624*
Paltrow, Gwyneth *294, 582,* **586**
Pandora 324, 384, 592
Pantoliano, Joe *188, 606*
Paquin, Anna *182, 762*
Parallax 140
Parallel montage **41**
Paramount 198, 358, 500, 540, 598, 686, 736
Paranoid cinema **483**
Paredes, Marisa *458, 614*
Parfit, Davit *582*
Parker, Alan *76*
Parker, Laurie *30*
Parker, Michael *30*
Parker, Nicole *452*
Parker, Sarah Jessica *214, 394*
Parkes, Walter F. *474*
Pasolini, Uberto *484*
Paton, Angela *148*
Patrick, Robert *66*
Pattison, Paul *284*
Pau, Peter *700*
Paxton, Bill *266, 272, 500*
Pearce, Craig *400*
Pearce, Guy *440*
Peck, Bob *130*
Peck, Gregory *18*
Pederson, Steve *272*
Peguero, Yakiru *308*

Pei-Pei, Cheng *700*
Peldon, Courtney *496*
Peña, Candela *614*
Penn, Chris *192*
Penn, Michael *452*
Penn, Sean *300, 546*
Peoples, David Webb *86, 312*
Peoples, Janet *312*
Pepper, Barry *598*
Percy Main Productions 56
Perez, Vincent *242*
Permut, David *490*
Pernel, Florence *156*
Perrineau, Harold *400*
Pesci, Joe *22, 316*
Peterman, Donald *46, 474*
Petersen, Wolfgang *152,* **154**
Petri, Nina *534*
Petty, Lori *46*
Pfeiffer, Michelle *120, 720*
Philbin, John *46*
Phoenix 428, 546
Phoenix, Gemma *140*
Phoenix, Joaquin *724*
Phoenix, River *30*
Piccoli, Michel *52*
Pickering, Marc *686*
Pickles, Christina *400*
The Picture Factory 654
Pierce, Justin *308*
Pierce-Roberts, Anthony *248*
Pierre Grise Productions 52
Piesiewicz, Krzysztof *156*
Pileggi, Nicholas *316*
Pink, Steve *752*
Pinon, Dominique *62*
Piovani, Nicola *458*
Pisani, Anne-Marie *62*
Pitt, Brad *56, 228, 294, 312, 624,* **627**
Piven, Byrne *672*
Pixar Animation Studios 304
Pixar Studios **307**

Place, Mary Kay *672*
Plimpton, George *368*
Plummer, Amanda *234*
Plummer, Christopher *312, 648*
Plummer, Glenn *256*
Pole Star 618
– Police film *188, 346, 440*
– Political thriller *22, 152, 756*
Polk, Mimi *56*
Pollack, Sydney *102, 126, 172, 618*
Pollak, Kevin *106, 316*
Polley, Sarah *522*
Polson, John *736*
Polygram 136, 312
Pook, Jocelyn *618*
Poon, Alice *434*
Pop, Iggy *72, 324, 388*
Pope, Bill *606*
Porizkova, Paulina *112*
Portman, Natalie *210, 394, 692*
Portobello Pictures 384
Portuondo, Omara *566*
Posey, Parker *570*
Post, Markie *578*
Postlethwaite, Pete *400*
Potente, Franka *534*
Potts, Annie *304*
Pounder, CCH *490*
Powell, John *490*
Powell, Sandy *582*
Pratt, Roger *312*
Predawn 448
Preisner, Zbigniew *156*
Prejean, Sister Helen *300*
Presnell, Harve *372, 490*
Pressman, Edward R. *116*
Preston, Carrie *448*
Preston, J.A. *106*
Prévost, Albert *72*
– Prison film *218*
Prochnow, Jürgen *420*
Proctor, Emily *342*

GENERAL INDEX

Les Productions Lazennec 278
Propaganda Films 672
Prosky, Robert 300
Pseudonyms **555**
Pullman, Bill 406
Pulp **240**
Purcell, Dominic 736

Q
Qi, Lu 176
Quaid, Dennis 756
Quertier, Jill 582
Quester, Hugues 156
Quinlan, Kathleen 272
Quinn, Declan 342

R
Rabe, David 172
Ragas, Roef 416
Ralston, Ken 198
Ramis, Harold 148, 526
Randall-Cutler, Roger 76
Randolph, John 570
Rane, Alexia 112
Raphael, Frederic 618
Raphaelson, Samson 570
Ratner, Suzy 574
Ratzenberger, John 304
Rauth, Héloïse 278
Ravey, Ronnie 140
Rawlins, Adrian 416
Rayfiel, David 172
RCS Films & TV 242
Rea, Stephen 228
Red Herring **723**
Redgrave, Vanessa 358
Redwave Films 484
Reed, Lou 388, 708
Reed, Oliver 724
Reeves, Keanu 30, 46, 256, 606
Regen, Elizabeth 210
Regency Enterprises 346, 440,
    624

Régent, Benoît 156
Reilly, John C. 452, 678
Reinartz, Judith 252
Reiner, Rob 106
Reinert, Al 272
Reitz, John T. 606
Remake 18, **269**
Remar, James 720
Remili, Leila 52
Renn Productions 242, 614
Reno, Jean 210, 358, **362**
The return of the melodrama **422**
Revell, Graeme 378, 648
Reyes, Julian 46
Reynolds, Burt 452
Rhames, Ving 234, 358, 556, 736
Ribisi, Giovanni 406, 598
Ricci, Christina 496, **498**, 510,
    686
Rice, Anne 228
Rice, Tim 260
Rich, Allan 248
Richards, Ariana 130
Richardson, Marie 618
Richardson, Miranda 686
Richardson, Robert 22, 106, 222,
    316
Richert, William 30
Richman, Jonathan 578
Rickles, Don 304, 316
Rickman, Alan 336
Ridings, Richard 630
Riemann, Katja 252
Rifkin, Ron 440
Rinzler, Lisa 566
Les Rita Mitsouko 72
Ritchie, Guy 574
Riva, Emmanuelle 156
Rivera, Louis 304
Rivette, Jacques 52
Roach, John 654
– Road movie 30, 56, **60**, 222,
    654

Road Movies 566
Robards, Jason 144, 678
Robards, Sam 636
Robbins, David 300
Robbins, Tim 102, 192, 218, 300,
    752
Roberdeau, John 546
Roberts, Joe 582
Roberts, Julia 448, 480, 658, 714,
    718
Robertson, Robbie 316
Robinson, J. Peter 352
Robinson, James 284
Robinson, Keith 368
Rodat, Robert 598
Rodriguez, Robert 378
Rodriguez, Valente 714
Roebuck, Daniel 188
Roger, Marie-Claude 52
Rohde, Armin 252, 534
Roll, Gernot 252
Rollins, Henry 406
Rollins, Jack 126
Rolston, Mark 218
– Romance 510, 556
– Romantic comedy 448, 526,
    570, **572**, 658
Romero, George A. 34
Rooker, Michael 22
Rose, Gabrielle 522
Rosenbaum, Stephen 198
Rosenberg, Scott 752
Ross, Chelcie 80
Rossignon, Christophe 278
Roth, Ann 420
Roth, Cecilia 614
Roth, Eric 198, 648
Roth, Tim 234
Roundtree, Richard 294
Rourke, Mickey 510
Rousselot, Philippe 228, 242, 428
Roven, Charles 312
Roxburgh, Richard 736

Rubin, Danny 148
Rubinek, Saul 86
Ruck, Alan 256
Rudin, Scott 172, 540, 686
Rudloff, Gregg 606
Rudolph, Lars 534
Rudrüd, Kristin 372
Ruggiero, Anthony 116
Rukov, Mogens 530
Rummel, John 510
Rush, Geoffrey 582
Russo, James 30
Russo, Rene 152
Rutowski, Richard 222
Ryan, Meg 570
Rydstrom, Gary 66, 130, 500, 598

S
Sadler, Nicholas 248
Sadler, William 218
Šafránková, Libuše 384
Sagall, Jonathan 162
Salerno, Tiffany 198
San Juan, Antonia 614
Sanchez, Eduardo 642
Sanchez, Sandra 642
Sanders, Jay O. 22
Sands, Julian 342
Sarandon, Susan 56, 300
Sardà, Rosa María 614
Sarde, Alain 654
Sarelle, Leilani 80
Sarossy, Paul 522
– Satire 102, 222
Saul Zaentz Productions 420
Savini, Tom 378
Sawiris, Jackie 618
Saxon, Edward 34, 144
Scacchi, Greta 102
Scalia, Pietro 22
Scanlan, Neal 290
Scarwid, Diana 720
Schamus, James 496, 700

Scheinman, Andrew *106*
Schellhardt, Mary Kate *272*
Schiavelli, Vincent *120, 428*
Schifrin, Lalo *358, 736*
Schipper, Sebastian *534*
Schmidt, Arthur *198*
Schmidt, Benno *126*
Schmitt, Sarah Kathryn *330*
Schnabel, Julian *708*
Schnitzler, Arthur *618*
Schreiber, Liev *412*
Schroeder, Adam *540, 686*
Schulman, Ann *112*
Schumacher, Thomas *260*
Schwartzman, John *480*
Schwarzenegger, Arnold *66, 266*
Schweiger, Til *252*
– Science fiction *98, 120, 312,*
   394, 464, 474, 540, 606, 692
Scorsese, Martin *18, 316*
Scott, Deborah Lynn *500*
Scott, Dougray *736*
Scott, Ridley *56, 724*
The *scream* trilogy **414**
Screening **213**
Seale, John *172, 420*
Seda, Jon *312*
Seelig, Mike *228*
Segundo, Compay *566*
Seko, Mobutu Sese *368*
Sekula, Andrzej *234*
Sellar, Joanne *452, 678*
Serbedzija, Rade *618, 736, 748*
Serra, Eric *210, 630*
Severdzan, Bajram *592*
Sevigny, Chloë *308*
Seymour, Cara *742*
Shaiman, Marc *106*
Shakespeare, William *400*
Shakespeare at the movies **404**
Shalhoub, Tony *474*
Shamberg, Michael *464, 556, 714*
Sharp, Lesley *484*

Sharrock, Ivan *420*
Shawn, Wallace *304*
Shaye, Lin *578*
Sher, Stacey *464, 556, 714*
Shore, Howard *34, 144, 214, 294,*
   434, 752
Short, Martin *394*
Shostakovich, Dmitri *618*
Shue, Elisabeth *342*
Shuler Donner Productions 480,
   570
Shuyuan, Jin *26*
Shyamalan, M. Night (Manoj
   Nelliyattu Shyamalan) *662*
Sidney, Sylvia *394*
Sihung, Lung *700*
Silva, Sebastian *708*
Silver Productions 480, 606
Silver, Joel *480, 606*
Silvestri, Alan *198, 720*
Simmons, Rudd *300, 752*
Sindall, Philip *136*
Sing, Chan Man *352*
Singer, Lori *192*
Singer, Rachel *624*
Single Cell Pictures 672
Singleton, John *42*
Sinise, Gary *198, 272*
Sirrs, Janek *606*
Sit, Ailen *352*
Sizemore, Tom *222, 346, 598*
SKA Films 574
Skarsgård, Stellan *416, 470*
Sklar, Zachary *22*
Skotak, Robert *66*
Slade, Max Elliott *272*
Slate, Jeremy *98*
Slater, Christian *228*
Slezak, Victor *330*
Smith, Brooke *34*
Smith, Kevin *470*
Smith, Larry *618*
Smith, Lois *300*

Smith, Pete *182*
Smith, Will *474*
Smoljak, Ladislav *384*
Smothers, Dick *316*
Smutný, Vladimír *384*
Snipes, Wesley *588,* **590**
Sobieski, Leelee *618*
– Social study *278*
Soderbergh, Steven *556, 668,*
   714, 756
Sokolow, Alec *304*
Solomon, Ed *474*
Solondz, Todd *526, 562*
Songshen, Zuo *204*
Sonnenberg, David *368*
Sonnenfeld, Barry *474,* **479**
Sony 700
Sorkin, Aaron *106*
Sorvino, Paul *400*
Sotirov, Stojan *592*
Soukup, Ondřej *384*
Sound design **134**
Space travel in the cinema **275**
Spacek, Sissy *22, 654*
Spacey, Kevin *294, 440, 636,* **639**
Spader, James *434*
Spalková, Petra *384*
Sparavalo, Dejan *592*
Speer, Hugo *484*
Spelling Entertainment 102
Spelling Films 192
Spielberg, Steven *130, 162,* **165,**
   598, 724
Spinotti, Dante *346, 440, 648*
Splendid Medien AG 756
Spradlin, G. D. *214*
Springsteen, Bruce *144*
Spyglass Entertainment 662
St. John, Marco *56*
Staenberg, Zach *606*
Stafford, Bill *30*
Stalens, Marion *72*
Stamp, Terence *668, 692*

Stanton, Andrew *304*
Stanton, Harry Dean *94, 654*
Stapleton, Jean *570*
Starkey, Steve *198*
Starr, Mike *214*
Starsky, Allan *162*
Statham, Jason *574*
Steadycam **51**
Steen, Paprika *530*
Steenburgen, Mary *144*
Steiger, Rod *394*
Steinberg, Michael *578*
Stern, Sandy *672*
Sternberg, Tom *406*
Steve Tisch Co. 574
Stevenson, Cynthia *562*
Stewart, Annie *342*
Stewart, Lisa *762*
Stewart, Patrick *480*
Stiller, Ben *578*
Sting *574*
Stipe, Michael *672*
Stockbridge, Sara *228*
Stockwell, Dean *102*
Stoltz, Eric *234*
Stone, Oliver *22, 222, 428*
Stone, Sharon *80, 316*
Stoppard, Tom *582*
Stormare, Peter *372, 552, 742*
Stowe, Madeleine *192, 312*
The Straight Story Inc. 654
Strathairn, David *172, 440*
Strauss, John J. *578*
Strawinsky, Igor *52*
Streep, Meryl *330*
Strick, Wesley *18*
Strong Heart Productions 34
Strother, Fred *312*
Stuart, Gloria *500*
Stuart, Jeb *188*
Stubbs, Imogen *336*
Studi, Wes *346*
Studio Canal 730

Le Studio Canal+ 80, 654
Sucharetza, Marla 198
Sulejmani, Sabri 592
Sullivan, Susan 448
Summers, Gary 66, 130, 500, 598
Suo, Masayuki 364
Suo, Yoshikazu 364
Surrealism – Cinema as dream **64**
Suschitzky, Peter 394, 434
Sutherland, Donald 22, 248, 748
Sutherland, Kiefer 94, 106
Suvari, Mena 636
Svěrák, Jan 384
Svěrák, Zdeněk 384
Swain, Dominique 490
Swanson, Ed 642
Swarts, Cheryl 434
Swayze, Patrick 46
Swedish Film Institute 742
Sweeney, Mary 406, 654
Sweeney, Steve 574
Syalis 316
Szarabajka, Keith 168
Szubanski, Magda 290

T
Taghmaoui, Saïd 278
Taguchi, Hiromasa 364
Takenaka, Naoto 364
Takeshi, Kaneshiro 204
Tally, Ted 34
Tambakis, Peter Anthony 662
Tambor, Jeffrey 578
Tang, Edward 352
Tarantino, Quentin 222, 234, 378, **382**, 516
Tattersall, David 692
Tattersall, Gale 76
Taurus Film 624
Taussig, Pavel 384
Taylor, Holland 540
Taylor, Lili 112, 192, 752
Taylor, Noah 762

Telefilm Canada 522
Teper, Meir 378

Thomas, Bradley 578
Thomas, Jeremy 434
Thomas, Jessie 30
Thomas, Kristin Scott 136, 358, 420
Thomas, Leonard L. 116
Thompson, Anna 86
Thompson, Danièle 242
Thompson, Emma 336, **338**
Thompson, Fred Dalton 18, 152
Thomsen, Ulrich 530
Thorn, Frankie 116
Thornton, Billy Bob 324
– Thriller 18, 34, 98, 102, 106, 172, 188, 294, 358, 406, 434, 480, 574, 624, 648, 662, 720, 736
Thum, Jon 606
Thurman, Uma 234, 464, **469**
Tinayre, Gilles 72
Tippett, Phil 130
Tisch, Steve 198
Tobolowsky, Stephen 56, 148, 648
Todde, Mickael 62
Todorovic, Srdan 592
Tokui, Yu 364
Tokuma, Yasuyoshi 364
Tolkin, Michael 102
Toll, John 284, 546, 762
Tomlin, Lily 192
Tomlinson, Ricky 140
Tomson Films 176
Tong, Stanley 352
Tong, Su 26
Tor Studio 156
Torn, Rip 474, 648
Touchstone 214, 648, 730, 752
Toussieng, Yolanda 214
Towne, Katharine 720

Towne, Robert 172, 358
Townsend, Clayton 222, 260
– Tragicomedy 112, 384, 458
Travolta, John 234, 490, **494**, 546
Trégouët, Yann 156
Trejo, Danny 378
Tribeca Productions 18
Tripplehorn, Jeanne 80, 172
TriStar 126, 144, 448, 526
Truffaut, Hervé 72
Trust Film 742
Tucker, Chris 516
Tufano, Brian 388
Tung, Barbie 352
Tung, Bill 352
Turturro, John 552, 730
12-Gauge Productions 324
20th Century Fox 46, 256, 266, 400, 500, 578, 720
Twohy, David N. 188
Tykwer, Tom 534
Typecasting **259**

U
UFA Non Fiction 368
UGC 62, 112
Uhls, Jim 624
Ulano, Mark 500
Ulrich, Skeet 412, 526
Underwood, Blair 464
Underworld 388
Unger, Deborah Kara 434
United China Vision 700
Universal 18, 162, 312, 316, 556, 714, 724, 730
USA Films 756
Utt, Kenneth 34

V
Vachon, Christine 562
Valdes, Billy 308
Valdes, David 168

Valentine, Jane 630
Valletta, Amber 720
Vampire films **231**
van de Sande, Theo 588
van der Knaap, Nico 252
Van Dien, Casper 686
Van Sant, Gus 30, 470
Vance, Courtney B. 748
Varney, Jim 304
Vaughn, Matthew 574
Vawter, Ron 144
Veloz, David 222
Venora, Diane 346, 648
Verhoeven, Paul 80, **85**
Véry, Charlotte 156
Vetchý, Ondřej 384
Viard, Karin 62
Vidal, Gore 464
Vidler, Susan 388
Village Roadshow Productions 748
Vincent, Frank 316
Vincent, Hélène 156
Vincent, Jan-Michael 510
Vinterberg, Thomas 530
Vinyl Films 762
Voe, Sandra 416
Voges, Torsten 552
Voice over **755**
Voight, Jon 346, 358
Volter, Philippe 156
von Bargen, Daniel 730
von Borsody, Suzanne 534
von Sinnen, Hella 260
von Trier, Lars 416, **418**, 742

W
Wachowski, Andy 606
Wachowski, Larry 606
Wadham, Julian 420
Wagner, Natasha Gregson 406, 752
Wagner, Paula 358

Wahl, Bob 510
Wahlberg, Donnie 662
Wahlberg, Mark 452
Waits, Tom 192
Wajsbrot, Rywka 278
Waldeman, Billy 308
Walken, Christopher 120, 234, 686
Walker, Andrew Kevin 294, 686
Walker, Kerry 182
Walker, Timothy 136
Wallace, Randall 284
Waller, Robert James 330
Walls, Kevin Patrick 588
Walsh, J.T. 106
Walsh, M. Emmet 400, 448
Walt Disney 260, 304
Walter, Harriet 336
Walters, Melora 678
Wang, Du Lu 700
– War Film 546, 598
Warbeck, Stephen 582
Ward, Fred 102, 192
Ward, Sela 188
Warner Bros. 120, 168, 188, 228, 394, 618
Warner, David 500
Warner, Rick 312
Warren Jr., Gene 66
Warren, Lesley Ann 668
Washington, Denzel 144
Watanabe, Eriko 364
Waters, Daniel 120
Watson, Alberta 522
Watson, Emily 416
Waxman, Michael 648
WCG Entertainment 490
WDR 534
Weaver, Sigourney 496
Weaving, Hugo 606
Webb, David 290
Webb, James R. 18

Weber, Steven 342
Wechsler, Nick 102
Weimin, Ding 26
Weinstein, Bob 420
Weinstein, Harvey 420, 582
Weir, Peter 540
Welsh, Irvine 388
Wenders, Wim 566
Werb, Mike 490
Wessler, Charles B. 578
West, Timothy 630
– Western 86, 324
Westlake, Nigel 290
Weston, Celia 300
Weston, Ken 724
What Else? 742
Whately, Kevin 420
Whedon, Joss 304
Whiteford, Bradley 168
Whitmore, James 218
Wick, Douglas 724
Widmer, Jörg 566
Wieggert, Donald 654
Wiesinger, Kai 252
Wilcke, Alexandra 260
Wildgruber, Ulrich 242
Wilkinson, Tom 336, 484, 582
Williams, Brian J. 480
Williams, John 22, 130, 162, 598, 692
Williams, Michael 642
Williams, Olivia 662
Williams, Robin 470
Williamson, Fred 378
Williamson, Jeffrey 144
Williamson, Kevin 412
Williamson, Mykelti 198, 346
Willis, Bruce 234, 312, 662
Wilson, Nancy 762
Wilson, Scott 300
Wincott, Michael 324, 708
Windeløv, Vibeke 416, 742
Winslet, Kate 336, 500

Winston, Stan 66, 130
Wise, Greg 336
Wise, Ray 94
Wisher, William 66
Wong, B.D. 130
Wong, Faye 204
Wong, Jonathan 352
Woo, John 490, 736, 741
Wood, Ed 217
Wood, Elijah 496
Wood, Oliver 490
Wood, Tom 188
Woods Entertainment 412
Woods, Cary 308, 412
Woods, James 316
Woodward, Joanne 144
Woof, Emily 484
Wooley, Stephen 228
Woolvett, Jaimz 86
Working Title 136, 300, 372, 552, 658, 730, 752
Wortmann, Sönke 252, 255
Wright, Jenny 98
Wright, N'Bushe 588
Wright, Robin 198
Wyatt "Cherokee", Lucius 210
Wyman, Dan 98

X
X Filme Creative Pool 534
Xian, Gao 700
Xiao, Chu 26

Y
Yakusho, Koji 364
Yan, Hai 700
Yang, Janet 428
Yared, Gabriel 420
Yates, Janty 724
Yeoh, Michelle 700
Yi-Kan, Chan 204
Yimou, Zhang 26
Yip, Françoise 352

Yip, Tim 700
Yost, Graham 256
You, Ge 176
Young, Bruce A. 80
Young, Neil 324
Young, Peter 686
Young, Roderick 368
Yun-Fat, Chow 700

Z
Zabriskie, Grace 30
Zaentz, Saul 420
Zahn, Steve 556, 570
Zaillian, Steven 162
Zane, Billy 500
Zapp and Roger 278
Zázvorková, Stella 384
Zea, Kristi 526
Zemeckis, Robert 198, 720
Zentropa 416, 742
Zeta-Jones, Catherine 752, 756
Zhen, Liang 204
Zhen, Ni 26
Zhengyin, Cao 26
Zhihgang, Cui 26
Zhiming, Huang 204
Zimmer, Hans 56, 260, 526, 546, 724, 736
Ziyi, Zhang 700
Zubernis, Jeffrey 662
Zucker, Jerry 448
Zwick, Edward 582, 756

ABOUT THE AUTHORS

Ulrich von Berg (UB), *1955, degree in American and Media Studies. Many years' experience as a movie journalist in all branches of the media. Editor and author of various books on film. Lives in Berlin.

Malte Hagener (MH), *1971, degree in Literature and Media Studies. Editor and author of numerous academic articles. Lecturer in Film History at Amsterdam University. Lives in Hamburg and Berlin.

Steffen Haubner (SH), *1965, studied Art History and Sociology. Has written many academic and press articles. Collaborator on the science and research section of the Hamburger Abendblatt. Lives in Hamburg.

Jörn Hetebrügge (JH), *1971, studied German Literature. Author of many academic and press articles. Lives in Berlin.

Annette Kilzer (AK), *1966, degree in Theatre Studies, German Studies and Philosophy. Has written many books and press articles. Lives in Berlin.

Heinz-Jürgen Köhler (HJK), *1963, deputy editor-in-chief of the movie program for TV Today. Author of many academic and press articles. Lives in Hamburg.

Steffen Lückehe (SL), *1962, Film Theorist. Member of the German Standards Committee for children's and young people's videos. Author of many articles in various papers and magazines. Lives in Mannheim.

Nils Meyer (NM), * 1971, studied German Literature and Politics. Has written many articles in various papers and magazines. Lives in Berlin.

Olaf Möller (OM), Author, translator, program curator. Writes for the national press. Lives in Köln.

Anne Pohl (APO), *1961, active as a journalist since 1987. Author of numerous academic articles. Lives in Berlin.

Burkhard Röwekamp (BR), *1965, researcher at the Institute for Contemporary German Literature and Media at the Philipps University in Marburg. Has taught numerous courses and published many articles on the aesthetics and theory of contemporary film. Lives in Marburg.

Markus Stauff (MS), *1968, researcher at the Institute for Film and Television Studies at the Ruhr University in Bochum. Author of many academic articles. Lives in Bochum.

Rainer Vowe (RV), *1954, historian, works for the EU Directorate General XII (Audio-Visuelles and the Institute for Film and Television Studies at the Ruhr University in Bochum. Numerous articles about the history of cinema and television. Lives in Bochum.

Our thanks to the distributors, without whom many of these films would never have reached the big screen.

ARSENAL, ARTHAUS, BUENA VISTA, C/I VERTRIEBSGEMEINSCHAFT, COLUMBIA TRI STAR, CONCORDE, CONSTANTIN, HIGHLIGHT FILM, JUGENDFILM, KINOWELT, NIL FILM, PANDORA, POLYGRAM FILMS, PROKINO, SCOTIA, SENATOR, TOBIS, 20TH CENTURY FOX, UIP, WARNER BROS.

Academy Award® and Oscar® are the registered trademark and service mark of the Academy of Motion Picture Arts and Sciences.

We deeply regret it if, despite our concerted efforts, a distributor has been unintentionally overlooked and omitted. Obviously we will amend any such errors in the next edition if they are brought to the attention of the publishers.

ACKNOWLEDGEMENTS

The creation of this book was made possible by the collaboration of a number of people. Heartfelt thanks go to *Thierry Nebois* of TASCHEN Verlag for the coordination work and his ability to keep track of everything. *Birgit Reber* and *Andy Disl* came up with a design concept that gives pride of place to the pictures, which are the true capital of a film book. My thanks to *Herbert Klemens* from the *Filmbild Fundus* for his help in accessing the original stills. But this book was only first made really possible by the stimulating texts from the authors. The keen-eyed editing work was done by *Corinna Dehne* and *Lioba Waleczek*. *Malte Hagener* attended to the technical editorial work with his customary meticulousness. The fact that this book got off the ground is thanks to the commitment and initiative of *Petra Lamers-Schütze*. And last but not least *Benedikt Taschen* has included the book in his programme and enthusiastically followed the publication's progress from start to finish. My personal thanks to him and everyone else mentioned here.

ABOUT THIS BOOK

The 141 films selected for this book represent a decade of cinema. It goes without saying that this particular selection is based on a decision that could have turned out differently. Each film is presented by an essay, and additionally accompanied by a glossary entry devoted to one person or a cinematographic term. To ensure optimal access to all this information, an index for the films and a general index are provided at the back of the book.

IMPRINT

ENDPAPERS, PAGE 1 AND PAGES 768–769	LOST HIGHWAY / David Lynch / SENATOR FILM / OCTOBER FILM
ILLUSTRATIONS PAGES 2–15	THE SILENCE OF THE LAMBS / Jonathan Demme / COLUMBIA / TRI STAR / ORION PICTURES
ILLUSTRATIONS PAGE 16	EDWARD SCISSORHANDS / Tim Burton / 20TH CENTURY FOX

© 2002 TASCHEN GMBH
Hohenzollernring 53, D–50672 Köln
WWW.TASCHEN.COM

PHOTOGRAPHS	FILMBILD FUNDUS ROBERT FISCHER, Munich
PROJECT MANAGEMENT	PETRA LAMERS-SCHÜTZE, Cologne
EDITORIAL COORDINATION	THIERRY NEBOIS, Cologne
DESIGN	SENSE/NET, ANDY DISL and BIRGIT REBER, Cologne
TEXTS	ULRICH VON BERG (UB), MALTE HAGENER (MH), STEFFEN HAUBNER (SH), JÖRN HETEBRÜGGE (JH), ANNETTE KILZER (AK), HEINZ-JÜRGEN KÖHLER (HJK), STEFFEN LÜCKEHE (SL), NILS MEYER (NM), OLAF MÖLLER (OM), ANNE POHL (APO), BURKHARD RÖWEKAMP (BR), MARKUS STAUFF (MS), RAINER VOWE (RV)
TECHNICAL EDITING	MALTE HAGENER, Berlin
ENGLISH TRANSLATION	DEBORAH CAROLINE HOLMES, Vienna (Texts), HARRIET HORSFIELD in association with FIRST EDITION TRANSLATIONS LTD, Cambridge (Introduction), KATHARINE HUGHES, Oxford (Captions)
EDITING	JONATHAN MURPHY, Brussels
COLLABORATION	BRIGITTE LÖBACH, Cologne
PRODUCTION	UTE WACHENDORF, Cologne

PRINTED IN SPAIN
ISBN 3–8228–5878–1